World Security

CHALLENGES FOR A
NEW CENTURY

THIRD EDITION

World Security

CHALLENGES FOR A
NEW CENTURY

THIRD EDITION

*A Project of the Five College Program
in Peace and World Security Studies*

Michael T. Klare

HAMPSHIRE COLLEGE

Yogesh Chandrani

HAMPSHIRE COLLEGE

**ST. MARTIN'S PRESS
NEW YORK**

Sponsoring editor: Beth A. Gillett
Development editor: Susan Cottenden
Manager, publishing services: Emily Berleth
Senior editor, publishing services: Douglas Bell
Project management: Publisher's Studio
Production supervisor: Scott Lavelle
Cover design: Patricia McFadden
Cover photo: Mark LaFavor/Parallel Productions, Inc.

Library of Congress Catalog Card Number: 97-65191

Manufactured in the United States of America.

3 2 1 0 9 8
f e d c b a

For information, write:

St. Martin's Press, Inc.
175 Fifth Avenue
New York, NY 10010

ISBN: 0-312-14990-5 (paperback)
      0-312-17635-X (hardcover)

Acknowledgments

It is a violation of the law to reproduce these selections by any means whatsoever without the written permission of the copyright holder.

An earlier version of James N. Rosenau's chapter, "The Dynamism of a Turbulent World," appeared in *The United Nations in a Turbulent World,* an Occasional Paper of the International Peace Academy. Copyright © 1992 by Lynne Rienner Publishers.

An earlier version of Michael Klare's chapter, "The Era of Multiplying Schisms," appeared in *Current History,* Volume 95, Number 604 (November 1996), pp. 353–58. Copyright © 1996 by Current History, Inc.

An earlier version of Karen Dawisha's chapter, "The Imperial Impulse: Russia and the 'Near Abroad,'" appeared in Karen Dawisha and Bruce Parrot, eds., "The End of Empire? Comparative Perspectives on the Soviet Collapse," *The International Politics of Eurasia,* Volume 9 (1997). Reprinted by permission of M. E. Sharpe, Inc.

An earlier version of the chapter by Barry Buzan and Gerald Segal, "Rethinking East Asian Security," appeared in *Survival,* Volume 36, Number 2 (Summer 1994), pp. 3–21. Reprinted by permission of Oxford University Press.

An earlier version of Michael Hudson's chapter, "The United States and the Middle East," originally appeared in Hudson, "To Play the Hegemon: Fifty Years of U.S. Policy Toward the Middle East," *The Middle East Journal,* Volume 50, Number 3 (Summer 1996), pp. 329–43. Reprinted by permission of The Middle East Institute.

Michael Brown's chapter, "The Causes of Internal Conflict," originally appeared in Michael Brown, editor, *Nationalism and Ethnic Conflict* (Cambridge: MIT Press, 1997), pp. 3–25. Reprinted by permission of MIT Press.

Portions of the chapter by Margaret Karns and Karen Mingst, "The Evolution of UN Peacekeeping and Peacemaking," appeared in Karns and Mingst, *The United Nations in the Post-Cold War Era* (Boulder, CO: Westview Press, 1995). Reprinted by permission of Westview Press.

Portions of the chapter by Phil Williams, "Transnational Criminal Organizations and International Security," appeared in *Survival,* Volume 36, Number 1 (Spring 1994), pp. 96–113. Reprinted by permission of Oxford University Press.

Portions of Thomas Homer-Dixon's chapter, "Environmental Scarcity and Intergroup Conflict," originally appeared in Homer-Dixon's "On the Threshold: Environmental Changes As Causes of Acute Conflict," *International Security,* Volume 16, Number 3 (Fall 1991), pp. 76–116. Reprinted by permission of MIT Press.

Contents

Preface

Like many of our colleagues in the field of international relations and world security, the editors of this volume have come to realize that the onset of the post-Cold War era in 1990 entailed far more sweeping and revolutionary changes than were even apparent at the time. The end of U.S.-Soviet hostility and the breakup of the former Soviet Union seemed momentous enough—but, since then, we have witnessed the Gulf War, the carnage in Bosnia, the genocide in Rwanda, the rise of China as a major power, and other dramatic developments. More than this, we have seen the emergence of entire new *categories* of security challenges: environmental degradation, resource scarcities, transnational criminal activities, mass human migrations, and so on. Clearly, human civilization is experiencing a transformation every bit as profound—perhaps even more so—than that which occurred at the end of World Wars I and II.

This transformation engenders both risks and opportunities for the world community. On the risk side, it poses a wide range of traditional and nontraditional threats to world peace and stability. As in the past, nations and peoples will arm for war and, on occasion, provoke armed hostilities with their neighbors; in many such cases, however, these forces will use weapons of a type unknown in the past, or employed only by a handful of major powers. Economic and environmental forces are also likely to generate new threats to global security, most probably in ways that cannot be foreseen. At the same time, the very magnitude of the changes now under way will allow for a great deal of experimentation in the design and implementation of strategies for global peace and security. Existing international organizations like the United Nations are likely to be reconfigured in response to changing needs, and new organizations will be established.

The interplay of these two sorts of phenomena—the emergence of new threats and the development of new responses—will dominate the world security agenda for decades to come. It is possible, of course, that some *particular* threat will come to dominate the global security landscape of the twenty-first century, just as U.S.-Soviet hostility dominated the landscape of the Cold War era. Far more likely, however, is a security environment characterized by the presence of *many* threats, each demanding the attention of international policymakers. These perils—arms proliferation, ethnic warfare, criminal violence, human migrations, climate change, and so on—will undoubtedly experience periodic highs and lows in perceived importance as developments unfold, but *all* are likely to figure prominently in the global discourse on international peace and security.

The aim of this edition of *World Security* is to introduce readers to the most significant of these emerging challenges. Given space limitations, it is impossible to examine each of them in great detail; nevertheless, we have attempted to provide some background on those security threats that are most likely to command international attention in the years ahead. In doing so, moreover, we have sought to identify the underlying forces that are now transforming the human landscape and producing these various perils. At the same time, we have tried to suggest ways in which the world community can act to overcome or minimize the emerging threats to international peace and stability.

To accomplish all this, the editors of *World Security* undertook a complete and thorough overhaul of the previous (second) edition of the book. Although some of the authors and topics remain the same, the essays that appear below were either written specifically for this edition or substantially revised and updated. Furthermore, to ensure coverage of key emerging themes in international security, new essays were secured or commissioned from leading experts in the field. The result is a completely new book, fully geared to the world security agenda of the twenty-first century.

Among the distinctive features of this new edition are:

- An expanded discussion of **underlying forces** in international security affairs, with contributions by James Rosenau, Daniel Nelson, and Michael Klare.
- An entirely new section on **regional developments** in international security, with essays on Eurasia by Karen Dawisha, on East Asia by Barry Buzan and Gerald Segal, and on the Middle East by Michael Hudson.
- The addition of new chapters on **emerging themes** in world security, including transnational criminal operations, global economic inequity, trade conflict, and international environmental politics.
- The revision and updating of existing chapters on nuclear proliferation, conventional arms trafficking, UN peacekeeping, global violence against women, and worldwide demographic change.

As for the structure of the book, we have retained all of the successful features of the first and second editions. The book begins with several analytical essays on current trends in international affairs, followed by more descriptive essays on a wide range of specific world security problems. Each of the latter is intended to provide a general overview of the topic at hand, covering all salient features of the problem and giving an assessment of likely developments in the years to come; each, moreover, covers both the nature of the problem and possible approaches to its control and amelioration. As in the past, the book concludes with a capstone essay on new approaches to world peace and security.

In selecting authors for these essays, the editors sought scholars who are known for their expertise in the particular field involved. At the same time, we aimed to produce a volume that, on the whole, reflects what might be called a *world security* approach to international affairs. That is, we sought to demonstrate that truly *global* problems, like environmental degradation, arms proliferation, and transnational criminal activity, are best addressed at the international level. There are, of course, many problems that are best addressed at the local or national level; we do not question that. But the problems raised in this volume *cannot* be solved in this fashion; they must entail cooperation at the global level. While the authors of particular essays in this book may not agree on the specific *strategies* to be employed in addressing these problems, they generally share a belief in the need for international cooperation.

It is our hope that readers of this volume will gain a strong general knowledge of the basic trends in world security affairs and a deeper understanding of some of the most critical problems facing human society today. We hope, in addition, that they will be motivated to do additional research on these issues, to join in the international discourse on global security affairs, and to participate in the worldwide search for constructive solutions. Only through such involvement and cooperation, we believe, can the world community succeed in overcoming the major threats to international peace and security in the twenty-first century.

*   *   *

Because we sought to be comprehensive in our coverage of contemporary world security affairs, the editors of this volume relied on the advice and suggestions of many other scholars in the field. In some cases, this reliance entailed intensive discussion of the book and its contents; in others, it was more a matter of ongoing conversations about international processes in general. Whatever the case, we gained enormously from all of these encounters—and if we cannot always identify our benefactors by name, we are no less grateful for their suggestions and insights.

In acknowledging such assistance, a major debt of gratitude is owed to Daniel C. Thomas, the co-editor of the first two editions of *World Security* and an important figure in the design of the third. Although Dan's new responsibilities, as assistant professor of political science at the University of Illinois at Chicago, precluded his participation as a co-editor of this edition, he provided us with invaluable advice on new themes and authors. To a great extent, the shape of the current volume reflects his wisdom. We are very grateful for his assistance.

Next, we wish to acknowledge the important and always illuminating conversations we have had with our colleagues at the Five Colleges, especially the members of the Faculty Steering Committee of the Five College Program in Peace and World Security Studies (PAWSS), with which we are associated. In particular, we wish to commend Pavel Machala and Ronald Tiersky of Amherst College; Eqbal Ahmad, Elizabeth Hartmann, Frank Holmquist, and Ali Mirsepassi of Hampshire College; Vincent Ferraro and Kavita Khory of Mount Holyoke College; Mary Geske and Gregory White of Smith College, and Neta Crawford, James Der Derian, Eric Einhorn, and Peter Haas of the University of Massachusetts at Amherst. Each time we get together to talk with these wonderful colleagues—whether at a panel discussion, a seminar, or just a meal—we gain some new insight into the larger scheme of things. Our thanks to you all!

We could not have produced this book without the involvement and support of the individuals—all of whom are engaged in other time-consuming and important projects—who wrote the various essays found within. In many cases, they devoted considerable time and energy to this project despite many other pressing duties. Busy as they are, they still took time to answer the various queries we sent, along with requests for revisions of one sort or another. It is a testament to their commitment to undergraduate education that this collection has appeared. We cannot thank you enough.

We also wish to express our gratitude for all the support we receive from Hampshire College, the Five Colleges Inc., and the staff of PAWSS. At Hampshire College, which houses the PAWSS program, we are especially grateful to President Gregory Prince, Dean of Faculty E. Francis White, the deans of the School of Social Sciences, Margaret Cerullo and Michael Ford, and to all of the many wonderful and dedicated people who work and teach at the College. We couldn't be in a finer place! At the Five College Center, special thanks are due to Lorna Peterson, the coordinator of the Five Colleges, and to her colleagues Carol Aleman, Carol Angus, Susan Bronson, Elizabeth Loudon, Jean Stabell, and Nate Therien. And particular thanks are due to our colleague on the PAWSS staff, Assistant Director Adi Bemak, and to the wonderful student assistants who have served us loyally over the years.

As with the first two editions of *World Security,* we received outstanding cooperation from the fine people at St. Martin's Press. Particular gratitude is due to Beth Gillett, the sponsoring editor, Susan Cottenden, development editor, and Jayme Heffler, assistant editor. Finally, for offering comments to St. Martin's about the book in various stages of its development, we wish to thank Erica G. Alin, Hamline University; Laura Bloodgood, George Washington University; Bill Felice, Eckerd College; Michael Gold-Biss, St. Cloud State University; H. M. Mokeba, Louisiana State University—Baton Rouge; Jeffrey S. Morton, Florida Atlantic University; Brian M. Pollins, The Ohio State University; Timothy J. Schorn, University of South Dakota; Gary L. Scott, Portland State University; Bob Switky, SUNY College at Brockport; Barbara F. Walter, University of California, San Diego; B. Welling Hall, Earlham College; and Daniel J. Whiteneck, U.S. Air Force Academy.

Michael T. Klare and Yogesh Chandrani
Amherst, Mass.

About the Contributors

Janet Welsh Brown is a senior fellow of the World Resources Institute in Washington, D.C., and co-author of *Global Environmental Politics* (1995). She has also served as executive director of the Environmental Defense Fund and has taught at the University of Washington (Seattle), Howard University, the University of the District of Columbia, and Sarah Lawrence College.

Michael E. Brown is associate director of the International Security Program of the Center for Science and International Affairs of the John F. Kennedy School of Government of Harvard University. He is managing editor of the journal *International Security* and the editor of several books on internal conflict, including *Ethnic Conflict and International Security* (1993) and *The International Dimensions of Internal Conflict* (1996).

Seyom Brown is Wien Professor of International Cooperation and chair of the Department of Politics at Brandeis University, and an associate at the Center for International Affairs at Harvard University. His published works include: *International Relations in a Changing International System* (1996); *The Causes and Prevention of War* (1994); and *New Forces, Old Forces, and the Future of World Politics* (1995).

Charlotte Bunch is the director of the Douglass College Center for Women's Global Leadership and a professor in the Bloustein School of Planning and Public Policy at Rutgers University. She has edited seven feminist anthologies and is the author of *Passionate Politics: Feminist Theory in Action* (1987) and *Demanding Accountability: The Global Campaign and Vienna Tribunal for Women's Human Rights* (1994).

Barry Buzan is professor of International Studies at the University of Westminster in London and director of the European Security Project at the Copenhagen Peace Research Institute. He is the author of many books and articles on international security, including *Peoples, States and Fear* (1991), *Security: A New Framework for Analysis* (1997, with Ole Waever and Jaap de Wilde), and *The Arms Dynamic in World Politics* (1998, with Eric Herring).

Roxanna Carrillo is the Human Rights Advisor at the United Nations Development Fund for Women (UNIFEM) and director of UNIFEM's Human Rights Programme. A Peruvian activist in the international women's movement for many years, she was one of the founders of Centro de la Mujer Peruana Flora Tristan in Lima.

Zachary S. Davis is a specialist in international nuclear policy in the Environment and Natural Resources Policy Division of the Congressional Research Service of the Library of Congress. He has lectured and written widely on issues of nuclear proliferation and international security.

Karen Dawisha is professor of government and politics and director of the Center for the Study of Post-Communist Societies and the Russian Littoral Project at the University of Maryland at College Park. She is the author of many books and articles on Soviet and Russian affairs, and is the co-editor of *The End of Empire?: Comparative Perspectives on the Soviet Collapse* (1997).

Vincent Ferraro is the Ruth Lawson Professor of International Politics at Mount Holyoke College and the author of many articles on strategic doctrine and international political economy.

Julie Ginocchio is a student at Mount Holyoke College.

Michael C. Hudson is the Seif Ghobash Professor of Arab Studies and professor of international relations in the School of Foreign Service of Georgetown University and former director of Georgetown's Center for Contemporary Arab Studies. He is also the author of numerous books and scholarly articles on Middle Eastern politics and is the editor of *The Politics and Economics of Integration in the Arab World* (1998).

Thomas Homer-Dixon is assistant professor of political science and director of the Peace and Conflict Studies Programme at the University of Toronto and associate fellow of the Canadian Institute for Advanced Research. He is the author of *Environment, Scarcity, and Violence* (1998) and several scholarly articles on global environmental politics.

Robert C. Johansen is the director of graduate studies at the Kroc Institute for International Peace Studies and a professor of government at the University of Notre Dame. He is the author of numerous articles on world affairs and *The National Interest and the Human Interest* (1980), and is co-editor of *The Constitutional Foundations of World Peace* (1993).

Margaret P. Karns is professor of political science at the University of Dayton. She is the co-author, with Karen Mingst, of *The United States and Multilateral Institutions* (1990) and *The United Nations in the Post-Cold War Era* (1995).

Michael T. Klare is the Five College Professor of Peace and World Security Studies (a joint appointment at Amherst, Hampshire, Mount Holyoke, and Smith Colleges and the University of Massachusetts at Amherst) and director of the Five College Program in Peace and World Security Studies (PAWSS). He is the author or editor of several books and articles on international security affairs, including *American Arms Supermarket* (1985), *Low-Intensity Warfare* (1988, with Peter Kornbluh), and *Rogue States and Nuclear Outlaws* (1995).

Lora Lumpe is director of the Arms Sales Monitoring Project at the Federation of American Scientists in Washington, D.C. She has lectured and written widely on the arms trade and U.S. foreign policy.

Karen A. Mingst is a professor of political science at the University of Kentucky. She is the author of *Politics and the African Development Bank* (1990) and, with Margaret Karns, the co-author of *The United States and Multilateral Institutions* (1990) and *The United Nations in the Post-Cold War Era* (1995).

Daniel N. Nelson is professor of international studies at Old Dominion University, where he was founding director of the Graduate Program in International Studies. He is also president of Global Concepts, Inc., an internatonal consulting firm in Alexandria, Virginia, and editor of the journal *International Politics;* previously, he served as Senior Foreign Policy Advisor for then House Majority Leader Richard Gephardt.

Dennis Pirages is a professor of government and politics and director of the Harrison Program on the Future Global Agenda at the University of Maryland. He is the author or editor of nine books, including *Global Ecopolitics: A New Framework for International Relations* (1978), *Global Technopolitics: The International Politics of Technology and Resources* (1989), and *Building Sustainable Societies: A Blueprint for a Post-Industrial World* (1996).

Michael Renner is a senior researcher at the Worldwatch Institute in Washington, D.C. and a regular contributor to the Institute's annual publications, *State of the World* and *Vital Signs.* He is the author of *Fighting for Survival* (1996) and several Worldwatch Papers, including *Budgeting for Disarmament: The Costs of War and Peace.*

James N. Rosenau is University Professor of International Affairs at George Washington University. He also is the author of many books and articles on international relations, including *Turbulence in World Politics: A Theory of Change and Continuity* (1990) and *Along the Domestic-Foreign Frontier: Exploring Governance in a Turbulent World* (1997).

Ana Cristina R. Santos is a financial analyst at Lehman Brothers in New York.

Gerald Segal is a senior fellow at the International Institute for Strategic Studies in London, and director of Britain's Pacific Asia Programme. He is also the author of numerous books and articles on Asian security issues.

Phil Williams is professor of international affairs and director of the Ridgway Center for International Security Studies at the University of Pittsburgh. He is also the editor of the journal *Transnational Organized Crime* and is the author or editor of several books, including *Superpower Competition and Crisis Prevention in the Third World* (1990) and *Security in Korea: War, Stalemate, and Negotiation* (1994).

1 / World Interests and the Changing Dimensions of Security

SEYOM BROWN

The security predicaments featured in the following chapters are largely symptoms of the structural crisis in contemporary world society—the incongruence between the traditional state-sovereignty system and the increasing interdependence of peoples. The so-called "realist" view of international relations which takes the anarchic system of world politics as basically unalterable, and regards the pursuit of national interests as the essence of rational statecraft, is unable to comprehend, let alone counter, the structural contradictions underlying the contemporary security threats.[1] Policies and institutions for dealing effectively with the threatening incongruities need to be informed by a concept of *world interests* that focuses on the needs of humankind as a whole and that can provide a basis for reconciling or arbitrating among conflicting national, international, and subnational interests.

THE INADEQUACY OF "REALISM"

The major contribution of the "realists" has been their virtually exclusive focus on nation-states (meaning, for the most part, national governments) as both agents and objects of the most significant occurrences in world politics.[2] The justification for this focus is that in the anarchic world polity, individuals and peoples must rely ultimately on the power and authority of the national government in whose jurisdiction they reside to secure their basic needs and amenities. Accordingly, national statespersons in every country are obligated first and foremost to do all they can to serve "the national interest"—the safety and well-being of the nation as a whole.

But the narrowly focused "realist" lens fails to illuminate many of the momentous developments occurring within, above, and across the jurisdictions of the nation-states that are creating dangerous incongruities in world politics and society. The peaceable and just amelioration of these incongruities will require enhancement of the authority of norms and institutions to which the nation-states themselves must be held accountable—a development considered infeasible, to the extent it is addressed at all, in most "realist" treatises on international relations.

Another contribution of the "realists" has been their persistent attention to the international distribution of coercive power, especially military capabilities and resources, but also other resources that can be used coercively. Citing as the essence of political wisdom Thucydides's account of the Athenian warning to the Melians that the strong can have their way with the weak, contemporary "realists" confidently invoke the historical record in support of the proposition that force is *ultima ratio* of international relations. Presumably, no nation can reliably secure its existence and well-being unless it can fend off or overwhelm the coercive capabilities of its rivals—if not by itself, then in combination with the capabilities of its allies. As Hans Morgenthau taught, in the anarchic world polity, rational statecraft requires the pursuit of the national interest defined in terms of power. Foreign policy, from this perspective, is essentially national security policy, which in turn is predominantly military policy (that is, about the threat and use of force); and international relations analysts and theorists are doing their job when they give heavy emphasis to military balances of power and alliance relationships.

To be sure, attention to the distribution of coercive power among countries is a necessary aspect of statecraft in the anarchic world polity, and those concerned with national or world security ignore this dimension of international relations at their peril. Necessary yes; sufficient no. For while war continues to be available as an ultimate arbiter of international disputes, most of the issues over which peoples must deal with each other across national borders in this age of burgeoning interdependence (import barriers and export subsidies; rules for the investment, transfer, and exchange of money; interest rates; regulations on international transportation and communication; migration; the use of transborder and global ecologies) are best handled—and usually handled—at levels of bargaining far removed from the exchange of threats of military action.

There may well be the temptation for those dissatisfied with bargaining outcomes in the normal arenas to "up the ante" to threats of violence; particularly if the dissatisfied parties have access to powerful military or paramilitary forces. But this is precisely the problem with a model of international relations that attributes negotiating outcomes largely to the distribution of coercive capabilities, and that is morally neutral with respect to crossing the threshold between nonviolent bargaining and the use of force. The "realist" model, to the extent that it influences the way officials and policy analysts view their options, tends to be self-confirming, in that it perpetuates a picture of an international system in which it is futile to attempt to substantially reduce the reliance on military power.

But is this model of the way the world works truly *realistic?* Does it provide a conceptual framework that can assist contemporary statespersons and citizens in making policy choices that are rational (let alone morally tenable) in the sense of servicing their basic interests and values?

Perhaps the "realist" model did essentially correspond to the reality of world politics during most of the three centuries preceding World War II. The dominant statecraft then operated on the premise that the most intensive patterns of human interaction would take place *within* territorially demarcated countries. Each of these presumably sovereign states would control interpersonal and intergroup behavior within its jurisdiction to provide at least the minimum personal and institutional security necessary for the performance of basic societal functions: the protection of persons and property from physical attack; the enforcement of laws and contracts; the orderly exchange of goods and services; the husbanding of resources essential to the healthy survival of the population; and the maintenance of the society's cultural, moral, and legal norms, including the rights and obligations of individuals and standards of distributive justice. Interstate and transborder interactions would be relatively sparse and could be managed, for the most part, by diplomacy, or by war when conflict was unresolvable by peaceful bargaining. Most countries would be willing to take their chances in this anarchic world polity when it came to handling international relations, in preference to subordinating the sovereignty of their territorial unit to "supranational" governing bodies purporting to act on behalf of some larger inchoate international community.

The contemporary world system, however, departs considerably from the traditional picture of sovereign nation-states warily interacting with each other only at the margins of their existence. As will be argued below, and as other chapters in this book show in greater detail, the separate nation-states have become ever-more impotent in dealing on their own (that is, mainly through *national* laws and *national* institutions) with material and political realities that are increasingly threatening the safety and well-being of their citizens.

At best, the "realist" model, while continuing to generate elegant theoretical discourse, has become largely irrelevant to policy analysis because of its failure to comprehend some of the most serious predicaments of contemporary society.[3] At worst, the effort to conduct statecraft-as-usual in terms of this model can jeopardize the healthy survival of the human species. It has become an anachronistic, if not counterproductive, frame of reference for individuals as well as for collectivities, since the attempt to secure the power of the nation-state of which one is a citizen is no longer, in many areas of one's life, a sufficient, or even the best, means for protecting or advancing one's interests and basic values.

THE INCONGRUENCE OF SOCIETY AND GOVERNANCE IN THE NATION-STATE SYSTEM

The "realist" model, in short, diverts our attention from the most profound structural problem of contemporary world society: the widening gap between (a) the emergent realities of material interdependence and patterns of interaction among peoples and (b) the inherited legal/political structure of the nation-state system.[4] This incongruence is creating dangerous instabilities along at least five interrelated dimensions of civil society: the peace and public order dimension, the commercial dimension, the ecological dimension, the cultural dimension, and the human rights dimension. Political systems owe their viability and legitimacy to their effectiveness in servicing the public order, commercial, ecological, cultural, and justice needs of communities. Where a society's highest agencies of governance— the national governments, in the case of world society—neither adequately control, represent, nor are accountable to the most active human groupings in these fields, the society's political system is in crisis and the values of civil society are insecure.

The Crisis in World Public Order

Many of the post-Cold War headline-grabbing events—violent secessionist and self-determination movements; xenophobic attacks against refugee and immigrant groups; contraband in nuclear, chemical, and biological weaponry; criminal activities of transnational drug syndicates; international terrorism—are symptoms of the incongruence of society and governance in the international system. Sovereign national enclaves of security and order, fenced off from the "chaos" of the world at large, are becoming unviable. Affluence, cultural homogeneity, and powerful national armies and navies are no longer sufficient bases for sustaining barriers against one's country being penetrated, if not engulfed, by hostile or unwanted people, substances, or ideas that can disturb the domestic peace.[5]

Human society cannot return to the simpler political configurations for assuring public order that prevailed before the twentieth-century revolutions in transportation and communication technology. Efforts to strengthen national border controls against waves of migrants escaping from political persecution or economic destitution, for example, are not only very expensive but also demand levels of policing contrary to the open-society traditions of most of the advanced industrial democracies. Nor can the growing transboundary contraband in weapons, drugs, and other harmful substances be effectively suppressed simply by tightening surveillance by customs officials at standard points of entry. An unprecedented degree of multilateral cooperation (and trust) between policing agencies at operational levels is required for apprehending the deftly evasive and transnational criminal syndicates, themselves utilizing highly sophisticated communications systems and countersurveillance technologies.

Political terrorism, too, is facilitated by the new technologies for moving people, materials, and messages. The governments that are often the prime objects of terrorist coercion are more heavily involved than ever in global commerce, exposing and making vulnerable their citizens and officials to hit-and-run violence and hostage taking. By contrast, the secret terrorist networks have the luxury of stealth and surprise, sometimes aided clandestinely by paramilitary and spy agencies of disaffected states. Counterterrorism, even when engaged in the relatively narrow mission of meeting force and brutality with counterforce, is unlikely to be very effective against such transnational networks if it is conducted, for the most part, unilaterally through national agencies.

Meanwhile, new technologies of warfare have been overwhelming and rendering dysfunctional even the traditional alliance and power-balancing processes of the nation-state system—the system's principal means of protecting relatively weak and small countries from attack and bullying by more powerful adversaries. When going to war can place the national community at high risk of virtually total destruction (which can happen readily today, even with "conventional" weapons), an intolerable strain is put on alliance relationships. Publics and parliaments begin to question whether any foreign interests, save perhaps those deemed essential to the defense of the homeland itself, are worth the destruction of the entire national community. Countries lacking sufficient military force of their own to deter provocations from a great power armed with awesome destructive capabilities are no longer able to count on allies to redress the imbalance of power. Formal "mutual security" pacts are suspected of being hollow commitments, unlikely to be honored at moments of truth. Even before the end of the Cold War, NATO and the Warsaw Pact, under the impact of the Mutual Assured Destruction capabilities of the superpowers, were experiencing this profound crisis of credibility.

The post-Cold War initiative of the United States to enlarge NATO's membership to include East European countries that had been Soviet allies, while viewed by many Russians as an effort to perpetuate and tighten their encirclement by a band of hostile states, has been advertised by the U.S. government as a venture in East-West cooperation to facilitate and secure peaceful transitions to democracy, not a power-balancing move against Russia. In actuality, Russian suspicions of a continued "containment" motive behind NATO expansion are warranted (Western geostrategic planners *do* want to hedge against the prospect of a revival of Russian ambitions to reassert hegemony over Eastern Europe and the Balkans); but the popular distaste for long-term military commitments has compelled Washington to cloak its realpolitik purposes under idealistic rhetoric.

Could an enhancement of the collective security features of the United Nations ameliorate those aspects of the world public-order crisis that result from the declining credibility of military alliances? Not unless there were a collateral change in the constitutive national sovereignty norms of the nation-state system—norms that remain deeply imbedded in the United Nations Charter. For as long as the military forces that can be deployed under direct command and control of the United Nations organization will be clearly inferior to the military forces remaining under the sovereign control of national governments who might be adversaries in future international conflicts, the actual implementation of United Nations collective security decisions will continue to fall to particular militarily well-endowed countries; and these countries will still have to generate national decisions that incur the prospect of terrible war costs, including having to absorb retaliatory strikes on their homelands from the aggressor states. The contemplation of such costs and risks are still likely to prompt the militarily capable guardians of world order to work against true UN collective security responses in particular cases, and certainly against giving any UN agencies standing authority to *order* members' forces into action.

The role of the United Nations in response to Iraq's 1990 invasion of Kuwait might seem to contradict this pessimistic assessment. But the functioning of the world organization in the 1990–91 Gulf war, like the UN action in Korea forty years earlier, was an anomaly—brought on by circumstances unlikely to recur. The aggressor, Iraq, had no allies among the permanent members of the UN Security Council in 1990 who might be willing to oppose the Bush administration's desire to obtain international legitimacy for its plans to remove Iraq from Kuwait by force. The Bush administration had convinced itself and a majority of the American public that allowing Saddam Hussein to keep control of Kuwait would put a Hitler-like aggressor in a position to control the economically and strategically crucial energy resources of the Middle East. Moreover, the ensuing military action against Iraq, as happened in Korea in 1950, was not really a "collective security" operation; it was, by design of the Bush administration, undertaken by only a handful of countries acting in the mode of a traditional ad hoc military coalition, and mobilized and directed by the coalition leader, the United States.

Even in the less risky field of "peacekeeping," hopes that the United Nations would fill the world public order vacuum created by the collapse of the Cold War alliance system have been dashed by disputes over the financing, contributions of military personnel, and command and control of UN forces. The growing disaffection with the United Nations in the United States (which President Clinton pandered to in the 1996 elections in order to outflank his Republican opponents) makes it unlikely that the world organization, in the near future at least, will have sufficient resources to perform in the global conflict control role that its champions have envisioned.

In short, the world is still operating basically under a national self-help, military power-balancing mode of enforcing minimum global order, while the threats to community and individual security are becoming increasingly transnational. Ultimately, weakly armed states may still have to rely on the old type of alliance commitments to secure themselves against powerful aggressors, while most people know (like the child who shouted "the emperor has no clothes") such commitments, given the society-devastating effects of modern war, are becoming less and less credible.

Transnational Economy versus National Polity

The ability of individuals and communities to secure what they value for themselves and their posterity is also jeopardized by the growing incongruence between the world's most dynamic contemporary economic relationships and its traditional political structure (the nation-state system and its legal norms of national sovereignty and noninterference by foreigners in a country's domestic affairs).

Government agencies, commercial enterprises, political movements, and criminal syndicates in possession of (or able to use) advanced transportation and communication systems can leapfrog many of the controls on the movements of people, goods, and information across international borders, by which countries traditionally have attempted to retain sovereignty over their national economies. More than ever before, in fields crucial to the functioning of a country's system and the well-being of its people, investors and producers and buyers and sellers are thickly linked in networks of interdependence with their customers or suppliers in other countries. In some fields the interdependencies give rise to collusion across national borders, with transnational interests conspiring, as it were, in price, supply; and market-sharing arrangements and to bring pressure on their respective national governments.

Decisions of giant multinational/multiproduct firms to invest in new plants here or there, to build roads and seaports, or to pull up stakes for a more congenial locale, can drastically affect (positively and negatively) the life chances of people the world over. Constituting a family of firms located in different countries, and joined together by a head office usually located in one of the advanced industrial countries, many multinational corporations have greater impact on the world economy than do some of the important nation-states.

The emergent breed of powerful transnational entrepreneurs comprises more than producers and marketers of goods and services. The movers and shakers also include banks, investment houses, and money brokers engaged in the global distribution of capital, the lifeblood of every country's economy. The most effective entrepreneurs in this money arena often operate through multiple partnerships, and have financial ties to and strategic information on all the world's major money markets and to firms in numerous countries—"enterprise webs," Robert Reich calls them—that enable them to obtain early information on changes in demand for products and services and contemplated shifts in interest rates or currency values.[6] These transnational enterprise webs frequently transfer huge financial investments in and out of countries to take advantage of demand shifts and in anticipation of currency devaluations or upward revaluations by particular countries. The tremendous amounts of money circulating around these networks of currency speculators now changes national hands so fast that the whole thrust of a country's domestic policy can be overthrown, literally overnight, by nongovernmental financial transactions.

By comparison, the national official agencies operating in the fields of commerce and banking are sluggish and lack spans of control congruent with the global scope of operation of the most dynamic transnationals. The ascendancy of the new breed of globally active transnational entrepreneurs is generating new insecurities among other groups. Some have ample reason to worry. When a country's policies for regulating national markets can be avoided or overwhelmed by transnational buyers, sellers, and investors, the national polity is eroded at its very essence: the capacity to sustain, within the country's jurisdiction, national standards of health and safety, orderly commerce, social justice, and the integrity of the national culture.

Mismatch between Ecology and Polity

It is now common knowledge that nature-altering technologies employed by humans in their pursuit of economic and political security are jeopardizing ecological conditions required for the sustenance of healthy human life on the planet. Yet human society has been dangerously slow, if not baffled, when it comes to developing political/legal instruments to effectively counter even the most serious and widely recognized ecological threats—cancer-producing sun rays flooding through the depleted ozone layer, and excessive global warming from the thickening of greenhouse gases in the atmosphere.

This new security predicament results to a large extent from the lack of sufficient correspondence between the basic political structure of world society (built on the foundation of autonomous nation-states) and the structure of the natural environment (which is unavoidably transnational in many of its dimensions). Originally formed in part to harness an area's natural ecologies, many of the world's territorially specific political jurisdictions are not at all congruent with dimensions of the ecologies now being perturbed.

Some of the most tangible and immediately visible disturbances are against natural ecologies that, while transnational in scope, are still located in particular regions of the globe. And many of these, as forecast in Chapter 17 by Thomas Homer-Dixon and Chapter 18 by Dennis Pirages, will be exacerbated over the coming decades as population growth and industrialization strain and deplete essential environmental resources. The resulting conflicts over access to and control of scarce resources are likely to be of the kind that historically have been least susceptible to noncoercive diplomatic resolution in the anarchic world polity.

To the traditional war-provoking disputes over rights to navigate, fish, or divert the waters of rivers, lakes, or seas used in common by various countries we now have added conflicts over the pouring of effluents in such bodies of water that can degrade their value for other users. Similarly, the growing awareness of how the injection of industrial by-products into the planet's other highly mobile medium—the atmosphere—can severely injure agricultural productivity, as well as cause life-threatening human illness in neighboring populations, has multiplied the opportunities for nations to get angry with one another. In addition, transborder injuries caused by mega-accidents, such as nuclear power-plant meltdowns and oil-tanker spills, further expose the inadequacy of the existing political/legal order to handle the interdependencies and mutual vulnerabilities of peoples across national lines.

Nations without States

Humans characteristically seek to secure not only their physical survival, health, and material possessions, but also a way of life—meaning, a set of beliefs about good and bad behavior, folkways, language and art forms, and religious views about their place in the universe. This typically translates into membership in a national community with others committed to essentially the same way of life, usually as a result of similar ancestral ties and historical experiences. National communities located within states whose territorial boundaries are essentially congruent with them tend to have a better chance of securing their way of life than do national communities that are minorities in states run by other national communities. Understandably, most nations would prefer to have states of their own; and throughout history, wars have been initiated by nations attempting to realize this goal against states within which they feel unjustly subordinated.

A stable world polity, in theory, would be one in which most large nations lived within their own states. Conversely, a system of presumably sovereign states characterized by a high degree of incongruence between state boundaries and the location of major nationality groups would be inherently unstable. If true, this augurs poorly for the stability of the contemporary world polity, given the wide dispersal of nationality groups across state boundaries—political demarcations that, more often than not, have been drawn by powerful multinational states for reasons of their military and economic security, largely indifferent to the desires of the peoples affected. Indeed, the notion of a stable nation-state system has turned out to be an oxymoron—and an increasingly dangerous one, conducive to neither individual security, national security, nor world security, especially given the wide dispersal of weapons of mass destruction.

Human Rights versus State Sovereignty

The efforts of many people around the world to secure for themselves and their families what are widely claimed to be their fundamental human rights—"life, liberty, and the pursuit of happiness [variously defined]"—and, in some places, certain minimum levels of economic welfare, often contradict the foundational norms of the nation-state system: the sovereignty of each country and the prohibition against intervention by foreigners in a country's internal affairs. On the one hand, we have the insistence that every human being, simply by virtue of being human, has certain basic rights vis-à-vis all other humans and that governments are created to secure these rights—in other words, all human beings are "naturally" endowed with rights, but governments and other collectivities possess merely artificial and recallable powers. On the other hand, we have the prevailing state-centric view that a stable and durable community is at least the necessary context for, if not the source of, individual human rights, and that, therefore, the existing governing institutions of the recognized national states must be respected as agencies of public order and justice and also as the legitimate authorities for arbitrating among competing human rights claims.

The debate is more than abstract and philosophical. In the years ahead, as has happened many times in history (from the French Revolution in 1789 to Tiananmen Square in 1989), the tensions between the champions of elementary human rights and the defenders of the prerogatives of established states can ignite lethal confrontations that, before they run their course, can destroy the most basic security of the individuals and communities that are drawn into the fray.

THE CONCEPT OF WORLD INTERESTS

An enhancement of norms and institutions that express the interests of *world* society is essential if the growing incongruities between the inherited state-sovereignty system and the expanding interdependence of peoples are to be kept from destroying the conditions of civilized life on the planet.[7] We can conceive of the norm-building and institution-building process as the contemporary counterpart of the process that began in earnest some three hundred years ago to rectify the incongruence between the medieval feudal polity and the emerging patterns of nationwide commerce and cultural identity. Just as in the previous era when the time had come to give national interests primacy over the interests of manor, town, parish, and mosque, so in the contemporary era the time has come to give certain world interests primacy over various national, local, religious, and special economic interests.

The challenge to contemporary political theorists is to elaborate an appropriate concept of such world interests—a concept capable of commanding wide assent among the world's peoples—that can provide a basis for controlling and arbitrating the conflicts among lesser interests (national, subnational, and transnational) that otherwise threaten to undermine the security of us all.

The conceptual framework should lay out assumptions about what is good (or bad) for the world as a whole. Just as much of the foreign and domestic policy discourse within countries assumes that there are "national interests" (meaning conditions that are desirable for the whole country viewed as an entity), there is ample reason to consider as "world interests" those conditions that are desirable for the entire planet Earth viewed as an entity.

This is not to say that everyone will agree on which interests deserve to be placed in the category of world interests that must be secured (there are, after all, continuing debates in most countries over what interests ought to be considered national interests[8]); nor will there be universal agreement on their definition, let alone on policies for implementing them. What is claimed here, as a minimum, is that there *are* world interests that have high value in their own right; that such interests, in addition to national and special interests, need to be taken into account in evaluating and managing the behavior of states and other actors in world society; and that the question of what ought to be the priority world interests is crucially important to debate.

My candidates for the highest-value world interests are listed below, rank ordered. Those that I rank highest, I contend, would also command the widest support among the world's peoples. Those lower on my list are likely to be more controversial—all the more reason, then, to present them for domestic and international debate.

1. *Survival of the human species.* Few would contest that this should be the cardinal world interest, since humankind's survival is the necessary condition for the realization of every other value (except, perhaps, salvation in the afterlife). "Survival" should be taken to mean "in a reasonably healthy condition of body and mind," so that at least the reproduction of healthy offspring can be sustained across generations.

This world interest cannot be taken for granted, however. Modern weapons of war powerful enough to jeopardize the survival of the human species are deployed around the globe; and there are no reliable guarantees against their use in a world polity where force continues to be the *ultima ratio* of who gets what, when, and how, and in which war is still widely regarded as "a continuation of politics by other means."

The survival of the species is also placed at risk by nature-altering agricultural and industrial processes capable of severely disturbing the natural balances of the Earth's biosphere that sustain human life. The life-threatening activities are undertaken by national agencies, corporations, or other special entities in the service of their particular interests, usually with no hostile intent whatsoever to others, but also with little or no reference to larger community interests. Even "external" ecological effects that are not always immediately evident or calculable can, through cumulative increments, eventually degrade or reduce the value of the entire human population's life-sustaining resources.

It is now becoming widely understood (as demonstrated by the Rio Earth Summit of 1992) that a more active assertion of this overriding world interest—through processes and institutions that compel taking it into account when more particularistic decisions are made—is needed to prevent irreversible catastrophes.

2. *Reduction in the amount of killing and other extremely brutal treatment of human beings.* Human society in most places has evolved to the point where killing and torture of one's fellows *within* the national community are generally regarded as evil and are discouraged through stringent legal penalties (except during periods of revolution or civil war), unless they can be justified by the necessity of preventing even greater amounts of killing or torture. A universal extension of the imperative of reducing physical violence to include actions that would inflict death and pain on people with whom one has no ethnic or other primordial bonds would represent a further stage in the evolution of humankind.

It is questionable, however, whether most of the world's peoples are ready to embrace the minimization-of-violence ethic a priori—as a self-evident good requiring no other justification. The existence of cauldrons of interethnic and communal violence on virtually every continent is testimony to the fact that many groups and individuals continue to give higher priority to other values, despite their governments having become parties to international covenants prohibiting genocide and torture.

Efforts to make the reduction of violence anywhere a high-priority world interest (and to give it clout in the form of well-funded and equipped world conflict-resolution and peacekeeping institutions) must rely mainly on the consequentialist argument that violence tends to feed upon itself, drawing increasing numbers of people into its contagious vortex, particularly in the contemporary world where instruments of violence with wide ranges and radii of lethal effects have fallen into many hands.

This world interest is the primary rationale for the international tribunals set up to prosecute the perpetrators of genocide in Bosnia and Rwanda, and for the deployment of United Nations peacekeeping (and "peace*making*") units into situations of intense local conflict, such as the former Yugoslavia, Cyprus, Cambodia, and Mozambique. It also underlies proposals for a permanent international criminal court and a standing UN police force.[9] And it is a central assumption of the analysis in the chapter by Margaret Karns and Karen Mingst.

3. *Provision of conditions for healthy subsistence to all people.* The elevation of this objective to the level of a world interest emanates from the fundamental ethical premise that the most basic human right is the right to live one's naturally given life (the sine qua non of all other rights)—a right that can be negated not only by physical violence but also by the denial of the requisites for human survival: uncontaminated and adequate water, food, and air; shelter against climatic extremes; and protection against disease.[10]

Basic utilitarian security considerations can also be invoked on behalf of this world interest. Some of the most lethal diseases that feed on poverty (AIDS, for example) cannot be readily quarantined, and therefore extreme poverty anywhere threatens the well-being of even those who would confine themselves to enclaves of affluence. It is also in the interest of the affluent to make good-faith efforts to ameliorate the suffering of the desperately poor, lest the latter become so alienated and angry at those better off that they organize revolutionary movements and wars to forcibly rectify the maldistribution of resources and wealth. Third World poverty has been enlarging the flow of job-seeking migrants and their families into the advanced industrial countries, producing in turn a wave of ugly nationalistic and xenophobic backlashes, particularly in Western Europe, among middle-class workers fearful of losing their jobs. Moreover, a situation of chronic political alienation and instability in the poor countries, even if confined primarily to the Third World, can threaten the economic security of the more-affluent countries and communities. Major manufacturing and marketing sectors of the economies of the United States, Japan, and the European Union are crucially dependent upon stable commercial relationships with a wide array of developing countries.

Finally, countries convulsed and consumed by the misery of their desperately impoverished populations are unlikely to be willing partners in the international cooperative projects required to sustain the world's essential ecological systems.

4. *Protection of citizen rights.* This world interest embraces the exercise by individuals of the standard civil, political, and economic rights—in addition to survival and basic subsistence—now claimed by persons all around the world simply by virtue of being human. To elevate the protection of such citizen rights to a world interest, even though ranked fourth, is to take issue with the traditional normative basis of the nation-state system that puts a higher value on the sovereign autonomy of the recognized nation-states than on the rights of individuals vis-à-vis one another or vis-à-vis governments. It also thereby challenges the associated rule against interference by outsiders in the domestic affairs of countries.

Even though moral philosophers continue to debate whether the rights of individuals ought to take precedence over the imperatives of community, the universalization of the claim to basic participatory citizenship is now an unavoidable fact of life. Global security, national security, and individual security require that national governments and international agencies be responsive to this claim, for a major source of violence within countries and international military interventions in the contemporary world is the failure by governing elites to base their policies on the uncoerced consent of the governed. The particular means for assuring that governments are accountable to their citizenry will, of course, vary from country to country, but governments and ruling elites ignore this requirement for durable domestic peace at their peril, and ultimately to the peril of a peaceful world order.

5. *Preservation of cultural diversity.* Lower on this list, but nonetheless a world interest deserving of great respect, is the right of peoples to practice and experiment with different ways of life and societal organization. It is in the interest of humankind as a whole that this basic right not be sacrificed in the pursuit of what some might see as the security imperative of a centralized and unitary world state or the moral imperative of a totally open, borderless world society.

The human species—only recently evolved, and still evolving as nature and human volition select the traits worth preserving—has yet to find *the* form of polity most conducive to the realization of basic human needs and wants. This argues for maintaining considerable political pluralism and decentralization in the world system; then, even if those in control of particular states repress the minorities in their midst, the repressed minorities have the possibility of migrating to another state where they will be better treated, or perhaps even constitute the majority culture. Decentralization of the polity in the service of cultural pluralism remains not only a stimulus to creativity but also a crucial safety valve for world society, allowing for the deflation of dangerously combustible domestic situations that otherwise could lead to a full-scale civil war and international intervention on behalf of the warring parties.

6. *Preservation of the planet's basic natural ecologies and environment.* In addition to the self-evident world interest in protecting those biospheric conditions required for the sustenance of human life on earth, there is good reason for humans to respect, if not stand in awe of, nature's givens. We are still very primitive in our understandings of the connections in the universe—what causes what, both concretely and transcendentally in space and time—and therefore ought to be highly reluctant to cause changes in the natural order (or disorder).

The objective, accordingly, should be to preserve as much of the basic natural environment as possible without crucially sacrificing other, higher priority, world interests; and vice versa, to serve the other world interests while minimizing any probable damage to important natural conditions of the known universe.

7. *Enhancement of accountability.* These world-interest imperatives are likely to remain largely unrealized statements of principle unless authority to facilitate their implementation is lodged in appropriate agencies. This returns us to the central structural deficiency of the nation-state system: the incongruence between its dominant institutions of governance and many of the most dynamic interactions of peoples. Even with widespread assent on the substance of what the world interest demands in a particular field, the lack of public accountability by states or private actors for harms they inflict on people across national borders means that the traditional business-as-usual avoidance of responsibility for the well-being of humankind will persist, and the "realist" prognosis will be vindicated.

Being a necessary means for giving flesh and blood to the concept of world interests, international accountability itself deserves to be championed as a high-priority world interest. Such accountability, as pointed out by Robert Johansen in Chapter 19, needs to be elaborated in "horizontal" (transborder) and "vertical" (democratic representation) dimensions. Consistent with Johansen's recommendations, I offer the following principle for determining the appropriate locus and functions of institutions along both of these dimensions: *Those who can or do substantially affect the security or well-being of others (especially by inflicting harm) are assumed to be accountable to those they can or do affect.*

Morally appropriate and politically feasible accountability arrangements will inevitably range across a wide spectrum of configurations—from ad hoc meetings between those who can affect one another (meetings in which information and/or threats are exchanged and/or behavioral adjustments are negotiated, after which the parties go home) to permanently sitting decision-making institutions. The configuration of such institutional arrangements will also vary with respect to the *degree* of accountability members are willing to accept, ranging from the most minimal of obligations to keep the affected or potentially affected informed of what is being (or will be) done to them, to enforceable agreements not to act without the approval of the affected parties.

Fortunately, we need not start from totally unprepared ground in attempting to build such accountability relationships into the world system. Rudimentary accountability relationships already exist in the fields of arms control, international commerce, environmental management, international transportation and communications, and human rights—serving as a scaffolding, as it were, on which more elaborate structures can be built to meet emerging needs. Although progress has been slow, the countries of the European Union, by fits and starts, but nonetheless inexorably, have been leading the way in constructing such accountability regimes congruent with their thickening day-to-day interactions—both interstate and intersectoral.

Nor is the academic discipline of international relations entirely fallow with respect to what Johansen and I call accountability. A considerable amount of fruitful empirical and conceptual work during the past two decades has been devoted to understanding the proliferation of global and regional "regimes" for coordinating trade, monetary affairs, banking, communications, and transportation, and the management of the commons (oceans and seas, rivers, the atmosphere, and outer space). Concentrated mainly among scholars in the subfield of international political economy, however, the analysis of regime formation and maintenance, with a few notable exceptions, has not significantly engaged the energies of scholars whose province has been "security affairs" as traditionally defined.[11] But in the words of a song by the troubadour Bob Dylan, "The times, they are a-changin'."

THE EXPANSION OF SECURITY

The field of "security studies," having come of age in the United States in the late 1940s at the start of the Cold War, relegated international organizations, international law, and universal collective security to the back burner. For nearly four decades, most foreign policy officials and scholars, to the extent that they did concern themselves with world security, tended to regard what was good for the security of the United States as good for the world. If there *were* world interests, they were derivative of national interests—the conceit of "nationalistic universalism" that enlightened "realists" like Hans Morgenthau warned against, and which persists, even today, in some of the Pax Americana premises of U.S. policy.

But as the incongruities of the state-centric system of world politics have become increasingly evident to officials, laypersons, and scholars alike, the need for a broader and deeper basis for securing the safety and well-being of peoples has begun to be more widely recognized.

The chapters in this book are part of the current of scholarship and writing—rapidly becoming mainstream—that has been expanding the definition of security. This thinking challenges the notion that the pursuit of the country's national interests, as narrowly defined by the "realists," is essentially the only obligation of the statesperson, and that such putative world interests as may exist are in any case best serviced as a by-product of statespersons rationally pursuing their national interests.[12] The post-"realist" analysis shows that more often than not the opposite is true: The securing of world interests of the kind outlined above is the necessary condition for maintaining many of the national and special interests that continue to be highly valued.

The broadening of views about *whose* interests are to be secured is complimented by an enlargement of the definition of *what* interests are the legitimate domain of world security policy. My outline of world interests reflects this growing awareness that whatever the scope of the polity—city, province, country, the entire planet—the fundamental human interests that deserve to be accommodated and reliably secured include not only physical safety and minimum public order, but also economic subsistence and basic health of the population (which implies a sustainable ecological environment), individual civic and property rights, and opportunities for cultural and religious communities to develop their own ways of life.

World security policy thus breaks out of the confines of "geopolitics" and its focus on military balances of power, alliance relationships, and traditional "collective security" measures. Its expanded definition encompasses economics as well as politics, cultural as well as material values, ethical altruism as well as amoral self-interest, and nongovernmental actors as well as states.

Those who choose to work in this field—in the arenas of either policy or scholarship—must be prepared, more than their predecessors, to deal with the complexities of world society.

QUESTIONS FOR FURTHER STUDY

1. Why does Brown believe that the "realist" approach to international relations has become "largely irrelevant to policy discourse"?
2. Why does Brown believe that the nation-state system is dangerously out of sync with the realities of contemporary world society? Is his argument persuasive?
3. What does Brown mean by "world interests"? Are world interests likely to supplant national interests in setting U.S. foreign policy objectives?
4. Brown lists seven basic "world interests" that he believes should govern international relations. Are these seven truly the most important world interests? Should other interests be added, or any of Brown's seven be excluded?

Notes

1. I use quotation marks around the terms "realist" and "realism" throughout this essay to remind the reader that those adhering to this school of thought are simply making a *claim* of realism, which, according to my lights, is not sufficiently merited.

2. The most influential recent exposition of international relations "realism" is Kenneth N. Waltz's *Theory of International Politics* (Reading, MA: Addison-Wesley, 1979). Waltz

attributes the behavioral characteristics of states to the anarchic structure of the international system, and for that reason calls his theory "structural realism." Waltz's progenitor (often called the father of modern "realism") was Hans J. Morgenthau, whose seminal treatise *Politics Among Nations: The Struggle for Power and Peace* (New York: Alfred A. Knopf, 1954), also gave determinative weight to international anarchy; but Morgenthau, like the philosopher Thomas Hobbes, located the source of the anarchic world polity in the human animal's "lust for power." Domestically suppressed in the modern nation-state, this power drive, Morgenthau taught, was projected into the international arena where, given the holocaust potential of modern weapons, it would lead to the destruction of the human species unless (again echoing Hobbes) it could be disciplined by a centralized world government—a development that presumed the prior development of a genuine world community (which Morgenthau considered highly unlikely). For an analysis of the larger corpus of "realism," of which Waltz and Morgenthau are only partial expressions, see Michael Joseph Smith, *Realist Thought from Weber to Kissinger* (Baton Rouge: Louisiana State University Press, 1986). See also David Baldwin, ed., *Neorealism and Neoliberalism: The Contemporary Debate* (New York: Columbia University Press, 1993).

3. A similar (but considerably more detailed) criticism of the "realist's" failure to capture the complexity of contemporary world politics is provided in James Rosenau's *Turbulence in World Politics: A Theory of Change and Continuity* (Princeton: Princeton University Press, 1990). See especially his Chapter 2: "Justifying Jailbreaks: The Limits of Contemporary Concepts and Methods."

4. This section draws on Chapter 7 of my *International Relations in a Changing Global System: Toward a Theory of the World Polity* (Boulder: Westview Press, 1997), pp. 107–118.

5. For an analysis of the expanded range of international and transnational public-order problems characteristic of the post-Cold War era, particularly the increasing salience of "North-South" (rich vs. poor) issues, see Donald M. Snow, *Distant Thunder: Third World Conflict and the New International Order* (New York: St. Martin's Press, 1993).

6. Robert B. Reich, *The Work of Nations: Preparing Ourselves for 21st-Century Capitalism* (New York: Alfred A. Knopf, 1991), pp. 87–135.

7. This section draws on Chapter 8 of my *International Relations in a Changing Global System*, pp. 121–129.

8. An excellent discussion of the problem of achieving agreement in the U.S. policy community on the nature of the country's national interests is provided by Alexander L. George and Robert O. Keohane, "The Concept of National Interests: Uses and Limitations," in Alexander L. George, *Presidential Decisionmaking in Foreign Policy: The Effective Use of Information and Advice* (Boulder: Westview Press, 1980), pp. 217–237.

9. See Boutros Boutros-Ghali, *An Agenda for Peace: Preventive Diplomacy, Peacemaking and Peace-keeping* (New York: United Nations, 1992).

10. The argument that subsistence is a basic human right equal to the right to life itself is made persuasively by Henry Shue, *Basic Rights: Subsistence, Affluence, and U.S. Foreign Policy* (Princeton: Princeton University Press, 1997).

11. The "regime" literature in the field of international political economy is well represented in Stephen D. Krasner, ed., *International Regimes* (Ithaca: Cornell University Press, 1983). Concerns about ecological management are also generating important studies on the development and operation of international regimes, such as Peter M. Haas, *Saving the Mediterranean: The Politics of International Environmental Cooperation* (New York: Columbia University Press, 1990); and Oran R. Young, *International Cooperation: Building Regimes for Natural Resources and the Environment* (Ithaca: Cornell University Press, 1989). Mainline "security affairs" specialists who have contributed prominently to the "regime" literature include Robert Jervis, the contributor of an essay on "Security Regimes" to the Krasner volume; Joseph Nye, co-author with Robert Keohane (a leading international political economy theorist) of *Power and Interdependence: World Politics in Transition* (Boston: Little, Brown, 1977); and Robert M. Axelrod, whose *The Evolution of Cooperation* (New York: Basic Books, 1984) applies game-theoretic analysis to the explanation of how enemies can learn to escape from mutually destructive patterns of behavior and regularize patterns of cooperation.

12. A foreshadowing of how mainstream international relations thinking would soon be moving is found in Stanley Hoffmann's *Duties Beyond Borders: On the Limits and Possibilities of Ethical International Politics* (Syracuse: Syracuse University Press, 1981).

2 / The Dynamism of a Turbulent World

JAMES N. ROSENAU

While there is no dearth of indicators that highlight the many ways world politics is marked by continuity, it is hardly less difficult to demonstrate that huge changes have been at work in the global system, changes that are of sufficient magnitude to suggest the emergence of new global structures, processes, and patterns.[1] The seemingly daily occurrence of unexpected developments and the numerous uncertainties that prevail in every region, if not every country, of the world are so pervasive as to cast doubt on the viability of the long-established ways in which international affairs have been conducted. It almost seems as if the anomalous event has replaced the recurrent pattern as the central tendency in world politics.

That a deep sense of uncertainty should pervade world affairs since the end of the Cold War is hardly surprising. The U.S.-Soviet rivalry, for all its tensions and susceptibility to collapsing into nuclear holocaust, intruded a stability into the course of events that was comprehensible, reliable, and continuous. The enemy was known. The challenges were clear. The dangers seemed obvious. The appropriate responses could readily be calculated. Quite the opposite is the case today, however. If there are enemies to be contested, challenges to meet, dangers to avoid, and responses to be launched, we are far from sure what they are. So uncertainty is the norm and apprehension the mood. The sweet moments when the wall came down in Berlin, apartheid ended in South Africa, and an aggression was set back in Kuwait seem like fleeting and remote fantasies as the alleged post-Cold War world order has emerged as anything but orderly. Whatever may be the arrangements that have replaced the bipolarity of U.S.-Soviet rivalry, they are at best incipient structures and, at worst, simply widespread disarray.

Put differently, a new epoch is evolving. It is an epoch of multiple contradictions: The international system is less dominant, but it is still powerful. States are changing, but they are not disappearing. State sovereignty has eroded, but it is still vigorously asserted. Governments are weaker, but they can still throw their weight around. At times publics are more demanding, but at other times they are more compliant. Borders still keep out intruders, but they are also more porous. Landscapes are giving way to ethnoscapes, mediascapes, ideoscapes, technoscapes, and finanscapes, but territoriality is still a central preoccupation for many people.[2]

Sorting out these contradictions raises difficult questions: How do we assess a world pervaded with ambiguities? How do we begin to grasp a political space that is continuously shifting, widening and narrowing, simultaneously undergoing erosion with respect to many issues and reinforcement with respect to other issues? How do we reconceptualize politics so as to trace the new or transformed authorities that occupy the new political spaces created by shifting and porous boundaries?[3]

The cogency of such questions—and the uncertainty they generate—reinforce the conviction that we are deeply immersed in an epochal transformation sustained by a new worldview about the essential nature of human affairs, and a new way of thinking about how global politics unfold. At the center of the emergent worldview lies an understanding that the order which sustains families, communities, countries, and the world through time rests on contradictions, ambiguities, and uncertainties. Whereas earlier epochs were conceived in terms of central tendencies and orderly patterns, the present epoch appears to derive its order from contrary trends and episodic patterns. Whereas the lives of individuals and societies were once seen as moving along linear and steady trajectories, now their movement seems nonlinear and erratic, with equilibrium being momentary and continuously punctuated by sudden accelerations or directional shifts.

Accordingly, the long-standing inclination to think in either/or terms has begun to give way to framing challenges as both/and problems. People now understand, emotionally as well as intellectually, that unexpected events are commonplace, that anomalies are normal occurrences, that minor incidents can mushroom into major outcomes, that fundamental processes trigger opposing forces even as they expand their scope, that what was once transitional may now be enduring, and that the complexities of modern life are so deeply rooted as to infuse ordinariness into the surprising development and the anxieties that attach to it.

To understand that the emergent order is rooted in contradictions and ambiguities, of course, is not to lessen the sense of uncertainty as to where world affairs are headed and how the course of events is likely to impinge on personal affairs. Indeed, the more one appreciates the contradictions and accepts the ambiguities, the greater will be the uncertainty one experiences. And the uncertainty is bound to intensify the more one ponders the multiplicity of reasons why the end of the Cold War has been accompanied by pervasive instabilities. Clearly, the absence of a superpower rivalry is not the only source of complexity. Technological dynamics are also major stimulants, as are the breakdown of trust, the shrinking of distances, the globalization of economies, the explosive proliferation of organizations, the information revolution, the fragmentation of groups, the integration of regions, the surge of democratic practices, the spread of fundamentalism, the cessation of intense enmities, and the revival of historic animosities—all of which in turn provoke further reactions that add to the complexity and heighten the sense that the uncertainty has become an enduring way of life.

This is not the place to enumerate the many anomalous developments that underlie the pervasive uncertainties and rapid changes, but it is useful to recall the utter surprise that greeted the abrupt end of the Cold War. Pundits, professors, politicians, and others conversant with world politics were literally stunned, with none claiming to have anticipated it and all admitting to ad hoc explanations. Since the sudden collapse of the communist world culminated dynamics that had been subtly at work for a long time, the intensity and breadth of the surprise it evoked can only be viewed as a measure of the extent to which our understandings of world politics have lagged behind the deep transformations that are altering the global landscape.[4] Signs of profound transformation appeared well before the end of the Cold War, but only when a series of events late in 1989 manifestly transformed Eastern Europe did attention focus on the presence of powerful agents of change.[5]

But how do we account for the accelerating pace of change? What dynamics fostered and are still sustaining the profound processes that are transforming life at all levels of community? And which dynamics are especially geared to generating change at those levels that extend beyond the boundaries of societies and states? Even more specifically, how do individuals contribute to the pace, scope, and rapidity of global transformations? Indeed, since world politics is usually conceived to be about the conduct of states and other large collectivities, how is it possible to delineate a meaningful role that individuals other than leaders play in the course of events? The ensuing analysis provides a brief overview of a line of reasoning that offers answers to such questions.

TURBULENCE IN WORLD POLITICS

In order to assess some of the major ways in which individuals may contribute to the ongoing processes of global transformation, it is useful first to identify the larger context in which these contributions can be made. This context is elaborated at length elsewhere,[6] but even this summary of the main transformative sources of our turbulent times suggests there are many subtle ways in which people everywhere are playing a crucial role in the change dynamics.

As is the case for any human system, the parameters of the global system serve as the sources of constancy, as boundary conditions within which variations may occur, but never so greatly as to alter the underlying structures of the system. However, at rare moments in history the system's parameters undergo enormous stress and change. In effect, they become variables until such time as new boundary conditions emerge. Such is the case late in the twentieth century. The prime parameters that have long bound and sustained world affairs have been overcome by high degrees of complexity and dynamism—that is, the global stage is now occupied by increasingly numerous, interdependent, and volatile actors—a condition that has moved world politics into a highly turbulent state.[7]

In attempting to analyze this turbulence, three parameters may be considered primary: the distribution of power in world politics, according to which states, international organizations, and other key actors respond to each other (a macroparameter); authority relationships, through which governments, multinational corporations, ethnic groups, and other large collectivities are linked to individual citizens (a macro-microparameter); and the analytical and emotional skills citizens possess, through which they respond to the course of events (a microparameter). All three parameters are presently undergoing substantial expansion in their complexity and dynamism, thus leading to the conclusion that the world order is presently experiencing its first period of turbulence since the birth of the state system some 350 years ago. Perhaps more to the point, the relative simultaneity that marks the impact of much greater complexity and dynamism on all three parameters has given rise to what might well be the central characteristic of world politics today, namely, persistent tension between opposing tendencies toward fragmentation and integration. I have called this phenomenon "fragmegration," a term that is perhaps grating but that captures well the interactive and causal links between the globalizing and localizing forces that are altering the underlying structures of world affairs.[8] As will be seen, these interactive "fragmegrative" tensions are especially evident in the transformation of each of the three prime parameters.

Incisive insights into the turbulence of world politics depend on an appreciation of the continuing overlap among the three parameters—on recognizing that even as individuals shape the actions and orientations of the collectivities to which they belong, so the goals, policies, and laws of the latter shape the actions and orientations of individuals. Out of such interactions a network of interdependence is fashioned that is so intermeshed as to make it difficult to separate causes from effects. Indeed, much of the rapidity of the transformations at work in world politics can be traced to the ways in which the changes in each parameter stimulate and reinforce the changes in the other two.

A Skill Revolution

The transformation of the microparameter lies in the shifting capabilities of citizens everywhere. Individuals have undergone a skill revolution. For a variety of reasons—ranging from the advance of communications technology to the greater intricacies of life in an ever more interdependent world—people have become increasingly more competent in assessing where they fit in international affairs and how their behavior can be aggregated into significant collective outcomes.

Put differently, it is an error to assume that citizenries are a constant in politics, that the world has changed rapidly and its complexity increased greatly without consequences for individuals everywhere. As long as people were uninvolved in and apathetic about world affairs, it made sense to look at the macro level for explanations of events in world politics. Today, however, the skill revolution has expanded the learning capacity of individuals, enriched their cognitive maps, and elaborated the scenarios that they anticipate for the future. It is no accident that late in the twentieth century the public squares of the world's cities have been filled with large crowds demanding change.

It is tempting to affirm the impact of the skill revolution by pointing to the many restless publics that have protested authoritarian rule and clamored for more democratic forms of governance. While the worldwide thrust toward an expansion of political liberties and a diminution in the central control of economies is certainly linked to citizens and publics having greater appreciation of their circumstances and rights, there is nothing inherent in the skill revolution that leads people in more democratic directions. The change in the microparameter is not so much one of new orientations as it is an evolution of new capacities. The world's peoples are not so much converging around the same values as they are sharing a greater ability to recognize and articulate their values. This change is global in scope; it enables Islamic fundamentalists, Asian peasants, and Western sophisticates alike to better serve their respective orientations. Thus, the convergence of protesters in public squares has not been confined to cities in any particular region of the world. From Seoul to Prague, from Soweto to Beijing, from Paris to the West Bank, from Belgrade to Yangon (Rangoon), from Hong Kong to Toronto, the transformation of the microparameter has been unmistakably evident.

Equally important, evidence of the skill revolution can be readily discerned by looking at trends in education, television viewing, computer usage, travel, and a host of other situations in which people employ their analytic and emotional skills. And hardly less relevant, a number of local circumstances—from traffic jams to water shortages, from budget crises to racial conflicts, from flows of refugees to threats of terrorism—people are relentlessly confronted with social, economic, and political complexities that impel them to forego simplistic premises and replace them with more elaborate conceptions of how to respond to the challenges of daily life.

This is not to say to that people everywhere are now equal in the skills they bring to bear on world politics. Obviously, the analytically rich continue to be more skillful than the analytically poor. But while the gap between the two ends of the skill continuum may be no narrower than in the past, the advance in the competencies of those at every point on the continuum is sufficient to contribute to a major transformation in the conduct of world affairs. More important for present purposes, the skill revolution highlights the extent to which scientific and technological advances have facilitated new opportunities for citizens to extend their influence—if they seize them.

Let us be more precise as to the foundations of the skill revolution. It consists of two dimensions: analytic skills and emotional skills. The former springs from a growing ability to construct scenarios as to how distant events feed back into people's pocketbooks and living rooms, while the latter involves a deepening capacity for focusing emotions and making judgments as to whether the scenarios are to be welcomed or feared. It follows that the skill revolution does not necessarily entail an increase in information. It is perfectly possible to be well informed and lacking in analytic and emotional skills, just as wise Vermont farmers or Asian peasants can grasp where they fit in the course of events even if they do not possess extensive and up-to-date information about what is happening. People may not know, for example, the name of the capital of Pakistan even though they understand that an upheaval in that country may have consequences that can circuitously feed back and affect their well-being. Stated differently, the skill revolution derives from an extension of people's working knowledge, from an elaboration of understanding that is not so much memorized or calculated as it is intuitively grasped. In sum, and to use a colloquial phrase, it is a revolution that derives as much from an enlargement of "street smarts" as from an advance in detailed information.

A Relocation of Authority

The macro-microparameter consists of the orientations, practices, and patterns through which citizens at the micro level are linked to their collectivities at the macro level. In effect, it encompasses the authority structures whereby large aggregations—private organizations as well as public agencies—achieve and sustain the cooperation and compliance of their memberships. Historically, these authority structures have been founded on traditional criteria of legitimacy, derived from constitutional and legal sources: individuals were habituated to comply with the directives issued by higher authorities. People did what they were told to do simply because it was expected. As a result, authority structures remained in place for decades, even centuries, as people tended to yield unquestioningly to the dictates of governments or the leadership of any other organizations with which they were affiliated.

For a variety of reasons, including the expanded analytic skills of citizens, the foundations of this parameter have been eroded. Throughout the world today, in both public and private settings, the sources of authority have shifted from traditional to performance criteria of legitimacy. Where the structures of authority were once stable, in other words, they are now in crisis, with the readiness of individuals to comply with governing directives very much a function of their assessment of the performances of the authorities. The more the authorities' performance record is considered appropriate by citizens—in terms of satisfying needs, moving toward goals, and providing stability—the more they are likely to cooperate and comply. The less they approve of the performance record, the more they are likely to withhold their compliance or otherwise complicate the efforts of the authorities.

As a consequence of the pervasive authority crises, states and governments have become less effective in confronting challenges and implementing policies. They can still maintain public order through their police powers, but their ability to address substantive issues and solve substantive problems is declining as people find fault with their performances and thus question their authority, redefine the bases of their legitimacy, and withhold their cooperation. Such a transformation is being played out dramatically today in Russia, as it did only a few years earlier within all the countries of Eastern Europe. But authority crises in the former communist world are only the more obvious instances of this newly emergent pattern. It is equally evident in every other part of the world, albeit taking different forms in different countries and among different types of private organizations. In

Canada the authority crisis is rooted in linguistic, cultural, and constitutional issues, as Quebec seeks to secede or otherwise redefine its relationship to the central government. In France the devolution of authority has been legally sanctioned through legislation that privatized several governmental activities and relocated authority away from Paris and toward greater jurisdiction for the provinces. In China the provinces enjoy wider jurisdiction by, in effect, ignoring or defying Beijing. In Yugoslavia a devolution crisis led to violence and civil war. In countries of Latin America the challenge to traditional authority originates with insurgent movements or the drug trade. And in those parts of the world where the shift to performance criteria of legitimacy has not resulted in the relocation of authority, uneasy stalemates prevail in the form of either slim majorities or, more frequently, divided governments. The United States, Israel, Italy, and Japan are but the more obvious examples of governments immersed in continuing policy stalemates and, sometimes, in paralysis. Viewed in this way, it is less surprising that the U.S. government closed down twice late in 1995.

Nor are global authority crises confined to states and governments. They are also manifest in subnational jurisdictions, international organizations, and nongovernmental transnational entities. Indeed, in some cases the crises unfold simultaneously at different levels. For example, when the issue of Quebec's place in Canada became paramount, the Mohawks in Quebec also pressed for their own autonomy. Similarly, just as Moldava rejected Moscow's authority, so did several ethnic groups within Moldava seek to establish their own autonomy by rejecting Moldava's authority. And among international and transnational organizations, UNESCO, the PLO, and the Roman Catholic Church have all experienced decentralizing dynamics that are at least partly rooted in the replacement of traditional with performance criteria of legitimacy.

The relocation of authority occurs in several directions. In many instances, it has involved a "downward" relocation toward subnational groups—notably ethnic minorities, local governments, single-issue organizations, religious and linguistic groupings, political factions, trade unions, and the like. In some cases the relocation process has moved "upward" toward more encompassing collectivities that transcend national boundaries. The beneficiaries of this upward relocation of authority range from supranational organizations like the European Union to intergovernmental organizations like the International Labor Organization, nongovernmental organizations like Greenpeace, professional groups such as Doctors Without Borders, multinational corporations like IBM, and inchoate transnational social movements such as those concerned with environmental protection or women's rights. These upward and downward relocations reinforce the "fragmegrative" tensions that underlie the turbulence presently at work in world politics.

Associated with these crises is an undermining of the principle of national sovereignty. To challenge the authority of the state and then to redirect legitimacy sentiments toward supranational or subnational collectivities is to begin to deny that states have the right to resort to force. Since authority is layered such that many levels of governance may have autonomy within their jurisdictions, there is no one-to-one relationship between the location of authority and sovereignty. Nevertheless, trends toward the relocation of authority are bound to contribute to the erosion of sovereignty. If a state is thwarted in its efforts to mobilize effective armed forces, then its sovereignty is hardly a conspicuous feature of its existence as an independent collectivity. If it cannot prevent one of its subjurisdictions from seceding, then the reach of its sovereignty is certainly reduced.

It is useful to note that the undermining of the sovereignty principle began with its redefinition during the decolonizing processes of the former European empires after World War II, processes that "amounted to nothing less than an international revolution . . . in which traditional assumptions about the right to sovereign statehood were turned upside down."[9] In using self-determination as the sole criterion for statehood—irrespective of whether a former colony had the consensual foundations and resources to govern—a number of sovereign states were created, recognized, and admitted to the UN even though they were unable to develop economically and manage their internal affairs without external assistance. Thus, sovereignty often seemed to be less a source of independence than an invitation to interdependence.

A Bifurcation of Global Structures

For some three centuries the overall structure of world politics—the macroparameter—has been founded on an anarchic system of sovereign nation-states that did not have to answer to any higher authority and that managed conflict through accommodation or war. States were not the only actors on the world stage, but traditionally they were the dominant collectivities that set the rules. The resulting state-centric world evolved its own hierarchy based on the distribution of military, economic, and political power. Depending on how many states had the greatest concentration of power, at different historical moments the overall system was varyingly marked by hegemonic, bipolar, or multipolar structures.

Today the state-centric world no longer predominates. The skill revolution, the worldwide authority crises, and other sources of turbulence (noted below), have led to a bifurcation of the international system into two global structures, one the long-standing state-centric world of sovereign states and the other a complex multi-centric world of diverse, relatively autonomous actors replete with structures, processes, and rules of their own. The sovereignty-free actors of the multi-centric world consist of multinational corporations, ethnic minorities, subnational governments and bureaucracies, professional societies, political parties, transnational organizations, and the like. Individually, and sometimes jointly, they compete, conflict, cooperate, or otherwise interact with the sovereignty-bound actors of the state-centric world. Table 2.1 delineates the main differences between the multi-centric and state-centric worlds.

Table 2.1 / Structure and Process in the Two Worlds of World Politics

	State-Centric World	Multi-Centric World
Number of essential actors	Fewer than 200	Hundreds of thousands
Prime dilemma of actors	Security	Autonomy
Principal goals of actors	Preservation of territorial integrity, physical security	Increase in world market shares, maintenance of integration of subsystems
Ultimate resort for realizing goals	Armed force	Withholding of cooperation or compliance
Normative priorities	Processes, especially those that preserve sovereignty and the rule of law	Outcomes, especially those that expand human rights, justice, and wealth
Modes of collaboration	Formal alliances whenever possible	Temporary coalitions
Rules governing interactions among actors	Diplomatic practices	Ad hoc, situational
Distribution of power among actors	Hierarchical by amount of power	Relative equality as far as initiating action is concerned
Locus of leadership	Great powers	Innovative actors with extensive resources
Institutionalization	Well established	Emergent
Susceptibility to change	Relatively low	Relatively high
Control over outcomes	Concentrated	Diffused
Bases of decisional structures	Formal authority, law	Various types of authority, effective leadership

Source: Reproduced from James N. Rosenau, *Turbulence in World Politics: A Theory of Change and Continuity* (Princeton: Princeton University Press, 1990), p. 250.

In sum, although the bifurcation of world politics has not pushed states to the edge of the global stage, they are no longer the only key actors. Now they are faced with the new task of coping with disparate rivals from another (multi-centric) world as well as the challenges posed by counterparts in their own (state-centric) world.

SOURCES OF GLOBAL TURBULENCE

Thus far we have defined turbulence and indicated the sites at which its consequences are likely to be most extensive and enduring, but we have not accounted for the dynamics that underlie the parametric transformations. What drives the turbulence? Although a variety of factors have contributed to its onset, several are particularly salient. Some are external to the processes of world politics and some are internal. Together they go a long way toward explaining why what once seemed so anomalous now appears so patterned.

Proliferation of Actors

The world's population exceeded 2.5 billion in 1950; it is more than 5 billion today and is projected to reach 8 billion by 2025. This demographic explosion lies at the heart of many of the world's problems and is also a continual source of the complexity and dynamism that has overwhelmed the parameters of the global system. Ever greater numbers of people have exerted pressure for technological innovations. They have meant larger, more articulate, and increasingly unwieldy publics. They have contributed to the unmanageability of public affairs that has weakened states, stimulated the search for more responsive collectivities, and hastened the advent of paralyzing authority crises. And through the sheer weight of numbers, the population explosion has created new and intractable public issues, of which famines and threats to the environment are only the more conspicuous examples.

But the proliferation of relevant actors is not confined to people. No less important has been the vast increase in the number and types of collective actors whose leaders can clamber onto the global stage and act on behalf of their memberships. Indeed, to note that the mounting complexity of world affairs springs in part from the deepening density of the global system is to stress not so much the unorganized complexity fostered by the population explosion as it is to refer to an organized complexity consisting of millions of factions, associations, parties, organizations, movements, and interest groups that share an aspiration to advance their welfare and a sensitivity to the ways in which a rapidly changing world may require them to network with each other.

The dizzying increase in the density of actors that sustain world politics stems from a variety of sources. In part it is a product of the trend toward ever greater specialization—the hallmark of industrial and post-industrial economies—and the greater interdependence these economies foster. In part it stems from worldwide concerns about the environment and efforts in communities everywhere to mobilize publics to meet ecological challenges. In part, too, it is a consequence of widespread dissatisfaction with large-scale collectivities and the performance of existing authorities, a discontent that underlies the turn to less encompassing organizations that are more fully expressive of immediate needs and wants.

Impact of Dynamic Technologies

Just as population growth has led to the crowding of geographic space, technological development has fostered the narrowing of social and political space: travel times have been shortened, social distances have been narrowed, and economic barriers have been circumvented. And as people have thus become more interdependent, enormous consequences have followed for the skills of individuals, the conduct of their relations with higher authorities, and the viability of their collectivities. In short, it is highly doubtful whether world politics would have been overtaken by turbulence without the explosion of innumerable technologies.

The nuclear and communications revolutions stand out as especially relevant. The extraordinary advances in military weaponry after World War II, marked by nuclear warheads and the rocketry to deliver them, reduced the probability of a major global war. The nuclear revolution thus had the ironic consequence of depriving states of one of their prime instruments for pursuing and defending their interests. To be sure, the arms race and events like the Cuban missile crisis infused this context with a high degree of volatility that often made it seem fragile. Nevertheless, even as the nuclear context emphasized the extraordinary capacities several states had acquired, it also pointed up the limits of state action and thereby opened the door for challenges to state authority. It is no accident that as states added substantially to their nuclear arsenals, a series of transnational, large-scale, and powerful social movements—in the realms of peace, ecology, and women's rights—acquired momentum and posed serious challenges to governments.

The communications revolution is equally central as a source of global turbulence. The rapidity and clarity with which ideas and information now circulate through television, VCRs, the Internet, fax machines, satellite hook-ups, fiber-optic telephone circuits, and many other microelectronic devices have rendered national boundaries ever more porous and world politics ever more vulnerable to cascading demands. Today the whole world, its leaders and its citizenries, instantaneously share the same pictures and descriptions (albeit not necessarily the same understandings) of what is occurring in any situation.

Examples of the cascading impact of science and technology through the communications revolution abound. Most conspicuous perhaps is the influence of the Cable News Network (CNN), which is said to be continuously watched in every embassy and every foreign office of every country in the world and which served as the bases for diplomatic and military action on both sides of the conflict during the Gulf War. No less telling is the example of the French journal, *Actuel,* which reacted to the crackdown in Tiananmen Square by compiling a mock edition of the *People's Daily* containing numerous accounts the Chinese leadership did not want their people to read, and sending it to every fax machine in China in the fall of 1989.[10] Or consider the far-reaching implications of the fact that whereas only 5 percent of Brazil's households had television sets when its 1960 presidential election was held, this figure had swollen to 72 percent at the time of the next presidential contest in 1989.

Given the magnitude of the changes the communications revolution has wrought, it is not surprising that people everywhere have become more skillful, more ready to challenge authority, and more capable of engaging in collective actions to press their demands. Their information may be skewed and their understanding of what is at stake in situations may be loaded with bias, but the stimuli to action are now ever present. Today individuals can literally see how the participation of their counterparts elsewhere can have meaningful consequences. Likewise, the availability of high-tech communications equipment has enabled leaders in the public and private sectors to turn quickly to their memberships and mobilize them.

The Globalization of National Economies

If the communications revolution has been a prime stimulus of tendencies toward *decentralization* through the empowering of citizens and subnational groups, the dynamics at work in the economics realm are equally powerful as sources of *centralizing* tendencies. Starting in the most technologically advanced sectors of the global economy, a new kind of production organization—geared to limited orders for a variety of specialized markets—began to replace the large plants that produced standardized goods. Consequently, businesses began to restructure capital to be more effective in world markets. And as capital became increasingly internationalized, groups of producers and plants in different countries became linked in order to supply markets in many countries. This process fostered and sustained a financial system global in scope and centered in major cities such as New York, Tokyo, and London.

In short, capital, production, labor, and markets have been globalized and are deeply enmeshed in networks of the world economy that have superseded the traditional political jurisdictions of the state. Such a transformation was bound to affect the established parameters of world politics. It has loosened the ties of producers and workers to their states, expanded the horizons within which citizens ponder their self-interests, and fostered the formation of transnational organizations. The rapid growth and maturation of the multi-centric world can in good part be traced to the extraordinary dynamism and expansion of the global economy. And so can the weakening of the state, which is no longer the manager of the national economy and has become instead an instrument for adjusting the national economy to the exigencies of an expanding world economy.

The Advent of Interdependence Issues

But the evolution of the world economy is not the only source of centralizing tendencies at work in global life. There are also a number of new transnational problems that are crowding high on the world's agenda.

Whereas the political agenda used to consist of issues that governments could cope with on their own or through interstate bargaining, now these issues have been joined by challenges that do not fall exclusively within the jurisdiction of states and their diplomatic institutions. Six current challenges are illustrative: environmental pollution, currency crises, the drug trade, terrorism, AIDS, and the flow of refugees. Each embraces processes that involve participation by large numbers of citizens and that inherently transgress national boundaries. The winds from the nuclear accident at Chernobyl in 1986, for example, carried radioactive pollution into many countries and had immediate and long-term effects on the people living there. It was then impossible for governments to treat them as domestic problems or to address them through conventional diplomatic channels.

Since such problems are essentially the product of dynamic technologies and the shrinking social and geographic distances that separate people, they can appropriately be called "interdependence" issues. And, given their origins and scope, they can also be regarded as important centralizing dynamics in the sense that they require cooperation on a transnational scale. Each of the six issues, for instance, is the focus of either transnational social movements or ad hoc international institutions forged to ameliorate, if not to resolve, the boundary-crossing problems they have created.

The advent of interdependence issues has contributed to the present era of turbulence in world politics in several ways. First, they have caused citizens to doubt that their states are the ultimate problem solvers and, in the case of those who join social movements, they have led people to ponder a restructuring of their loyalties. In doing so, interdependence issues have also fostered the notion that transnational cooperation can be as central to world politics as interstate conflict. Equally important, given their diffuse, boundary-crossing structure, these issues are spawning a range of transnational associations that are likely to serve as additional challenges to the authority of states.

The Weakening of States and the Restructuring of Loyalties

States have not become peripheral to global affairs; they continue to maintain the international system and infuse it with vitality and a capacity to adapt to change. Moreover, states have been and continue to be a source of the turbulent changes that are at work. After all, it was the state-centric and not the multi-centric world that created multilateral organizations, that contained the nuclear revolution, and that responded to the demands for decolonization by producing the hierarchical arrangements that have enabled the industrial countries to dominate the developing world.

Accordingly, some analysts see states as increasingly robust and explicitly reject the patterns highlighted here. They see the state as so deeply ensconced in the routines and institutions of politics that the erosion of its capabilities and influence is unimaginable. The state has proved itself, the argument goes, by performing vital functions that serve the needs of people, which is why it has been around for more than three hundred years. During this time the state has overcome all kinds of challenges, many of which are far more severe than the globalization of national economies and the emergence of new types of collectivities. Indeed, the argument concludes, there are many ways in which states may actually be accumulating greater capabilities.

However, it seems just as erroneous to treat states as constants as it is to view the skills of citizens as invulnerable to change. States are not eternal verities; they are as susceptible to variability as any other social system. This includes the possibility of a decline in the sovereignty principle from which they derive their legitimacy as well as an erosion of their ability to address problems.

Viewed from the perspective of vulnerabilities, the growing density of populations, the expanding complexity of the organized segments of society, the globalization of national economies, the constraints of external debts, the relentless pressure of technological innovations, the challenge of subgroups intent on achieving greater autonomy, and the endless array of other intractable problems that comprise the modern political agenda, it seems evident that present circumstances lessen the capacity of states. Their agendas are expanding, but they are short on the will, competence, and resources to expand correspondingly. Consequently, most states are overwhelmed to the point where effective management is largely impossible. Added to these difficulties is the fact that citizenries, through the microelectronic revolution, are continuously exposed to authority crises elsewhere in the world. Such scenes are bound to give rise to doubts and demands in even the most stable of polities and thus to foment a greater readiness to question the legitimacy of government policies. There is considerable evidence, for example, that the collapse of authority in East Germany in the fall of 1989 was stimulated by the televised scenes of authority being challenged in Tiananmen Square several months earlier.

Accordingly, while states may not be about to exit from the political stage, and while they may even continue to occupy the center of the stage, they do seem likely to become increasingly vulnerable and impotent. And as ineffective managers of their own affairs, they also serve as stimuli to turbulence in world politics.

But this argument for diminished state competence is subtle and depends on many intangible processes for which solid indicators are not easily developed. Perhaps most notable in this regard are subtle shifts in loyalties that accompany the globalization of national economies, the decentralizing tendencies toward subgroup autonomy, and the emergence of performance criteria of legitimacy. Such circumstances seem bound to affect loyalties to the state. That is, as transnational and subnational actors in the multi-centric world become increasingly active and effective, as they demonstrate a capacity to deal with problems that states have found intractable or beyond their competence, citizens will begin to look elsewhere than the national capital for assistance. Examples abound. Most notable recently are the difficult choices Russians have had to make between their long-standing orientations toward Moscow and the "downward" pull of the particular republics or ethnic minorities of which they are also members. With Moscow unable to provide effective leadership, and with their subnational attachments being thereby heightened, individuals throughout that troubled land are having to face questions about distant attachments they have long taken for granted. Chechnya is only the most recent example of this dynamic.

It would be a mistake, however, to regard the loyalty problem as confined to multi-ethnic systems. Relatively homogeneous societies are beset with the same dilemma, as was so clearly evident in European countries during the debates and plebiscites over whether to accept membership in the European Union.

This is not to say that traditional national loyalties are being totally abandoned; such attachments do not suddenly collapse. Rather, there are subtle processes whereby what was once well-established and beyond question is now problematic and undergoing change. It seems reasonable to presume that the diminished competence of states to act decisively, combined with the processes of loyalty transformation, are rendering more complex each of the three prime parameters of world politics.

Subgroupism

Since there is a widespread inclination to refer loosely to "nationalism" as a source of the turbulent state of world politics, it is perhaps useful to be more precise about the collective nature of those pervasive decentralizing tendencies wherein individuals and groups feel readier to challenge authority and reorient their loyalties. As previously noted, the authority crises that result from such challenges can be either of an "upward" or a "downward" kind. In both kinds of relocation, the motivation that sustains them may not be so deeply emotional as to qualify as an "ism." The creation of subnational administrative divisions, for example, can stem from efforts to rationalize the work of a governmental agency or private organization, and the process of implementing the decentralized arrangements can occur in the context of reasoned dialogue and calm decision making. Often, however, intense concerns and powerful attachments can accompany the press for new arrangements—feelings and commitments strong enough to justify regarding the upward relocations as evoking "transnationalism," "supranationalism," or "internationalism." The downward relocations marked by comparable intensities are perhaps best labeled with the generic term, "subgroupism."

Subgroupism refers to those deep affinities which people develop for the associations, organizations, and subcultures with which they have been historically, professionally, economically, socially, or politically linked, and to which they attach their highest priorities. Subgroupism values the in-group over the out-group, sometimes treating the two as adversaries and sometimes positing them as susceptible to extensive cooperation. Subgroupism can derive from and be sustained by a variety of sources, not the least being disappointment in—and alienation from—the performances of the whole system in which the subgroup is located. Most of all, its intensities are the product of historical roots that span generations and are reinforced by the lore surrounding past events that the subgroup survived.

That subgroupism can be deeply implanted in the consciousness of peoples is manifestly apparent in the resurfacing of strong ethnic identities throughout Eastern Europe and Russia. These subgroups were historic nations and the accompanying feelings can thus be readily regarded as expressions of nationalism. Not all, nor even a preponderance, of these decentralizing tendencies attach to nations, however. Governmental subdivisions, political parties, labor unions, professional societies, and a host of other types of subgroups can also evoke intense attachments, and it would grossly understate the relevance of the decentralizing tendencies at work in world politics to ignore these other forms of ties. Accordingly, it seems preferable to regard the emotional dimensions of the generic decentralizing tendencies as those of subgroupism and to reserve the concept of nationalism for those subgroup expressions that revolve around nations and feelings of ethnicity.

The Spread of Hunger, Poverty, and the Developing World

Underlying the bifurcation of world politics into state- and multi-centric worlds has been another split—between industrially developed and underdeveloped countries—that has also contributed substantially to the onset of turbulence. The many and diverse countries of the developing world have added to the complexity and dynamism of global structures, sharpened performance criteria of legitimacy, enriched the skills of the underprivileged, hastened the transnationalization of economies and social movements, limited the authority of developed states over their production facilities, intensified the flow of people from South to North, lengthened the list of interdependence issues, and strengthened the tendencies toward subgroupism.

The impact of the split fostered by the breakup of Europe's colonial empires is perhaps most obvious with respect to the global distribution of power. Decolonialization not only resulted in the proliferation of actors in the state-centric world, but also infused a greater hierarchical rigidity in global structures. The process whereby ever greater power accompanied the emergence of industrial states in the developed world was not matched when statehood came to Africa and Asia. As was noted earlier, the newly established states of the developing world acquired sovereignty and international recognition even though they lacked the internal resources and consensual foundations to provide for their own development, a circumstance that led the states themselves into a deep resentment over their dependence on the industrialized world for trade, technology, and many of the other prerequisites necessary to fulfill their desire for industrial development. Their sovereignty, in effect, is "negative" in that it protects them against outside interference but does not empower them to address their problems successfully. The result has been a pervasive global pattern in which the industrial world has continued to prosper while the developing world has languished, thus endlessly reinforcing the inequities that underlie the hierarchical structures of world politics. And having long remained at or below the poverty line, most of these quasi-states have been keenly aware of the inequities and have sought vainly to overcome them.

As the advent of the Third World has solidified the hierarchical structure of the state-centric world, it has also added to the decentralizing tendencies in the multi-centric world. Composed of tribes and ethnic groups artificially brought together under state banners during decolonization, besieged by multinational corporations seeking to extend their operations and markets, and plagued with internal divisions and massive socioeconomic problems, many developing countries have added greatly to the breadth and depth of the multi-centric world. Their quasi sovereignty keeps them active in the state system, but the multi-centric world has been hospitable to their fragmenting dynamics and thereby contributed to the process wherein subgroup networks are proliferating.

It must be noted, on the other hand, that a handful of developing countries have dramatically raised their productivity and living standards to the point where they are now regarded as forming a new category—that of newly industrializing countries, or NICs. South Korea, Taiwan, Hong Kong, and Singapore are especially illustrative in this regard, but a few others are also showing signs of increasingly successful development. Once again, generalization is difficult as contradictions and ambiguities have come to pervade the developing world.

DYNAMIC OUTCOMES

Where are the conditions of turbulence taking world affairs? Do they add up to a gloomy assessment of the prospects for peace and stability? Or do they point to a trend wherein shared norms evolve on a global scale and facilitate an eventual decline in upheaval and disarray?

Surely there are no simple answers to these questions. Positive scenarios in which cooperation among communities, societies, and states steadily increases can be constructed as easily as scenarios that envision a continuing breakdown of intergroup relations, deepening authority crises, and a worsening of humankind's lot. The turbulence model suggests that at present the integrating and fragmenting forces are roughly in balance, allowing world affairs to limp from situation to situation, some of which get resolved while others persist and fester. Much depends, in the end, on the kind of leaders that come to power in the state-centric and multi-centric worlds and the quality of the demands that ever more skillful publics make upon them.[11]

In all probability, both scenarios are likely to play out in the years ahead. The turbulence model does not anticipate that the parametric changes will occur at the same pace in the same direction everywhere in the world. "Fragmegrative" processes are anything but uniform. They are uneven, with cooperative dynamics prevailing in some regions and conflictual tendencies holding sway in other areas. In an era of ever more skillful and challenging citizenries, however, it seems doubtful that ruthless, conflict-ridden regimes will be able to hold on to power for very long. It may be decades before the world's transformed parameters settle into place and again serve as boundary conditions for the global system, but in the meantime it is likely the world will manage to move from crisis to crisis without collapsing into calamitous war.

QUESTIONS FOR FURTHER STUDY

1. How does Rosenau distinguish the current period from past epochs of human history? Is his contention that this era is markedly different from those that preceded it persuasive?
2. What does Rosenau mean by his assertion that individuals have "undergone a skills revolution"? What consequences does he attribute to this revolution?
3. In what ways, according to Rosenau, is political authority in the international system being "relocated"?
4. What, according to Rosenau, are the "sources of global turbulence"? Are there other important sources that he has left out?

Notes

1. This is a considerably revised version of an article that originally appeared under the title, "Security in a Turbulent World," *Current History*, Vol. 94 (May 1995), pp. 193–200.
2. For a discussion of the nature of these diverse "scapes," see Arjun Appadurai, "Disjuncture and Difference in the Global Cultural Economy," *Public Culture*, Vol. 2 (1990), pp. 1–23.
3. An extended effort to answer these questions is provided in James N. Rosenau, *Along the Domestic-Foreign Frontier: Exploring Governance in a Turbulent World* (Cambridge: Cambridge University Press, 1997).
4. In this connection, see John L. Gaddis, "International Relations Theory and the End of the Cold War," *International Security*, Vol. 17 (Winter 1992/93), pp. 5–58.
5. An extensive enumeration of the signs of change that surfaced in the 1980s can be found in James N. Rosenau, *Turbulence in World Politics: A Theory of Change and Continuity* (Princeton: Princeton University Press, 1990).
6. Rosenau, *Turbulence in World Politics*, op. cit.
7. This definition of turbulence is elaborated in Rosenau, *Turbulence in World Politics*, op. cit., pp. 59–65, 78.
8. Development of the "fragmegration" approach has occurred in fits and starts. See James N. Rosenau, "'Fragmegrated' Challenges to National Security," in Terry L. Heyns, ed., *Understanding U.S. Strategy: A Reader* (Washington: National Defense University, 1983), pp. 65–82; James N. Rosenau, "Distant Proximities: The Dynamics and Dialectics of Globalization," in Björn Hettne, ed., *International Political Economy: Understanding Global Disorder* (London: Zed Books, 1995), pp. 46–64; and Rosenau, *Along the Domestic-Foreign Frontier*, op. cit., Chapter 6.
9. Robert H. Jackson, *Quasi-States: Sovereignty, International Relations and the Third World* (Cambridge: Cambridge University Press, 1990), p. 85.
10. An account of *Actuel*'s efforts can be found in *Europe: Magazine of the European Community* (April 1990), pp. 40–41.
11. For an effort to assess the kind of leadership conducive to movement in cooperative directions, see James N. Rosenau, "Notes on the Servicing of Triumphant Subgroupism," *International Sociology*, Vol. 8 (March 1993), pp. 77–90.

3 / Threats and Capacities: Great Powers and Global Insecurity

DANIEL N. NELSON

INTRODUCTION

When this millennium began, Europe had yet to emerge from the inchoate debris of the Roman Empire. In the same epoch, other continents' empires had persevered for centuries and ruled great land masses, but did not organize as nation-states. A discernible international system emerged only when the European idea of a state[1] was imposed around the world through war, economic dominance, and colonialism,[2] most often overlaying values, laws, and authority structures that were far more durable. Nation-states—territorially defined political units in which one people and their language predominate—began to form the core units of an international system in the seventeenth century, but did not achieve overwhelming dominance until the nineteenth century.

At the turn of the twentieth century, the state had no rival, having pushed aside religion, land-owning aristocrats, and nobility. Rivalries between states and their alliances, however, had led inexorably to a precipice from which there would be no retreat; twice in the twentieth century the world was plunged into global warfare. Then, when weapons of mass destruction imposed a distance between "great power" antagonists, countless regional and local conflicts were fought by proxies using the money, weapons, and ideologies of the most powerful.

But what will be the role of states—particularly the largest and most powerful—in the global affairs of the twenty-first century? Commencing a new century and millennium, states retain a principal role in human affairs not because of their vitality but because there is yet no clear successor. From above and outside, states are now far more permeable and less autonomous, while from inside and below states confront demands for empowerment, self-determination, and devolution.

"Postinternational" dynamics might be said to lie beyond, beneath, or behind states—dynamics that evoke "turbulence," rendering their institutions, processes, and laws archaic.[3] Matters of state—most notably, national security—are increasingly not seen in terms of the nation-state alone; if there are national interests, they are more and more not the business of the state but, rather, of subnational or transnational businesses and institutions that can address critical issues such as employment and the environment.[4]

States aren't what they used to be. The "real stuff" of politics that involves the authoritative allocation of values and resources is less and less vested in the state and its institutions. These critical functions have been shifted to multinational businesses, worldwide crime syndicates, global media, international financial institutions, and a stratum of advocacy-focused nongovernmental organizations.[5] A "gross criminal product" from global organized crime, for example, may have reached $1 trillion in 1996, more than any sovereign state except the United States and Japan.[6]

In many cases, these extrastate institutions perform functions more efficiently than the state itself. The state's institutions continue to operate, but with less efficiency, fewer resources, and reduced legitimacy.[7] In Africa, states have been destructive, preventing development and democracy, while in Latin America, the continuing dominance of land owners, business elites, drug traffickers, armies, and the church has meant that political systems and particular regimes may come and go with little effect. A number of Islamic states have had a somewhat different fate, being co-opted or subsumed by fundamentalist clergies or dominated by militarized one-party regimes. Where strong central government does not prevail, "quasi-states"[8] proliferate and micro-self-determination—where small minorities insist on separate, sovereign political authority—leads to state fragmentation. As the imperatives of the world capitalist order weigh in on every country, moreover, the fracturing of states leads to more peripheral economies with substantial dependence on or absorption into dominant economies.[9]

At the very least, political, economic, and social functions of human organization are no longer vested in the territorial control exerted by states.[10] And, when political leaders stubbornly insist that greater sovereignty is their aim, reduced economic performance usually follows.[11]

States nevertheless remain the principal organizational unit of human society and a key structure on which global peace and prosperity depend. Overtaken and underthrown, states hold fewer cards than ever before, but are still important players. Between the most powerful states and groups of states will rest the potential to build or destroy security for the foreseeable future. In large part, this is because states still control most large armies and modern weapons and still maintain large bureaucracies for obtaining and distributing resources.

The United States, China, Russia, Japan, and the European Union are, for now, the only states or associations of states that might be labeled "great powers," and it is on these five key actors that this essay is focused. Although other analysts have preferred to use such terms as "potential challengers" or "major contenders" for those states with substantial military or economic capacities, the same five were identified in 1990 as principal actors on the global stage.[12] Adjustments in the capacities of each to "control their political environment and to get other nations to do what [they] want"[13] have clearly occurred—Russia as the principal successor to the former USSR is certainly far weaker, whereas China has accumulated added economic and military resources and the European Union is likely to become more of a unified economic actor—but all remain in the great power category.

But the real issue here is broader: How will these major states and relations among them affect the prognosis for global security in the twenty-first century? While such a far-reaching question has no definitive answer, the following discussion considers the potential role of these principal actors in maintaining a regional and global balance between threats and capacities—the ratio that lies at the core of what we mean by "security."[14] Such an imprecise ratio implies the degree to which military, economic, or political resources possessed by an actor address or ameliorate dangerous conditions. Although this ratio cannot be reduced to a science, neither is it a matter for mere speculation. States have resources and capacities; if they are substantial, threats from domestic or foreign origins can be balanced and neutralized.

Disorder and conflict inherent in human nature require (if one accepts a vision about which the seventeenth century English philosopher Thomas Hobbes wrote at length) the creation of an authority—the state—to ensure physical security and socioeconomic well-being. Only derivatively are states providers of justice, equality, and other "political goods."[15] States affiliate with one another in alliances not because of principles but because there are tangible military and political rewards that outweigh costs. Alliances are formed essentially because of a common threat, not because of shared values, and they operate as "self-help systems" in which states cooperate to enhance their capacities to deter or defeat an actor that poses a common threat.[16]

Are the world's great powers, their associations, and their alliances willing and able to fulfill such a role as we inaugurate a new century and millennium? Do principal states and their bilateral and multilateral relations provide humankind with greater order, more peace, or enhanced prosperity? States are unquestionably involved in matters of security, but achieving a balance between threats and capacities depends less and less on actions by, or decisions within, the state. For the most part, states are *capacity-driven,* concentrating on the accumulation of wealth, the expanding markets, the strengthening of defense, and the protecting of interests. They have yet to fashion effective mechanisms for conflict avoidance or resolution. Instead, states are a milieu in which resources are amassed for conflict and, thereby, they encourage precisely such behavior.

THREATS AND CAPACITIES

For individuals, groups, a regime, a political system, or a nation and its people, danger can be physical or psychological, real or perceived, imminent or latent, internal or external.[17] The degree to which individuals, groups, and societies confront economic distress, social malaise, political violence, dangers to environment and health, and the specter of armed attack, and the *immediacy* with which these and other perilous conditions are perceived, both contribute to insecurity unless they can be abated, or capacities enlarged, to achieve a balance.

Table 3.1 / Behavioral Consequences of Threat

Threat-to-Capacity (T/C) Ratio	Nation	State	Political System	Regime	Group	Individual
T/C Ratio more than 1.00: more threats than capacities	xenophobia	invasion, annexation, absorption	revolution, anarchy	political turmoil, indecision, policy fluctuation	dissolution	fear, evasion
T/C Ratio 1.00: balance between threats and capacities	integration	cooperation	democracy, egalitarianism	alliances, collective endeavors	negotiation/ accommodation	cooperation/ joining
T/C Ratio less than 1.00: more capacities than threats	ethnic cleansing, genocide	militarism, aggression	dictatorship/ authoritarianism	elitist and unitary, eschews alliances	demands and confrontation	abuse, violence

Physical or psychological threat can rise or fall, but it is never that which determines net security. Rather, the ratio of threats to capacities defines security. When threats exceed capacities, and the ratio is larger than 1.00, one can expect—at any level of analysis—suspicion, vulnerability, turmoil, indecision, dissolution, and evasion. When capacities exceed threats, and the ratio is less than 1.00, the inverse can be expected—aggressiveness, authoritarianism, elitism, autarky, confrontation, and abuse. Although many intervening variables may affect the qualities of such behavioral consequences, Table 3.1 suggests a typology of such responses to threat.

Security lies at the intersection of threats and capacities. From nations and their organization into states down to individuals, an equilibrium between threats and capacities offers the potential of peace and prosperity. When threats exceed the capacities of states, they become inviting victims of those with greater capacities; when capacities exceed threats, a classic "security dilemma" ensues, wherein states will seek to bolster their defenses or form alliances to deter the strong.[18]

Ambient threat for a state may be generated by other states. In the twenty-first century, however, cumulative threat is far more likely to derive from forces above, below, or within the state. Indeed, for the United States, the European Union, Russia, China, and Japan, other states are not "the problem" in the security realm, even if old thinking continues to insist that danger looks the way it always did. Even these great powers confront forces bigger and more pervasive than their own budgets can address, yet too elusive for their armies or police to target. Criminal syndicates burrowed deeply within society and bureaucracy, and transnational links among extremist and anarchist groups add to social violence, the prevalence of drugs, and the danger of terrorist attacks.[19] Ethnic hatreds, massive refugee flows, and ecological devastation and other phenomena lie well beyond what one state alone could stop with traditional tools of diplomacy, economic sanctions, or military action.[20] Speculation about "information warfare" and cyber attacks suggests, as well, that states no longer have borders denoted by territorial control and defended with divisions, flotillas, laws, or courts.[21] And, most broadly, the world economy and effects of technological diffusion can no longer be redirected through the policies of a major state or alliance.[22]

Capacities are resources with which an actor can pursue desired outcomes. Security is a universally desired outcome, and capacities are used to deter threats (with counterthreats) or defeat those who try to implement their threats.

Among the five powers discussed below, capacities are proportionately greater than other states in the contemporary international system. But, by no means are the resources of these powers either complete or uniform. As Joseph Nye observed in 1990,[23] and as was apparent in earlier attempts to quantify states' "power," the capacities of great powers are highly varied and, to different degrees, partial.[24] We can, however, recognize that resources in economic, social, political, and military realms can gain credibility and utility if they are more autonomous, unique, large, flexible, durable, and qualitatively superior. Self-sufficiency in microchips or satellite imagery can, therefore, prove to be a highly useful and applicable resource. A unique missile defense system, a very large army, a small but flexible police strike force, long-term economic or political stability, advanced or precise technology, or social cohesion—any or all of these can add to capacities that may be deployed as a balance against real or perceived threats.

Among great powers at the end of this century, however, capacities are increasingly missing the mark. The sheer weight of accumulated power indicators can no longer pin down security. Or, to put it another way, states that pursue a "national security strategy" through capacity-driven behavior deploy armies, defense industries, and intelligence agencies all dressed up but with no place to go. Much of the surge in peacekeeping, peacemaking, and humanitarian intervention, as well as NATO's metamorphosis and enlargement and other late-century multilateral trends may, in retrospect, be understood as new activities for old capacities.

THE UNITED STATES AND GLOBAL INSECURITY

Hubris hung thickly in the air of Washington, D.C. during the years immediately following the fall of the Berlin Wall. European communist regimes had come apart at the seams, as popular movements led ruling parties to hand over the reins of power through a nonviolent, "velvet" revolution. To many in the U.S. national security establishment and business elite, this was a victory over evil denied on the battlefields of Korea, the Bay of Pigs, and Vietnam—a vindication of military expenditures, global competition, and, ultimately, American values, will, and strength.

Then, in the fall of 1990, an unequivocally vicious Middle Eastern dictator decided to invade a small, neighboring undemocratic state that happened to supply much of the industrialized West with critical oil supplies; with interests joined, consciences clear, and ample Cold War weapons at the ready, the American-led coalition provided a convincing victory in the brief 1991 Gulf War. When the Soviet Union itself fractured at the end of 1991, and Washington's archnemesis of the Cold War appeared defeated, no tangible threats seemed to loom on the horizon.

No sooner had the last floats and bands of victory parades exited from America's main streets, however, than the horizon quickly began to darken. Yugoslavia's dissolution was anything but velvet, erupting into Europe's most deadly conflict since World War II. Fighting began in 1991, pitting Serbia briefly against Slovenia, and then in months of vicious warfare against Croatia. In 1992, warfare spread further into Bosnia-Herzegovina, which continued to suffer from combat until the U.S.-led NATO intervention of 1995.

Further, military intervention to overthrow elected politicians in Haiti, renewed warfare in Afghanistan, and terrorist incidents in many locales gave the U.S. leadership and public little respite. That these challenges were perceived as distant by most American voters was evident in the tenor of the 1992 presidential campaign, which focused almost exclusively on domestic issues. But the persistence of perils affecting the United States, and the increasingly diffuse nature of such threats—no longer presumed to be primarily political and military or emanating from one source as in the Cold War era—was worrisome nonetheless.

Between late 1992 and late 1997, the litany of international crises in which American lives were at stake was lengthy, and tragic outcomes were many. The deaths of eighteen U.S. troops on one day in Mogadishu effectively ended U.S. participation in the UN intervention in Somalia, and led to the eventual withdrawal of all foreign forces in the next year. Meanwhile, the 1994 U.S. intervention in Haiti obtained uncertain success, with democracy hardly ensured and neither social peace nor economic recovery evident thus far; both supporters and opponents of U.S. action agree that little economic improvement was evident in Haiti three years later, and that the threat of violence still permeates the country's politics.[25]

Elsewhere, the picture looked no better. American, French, and other forces entered central Africa about the same time to ensure relief for hundreds of thousands of refugees from war and genocide in Rwanda; two years later, a regional war ensued that spread into Zaire. U.S.-brokered negotiations between Israel, Palestinians, and Syrians have ended neither violence nor fear of renewed war. In Bosnia, a threat-laden environment remained after the signing of the Dayton peace accords and the prolonged deployment of U.S. and NATO forces; refugees did not return, weapons were still plentiful, war criminals carried on with impunity, poverty was endemic, and the economy lay in shambles.

In these instances, American "power" was deployed through the injection of military force. Success was always incomplete and transient. U.S. armed forces have both the equipment and training to constitute a formidable instrument of international policy. Yet, American military force offers no "silver bullet"; marines do not wade ashore as midwives to democracy, and cruise missiles make poor diplomats. A show of force might have some temporary utility to delay or redirect action; but it will not change minds, spawn a new political culture, or make friends out of enemies.

Most conditions that set American nerves on edge cannot be ameliorated with the strengths amassed by the United States during generations of confrontation with the "communist menace." Post-Cold War wars, fought with the cast-off weapons of erstwhile superpowers and their erstwhile allies, have turned out to be vicious affairs, in which there are few opportunities to identify sympathetic victims led by noble heroes. And most contemporary security threats have little to do with overt aggression and much more to do with incremental processes that enfeeble, undermine, and erode the social fabric and political institutions within a state.

In the United States, neither elites nor the public see America as "threatened" in the same manner that it was for two generations after World War II.[26] But unease can be felt from Main Street to Pennsylvania Avenue—a palpable concern that arsenals and command centers do little good when endangered by organized crime organizations from Asia, Russia, or South America that export violence with a plutonium or cocaine bonus. At the top of Americans' foreign policy goals during much of the 1990s was "stopping the flow of drugs."[27] More broadly, Americans are confronted by images of a tidal wave of boat people, by whispers of terrorists' intentions, or by probabilities of a nuclear catastrophe. To combat such frightening notions, Americans see their own capacities as limited and their vulnerability as considerable. Regarding drugs alone, a typical news day of the late 1990s suggested a very limited U.S. capacity to deter or deflect drug imports from Latin America.[28]

In the 1990s, under both Republican and Democratic presidents, the United States has "stayed the course" in national and international security policy. While American armed forces have been thoroughly reviewed, downsized, and redeployed since 1989 and 1990, most of the commands, types of weapons, and missions retain greater similarities to than differences from those of a decade ago. The United States continues to order new ships and aircraft for global force projection and worldwide intervention. Our allies remain those with which Americans have been joined since the end of World War II, and U.S. links to NATO have gained added weight given promises to enlarge the Alliance's functions and membership. Not surprisingly, U.S. military expenditures remained at levels of about 92 percent of the Cold War average, expressed in 1997 dollars.[29]

From the "quiet cataclysm" of the late 1980s, when European communism was pushed aside peacefully, through a period of post-Cold War turmoil evident in the Balkans, Central Africa, and elsewhere, the United States has sought to maintain its preeminent role.[30] To do so, Washington has relied on the same capacities, among which are the same friends in the same organizations backed by a military force structure that looks like a smaller version of its Cold War antecedent. American security policy remains dominated by a capacity-driven strategy.

This is a risky game made even more risky because we do not seem to know we are playing it. When the Cold War ended, the United States was the only player holding any cards. Less than a decade after that watershed, that is no longer the case; having intervened militarily to restart democracy, enforce peace, feed refugees, and assert order, options have become more limited as the century draws to a close. The American public is wary of overseas involvement and money is scarce. But it is the waning credibility—and thus reduced efficacy—of such intervention that makes it harder to revisit the military option with each new crisis.

During the 1992 presidential campaign and in the heady first days of the first Clinton Administration, talk of "assertive multilateralism" was heard from novice policymakers.[31] A first draft of a 1993 Presidential Decision Directive (eventually issued as "PDD-25") would have sanctioned U.S. military participation in UN or other peacekeeping efforts not under American command. But the Somalia imbroglio, the intractable crises of Yugoslavia and Haiti, the dangers in Korea and the Middle East, and innumerable other post-Cold War tensions generated harsh criticism of U.S. commitments to supranational authorities. Clinton's foreign policy advisors spent most of the next three years trying to find firm strategic and political footing—offering a variety of soundbite notions such as "engagement and enlargement" from 1994 to 1996, and then "integration" in lieu of the Cold War theme of "containment," while backing away from fundamental principles (e.g., human rights vis-à-vis China or other states) for which they could not generate political support.[32]

In this first post-Cold War decade, American relations with the world were like the efforts of a physician who, believing that he has just cured the world of a devastating disease, tries to apply the same analysis and techniques against all other illnesses everywhere. Clinton's foreign and defense team spoke, instinctively, about the changes the world had seen in the 1980s and early 1990s, but had no new strategy and no new tools. In part because they were unable to create adequate political support, in part because they lacked a vision of anything else, they fell back to adapting old capacities and instruments, applying them as Band-Aids to address gaping wounds made by new, transnational threats.

For Bosnia, the United States urged a "lift and strike" option—lifting the UN arms embargo with respect to the Bosnian Muslim-led government, and employing air strikes to halt Serb aggression. Secretly, Washington tacitly aided the arming of Croatian and Muslim armies through a secret pipeline of money and weapons from other sources. The key to America's response was military, not participation in the UN Protection Force (UNPROFOR)—much less any farsighted effort in 1991 and 1992 to deploy peacekeepers when there was a peace to keep. For the nascent democracies of east-central and southeastern Europe, the enlargement of a Cold War military alliance has been the core of U.S. policy in the late 1990s. For Latin America, the message has been the "war" on drugs carried out with U.S. military assistance and the coercive Helms-Burton Act that threatens retribution in U.S. courts against any foreign company that does business with Cuba involving expropriated U.S. assets.

Meanwhile, with those great powers against which Washington could not exert direct military pressure, the word was accommodation at any cost. Business must be conducted as usual with Beijing no matter what human rights violations occurred, regardless of illicit missile sales and technology transfers, and despite an extraordinary trade imbalance assisted by deplorable labor conditions in China.[33] Russia can, with impunity, bomb civilians in Chechnya, sell arms to China and Iran, and allow deep and pervasive mafia control—anything, so long as Moscow ultimately plays ball on NATO enlargement and the control of its own nuclear arsenal. Japan can ignore or comply minimally with bilateral trade agreements, pursue regional economic dominance, and voice attitudes of ethnic superiority, provided that Tokyo accepts minimal changes to the U.S.-Japan status-of-forces agreement and supports U.S. policy vis-à-vis China and Russia.

Abandoning any alternatives that might have addressed the world's changing panoply of threats, the United States ends the century and millennium with the rhetoric of American leadership plus "enlargement and engagement." All the while, Washington accommodates the presumed interests of the great powers while dealing with the rest of the world on a crisis-by-crisis basis, using familiar resources—cruise missiles to send diplomatic messages, airborne divisions to deliver democracy, mechanized brigades to ensure peace, and arms transfers to balance power.[34] That the United States has ample capacities of different kinds—dominance in technology and information science, for example[35]—seems lost on policymakers, just as the option of a security strategy focused on threat-abatement instead of capacities appears to be beyond the ken of these same political elites.

GREAT POWERS' POWERS AND GLOBAL SECURITY

Do any of the world's other major principal states, or associations of states, use their "powers" to enhance global security? Is a balance between threats and capacities more or less likely as a consequence of policies pursued by the European Union's largest members, or by Russia, China, or Japan?

Among the large powers with a "reach" beyond their immediate area—by virtue of some combination of economic strength, population and geographic size, military prowess, possession of nuclear arms, or cultural influence—the end of the millennium finds varying degrees of democracy, market principles, and other measures of adherence to higher standards. In each, however, leaders continue to apply political, economic, and military capacities in ways oblivious to the limits of state efficacy. The dysfunctional role of great powers in global security is, indeed, the "story" of the post-Cold War era. Each struggles to preserve the prerogatives its elites expect and its masses viscerally believe in, relying on makeshift policies, recycled capacities, and techniques that no longer fit specifications. And, by doing so, they help no one, including their own populations.

In the European Union (EU), key members such as Germany and France pursue foreign policy trajectories that, at the very least, offer little chance for a "common foreign and security policy" (CFSP) for Europe and a rocky road at best for European Monetary Union (EMU), to which EU members agreed in their 1992 summit at the Dutch city of Maastricht. Elites and publics evince little sympathy for CFSP or EMU. Some observers, indeed, think that "the impending crisis in Europe" will be sparked by "the eventual failure of EMU."[36] Still, the EMU has certain identifiable standards and a timetable, while the CFSP has none and is unlikely ever to materialize. Europe's potential to unravel, rather than to progress further toward integration, was being given serious thought by 1997, in part because of the difficulties over EMU and partly because of the obvious inability of European countries to act in concert in addressing the crisis in Bosnia.[37]

Even in the case of Helmut Kohl's Germany, where the government speaks as if it were a staunch advocate of foreign and defense policy coordination, public support is dwindling for such multilateralism.[38] Despite its rhetoric as the most European of Europeans, Kohl's Christian Democratic government has fashioned a distinctly traditional foreign and defense policy since reunification, using its new constitutional latitude to deploy military assets in Bosnia, employ arms transfers to further German contacts in such countries as Turkey, provide only support to international peacekeeping, and vigorously press ahead with the expulsion of refugees in order to placate extremist public opinion. The German government has not, thus far, utilized anything other than the standard resources of a powerful state, for which the *Weltanschauung* is viewed through the Realists' lens.[39] And, notwithstanding a lot of Maastricht rhetoric, Kohl has been unable or unwilling to roll back a strong public desire to delay or scrap the EMU.[40]

For France, too, security issues have been framed in unilateral terms. President Jacques Chirac, former Foreign Minister Herve de Charette, and ex-Defense Minister Charles Millon often spoke in the late 1990s of their concerns for Mediterranean security and "conflicts in the south"—i.e., terrorists of Islamic origin or uncontrolled migration from Northern Africa.[41] (The latter concern, it should be noted, flew in the face of data that clearly refuted any notion of an immigration "surge" into France; the proportion of foreigners within France's population remained stable between 1975 and 1995 at about 6.5 percent.[42]) In the public mind, immigration destroys national culture, and, with "globalization," takes away jobs.[43] French elites also fret over the continuing inroads of American cultural influence. In response to all this, French leaders emphasized the need to restructure and modernize the French military and to rejoin NATO's military councils. The latter step, however, can occur only on terms recognizing the importance of France, e.g., by transferring leadership of NATO's Southern Command at Naples from an American to a European.[44] Despite words of conciliation in early 1997, this loggerhead continued to fester after NATO's decision on enlargement into Eastern Europe—meaning that the alliance confronts its biggest issues without unity among its oldest members.

The doubt and fear that underlie such issues have not, however, generated fundamental change. Instead, the French have tended to retreat into a culturally defensive posture and to political conservatism without vision, à la President Chirac, or reactionary politics à la Jean-Marie Le Pen's National Front. In the face of clear and present evidence that domestic socioeconomic conditions—13 percent unemployment in 1997, social unrest, and a growing appeal of extremist politics—are moving in perilous directions, the weak French state has little to offer.[45]

Through such behavior, the Germany and France of the 1990s have evinced many of the dysfunctional roles played by major states within associations of states. While governments seek to protect sovereignty and territoriality by, for example, expelling refugees, or by expanding their role in alliance structures, they pander to the same fears that stoke neofascist flames in France and an insidious rightward drift in Germany while dismissing the underlying issues that are generating fear and political volatility.[46]

From the standpoint of public opinion, these fears are rooted in socioeconomic conditions. "Profound changes in trade, finance, and technology" have given us an "age of widespread economic insecurity" and worker disaffection, notes Ethan Kapstein in *Foreign Affairs*.[47] In Europe, joblessness soared from the very low levels of the first decades after World War II to 12 percent by 1994 and more than 13 percent by 1996. To make matters worse, a large part of Europe's jobless have been unemployed for a year or longer.[48] In Germany, the 1996 unemployment rate of 12.2 percent was the highest recorded since the 1930s.

Socioeconomic crises will soon assume an added dimension in Europe as the percentage of pensioners in the population exceeds 20 percent in much of the EU by the year 2020, when worker-to-retiree ratios will be only about 1.5:1 (versus 2:1 in the United States).[49] Such ratios mean that more retired people will be supported by fewer wage-earners, putting greater strain on taxes, budgets, and the allocation of scarce resources (especially health care). To these concerns, European states—whether singly or conjoined in the EU—have thus far offered no solution or strategy. The nation-state's inability "to keep unemployment at a tolerable level while maintaining the social safety net," writes John Newhouse, "has accelerated Europe's growing devolution of authority."[50]

Such current or impending threats, when joined with anti-immigrant sentiment, provide the nutrients for demagogues of the right and left and weaken interest in or commitment to further European integration. Germany's intellectual debate now resonates with voices from a resurgent "new right" that speak the language of national "self-confidence," which, in practice, provides a theoretical defense of neo-Nazi actions. Rejection of the postwar Bonn government and its participants, and glorification of renewed "Germanness" are recurrent themes. And, while the views of controversial figures like Botho Strauss are not those of the governing party, "new right" messages are readily seen in the nationalism of the CDU's youth movement, in major newspapers which now print characterizations such as "the Jew Rifkind" (to refer to then British Foreign Minister Malcolm Rifkind),[51] and in writings of Kohl's heir apparent, Wolfgang Schauble, who talks about German identity being derived from the "emotional, connective power of the nation."[52] The rumblings of unrest in Germany, although still distant, are no longer possible to ignore.[53]

These narrow interests and the rhetoric of national identity do not sound much like the promised "new Europe." Fueled by economic insecurity and immigration, such views slow momentum toward integration and make the ascent toward a united Europe longer and steeper. The European Union, far from being a strong partnership, has a gossamer-like visage in global security.

GREAT POWER DILEMMAS IN ASIA

Major Asian states, out of the great power business for more than two generations, are now members of the club again. China's economic surge of the 1980s and 1990s has initiated a trend that could make it the world's largest economy—surpassing even the United States—before 2020.[54] Although per capita measures would still place China among the "developing" countries, its gross output (GDP at "purchasing power parity") might reach more than $20 trillion in 2020, versus $13.5 trillion for the United States and $5 trillion for Japan. These projections assume a continuation of China's extraordinary growth rate—9.7 percent in 1996 and 8 percent anticipated for 1997[55]—and trouble-free incorporation of Hong Kong. Regardless of the exact pace of China's economic expansion, this growth has been accompanied by a significant enlargement of China's military capacity, supported by a bigger defense budget. Purchases of advanced Russian aircraft, the transfer of U.S. missile and avionics secrets via Israel, the addition of blue-water surface and submarine fleets, and more professional ground forces all add up to a regional if not global presence in the twenty-first century.[56]

Chinese nationalism is a predictable, if not comfortable, counterpoint to domestic uncertainty and flux. "No one dares to be anything but a strong nationalist in such circumstances," said Michel Oksenberg of China in the mid-1990s.[57] Having lunged into "state capitalism" while trying to retain political control, the Chinese Communist Party cannot be sanguine about its

own future. The death of Deng Xiaoping in February 1997 did not precipitate turmoil, collapse, or any other cataclysm, in part because he had been
on the precipice of death for years and partly because Chinese reform had
generated its own "conservative but energetic" foundation.[58]

Nevertheless, high officials such as Party Chairman Jiang Zemin,
Premier Li Peng, and National People's Congress Chairman Qiao Shi can no
longer dictate; rather, they must manage, in a very political fashion, all of
the social, economic, and cultural tensions that accompany rapid change.
The suppression, with military force, of student democrats in the spring of
1989 killed hundreds or thousands, but did not eradicate visions of a more
plural and tolerant China.

Regardless of rhetoric, China's stance is one of unreconstructed Realism—
defense of the state, its interests, and its power against all threats. As "the
high church of realpolitik in the post-Cold War world . . . [whose] analysts . . . think more like traditional balance-of-power theorists than do most
contemporary Western leaders," China eschews normative ends or multilateral means.[59] Instead, Beijing acts unilaterally to accumulate comprehensive
national power through military and economic capacities with which to
intimidate, aggrandize, and support the enemies of its enemies.

Beijing's principal approach to Taiwan, which it regards as a renegade
province, is the path of military intimidation. The most egregious example
was during 1996 Taiwanese presidential elections, when China conducted
military exercises and fired missiles from Taiwan's coasts, but similar techniques were used earlier.[60] Similarly, when the Paracel and Spratly Island
groups of the South China Sea became a matter of competing claims in the
early 1990s, China resorted quickly to the deployment of warships in the
region. To counterbalance India—still seen in Beijing as a challenge to
Chinese regional security—China has sold M-11 ballistic missiles to Pakistan
in clear violation of its pledges to the United States.[61] Although Deng's
counsel of "acting calmly" and "not seeking confrontation" can be traced in
cases where China reacted rhetorically, rather than militarily, to perceived
external provocation,[62] Party conservatives and the People's Liberation
Army (PLA) have criticized moderation and pulled China inexorably
toward a more hard-line position. China's military capabilities still pose no
imminent threat to the United States, but its military buildup and assertive
regional role is not reassuring.[63]

China's leaders talk and act with militaristic bravado. But just beneath
and behind this image of strength lies a weak state with a ruling elite enjoying uncertain political legitimacy.[64] Turmoil such as the June 1989
Tiananmen Square incident led quickly to a reemergence of China's old
"anti-hegemonist" theme, stressing the threat of "international policemen"
and foreign intervention. Chinese leaders warn of Japanese militarism,
American commitments to Japan or Taiwan, Taiwanese moves toward independence, and an international "China threat" conspiracy to isolate and
contain Beijing.[65] But they also worry about labor unrest if the economy
ceases to grow rapidly, the growing migration of peasants to the cities in

search of (often nonexistent) factory work, and political and cultural dissent among urban intellectuals. By the late 1990s, Chinese authorities also had to contend with minority uprisings, as erupted in early 1997 among Uighurs in Xinjiang Province, and a series of terrorist bombing incidents in Beijing.[66] Any of these could begin to tear away the shroud that conceals a China far less unified and far more questioning than Western observers typically assume.

Japan, an American ally by treaty and historical exigency, is often in conflict with the United States. The conflicts are nonviolent, but vehement, and stir public antipathies in both countries. Disputes about trade have been the most frequent, but increasing friction was created in the late 1990s because of sexual attacks by U.S. armed forces personnel on Japanese women on the island of Okinawa and elsewhere, and the harm (and sometimes death) suffered by Japanese visitors in the United States.

That the United States and Japan both saw the Soviet Union and Communist China as threatening helped to ensure their defense cooperation for several decades after the end of the post-World War II U.S. military occupation. But signs that the two countries view their security differently—and that the disagreements are rather substantial—are evident. Japan said "no" to working with the United States in jointly developing a theater missile defense (TMD) system, for example, not only because burden-sharing with the United States has little political benefit but also because other threats are perceived. While Americans' difficulties with the unsophisticated Iraqi "Scud" missiles in the 1991 Gulf War led U.S. officials to view North Korea's tests of a Rodong medium-range ballistic missile in the mid-1990s as cause to accelerate a TMD system for Northeast Asia, Japan considered such a system too costly, given the potentially negative signals that this would send to China.[67] Yet, Japan has meanwhile begun to reconsider unilateral measures that might someday be required to protect its security with military means, including the development of nuclear weaponry.[68]

By 1997, the luster of Japan's economy had diminished considerably; growth had slowed, small and medium banks had begun to fail, unemployment had appeared and grown (although still far below any European country), and the Tokyo stock market had lost almost half its value as compared with the late 1980s. The "beginning of the end" of "Japan, Inc." was being foreseen by some observers.[69] A March 1995 terrorist attack on the Tokyo subway using Sarin nerve gas killed twelve people and injured several thousands more; although the Aum Shinrikyo cult leader, Shoko Aasahara, was subsequently taken into custody, the shaken Japanese public found that it had been targeted for mass terrorism.[70] Fears accompanying these developments had led to a rollback of voter interest in alternative political leadership and much of what passes for political reform. Prime Minister Ryutaro Hashimoto's Liberal Democratic Party (LDP) government, installed in 1996, constitutes a return to power of the "old guard," albeit a new generation of faction leaders. As in other states, elites and masses reach for the familiar and comfortable when uncertain conditions loom.

As states are wont to do, Japan and its leaders have been drawn inexorably toward what appear to be Japan's problems—economic malaise (where such an idea was unheard of for two generations), domestic terrorism, and a visceral reaction against an American "presence." Husbanding resources, while responding to voters' fears and resentments, Japan fulfills far less of an international or multilateral role than its extraordinarily important and "powerful" economic role would otherwise lead one to expect.

RUSSIA'S INSTABILITY

Russian capacities have eroded to the point that, except within certain localities such as Moscow and its mafia-ridden government, few things "work" at all. As a state, Russia functions poorly, although economic activity in Russia began its recovery by 1995 and seemed, by the end of 1997, to hold some promise.[71] But new prosperity has thus far affected only a narrow stratum of the population in a positive direction, and economic woes of various kinds dominated the top worries for the Russian population as a whole in 1997. For ordinary Russians, where there was once a fear of the centralized state and its security organs, one now finds a new demon—the "decentralization of fears."[72] With mafia violence, intimidation, and assassinations on the rise, anyone with talent or ambition in any field is vulnerable as a target to be frightened into submission. In the threat-rich, capacity-poor environment of Russia at the end of the century, questions are being raised à la 1917 about how long the Russians will tolerate the situation, and to what they might turn.

A Russia thus enfeebled still deploys thousands of nuclear warheads, exports vast quantities of sophisticated weaponry to governments with uncertain intentions, and has a capacity to punish neighboring peoples with violence or a cutoff of energy supplies. Several "Kilo"-class diesel submarines and extensive nuclear technology have been provided to Iran; to China, Russia has provided scores of Su-27 fighters, plus tanks, missiles, and other weapons.[73] The vicious air and artillery attacks by the Russian military against Chechen cities and towns did not lead to victory, but did kill tens of thousands. Less directly, Russian pressure through the control of energy supplies can be a potent weapon against Ukraine, the Baltic states, and other former components of the USSR.

A Russia propelled by fear may not engage in direct military provocations, but could well obstruct multilateral efforts (using its UN veto), support unfriendly, "rogue" governments (by selling weapons, oil, or gas), or by using pressure and intimidation on vulnerable targets such as the Baltic states. And, domestically, a Russia full of fears could easily turn toward the authoritarianism of Lebed or others like him.

The United States and, to an even greater extent, Germany have sought to "deal" with Russia in this delicate and perilous period by first supporting and then relying on the presidency of Boris Yeltsin. Such a one-man policy, followed almost unflinchingly through 1995, may have been derived from the romantic vision of Yeltsin atop the tank in August 1991, when he resisted a coup by pro-Soviet generals, reinforced by the absence of strategic thinking in the West. This dependency on one leader in Moscow was criticized by many, and broader and far-reaching engagement was advocated—but to little avail.[74]

As the United States and NATO's other principal members pressed ahead with plans to extend invitations to some former Warsaw Pact members to join the Alliance, Russian objections became increasingly strident in 1996 and 1997. Although, in Washington and Western Europe, enlarging the venerable Western alliance seemed unthreatening—a benign and an appropriate reward for the anti-communist struggles and democratic transitions of Poles, Czechs, and their Central European neighbors—the view from Moscow was another thing altogether. From the Kremlin walls, it appeared that a victorious military alliance, already in a dominant position, sought to edge closer and perhaps forward-deploy its weapons and troops on Russia's periphery. Even among savvy Russians who rejected such a simplistic interpretation of NATO's motives, there was no way to depoliticize NATO enlargement; opposition to NATO's growth became de rigueur—a ticket that every national figure had to punch to remain credible. Consequently, Moscow's demands for compensatory security gestures—revision of the Conventional Forces in Europe (CFE) treaty, more military collaboration with the United States, and other structural ties codified in a binding NATO-Russian "charter"—escalated as Russian politicians and generals outbid each other in their condemnation of enlargement. The vague Cooperation Council, established by the May 27, 1997 "Founding Document" signed by Russia and NATO, provides no assurance of lasting accord and tranquillity within Russia, or between Russia and the alliance.

In the months leading up to the Madrid NATO summit of July 1997, U.S. and Western European leaders sought to mollify Russian concerns. The CFE revisions sought by Moscow, permitting greater Russian deployments in flank areas such as the Caucasus, were given grudging approval. But in these and other Western initiatives, the core insecurities of Russia remained unattended; CFE changes, joint brigades, and a host of joint fora in Brussels neither reduced domestic insecurity nor abated the sense of impotence that generates the rhetoric of extremism.

STATES' DYSFUNCTION

This cursory survey of great power behavior tests no hypothesis. Yet, such observations evoke the dilemma of large and ostensibly influential states at the close of the twentieth century. For all that they may intervene in far-flung corners of the world, rattle their sabers, or throw around their economic weight, such states are neither very strong nor very secure. Some have far greater capacities than others. But their insecurity derives less from having too few capacities than from a failure to abate genuine threats. Transfixed by the flamboyance of their militaries on parade, or compelled to advocate economic growth and territorial control, rulers still push the same old buttons of power whether they work or not.

And, increasingly, they do not work well at all. In large, muscle-bound powers, the state itself may be weak—that is, lacking in sociopolitical cohesion.[75] In that condition, trying to push the buttons of power may precipitate a performance crisis from which a regime, government, or system will not recover. Even a strong state that is well-endowed with the accoutrements of industry and armies has no guarantee of security. The Soviet Union had the world's largest nuclear arsenal, but nonetheless rotted from within—a weak state with huge military and industrial capacities that proved irrelevant or counterproductive to its political survival. Or, to put it another way, the security of such a system rested on its ability to contain the threat within, not on its accumulation of military-industrial capacities.

By comparison, the United States is still in the business of global leadership, enlargement, and engagement; it looks and acts like the sole remaining "superpower." But the victor of the Cold War and guardian of the world's freedom for almost fifty years is unwilling to pay for its foreign policy establishment, is unable to slow—much less halt—the drug trade, confronts mounting incidents of domestic terrorism, remains at the pinnacle of murders per capita among advanced industrial countries,[76] and mutely accepts social stratification that excludes tens of millions from health care and educational opportunities. Perhaps the United States is a strong state relative to others, but the direction of its internal evolution might be questioned even by the most ardent patriot.

Externally, the stronger the state, the more it is likely to be engaged elsewhere and thus become enmeshed in tensions, disputes, or conflicts. In other words, strong states may not be good news for security—their own or their neighbors'. Yet, when the strength of great powers wanes, there is still no good news. Hemorrhaging political legitimacy, ebbing social cohesion, faltering economic momentum, or a combination of these deadly ills for states can be harbingers of conflicts, cold or hot. The potential for violent conflict between the largest, most well-endowed states may increase not when great powers cease to be great but when leaders of major states fear that their domain may soon become less great. When a loss of capacity can be foreseen or inferred—for example, due to the diminished availability of vital resources such as energy supplies, water, critical minerals, and so on, confrontations and military clashes are more, not less, likely to occur.

Insecurity follows from an inability to use resources that states typically accumulate—wealth, military assets, cultural influence, diplomatic skills—to address the threats of the new millennium. Capacities that states garner are fungible when threats are unequivocal and univariate (that is, primarily and consistently of one type, as was the Soviet and Warsaw Pact military danger). When capacities can be targeted at a particular type or source of threat, its effects can be deterred or defeated. But the convenient image of a "communist menace" emanating from a central command post in the

Kremlin is no longer present. And against the complex, diffuse threats of the current era, such strategies of capacity accumulation have minimal effect. Moreover, alternative methods of mitigation of internal or external peril—negotiation, arbitration, redistribution of material or political resources, confidence-building, and peacekeeping—are done less effectively or ignored altogether.

Because states are capacity-driven, relations between and among great powers will be less and less relevant to preserving twenty-first-century security. Indeed, states may get in the way. Should the United States and other principal states plan military forces and economic development into the twenty-first century thinking only of worst-case scenarios, we are likely to get the international environment for which we plan. When states persist in building capacities (military, economic, or political) for power projection, the global environment responds as other actors restructure their capacities in similar fashion. By shunning the international system's interactive character, we may be blinding ourselves to promising insights regarding how capacity-driven policies "construct" threats which, if not thought to be balanced by further capacities, generate dangerous behavioral consequences. [77]

Balancing threats and capacities will not be achieved soon without states. But it is becoming increasingly difficult to do it with them. More and more, states are the harbingers of global insecurity, be they "rogue" actors or great powers. For supranational and subnational agents in pursuit of peace and prosperity, getting around the obstacle of states that traffic in arms, harbor criminals, enlarge inequalities, or suppress expression has become a raison d'être.

Left to their own devices, states conduct bilateral relations, and form associations or alliances based on balance-of-power machinations among territorially defined sovereign actors—a calculus offering a counterthreat to potential or perceived enemies, not a strategy for avoiding conflict. States using traditional instruments of power, guided in a vague fashion by presumed national interests, lurch toward an illusive security, trying to accumulate the capacities they know best. And, as they do so, the biggest and most capacity-endowed states inexorably generate security dilemmas for the next generation; as the ratio of threats to capacities falls under 1.00 (as described in Table 3.1), what had seemed a chimera of security for one power becomes a harbinger of threat for others. The more one actor stockpiles capacities, the more neighbors will begin to exhibit "security envy."

Opportunities and solutions lie elsewhere—with shared resources and inclusive institutions to confront global problems. Balancing threats and capacities—not ensuring that one's own strengths exceed all adversaries—is a forward-thinking route to the next century's security challenges. No longer utopian, but rather urgent and pragmatic, this wider security perspective for the twenty-first century may allow states to retain a role in the global quest for a balance between threats and capacities, by becoming agents of threat-abatement instead of capacity enhancement. But, to do so, there is much to be learned and few signs that the great powers are ready to begin.

QUESTIONS FOR FURTHER STUDY

1. What, according to Nelson, is the relationship between threats and capacities in shaping the security policy of nation-states? What is likely to occur when threats exceed capacities? When capacities exceed threats?

2. Why, in Nelson's view, have America's vast military capabilities proved only marginally useful as a tool of foreign policy in the post-Cold War era? Are his arguments on this score persuasive?

3. What are the socioeconomic factors that are undermining the effectiveness of state policy in France and Germany? In China and Japan?

4. What does Nelson mean by saying that the great powers of today are "capacity driven"? Why does he believe that this orientation is likely to prove increasingly dysfunctional? Do you agree with this assessment?

Notes

1. A succinct but useful definition of the state is in John Holden, *The State and the Tributary Mode of Production* (London: Verso, 1993), pp. 32–33: ". . . a set of institutions and personnel, concentrated at a single point, and exerting influence over a territorially distinct area."

2. Adam Watson, "European International Security and Its Expansion," in Adam Watson and Hedley Bull, eds., *The Expansion of International Society* (Oxford: Oxford University Press, 1984), pp. 13–32.

3. James N. Rosenau, *Turbulence in World Politics: A Theory of Change and Continuity* (Princeton: Princeton University Press, 1990), pp. 12–13. Rosenau discusses five forces that characterize the world's transition from international to postinternational. These are, briefly, (1) the dynamics of technology, (2) transnational issues, (3) reduced capacity of governments to provide satisfactory solutions to major issues, (4) international and national tendencies towards decentralization and subgrouping, and (5) populations with enhanced analytical skills that can less easily be manipulated by governments. The threat to states from within, not from the anarchical nature of the international system, is an important related theme developed superbly by Heinz Gartner, "States without Nations: State, Nation and Security in Central Europe," *International Security*, Vol. 34, No. 1 (April 1997).

4. John Newhouse makes this point in his article "Europe's Rising Regionalism," *Foreign Affairs*, Vol. 76, No. 1 (January/February, 1997), pp. 67–84.

5. A similar theme is echoed in Jessica T. Matthews, "Power Shift," *Foreign Affairs*, Vol. 76, No. 1 (January/February, 1997), pp. 50–66. Matthews cites an estimate by McKinsey and Company that global financial markets will expand to reach $84 trillion by 2000, ". . . triple the aggregate GDP of the affluent nations of the [OECD]" (p. 57).

6. Vincent Boland, "Earnings from Organized Crime Reach $1,000 Billion," *Financial Times* (February 15, 1997), p. 1.

7. One examination of the state's dwindling functionality is John W. Meyer, "The World Polity and the Authority of the Nation-State," in Albert Bergesen, ed., *Studies in the Modern World System* (New York: Academic Press, 1980), pp. 109–137.

8. Robert H. Jackson, *Quasi-States: Sovereignty, International Relations and the Third World* (Cambridge: Cambridge University Press, 1990).

9. Edward A. Kolodziej, "Order, Welfare and Legitimacy," *International Politics*, Vol. 34, No. 1 (March 1997).

10. David J. Elkins, *Beyond Territoriality: Territory and Political Economy in the Twenty-First Century* (Toronto: University of Toronto Press, 1995), pp. 121–146.

11. Branko Milanovic, "Nations, Conglomerates, and Empires: The Tradeoff Between Income and Sovereignty," World Bank Policy Research Working Paper 1675 (October 1996).

12. See, for example, Joseph S. Nye's listing of "Major Contenders" according to his estimate of their power resources in 1990 in *Bound to Lead: The Changing Nature of American Power* (New York: Alfred A. Knopf, 1990), p. 173.

13. Ibid., p. 174.

14. Concerning the notion of security as a balance between threats and capacities, see Daniel N. Nelson, "Civil Society Endangered," *Social Research*, Vol. 63, No. 2 (Summer 1996), pp. 345–368, and the same author's "Great Powers and World Peace," in Michael Klare and Daniel Thomas, eds., *World Security: Challenges for a New Century*, 2nd ed. (New York: St. Martin's Press, 1994), pp. 27–42. An alternative, somewhat ironic view of security is that of the author Germaine Greer, for whom "Security is when everything is settled—when nothing can happen to you. Security is the denial of life." But, for most people, risk is not life-enriching; Greer's notion of security qua death won't wash.

15. J. Roland Pennock, "Political Development, Political Systems, and Political Goods," *World Politics*, Vol. 18, No. 2 (April 1966).

16. This realist perspective on alliances is, for example, clear in George Liska, *Nations in Alliance* (Baltimore: Johns Hopkins University Press, 1962).

17. Davis B. Bobrow, "Complex Insecurity: Implications of a Sobering Metaphor," *International Studies Quarterly*, Vol. 40, No. 4 (December 1996).

18. See, for example, Robert Jervis, "Cooperation under the Security Dilemma," *World Politics*, Vol. 30, No. 1 (January 1978), pp. 167–214. Generally, Jervis and a long lineage of other authors see such a dilemma as arising when one state's efforts to achieve unassailable protection from threats pushes other actors to seek added capacities (e.g., by arming more heavily) to counter the first state's actions.

19. Despite years during which the U.S. pursued a "war on drugs," the State Department concluded, in early 1997, ". . . that it [the war on drugs] has had 'little discernible effect' on the price or availability of narcotics on North American streets," *The Economist* (March 8, 1997), p. 44.

20. The number of refugees, for example, expanded by over six times between the mid-1970s and the mid-1990s—from about 2.4 million in 1975 to over 18.2 million in 1993. States, unable to respond, have thrown the problem to a once-tiny UN agency, the High Commissioner for Refugees, or UNHCR, the budget of which rose from a mere $69 million in 1975 to $1.3 billion in 1993. See *World Refugee Report* (New York: UNHCR, 1995).

21. Regarding cyber-conflict, see Richard E. Haynes and Gary Wheatley, "Information Warfare and Deterrence," *Strategic Forum*, No. 87 (Washington: Institute for National Strategic Studies, October 1996).

22. Good, if cursory, discussions of these many new threats and their effects at the end of the twentieth century are in Karl Kaiser and Hans-Peter Schwarz, eds., *Die neue Weltpolitik* (Baden-Baden: Nomos Verlagsgesellschaft, 1995), particularly articles in Section II, "Determinanten der neuen Weltpolitik," pp. 73–300.

23. Nye, op. cit.

24. One novel effort to quantify measures of relative power was attempted by Ray S. Cline in *World Power Trends and U.S. Foreign Policy* (Boulder: Westview Press, 1980).

25. John Sweeney, "Stuck in Haiti," *Foreign Policy*, No. 102 (Spring 1996) and Robert I. Rotberg, "Clinton Was Right" in the same journal.

26. Gallup polls regularly ask, "What do you think is the most important problem facing this country today?" The proportion of Americans who said that superpower confrontation, nuclear weapons, or related issues was "most important" dropped from 20–27 percent in the mid-1980s to 2 percent at the beginning of 1996. See Jeremy D. Rosner, "The Know-Nothings Know Something," *Foreign Policy*, No. 101 (Winter 1995/96), pp. 124.

27. See, for instance, the Chicago Council on World Affairs annual survey of public attitudes in 1995.

28. See, for example, Douglas Farah, "Colombia Suspends Anti-Drug Crop Effort" and Molly Moore and John Ward Anderson, "U.S. Officials Visit Mexico for Parlay on Drug Policy," both in the *Washington Post* (March 6, 1997).The same month, other reports carried similar ominous messages, e.g., Doug Farah and Molly Moore, "Mexican Drug Traffickers Eclipse Colombian Cartels," *Washington Post* (March 20, 1997).

29. As calculated by the Center for Defense Information, Washington, D.C., and cited in CDI's *Defense Monitor* (April 1997).

30. See John Mueller, *Quiet Cataclysm: Reflections on the Recent Transformation of World Politics* (New York: HarperCollins, 1995).

31. In Madeleine Albright's confirmation hearings in the U.S. Senate for the post of Ambassador to the United Nations in January 1993, she used this phrase which was later repeated in private conversations before various think-tank audiences.

32. See *A National Strategy of Engagement and Enlargement* (Washington: The White House, February 1995). Also, regarding the newer theme of integration, see Jonathan S.

Landay, "Clinton Team Forges Foreign Policy Vision," *Christian Science Monitor* (April 2, 1997).

33. David M. Lampton, "America's China Policy in the Age of the Finance Minister: Clinton Ends Linkage," *The China Quarterly*, No. 139 (September 1994), pp. 597–621.

34. On the latter point, see "USA: Arms Sales Superpower," *Boston Globe* (February 11, 1996), p. B-2.

35. Joseph S. Nye, Jr., and William A. Owens, "America's Information Edge," *Foreign Affairs*, Vol. 75, No. 2, (March/April 1996), pp. 20–36.

36. These comments were made by Lucio Caracciolo, editor of *Li Mes*, at a seminar at the Eurowatch Group, Center for Strategic and International Studies, Washington, D.C. (December 2, 1996). See also, "Sweating for that Euro," *The Economist* (February 15, 1997), wherein it is opined that ". . . some of the single currency's keenest proponents are starting to doubt that it will take shape on time" (p. 45).

37. George Soros, "Can Europe Work?" *Foreign Affairs*, Vol. 75, No. 5 (September/October 1996), pp. 8–14.

38. German public opposition to a common European security identity rose to 28 percent in 1995 and 31 percent in 1996. Although still a minority, this trend was clearly different than elsewhere on the continent. See USIA, *The New European Security Architecture* (Washington: USIA Office of Research and Media Reaction, September 1995), p. 31 and *Eurobarometer* reports in 1996.

39. For a more detailed discussion, see Daniel N. Nelson, "Germany and the Balance between Threats and Capacities in Europe," *International Politics*, Vol. 34, No. 1 (March 1997).

40. See the Lou Harris poll in *The Independent* (June 19, 1996) that reported 67 percent of the German public opposed to the EMU. Some other polls found even greater opposition.

41. This French view was noted by Jim Hoagland, "South of Europe," *Washington Post* (March 6, 1997).

42. Barry James, "Immigration to France Unchanged in Twenty Years," *International Herald Tribune* (February 28, 1997).

43. See Jim Hoagland, "Debating Immigration the French Way," *Washington Post* (March 2, 1997).

44. On French foreign and defense policy priorities, see R. P. Grant, "France's New Relationship with NATO," *Survival*, Vol. 38, No. 1 (Spring 1996), pp. 58–60.

45. Two reports that convey this mood are Roger Cohen, "A Somber France, Racked by Doubt: Under Pressure to Modernize, Nation Clings to the Old Ways," *International Herald Tribune* (February 12, 1997) and Barry James, "New Victory of Far Right Stirs Doubts in France," *International Herald Tribune* (February 11, 1997).

46. In the French case, Prime Minister Alain Juppe has advocated that intellectuals not protest a government bill against illegal immigration because their protests would "undermine democracy" by giving arguments to the extreme right. Essentially, then, the government must do much of what the extremists want to prevent them from becoming stronger. Such pandering to extremism understandably drew the wrath of French intellectuals. See Barry James, "French Face Off Over Immigration," *International Herald Tribune* (February 18, 1997).

47. Ethan B. Kapstein, "Workers and the World Economy," *Foreign Affairs*, Vol. 75, No. 3 (May/June 1996), p. 37.

48. Ray Marshall, "The Global Job Crisis," *Foreign Policy*, No. 100 (Fall 1995), p. 50.

49. These data are from the World Bank and U.S. Department of Commerce as reported by Marshall N. Carter and William G. Shipman, "The Coming Global Pension Crisis," Special Supplement to *Foreign Affairs*, Vol. 75, No. 6 (November/December 1996).

50. Newhouse, op. cit., p. 67.

51. The *Frankfurter Allgemeine Zeitung*, perhaps Germany's most respected conservative newspaper, used such a phrase in late February 1997, as reported in the *Washington Post* (February 23, 1997).

52. Wolfgang Schauble, *Und der Zukunft zugewandt* (Berlin: Siedler Verlag, 1994).

53. A journalist's reflections on such troublesome indicators is E.J. Dionne, Jr.'s "Germany's Problems Should Trouble Us, Too," *International Herald Tribune* (February 11, 1997).

54. Central Intelligence Agency, *World Factbook* (Washington: CIA, 1995).

55. Steven Mufson, "Major Speech Puts Li Peng in Spotlight," *Washington Post* (March 2, 1997), p. A-22.

56. On the Chinese defense budget, see: "Soldiering Pays," *The Economist* (July 4, 1994); and Nicolas Kristof, "China Raises Military Budget," *The New York Times* (March 17, 1993).

The Sukoi (Su)-27, one of the best Soviet (Russian) combat aircraft to be developed in the 1980s, was sold to China in large numbers during the mid-1990s—perhaps as many as forty-eight units in two batches. Russia, eager for exports and to repair relations with China, apparently agreed to transfer Su-27 technologies to China and to license Beijing's production of this potent supersonic aircraft. See "Russia: Largest Aircraft Deal to Be Signed with PRC," *Kommersant Daily* (February 7, 1996) as translated in FBIS-SOV-96-028 (February 9, 1996), p. 21. The Israeli-China connection has long been rumored. CIA briefings in 1991 to Congressional leaders and, later, newspaper reports based on those CIA findings suggested that Israel had supplied missile and avionics technology to China in the late 1980s and early 1990s. See, for example, "China Has U.S. Missile Secrets," *Washington Times* (January 5, 1993), regarding the Patriot system used in the Gulf War. Israel has also helped China develop its J-10 fighter, a system based on the Israeli "Lavi" which, in turn, had benefitted greatly from avionics in the best American fighter-bombers of the late 1980s. See "Israel Co-operates with China on Secret Fighter," *Flight International* (November 2–8, 1994). On naval expansion, see Ben Barber, "Beijing Eyes China South Sea with Sub Purchase," *Washington Times* (March 7, 1995).

57. Oksenberg, quoted in the *New York Times* (December 19, 1994).

58. An upbeat assessment of China's evolution is William H. Overholt, "China After Deng," *Foreign Affairs*, Vol. 75, No. 3 (May/June 1996), pp. 63–78.

59. See Thomas J. Christensen, "Chinese Realpolitik," *Foreign Affairs*, Vol. 75, No. 5 (September/October 1996), p. 37.

60. "Chinese Weapons Tests Seen Targeting Taiwanese Politics," *New York Times* (August 16, 1995). Before and during the 1996 Taiwanese election, the Chinese held huge military exercises just across the straits between the island and mainland, and repeatedly fired ballistic missiles into target areas less than thirty miles from the Taiwanese coast.

61. Many sources have reported these sales. See, for example, Martin Sieff, "U.S. Probes China on Missiles," *Washington Times* (July 9, 1995) and Dougles Jehl, "China Breaking Missile Pledge," *Washington Times* (May 6, 1993).

62. This more charitable view of Chinese foreign policy intentions is exemplified by Joseph Yu-shek Cheng, "China's America Policy," *Journal of Chinese Political Science*, Vol 2, No. 2 (Summer 1996), especially pp. 58–61.

63. A well-written example of concern and scenarios of impending conflict between the U.S. and the Beijing regime is Richard Bernstein and Ross Munro, *The Coming Conflict with China* (New York: Alfred Knopf, 1997).

64. An insightful discussion of this thesis is Samuel S. Kim, "China's Quest for Security in the Post-Cold War World," Strategic Studies Institute Monograph, U.S. Army War College, Carlisle, PA (July 29, 1996).

65. On post-Tiananmen commentaries, see, for example, the *South China Morning Post*, Hong Kong (September 25, 1989) which quotes the official Beijing daily *Remin Ribao* (September 24, 1989) in this regard. By mid- and late 1995, there was substantial talk of a new U.S. "containment" strategy and "hegemonist" policy toward China. See Cheng, op. cit., p. 66. Japanese militarism is a theme, for example, in *Jiefangjun Bao* (April 2, 1996), p. 1. On the "China threat" theme, see Cheng, op. cit., p. 69–70, and his citations of *Renmin Ribao* (December 22, 1995 and January 26, 1996).

66. See Steven Mufson, "Ethnic Turmoil Roils Western China," *Washington Post* (February 23, 1997).

67. Clifford Krauss, "U.S. Doubtful Japanese Will Join Plan for Missile Defense," *New York Times* (February 14, 1997).

68. Charles J. Hanley, "Japan Keeps Open Unthinkable Option," *Washington Times* (May 12, 1995) and "Japan Shifts Its Stand on Ruling Out A-Bomb," *Los Angeles Times* (July 9, 1993).

69. Sandra Sugawara, "Japanese Face Up to Need for Change," *International Herald Tribune* (March 10, 1997).

70. A good account of this episode was in *Jane's Intelligence Review*. See E. Croody, "Urban Terrorism: Chemical Warfare in Japan," Vol. 7, No. 11 (November 1995), p. 521.

71. A more upbeat economic assessment of Russia was conveyed in Avraham Shama, "Inside Russia's True Economy," *Foreign Policy*, No. 103 (Summer 1996), pp. 111–127.

72. *The Economist* (March 8, 1997) cites data from a "Visions" survey in which the top ten "worries" were, with the exception of crime, dominated by strictly economic matters (p. 55). "The decentralization of fears" is Vladimir Shlapentokh's term from his article "Decentralization of Fears: Life in Post-Communist Society," unpublished manuscript, Department of Sociology, University of Michigan, January 1997.

73. "Sino-Russian Arms Bazaar," *Jane's Intelligence Review*, Vol. 8, No. 7 (July 1996), p. 30.

74. See, for example, Senator Bill Bradley's "A Misguided Russia Policy," *Foreign Policy*, No. 101 (Winter 1995/96), pp. 81–101.

75. Barry Buzan discusses this notion in detail in *People, States, and Fear* (Hemel Hempstead: Harvester Wheatsheaf/Lynne Rienner, 1991), Chapter 2.

76. World Bank data on murder rates per 100,000 population for the late 1980s and early 1990s ranked the U.S. ninth in the world, lower than eight Latin American states, but far higher than any other advanced industrial democracy (at 10.1 murders per 100,000).

77. This is the argument of constructivists like Alexander Wendt. See his "Collective Identity Formation and the International State," *American Political Science Review*, Vol. 88, No. 2 (June 1994), pp. 384–396.

4 / The Era of Multiplying Schisms: World Security in the Twenty-First Century

MICHAEL T. KLARE

From a world security perspective, the post-Cold War era—the name popularly given to the period that commenced with the fall of the Berlin Wall in November 1989—has drawn to a close. Although widely viewed as the beginning of a new epoch, the post-Cold War era proved to be a relatively short-term transitional period, lasting only until the late 1990s. Now that the major aftershocks of the Cold War's demise have passed, it is time to abandon this transitional mentality and look ahead to the challenges and crises that are most likely to preoccupy international policymakers in the twenty-first century.

The conclusion of the Cold War was one of the most tumultuous and significant events in modern human history. For the peoples of the former Soviet Union (FSU) and the ex-communist states of Eastern Europe, this event entailed traumas that resembled, in many respects, the consequences of a major military defeat. The Soviet Union itself broke up into an unstable constellation of fifteen independent states—some lacking the resources to survive alone and others harboring ethnic minorities (like the Chechens of Russia) that have sought independence on their own. The trauma of dissolution was also felt in the former Yugoslavia, where disputes between ethnic communities over the nature of post-communist rule led to bloody fighting in Croatia and Bosnia.

To a considerable extent, these post-Cold War crises diminished in intensity in the mid-1990s. This reflects, most of all, the relatively tranquil 1996 presidential election in Russia, which ensured the continued implementation of post-communist reforms. Although there was much about the election that was disconcerting, such as the monopolization of the national media by pro-Yeltsin forces, it nevertheless provided a mandate of sorts for the "normalization" of Russian society along modern, Western lines.[1] Progress in arms control also led to the establishment of reasonably effective controls over the remnants of the USSR's nuclear arms complex, while NATO intervention and vigorous U.S. diplomacy produced a degree of peace and stability in the Balkans.

It is true, of course, that many of the problems unleashed by the Cold War's demise will remain significant features of the world security environment for many years to come. Certainly the status of the FSU's nuclear weapons—and of all the fissionable materials still in Russia's possession—

will be a matter of long-term concern. Russia's continuing sales of modern arms and nuclear technology to contentious Third World countries like Iran will also pose a danger. But these problems will no longer *dominate* the security agenda, as they did in the past; rather, they will take their place among an *array* of dangers that will compete for the attention of international policymakers.

It is possible, of course, that some new threat, or combination of threats, will prove so severe in the years ahead as to define the historical era we are now entering. Just as the rise of Nazism in Germany came to define the security environment of the 1930s, some future danger—the outbreak of a major arms race in Asia, perhaps, or the emergence of some new ecological threat—may come to define the early decades of the twenty-first century. At this point, however, no such overarching threat can be discerned. Rather, we face a security environment composed of *many* perils, none of which poses an overwhelming threat to world survival but all of which have the potential to cause considerable harm and suffering.

In considering these perils, it is important to note that the emerging world security environment is, on the whole, less menacing than that of the Cold War period, when the world faced a very real threat of nuclear Armageddon. But while the risk of a global nuclear war has not disappeared altogether (and will not disappear until all or most of the world's nuclear munitions have been disabled), the likelihood of such a disaster has been significantly diminished. With the dissolution of the Warsaw Treaty Organization, moreover, the risk of a continental-wide clash in Europe has become negligible. East-West military competition in other areas has also come to an end, significantly reducing the danger of a major conflagration in the Third World.

The risk of major international conflict is also diminished by the fact that none of the world's existing great powers—the United States, Russia, China, Japan, and the major Western European states—are currently engaged in an all-out military competition with any of the others. Great-power rivalries of this sort were a conspicuous feature of the global security landscape during much of the twentieth century, provoking two world wars and a succession of lesser conflicts. Today, however, all of the great powers are members of the United Nations and are further linked through a complex web of economic, diplomatic, and arms-control regimes. While sharp disagreements are likely to arise among these states in the years ahead, and a future military competition between some combination of them cannot be ruled out, the world does not appear to face the immediate prospect of a great-power conflict.

All this having been said, it must be noted that many types of lesser conflicts remain a significant threat to global security and that other types of security threats are likely to arise in the years ahead. While the likelihood of a major conventional conflict has declined, the world faces an increased risk of ethnic, religious, and sectarian conflict. Wars of these types, such as those now (or recently) under way in Afghanistan, Algeria, Angola, Bosnia,

Burma, Chechnya, Kashmir, Liberia, Rwanda, Sierra Leone, Somalia, Sri Lanka, Sudan, and Zaire, do not threaten global stability in the way that a major war in Europe would, but can produce huge numbers of civilian casualties and force millions of people to flee their homelands.

The new era is also likely to witness the emergence or intensification of other types of security threats. These range from illegal drug trafficking and transnational criminal activity to environmental degradation, economic and trade disputes, resource scarcities, mass human migrations, and excessive population growth. Again, these threats do not constitute a peril on the scale of global thermonuclear war—but they *are* significant in their own right, and could prove far more severe in the decades ahead. They can also interact with one another in such a way as to erode and eventually shatter the social fabric in many countries.

The proliferation of low-level conflict and the intensification of other security threats is producing a new international configuration of social, political, and economic cleavages. Just as the world security environment was once defined by the deep, continent-spanning divide between East and West, it can now be characterized by a complex pattern of interlacing schisms—each of which represents a potential site of ferment and violence. And while none of these fault lines is as deep or wide as those seen in Europe and Asia at the height of the Cold War, they appear to be branching out across the globe and intersecting with one another in an unstable and menacing fashion.

To define this new period, I propose the term "era of multiplying schisms." While not a particularly elegant term, it aptly describes the emerging situation: a world in which multiple pressures are being brought to bear upon human society, producing new social cleavages and widening existing ones. These schisms are more concentrated in some areas than in others, but no section of the globe is entirely free of their presence. As these rifts widen and grow, societies experience more and more tension until the social fabric unravels and trauma of one sort or another ensues.[2]

These traumas can take many forms. Most common, perhaps, is the outbreak or intensification of nationalist struggles conducted by ethnic groups seeking to carve out their own nation-states in territories controlled or claimed by existing states. Examples include the separatist drives being waged by the Kurds, the Chechens, the Tamils of Sri Lanka, the Karens of Burma, the Kashmiris, and the Palestinians. Also common is the outbreak of fighting between various ethnic and religious groups over control of the state apparatus in lands where such control is seen as a vital source of jobs, housing, and business opportunities. This appears to be the case in such war-torn societies as Liberia, Rwanda, Somalia, and Tajikistan. Yet another widespread response to social breakdown is the flight of entire communities to other, more stable regions—often producing a hostile response from the permanent residents of the receiving area.

As these examples suggest, the multiplying schisms of the current era do not always fall along established national boundaries. Indeed, they are more likely to fall along *internal* boundaries within states, such as those between ethnic, religious, and economic constituencies. In the Middle East, for example, the most volatile boundaries are not those between Israel and neighboring Arab states, but those between Jewish and Palestinian communities in the West Bank—a fact that has hugely complicated the task of implementing the Oslo peace accords. A similar pattern is visible in Bosnia, where Serbs, Croats, and Muslims had lived for generations in the same neighborhoods and villages before the outbreak of ethnic violence in 1992.

While these cleavages are more frequently found within societies than along a nation's borders, it is also true that they often extend *across* international boundaries, producing transnational schisms with offshoots in several states. The bitter fighting between Hutus and Tutsis, for instance, cuts through Burundi, Rwanda, and Zaire (now Congo). Similarly, the Kurdish struggle for autonomy extends from northern Iraq into parts of Iran, Syria, and Turkey. Environmental perils also tend to stretch across international boundaries. Thus, the southern fringe of the Sahara is pushing ever deeper into Chad, Mali, Mauritania, Niger, and Sudan, while the shrinkage of Southeast Asia's tropical forests is occurring simultaneously in Cambodia, Myanmar, Thailand, and Vietnam.

What is most common, in fact, is the *intersection* of internal and transnational schisms. That is, internal divisions between ethnic and religious groups are often connected, in various ways, to regional and global fissures. The fighting in Algeria, for instance, nominally revolves around the efforts of militant Islamists to establish a theocratic state on the model of Iran; much of the discontent that fuels this conflict, however, is derived from Algeria's sluggish economic performance, endemic political corruption, and high unemployment rate—factors that have been exacerbated in recent years by rapid population growth, mounting environmental decline, and a changing world economy.[3] High unemployment and continuing internal disorder have also prompted many Algerians to flee—often by illicit means—to France and other Western European countries, producing new social schisms in areas where unemployment is already high within the indigenous population. A similar pattern of interlocking schisms can be seen in other regions of conflict, including southeastern Europe and the Great Lakes region of Africa.[4]

The multiplying schisms of the current era will pose new and formidable challenges to the world community. The intervals between major international crises are likely to become shorter and shorter, allowing little time for careful analysis and planning. Concurrently, the scope and *complexity* of future crises is likely to grow, making their solution more and more difficult. As a consequence, the systems of international governance set up to deal with the exigencies of the Cold War era are not likely to cope successfully with the challenges of this new period; instead, new or transformed systems will be needed to deal with these new dangers, along with new methods of mediation, reconciliation, and conflict prevention.

Before these new systems can be established, however, the world community will require a sophisticated understanding of the new perils and the ways in which they interact. Developing such an understanding will, in fact, represent a major challenge for international security analysts in the years ahead. One way to approach this task is to examine the multiple pressures that are being exerted on human societies and the various types of cleavages they are producing. Five such categories, in particular, merit our attention: regional rivalries and antagonisms; ethnic, religious, and sectarian conflicts; economic schisms; demographic schisms, and environmental schisms.

REGIONAL RIVALRIES AND ANTAGONISMS

With the Cold War over, the bipolar division of the world into two great "camps" or alliance systems has come to an end, and no similar configuration of military blocs has come to take its place. However, some of the regional rivalries that emerged during the Cold War era—often as a by-product of superpower competition—continue to fester. Furthermore, new rivalries have begun to develop in some areas. Although not as menacing as the antagonism between NATO and the Warsaw Pact, these regional antagonisms—both old and new—pose an enduring and significant threat to world security. Indeed, any major outbreak of large-scale combat in the years ahead is most likely to arise out of a rivalry of this type.

Of all of the dangers of the current era, these regional rivalries are most akin to those of the Cold War period. As in other areas of international affairs, however, these antagonisms are being reshaped by the powerful forces of global change. These forces are also responsible for the emergence of new rivalries. Thus, as we look into the future, we need to ask two vital questions: (1) How, and to what extent, have existing rivalries been affected by changing world conditions? (2) What new antagonisms have emerged in recent years, or are likely to do so in the future?

Because the existing rivalries have persisted for so long in their present guise, it is often difficult to detect fundamental changes that might become more obvious to future observers. Nevertheless, the immense upheavals of the past few years do seem to have had considerable impact on a number of these rivalries. In particular, the disappearance of the Soviet Union as a major military patron and the simultaneous emergence of the United States as the world's paramount power has encouraged some potential adversaries to adopt a more flexible and conciliatory stance than they might have otherwise.

The loss of Soviet military support has proved especially onerous for Syria and North Korea—both of which were heavily dependent on Soviet arms transfers, and now find themselves without a major superpower patron. Although neither of these states has indicated that it is willing to abandon the military option entirely, both have engaged in a new round of peace talks with their traditional foes. Syria has agreed to participate in the U.S.-sponsored Middle East peace process, and to consider a permanent peace settlement with Israel; North Korea has agreed to dismantle its nuclear weapons program, and to engage in peace talks with the United States and South Korea.[5] Future developments could, of course, block progress on either or both of these peace initiatives, but the mere fact of their existence represents a significant change from just a few years ago.

The disappearance of the Soviet Union and the resulting prominence of the United States has also had an effect on other regional rivalries. In South Asia, for instance, India and Pakistan can no longer play one superpower against the other in their efforts to fuel their own military competition, as they did in the past. Both, in fact, now seek to maintain close ties with Washington, and so are unlikely to engage in aggressive behavior that might alienate U.S. policymakers.

Another aspect of the changing security environment that may affect the future evolution of existing regional rivalries is the explosive growth in international trade and commerce. This expansion could prompt some antagonists to overlook their political differences in order to benefit from advantageous trade relationships. This factor is particularly salient in the case of China and Taiwan, both of which seek to increase their commercial linkages even while quarreling over a wide range of political and military issues. It is possible that increased trade and investment will lead to further accommodation between these two historical adversaries; however, the process is not, at this point, so far advanced as to preclude a return to a more fractious and hostile relationship. Elsewhere, the attraction of increased trade and investments may induce other pairs or groups of adversaries to moderate their mutual hostility in the years ahead.[6]

How all of this will play itself out in the future is something that can only be determined with time. It is evident, however, that new forces are at work in the international arena, and that these forces will have an effect on the long-term evolution of existing regional rivalries. At the same time, these forces are contributing to the emergence of *new* conflict systems. Among these, two stand out as deserving special attention: the growing tension between Russia and its neighbors to the south and west (including other former republics of the Soviet Union), and that between China and its neighbors in Southeast Asia and the western Pacific.

The dissolution of the Soviet Union in 1992 produced one large successor state—the Russian Federation—and fourteen smaller states that had long existed in the shadow of Moscow. While Russian leaders have pledged to respect the independence of these states, many politicians and pundits argue that Russia has a historical or a geopolitical mandate to exercise a form of dominion over them. Some Russian politicians go further, calling for the reconstitution of the Soviet Union or the Russian empire. While Moscow may, at present, lack the resources and the military might to act on these impulses, the very popularity of these views will produce continuing tension between Russia and the other former republics of the Soviet Union.

The risk of future conflict between Russia and the other republics is heightened, moreover, by the existence of a number of important irritants in their mutual relationships. Most significant, perhaps, is the existence of large communities of ethnic Russians in the Baltic states, Belarus, Kazakhstan, Ukraine, and several of the other ex-Soviet republics. These communities include many Russian natives who migrated there during the Soviet era to pursue job opportunities—often in the context of a deliberate effort by Moscow to dilute the non-Russian populations of these areas (and thereby reduce the risk of ethnic revolt). While these Russians once enjoyed special privileges as members of the Union's dominant group, they are now being subjected to various forms of discrimination by these states' majority group—a factor that is fueling some of the neoimperial sentiment in Russia itself. Further complicating this picture is the emergence of territorial disputes between Russia and its new neighbors, including a dispute with Ukraine over the Crimea (until the Khrushchev era a part of the Russian Federation) and with some of the Caucasian and Central Asian republics over control of the Caspian Sea (which is believed to lie atop vast deposits of oil).[7]

The evolution of Russia's ties with the other ex-Soviet states is likely to be heavily influenced by another set of uneasy relationships—those involving Russia and the emerging powers of Southwest Asia, particularly Iran and Turkey. In the wake of the USSR's collapse, these powers have adopted a more assertive foreign policy in the region, particularly with respect to the ex-Soviet republics of the Caucasus and Central Asia, which harbor significant Turkic- and Persian-speaking populations. Iran and Turkey have both begun to compete with Russia for influence in the newly independent states, and, in some cases, have sought to interest them in joint economic endeavors, particularly in the energy field. This has provoked considerable ire from Moscow, which seeks to dominate the region and to control its economic development.[8]

A somewhat similar pattern of conflictive relations is also emerging in East Asia, where the ascension of China as a major power has produced new regional tensions. With a booming economy and growing military strength, China is poised to play an increasingly assertive role in Asian affairs—a prospect that has produced considerable anxiety in neighboring countries. For Taiwan, of course, this is nothing new; for the newly industrializing countries (NICs) of Southeast Asia, however, the rise of China poses new and unfamiliar dangers. In particular, these states are troubled by China's unyielding claim to control over the islands of the South China Sea—a region claimed in part by several of the NICs, and used by every country in the region as a vital trade route.

The islands at stake in this dispute are the Paracel and Spratly archipelagos. For the most part uninhabited, these islands are thought to sit astride vast undersea oil reserves—and so have been the subject of competing claims by China, Vietnam, Taiwan, the Philippines, Malaysia, Indonesia, and Brunei. Although professing to welcome negotiations on the fate of the islands, Beijing has claimed them as part of China's national territory and has periodically sent warships into the area to assert its sovereignty and to chase off vessels belonging to the other claimants—on several occasions provoking a firefight.[9] In response, the nations of the area have begun to expand their own air and naval capabilities, producing a regional arms race and a recurring risk of conflict.[10]

New antagonisms are also likely to emerge in other regions, particularly in those areas where—as in Caspian and South China Seas—several states have staked out conflicting claims to major sources of oil. Fresh water is another vital resource that may figure in future rivalries of this sort. As population and industrial growth continues in areas of scarce or limited water supplies, countries are likely to clash over the utilization of shared rivers and aquifers. Thus, Turkey's decision to dam the Tigris and Euphrates Rivers and to divert their waters to new irrigation projects has provoked fresh tensions with Syria and Iraq, which are largely dependent on these two rivers for their own water requirements. Disputes over water usage could also provoke conflict among states that jointly rely on other major river systems, including the Ganges, the Jordan, and the Nile.[11]

ETHNIC, RELIGIOUS, AND SECTARIAN SCHISMS

One of the most prominent features of the contemporary world security landscape is the proliferation of ethnic, religious, and insurgent conflicts *within* states. Such conflicts typically involve fighting between irregular units—ethnic militias, guerrillas, terrorists, and so on—and the armed forces of the state, or between one irregular unit and another (or several others). Combat of this sort rarely entails large set-piece battles like those seen in major interstate conflicts, but can produce endemic violence of a particularly brutal nature—often involving attacks on civilian populations and/or the basic resources (fields, forests, factories) on which they depend. In many cases, such fighting is accompanied by widespread hunger, the destruction of homes and villages, and the flight of fearful survivors to other regions or countries.

Internal conflicts of this sort can arise from a variety of causes. In some cases, ethnic or religious minorities seek to break off a section of the country they presently inhabit and use it to establish their own national homeland. This is evident, for instance, in the struggles of the Kurds in Iraq and Turkey, the Tamils in Sri Lanka, the Chechens in Russia, and the Palestinians in Gaza and the West Bank. Ethnic groups may also seek to gain greater political or economic power within an existing state, or to enlarge the borders of their present homeland in order to include others of their kind living in neighboring countries (as seen, for example, in the efforts of the Serbs of the former Yugoslavia to incorporate parts of Croatia and Bosnia in a "greater Serbia"). Still other groups seek to transform their societies by imposing a certain political system (for example, Marxism in the case of the Shining Path guerrillas of Peru) or a particular religious system (fundamentalist Islam in the case of the Taliban of Afghanistan). Such motives, according to the Stockholm International Peace Research Institute (SIPRI), figured in all thirty of the major armed conflicts under way around the world in 1995.[12]

It is true, of course, that many of the ethnic and sectarian conflicts of the current period have their roots in clashes or invasions that occurred many years ago. It is also true that the violent upheavals that broke out in the former Yugoslavia and the former Soviet Union in the early 1990s drew upon deep-seated hostilities, even if these cleavages were not generally visible during much of the communist era (when overt displays of ethnic antagonism were prohibited by government decree). In this sense, the ethnic fissures that are now receiving close attention from international policymakers cannot be said to represent a truly "new" phenomena. Nevertheless, many of these schisms have become more pronounced since the end of the Cold War or have exhibited characteristics that are unique to the current era.[13]

Greatly contributing to the intensity of recent ethnic and sectarian conflicts is the erosion or even disappearance of central state authority in poor Third World countries experiencing extreme economic, political, and environmental stress. As these stresses accumulate, the flimsy state structures established at the time of independence—often following years of colonial exploitation and neglect—are simply not capable of coping with the demands of housing and feeding their growing populations with the meager resources at hand. In such circumstances, people lose all confidence in the state's ability to meet their basic needs and turn instead to more traditional, kinship-based forms of association for help in getting by—a process that often results in competition and conflict among such groups over what remains of the nation's scarce resources.[14]

This shift in people's loyalty from the state to clan or ethnic identity is particularly evident in Somalia, where a national rebellion against the government of former dictator Mohammed Siad Barre degenerated into a contest between clan-based militias for control of the nation's crumbling infrastructure.[15] When UN peacekeepers attempted to disarm these factions in 1993, they came under attack from one of the most powerful of these militias—one led by General Mohammed Farrah Aidid—and, after suffering a number of casualties, elected to withdraw. A very similar pattern can be seen in Liberia, where several competing militias, organized largely along tribal lines, fought for control of the country until a peace agreement was signed in 1996. Here, too, international peacekeepers failed to disarm the major combatants and so fighting continued for many years between regional warlords who extracted what they could from the local population to pay for arms and ammunition.[16]

Also contributing to the intensity of ethnic and sectarian conflict in the current era is the spread of mass communications and other instruments of popular mobilization. Such advances have accelerated what James Rosenau calls a worldwide "skill revolution," whereby individual citizens "have become increasingly competent in assessing where they fit in international affairs and how their behavior can be aggregated into significant collective outcomes."[17] (See Chapter 2.) This competence can translate into calls for greater personal freedom and power, leading to the spread of democracy. It can also lead, however, to increased popular mobilization along ethnic, religious, and linguistic lines—often producing great friction and disorder within heterogenous societies. A significant case in point is India, where Hindu nationalists have proved adept at employing modern means of communication and political organization to whip up anti-Muslim sentiment and thereby erode the authority of India's largely secular government.

To a greater degree than ever before, ethnic and internal conflicts have entailed or aroused a significant degree of international involvement. In many cases, members of diaspora communities living outside the zone of conflict have contributed to the intensity of combat by supplying the beligerents with funds, arms, or medical supplies, or by engaging in terrorist actions against embassies and other outposts of the enemy in their own territory.[18] These conflicts have also produced vast numbers of international refugees, producing great strain on humanitarian aid agencies and on the populations of receiving countries. For these and other reasons, the international community has intervened in these conflicts in a variety of ways—through diplomacy and mediation, the deployment of peacekeeping forces, and the delivery of emergency food assistance.

Recent experience suggests that ethnic and sectarian violence *can* be curtailed if the international community is willing to make the necessary effort. However flawed, the Dayton peace accords brought a measure of calm to Bosnia and provided the political space for sustained attempts at mediation and conflict resolution. A similar process may result in the termination or abatement of long-standing conflicts occurring elsewhere. But the conditions that led to the proliferation of sectarian warfare in the early 1990s have not disappeared, and could grow more severe in the years ahead—producing a fresh round of ethnic and internal conflicts.

ECONOMIC SCHISMS

When viewed as a whole, the world has grown much richer over the past 25 years. According to the Worldwatch Institute, the world's total annual income rose from $10 trillion in 1970 to approximately $20 trillion in 1994 (in constant 1987 dollars).[19] This increase has been accompanied, moreover, by an improved standard of living for many of the world's peoples. But not all nations, and not all people in the richer nations, have benefitted from the global increase in wealth. Some nations (mostly concentrated in Africa and Latin America) have experienced marginal growth or even a net *decline* in gross domestic product (GDP) over the past few decades, while many of the nations that did achieve a higher GDP also experienced an increase in the numbers of people living in extreme poverty. Furthermore, the gap in national income between the richest and the poorest countries continues to increase, as does the gap between rich and poor people within most societies.[20]

The growing disparities between rich and poor societies are amply demonstrated in the UN figures on global income rates. Between 1960 and 1990, the average annual per capita GDP in the developed market economies rose from $5,501 to $12,490 (in 1980 dollars), an increase of 127 percent; for the developing nations, per capital GDP rose by only 76 percent, from $556 to $980. This meant that the *ratio* of the rich states' per capita GDP to that of the developing countries grew significantly, from approximately 10:1 in 1960 to 13:1 in 1990. Furthermore, many areas of the Third World experienced negligible or even negative growth during this period. The per capita GDP of sub-Saharan Africa, for instance, actually declined between 1960 and 1990, from $514 per year to $440.[21] Thus, while many people in the world are enjoying higher standards of living, a very large proportion of the human community—well over one billion people—continue to live in dire poverty. (See Chapter 14.)

These differentials in economic growth rates, along with the widening gap between rich and poor, is producing dangerous fissures in many societies. As the masses of poor see their chances of escaping acute poverty diminish, they are likely to grow increasingly resentful of those whose growing wealth is painfully evident around them. This resentment is especially pronounced in the impoverished shantytowns that surround many of the seemingly prosperous cities of the Third World. In these inhospitable surroundings, large numbers of people—especially among the growing legions of unemployed youth—are becoming attracted to extremist political and religious movements, such as the *Sendero Luminoso* (Shining Path) of Peru and the Islamic Salvation Front of Algeria. Many others, meanwhile, have been recruited into criminal gangs or drug trafficking syndicates. The result, in all too many countries, is an increase in urban crime and violence.[22]

The risk of such disorder arising from economic inequities is further enhanced by the growing inability of state authorities—especially in poor and underdeveloped countries—to minimize the hardships of poverty or to generate new employment. In order to secure the funds needed to pay for vital imports of food and fuel, or to retire past debts, many Third World governments have had to impose "structural adjustment programs" devised by the World Bank and the International Monetary Fund (IMF)—programs that typically entail the privatization of government-owned industries, the contraction of state services, and the elimination of subsidies for basic necessities like food and transportation. To attract foreign investment, moreover, these governments are often under pressure to reduce taxes, keep wages low, and overlook occupational and environmental standards. All this, in turn, greatly diminishes the state's ability to meet the needs and expectations of those on the bottom and middle rungs of society—thus increasing the attraction of extremist movements and criminal occupations.[23]

Also contributing to social instability in many countries is the persistent growth in permanent unemployment—a phenomenon that has been called the "global jobs crisis."[24] An estimated one-third of the world's 2.8 billion working people are either jobless or underemployed, and the millions of young adults who will enter the labor market in the years ahead are likely to further swell the legions of unemployed.[25] Economists differ on the causes of this phenomenon, but most agree that the growing competitiveness of the world economy will place a premium on corporate "downsizing" and the elimination of public-sector jobs—processes that are certain to keep unemployment high. In such an environment, jobless and insecure workers are likely to prove highly susceptible to extremist appeals of a racist or xenophobic character (such as the anti-immigrant polemics of Le Pen and others like him in Western Europe), or to pursue alternative forms of employment in banditry, drug trafficking, and other forms of criminal (and often violent) behavior.

These various patterns are evident in all areas of the world, but have become particularly noticeable in the former Soviet Union, China, and the once-communist states of Eastern Europe. Until the recent introduction of market reforms in these countries, unemployment was almost nonexistent and the income gap between rich and poor was kept relatively narrow by state policy. With the onset of capitalism, however, the economic plight of the lowest strata of these societies has become considerably worse, while the newly formed entrepreneurial class has been able to accumulate considerable wealth—and to display it in highly conspicuous ways (as, for example, through the ownership of imported luxury cars). This has generated new class tensions and provided ammunition for those who, like Gennadi Zyuganov of Russia's restyled Communist Party, seek the restoration of the old, state-dominated system.

Class tensions are less visible in China, but no less explosive in their implications. Although many residents of China's prosperous coastal areas (especially around Guangzhou and Shanghai) have attained a relatively high standard of living, hundreds of millions of rural Chinese continue to live in poverty. According to a 1996 World Bank report, some 300 million Chinese earn less than $1 per day, the minimum needed to escape extreme hardship and starvation. This has triggered rioting in some areas and led millions of rural inhabitants to migrate to the cities—producing a sharp increase in urban unemployment, crime, and homelessness, with all of their attendant problems.[26] As yet, none of this has found expression in overt political opposition, but Communist Party officials—obviously mindful of the government's revolutionary origins—are clearly fearful of such a move, and so have moved swiftly to suppress any signs of political unrest.

Economic unrest has also emerged in other societies where the gap between rich and poor has become conspicuously wider. In South Korea, for instance, newly active trade unions have proved surprisingly militant, paralyzing Seoul and other major cities in a campaign to raise wages and improve job security.[27] Economic discontent has also fueled protests and rioting in Indonesia, where rising national income has failed to improve the lives of millions of low-paid factory workers.[28] Similar unrest can be seen in Brazil, Mexico, Thailand, and other newly industrialized nations.

DEMOGRAPHIC SCHISMS

Global population growth, and regional variations in such growth, represent another potential source of discord. According to recent UN estimates, total world population is expected to soar from approximately 5.6 billion people in 1994 to somewhere between 8 and 12 billion people by the year 2050[29]—an increase that will undoubtedly place great strain on the Earth's food production and environmental capacity. But the threat to the world's environment and food supply is not all that we have to worry about. Because population growth is occurring unevenly in different areas, with some of the highest rates of growth to be found in countries with the slowest rates of economic growth, future population increases could combine with other factors to exacerbate existing cleavages along ethnic, religious, and class lines.

Data collected by the United Nations provides clear evidence of worldwide variations in population growth. Overall, the less-developed countries (LDCs) are growing at a much faster rate than the advanced industrial nations. As a result, the share of world population accounted for by the LDCs rose from 69 percent in 1960 to 74 percent in 1980, and is expected to jump to nearly 80 percent in the year 2000. Among the LDCs, moreover, there have been marked variations in the rate of population growth: while the newly industrialized nations of East Asia have experienced a sharp decline in the rate of growth, Africa and parts of the Middle East have experienced an increase. If these trends persist, the global distribution of population will change dramatically over the next few decades, with some areas experiencing a substantial increase in total population and others moderate or even negligible growth.[30] (See Chapter 18.)

This is where other social and economic factors enter the picture. If the biggest increases in population were occurring in areas of rapid economic growth, the many young adults entering the job market each year would have a good chance of finding productive employment and would, therefore, be able to feed and house their growing families. In many societies, however, large increases in population are coinciding with low or stagnant economic growth—meaning that a large proportion of future job-seekers is not likely to find adequate employment. This, in turn, is likely to increase social instability in many areas. At the very least, it is bound to produce increased migration from rural areas (where population growth tends to be greatest) to urban centers (where most new jobs are to be found), and from poor and low-growth countries to faster-growing and more affluent ones. The former process is resulting in the rapid expansion of many Third World cities, with an attendant increase in urban crime and intergroup friction (especially where the new urban dwellers are of a different ethnic or tribal group from the original settlers); the latter is producing huge numbers of new immigrants, often sparking hostility—and sometimes violence—from the indigenous populations.[31]

Rapid population growth in poor countries with slow or stagnant economic growth has other significant implications. In many societies, it is leading to the hyperutilization of natural resources, particularly arable soil, grazing land, and forests—a process that severely complicates future economic growth (as vital raw materials are depleted) and accelerates the pace of environmental decline. It can also overwhelm the capacity of weak or divided governments to satisfy their people's basic needs, leading eventually to the collapse of states and to the sort of intergroup conflict described previously. Finally, it could generate fresh interstate conflicts as leaders of nations with exploding populations consider the seizure of less-crowded land in neighboring countries, or when states with relatively slow population growth employ stringent measures to exclude immigrants from nearby countries with high rates of growth.[32]

ENVIRONMENTAL SCHISMS

Worldwide environmental degradation and resource scarcities pose additional threats to global security. Even if dramatic and far-reaching measures are adopted by the world community to overcome future environmental perils—and this is by no means certain—the planetary ecosphere will continue to suffer from the legacy of past and current human activity. The buildup of carbon dioxide and other gases in the Earth's atmosphere, for example, is impeding the natural radiation of heat from the planet and thereby producing a gradual increase in global temperatures—a process likely to be accompanied by rising sea levels and the desiccation of once bountiful agricultural zones. Other forms of environmental degradation— the thinning of the earth's outer ozone layer, the poisoning of rivers, lakes, and oceans, the blight caused by "acid rain," and so on—will imperil human health and safety in other ways. And the steady depletion of such vital resources as oil, timber, and natural fisheries is likely to produce widespread human hardship.

As with population pressures, however, the damaging effects of environmental decline will not be felt uniformly by all peoples but will threaten some states and groups more than others—producing sharp cleavages in human society that could prove more destabilizing than the effects of the environment itself.[33] In many cases, the first to suffer from environmental decline are those living in marginally habitable areas such as tropical forests, arid grazing lands, and coastal lowlands. As drought persists, sea levels rise, and forests are harvested, these lands become increasingly uninhabitable. The choice, for those living in such areas, is often grim: to migrate to the cities, with all of their attendant problems, or to occupy the lands of neighboring peoples—often provoking fresh outbreaks of intergroup violence. (See Chapter 17.) The civil war in Mali, for instance, was ignited when the Tuareg people from the Sahel (the southern fringe of the Sahara) migrated into the more verdant lands of the Bambara.

The uneven impact of environmental decline has fallen with particular severity on indigenous peoples, who in many cases were originally driven into marginal habitats by more powerful groups. A conspicuous case in point is the Amazon region of Brazil, where systematic deforestation is destroying the habitat and lifestyle of the indigenous population—producing death, illness, and unwelcome migration to the cities. Deforestation and soil erosion was also a factor in the 1994 rebellion in Chiapas, spearheaded by Mexico's impoverished Mayan minority.[34] Similarly, in Nigeria, environmental damage caused by oil production in the Niger River Delta has led to protests by the Ogoni people who inhabit the region—protests that were violently crushed by the Nigerian military regime.[35]

Environmental pressures also place an especially heavy burden on poor Third World countries that lack the resources to respond effectively. While the wealthier nations are able to rebuild areas damaged by flooding or other disasters, to procure alternative sources of vital materials, and to relocate displaced citizens to safer regions, the poorer countries are much less capable of doing these things. As Thomas Homer-Dixon has noted, environmental decline "sharply raises financial and political demands on government by requiring huge spending on new infrastructure." For many Third World countries, this results in "a widening gap between demands on the state and its financial ability to meet these demands." This, in turn, can lead to state collapse and the outbreak of fighting among competing ethnic groups—accompanied, in many cases, by widespread migration to countries better able to cope with environmental damage.[36]

The worldwide scarcity or depletion of vital resources is also likely to produce strains and conflict in the human population. Although the global demand for energy is expected to grow steadily in the years ahead, the world's most important source of energy—liquid petroleum—is a finite commodity that could begin to run out in second or third decade of the twenty-first century.[37] As natural petroleum becomes more scarce, the major oil-consuming countries are likely to become frantic in their efforts to control or gain access to major sources of supply—a process that could easily lead to war. Indeed, the large U.S. military presence in the Persian Gulf region is primarily intended to protect U.S. access to the region's vast oil reserves—the source of approximately half of current world oil exports. And because the Gulf is expected to provide an even larger share of oil exports in the twenty-first century (as much as 70 percent), the United States can be expected to resist by force any effort by a hostile power to gain control of the region.

Scarcities of other vital resources, including fresh water, fish stocks, and timber, could also provoke fighting between competing states and peoples. Although fresh water is abundant in some (mostly northern) regions, it is not available in sufficient quantity in many areas with large and growing populations—leading, conceivably, to recurring conflict over access to vital sources of supply. The potential for conflict between Iraq, Syria, and Turkey over the Tigris and Euphrates Rivers has already been noted. Similarly,

Egypt has threatened to intervene in Ethiopia and the Sudan if either of these countries divert significant quantities of water from the Nile, the source of most of Egypt's supply.[38] The worldwide depletion of the world's natural fisheries has also led to conflict as coastal states seek to exclude foreign fishing fleets from their offshore waters. And the growing shrinkage of the world's tropical forests has triggered battles between the indigenous peoples (and others who inhabit the forests) and those who would log the timber for profit.

THE NEW CARTOGRAPHY OF WORLD SECURITY: IMPLICATIONS FOR WORLD SECURITY

These multiplying schisms of the current era are constructing a new map of global security affairs. Whereas earlier maps of this type depicted only one type of cleavage—the political divisions between major military blocs—the new map would show a much wider array of fissures, some penetrating deep within states and others slicing straight across international boundaries.

A map of global schisms would reveal another critical characteristic of the emerging security environment: in many areas of the world, the various types of schisms overlap and intersect one another, producing zones of profound and chronic instability. In such areas, already divided societies are experiencing severe economic, demographic, and environmental pressures, greatly increasing the risk of state collapse and social disintegration. The intersection of these schisms is also producing new instabilities at the regional level, particularly where long-standing political divisions coincide with disputes over the possession of vital resources or the use of shared water supplies.

Such a map would also show that these fissures are to be found in every part of the world, not just in the poorer and less-developed areas. Although it is certainly apparent that the greatest concentrations of schisms are to be found in parts of Africa and Asia, where existing social cleavages coincide with economic, environmental, and demographic fissures, significant rifts can also be found in other regions. As unemployment has risen in Western Europe, for instance, there has been an accompanying increase in anti-immigrant violence. The United States has also experienced periodic outbreaks of anti-immigrant violence, along with other forms of ethnic strife.

Given the continuing multiplication and spread of these various types of cleavages, the world system is likely to experience increased tension and strife in the years ahead. The resulting upheavals may be localized in their immediate effects, but inevitably the world as a whole will suffer from the chronic and ubiquitous disorder. The proliferation of conflict will also impede international efforts to address the underlying causes of instability, including underdevelopment, hunger, and environmental decline. While some regions of the world may remain relatively stable when compared to areas of recurring disorder, no portion of the globe will be entirely immune to the stresses described above.

All of this has profound implications for global governance and the management of national and international security. No longer will it be possible to manage major crises by arranging a deal among leaders of the major powers. The emerging problems are too complex, and involve too many parties of various types (including nonstate actors and a variety of transnational institutions, like the World Bank and the International Red Cross), to be solved by a few leaders meeting in isolation. Instead, the world community will have to devise new instruments of governance and crisis control, allowing for the input and participation of many types of actors.

The success of these new instruments will depend, to a considerable extent, on their ability to promote cooperation—or, at the very least, mutual acceptance and tolerance—among the parties to international and internal disputes. This is because any resort to the use of violence by any of these parties is likely to prove self-defeating in the attainment of their ultimate objectives; modern weapons are simply too effective, and too widely disseminated, to permit a rapid and cost-free victory for either side in any conflict among one armed group and another. Instead, they will discover that a negotiated solution is the only way to attain at least some of their vital objectives—and that arriving at such a solution *requires* that they make some concessions to their foes. This is the painful but inescapable lesson of the Dayton peace process and the ongoing Israeli-Palestinian dialogue.

The resolution of future crises will also require the integration of economic, social, and environmental measures with more traditional security arrangements. Certainly security issues will play a central role in most agreements, as it is not possible to move forward on other objectives when the security environment is unstable: people will not return to their abandoned villages and begin planting crops again if they are afraid of being shot. By the same token, however, people will not agree to complex peace arrangements (like the Dayton agreement and Israeli-Palestinian accords) unless they believe that peace will bring with it an improvement in their basic living conditions. In most cases, this will entail not only the provision of substantial reconstruction assistance, but also the establishment of new schools, health facilities, job programs, irrigation projects, and so forth.

It is not the purpose of this essay to identify all of the new instruments and programs that will be needed. That can only come from further study of the world security environment and exhaustive consultation among representatives of all interested parties. But the starting point of any such effort must be the mapping and evaluation of the multiple schisms that are likely to jeopardize world peace and stability in the decades ahead. Only through such an analysis will it be possible to identify the major threats to international peace and stability, and to assemble the many types of expertise that will be needed to design and implement effective responses.

QUESTIONS FOR FURTHER STUDY

1. On what basis does Klare contend that the post-Cold War era has drawn to a close? Is his argument persuasive?
2. Why does Klare believe that "era of multiplying schisms" is an appropriate name for the historical period that we are now entering? What are the distinctive characteristics of this new era?
3. What, according to Klare, are the major types of global schisms that can be found in this new era? How are they different from those of the Cold War period? Is this distinction valid?
4. What are the implications for global governance and crisis management of the "new cartography" of international security?

Notes

1. For a similar analysis, see Angela Stent and Lilia Shevtsova, "Russia's Election: No Turning Back," *Foreign Policy,* No. 103 (Summer 1996), pp. 92–109.
2. The author first discussed the emergence of multiple schisms of these types in "Redefining Security: The New Global Schisms," *Current History* (November 1996), pp. 353–58.
3. For background on Algeria, see Andrew J. Pierre and William B. Quandt, *The Algerian Crisis* (Washington: Carnegie Endowment for International Peace, 1996).
4. For further discussion of the ways in which these various types of schisms intersect, see Michael Renner, *Fighting for Survival: Environmental Decline, Social Conflict, and the New Age of Insecurity* (New York: Worldwatch Institute and W.W. Norton, 1996). See also Thomas F. Homer-Dixon, "Environmental Scarcity, Mass Violence, and the Limits to Ingenuity," *Current History* (November 1996), pp. 359–65; and Robert D. Kaplan, "The Coming Anarchy," *The Atlantic Monthly* (February 1994), pp. 44–75.
5. On North Korea, see Nicholas D. Kristoff, "In the Two Koreas' Ice Rivalry, Signs of a Thaw," *The New York Times* (January 26, 1997) and Steven Lee Myers, "U.S. Reports Foes in Korea Willing to Discuss Peace," *The New York Times* (December 31, 1996).
6. For further discussion of the implications of economic globalization for regional peace and conflict, see Benjamin R. Barber, *Jihad vs. McWorld* (New York: Ballantine Books, 1996).
7. For further discussion of these issues, see Karen Dawisha, "Russian Foreign Policy in the Near Abroad and Beyond," *Current History* (October 1966), pp. 330–34. On the Caspian Sea dispute, see Elaine Holoboff, "Russia and Oil Politics in the Caspian," *Jane's Intelligence Review* (February 1996), pp. 80–84.
8. On the competition between these states in the energy field, see Hugh Pope, "Great Game II: Oil Companies Rush into the Caucasus to Tap the Caspian," *The Wall Street Journal* (April 25, 1997).
9. For background on these disputes, see Mark K. Valencia, "Troubled Waters," *Bulletin of the Atomic Scientists* (January/February 1997), pp. 49–54.
10. See Michael T. Klare, "The Next Great Arms Race," *Foreign Affairs,* Vol. 72, No. 3 (Summer 1993), pp. 136–52.
11. For background on these disputes, see Kent Hughes Butts, "The Strategic Importance of Water," *Parameters,* Vol. 27, No. 1 (Spring 1997), pp. 65–83 and Peter H. Gleick, "Water and Conflict," *International Security,* Vol. 18, No. 1 (Summer 1993), pp. 79–112.
12. Stockholm International Peace Research Institute, *SIPRI Yearbook 1996: Armaments, Disarmament, and International Security* (Oxford and New York: Oxford University Press, 1996), pp. 16–30. For discussion, see Ted Robert Gurr, "Communal Conflicts and Global Security," *Current History,* Vol. 94, No. 592 (May 1995), pp. 212–17.
13. For further discussion of contemporary forms of ethnic conflict, see the essays in Michael E. Brown, ed., *Ethnic Conflict and International Security* (Princeton: Princeton University Press, 1993). See also Michael E. Brown, Owen R. Coté, Jr., Sean M. Lynn-Jones, and Steven E. Miller, eds., *Nationalism and Ethnic Conflict* (Cambridge: M.I.T. Press, 1997).
14. For discussion, see Ronald K. McMullen and Augustus Richard Norton, "Somalia and Other Adventures for the 1990s," *Current History,* Vol. 92, No. 573 (April 1993), pp. 169–74.

15. For background, see Rakiya Omaar, "Somalia: At War with Itself," *Current History* (May 1992), pp. 230–34.

16. For discussion of this process, see William Reno, "Reinvention of an African Patrimonial State: Charles Taylor's Liberia," *Third World Quarterly,* Vol. 16, No. 1 (1995), pp. 109–120.

17. James N. Rosenau, "Security in a Turbulent World," *Current History,* Vol. 94, No. 592 (May 1995), p. 194.

18. On the role of ethnic diasporas, see Gabriel Sheffer, "Ethno-National Diasporas and Security," *Survival,* Vol. 36, No. 1 (Spring 1994), pp. 60–79.

19. Lester R. Brown, et al., *Vital Signs 1995: The Trends That Are Shaping Our Future* (Washington: Worldwatch Institute, 1995), p. 71.

20. For analysis of these trends, see United Nations Development Program, *Human Development Report 1996* (Oxford and New York: Oxford University Press, 1996).

21. United Nations, *Global Outlook 2000* (New York: UN Publications, 1990), p. 10.

22. For further discussion of this point, see Ivan L. Head, "South-North Dangers," *Foreign Affairs* (Summer 1989), pp. 71–86.

23. For further discussion of this point, see Vincent Cable, "The Diminished Nation-State: A Study in the Loss of Economic Power," *Daedalus* (Spring 1995), pp. 23–53; and Susan Strange, "The Defective State," *Daedalus* (Spring 1995), pp. 55–74. See also Michael Renner, *Fighting for Survival* (New York: W.W. Norton, 1996), pp. 85–89.

24. See Ray Marshall, "The Global Jobs Crisis," *Foreign Policy,* No. 100 (Fall 1995), pp. 50–68.

25. Ibid., pp. 50–52.

26. See "How Poor Is China?" *The Economist* (October 12, 1996) and Patrick E. Tyler, "In China's Outlands, Poorest Grow Poorer," *The New York Times* (October 26, 1996).

27. See Nicholas D. Kristof, "Clashes in Seoul As Strike Widens Its Grip," *The New York Times* (December 29, 1996).

28. See "Signs of Danger," *The Economist* (January 4, 1997), p. 40.

29. As reported in Brown, et al., *Vital Signs 1995,* p. 94.

30. For background and statistics, see United Nations, *Global Outlook 2000,* op. cit., pp. 202–217, 228.

31. For discussion, see ibid., pp. 217–45.

32. For discussion, see Thomas F. Homer-Dixon, "Environmental Scarcities and Violent Conflict: Evidence from Cases," *International Security,* Vol. 19, No. 1 (Summer 1994), pp. 5–40.

33. For background and discussion, see Thomas F. Homer-Dixon, "On the Threshold: Environmental Changes As Causes of Acute Conflict," *International Security,* Vol. 16, No. 2 (Fall 1991), pp. 76–116.

34. See Michael Renner, "Chiapas: An Uprising Born of Despair," *World-Watch* (January/February 1997), pp. 12–23.

35. See Renner, *Fighting for Survival,* op. cit., pp. 57–59.

36. Thomas Homer-Dixon, "Environmental Scarcity and Intergroup Conflict," in Michael T. Klare and Daniel C. Thomas, eds., *World Security: Challenges for a New Century* 2nd. ed. (New York: St. Martin's Press, 1994), pp. 298–99.

37. See James J. MacKenzie, "Heading Off the Permanent Oil Crisis," *Issues in Science and Technology* (Summer 1996), pp. 48–54.

38. For background on these disputes, see Butts, "The Strategic Importance of Water," Gleik, "Water and Conflict," and "Water Resources: Scarcity and Conflict," in International Institute for Strategic Studies, *Strategic Survey 1991–92* (London: Brassey's, 1992), pp. 219–30.

5 / The Imperial Impulse: Russia and the "Near Abroad"

KAREN DAWISHA

The contemporary debate about the future of politics in Eurasia comes back again and again to "the Russian question": will the Soviet Union, having collapsed, reassert itself—this time as a new Russian empire? Analysts in the West and elsewhere moved quickly from euphoria over the independence of the long-suppressed ex-Soviet republics to concern over whether they would be able to resist or survive in the face of any renewed Russian imperial drive. Within two years of the Soviet collapse, books and articles began to fill the shelves analyzing Russia's potential strength, speaking of the Russian impulse to empire, and chronicling the near-total obsession that elites in neighboring countries have with managing their relationship with Moscow.[1]

Many of these authors point to the difficulties faced by elites in all the newly independent states—including Russia—in developing a conception of national interest that would orient their foreign policies beyond the Eurasian heartland.[2] But the frailties of both the new states themselves and the foreign policy institutions within them limit their ability to extend the focus of their external politics outside the Eurasian orbit. The fact that the interrelationships among these fifteen states is likely, for the foreseeable future, to occupy the first rank of their concerns means that the larger international system will also interact with them through the prism of these relationships. Consequently, the ability of the world community to effect change in these relationships will depend on having a clearer understanding of their essential nature.

This task can best be approached by posing a number of questions about the whole range of possible relationships between Russia (as a potential future imperial power) and the other ex-Soviet states:

For Russia: What are the prerequisites for the emergence of an imperial power? Could a country with low state capacity and no avowed official ideology of imperialism nevertheless become an empire? Does Russia, even if it rejects a renewed imperial role, have either rights or responsibilities in the new states? What would Russian imperialism look like today? How could Russia's reemergence as a major regional and international power be distinguished from a reassertion of imperial power?

For the other new ex-Soviet states: How dependent on Moscow are the former republics? Can these newly independent states break out of a cycle of dependence on Moscow? Could the dependence of some become so great as to constitute what might be called "autocolonization," or the voluntary acquiescence of populations and elites in the other republics to imperial rule by Moscow?

For the international system: Can the international system prevent Russian imperialism from emerging? What measures can be used to both decrease the temptation of empire in Russia and increase the former republics' independence from Moscow? Is the republics' dependence on Russia sometimes in the interest of the West and other external powers? Can one distinguish between imperial domination and (voluntary) economic dependency of the sort found in much of the Third World?

These are the questions that are likely to govern Western discourse on Russia's international role in the years ahead, and will also guide the discussion that follows.

IMPERIAL PREREQUISITES

An empire as a *polity,* and imperialism as a *system of ideas* that guides the policies of imperial states, intersect conceptually, in that the first is an outgrowth, a result, of the latter. This apparently trivial and obvious point gets to the heart of the first requirement of empires: namely, that they be established *on purpose,* with the objective of the elites in the center gaining unfair advantage—through coercion or its threat—over countries or territories on their periphery. Hence the definition of imperialism provided by Schumpeter in his earliest works as "the objectless disposition on the part of a state to unlimited forcible expansion,"[3] or the old argument that the British empire expanded "in a fit of absentmindedness," miss the fundamental point that states *do not expand for no reason.* While there have been a wide variety of motivations for imperial expansion, and those motivations may have differed from empire to empire and from period to period, *intent* is clearly central to the imperial temptation.

Jack Snyder, in *Myths of Empire,* has perceptively explored the various and often conflicting explanations for expansion.[4] As he demonstrates, such an expansion may, in the fullness of time, prove to have been irrational or unwise, and often results in an eventual pullback from the colonies after new elites realize that the capabilities of the imperial state are overextended. Nevertheless, the impulse to expand has always been a conscious one on the part of dominant elites in the pursuit of what they perceived to be state interests at the time.

A policy of imperialism pursued by elites at the center need not, of course, be advertised as such (although one can find countless instances in which it has been). Yet it is important to include in one's conceptualization of imperialism the conscious effort by one state to wrest formal sovereignty from another. The concept also presupposes that an entire structure of governance from the center has been put in place in the colony. Imperialism, then, is more than military expansion during wartime, and certainly more than the exercise of influence over the policies of another country.

Accordingly, while it is not necessarily the case that elites in a particular state would openly declare in advance that they were going to create an empire, it should be possible to determine whether a state has the *interest,* the *capacity,* and the will or *motivation* necessary to pursue such a course.

While there are great differences on other issues pertaining to imperialism, scholars generally agree that the drive to empire has to serve some set of overarching interests, whether economic (as with the British drive to colonize India), geopolitical (as with the nineteenth century competition among Russians, Turks, Germans, and Austrians for "the lands between" in Eastern Europe), messianic (as with the missionary expansionism of Iberian Catholicism), or ideological (as with Bolshevism in the USSR).

Similarly, while elites in many countries may contemplate expansion to increase their state's well-being, only states with excess capacity can fruitfully undertake imperial expansion. This perspective, articulated by numerous analysts from Lenin on down, focuses on the notion that only those states already among the most powerful in the international system can garner the relevant military and economic capability both to expand beyond existing state boundaries and to sustain and administer an empire in new territories. The extent of capability required to establish and sustain an empire is variable, depending as it does upon the extent of resistance met both locally and from other major powers. But the general principle remains the same: the state must possess significant excess capacity in order to launch and sustain imperial expansion.

Finally, while the motivations for expansion may vary from case to case, they must be present in order for the foreign policy of a state to be characterized as imperialistic. That is, significant elites within the center must consciously seek to extend the state's dominion into new territories on the periphery. In this sense, Winston Churchill's statement that "the empires of the future are the empires of the mind" informs the discussion by pointing to the central aspect of intent.[5] The elites must be motivated by what Ghita Ionescu called a "historical mission of expansion," and possess a sense of "final purpose."[6]

RUSSIAN IMPERIALISM

In Russia, were imperialism to reassert itself, it would require capability, motive, and context. Russia's continuing preeminence in Eurasia as the dominant geographic and economic power gives it enormous natural advantage over its neighbors. Comprising over three-quarters of the territory of the former Soviet empire, over one-half of its total population (a figure that rises to almost two-thirds if ethnic Russians residing in the other former republics are added), and controlling most of the international transportation routes and energy pipelines, Russia certainly can be expected to continue to exert an enormous presence in the calculations of its neighbors.

To conclude from this, however, that Russia will "naturally" exercise imperial ambitions over the other newly independent states is both to overdetermine for geography and to focus exclusively on the positive bene-fits of Russia's size. In fact, the cost for the central government of maintain-ing Russia within its current boundaries has been considerable, as both the war in Chechnya and the failure of Moscow to negotiate favorable revenue-sharing agreements with some of the richest of its non-Russian internal republics have shown.[7]

Where geography becomes a factor is in enhancing capacity. When pos-sessed of the political will to create an empire, the size and extent of natural resources are important inputs into any state machine bent on imperial expansion. Leaders seeking expansion may be motivated by the lure of wealth, but to actually launch a successful and sustained policy of expan-sion states must themselves possess significant capacity: full coffers, large armies and navies, and extensive excess production capabilities large enough to support wars of conquest and occupation.

The level of capacity needed to sustain an expansionist campaign is rela-tive, and not absolute: the resources required are in inverse relationship to the resistance offered both by the population in the area invaded and also by other great powers and the international system as a whole. All the European imperial powers of the late nineteenth century, including Russia, were already powerful when they entered the so-called golden age of empires: an age in which all of the European powers supported each other in the scramble for low-risk, high-yield gains in Africa and elsewhere. Indeed, the concert of Europe's balance of power was maintained at the same time, and largely as a result of, the great powers' abilities to vent their competitive spirit in Africa, the Middle East, and southern Asia.

When the empire costs more than it yields, institutional interests and ideas like prestige and *mission civilisatrice* often come to the forefront. However, once the general population in the metropolis begins to shoulder the heavy costs of expansion, a vital domestic constituency for empire is likely to disappear. The collapse of internal support for empire forced Britain to withdraw from its bases to the west of Aden in 1971, and Portugal to withdraw from its colonies in Africa in 1975. And it was this recognition of the cost of empire that informed popular Russian support for the withdrawal from both the "external" empire in Eastern Europe after 1989 and the "internal" empire in the Soviet Union after 1991.

From this perspective, it is clear that Russia currently lacks both the capacity and the will to launch a major military campaign to reassert imper-ial control over the newly independent states of its former empire. In the years since the breakup of the USSR, the Russian military has shrunk to less than half of its peak mid-1980s level, and the war in Chechnya—a war to maintain Russia's territorial integrity, not an imperial war of conquest—produced widespread failure on the part of Russian males of draft age to heed official call-up notices for compulsory military service. Moreover, pub-lic opinion polls have shown that while nostalgia for the Soviet era is wide-spread, revulsion for the loss of Russian life in the fight against the Chechens runs much deeper. This revulsion has also shaped popular sentiment against imperial expansion abroad: polls have repeatedly shown that almost three-quarters of the Russian population rejects any form of reestablishment of the Union, and that, of those who support such an end, only a very small number—usually not exceeding 5 percent—sanction the use of military means for this purpose.[8] The costs of empire—if it must be established by force—appear too high for Russia to bear at this moment in its history.

This is implicitly recognized in the military doctrine adopted by Russia in 1993. The doctrine emphasizes war prevention and the maintenance of military sufficiency, and eschews the earlier, Soviet-era commitment to war-fighting in forward areas; instead, it sees the military's major role to be the prevention of local wars that might arise from claims on Russian territory (as in Chechnya) and the deescalation of conflicts in lands adjacent to Russian territory that could imperil Russian interests or spill over into Russia proper (as in Georgia). Clearly, the doctrine that currently drives their force posture does not emphasize force projection beyond national boundaries.[9]

Is it possible that the imperial idea will be reborn in Russia, even if the capacity to pursue an imperial policy is limited? History suggests that this would require a concerted effort on the part of significant figures or groups within Russia. Certainly, in all past empires, prominent individuals and political groups have acted as the agents for the germination of the imperial idea. Whether considering Cecil Rhodes (whose own personal vision of cap-italist imperialism in South Africa came to be adopted by the British) or the pan-Turanists in Ottoman Turkey (who sought unsuccessfully in the dying days of the Ottoman empire to revive it on the basis of the unity of all Turkish-speaking peoples), such groups and individuals have mobilized society and its elites to commit the resources necessary for expansion. They have worked with the intelligentsia to develop the essential myths that have legitimized and sustained expansion, and they have fostered an intellectual climate in which any challenge of these myths is seen as subversive of the broadest goals of society.

Clearly, groups and individuals who espouse expansionist views can be found in Russia today. Numerous right-wing figures ran in the December 1995 parliamentary elections on a platform of supporting the redrawing of Russia's borders to encompass an area larger than its current boundaries, including leaders of the Liberal Democrats, the Communists, the Agrarians, the Congress of Russian Communities, and the Derzhava party. These groups and individuals are important in Russia today, in that to a certain extent they have become politically influential and their ideas have become "the ruling ideas." None of the parties has promoted—or received public support for—an immediate military drive to retake any part of the old Soviet empire. Nor would Russia's low state capacity allow such an expan-sion to be undertaken today or, without enormous cost, for the foreseeable future. Observers worry, however, that if economic and internal conditions continue to deteriorate, and if the public comes to reject Russia's further integration into an international economic system dominated by the West, public support for the essentially Western institutions of democracy may decline.

The electoral success of Russian parties and leaders on the right wing of the political spectrum who served up a steady stream of anti-Western and pro-imperial rhetoric must be seen in this light. Both the 1993 and the 1995 elections indicated that pro-imperial rhetoric has solid resonance among the population and constitutes a political reserve capable of winning votes. On two occasions, in 1991 and 1993, these groups also attempted to take power by force, and some elements among them continue to espouse not only imperialistic but also anti-democratic slogans—making the evident popular support for their positions both perplexing and worrying from a Western standpoint.

It is regrettable, but not entirely surprising, that in Russia today—where government leaders can point to few signs of economic progress—political life should incorporate trends that could endanger the survival of democratic institutions. The success of rightist forces in both the 1993 and 1995 elections stimulated the general movement of the political center toward the right, and led to the adoption of numerous resolutions in the Duma that did not carry the weight of law but that nevertheless clouded the political environment. These included calls for the signing of military basing agreements with all states on Russia's borders, the promotion of dual-citizenship agreements with Russia's neighbors, the elimination of Belarus's central bank as a precondition for accepting Belarus's request for economic union with Russia, and the declaration of Sevastopol in Ukraine as a Russian city. At the same time, government officials have been increasingly reluctant to issue formal disavowals of Russian "rights" in the other ex-Soviet republics. All of this suggests that an elite consensus could form around the desirability of reestablishing the Union or otherwise restoring Russian power, rights, and duties in what is viewed from Moscow as the "near abroad."

But while the nucleus of such a consensus can be seen in Russia today, it is unclear how much support such a position could elicit from the masses of the population. While significant sectors of the electorate have voted for parties that promise a turn away from Russia's present economic course, it is not clear that these voters also support strong measures to restore Russia's imperial dominion. Public opinion polls have consistently revealed respondents' preference for the parties that they felt would be most capable of dealing with Russia's domestic economic problems, followed by those considered strong on crime and the rule of law, and only then for those noted for their views on foreign policy. Even though General Lebed's Congress of Russian Communities was identified in one poll as the party most capable of resolving domestic and international military conflicts involving Russian soldiers, the lower popular perception of the party's ability to handle what was regarded as the more important issue of the economy meant that it did not even break the 5 percent electoral threshold required by the Constitution to ensure representation in the Duma.[10]

At present, then, it appears that there is insufficient state capacity and political will to implement a sustained policy of imperial expansion, particularly if military force were required. Moreover, with Bolshevism discredited as a mobilizing ideology and most of the other new states in worse economic conditions than Russia itself, it is hard to discern what vital interests might spur Russian expansionism. Indeed, it would appear that much of the state's capacity in the foreseeable future will be focused on preventing the boundaries of Russia from shrinking even further, especially given the existence of so many restless national minorities at the periphery—notably in Chechnya, but also elsewhere in the North Caucasus and in Siberia. Russia's involvement in Chechnya turned into a political quagmire because of the public's rejection of costly military entanglements. Obviously, this suggests that little public support would be forthcoming for future military ventures on Russia's periphery.

Yet history has shown that the political culture of a country can change rather swiftly from the politics of humiliation to the politics of revenge, as in France after 1870, Germany in the 1930s, and Egypt after 1967. Unfortunately, the presence of an impoverished and defeated population has often in the past assisted in the reemergence of a fascistic regime devoted to the icons of heroic nationalism—even in countries like France, Italy, and Spain that were the birthplaces of Western liberal democracy. It cannot be excluded that the political culture in Russia may see an equally swift transformation.

AUTOCOLONIZATION

In assessing the potential for the reassertion of the Russian empire in the Eurasian space, it is not sufficient to consider developments in Russia alone; one must also examine developments in the other former republics that could contribute to Russian expansionism. In particular, we need to consider the possibility of empire being reasserted at the behest of local elites— that is, autocolonization.

I define autocolonization as the process whereby elites or populations in a target country seek and accept a diminution in their state's sovereignty in hopes of receiving enhanced material wealth, security, or other benefits from an external power, thereby lowering the costs to that power of becoming an imperial state. This concept, it should be noted, is not confined to Russia and the other new states; nor should it be seen as a purely contemporary phenomenon. The history of imperialism is full of examples of colonial processes in which elites or social subgroups have been willing to extend sovereign rights to external powers, trading certain kinds of authority and independence for other benefits.

Take, for example, relations between Great Britain and Iraq before and after Iraq gained independence in 1932. Prior to independence, when Iraq was mandated by the League of Nations to Britain, the country was indeed ruled as an administrative outpost of Britain. After independence was formally granted, however, the British remained in Iraq as the result of a mutually beneficial relationship between the British and the local Iraqi elites. The pro-British ruling elites sought to maintain Britain's role in protecting their political and economic preeminence and in return were willing to grant the British an exclusive oil concession, as well as military basing rights and other privileges. This expression of Iraqi autocolonization operated in tandem with the establishment by Britain of an informal empire in several of its former colonies.

One can also cite many contemporary examples of autocolonization. During the Soviet era, for example, nondemocratically elected elites in Eastern Europe adopted a pro-Soviet stance in order to receive security assistance that would keep them in power. The argument has often and justifiably been made that the Soviet Union imposed communism as a system of power on Eastern Europe. Armed with this system, however, local communist leaders like Todor Zhivkov of Bulgaria, Eric Honecker and Walter Ulbricht of East Germany, and Gustav Husak and Klement Gottwald of Czechoslovakia constructed security services and systems of rule that served Moscow's needs while also maintaining their own power. Their willingness even to use force to sustain their regimes, as became apparent in East Germany and Czechoslovakia in the late 1980s, while *glasnost* and *perestroika* were being promoted in Moscow, is indicative of the desire of these elites to maintain their autocolonial status even as the impulse for empire was receding in the Kremlin under Mikhail Gorbachev. The same holds true of Moscow's allies in the Third World, who clung to their relationship with Moscow long after Soviet elites had begun to openly criticize them for their failure to implement domestic reforms.

One can also find contemporary examples of autocolonization in the West. Frequently, these are cases in which the nation's economic well-being and independence is suppressed in the interests of the personal enrichment of the elite. In the Philippines, there were those who argued that Ferdinand Marcos used American involvement to secure his corrupt regime in preference to instituting democratic measures that in short order would have ousted him from power. In Francophone Africa, elites often have preferred to rule with French security assistance while plundering their own country's national wealth; and as Miles Kahler points out, of the more than thirty instances of French military intervention in postcolonial Africa, most have been spurred by pressure from its clients in the region.[11]

The success of autocolonization depends on the ability of local elites to convince their great power protector that the costs of the relationship are less than the benefits. It also depends on the ability of the local elites to help shape the debate in the metropolis as much as possible, by creating nostalgia for the center's rights as a great power, promoting an imperial identity, warning of the dire consequences of inaction, and appealing to the duty and, if all else fails, the sheer vanity of the ruling elite. Throughout history, the Serbs have been masters at inculcating in Russian elite opinion the view that Serbia was Russia's only true ally in southeastern Europe. Seeing Serbia as permanently beleaguered in the Balkans, they have traditionally argued that not only was it Russia's duty to respond to Serb appeals, but that Russia's very ability to call itself a great power was dependent upon maintaining the dominance of Slavic and Orthodox brothers in Belgrade.[12]

Of course, this is a high stakes game, since the elites in the periphery risk being swept from power themselves if they invite intervention and then become subject to its rules. Thus, the Georgian monarchy, when concerned about a Persian invasion, ceded sovereign rights to Catherine II and became a protectorate of Russia in 1783; seventeen years later, however, Paul I ended whatever rights the local elite still maintained by directly annexing the entire country and abolishing the monarchy.[13] As this case suggests, autocolonial policies pursued by elites in the periphery are often reactive: chosen out of fear or driven by the necessities of war. In such cases, the external power can be called in to impose social order and assist in reasserting stability. If successful, such policies can accrue benefits for elites in the periphery while transferring the cost of imposing order to the great powers. Clearly, however, the great power maintains significant advantage.

While the concept of autocolonization should normally be associated with action on the part of local elites, one should not assume that their actions never have a social basis. Protestants among the population of Northern Ireland, for example, have preferred union with Britain, even with direct rule, to an independence that might leave them open to what they believe would be inevitable pressure for union with the Catholic South. Likewise, the Christian Maronites in Lebanon welcomed Syrian intervention to balance the growing power of Palestinian and Shiite groups in their society. Many other examples exist, and it is certainly possible that there might be parallels now or in the future in the relations among Russia and the rest of the new states, as discussed below.

AUTOCOLONIZATION IN THE EURASIAN SPACE

When analysts consider the prospect of a reassertion of Russian imperial activities beyond the mere expression of sentiment, they primarily deal with scenarios in which the newly independent states, struggling to establish and maintain their independence, resist such efforts by all means available, including force of arms. And, to be sure, many of Moscow's actions in the period since independence have met with a stern rebuff. Indeed, it could be said that a central feature in the national identity of many of the new states is the imperative of resistance to any renewed Russian drive.

This resistance to Russian control is particularly apparent in Latvia and Estonia, in western Ukraine, in western Moldova, in Azerbaijan, and, unfortunately for Russia, also within Russia itself (especially in the north Caucasus). However, such resistance is less a part of the central governing raison d'être in Armenia, Georgia, eastern and southern Ukraine, eastern

Moldova, Belarus, Lithuania, and the states of Central Asia. Whereas, in the first group, there is a solid consensus among the elites and the population that independence for their countries means independence from Russia, the situation in the latter group is not so clear-cut. The existence of historic memories of Russia as a savior of local populations, common Slavic and Orthodox roots, a common economic infrastructure still centered in Russia, Russophone elites, and/or large numbers of Russian nationals living among and often intermarried with the local population are just some of the factors that favor a continued Russian influence.

But how do conditions that favor Russian influence translate into circumstances that produce autocolonization? There would appear to be two primary motivations for autocolonization: security and economics. In the first, local leaders are so absorbed in a military conflict, whether civil or interstate, that they see a Russian presence as a means of either tipping the conflict in their favor or suppressing it altogether. In the second, elites see a reunification with Russia as a better means of ensuring economic improvement for themselves or the population.

In Georgia, both the Abkhaz separatists and the Georgian state authorities called on Russian military support to tip the balance in their favor and then to maintain the peace once the threat of separatism had subsided. In the process, the Georgian government acceded to Russian demands for military basing rights in the country—bases that would be used both to promote Russia's interests and to support President Shevardnadze's own embattled position if needed.

In Armenia, the government has repeatedly tried to enlist Russian military support in its conflict with Azerbaijan over Nagorno-Karabakh, receiving critical supplies of oil for its 1994 offensive into western Azerbaijan. Both Armenia and Russia have sought the weakening of Azerbaijan, Armenia so as to promote its own claims to Nagorno-Karabakh and Russia so as to gain access to Azerbaijan's oil and weaken Baku's potential for reasserting its historic role as the beacon for the spreading of pan-Turkic and Islamic appeals north and east from the Middle East.

Azerbaijan has been thrown onto the defensive in the face of this dual pressure. The Azerbaijani Popular Front and its leader, President Elchibey, long objects of Russian concern, lost power to Gaidar Aliev, an old-time apparatchik who made his career in the old Soviet system. Aliev's strategy since coming to power has been to protect the country from Armenia by acceding to virtually all Russian demands, including ceding ever larger percentages of stock in Azerbaijan's oil industry to Russian firms. The Azerbaijanis had decided that the only way to buy security from Armenian attacks was to recognize Russian economic interests in the area.

Clearly none of the states in the Caucasus has become a colony of Russia; rather they have accepted an increase in Russia's presence in return for economic and security benefits for their own regimes. In so doing, they have increased their own dependence on Russia and made it possible for Russia to exert continuing and increased pressure on the politics of the region at a lower cost than would be required if Caucasian elites had not so easily accepted—even invited—an increased Russian presence.

In Belarus, however, the situation is different. President Lukashenka ran on a platform that promised a closer relationship and, indeed, reunification with Russia.[14] Public opinion polls in Belarus even four years after the breakup of the Soviet Union showed continuing support from almost half the population for significantly closer relations with Russia, and a popular referendum supported by the president called for union as well.[15] Belarus stands alone among the new states in actively favoring reunification with Russia; and, although elites in other ex-Soviet states (including Kazakhstan and Kyrgyzstan) have sought improved ties with Russia, Belarus is the best and clearest example among the newly independent states of the phenomenon of autocolonization.

As evidence of its unique position in this regard, Belarus has dismantled border posts along the frontier with Russia, restored Russian as the official language, agreed to continue paying pensions to the thousands of retired Soviet-era officers residing in Belarus, and granted Russia leases for two bases on its territory. In February 1996, the two countries signed an agreement renouncing mutual debts, including the $600 million (plus millions in penalties) that Belarus owed to the Russian natural gas monopoly Gazprom. President Lukashenka in March 1996 announced that the two countries would sign a treaty creating a single "unified state," a position favored by many in Belarus; however, lawmakers on both sides expressed skepticism that Russia would choose to undertake the economic burden of reincorporating Belarus or that authorities in Minsk would surrender the country's sovereignty completely.[16]

In Central Asia, the elites were clearly unprepared for the collapse of the Union and spent much of the first year of independence trying to convince Russia to form a commonwealth.[17] In the region as a whole, significant elites have appeared unable or unwilling to act on their economic independence from Russia.[18] Those elites trained in central planning continued to see Moscow as the center, and Russia has been able to maintain its relative economic advantage with relative ease. However, in none of the Central Asian countries is there a strong or increasing indigenous trend favoring the surrender of political sovereignty; national elites in most countries have become more, not less, committed to maintaining their countries' formal independence, while continuing to rely on Moscow for economic and military support.[19] The exception, of course, is Tajikistan, where after a brief but very bloody civil war, pro-Moscow elites gained the ascendancy and established a regime strongly in favor of a continued Russian presence in the country.[20]

Needless to say, the trend toward autocolonization in some of these states may be transitory. Given the speed and circumstances of the collapse of the USSR, the presence of so many elites and populations so unprepared for independence is historically unique. It may be that, with the passage of time, these elites or the next generation may come to value independence more highly, particularly if they are able to savor the national, cultural, psychological, and security benefits of independence. It is also possible, however, that some of the new states may fail to make the transition successfully, and so their populations—especially the Slavic groups within them—will look to Moscow to generate such benefits.

RUSSIA'S NATIONAL SECURITY ZONE

Russia has moved from pursuing an inchoate policy toward the countries on its border to one that has clearly marked the area as a region of vital interest, akin to Michael McGwire's concept of a "national security zone."[21] While Russia may not move to reestablish empire, the area surrounding its state borders will remain critical to its well-being and security. All states have national security zones; only the strongest have the capability to delineate such zones beyond their borders and promote their interests within them. The conceptual distinction between an empire and a national security zone is more than a difference of degree: the former has no basis in current international norms or laws, the latter allows one to focus on the natural interplay of relations between great powers and smaller states—an interplay in which great powers are infinitely more constrained than imperial powers, and small states have significantly more leeway than colonies. In policy terms, whereas it is highly unlikely that the international community would support a reassertion of Russian imperialism, it is by no means certain that all Russian activities in its national security zone would be condemned.

The distinction between empire and a national security zone is blurred somewhat, however, in some cases or types of autocolonization. If, for example, Belarus chooses to reunify with Russia, and if the reunification is recognized by the international community, then an autocolonized imperial expansion would have acquired a basis in international law and at least some legitimacy within the international community. The international community has also been relatively accepting of Russia's manipulation and domination of its neighbors when they were experiencing acute civil conflict, as in Georgia and Tajikistan. In such cases, where weaker neighboring states descend into chaos and civil war, renewed imperial or neo-imperial control by a more powerful state may be interpreted more as foreign policy within a security zone than as the reassertion of empire.

As the largest and strongest country of the former USSR, and the one that benefited the most from the institutional inheritance of the Soviet state, Russia is in a position of enormous comparative advantage. Russian leaders have often but not always exercised this advantage to the detriment of the other new states. Thus, Russia has used its position as the least dependent economy in the former Soviet space to exert economic pressure, particularly through the supply or withholding of energy or access to Russian-controlled pipelines. Russian leaders encouraged all the new states to join the Commonwealth of Independent States (CIS), which originally included a joint military command dominated by Russia. And the Russian military, via a network of formal basing agreements, units "temporarily" stationed abroad, loan-service personnel, and peacekeeping missions sanctioned by regional treaties, is the only force in the Eurasian space capable of sustained independent action beyond its borders.

Because of the fragility and comparative weakness of most of the new states, Russia is able to exert enormous leverage with relatively little effort. The way in which Russia has been able to shift between the Armenians and the Azerbaijanis, by supplying arms or energy to one side and then another, or by withdrawing relatively small numbers of forces here and then deploying them there, shows its ability to alternatively punish and reward without itself suffering significant or proportionate loss.[22]

Russia's military presence in Tajikistan, its legal claims to Crimea, and the protection accorded in Russia's military doctrine to ethnic Russians living abroad are issues that spring from different situations and political motivations. But they nevertheless reflect an overall consensus in Russia that, at a minimum, the former Soviet area constitutes a natural Russophone zone over which Moscow has "always" been able to exercise influence. Even President Yeltsin, who initially supported a foreign policy that emphasized international and especially Western links, has come to embrace the notion that "the sphere of Russia's economic, political, and humanitarian interests extends to the entire post-Soviet space."[23]

The central point is that the other new states, however hostile to Russia, being weaker and more fragile, *need* Russia. The fact that Russia has been willing to provide substantial and continued energy and trade subsidization—to the tune, according to International Monetary Fund estimates, of $17 billion in 1993 alone (making Russia the single largest aid donor to the other newly independent states)—shows the extent to which Russia is both aware of these needs and concerned enough to help stabilize these countries.

Certainly, not all the new states regard Russia as inherently untrustworthy as a partner. Belarus, with an economy that is even more inflation-ridden than Russia's, has been at the forefront of efforts to forge a stronger union with Moscow. And, while Belarus has been the most extreme example, all of these states have continued to rely on Moscow in varying degrees for continued trade, expertise, security assistance, and as the center of Eurasia's communications network. This reliance comes about not necessarily because of any nefarious design by the current Russian government, but because these countries (with the partial exception of Estonia) have yet to be incorporated into any regional or global network that bypasses Moscow. One is reminded in this context of the words of British Conservative politician, later prime minister, Benjamin Disraeli who said in a speech before Parliament in 1863, "colonies do not cease to be colonies just because they are independent."

In this context, therefore, it is necessary to distinguish between the fact of Russia's self-perception as the dominant power in the region and the other countries' objective dependence. The legacy of the Soviet empire has left them dependent, but overcoming the consequences of that dependence is primarily the responsibility of the new states themselves. Much the same phenomenon that was witnessed following the emergence of postcolonial states in Africa and the Middle East can be expected in Eurasia. Many leaders in these states, faced with almost intractable problems, have chosen either to seek salvation in a renewed Russian embrace or to blame Moscow as an excuse for their inability to implement a credible development strategy.

Looking at the patterns that have emerged in the decades since decolonization began in the developing world, one can find many reasons to conclude that the process in Eurasia will be equally difficult but substantively different. The proximity of the former colonial power and the harsh economic straits in which Russia and the other new states find themselves predispose one to conclude that the interrelationship between Russia and its neighbors is likely to be more intense than between most former colonial powers and their newly independent states. Russia will not have the "luxury" of a debate about casting off "the white man's burden," as the British did when discussing the benefits of withdrawal from India, because 25 million ethnic Russians found themselves in these new states after the breakup of the USSR, and because Russia's weak economy makes these states a more natural partner than India was for Britain. And, as for the other new states in Eurasia, they cannot easily form regional security systems to bolster their independence from their former colonial masters (as the newly independent African and Middle Eastern states did through the Organization of African Unity and the Arab League) because, whereas Britain, France, and Portugal withdrew over the horizon when these empires collapsed, Russia continues to reside in their midst.

Russia, too, lacks a regional alternative to cooperation with the other new states. While it is abundantly richer in natural resources than its neighbors, the psychological and organizational detritus of the Soviet era has created many barriers to cooperation with other regional alternatives in Europe or elsewhere. Whereas Britain and France could simultaneously pursue decolonization in Africa and Asia and integration in Europe, Russia has little alternative but to pursue decolonization in Eurasia as it simultaneously seeks regional reintegration with these same countries.

By far the most realistic course, therefore, to avoid both renewed imperialism in Russia and autocolonization among the new states, would be to promote interdependence and democracy. Such a course would be difficult for the reasons elaborated above: the legacy of *diktat* and distrust, a domestic political climate in which democratic institutions are skirted or assailed by former communist elites, and an international climate that alternately promotes Russia as a great power in its national security zone and punishes it for exercising the prerogatives of such a power. Moreover, states that are neither truly independent nor moving toward democracy cannot easily participate in an interdependent world—and until the states bordering Russia make further strides in this direction, their full participation will remain only a distant objective.

IMPERIALISM AND THE
INTERNATIONAL COMMUNITY

While empires have existed in both the modern and ancient worlds, the "age of empires" really lasted for the briefest period: from the mid-1800s to World War I. During this time, virtually all the European powers expanded their power, culture, and economic influence by means of formal acquisition of territories worldwide. The very essence of the international system was itself imperialist. The wars between empires that broke out in this period (as with the Crimean war, and the endless wars in the Balkans) were not about the nonacceptability of empire per se but about the fate of contested territories lying between empires.[24] Consequently, alliances among empires could be established, agreements not to attack one's flank when at war with another empire could be signed, and, all in all, discussions about the rights of nations and peoples to self-determination could be sacrificed to the interests of maintaining a balance of power within Europe.

But now that a century has passed, and the USSR (in many ways an empire itself) has collapsed, the discussion of empire—and particularly the possibility of the reemergence of a Russian empire—has resurfaced. The USSR succeeded in the early 1920s, in a weak and divided international community, to establish itself and incorporate by force many of the territories of the former Russian empire. Would the international community allow such a phenomenon to be repeated today?

Several important factors inhibit such a repetition. To begin with, as many scholars have noted, the post-1945 international system has come to recognize more fully as governing norms the principles of state sovereignty, national self-determination, and the inadmissibility of the use of force to change boundaries or replace legitimate, popularly elected governments.[25] The defense of the nation-state (not the imperial state) and the promotion of decolonization, democracy, and human rights (not the reestablishment of empire and authoritarian regimes) are the dominant norms upheld by the international community today, and constitute the foundation upon which international institutions derive their legitimacy. To the extent that force has been sanctioned by the international community through the United Nations, it has been to uphold these norms (as in Kuwait, Haiti, or Bosnia). It is virtually impossible to foresee a situation in which the use of Russian force against the wishes of a legitimately elected government would be formally sanctioned (as opposed to ignored or overlooked) by the international community and its organizations.

Unlike the Bolshevik expansion into other post-imperial territories (whether Russian, Ottoman, or Habsburg) in the aftermath of World War I, any renewed Russian imperial drive would entail the subordination of new sovereign states that have been recognized as such by the entire international community. It is inconceivable that the international community would support a wholesale Russian policy of using force to absorb states, or parts of states, that are recognized as sovereign and independent, or of systematically undermining democratically elected governments within those states. Not only would such a policy bring international censure, but it would prompt many of the Western-oriented international institutions (to which Russia has turned for assistance in its efforts to restructure the economy) to conclude that the increased costs of empire would so weaken Russian economic recovery as to negate the very basis on which the original loans and investments were made. In this way, the international community could both isolate Russia and punish it economically for any policy of expansion.

The success of an international policy aimed at preventing any renewed imperial drive from succeeding is obviously highly conditional; it would depend, first of all, on the extent to which the policy has domestic support within Russia that could be sustained even with hardships. This obviously depends on the regional context—if Russian nationals are being subjected to fierce repression abroad, then sentiment in Russia itself might indeed support military action regardless of the consequences. Yet, unlike in the past when Russia could break with the West and seek alternative trading partners within a bloc of communist and left-leaning developing states, such a bloc cannot be reconstructed today and so a turn toward communism, ultranationalism, and empire in Russia would leave the country isolated as never before.

It appears, then, that a Russian drive to reestablish an empire in the "near abroad" is neither inevitable nor likely. Certainly we are likely to see further efforts by Moscow to influence and manipulate developments in the other former Soviet republics, and these moves are likely to be supported by at least some social subgroups within these states. It is also conceivable that some of these states, most notably Belarus, will eventually be reabsorbed into an expanded Russia with the support of the populations involved. Should economic conditions in Russia continue to deteriorate, moreover, it is possible that political parties with a neo-imperial platform will rise to prominence and assume control of major government organs. Even in these circumstances, however, it is unlikely that Russia will engage in action that would provoke determined resistance from the populations of the new states (as in Chechnya) and therefore require a significant commitment of military force—with the attendant risk of significant Russian casualties and/ or the imposition of economic sanctions by the international community. The appeal of empire will no doubt remain strong, but the other prerequisites of expansionism—interests, capacity, and political will—are not present in sufficient strength to launch and sustain a new imperial quest.

QUESTIONS FOR FURTHER STUDY

1. What, according to Dawisha, constitutes the necessary prerequisites for imperial expansion?

2. What are the factors that might lead Russia to adopt a policy of imperial expansion in the years ahead? What are the factors that would oppose the adoption of such a policy? Which appear stronger today?

3. What does Dawisha mean by "autocolonization" in the Russian periphery? What forms has it taken in the past, and what forms might it take in the future?

4. What is the distinction, in Dawisha's view, between a "national security zone" and a policy of imperial expansion? Is this distinction valid?

5. What policies should the international community adopt to discourage Russia from pursuing a policy of imperial expansion in the space of the former Soviet Union?

Notes

1. Fiona Hill and Pamela Jewett, "'Back in the USSR': Russia's Intervention in the Internal Affairs of the Former Soviet Republics and the Implications for United States Policy toward Russia," Ethnic Conflict Project, Strengthening Democratic Institutions Project, John F. Kennedy School of Government, Harvard University (January 1994), pp. 1–90; Richard Pipes, "Imperial Russian Foreign Policy," *Times Literary Supplement,* No. 4755 (May 20, 1994), pp. 3–5; Peter Reddaway, "The Role of Popular Discontent," *The National Interest,* Vol. 31 (Spring 1993), pp. 57–63; Peter Reddaway, "Russia on the Brink," *New York Review of Books,* Vol. 40, No. 3 (January 28, 1993), pp. 30–36; and Peter Reddaway, "Yeltsin and Russia: Two Views," *New York Review of Books,* Vol. 40, No. 8 (April 22, 1993), pp. 16–19. From a completely different perspective some Russian intellectuals joined in the debate, arguing that Russia's "natural" superiority in culture would produce a reuniting tendency. See, for example, Tatyana Tolstaya, "Intellectuals and Social Change in Central and Eastern Europe," *Partisan Review,* Vol. 59, No. 4 (1992), pp. 568–73, and Tatyana Tolstaya, "The Struggle for Russia," *New York Review of Books,* Vol. 41, No. 12 (June 23, 1994), pp. 3–7.

2. Elena Bonner, "Yeltsin and Russia: Two Views," *New York Review of Books,* Vol. 40, No. 8 (April 22, 1993), pp. 16–19; Suzanne Crow, "Why Has Russian Foreign Policy Changed?" *RFE\RL Research Reports,* Vol. 3, No. 18 (May 6, 1993); Karen Dawisha and Bruce Parrott, *Russia and the New States of Eurasia: The Politics of Upheaval* (Cambridge: Cambridge University Press, 1994), Chapter 6; Adeed Dawisha and Karen Dawisha, eds., *The Making of Foreign Policy in Russia and the New States of Eurasia* (Armonk, NY: M.E. Sharpe, 1995); and John Lough, "The Place of the 'Near Abroad' in Russian Foreign Policy," *RFE\RL Research Reports,* Vol. 2, No. 11 (March 12, 1993).

3. Joseph A. Schumpeter, *Imperialism and Social Classes,* rev. ed. (New York: Kelley, 1951), p. 7.

4. Jack Snyder, *Myths of Empire: Domestic Politics and International Ambition* (Ithaca: Cornell University Press, 1991).

5. Winston Churchill, speech at Harvard, September 6, 1943, in *Onwards to Victory* (Boston: Little Brown, 1944), p. 238.

6. Ghita Ionescu, *The Breakup of the Soviet Empire in Eastern Europe* (Baltimore: Penguin, 1995), p. 7.

7. Christine Wallich, "Reforming Intergovernmental Relations: Russia and the Challenge of Fiscal Federalism," in Bartlomiej Kaminski, ed., *Economic Transition in Russia and the New States of Eurasia* (Armonk, NY: M.E. Sharpe, 1996).

8. U.S. Information Agency, *Briefing Paper* (Washington, September 13, 1994).

9. For a fuller discussion of the doctrine, see Raymond L. Garthoff, "Russian Military Doctrine and Deployments," in Bruce Parrott, ed., *State Building and Military Power in Russia and the New States of Eurasia* (Armonk, NY: M.E. Sharpe, 1995), pp. 44–64.

10. See Sarah Oates, "Vying for Votes on a Crowded Campaign Trail," *Transition,* Vol. 2, No. 4 (February 23, 1996), pp. 26–30.

11. Miles Kahler, "Empires, Neo-Empires and Political Change: The British and French Experience," in Karen Dawisha and Bruce Parrott, eds., *The End of Empire? The*

Transformation of the USSR in Comparative Perspective (Armonk, NY: M.E. Sharpe, 1996), pp. 299–300.

12. This relationship is the subject of an interesting article by Sergei A. Romanenko, "The Yugoslav Question in the Foreign Policy of Russia at the Beginning of the Twentieth Century," in S. Frederick Starr, ed., *The Legacy of History in Russia and the New States of Eurasia* (Armonk, NY: M.E. Sharpe, 1994), 41–61.

13. Ronald Grigor Suny, *The Making of the Georgian Nation,* 2nd ed. (Bloomington: Indiana University Press, 1994), pp. 58–9.

14. Kathleen Mihalisko, "Democratization in Belarus," paper presented at UMCP/SAIS Conference on Democratization in Post-Communist Countries (November 1995).

15. See Foreign Language Broadcast Information Service (FBIS), *Central Eurasia Daily Report* (March 20, 1996), p. 65, for details of an opinion poll showing that 47 percent of the Belarusian respondents supported a call for unification (integration) of the two countries, and of those 33 percent spoke in favor of "complete fusion" as in Soviet times.

16. Details are from FBIS, *Central Eurasia Daily Report* (March 5, 1996), pp. 55–6; Ibid. (March 6, 1996), p. 50; and *Washington Post* (March 24, 1996).

17. Martha B. Olcott, "Central Asia's Catapult to Independence," *Foreign Affairs,* Vol. 71, No. 3 (Summer 1992), pp. 108–31.

18. Bartlomiej Kaminski, "Factors Affecting Trade Reorientation of the New Independent States," in Kaminski, ed., *Economic Transition in Russia and the New States of Eurasia* (Armonk, NY: M. E. Sharpe, 1996).

19. The extent of the economic, military, political, and cultural ties between Central Asian states on the one hand and both Russia and the Middle East on the other is the subject of a Ph.D. thesis by Ibrahim Arafat, University of Maryland, College Park (1996). Arafat shows the trend toward increased ties with Russia after a brief period of decreased ties beginning in 1993 for all Central Asian states with the exception of Turkmenistan, whose ties with the Middle East became more significant.

20. Muriel Atkin, "Democratization in Tajikistan," paper presented at UMCP/SAIS Conference on Democratization in Post-Communist Countries (November 1995).

21. Michael McGwire, *Perestroika and Soviet National Security* (Washington: Brookings Institution, 1991).

22. A partial catalogue of Russian activities abroad and a full justification of all such activities was presented in a report by then Director of the Russian Foreign Intelligence Service, Yevgeny Primakov, and published in full in *Rossiyskaya Gazeta* (September 22, 1994).

23. *Segodnya* (September 30, 1994).

24. See Marcus Cunliffe, *The Age of Expansion: 1848–1917* (Springfield, MA: G. & C. Merriam, 1994).

25. Peter J. Katzenstein, "Coping with Terrorism: Norms and Internal Security in Germany and Japan," in Judith Goldstein and Robert Keohane, eds., *Ideas and Foreign Policy: Beliefs, Institutions, and Political Change* (Ithaca: Cornell University Press, 1993).

6 / Rethinking East Asian Security

BARRY BUZAN and GERALD SEGAL

As in other regions, international security in East Asia has been transformed by the end of the Cold War. Yet debate about the direction of change, let alone the reality of the transformation, has been much slower to develop in this region than in Europe. The reasons for these tardy reactions suggest that East Asians, and an interested wider world, have serious cause for concern about the risks of conflict in East Asia.

The debate about East Asian security is dominated by two theories of the future. On the one hand, there is the "back to the future" view espoused by realists, who argue that the end of the Cold War has released indigenous conflicts that were previously suppressed. It is argued that Asia could easily destabilize, with classic balance-of-power politics coming to dominate the international relations of the region. On the other hand, the more liberal view argues that the complex interdependence of the late twentieth century has curtailed military rivalry between industrialized states. The East Asian states, especially Japan and the newly industrializing countries (NICs), are ensnared in this web of trading and financial dependencies. Combined with the decline of the divisive influence of the Cold War, this interdependence can eradicate serious conflict in the region. Both of these arguments are persuasive, but the fear is that the pessimists may be closer to the truth. Assessing the balance between them is complicated by the aversion of Asians to being open about their security concerns.

The analysis that follows will assess the main arguments of the protagonists in order to identify the greatest risks of conflict. Trying to peer into the future is a notoriously hazardous business and those attempting it usually draw on both history and theory for guidance. That will also be our strategy. In each of the following sections we will take one perspective and use it as a lens through which to examine security relations in East Asia. Any lens tends to highlight some features of the object under scrutiny and exclude others. By adding several such examinations together, we hope to assemble a reasonably clear picture of the security situation in East Asia as a whole. The next section employs the historical lens to examine the legacy from which the future international relations of East Asia might draw. Following that we turn to theory, looking first through the realist lens at the balance of power and military security, then through the international political economy lens at economics and security, and finally through the lens of international society as a framework for regional order. We conclude by asserting that a movement "back to the future" is a distinct possibility in Asia, and by considering the nature of balance-of-power politics in the early twenty-first century and its place in the wider world order.

HISTORY

The lessons of history are seldom clear and often deceptive. Recent conditions always differ significantly from older ones even when tempting similarities invite comparison. And, of course, there are several layers of history to choose from. It is clear that Cold War history is not entirely obsolete. There are still four states ruled by communist parties, and the Korean conflict is the same explosive cocktail of an ideological and civil war. Relations between Taiwan and China fall into a similar category, as do aspects of the Cambodian conflict. The boundary dispute and status rivalry between India and China also remain unaltered. Although this relationship did not have its origins in Cold War ideology or superpower competition, it did develop during the Cold War and was in part shaped and reinforced by it. Thus, one legacy of the Cold War for contemporary Asia is a set of unresolved rivalries and flashpoints. A second, stemming in part from the particular way in which the region was divided up by the Cold War, is the almost complete absence of significant multilateral political organizations, be they regional forums or military alliances. Unlike in Europe, where both superpowers cultivated such organizations, in East Asia they both constructed largely bilateral relationships. A third legacy, echoing much older history, is a widespread fear of potential Chinese expansionism in many of the countries around its periphery.

The first half of the twentieth century was dominated by the rise of Japan, its clash with Russian imperialism and Japan's briefly successful bid to subjugate virtually the whole region to its military power and industrial economy. In this history is rooted the still strong and politically active fear and hatred of Japan in many countries. China and Korea, in particular, still remember the cruelty and arrogance of Japanese occupation, as do many of the countries of Southeast Asia, to a lesser extent. Russia remembers the humiliation of being the first European power to lose a major war to a non-white people and the threat to its sparsely populated holdings in Siberia.[1] One legacy from this period is a politically hamstrung Japan, which is unable to play a leadership role in the region commensurate with its power.[2] Another is the smoldering hostility between Japan and Russia, which might seem to be a Cold War leftover but has its roots further back in history. A third is a set of disputes over islands between Japan and Korea, and between Japan and China/Taiwan. These regularly flare into confrontation, most recently during 1996.

The eighteenth and nineteenth centuries were dominated by the clash between the Asian and European civilizations. This was the start of the ancient Sinocentric civilization being penetrated and eventually dominated by the military and economic power of the European "barbarians." The belief that it must right the wrongs of the humiliating history that began during this time is the main reason why China does not see itself as a status quo power. Furthermore, it is not simply a question of remaking China as a great power, but also one of resolving territorial disputes. China's ruthlessness, sometimes even at the cost of damaging its reputation and economic interests, has been evident in its handling of the takeover of Hong Kong[3] and its determination to acquire islands in the South China Sea. China's claim over Taiwan has also not been resolved and any sign that Taiwan might survive as an independent entity is firmly opposed by China, as was most recently illustrated by its military threats and demonstrations in the time preceding Taiwan's elections early in 1996. In short, China feels it is fully within its rights to change the territorial status quo, even though most other countries view such action as aggressive and dangerous.

China's acute concern with traditional notions of sovereignty is in sharp contrast to Japan, which, by virtue of its far greater interdependence with the global market economy, is moving toward what can be termed a "postmodern" definition of sovereignty.[4] This fundamental difference in how the international system is perceived is related to the cultural problems of how to modernize and how much to westernize. This is the basis of the successful Japanese adaptation, which led to Japan first joining and then superseding European imperial power in East Asia.

There are two legacies from this period. One is the uncertainty over Russia's colonial borders, which remained geographically fixed when other European powers withdrew from Asia. The other, which is more diffuse, is the fact that some Asian states have coped better than others with the challenge of modernization.

Before European powers had penetrated Asia, a Sinocentric imperial power had dominated the region. This power was remarkably durable, though it did wax and wane over the millennia. What was also remarkable was the degree of detachment of this civilization from those that developed further west. A few people, bearing ideas and luxury goods, traveled the silk roads but there was no sustained strategic interaction between China and the classical civilizations in South Asia, Mesopotamia, or the Mediterranean. The main legacy from this is a fear of Chinese domination, in Southeast Asia as a whole and Vietnam in particular. One might also see a shadow of the future in the rival penetrations by cultural, religious, and ethnic influences from India and China into Southeast Asia.

All of these historical legacies remain and, taken together, they suggest that political fragmentation and hostility characterize the region's international relations. There is little that binds its states and societies together but much that divides them. Any chance of finding unifying common ground against the West has long since disappeared. As the particular distortions imposed by the Cold War unravel, many historical patterns that were either suppressed or overridden by ideological and superpower rivalry are reappearing. Sino-Japanese rivalry is perhaps the most worrying because it involves the two biggest powers in the region. There is the potential for

Sino-Indian rivalry as the two giants of Asia slowly consolidate their modernizations and extend their military power. Although the United States may potentially be able to hold a stable balance of power in the region, this depends upon the extent of the relative decline of American power and the country's isolationist tendency when faced with intense local rivalries unmediated by some overriding ideological cause. History, therefore, strongly reinforces the view that Asia is in danger of heading "back to the future."

MILITARY SECURITY AND THE BALANCE OF POWER

What do the traditional realist concerns with the balance of power and military strength suggest about the future of Asia? Without a doubt, of fundamental importance is the lifting of the superpower overlay and the withdrawal of Soviet/Russian and American power and engagement from the region. This process is broadly comparable to that in Europe, though the particular details are quite different.[5] For four decades Asia, like Europe, was in the grip of the rival containment and countercontainment strategies of the two superpowers. This grip created its own pattern of ideological and military alignments, and drew American power deeply into East Asia. Although the Sino-Soviet split and intercommunist rivalry gave it a unique twist, security relations in East Asia were nonetheless deeply affected by the Cold War. Now Soviet power has imploded, the global ideological confrontation has collapsed into a few local pockets, and America has reduced its military power in response to domestic demands and the end of the Cold War.

The realist can argue, citing historical precedent, that the breakup of the superpower overlay allows, and indeed compels, local patterns of amity, enmity, and balance of power to reassert themselves. For East Asia, the cost of its freedom from foreign rivalries is that it now has to deal with regional insecurities that have deep roots of their own. The interesting, and in some ways alarming, fact about this analysis of East Asia is that we have little historical experience to guide us: there is no record of indigenous modern international relations in the region. For almost all of this century Asia has been dominated by foreign powers: first the European empires and later the superpowers. The Japanese expansion was certainly indigenous, but it occurred while China was in chaos and most of the rest of the region was under European occupation or control, and so does not provide a model for post-Cold War security dynamics.

During the Cold War a whole set of Asian states achieved independence, and some of them have become industrial and commercial powers. But they developed with their international relations much constrained and shaped by the Cold War. With the lifting of these restraints the regional pattern of security relations is no longer clear. These states have almost no modern experience of how to relate to each other on terms largely defined by the local dynamics of regional relations. In this sense, speculation about the future of Asia is profoundly different from that in Europe, where pre-Cold War patterns of power (im)balance play a significant role in post-Cold War relations.

One possible parallel is with the international relations emerging out of the wreckage of the Soviet Union, where a group of wholly new states have both to find their feet and work out their interrelationships. Another is with nineteenth-century Europe, where a cluster of powerful, nationalistic, and industrializing states had to deal with boundary disputes, historical fears, and status rivalries. In East Asia, the question is: what kind of regional patterns will fill the power vacuum left by the superpowers? For the realist, of central importance will be China's growing strength and the uncertainty about whether Japan will challenge China for regional influence.

The withdrawal of the superpowers and the rise of China and Japan (and further in the background, India) is in part matched by increases in defense spending and arms acquisition. China's defense budget (as a percentage of GDP) is up by 40 percent over the past five years, at a time when those of all the other permanent members of the United Nations Security Council have decreased. China has embarked on a major military modernization program, spurred on by the lessons of the 1990–91 Gulf War. It has acquired in-flight refueling technology, modern weapons, and coproduction facilities for state-of-the-art weaponry from Russia.

China is the most important part of the local arms dynamic. Taiwan has responded by purchasing modern fighter aircraft and ships from the United States and France. Southeast Asian countries concerned about Chinese intentions in the South China Sea are also buying new weapons systems. Many of these countries are increasingly able to afford the expensive advanced technology of modern warfare and their rapid pace of economic growth often hides the extent to which defense spending has increased, since it is not expanding as a percentage of their GDPs (see Table 6.1).[6] South Korea, threatened by both the increasingly aggressive and unstable policy of North Korea and the general withdrawal of American power, is also spending more on its armed forces.

So far this is more of an arms buildup than an arms race. States in the region are responding to the uncertainty about future threats, their own rapidly expanding economic strength, and the diminishing security commitments of the superpowers. There are as yet no highly focused competitive arms accumulations (except the long-standing one in Korea) and it is still rare for military expenditure to rise as a percentage of GDP. But this can easily change, as happened in the Gulf during the 1970s when the arms buildup that followed British withdrawal and the rise in oil prices turned into the arms race and wars of the 1980s and 1990s. In East Asia, the trend is clearly toward the development of more powerful indigenous arms industries, making the states less dependent on external supplies.

Japan views this arms buildup with growing concern. Although its defense spending has remained low as a percentage of GDP, the size of the

Table 6.1 / East Asian Military Expenditure 1985, 1990–1996
(in constant 1993 U.S. dollars)

	1985	1990	1992	1993	1994	1995	1996
Australia	7,155	6,383	7,364	7,448	8,096	8,120	8,200
Brunei	269	333	260	230	252	255	284
Cambodia	n.a.	n.a.	95	67	128	136	107
China	26,083	25,433	24,756	27,390	27,818	30,154	31,000
Fiji	18	37	31	32	33	34	36
Indonesia	3,076	1,854	1,880	2,031	2,267	2,495	2,696
Japan	28,240	31,100	36,645	41,732	44,822	47,723	45,091
Korea, North	5,461	6,486	5,649	5,305	5,439	4,972	4,500
Korea, South	8,268	10,609	11,368	11,994	12,266	13,645	15,632
Laos	72	70	69	70	74	69	77
Malaysia	2,318	2,358	2,786	2,905	3,019	3,339	3,500
Mongolia	45	68	28	10	17	18	22
Myanmar	1,583	1,100	1,275	1,600	1,752	1,840	1,900
New Zealand	849	818	636	628	705	872	890
Papua New Guinea	47	84	88	87	93	89	74
Philippines	623	1,146	1,139	1,067	1,074	1,094	1,107
Singapore	1,561	2,136	2,374	2,682	2,997	3,773	4,047
Taiwan	8,461	10,847	10,350	12,042	11,011	12,483	13,576
Thailand	2,462	2,504	2,938	3,232	3,489	3,702	4,167
Vietnam	3,154	789	735	720	954	865	860
Total	99,746	104,155	110,464	121,275	126,307	135,677	137,767
Percent change	—	+4.4	+6.1	+9.8	+4.1	+7.4	+1.5
Percent change 1985–96	+38.1						
Percent change 1990–96	+32.3						

Source: International Institute of International Studies, The Military Balance, various years.

GDP and the modernity of its economy gives Japan a formidable purchasing power and the ability to develop a threatening arsenal at relatively short notice. So far, Tokyo has avoided acquiring such offensive systems as in-flight refueling or aircraft carriers, but it has already warned China that by acquiring such weapons Beijing risks destabilizing the region. As the United States continues to reduce its forces in the Pacific, doubts will rise in Japan about the reliability of the American strategic umbrella and the consequent need to fill a perceived strategic vacuum. Such a change in Japanese policy would not only spur China to even greater efforts but would provoke fears in the Koreas and in Southeast Asia, where memories of Japanese imperial-ism are still assiduously cultivated by political elites.

Paradoxically, a crucial part of the momentum for the arms race comes from the American intention to cut back its forces. The United States fuels arms races by creating a power vacuum instead of establishing a structure of arms control or collective security. By seeking to arm states, for example in Southeast Asia, Taiwan, or South Korea, to lessen their fears about an American withdrawal, regional insecurities are often exacerbated. As Washington becomes ever more desperate to secure markets for American weapons as the Europeans cut back their purchases, the United States is making it easier for local states to increase the pace and lethality of the arms buildup and consequently heighten the risk of creating an arms race.

Looming behind the buildup of conventional arms is the specter of nuclear proliferation. Rising concern about nuclear security parallels that about conventional arms and has the same origin: local responses to the weakening or withdrawal of superpower nuclear umbrellas. China has, of course, been a nuclear weapon state since 1964. India became a threshold nuclear power with its test explosion in 1974 and Pakistan acquired a threshold nuclear weapon capability during the 1980s. The proliferation "chain" that led from China to India to Pakistan has the potential to spread further, both east and west, should India and Pakistan seek overt nuclear weapon status. In East Asia, there is evidence that North Korea has moved toward nuclear weapon capability, and no certainty that it will not resume doing so.[7] South Korea, Taiwan, and Japan are all wealthy, advanced industrial economies with substantial civil nuclear industries. Although South Korea and Taiwan have renounced the weapon-potential technologies of enrichment and reprocessing, both have the basis of a military nuclear program that could produce weapons within a few years. Japan has what might be called a policy of "recessed" deterrence.[8] It has civilian rockets and guidance systems capable of being converted into nuclear missiles, and has a nuclear industry with large stockpiles of fissile material that can be used in nuclear warheads. All three of these countries are signatories of the Nuclear Non-Proliferation Treaty. What their posture, especially that of Japan, seems to say is: "Don't push us around. Our intentions are peaceful, as indicated by our restraint in acquiring nuclear capability. But if circumstances change we command the technology and the wealth to become a formidable nuclear power in a short space of time. If pushed, we will mobilize these capabilities."

Circumstances, of course, are changing. The weakening of the American nuclear umbrella over East Asia confronts these states with choices that may be much harder than those they faced during the cocooned decades of the Cold War. If the restraints against proliferation break down, Asia could quite quickly contain several new nuclear powers. The possibility of a proliferation chain running outward from North Korea is particularly disturbing.

The military-strategic outlook is not all threatening, however. Japan is still highly constrained from any serious remilitarization by its internal politics. It has a well-embedded tradition of nonoffensive defense and, unlike the 1930s, would now have great difficulty recruiting large armies from its aging population. The Association of Southeast Asian Nations (ASEAN) states have constructed a durable security regime that has allowed them to solve and demilitarize a variety of disputes among them. There is a great flow of money and people from Taiwan into mainland China. India and China are on polite terms despite their unresolved border dispute. Furthermore, large parts of Asia, unlike most of Europe, have the benefit of being strategically insulated from each other by water. These factors are not insignificant, but neither are they by any means sufficient to lay to rest the concerns we have outlined.

THE ECONOMICS OF SECURITY

There is a remarkable "econophoria" when most people talk about East Asia and the Pacific. The optimists do not deny the risks in the region, but they do suggest that the depth and complexity of economic interdependence between its states makes the outbreak of war very unlikely. This outlook stems from liberal views of how the international political economy operates. It is argued that mutual dependencies in trade, finance, and technology both raise the costs of conflict and lower the incentives for war. Costs result from the disruption to markets, investments, and flow of goods. Economic dependence on others makes states more vulnerable to such dislocations, while at the same time fostering habits of communication and compromise between them. Incentives for conflict are lower because in a relatively open liberal international economy, access to raw materials, finance, and markets is obtained at less cost and on a greater scale than would be possible via military control of territory or spheres of influence. A liberal economic order divorces wealth and welfare from control over territory, and thereby removes one of the main reasons for the use of force.[9] The relative success of the pluralist market economies, and their victory in the Cold War, can be attributed to their pursuit of a liberal economic order, which has virtually eliminated the possibility that they will ever again use force against one another. Such optimism in Asia rests on the fact that Japan, the NICs and, increasingly, parts of China are now firmly tied into this Western-inspired global economic order. The end of the Cold War, by breaking up the resistance of communism, has further opened up the region to penetration through economic interdependence.[10] Yet, there are at least four reasons to qualify the optimism that this scenario might otherwise suggest for Asia.

First, the level of involvement in this liberal, postmodern international interdependence varies a great deal in the region and even within states themselves. Unlike the European Union, where the differences in the extent of interdependence are less pronounced, there are states in East Asia that still take a more traditional view of economic sovereignty. Echoes of the North-South agenda for the redistribution of wealth can also still be heard. China and Taiwan are not yet members of the World Trade Organization (WTO), and even when they join China will certainly not conform to transparency in trade. The presence of nontariff barriers in many East Asian states, including the more interdependent ones such as Japan, is a problem for trade both within the region and with other parts of the global market economy. The process of creating greater transparency and openness is bound to be painful as it provokes resistance from powerful vested interests.

Second, while there has been rapid economic growth in East Asia, there is much debate about whether interdependence is growing more, or less, strongly within the region than between its various countries and the rest of the world.[11] Given the uneven levels of development in East Asia, it makes sense for the most developed economies to seek markets in other developed states, which naturally encompasses North America and, more recently, the EU. As the East Asian countries continue to develop, they should be better placed to provide markets for each other, but the shakeout as market share is contested is likely to be acrimonious. The absence of an effective regional economic institution means that, unlike even in the early days of the European Community, there is no mechanism to minimize disputes. Also unlike in Europe, there is no political reservoir of goodwill from which to draw to lubricate economic cooperation. The fact that the ASEAN countries can agree not to tax the importation of snowplows, but has failed to open up its markets to more "popular" products, illustrates the depth of the problem.

There are also doubts over how evenly the mutual dependencies are distributed in the region. As Keohane and Nye have pointed out, interdependence can be uneven and when it is, power relations reassert themselves.[12] Erroneous Japanese assumptions that they can control the rising power of their neighbors, including China, because the latter depend on inputs of Japanese capital and technology to sustain growth, are an example of the logic of uneven interdependence at work. If interdependence in Asia is uneven then it could mask new power relations of dominance and dependence. If interdependence in Asia is weaker than between individual Asian states and the rest of the world, then one has to ask how much restraint that will provide against balance-of-power behavior within the region.

It is probable that the rest of the world, particularly the United States and Europe, might actually welcome a deterioration in security relations within Asia. If Asian states increase military spending to arm against each other it might take some of the heat out of their economic challenge to the West, as well as providing, at least in the short term, a large market for the armaments and related technology in which the West still holds the advantage. The rise in tensions in Asia would prolong the West's view of itself as being more civilized than the rest of the world and would give it more leverage over Japan and China. The potential downside of this argument is that sustained military competition in Asia might stimulate nuclear proliferation. In the longer term it would lead to more advanced weapons producers and possibly even military threats to the West. Nobody familiar with the history of Europe can underestimate the danger of this process—it was the European anarchy that took over the world and conquered the Asian empires, not the other way around.

A third reason for doubting the logic of liberal optimism in East Asia is that economic interdependence is not necessarily a protection against tension and conflict. The U.S.-Japanese relationship, both before World War II and recently, is evidence of this. There have been arguments about "economic interests" as a cause of intervention rather than of abstention, as demonstrated by Japan in the 1930s. There are also concerns about geopoliticians arguing that "strategic waterways" are so economically important as to justify intervention and power projection capability. Chinese strategists make a similar case for resources in the South China Sea. Japan is dependent on other states partly because it relies on external energy supplies, which could lead Japan to extraordinary lengths to defend what it views as vital economic interests. South Korea and Taiwan suffer similar high dependencies on energy supplies and long sea-lines of communication.

Indeed, is a liberal economic order only a temporary escape from security dilemmas? The much-cited case of the 1930s can be used to argue that the instabilities of management in a global economy, which is far stronger than any available mechanisms for governance, is a recipe for periodic collapse. When such collapse comes, the accompanying disruption of markets and shrinkage of production can cause great pain and profound political upheaval. Optimists will argue that these lessons have been learned and that the shadow of the past is strong enough to prevent a return to the 1930s. They may be right, but the signs are not all encouraging. The difficulties of the last GATT round—the willingness of national political leaders in many developed countries to put domestic priorities above international ones, the ease with which blaming the "unfair" practices of foreigners became part of the domestic political debate, and the increasing difficulties of managing economic interdependence in a world beset by surplus capacity, intensifying competition, expensive capital, a flow of "hot" money and short tempers— all suggest otherwise. The move toward a more regionalized world economy has been boosted by the formation of the North American Free Trade Agreement and the European Union, and talk of regional economic blocs is common in Southeast Asia, Southern Africa, Latin America, and elsewhere, despite the establishment of the WTO.

For Asia, the concern is the absence of machineries or structures, or even the foundations for them, for regional cooperation. For the reasons discussed earlier, Tokyo is still unable to act as a regional leader. Memories of its imperial phase still evoke strong negative reactions that would impair any attempt to construct a regional bloc. If the liberal world economy suffers a major breakdown, Asia, of all the big industrial centers, will be in the weakest position to weather the crisis.

Fourth, there is a curious tendency to use Europe as an example that greater economic integration makes war less likely. But a crucial difference between East Asia and Western Europe is their form of government, which is the key to this theory. If it is true that democracies do not fight each other, then Europe is well placed.[13] But only a few of the market economies in Asia are democratic. Some of those are democratic only in a rather superficial sense, and some of the major states in the region, notably China and Indonesia, are not democratic at all. As Chinese behavior demonstrates with depressing regularity, corporatist or authoritarian states, even with market economies, may not be so inhibited about resorting to force. This leads to the complex argument that because East Asian political culture has never had an enlightenment, as in Europe and America, Asian politics leans towards authoritarianism and sudden changes of policy. What is certainly true is that these political and economic cultures are less transparent than Western models and, therefore, conflict and misunderstanding among them are more likely.

THE WEAKNESS OF
INTERNATIONAL SOCIETY

A fourth perspective on Asia's future can be viewed through the lens of international society. Hedley Bull and Adam Watson define international society as: "a group of states (or, more generally, a group of independent political communities) which not merely form a system, in the sense that the behavior of each is a necessary factor in the calculations of the others, but also have established by dialogue and consent common rules and institutions for the conduct of their relations, and recognize their common interest in maintaining these arrangements."[14] International society encompasses the more specific notion of regimes. It suggests a situation in which a whole set of regimes, multilateral organizations, and rules exists that enables states to communicate on a regular basis, to establish modes and habits of consultation and cooperation, to coordinate and manage their relations, and to prevent their disputes from escalating into conflict or war.[15]

Europe in particular, and the West in general, constitute advanced and richly developed international societies. Given the near universal acceptance of the diplomatic practice and membership of the United Nations, the international system as a whole can be seen as an international society, albeit one of a rather basic and thinly developed type. What is distinctive about Asia is its combination of several industrialized societies with a still very partial and tentative regional international society.

Perhaps the most alarming aspect of East Asian security is the virtual absence of any tradition of effective multilateralism. Such institutions that now exist, though certainly better than nothing, have shallow roots and unimpressive records. One might argue that Europe has a confused alphabet soup of institutions, but its problem is the lesser one of finding the most appropriate forum, rather than the greater one of developing a process of dialogue from scratch. East Asians have little experience of multilateral institutions. ASEAN has been relatively successful in establishing peace among its members, and since the end of the Cold War it has been expanding to draw its former enemies in Indochina into its security regime. It has also tried to create a superregional security forum (the ASEAN Regional

Forum, or ARF) embracing most (but not all) of the states of East Asia, as well as India, the United States and the EU. But the ARF has so far accomplished little except to engage China in a process of dialogue. It is indeed a symbol of the region's problems. That the small powers have had to take the lead in trying to create East Asian security institutions simply underlines the fact that neither great power in the region is acceptable as a leader. And since the great powers are the problem, the minor powers and the ARF can do little.

Asia-Pacific Economic Cooperation (APEC) is the most developed of the economic groupings, but it looks unlikely to become more than an unwieldy Pacific summit beloved by sherpas and journalists. Indeed, APEC can be viewed as an attempt to avoid confronting the consequences of the ending of the Cold War. Like the ARF, its objective is to keep the United States as guarantor of Asian security, which both flatters waning American power and keeps the Asian countries from having to come to terms with each other. There are two risks for Asia in this policy: first, that the United States is unwilling to become entangled in inter-Asian rivalries, and second, that it is willing, but only for reasons of self-interest. The result could be the United States playing the role to its own advantage, as "perfidious Albion" did in Europe before World War II. Economically, Japan and the United States are keen to limit the development of economic regionalism because they fear that its success would mean more trade barriers. Many ASEAN states fear that in a wider regional organization they would be overshadowed by the agendas of their great-power neighbors.

The virtual absence of multilateralism is a cause of deep concern for the security of the region. Japan, South Korea, and the United States have only now begun to hold talks about Northeast Asian security, let alone try to evolve an effective consultation mechanism for the region. Hopes for a Conference on Security and Cooperation in Asia, akin to the Conference on Security and Cooperation in Europe (CSCE), have foundered on regional rivalries and the inability of the ARF to deal with any significant security issues, even as Chinese troops continue to extend their grip on the South China Sea. While the Five Power Defence Arrangement (consisting of Malaysia, Singapore, Australia, New Zealand, and the UK) survives as a confidence-building measure between Singapore and Malaysia, it serves as evidence that more wide-ranging multilateralism in security requires the involvement of powers from outside East Asia. It is significant that Japan could only contribute to the peacekeeping operation in Cambodia because it was under the auspices of the UN. As with many regional economic issues, the East Asians are unable and unwilling to solve security issues between themselves and need outside assistance. This is rocky soil in which to plant the seeds of multilateralism and arms control.[16]

One of the most obvious causes of a weak international society is the presence or prevalence of weak states (those with low levels of sociopolitical cohesion).[17] The logic of the international "anarchical society" is based on decentralized political order.[18] For international order to prevail under these conditions, it is necessary (though not sufficient) for the states comprising it to be socially and politically stable. If they are not, as illustrated most obviously by the international relations of the Middle East and Africa, then the construction of stable, long-term relations among them is impossible. Where weak states exist, leaderships and ideologies are unstable, domestic turbulence spreads beyond borders, insecurity is endemic, and no state can rely on consistent patterns of attitude and alignment. Even the most casual observer of European security after the Cold War will identify weak states as a major cause of insecurity. The collapse of Yugoslavia, Czechoslovakia, and the Soviet Union are the most dramatic examples, but the painful reconstruction of state-society relations throughout Eastern Europe is also a cause of concern.

In East Asia, the collapse of the Soviet Union has had its own consequences, including the possibility of an independent Russian Far East and the destabilizing effects on the emergence of independent and unstable Central Asian states has had on China. One effect of the collapse of the Soviet Union was the Asian communists' acceleration of their domestic reforms through the extension of decentralization. Central authority is consequently weakening and it is now no longer unreasonable to talk of the fragmentation of China, albeit not in the same way as that of the Soviet Union. As China pulls in different directions, depending on its regional trade partners, serious questions have to be asked about the risks of conflict if or when China is no longer a single entity in a region that it once had the potential to dominate. Some states in the West and Asia might be pleased to see a fragmenting China, though probably not if the outcome was a violent civil war.[19]

Weakness in other states in East Asia takes on less dramatic but more varied forms. There is the special case of the two Koreas, with the ideological and military confrontations of the Cold War remaining and the existence of each state undermining the legitimacy of the other. Taiwan faces a similar lack of legitimacy in the eyes of China. Greater political pluralism, particularly in South Korea and Taiwan, may have an important impact on possible reunifications. Greater democracy may encourage ideas of independence in Taiwan and the debate in South Korea may be shaped by a population allowed to voice opposition to the inevitable costs of reunification. Indonesia remains corrupt and authoritarian, and the recent suppression of the opposition suggests that it is heading for an unpleasant succession crisis. The NICs of the region have achieved remarkable economic growth, but they are trying to combine expansion with a move away from authoritarian military rule, and toward increased pluralism and democracy. Recent mass killings of civilians by the military in Thailand show how far there is to go even in a prospering "dragon" economy. Neighboring Myanmar remains locked in a corrupt and repressive military dictatorship. In the face of ethnic divisions, boundary disputes, politicized armed forces, and deeply institutionalized corruption, most of the countries of Southeast Asia face serious problems in establishing stronger states, even though they are no longer suffering from the intense competing foreign interventions of the Cold War.

The presence of these weak states, with their spillover effects on the international relations of the region, partly explains the weakness of international society in Asia and the difficulty of remedying the situation. The lack of a well-developed international society means that Asia is peculiarly vulnerable to the "back to the future" scenario and a revival of balance-of-power behavior. Global international society may act as a restraint but, as argued above, the Western powers, whether mistakenly or not, may see little short-term benefit in preventing such a development.

FORWARD TO AN UNHAPPY FUTURE?

When added together, the views through our four analytical lenses reveal many weighty factors indicating a balance-of-power future for East Asia, with much sparser and less well-rooted forces favoring the interdependence view. While this pessimistic assessment does not suggest that large-scale conflict or war is inevitable, or even likely, an escalation of military spending and arms rivalry is a real possibility. Some military conflict is distinctly possible, though Asians, like Europeans, are constrained by the overriding fear of nuclear escalation. The point is not that the future is doomed to gloomy scenarios, but that despite the superficial Western orientation of its NICs, Asia is not an integral part of Western international society. It has dynamics of its own, which are becoming more prominent and raise serious doubts about the validity of optimistic assumptions of a benign future based on peaceful interdependence. While the Atlantic community and Japan have established an interdependent security community, it does not cover the rest of East Asia, suggesting that the West may choose to avoid squabbles in this region.

There are a number of specific security concerns in East Asia. The first is the potential for arms races. As was evident during the Cold War in Europe, even a sustained, high-level arms race does not necessarily result in war. Although it can be argued that this money may have been more effectively spent on other public needs, there is no simple trade-off between bombs and butter as suggested by talk of a "peace dividend." In addition, East Asia is becoming increasingly wealthy and, therefore, better able to endure high levels of defense spending. Although arms races represent political insecurity and may not necessarily lead to war, it is still of benefit to limit the risks and costs. This requires greater transparency of defense spending, arms transfers, defense doctrines, and military deployments. These are all elements of practice within the CSCE that could be adopted by East Asia.

The most obvious area where arms races signify political instability is in the South China Sea. China's pursuit of its territorial claims, as the United States reduces its forces and the ASEAN countries seem incapable of organizing a coherent response beyond rhetoric, suggests the urgent need for an international effort to establish a formal dialogue on conflicting claims. China is the main threat to stability and it needs to be subjected to more vocal and effective efforts to make Beijing aware of the risks it is running. It would be peculiar if aggression in East Asia is tolerated by the international community after it was opposed in the Persian Gulf. Yet, it is unlikely that the United States will oppose China's continuing to take territory by force in the South China Sea, preferring instead to leave the East Asians to their own devices.

A related and longer-term concern must be decentralization in China and the impact this will have on the settlement of disputes over Hong Kong and Taiwan. It was unthinkable that the Chinese takeover of Hong Kong would be contested by force, but the imposition of harsh political and economic restraints by Beijing could result in a large flow of refugees and damage to regional economic cooperation. It could also affect the settlement of the Taiwan issue, in which military conflict is far more likely. If the resolution of these unsettled issues of Chinese history are part of a larger challenge to the unity of the Chinese state, then all predictions about the stability and prosperity of East Asia must be reconsidered. The reluctance of many analysts to consider the risks of the implosion of the Chinese empire is as strong as it was with the Soviet empire.

There is concern over the unification of the two Koreas and the risk that it will become entangled with the issue of nuclear proliferation. The absence of any formal mechanism, let alone a two-plus-four system (like that established to oversee the unification of Germany) for discussing the risks, is troublesome. Suspicion in Northeast Asia of the motives of all the key states in the region is every bit as great as it was in Europe regarding Germany, but at least in the case of the latter there was a long-standing mechanism of crisis consultation that eased the transition.

The much-touted risk of U.S.-Japanese conflict seems far-fetched, especially as the former has reduced its military presence in East Asia. The risk of conflict in the short term is more likely to be due to an absence of American power (as the main anti-China balancer), than to its presence. Given a 1920s-like scenario of American withdrawal and relative isolationism, coupled with economic tensions, U.S. passivity may allow East Asians to confront each other more directly. A Japan that could no longer count on American deterrence of China would probably have to spend more on its own defense, including a nuclear capability.

The lessons of the 1920s and 1930s suggest that the only way in which a retreating United States can maintain its influence at a reduced cost is by establishing an effective multilateral security structure. Of course, in the 1920s and 1930s the United States failed to pursue effective multilateralism and had to use force to subdue Japanese imperialism. By helping to keep the protagonists apart and the United States engaged at least politically and economically, it is possible that ventures such as ARF and APEC will encourage the local states to evolve their own processes of dialogue and regional cooperation. So far, the evidence suggests that East Asians are unable to formulate effective regionalism without outside participation. Economic multilateralism quickly runs into opposition by states who are reluctant to surrender sovereignty. Multilateralism in the security sphere encounters worries about Chinese power and intentions. Should the United States fail to stay and help sustain a balance of power, or fail to help build a regional dialogue on security, and should East Asians fail to take up the challenge of multilateralism, the region may become the most important zone of conflict in the twenty-first century.

QUESTIONS FOR FURTHER STUDY

1. What do Buzan and Segal mean by saying that East Asia is "in danger of heading 'back to the future'" with respect to regional security affairs? On what basis do they make this claim? Are their arguments persuasive?

2. What are the historical legacies that bear most heavily upon the security environment in East Asia in the post-Cold War period? What is their likely impact?

3. How is the post-Cold War security environment in East Asia different from that of Europe? What are the consequences (in Asia) of these differences?

4. How does the growing power of China affect the security environment in East Asia?

5. Many analysts believe that growing economic interdependence will diminish the likelihood of military rivalry and conflict in East Asia, but Buzan and Segal question this logic. What are the arguments on each side of this debate, and which side do you think is most persuasive? Why?

Notes

1. Gerald Segal, *The Soviet Union and the Pacific* (Boston: Unwin Hyman for the Royal Institute of International Affairs, 1990).

2. Barry Buzan, "Japan's Future: Old History Versus New Roles," *International Affairs,* Vol. 64, No. 4 (1988), pp. 557–73; "Japan's Defense Problematique," *The Pacific Review,* Vol. 8, No.1, (1995), pp. 25–43; "International Security in East Asia in the Twenty-First Century: Options for Japan," *Dokkyo International Review,* Vol. 9, (1996), pp. 281–314.

3. Michael Yahuda, *Hong Kong: China's Challenge* (London: Routledge, 1996); Gerald Segal, *The Fate of Hong Kong* (London: Simon and Schuster, 1993).

4. Christopher Coker, "Post-Modernity and the End of the Cold War: Has War Been Disinvented?" *Review of International Studies,* Vol. 18, No. 3, (1992), pp. 189–98.

5. Stuart Harris and James Cotton, eds., *The End of the Cold War in Northeast Asia* (Melbourne: Longman, 1991).

6. Gerald Segal, "Managing New Arms Races in the Asia/Pacific," *The Washington Quarterly,* Vol. 15, No. 3, (Summer 1992); Andrew Mack and Desmond Ball, "The Military Build-up in Asia-Pacific," *The Pacific Review,* Vol. 5, No. 3, (1992); Paul Dibb, *Towards a New Balance of Power in Asia,* Adelphi Paper No. 295 (London: International Institute of Strategic Studies, 1995).

7. Andrew Mack, "North Korea and the Bomb," *Foreign Policy,* No. 83 (1991), pp. 87–104; James Cotton, "North Korea's Nuclear Ambitions," Adelphi Paper No. 275 (London: International Institute of Strategic Studies, 1993); Paul Bracken, "Nuclear Weapons and State Survival in North Korea," *Survival,* Vol. 35, No. 3 (1993), pp. 137–53; Christopher Hughes,

"The North Korean Nuclear Crisis and Japanese Security," *Survival,* Vol. 38, No. 2 (1996), pp. 79–103.

8. This term is Daniel Deudney's. See Daniel H. Deudney, "Nuclear Weapons and the Waning of the Real-State," *Daedalus,* Vol. 124, No. 2 (Spring 1995), pp. 226–27.

9. Barry Buzan, "Economic Structure and International Security: The Limits of the Liberal Case," *International Organization,* Vol. 38, No. 4 (1984).

10. For a discussion of "openness," see Barry Buzan and Gerald Segal, "Defining Openness as Reform," in Gerald Segal, et al., *Openness and Foreign Policy in Government States* (London: Routledge for the Royal Institute of International Affairs, 1992).

11. Marc Busch and Helen Milner, "The Future of the International Trading System," in Richard Stubbs and Geoffrey Underhill, eds., *Political Economy and the Changing Global Order* (Toronto: McLelland and Stewart, 1994), Chapter 15; Andrew Wyatt-Walter, "Regionalism, Globalism, and World Economic Order" in Louise Fawcett and Andrew Hurrell, eds., *Regionalism in World Politics* (Oxford: Oxford University Press, 1995), p. 104; Richard Grant, Maria Papadakis, and J. David Richardson, "Global Trade Flows: Old Structures, New Issues, Empirical Evidence," in C. Fred Bergsten and Marcus Noland, eds., *Pacific Dynamism and the International Economic System* (Washington, Institute for International Economics, 1993), p. 53; Stephan Hessler, "Regionalization of the World Economy: Fact or Fiction?" paper presented to International Studies Association Conference, Washington, D.C., March 24, 1994.

12. Robert O. Keohane and Joseph S. Nye, *Power and Interdependence* (Boston: Little Brown, 1977).

13. See Nils Petter Gleditsch, "Democracy and Peace," pp. 369–76, and Erich Weede, "Some Simple Calculations on Democracy and War Involvement," pp. 377–83, both in *Journal of Peace Research,* Vol. 29, No. 4 (1992).

14. Hedley Bull and Adam Watson, eds., *The Expansion of International Society* (Oxford: Oxford University Press, 1984), p. 1.

15. Barry Buzan, "From International System to International Society: Structural Realism and Regime Theory Meet the English School," *International Organization,* Vol. 47, No. 3 (1993), pp. 327–52.

16. For a more optimistic view of multilateralism in security see Geoffrey Wiseman, "Common Security in the Asia-Pacific Region," *The Pacific Review,* Vol. 5, No. 1 (1992). For the critical view see Michael Leifer, *The ASEAN Regional Forum,* Adelphi Paper No. 302 (London: International Institute of Strategic Studies, 1996).

17. Barry Buzan, *People, States, and Fear: An Agenda for International Security Studies in the Post-Cold War Era* (Hemel Hempstead: Wheatsheaf, 1991), especially pp. 96–107.

18. Hedley Bull, *The Anarchical Society* (London: Macmillan, 1977).

19. This complex issue is the subject of a major research project at the International Institute of Strategic Studies, London (IISS). See Gerald Segal, *China Changes Shape,* Adelphi Paper No. 287 (London: IISS, 1994); and Gerald Segal and David Goodman, eds., *China Deconstructs* (London: Routledge, 1994).

7 / The United States and the Middle East

MICHAEL C. HUDSON

Even critics of American Middle East policy must agree that the United States today stands astride this unhappy region like a colossus. A half-century of involvement in every conceivable way—through diplomacy, aid, culture, education, espionage, subversion, and (not least) the projection of military power—has secured the "holy trinity" of American interests: Israel, oil, and anti-communism. Those who said it couldn't be done underestimated America's ability to achieve contradictory goals. Today the American president can summon the leaders of most Middle Eastern governments to endorse his regional (and domestic) political agenda. American financial officials can write the domestic economic policy for most governments in the region. The U.S. military enjoys unprecedented access and acceptance from North Africa to the Gulf. New information technologies expose Middle Eastern cultures and societies to American-dominated global values, fashions, and definitions of political "realities."

Why, then, do American embassies throughout the Middle East today resemble fortresses? Why do they fear for the security of ordinary American businesspeople and tourists? Why can't American citizens travel in a normal manner to no fewer than five countries in the area? Why does America's chief regional ally Israel—powerful as it is—suffer from suicide bombers and missile attacks? Why do friendly Arab regimes often find their American patronage a political liability? Why does the United States find it necessary to maintain a larger and more permanent military presence than it did forty years ago when American interests seemed far less secure than they do today? Why—in this era of an apparently viable "peace process" and security in the Gulf—do Americans traveling in the Middle East encounter more hostile criticism of U.S. policies than ever before?

This chapter first describes the triumph of American policy over the past fifty years. Second, it analyzes current challenges to U.S. policy in the region. Finally, it takes a critical look at some current and future issues and makes some policy recommendations.

THE PAST

World War II marked what the late ambassador Raymond Hare called "the great divide" in U.S. relations with the Middle East, "between our traditional national position of rejecting political responsibility in the Middle East and our postwar acceptance of responsibility on a global or great

113

power basis. . . . "[1] Hardened as we now are to American realpolitik, we imagine the earlier period as an age of innocence, characterized by a virtuous avoidance of political entanglement in local quarrels and European rivalries in the region. We enjoy reading James Field's amiable account of American missionary activities.[2] We are proud of the American University of Beirut and other educational enterprises that won lasting respect from Middle Easterners. We are flattered to learn from Harry Howard's study of the King-Crane Commission of 1919 that the United States was better liked than the European countries.[3] Even the periodic malicious depictions of "State Department Arabists" cannot hide the contributions to smoother U.S.-Middle East relations made by U.S. diplomats in the past.[4] The far side of Hare's "great divide" was marked by classical American idealism. The near side is more complex: idealism is still there, though selectively invoked and ideologized. Increasingly, however, America presents an imperious image as it sets about in pursuit of its three emerging concerns—containing Soviet communism, protecting access to Middle East oil, and finally, securing Israel's place in the region.

Containing Soviet Communism

In October 1947, as Hare tells it, American and British officials met at the Pentagon to sketch out a geopolitical blueprint for the Middle East in light of the new threats of Soviet expansionism and communist ideology. Gone was the "reverse Monroe Doctrine" of the interwar period during which the United States left the Middle East to Britain (in contrast to President Monroe's insistence on keeping Britain out of Washington's Latin America in the nineteenth century).[5] Already President Truman had extended aid to Greece and Turkey to help those governments stave off communist or Soviet challenges. While still conceding Britain "primary responsibility" for the Middle East and the Mediterranean, Secretary of State Marshall was already contemplating an eventual leadership role for the United States in the region.

A decade later John C. Campbell, with the help of a study group from the Council on Foreign Relations (CFR), published *Defense of the Middle East* (1958)—a revealing account of the concern with which the foreign policy establishment viewed trends in the region. The fundamental problem was the threat to the security, even the survival, of the United States in the face of the global Soviet challenge. As for the Middle East: "The entrenchment of Soviet power in that strategic region would bring a decisive shift in the world balance, outflanking NATO. Soviet control of Middle Eastern oil could disrupt the economy of the free world. And the triumph of communism in the heart of the Islamic world could be the prelude to its triumph through Asia, Africa, and Europe."[6] With the region "convulsed by national and social conflicts of its own,"[7] the Soviets had plenty of troubled waters in which to fish. The study group asserted that the Arab-Israeli conflict "hangs like a poisonous cloud over the entire Middle East . . . Time has not solved the problem of the Arab refugees. Something must be done about it . . . The American commitment to Israel is to its continued independent existence, not to its existing boundaries or policies."[8]

On the geostrategic level, American policy sought to contain the Soviets in the Middle East through military alliances, as it was containing them in Europe through NATO. But this approach largely failed, as the examples of the Middle East Command proposal and the Middle East Defense Organization in 1951 and 1952 indicate.[9] Even the Baghdad Pact (1955), an alliance of Turkey, Iraq, Iran, and Pakistan sponsored by Britain with American backing, generated more animosity than security in the Arab world. Nor were looser political/economic umbrella projects, such as the Eisenhower Doctrine (1957), any more successful. Under this doctrine Washington promised financial aid and security assistance to any Middle Eastern government requesting American protection from "international communism," but Lebanon was the only Arab state to accept the offer, a decision that brought more instability than security to that small country. Indeed, under Stalin's less doctrinaire successors, the Soviet Union and its satellites succeeded in leaping over the Baghdad Pact into the Arab heart-land through its arms deals with Syria and Egypt from 1954 to 1956. To these governments, the real geostrategic threat was Israel, not the Soviet Union; and therein lay a real problem for American diplomacy. The U.S.-Soviet "game" was not being played exclusively on the geostrategic level. It was also being played on the volatile ideological terrain of Middle East domestic politics.

The waning of European imperialism in the Middle East after World War II coincided with a powerful current of national assertiveness in Iran and the Arab countries, which were rapidly modernizing. Ascension to great-power status and close wartime cooperation with colonialist European allies had not extinguished American liberal idealism. Accordingly, there was great curiosity and not a little sympathy with the emergence of independent states in what came to be called the Third World. With these trends in mind, U.S. government officials, such as Loy Henderson, director of the State Department's Office of Near Eastern and African Affairs, and Secretary of Defense James Forrestal, had correctly prophesied that support for a Zionist state in Palestine would set the United States at odds with the emerging Arab nationalist currents. They were equally right in predicting that the Soviet Union would try to associate itself with this trend in order to advance its own interests throughout the region. Regimes friendly to Washington would be weakened. Regional developments during the 1950s and 1960s revealed the extent of the problem—nationalist coups or up-heavals took place in Egypt, Iran, Iraq, Jordan, Lebanon, Libya, North Yemen, South Yemen, Sudan, and Syria. Periodic crises and violent eruptions (1956, 1967, 1969–70) in the unsolved Arab-Israeli conflict did not help matters.

If the American response to all this was often improvised and contradictory, the results were not altogether negative. American diplomats tried to avoid a head-on confrontation with nationalist forces—U.S. efforts to deal with Nasser are a fascinating case in point. Even American presidents occasionally made a supportive gesture—for example, Dwight Eisenhower in the 1956 war, and John F. Kennedy, who as a senator had spoken positively on Algeria, and as president initiated a dialogue with Nasser and supported the republican revolution in Yemen. On the other hand, the United States worked to suppress Iranian nationalism by organizing the overthrow of Prime Minister Muhammad Mussadiq's government in 1953, and it opposed the nationalist upheavals in Syria and Iraq. While Kennedy had some temporary doubts about supporting a "traditional" regime in Saudi Arabia he did not hesitate to support the Saudis when they were challenged by Nasser in the 1960s.

U.S. diplomacy in the field, and the respected nongovernmental American presence, somewhat blunted the U.S. confrontation with Arab nationalism, but it could hardly eliminate it. The Palestine problem lay at the heart of the pan-Arab cause, and American support for Israel was too massive to allow for healthy relationships with most Arab states, let alone with Arab public opinion. The Soviet Union, therefore, had a clear field to plow. But the Soviets had their own problems and weaknesses. Communism and Arab nationalism did not mix well together, and the Soviets were often clumsy in their military and aid relationships. Nationalist Arab regimes complained about the low level and poor quality of Soviet support. Nevertheless, Soviet patronage enabled the nationalist, anti-Israel camp to pose a serious challenge to U.S. interests in the region.

The growing enfeeblement of the Soviet Union vis-à-vis the United States was increasingly evident from the 1970s on, even to Arab governments heavily dependent on Moscow for arms and diplomatic support. Following Israel's smashing victory over the Arabs in the 1967 "Six-Day War," an Arab "rejectionist bloc" emerged that included states such as Egypt, Syria, Iraq, Sudan, Algeria, Libya, and the two Yemens. These rejectionists, with Moscow's support, had refused American and international plans for a negotiated settlement that would require recognition of Israel. But gradually this bloc began to disintegrate, and with it the influence in Arab public opinion of the pan-Arab nationalist movement. Egypt's President Anwar al-Sadat was the first Arab leader to recognize Moscow's decline, and he displayed logical realpolitik behavior by throwing out his Soviet military advisors and dramatically turning toward Washington in search of a negotiated solution to the Arab-Israel conflict. Later, Iraq and Syria would engage in their own more cautious flirtations with the United States. By the time of the Soviet Union's collapse in 1990, Washington was able to enlist the one-time rejectionist governments in Egypt and Syria into the international coalition to remove Iraq as a threat to Kuwait and Saudi Arabia. The U.S.-Soviet Cold War in the Middle East was over, and the Arab nationalist camp (what was left of it) no longer had a superpower patron to constrain the United States and Israel.

Oil

U.S. commercial interest in Middle East oil predates Hare's "great divide." American companies got their foot in the door of the Middle East oil cartel with the Red Line Agreement of 1928.[10] Under the Red Line Agreement the major international oil companies—now including an American group—pledged in a "self-denying" clause to share proportionally the future oil discoveries in the former Ottoman Turkish territories, including the Arabian peninsula (except for Kuwait), Iraq, the Levant (except for Sinai), Cyprus, and Anatolia. A decade later in Saudi Arabia, having outmaneuvered their British rivals in Saudi Arabia, a subsidiary of Standard of California made a stupendous find at "Dammam No. 7" which, over the next forty-five years, was to produce over 32 million barrels of oil. But oil did not acquire a strategic security dimension until World War II. Just as the British at the beginning of the century had seen the military and economic value of Middle East oil, so too did the Americans, not only for prosecuting World War II but also as a cheap supplement to declining U.S. reserves, and the West's oil-driven postwar economic development. With the price of Middle East oil a mere two dollars per barrel up until 1971, it is hardly surprising that Western Europe and even the United States would become dependent on it.

While European and Japanese dependency was well over two-thirds of total consumption, Americans in the 1970s found that half their oil was imported and half the imports were from the Middle East. Given, then, the importance of a secure supply of cheap Middle East oil, U.S. policymakers determined that their main tasks were to exclude the Soviet influence from the region and prevent any internal force from nationalizing Western companies, restricting production and/or raising prices, and overturning established regimes. Clandestine involvement by the CIA and the British in a coup code-named "Operation Ajax," which returned the young shah to his throne in Iran in 1953, seemed to have been an effective object lesson for would-be nationalist challengers.[11] As for the U.S.-Arab oil relationship, ARAMCO (Arabian-American Oil Company, a consortium of U.S. companies active in Saudi Arabia) had mounted a remarkably effective, indeed amicable, working relationship that has endured up to the present, weathering even the transfer to Saudi ownership.

In 1960, following an abrupt decision by the oil companies to cut prices, outraged governments of oil-producing states established the Organization of Petroleum Exporting Countries (OPEC). OPEC, inexperienced and weakened by internal rivalries, had little success in defending the price of oil during its first decade. But the situation was about to change. Growing world demand, the proliferation of small independent companies, and domestic nationalist pressures in several oil-producing countries set in motion the "oil revolution" of the 1970s, which by the end of the decade had lifted the price to around thirty-five dollars per barrel. It also led to a shift in the balance of oil power from the companies to the producing countries, by breaking the cohesion of the producer cartel at a time when world oil demand was growing. Libya, following Colonel Mu'ammar Qadhafi's nationalist revolution in 1969, led the charge, followed by Iran. Then, during the 1973 Arab-Israeli war, King Faisal of Saudi Arabia did what Americans had thought was unthinkable: he imposed a partial boycott on U.S. and Western European consumers. Suddenly the Arabs had "the oil weapon" and, stung by America's emergency war aid to Israel, they had used it.

The shock in the United States and Europe was palpable, and it lent urgency to Secretary of State Kissinger's mediation of the war. In the long term it also led to a comprehensive new energy policy designed to blunt the oil weapon in the future through the Strategic Petroleum Reserve, a vast underground oil storage facility, and conservation measures.[12] Thus, by the time of the second major price hike in 1979, due to the Iranian revolution of 1979–80, and the Iraq-Iran war of 1980–88, the global oil market was far more stable. Moreover, Saudi Arabia was both able and willing to cushion these shocks.

With the collapse of world oil prices in 1986, OPEC and non-OPEC producers alike lost their collective effectiveness, and "the Arab oil weapon" basically disappeared. For U.S. policymakers the main oil problem now was ensuring that the newly formed (1981) Arab Gulf Cooperation Council (GCC), a loose association of the governments of Saudi Arabia, Kuwait, Bahrain, Qatar, the United Arab Emirates, and Oman, be "protected" from regional (Iranian) or exogenous (Soviet) inroads. Fortunately for Washington, the Iraqi president, Saddam Hussein, shared American concern over Ayatollah Rouhollah Khomeini's regional system-challenging proclivities. Iraq provided the military shield, the GCC states the money, and the United States the intelligence data to beat back the Iranian Islamist challenge.

Israel

So firm—indeed, fervent—has American support for Israel become since 1967 that it is easy to forget how bitter was the policy debate in the United States over Palestine in the 1940s and how evenly matched the antagonists. On the one side were the pro-Zionists in the domestic political arena, and on the other, the Executive Branch officials concerned with the global and regional implications of a U.S.-supported Jewish state. The debate actually began in 1922 with the Joint Congressional Resolution endorsing the Balfour Declaration, but the State Department subsequently issued a statement insisting that the resolution "did not constitute a commitment to any foreign obligation or entanglement."[13] By the end of the 1930s, with Hitler's persecution of Jews and the situation in Palestine worsening, the debate grew more heated. In a well-known article published in *The Middle East Journal* in 1948, Kermit Roosevelt, an American intelligence expert on the Middle East, described (and criticized) the Zionist lobbying effort, observing that "almost all Americans with diplomatic, educational, missionary, or business experience in the Middle East protest fervently that support of political Zionism is directly contrary to our national interests, as well as to common justice."[14]

But President Harry Truman, influenced by Zionist friends and desirous of Zionist political support in the 1948 election campaign, decided that the United States would support the establishment of a Jewish state in Palestine. Had he not taken that stand (and he himself wavered at one point), the Zionist enterprise in Palestine might have taken a weaker form and, indeed, might not have ultimately succeeded. It was not until 1967 that the Executive Branch diplomatic and defense establishment, impressed with Israel's military prowess and Arab weakness, was finally persuaded that Israel might be something more than a burden on the national interest. Since then the deeply committed supporters of Israel have managed not only to mobilize most of the American Jewish community but have helped win general public support for Israel and its policies in the region almost without reservation. Perhaps the best evidence for the political clout of Israel's supporters is the size of the annual U.S. aid package—upward of $3 billion.

Israel today is not only an established part of the Middle East landscape but has become a regional superpower: its GNP is more than twice that of the largest Arab state, Egypt, and it has a world-class military establishment. Yet the naysayers of the 1940s were not entirely wrong in their assessment. Indeed, they were correct in forecasting that the U.S. relationship with the Arab world would deteriorate, that repeated wars and immense suffering would result from the creation of a Jewish state, and that the Soviets would take advantage of this rancor and instability. The U.S. political leadership was prepared to accept these costs, and insisted that the Arabs do likewise. For American leaders the costs were bearable because they did not include loss of access to Arab oil nor the complete surrender of the Middle East to the Soviet Union. For that, they may thank the Arabs, who failed to respond collectively to the challenges facing them, and the Soviets who proved incapable of sustaining their empire.

As midwife to the birth of Israel in 1948, the United States faced the task of helping to arrange a settlement that would see the new nation through infancy and ensure it a prosperous life. To that end, the United States has supported over the years a variety of diplomatic initiatives and projects to normalize the new state's relations with its neighbors. But owing to the manner in which Israel had been established—basically by force of arms which led to the displacement of some 750,000 Palestinians into neighboring countries—these efforts were largely unsuccessful until 1978. They included the Lausanne talks of 1949 and the Palestine Conciliation Commission, which were intended, among other things, to facilitate the return of displaced Palestinians—without success. Washington backed the Tripartite Declaration of 1950 on arms limitation, hoping to minimize the possibilities of a new war, but another war occurred in 1956. On the theory that economic (and water) development projects might bring about Arab-Israeli peace, the United States promoted the Economic Survey Mission of 1949 and the Eric Johnston Jordan Valley Development Plan of

1955.[15] In the spring of 1956, Eisenhower's envoy Robert Anderson undertook secret shuttle negotiations between Nasser and Ben Gurion, which were unsuccessful, and war broke out a few months later.

The American government also backed various UN peacemaking efforts, including the negotiations in 1949 on the Greek island of Rhodes (which led only to an armistice and not full peace treaties), the United Nations Truce Supervision Organization (UNTSO), the United Nations Relief and Works Administration for Palestine Refugees (UNRWA) from 1949 to the present, the United Nations Emergency Force (UNEF) after the 1956 war, and the Palestine refugee project proposed by Kennedy's special representative, Joseph Johnson (1961–63). Following the 1967 Six-Day War, America backed the mission of Swedish diplomat Gunnar Jarring to implement the 1967 UN Security Council Resolution 242. This mission failed, as did the Soviet-American talks (1969), the Rogers Plan (1969), the Interim Settlement effort (1971), Secretary of State Henry Kissinger's "step-by-step" diplomacy after the 1973 war, and President Jimmy Carter's maiden Middle East initiative—the failed Geneva conference approach of early 1977. Only at Camp David (1978) did the American government finally make a significant dent in the problem.

The Camp David Accord is a milestone. There is no reason to suppose that Carter intended at the outset of the Camp David process to promote a separate peace between Egypt and Israel, leaving the crucial Palestinian question unresolved, but Menachem Begin proved to be the better bargainer. Egypt got back Sinai and a generous American aid package but at the cost of its leadership in the Arab world, which it has yet to reclaim. The Palestinians got nothing and Lebanon would soon be invaded by an Israeli army. Israel, the big winner, obtained geostrategic security and a stepping stone to regional hegemony. For the United States, Camp David brought at least three major benefits: Israel was secured; the Arabs' ability for collective action was definitively crippled; and the Soviets were once again marginalized.

Camp David is one of two pivotal events for American policy in securing the "normalization" of Israel in the Middle East. The other is the Madrid/Oslo "peace process" that began in September 1991. But the road from Camp David to Madrid was, to say the least, bumpy. The presidency of Ronald Reagan (1980–1988) was sterile with respect to the Middle East. The Reagan officials maintained a quixotic and unrealistic fixation on "strategic consensus," by which they meant agreement between Israel and its Arab neighbors to cooperate in rolling back what they saw as Soviet inroads in the Middle East. Reagan's first Secretary of State Alexander Haig is widely believed to have given "an amber light" for Israel's invasion of Lebanon in 1982 to liquidate the Palestine Liberation Organization, a bloody adventure that only intensified Israeli-Palestinian hostility. The Reagan administration also sought to resuscitate the perennial "Jordanian option" as a solution to the Palestine problem, even though Jordan's King Hussein was no longer in a position to represent Palestinian nationalism. So ill-equipped were the Reaganites to understand, let alone deal with, the

Middle East, that they allowed valuable years to go by during which the Arab-Israeli situation only worsened. This paralysis of policymaking set the stage for the Palestinian *intifada,* a mass uprising of young, stone-throwing Palestinians in the occupied territories, that began in December 1987 and refocused world attention on Palestinian national grievances as the heart of the Arab-Israeli conflict.

Whatever one's views about the current "peace process," one must be impressed by the diplomacy of President Bush and Secretary of State James Baker. Exploiting the consequences of the second Gulf war (1990–91), Baker played upon Palestinian and Arab weakness, Israel's enhanced security, and the disappearance of the Soviet Union to bring the contending parties together in Madrid in September 1991. Perhaps Baker's most impressive accomplishment was winning over the Syrians by promising the "comprehensive" approach that they demanded along with the face-to-face bilateral framework that the Israelis required. Equally impressive was the manner in which authentic but non-PLO Palestinian representatives were included, despite the obstacles imposed by the right-wing Israeli government of Yizhak Shamir.

Future students of diplomacy no doubt will study the elaborate, multi-track structure of negotiations that Baker created. Modeled on the Committee on Security and Cooperation in Europe (CSCE), the Madrid plan envisaged not only loosely parallel, bilateral negotiations between Israel and its several Arab antagonists, but also a multilateral, functional dimension involving states throughout the Middle East and the industrialized world. The broader regional focus appealed to the Israelis, and drew in countries like Saudi Arabia which could influence the Arab parties to the bilateral talks. The Madrid process, in short, was designed for bandwagoning, or developing a centrifugal momentum to create a new Middle East, in which Israel would play a central role. To be sure, the initial momentum of Madrid quickly flagged, and the subsequent set of bilateral talks in Washington between Israel and its contiguous neighbors bogged down so completely that by the spring of 1993, observers were confidently predicting that this initiative, like so many others before it, would soon fail. But these observers, like the Arab and Israeli negotiators in Washington, were unaware of what was going on in Oslo.

CHALLENGES TO U.S. POLICY

Considering the turbulent condition of the Middle East in the 1950s one can understand the alarm expressed by Campbell and his associates at the CFR. It was far from clear that U.S. interests would prevail. Nearly forty years later, however, the situation appears to be well under control. The Soviet Union is gone, Israel has not only survived but has become a regional superpower, pan-Arabism is a spent force, and Arab oil (most of it, anyway) is in the hands of friendly, dependent regimes. Defense of the Middle East has succeeded and America has achieved hegemony. Why, then, in this moment of triumph, does the situation in the Middle East look so problematic for American interests? Why, indeed, are American embassies throughout the region so fortified?

To be sure, there is a surface normality. Washington is on good-to-excellent terms with most governments in the area: Morocco, Mauritania, Tunisia, Egypt, Saudi Arabia, Kuwait, Bahrain, Qatar, the United Arab Emirates, Oman, Yemen, Turkey, Lebanon, Jordan, the Palestinian Authority, and of course Israel. It has mobilized most of these regimes to support the Arab-Israeli peace process. It has close military and lucrative arms-supply relationships with key states such as Israel, Turkey, Egypt, Jordan, and Saudi Arabia. It finds a substantial market in the Middle East for all manner of exports—agricultural, industrial, and high-tech. It has a major and seemingly permanent military presence in the Gulf to protect its Arab oil suppliers. There is no credible external challenger to the sphere of influence which the U.S. has achieved over most of the region.

But beneath the surface lies trouble. If the United States is on good terms with most states in the region it is on extremely bad terms with the two biggest states in the crucial Gulf area: Iran (population 65 million) and Iraq (population 20 million), both of which threaten the six small Arab oil states of the Gulf Cooperation Council (combined population around 24 million). The regimes in Sudan and Libya are also considered "rogues" by Washington, because of alleged support for "international terrorism." Syria is also on the U.S. "terrorism list" even though Washington realizes Syria's importance for the "peace process." The military government in Algeria is, to say the least, a "friend in need" but paralyzed by the brutal internal war it is waging against Islamist radicals. Relations with the government of post-civil-war Lebanon (a traditionally friendly state) are officially very good, but the United States has banned travel by its own citizens to Lebanon—fearing, it says, acts of terrorism against them. America's relations are either downright hostile or distinctly problematic with seven states whose populations total around 162 million, or some 40 percent of the region's total population. Four of them are major oil or gas exporters.

America's problems with the Middle East in the years ahead are rooted mainly (though not entirely) in the region's internal dynamics. Most obviously, there are serious "interstate problems" with the potential for erupting into war. But increasingly there are "intrastate problems" as well. There is the "social problem," arising out of population growth and economic stagnation. There is the "political problem," arising out of bloated bureaucracies, fading capabilities, and declining legitimacy. Finally, there is the problem of "the new Islamist populism"—a transnational force with an anti-Western, anti-American tilt.

As a region, the Middle East has had more than its share of interstate conflicts over the past half century. There have been no fewer than six Arab-Israeli wars and two considerably more violent wars in the Gulf—the Iran-Iraq war of 1980–88 and the U.S.-Iraq war of 1990–91. In addition there have been numerous smaller interstate skirmishes and crises such as the Sahara disputes involving Algeria and Morocco, and "miniwars" between the former North and South Yemen, and between Syria and Jordan. As we move into the twenty-first century is the Middle East regional system likely to become more stable? Much depends on the outcome of the Arab-Israeli "peace process." If it succeeds fully, then the region could develop a degree of harmony and integration unlike anything it has known.

While such a happy outcome remains so far unfulfilled, even if it were to occur there would still be interstate conflicts. The primary arena of conflict will be the Gulf, where the question of a "security regime" for this area is going to continue to be hotly contested between Iran, Iraq, Saudi Arabia, and the smaller Arabian states. Egypt and Syria will also vie for influence. In the Levant, even with a durable Arab-Israeli settlement, one may expect continuing rivalry involving Syria, Jordan, Palestine, and Lebanon, with strong involvement from neighbors such as Egypt, Saudi Arabia, and Iraq. Another zone of conflict may arise between Turkey, Syria, Iraq, and Iran over water, economic issues, the Kurds, and political subversion activities. In the Nile Valley, the interminable civil war in the Sudan between the Arab-Islamist government in Khartoum and opposition forces in the non-Arab, non-Muslim southern provinces, which has already become an interstate affair involving Eritrea, Ethiopia, Uganda, Egypt, Israel, and the United States, is not likely to be settled quickly. Cyprus—a slumbering but unsolved problem between Greece and Turkey—could well ignite a serious conflict between two NATO partners that could spread into the Aegean and even farther up into the Balkans, especially if the conflicts in former Yugoslavia are not decisively resolved. Finally, northern Africa presents uncertainties of its own. Much will depend on what kind of a government emerges in Algeria after the civil war: an Islamist government could provoke conflict with neighboring Morocco, Tunisia, and Libya.[16]

Turning now to the domestic arena, the social problem is the result of population pressure, stagnant oil prices, declining productivity, and insufficient external investment. Annual population growth in the region has averaged a very high 3 percent for decades, meaning that its total population increases by half every decade.[17] Such growth has increased the pressures on states and regimes to deliver prosperity and welfare. Populations are also very young: over half of all Middle Easterners are under twenty years of age, compared to around one-third in the United States.[18] Very young populations need education and employment that are in short supply, and they have not had much time to to be socialized into citizenship or prevailing political norms.

The social problem is greatly exacerbated by the economic crisis that the region has experienced since the mid-1980s. While the Middle East's aggregate economic growth over the period from 1960 to 1985 was actually higher than most other regions of the world, the collapse of oil prices since then has led to a drastic contraction of growth at a time when demographic pressures have relentlessly been rising. When oil revenues dropped by around 40 percent in the mid-1980s, the results were severe not only for the oil-exporters (Saudi Arabia and the smaller GCC countries, Iraq, Iran, Libya, Algeria, and Egypt), but also for the neighboring countries that had been benefiting indirectly from the oil boom, mainly by exporting labor to the oil-rich countries; these included Jordan, the Palestinian community, Lebanon, Yemen, Egypt, Sudan, and Tunisia. According to the World Bank, per capita income in the Middle East has fallen by 2 percent a year since 1986—the biggest decline in any of the developing areas.[19] Moreover, the state-dominated economies of the region, with their large and inefficient public sector enterprises, have proven to be increasingly unproductive in an increasingly competitive, global economy. Bedeviled by wars and political problems, the region has been unable to attract sufficient outside investment to restructure and modernize its enfeebled manufacturing infrastructure.

The political problem has several dimensions. The Middle Eastern state has grown dramatically in the post-World War II period, but its ability to "manage" society is increasingly open to question nonetheless. As the Egyptian political scientist Nazih Ayubi[20] has observed, some Arab states may be described as "fierce" by virtue of their suppression of internal opposition and dissent, but that does not mean that they are "strong"—i.e., capable of delivering economic growth and social services or of winning legitimacy and support from their populations. Nor are the regimes that control these states as firmly entrenched as they may seem. They often have a fairly narrow social base in a particular family, tribe, sect, ethnic group, region, or profession (such as the military). A number of Middle East political systems are dominated by a particular individual—a king, a president, a "leader." Some of these key leaders are getting old or are not in good health: King Fahd of Saudi Arabia, King Hussein of Jordan, President Hafiz al-Asad of Syria, and Shaykh Zayid of the United Arab Emirates come to mind. There is also the possibility of authoritarian leaders being assassinated or overthrown.

Will political successions in these cases and others be easy, or will they open the door to political instability? What would be the implications for the United States, for example, if a close ally such as President Mubarak of Egypt (who survived an assassination attempt in 1996) were to be replaced by a hostile Islamist military officer? Even the sudden demise of "enemy" leaders such as President Saddam Hussein of Iraq or Mu'ammar al-Qadhafi of Libya could have unexpected and negative consequences for American policy. To be sure, there has been substantial domestic political stability in Middle Eastern countries since the early 1970s (the most significant exception being the Iranian revolution of 1979), but contemporary sociopolitical strains suggest a rather more turbulent future.

The most important indication of such turbulence is what we may call the movement of Islamist populism that has swept across the entire region from Iran to Morocco. While the Islamic revolution in Iran undoubtedly gave strong impetus to this movement, it has deep indigenous roots in the Arab countries and, increasingly, Turkey as well. Today, there are significant underground Islamist movements in virtually every country in the region.

Algeria is in the throes of a brutal civil war between Islamist groups and a military government that denied an Islamist party its expected victory in parliamentary elections. Egypt has been fighting a war against Islamist groups for a number of years. The ruler of Tunisia was more successful in suppressing—for the time being, at least—the "Nahda" Islamist group. In Lebanon, a Shi'ite Islamist organization, Hizballah, kidnapped American citizens in the 1980s and carries out resistance to Israel's occupation of the southern border zone. In Palestine, the Islamist group Hamas opposes the American-sponsored "peace process" with Israel.

Political Islam, of course, is not confined to opposition movements. Islamist parties have been incorporated into the formal political institutions of Jordan, Yemen, and Turkey, much to the unease of secular liberal sectors in those societies. Furthermore, at least three Middle East regimes define themselves as fundamentally Islamist, in policy as well as in name: Iran, Saudi Arabia, and Sudan. The leader of the Islamic party in Turkey, Necmettin Erbakan, served as prime minister from 1996 to 1997 (when he was forced to resign by the military). The Islah Islamist party has been junior partner in the government of Yemen since 1993.

Scholars such as Dale Eickelman and James Piscatori, Nazih Ayubi, Saad Eddin Ibrahim, John Esposito, John Voll, and others have shed much-needed light on the origins and behavior of political Islam.[21] They tell us that the Islamist movement is not a single, homogeneous phenomenon but rather a collection of religiously conceived responses to specific sociopolitical conditions in particular countries. In general, however, the Islamists seek to create societies in which the moral principles of Islam are preeminent. They stress the need for fuller observance of Islamic law (the *shari'a*), greater attention to social equality, establishment of government informed and guided by experts in Islamic theology and law, and preservation of a culture which they feel is under massive, multidimensional assault from the secular West. They point to social dislocations, regime and elite corruption, the presence of Israel, and a perceived Western cultural invasion as among its causal forces.

To what extent is Islamism a problem for the United States? Many within the American foreign policy elite and policymaking community believe that the "Islamic threat" is significant, insofar as it endangers Israel, the Arab-Israeli "peace process," and Arab regimes friendly to the United States. It is also claimed that political Islam is anti-democratic and prejudicial toward non-Islamic minorities. While Islamist leaders in Saudi Arabia and Turkey try to assuage American fears, Islamist opposition leaders are often fiercely hostile to what they see as America's hegemony in the region. American perceptions of an "Islamic threat" may be exaggerated; nevertheless, it seems reasonable to suppose that any further spread of Islamists into positions of power in the Middle East will complicate the goals the U.S. government is trying to pursue in the region.

Notwithstanding the expansion of American influence throughout the Middle East and North Africa, this region continues to pose formidable challenges to Washington. There may no longer be a Soviet threat to Western access to Arab oil, but the main oil-producing area—the Persian (or Arab) Gulf—has recently experienced two major wars and remains only precariously secure. Israel seems more than secure by any normal measure, yet the Arab-Israeli conflict is far from over, notwithstanding the limited progress in the "peace process"—progress which may well be reversible. And myriad local disputes and domestic socioeconomic tensions regularly arouse animosities against the United States, justified or not.

PRESENT AND FUTURE: ORGANIZING A "NEW MIDDLE EAST"

By virtue of their superior strength, hegemons are—and should be—held to higher standards; their moral responsibilities increase with their power and influence. Writing in 1953, Albert Hourani explained the decline of an earlier Middle East hegemon—Great Britain—by observing that "the fundamental weakness of Britain's policy in the Middle East was that she never fully recognized the responsibility which her power and dominant influence imposed upon her."[22] Having now attained paramount influence throughout the region, with no close competition, how is the United States coping with its new status? A sketch of what appears to be the present administration's grand design for a new Middle East might help to answer this question.

Washington's "New Middle East"

There are two ways of looking at American Middle East policy today. One is a modest, self-effacing vision that comes mainly from diplomats in the field. This view holds that the policymaking process in Washington is too clumsy and irrational to be capable of long-term planning. To be sure, there has been no dearth of failings and miscalculations, be they in intelligence, foreign aid, diplomacy, or ideological competition. Nevertheless, this characterization is incomplete if not disingenuous. American policy was never simply reactive and ad hoc, and it is even less so today.

The other perspective interprets those at the top of the policymaking pyramid as pursuing a far-reaching agenda for shaping a new Middle East. Ironically, the most articulate statement of this agenda has been made not by an American official but by Israel's former prime minister, Shimon Peres.[23] The Clinton Administration appears to believe that there is now a historic opportunity to reshape the region, owing to the collapse of the Soviet Union, the defeat of Iraq in the second Gulf war, and the authentic Palestinian leadership's acceptance of the Madrid/Oslo peace process. If American policymakers have their way, a new Middle East will supercede the old Arab state system with a web of regional economic integration projects involving Israel, Turkey, and other Mediterranean states. New regional security agreements will also be concluded, and Israel will play a key role in protecting the vulnerable Arab Gulf states from Iraqi or Iranian threats since the Arab states seem incapable of setting up a viable collective security system.

Regimes designated by the United States "rogues," such as Iraq, Iran, and Libya, will be actively opposed through economic boycotts, diplomatic isolation, subversion, and even the threat or application of military force.[24] Vigorous efforts will be made to expose and combat terrorism from these countries. "Islamic fundamentalism" will be marginalized and domesticated, just as happened to radical pan-Arabism after 1967. A culture of moderation, pragmatism, and consumerism will be encouraged in place of the old militant transnational ideologies. The United States will also use its hegemony to reform domestic economic and financial policies to achieve market economies, strong private sectors, and global connections. Cultural openings to the West will be increased. And, although this is not a top-priority consideration, limited political liberalization—even some form of democratization—will be encouraged as long as it does not weaken friendly regimes.

The Peace Process

The Bush and Clinton Administrations have rightly claimed that the Arab-Israeli peace process that began in 1991 was a historic diplomatic achievement. Whatever one thinks of the terms of the agreement, bringing the authentic Palestinian leadership and the Israeli government into a significant negotiating process has been a major accomplishment that dozens of earlier American and other initiatives failed to achieve. The Jordan-Israel peace treaty and the continuing small breakthroughs in the multilateral tracks may well have set in motion the regional reconciliation so desired by the United States and Israel.

The United States was instrumental in getting the process started through the Madrid conference of 1991. But Washington has been less effective in maintaining or advancing the process since then. The Oslo phase, in which Israel and the PLO engaged in secret, direct negotiations parallel to the deadlocked "official" talks going on in Washington, rescued the process from collapse in the summer of 1993, but the credit for that belongs mainly to Norway, Israel, and the PLO, not the United States. While American mediation played an important part in the follow-up phases (notably the "Oslo II" agreement of October 1995), the United States was unable to sustain the peace process following the assassination of Israeli prime minister Yitzhak Rabin at the hands of a Jewish extremist in November 1995 and the Palestinian suicide bombings inside Israel in 1996 and 1997. The American response to the Hamas (Islamic Resistance Movement) suicide bombings inside Israel and the two-week war in April 1996 between Hizballah (Party of God) and Israel in Lebanon indicated an almost complete identity of views with Israel over terrorism and how to deal with it. Arab public opinion was outraged over what was widely seen as

Washington's collusion with Israel's fierce military action in South Lebanon, including an attack on a UN outpost in the village of Qana on April 18, 1996 that killed 102 Lebanese civilians, mostly women and children.

Although disappointed by the victory of a militant Likud-dominated coalition in the June 1996 parliamentary elections, the Clinton Administration was most reluctant to exert pressure on Prime Minister Binyamin Netanyahu. American policymakers seemed unconcerned about the negative implications of such a partisan stance on the stalled Syrian-Israeli track. After months of stalemate, in order to achieve an agreement on the withdrawal of Israeli forces from 80 percent of Hebron, the United States agreed to accept Israel's interpretation that Israel alone would determine the extent of rural Palestinian territory to be evacuated in the next phase of withdrawals, raising the likelihood of a new impasse. For their part, the Palestinians perceived a continuing erosion of American evenhandedness over the crucial "final status" phase of the peace process, over issues such as Jerusalem, Israeli settlements, and Palestinian statehood.

Gulf Security

The other big success story for U.S. policy appears to have been "Desert Storm"—the second Gulf war of January-February 1991. Not only was it a decisive and (for the United States) an inexpensive military victory, leading to the restoration of Kuwait, it also enhanced at least the short-term security of Saudi Arabia and its Gulf Cooperation Council neighbors by sharply reducing Iraq's power and influence. Since Iraq (with American help) had diminished Iran's power in the first Gulf war, both Gulf "superpowers" were now seemingly contained. Moreover, America's GCC allies now found themselves almost completely dependent for their security on a permanent American military presence, giving the American military a needed and not-too-costly new mission. But as suggested above, this view may be too optimistic.

The Clinton Administration's policy of "dual containment" in the Gulf is intended to topple the Saddam Hussein regime in Iraq and reform the regime in Iran. This is to be accomplished, it would seem, by speaking loudly and carrying a medium-sized stick. The stick consists of a small but quickly expandable military force in the Gulf and a battery of economic sanctions, tough in the case of Iraq, less effective in the case of Iran. The Administration rejected the strategy of exploiting the rivalry between Iran and Iraq, which its predecessors had done quite effectively, in favor of confronting both of these wounded big Gulf powers simultaneously. Is this a good policy for the long run? It is worrisome to hear so much sotto voce criticism of dual containment from those in the GCC countries who are presumably its biggest beneficiaries. As one official put it, "We have to live with our Iraqi and Iranian neighbors; you don't. Your protection gives us security, but when you continue to antagonize them you make us vulnerable to their anger. What happens to us if you decide to go away?"[25] Also troubling is the widespread perception of the United States as an insensitive, even brutal, hegemon because of its Iraq sanctions policy. American attempts to persuade regional opinion that the blame rests exclusively with Saddam Hussein have not been very successful. There are other, better options: with respect to Iran, there is much to be said for restoring diplomatic relations in order to exert more influence in Teheran, while exerting pressure against some Iranian government policies. As for Iraq, the severe American-inspired economic sanctions against the civilian population are not only morally repugnant but politically inefficacious: having won the Gulf War, the United States should be dealing directly with whatever regime rules in Baghdad, both to deter any future Iraqi aggression and to restore some normality to Gulf regional relations.

Political Islam

"The Islamic threat," like its big brother "the clash of civilizations" (the argument advanced by Samuel Huntington that the main fault lines in the post-Cold War era will be civilizational conflicts[26]), could well turn out to be a self-fulfilling prophecy. While, as we have seen, the academic discussion of political Islam generally has been enlightening, the public debate all too often has been marred by stereotypes and reductionist analysis. To be fair, State Department spokespeople have consistently tried to take a nuanced position even while their political superiors conflate Islamism with terrorism. In fact, today's radical Islamism is the ideological cutting edge and umbrella for a multifaceted, historically rooted resistance in Muslim societies against Western political penetration. At times the ideological rallying cry of this resistance has been indigenous liberal reform (fighting fire with fire, as it were), at other times nationalism; today, again, it is religion. The social constituency of resistance over time has been a shifting coalition drawn from the middle class intelligentsia, landed interests, the commercial middle class, the peasantry, the urban poor, the military, and the clerical establishment. During their "moment in the Middle East" (as Elizabeth Monroe put it), the British had to face this resistance; now it is the turn of the United States.[27]

Terrorism is but one of the instruments that some but not all of these movements employ. They also utilize cultural, social, economic, and political resources. An analysis that conceives of political Islam essentially as a "terrorism" problem is certain to yield poor policy recommendations. When the American president summons Middle East and world leaders to Sharm al-Shaykh (as he did in March 1996) to mount a campaign against terrorism, clearly he has in mind Islamist groups like Hamas, Hizballah, and the *Jama'at Islamiyya* (of Egypt), as well as the terrorism sponsored by "rogue" states like Iran, Iraq, Sudan, and Libya. But when America's chief regional ally—Israel—deploys the massive military power of the state to terrorize whole populations, and the United States excuses it, public opinion throughout the Islamic Middle East naturally becomes inflamed against America for employing a double standard.

The Democratization Puzzle

When Anthony Lake, the National Security advisor in the first Clinton administration, proclaimed in January 1994 the expansion of democracy throughout the world as a major American objective, he was echoing an idealist vision dating back at least to Woodrow Wilson's era. Democracy, many believe, has instrumental benefits as well: it can promote regional peace and capitalist economic growth. But even though there is a need for peace and economic growth in the Middle East, American policymakers are reluctant to press vigorously for democratic reform in the region. The reasons are clear. America's major allies in the region (Israel excepted) are undemocratic. Some of these regimes enjoy only modest legitimacy. American officials committed to the necessity of painful economic structural adjustment programs, involving downsizing of the public sector and cancellation of subsidies (among other things), wonder whether fragile new democratic experiments could generate the discipline to carry them out. Others, frightened by "the Islamic threat," shudder at the prospect of anti-American elements winning power or influence through democratic means. When Lebanon—the only enduring (albeit limited) example of democracy in the Arab world—collapsed, the United States suffered a costly and humiliating experience there that darkened its expectations about democracy elsewhere in the area. In a recent study, Colby College political scientist Guilain Denoeux observes: "More generally, in its policy toward the Arab world, America continued to apply the old Islamic maxim 'better sixty years of tyranny than one day of anarchy.'"[28]

Caught up by the contradiction between global principle and regional application, the United States is accused of meddling by undemocratic ruling elites who feel undermined by Washington's democratic evangelism, and of hypocrisy by indigenous liberal-democratic reformers and human rights advocates, who see the United States as paying only lip service to democratization when it comes to the Middle East, where most of America's allies are far from democratic. U.S. policymakers need to become aware of the political instability that lies ahead in countries facing economic stagnation, social ferment, and a potential crisis of political legitimacy. Broadened participation is the answer—in general. But how can it be achieved in particular cases, and what role (if any) should the United States play? American policy faces the delicate task of encouraging political openings without intruding imperialistically. Currently, the United States and U.S.-funded nongovernmental organizations (NGOs) do operate modest democratic support programs in several Middle East countries, for example by providing technical assistance to legislatures. This is helpful but insufficient. If we are to avoid accusations of yet another double standard, our top leadership should not exempt Middle Eastern regimes from the same kind of moral suasion that it metes out to others.

To Play the Hegemon

American hegemony in the Middle East is not going to disappear soon. The question is, what kind of hegemony will it be? Perhaps it will be benign. "What other country, having defeated its adversary and now striding the world unrivaled, would be so reluctant to extend its might, so uninterested in the satisfactions of empire and influence?" writes Fareed Zakaria, the managing editor of Foreign Affairs.[29] Most Americans genuinely want a peaceful, stable, and prosperous Middle East, and the U.S. government is not without generosity when it comes to helping refugees, aiding the fledgling Palestinian authority, contributing to a Middle East development bank, trying to end anarchy in Somalia, saving Kuwait, and providing technological know-how and cultural opportunities for thousands of Middle Easterners.

Or, will American hegemony be hurtful? Many Middle Easterners think it is already. They point, above all, to the tens of thousands of Iraqi children who appear to have died as a by-product (however undesired) of U.S.-led sanctions; according to UNICEF in 1996, some 4,500 children were dying every month from hunger and malnutrition.[30] Other examples of American heavyhandedness include: the air raids on Tripoli and Benghazi in Libya (1986) in retaliation for a Libyan-sponsored terrorist attack on U.S. soldiers in a Berlin nightclub; the battleship New Jersey firing 16-inch guns into the Lebanese mountains (1983) as Washington found itself drawn into the Lebanese civil war; another warship accidentally shooting down an Iranian civilian airliner over the Gulf (1988) during the Iran-Iraq war, when the U.S. Navy was trying to protect oil tankers from Iranian interference; massive support over many years for Israel, whose use of violence has repeatedly created huge refugee populations and immense human suffering; manipulation of a national movement (the Kurds in northern Iraq) for realpolitik advantage (1970s, 1991); the arming of *mujahideen* for Afghanistan during the Soviet occupation of that country with little regard for disastrous consequences (1980s); and the tendency (by some politicians and parts of the media) to demonize Islam.

Much depends on the quality of America's Middle East policymaking process. Common sense suggests that good information, open informed debate, diplomatic skill, a minimum of special interest pleading, and statesmanship are highly desirable in dealing with a region as complex and potentially explosive as this one. But does our Middle East policy process measure up to these standards? The record is not entirely encouraging. U.S. Middle East policy appears to be heavily shaped by domestic politics: the American Jewish constituency and the pro-Israel lobby are the most influential players, exerting substantial pressures on the White House and the Congress. U.S. businesses operating in the Middle East also exert influence but lack the electoral clout of the pro-Israel forces. It is hardly surprising, therefore, that Israel's interests are widely seen as essentially identical to those of the United States.

Does this policymaking structure allow for sufficient incorporation of alternative perspectives either from within or outside the government?

Government area specialists feel that their views are not given much weight. The quality of diplomatic reporting appears to have declined over recent years, in part because U.S. diplomats no longer have easy access to several key countries in the region, including Iraq, Iran, Sudan, and Libya. The American academic community specializing in the Middle East has relatively little input at the higher decision-making levels. With certain exceptions, U.S. press coverage of the Middle East lags behind Europe's in quality and quantity.

If history is any guide, hegemony by the United States or any other party in the Middle East tends to produce resistance. Under the most benign of scenarios there will be problems. But under the hurtful scenario the problems will be vastly worse. It behooves the hegemon, then, to play the game wisely. Among other things, wisdom suggests that the hegemon adopt a low profile by involving other outside players such as the European Union and Japan in regional issues. Wisdom suggests pursuing less confrontational and more balanced polices. It suggests that instead of "dual containment" in the Gulf, perhaps "multilateral engagement"—in which the United States, jointly with the European Union and Japan, would open a dialogue with "rogues" as well as allies—might provide more security over the long term. Instead of a partisan stance in the peace process, greater evenhandedness may bring the final status negotiations to a just and durable conclusion. Instead of mobilizing noisily against a poorly analyzed "Islamic threat," the United States might be better advised to undertake a vigorous initiative to promote dialogue which could reduce mutual fears and antagonisms. Instead of offering lip service on democratization and human rights, Washington might make a more serious effort to promote economic and political liberalization in order to enhance the legitimacy of Middle Eastern governments and in turn contribute to regional stability.

At the beginning of the twentieth century the United States was scarcely a player in Middle East regional politics. Indeed, we were only on the threshold of world-power status. Within mere decades, however, America had developed, for better or worse, both the strengths (economic, military, ideological) and the interests of a global power. In the Middle East three of these important interests—oil, Israel, and the Soviet threat—drew Washington into an increasingly active and (as Britain's influence declined) an increasingly dominant role. Notwithstanding the contradictory implications of these American interests, and the growth of sometimes hostile indigenous forces, the United States stood as the unchallenged hegemon in the region as the century drew to an end. What the new century may hold is problematic. On the one hand, there is the possibility of harmonious globalization, with the Americans guiding the powerful new economic, technological, cultural, and even political forces that will shape the region. On the other hand, there are powerful indigenous groups that understandably fear and even despise this "globalization, American-style." Notwithstanding its power and its victories, the U.S. government has not displayed commensurate skill or understanding, let alone magnanimity, in the conduct of its political affairs in this region. Indeed, while the United States is widely respected for its technological and economic achievements, its government is widely reviled throughout the Arab and Islamic Middle East for the policies it has pursued. Barring major improvement in its policies and diplomacy, the United States may find its hegemony painful in the years ahead.

QUESTIONS FOR FURTHER STUDY

1. How did problems arising from Soviet expansionism, the demand for oil, and the establishment of Israel affect American policy toward the Middle East during the Cold War era? To what extend did Washington succeed in attaining its policy objectives in the Middle East during this period? To what extent did it fail?
2. What, in Hudson's view, are the underlying factors that lead to instability in the Middle East today?
3. What are the prospects for the Israeli-Palestinian peace process? What can be done to enhance the prospects for this effort?
4. Much has been made about the threat to U.S. interests posed by the rise of Islamic fundamentalism. How does Hudson characterize this threat? Do you agree or disagree with his assessment of this phenomenon? Why?
5. What do you think should be the primary objectives of U.S. foreign policy in the Middle East? How would you go about attaining those objectives?

Notes

1. Paul J. Hare, *Diplomatic Chronicles of the Middle East: A Biography of Raymond Hare* (Washington: The Middle East Institute, 1993), pp. 31–32.
2. James A. Field, Jr., *America and the Mediterranean World, 1776–1882* (Princeton: Princeton University Press, 1969).
3. Harry N. Howard, *The King-Crane Commission: An American Inquiry into the Middle East* (Beirut: Khayat's, 1963).
4. Robert D. Kaplan, *The Arabists* (New York: The Free Press, 1993).
5. Hare, *Diplomatic Chronicles of the Middle East*, p. 20.
6. John C. Campbell, *Defense of the Middle East* (New York: Harper and Row, 1958), pp. 4–5.
7. Ibid., p. 4.
8. Ibid., pp. 351–52.
9. The Command Proposal involved establishing a U.S., British, French, and Turkish military command in Cairo, augmented by Egyptian forces. Egypt rejected it. In 1952, Britain and the United States floated the idea of a Middle East defense organization, involving, in addition, Australia, New Zealand, and South Africa. But after an initial expression of interest, Egypt's new military government declined to participate, and the project was abandoned. See Thomas A. Bryson, *American Diplomatic Relations with the Middle East, 1784–1975* (Metuchen, NJ: The Scarecrow Press, 1977), pp. 179–81.
10. The "Red Line" delimited the World War I Ottoman Empire (including Anatolia, the Levant, Iraq, and the entire Arabian Peninsula except for Kuwait). The signatories to the agreement, and their share of the oil, were: Royal Dutch Shell (23.75 percent), Anglo-Persian (23.75 percent), Compagnie Française des Pétroles (23.75 percent), the American Near East Development Company (23.75 percent), and Calouste Gulbenkian (5 percent). The signatories agreed to a "self-denying" clause requiring mutual agreement on oil operations in the area.

11. In August 1953, American operatives plotted the overthrow of the nationalist prime minister, Muhammad Mussadiq, who had nationalized the Anglo-Iranian Oil Company. When the shah, at American urging, tried to dismiss the popular prime minister, the effort backfired and the shah himself was forced to flee the country. But the U.S. agents organized a counter-coup in which Mussadiq was deposed and the shah restored. See James A. Bill, *The Eagle and the Lion* (New Haven: Yale University Press, 1980), pp. 86–94.

12. In 1977, the Carter Administration proposed a comprehensive energy policy, including the establishment of a 500-million-barrel Strategic Petroleum Reserve. Other industrialized societies established similar stockpiles. Other measures included encouraging usage of alternative forms of energy, and more fuel-efficient vehicles. As a result of these and other measures, U.S. dependence on OPEC oil was reduced.

13. Hare, *Diplomatic Chronicles*, p. 20.

14. Kermit Roosevelt, "The Partition of Palestine: A Lesson in Pressure Politics," *The Middle East Journal*, Vol. 2, No. 1 (1948), p. 1. Roosevelt, an author and Middle East intelligence specialist with the Office of Strategic Services during and after World War II, later became head of the Middle East Department of the CIA. He played a key role in "Operation Ajax."

15. The 1949 Economic Survey Mission was headed by Gordon Clapp of the Tennessee Valley Authority, and sought to apply economic relief measures to ease the Palestinian refugee problem. The "Johnston Plan" focused on the efficient allocation of Jordan River basin waters as a means toward solving the Arab-Israeli conflict.

16. For background on these subregional disputes, see, in general, Alasdair Drysdale and Gerald Blake, *The Middle East and North Africa: A Political Geography* (New York: Oxford University Press, 1985), and Bahgat Korany and Ali E. Hillal Dessouki, et al., *The Foreign Policies of Arab States,* 2nd ed. (Boulder: Westview Press, 1991). For coverage of current developments, see the fortnightly newsmagazine *Middle East International* (London).

17. The World Bank, *World Development Report, 1995* (Washington: The World Bank, 1995), p. 211.

18. Alan Richards and John Waterbury, *A Political Economy of the Middle East* (Boulder: Westview Press, 1990), pp. 91–95.

19. The World Bank, *Claiming the Future: Choosing Prosperity in the Middle East and North Africa* (Washington: The World Bank, 1995), p. 3.

20. Nazih Ayubi, *Over-Stating the Arab State* (London: I.B. Tauris, 1995), Chapter 12.

21. Dale Eickelman and James Piscatori, *Muslim Politics* (Princeton: Princeton University Press, 1996); Nazih Ayubi, *Political Islam: Religion and Politics in the Arab World* (London: Routledge, 1991); Saad Eddin Ibrahim, "The Anatomy of Egypt's Militant Islamic Groups: A Methodological Note and Preliminary Findings," *International Journal of Middle East Studies,* Vol. 12, No. 4 (December 1980), pp. 423–53; John L. Esposito, *The Islamic Threat: Myth or Reality?* (London: Oxford University Press, 1992), John L. Esposito, ed., *Voices of Resurgent Islam* (New York: Oxford University Press, 1983), and John Obert Voll, *Islam: Continuity and Change in the Modern World* (Boulder: Westview Press, 1982).

22. Albert Hourani, "The Decline of the West in the Middle East," *International Affairs* (London), Vol. 29 (1953), p. 157.

23. Shimon Peres (with Aori Naori), *The New Middle East* (New York: Henry Holt, 1993), especially Chapters 3–6.

24. See Anthony Lake, "Confronting Backlash States," *Foreign Affairs,* Vol. 73, No. 2 (March/April 1994), pp. 45–55, for the official rationale for dealing harshly with "rogues"; but see also a contrary view, F. Gregory Gause, III, "The Illogic of Dual Containment" in the same issue, pp. 56–66.

25. Interview conducted by the author with an official in the United Arab Emirates, March 14, 1996.

26. Samuel P. Huntington, "The Clash of Civilizations?" *Foreign Affairs,* Vol. 72, No. 3 (Summer 1993), pp. 22–49.

27. Elizabeth Monroe, *Britain's Moment in the Middle East, 1914–1971* (London: Chatto and Windus, 1981).

28. Guilain P. Denoeux, "The United States and the Challenge of Democratization in the Arab World," (Georgetown University, Center for Contemporary Arab Studies, Occasional Paper, April 1996), p. 8.

29. Fareed Zakaria, "Divining Russia," review of George F. Kennan's "Reflections, 1982–1995," *New York Times Book Review,* April 7, 1996, p. 6.

30. Barbara Crossette, "Unicef Head Says Thousands of Children Are Dying in Iraq," *The New York Times,* October 29, 1996.

8 / Nuclear Proliferation and Nonproliferation Policy in the 1990s

ZACHARY S. DAVIS

Despite the end of the Cold War, the potential use of nuclear weapons continues to pose one of the greatest dangers to world security. While the risk of a nuclear war between the United States and the former Soviet Union has been drastically reduced, and both superpowers have begun to retire large portions of their nuclear forces, other countries retain an interest in joining the nuclear weapons "club." Most of these countries are engaged in military rivalries with other rising powers, greatly increasing the risk of a regional nuclear conflict. Halting the spread, or "proliferation," of nuclear weapons thus remains a top priority for world security.

What are the dangers associated with nuclear proliferation? Even "small" or relatively unsophisticated nuclear weapons constructed with fifty-year-old technology can inflict massive death and destruction. The bombs that destroyed Hiroshima and Nagasaki in 1945 were small, crude weapons by today's standards.[1] As more nations acquire nuclear weapons, the likelihood of their use may increase. Nuclear weapons could be fired accidentally, change hands due to a coup d'état or shift in government, or fall into the possession of terrorist or subnational groups. The actual or threatened use of nuclear weapons could escalate regional conflicts and perhaps spark the use of chemical munitions or other weapons of mass destruction. Such "worst-case" scenarios might induce some nations to reverse previous decisions to forego the acquisition of nuclear weapons.

For these reasons, there has been a strong international consensus against the spread of nuclear weapons. Efforts to block proliferation can claim many notable successes; indeed, many people expected in the early nuclear era that more nations would to try to acquire nuclear weapons. At present, there are only five acknowledged nuclear weapons states: China, France, Great Britain, Russia, and the United States. In addition, three other nations—India, Israel, Pakistan—possess at least some undeclared nuclear weapons capabilities, and so are considered to be de facto nuclear weapons states. However, several other nations have recently abandoned their nuclear weapons programs. For example, Ukraine, Belarus, and Kazakhstan have transferred to Russia all of the nuclear weapons that remained on their territory following the demise of the Soviet Union. Furthermore, Argentina, Brazil, and South Africa—all of which conducted secret nuclear weapons programs in the 1970s and 1980s—have pledged to cancel their programs and to open their nuclear installations to international inspection.

Despite these successes, other countries have demonstrated an interest in developing a nuclear weapons option. Iraq, which signed the Nuclear Non-Proliferation Treaty (NPT) in 1969, maintained a secret nuclear program that was close to producing its first nuclear bomb before it was exposed following the 1991 Persian Gulf conflict. North Korea, which signed the NPT in 1985, is widely suspected of having established a clandestine nuclear weapons project. The construction of nuclear reactors in countries such as Iran, Algeria, and elsewhere raises questions about the possible military uses of their supposedly civilian nuclear development programs. It is possible that a decision by these or other nuclear-capable countries to develop nuclear weapons could cause neighboring countries to reconsider their decisions to sign the NPT and refrain from the acquisition of nuclear weapons.

These trends could signal hard times for international efforts to block the spread of nuclear weapons. Conversely, the end of the Cold War generated new hopes and opportunities for strengthening the international consensus against nuclear proliferation. In 1995, the member states of the NPT agreed to extend the life of the treaty indefinitely. Responding to revelations about Iraq's secret nuclear program and North Korea's refusal to allow inspections of suspected clandestine activities, many countries have renewed their interest in developing tight controls on exports of nuclear and nuclear-related technology. Nevertheless, hostility between regional powers can generate increased tensions and insecurity, leading some states to pursue the acquisition of nuclear weapons.

PROLIFERATION VS. NONPROLIFERATION

The United States developed its nuclear weapons during World War II under the tightest possible secrecy. After the war, some American officials believed that it was possible to maintain the U.S. monopoly on nuclear weapons by continuing to shroud the wartime nuclear bomb program, known as the Manhattan Project, in total secrecy. Many Manhattan Project scientists objected to this view; they thought that it was inevitable that other countries, especially the Soviet Union, would soon develop their own nuclear weapons. To prevent the spread of nuclear weapons, some U.S. scientists and policymakers favored putting all uses of nuclear technology under the control of the United Nations.

A proposal for the international control of atomic energy became official U.S. policy in 1946. The Baruch Plan, named after the U.S. negotiator, Bernard Baruch, who presented this proposal to the United Nations, called for all nations to turn over all nuclear materials (including weapons) to a special UN agency, after which the UN would oversee the peaceful and military applications of nuclear technology. However, the plan was probably doomed to fail, because it would have required the USSR to surrender its nuclear program before the United States would give up *its* nuclear weapons.[2] In any case, Moscow rejected the plan.

With hopes for the international control of atomic energy dashed, the United States resorted to a policy of secrecy and denial. This did not prevent the Soviet Union from testing its first nuclear weapon in 1949, nor did it discourage other nations from pursuing nuclear research and development. While the United States could guard its knowledge of the industrial processes used by the Manhattan Project to build nuclear bombs, knowledge of nuclear physics was impossible to control.

"Atoms for Peace"

The United States changed its nuclear policy in the early 1950s in conjunction with President Eisenhower's 1953 "Atoms for Peace" plan. This proposal was intended to promote the transfer of peaceful nuclear energy technology from the advanced industrial powers to developing nations in exchange for a commitment by recipients of such technology that it would not be used for military purposes. As part of this "nuclear bargain," nuclear reactors and fuel were widely disseminated by the United States and other suppliers subject to assurances that they would not be used to make nuclear weapons. These assurances were to be verified by a new UN-affiliated organization, the International Atomic Energy Agency (IAEA), created in 1957. As part of its mandate, the IAEA established a system of nuclear "safeguards" that included inspections of nuclear facilities and various accounting procedures to detect any diversion of nuclear materials from their intended purposes.[3]

The "Atoms for Peace" plan combined self-interest in helping U.S. companies to export nuclear technology, idealism about nuclear energy's potential for improving economic conditions in developing countries, and a pragmatic approach toward nonproliferation policy. In retrospect, the program overestimated the economic benefits of nuclear energy and underestimated the proliferation risks of disseminating nuclear technology.[4] Nevertheless, the "nuclear bargain" established the framework for international nuclear cooperation that remains at the heart of the existing nuclear nonproliferation regime today.

Some proliferation was probably inevitable. Great Britain acquired knowledge of nuclear weapons technology as a participant in the World War II Manhattan Project, and detonated its first nuclear bomb in 1953. France tested its first atomic bomb in 1960. In both cases, nuclear programs were motivated by doubts about the reliability of U.S. security guarantees and a desire for influence and prestige in the postwar world.[5] The Soviet Union initially offered nuclear assistance to China, but suspended its aid in the 1950s as relations between Moscow and Beijing turned sour; nevertheless, China became the fifth declared nuclear weapons state in 1964.[6] India tested what it called a "peaceful nuclear explosion" in 1974, but has not tested a nuclear device since then. No other nation has openly crossed the nuclear threshold by testing a nuclear weapon device, although there is good reason to believe that Israel and South Africa secretly tested such a device in the late 1970s.[7]

The Nuclear Non-Proliferation Treaty

The centerpiece of international efforts to stem the spread of nuclear weapons is the Nuclear Non-Proliferation Treaty, signed in 1968 and entered into force (for a term of twenty-five years) in 1970. The NPT's central provisions contain pledges by the nuclear weapons states—defined as nations having exploded a nuclear device prior to 1967—not to transfer nuclear explosive devices to any non-nuclear weapons state (Article I), and by the non-nuclear weapons states not to acquire such devices (Article II). Non-nuclear states also agree to accept IAEA safeguards on all of their nuclear facilities (Article III).

Two other key provisions of the NPT have been the subject of perennial controversy: Article IV, pledging support for international cooperation regarding peaceful nuclear energy, and Article VI, promising "good faith" efforts toward nuclear disarmament by the existing weapons states. Some NPT member states have complained that nuclear assistance has been in short supply; others have complained that the nuclear weapons states have ignored their obligations to reduce their own armaments. In particular, continued nuclear testing by the existing weapons states came to symbolize what was seen as the discriminatory nature of the NPT.

Some critics of the treaty threatened to block extension of the NPT in 1995, when it came up for renewal, unless the nuclear weapons states signed a comprehensive test ban treaty (CTBT) and renewed their commitment to reduce their arsenals.[8] Enough progress had been made toward negotiating a CTBT by the time the NPT review conference convened in 1995 to win support for permanent extension of the treaty. However, periodic five-year reviews of the treaty, starting in 2000, assure that there will be continuing pressure on all NPT members to live up to their obligations.

The NPT helped to create an international norm of nonproliferation, in effect delegitimizing the acquisition of nuclear weapons by additional countries. With France and China finally agreeing to sign the treaty in 1992, all of the declared nuclear weapons states are now members. South Africa, which had been conducting a secret nuclear weapons program, also signed in 1991. Following the disintegration of the Soviet Union, Russia inherited Moscow's NPT status as a nuclear weapons state while the other ex-Soviet republics pledged to remove all nuclear weapons from their territory and to sign the NPT as non-weapon members. By 1997, NPT membership had swelled to 185 countries, with only a handful of holdouts remaining.

Despite these developments, some nations still refuse to join the NPT. India, a long-standing critic of the treaty, claims the right to keep its nuclear options open unless all nations disarm. Pakistan will not sign the treaty unless India does. Israel will not sign the treaty while its neighbors possess other weapons of mass destruction. Still other nations have signed the NPT but have violated it—as in the case of Iraq's clandestine nuclear weapons program—or delayed its implementation, as in the case of North Korea.

Signing the NPT does not guarantee that a country has no interest in nuclear weapons, nor that it will refrain from seeking them in the future.[9]

The Nuclear Nonproliferation Regime

The NPT has not stopped all proliferation. Not long after the treaty entered into force in 1970, several developments indicated that the danger of proliferation was growing. First, India detonated a nuclear explosive device—which it called a peaceful nuclear explosion—using plutonium from a reactor supplied by Canada under an early "Atoms for Peace" project. This essentially signalled the emergence of India as a de facto nuclear power, and spurred Pakistan to initiate its own nuclear weapons program.

Second, several Western European countries, notably France, West Germany, and Italy, emerged as major suppliers of a broad range of sensitive nuclear technologies—including those required to produce weapons-grade uranium and plutonium.[10] In particular, Germany offered reprocessing and enrichment technology to Brazil as part of a multi-reactor sale, France agreed to supply reprocessing plants to Pakistan and South Korea, and Italy sold reprocessing technology to Iraq. (Enrichment technology makes it possible to enrich the level of fissionable uranium-235 from the 0.7 percent of natural uranium to over 90 percent as required for nuclear weapons; reprocessing technology is used to extract plutonium from uranium fuel that has been "burned" in nuclear reactors.)

Third, the oil crisis of the mid-1970s stimulated new interest in nuclear power, including the development of "breeder reactors" that would be fueled by recycled plutonium and produce still more plutonium as a waste product. The prospect of plutonium-fueled energy independence held a strong attraction for many nations, especially those with little oil or coal of their own. However, the extensive use of plutonium as an energy resource would involve the widespread transportation, storage, and handling of large quantities of fissionable materials that could be used in nuclear weapons.[11]

If these trends had continued, and many countries had acquired a nuclear weapons option through imports of civilian nuclear technology, the line between peaceful and military uses of nuclear energy would have become nearly indistinguishable. With ready access to bomb-making materials, even a country that had signed the NPT could quickly make nuclear bombs; those that refused to sign the treaty were not obligated to obey its restrictions on weapons-related activities. During the 1970s, evidence of clandestine nuclear programs in Argentina, Brazil, India, Pakistan, Iraq, Iran, Israel, South Africa, South Korea, Taiwan, and other countries underscored the weaknesses of existing international nonproliferation efforts.[12]

Growing recognition of the gaps in the nonproliferation regime prompted a U.S.-led effort to strengthen international nonproliferation controls. This effort entailed the formation by the leading Western industrial powers of the Nuclear Suppliers Group (NSG), which established more stringent international standards to guide and control exports of nuclear technology. In addition, the U.S. Congress passed the Nuclear Nonproliferation Act of 1978, tightening the legal guidelines for nuclear technology exports by the United States;[13] Congress also adopted several amendments to the Foreign Assistance Act, requiring a cutoff of U.S. aid to nations that sold or received enrichment or reprocessessing technology without accepting comprehensive IAEA safeguards.[14]

Not all nuclear suppliers agreed with every aspect of the tougher nonproliferation restrictions on exports. Several Western European countries rejected the proposed abandonment of breeder reactor technology and continued to support the development of a plutonium fuel cycle. France, which had not yet signed the NPT, maintained its right to sell reactors to countries such as Pakistan, which did not allow inspections of facilities widely suspected of housing a covert enrichment program. West Germany continued to sell advanced nuclear technology to Brazil, Iran, and Iraq.

The 1980s brought continued evidence of clandestine proliferation activities. Claiming that Iraq was engaged in a secret weapons program of this sort, Israel bombed the French-designed Osirak reactor at Baghdad in June 1981.[15] Critics of the attack condemned the preemptive bombing of a nuclear reactor as a dangerous precedent for future nonproliferation policy;[16] as it turned out, the attack may have encouraged Saddam Hussein to take greater precautions to hide his nuclear weapons project. In 1986, new evidence came to light regarding Israel's own nuclear program when Mordechai Vanunu, a former technician at Israel's Dimona reactor complex, divulged significant details of the Israeli bomb-making capability.[17] Evidence also continued to accumulate regarding ongoing covert nuclear weapons programs in Argentina, Brazil, South Africa, India, Pakistan, and North Korea.[18]

The continued advancement of nuclear proliferation in the 1980s outpaced the sometimes halfhearted attempts by nuclear suppliers to clamp down on the spread of technologies that could be used to manufacture nuclear weapons. Whereas the nuclear suppliers initially focused on tightening international controls on exports of uranium enrichment and plutonium reprocessing technology, many proliferators sought to circumvent these controls by giving false information on export license applications or by acquiring "dual-use" equipment—that is, equipment with both military and civilian applications—that was not subject to tight controls but could be employed in their bomb-making operations.

The proliferation activities of these states was facilitated, moreover, by the emergence of new nuclear suppliers in the Third World—notably Argentina, Brazil, China, India, Taiwan, and South Africa—that were willing to supply dual-use equipment with fewer restraints than the original nuclear suppliers.[19] As a result, controls on nuclear goods and technology often proved ineffective against countries like Iraq, Israel, and Pakistan that established sophisticated international procurement networks to acquire the resources necessary to build their own bomb-making facilities.[20]

REGIONAL PROLIFERATION DYNAMICS

The continuing proliferation of nuclear weapons technology in the 1970s and 1980s demonstrates that international nonproliferation norms are not sufficient to stop the spread of nuclear weapons when individual states determine that the possession of such weapons is essential to their long-term security. Proliferation is, in fact, closely related to the security environment in regions where heavily armed and often antagonistic states confront each other in close proximity. To fully understand the dynamics of proliferation, then, it is essential to review the regional context of nuclear weapons activities.

South Asia

India and Pakistan stand at the brink of a nuclear arms race. Although neither country openly admits to having assembled fully operational nuclear weapons, there is convincing evidence that both could complete the necessary steps very quickly following a decision to do so. Both nations have disavowed any interest in nuclear weapons and claim only peaceful applications for their unsafeguarded nuclear programs; however, both admit to having developed the capability to build nuclear weapons and assert their sovereign right to use whatever means are necessary to defend themselves. With a long history of conflict between them, and a number of outstanding disagreements which have periodically led to violence, the potential for nuclear conflict may be growing. Indeed, the former Director of the CIA, R. James Woolsey, testified in 1993 that "the arms race between India and Pakistan poses perhaps the most probable prospect for future use of weapons of mass destruction, including nuclear weapons."[21]

India has not tested another nuclear device since its "peaceful nuclear explosion" of May 1974. It has, however, continued to produce quantities of plutonium from unsafeguarded reactors and reprocessessing facilities at a rate sufficient for the production of as many as two hundred bombs, but more likely has produced a far lower amount.[22] Indian officials have confirmed that their country has the ability to make nuclear weapons, but steadfastly maintain that no decision has been reached to build a nuclear arsenal. India has defeated Pakistan in previous wars and could probably do so again; nevertheless, a Pakistani nuclear test would probably cause India's leaders to change their essentially ambivalent nuclear policy and deploy a nuclear arsenal. Furthermore, while New Delhi views Pakistan's nuclear program as a major cause for concern, it also sees China—which has possessed nuclear weapons since 1964—as a potentially more serious threat to its security.

Following India's 1974 test of a nuclear device, Pakistan made steady progress toward nuclear status. Using uranium centrifuge technology purloined from the West, Pakistan built an enrichment plant at Kahuta thought to be capable of producing enough enriched uranium for up to a few bombs per year. China reportedly supplied Pakistan with warhead design and test-ing data.[23] Pakistani officials confirmed in 1992 that their country possesses "cores" for nuclear weapons; former Senator Larry Pressler has placed the number of bombs that could be assembled by Pakistan within a matter of hours at seven.[24] These statements confirmed that halfhearted U.S. attempts to persuade Pakistan not to produce weapons-grade enriched uranium had failed.

The nuclear standoff in South Asia reflects not only the bitter rivalry between these two nations, but also the failure of external pressures in sup-port of nonproliferation objectives. For much of the past twenty years, non-proliferation came into competition with other superpower interests in the region. This was particularly acute with respect to the U.S. response to the USSR's 1979 invasion of Afghanistan, after which Pakistan's strategic value as a conduit for aid to the anti-Soviet Afghan rebels was judged to outweigh the risk of Pakistan's advancing nuclear weapons program. Washington had suspended military aid to Pakistan in 1979, as required by the Foreign Assistance Act, when it was determined that Islamabad was conducting a secret nuclear weapons program; in 1981, however, Congress amended the law to allow the president to waive the aid cutoff if U.S. national interests were at stake. President Reagan employed this provision to restore military aid to Pakistan in 1982, as part of a policy of supporting the Afghan rebels. Even when Congress required that the President "certify" that Pakistan "does not possess a nuclear explosive device," the Reagan and Bush Adminstrations chose to overlook Pakistan's continuing nuclear weapons efforts rather than jeopardize the Afghan supply effort.[25] Only in 1990, with the Soviets in retreat from Afghanistan, did Bush acknowledge the now well-advanced Pakistani nuclear effort and cut off U.S. aid.

At present, then, both India and Pakistan possess a significant nuclear weapons capability. On the diplomatic front, Pakistan insists that it will sign the NPT if India does, and has proposed regional nonproliferation arrange-ments that would make South Asia a nuclear weapons free zone. However, New Delhi rejects the NPT because it is discriminatory, and refuses to par-ticipate in regional arrangements that would leave Pakistan's close ally China with nuclear weapons while India disarmed. Despite any lack of progress on arms control, Pakistan and India signed an agreement in 1989 in which both sides pledged not to attack each other's nuclear installations.

Some observers of nuclear developments in South Asia agree with Indian and Pakistani expressions of optimism that a stable nuclear deterrent rela-tionship is evolving between the two countries, making the outbreak of nuclear war unlikely. Other observers warn of the dangers that may be encountered by attempting to recreate the type of nuclear deterrence prac-ticed by Washington and Moscow over the course of the Cold War and beyond. At best, a degree of stability might be derived from an arms race which is sure to cost both countries massive investments of scarce resources. At worst, deterrence modeled after the U.S.-Soviet experience could lead to nuclear crises, similar to the Cuban Missile Crisis of 1962, that promise to increase the risks of nuclear war.[26]

The Middle East

The Middle East presents an extremely complex set of political relationships that form the backdrop for nuclear developments in the region. In particular, the history of conflict between Israel and its Arab neighbors and rivalry between Iran and Iraq have stimulated interest in the acquisition of nuclear weapons and other weapons of mass destruction.

At present, only Israel is believed to possess nuclear weapons. Iraq was probably within a few years of acquiring a nuclear capability before its nuclear program was attacked in 1991 during Operation Desert Storm and dismantled by UN teams in its aftermath. Libya has expressed interest in nuclear weapons, but has not built the necessary equipment to launch its own nuclear program. Iran and Algeria have active civilian nuclear programs that could eventually give them the capacity to develop a nuclear weapon should they chose to do so. Syria has acquired nuclear technology from China, but has not accumulated the infrastructure to support a nuclear weapons program.

Israel developed nuclear weapons using technology acquired largely from France, which supplied the Israelis with a reactor during the 1960s. (The reactor and its related reprocessing and enrichment facilities are located at Dimona, in the Negev Desert.) Israel has built some minor nuclear facilities under IAEA safeguards, but has not signed the NPT. Estimates of Israel's arsenal range from around fifty to as many two hundred weapons, some of which may be hydrogen bombs.[27] Israel also possesses a nuclear-capable ballistic missile, the Jericho, which has a range of nine hundred miles.

Although the existence of Israel's nuclear weapons program is widely known, Israeli officials maintain a scrupulously ambiguous posture regarding its nuclear capabilities, saying only that "Israel will not be the first to introduce nuclear weapons" into the region. Most observers speculate that Israeli strategists view nuclear weapons as a deterrent which would only be used as a last resort should the continued existence of their nation face an imminent threat.[28] This policy of ambiguity enables Israel to avoid the diplomatic and political problems that would arise if it admitted to possessing nuclear weapons; it also keeps open the possibility that it will give up nuclear weapons if circumstances permit.

Iraq was a charter member of the NPT when it entered into force in 1970. It used its oil wealth to buy nuclear technology in the 1970s, which it submitted for regular inspections by the IAEA. After the 1981 Israeli attack on the Osirak reactor, however, Iraq established a clandestine nuclear weapons program separate from its declared nuclear facilities. To do so, it created a sophisticated international procurement network that was used to acquire a range of nuclear and nuclear-related goods, ranging from nuclear triggers to raw materials. Iraq also acquired nuclear weapon design information, equipment, and facilities from a variety of sources, including the United States.[29] With these imports, Iraq built its own Manhattan Project, complete with updated copies of fifty-year-old uranium enrichment equipment called calutrons, which were used by the United States to build its first atomic bombs.[30] Iraq also undertook an elaborate centrifuge enrichment program and experimented with small-scale plutonium separation. Experts believe that these various efforts may have been capable of producing enough material for one or two bombs per year by the end of 1993.[31]

Years of inspections of Iraq's known nuclear facilities did not detect convincing evidence of the full-blown, billion-dollar clandestine nuclear weapons project that was exposed after the 1991 Gulf War. However, some official and unofficial analysts tracked the advance of Iraq's covert nuclear program from its origins before the Israeli bombing of Osirak in 1981 through the UN inspections after the Gulf War.[32] While some specific aspects of the Iraqi bomb program may have come as a surprise, much was known. This fact highlights a familiar pattern in nonproliferation policy: the tendency of the United States and other states to overlook a country's proliferation activities in pursuit of other foreign policy objectives. In Iraq's case, Washington concluded that helping Baghdad to prevent an Iranian victory in the Iran-Iraq War of 1980–88 was more important than stopping the flow of nuclear-related technology.[33]

Israel and Iraq outpaced other Middle Eastern nations in seeking nuclear capabilities. However, Iran under Shah Mohammed Reza Pahlavi (deposed in 1979) laid the foundation for an extensive nuclear power and technology infrastructure. Many of Iran's nuclear facilities were damaged in the war with Iraq or were allowed to decay during the Islamic revolution. In the 1990s, however, Iran's clerical leadership attempted to revive their country's nuclear program, largely by seeking nuclear assistance from China, Russia, and Germany, and by inviting Iranian nuclear scientists who fled after the fall of the Shah to return home. Germany refused to repair the large reactors it originally built at Bushehr, but in 1992 Moscow agreed to rebuild them, stoking fears that Iran would exploit weak controls on nuclear materials in Russia to acquire bomb materials and expertise. Although Iranian officials have insisted that Tehran will abide by its NPT commitments, Iran has sufficient nuclear resources and expertise to build a nuclear technology infrastructure that would allow the eventual production of nuclear munitions. According to U.S. intelligence estimates, Iran could be capable of building nuclear weapons by the beginning of the twenty-first century.[34]

Other Middle Eastern countries lag even further behind in nuclear capabilities, but could eventually catch up. Algeria advanced its nuclear technology base during the 1980s through a combination of Argentinean expertise and a secret reactor deal with China. (The existence of the reactor was exposed in 1991, despite initial Chinese denials.[35]) However, the current political instability in Algeria raises questions about the future of its nuclear program. Syria also obtained a small reactor from China in 1991. This transaction was delayed by the IAEA until Syria, an NPT signatory, completed the required safeguard agreement. Egypt has often stated an interest in acquiring nuclear power technology, as has Turkey. While these sorts of purchases alone do not necessarily give a country nuclear weapons options, such programs can lay a foundation for the pursuit of nonpeaceful objectives under new leaders.

The nuclear equation in the Middle East is further complicated by the proliferation of chemical and biological munitions, advanced conventional weapons, and ballistic missiles throughout the region. Egypt, Iran, Iraq, Israel, Libya, and Syria are believed to have produced chemical weapons; all signed the 1925 Geneva Protocol, which bans the use but not the possession of chemical weapons. A number of these nations justify their possession of chemical weapons—often called "the poor man's nuclear alternative"—as a counter to Israel's suspected nuclear arsenal. In addition, Iran, Iraq, Libya, and Syria are among the nations thought to have developed biological weapons.[36] Many Middle Eastern countries have also acquired or developed ballistic missiles with ranges that would enable them to strike targets throughout the region. Thus, Egypt, Iran, Libya, Syria, and Yemen all possess Scud-B or modified Scud-type missiles capable of carrying a one-thousand-kilogram payload over a distance of at least three hundred kilometers. (Iraq's Scud missiles were to be destroyed under the terms of the 1991 UN cease-fire agreement; however, the full extent of Iraq's missile inventory was never precisely determined, and some hidden missiles may remain in Iraqi hands.) Israel and Saudi Arabia have missiles with significantly longer ranges and payloads that may give them a capability to strike targets beyond the Middle East.[37]

For many years the United Nations and the IAEA have passed annual resolutions supporting the establishment of a nuclear weapons free zone (NWFZ) in the Middle East. Nearly all nations in the region, including Israel, have endorsed the concept, though there are wide differences on the terms for bringing it about. Arab states have suggested in the past that their support for such a zone is contingent on Israel's dismantling of its nuclear weapons capabilities, but without reciprocal commitments for negotiations on chemical or conventional arms and without recognition of Israel's right to exist; Israel considers such proposals unacceptable. Clearly, Israel is unlikely to change its nuclear posture while its security is at stake and while its neighbors are still building up their own weapons of mass destruction.

East Asia

Nuclear proliferation has been held in check in several key Asian countries, mainly due to U.S. efforts. Thus, U.S. security arrangements with Japan, South Korea, and Taiwan have eased the security concerns of these countries sufficiently to avoid a nuclear arms race in East Asia. Nevertheless, these countries possess advanced nuclear power programs that give them the option of acquiring nuclear weapons should they deem them necessary. Furthermore, China and Russia—both nuclear weapons states—and North Korea make nuclear weapons a major factor in the region's security outlook.

North Korea's nuclear program presented the international community with its first major test of will over nuclear nonproliferation policy in the post-Gulf War era. North Korea obtained some nuclear technology and training from the Soviet Union, but that was gradually cut off in the late 1980s. Much of its nuclear infrastructure was designed and built indigenously, so the cutoff did not end its nuclear program. In 1985, under pressure from Moscow, North Korea joined the NPT; however, it did not permit IAEA inspectors to visit its nuclear facilities until 1992. These inspections revealed discrepancies in North Korea's required declaration of its past plutonium reprocessing activites, suggesting the diversion of fissionable materials for weapons use.[38]

In February 1993, North Korea denied access by IAEA inspectors to two sites that the IAEA (and U.S. intelligence) believed held evidence of clandestine nuclear weapons activities. The North Koreans then threatened to withdraw from the NPT and claimed "special status" under the treaty that exempted them from inspections. The UN Security Council urged North Korea to comply with its obligations, but declined to impose harsh economic sanctions. Despite great international pressure, Pyongyang continued to block IAEA inspections into May 1994, when it began unloading the fuel rods from its principal reactor at Yongbyon. Former CIA Director James Woolsey has indicated that North Korea probably had accumulated sufficient plutonium for two nuclear bombs by this date, and that the fuel rods unloaded from the Yongbyon reactor might contain enough plutonium for the manufacture of several more bombs.[39]

With tensions rising and pressure mounting from all sides, North Korea invited former President Jimmy Carter to visit Pyongyang in June 1994 to discuss the nuclear issue. Carter, in talks with North Korean leader Kim Il Sung, arranged a deal in which North Korea would freeze its nuclear program in exchange for high-level talks with the United States. Despite the unexpected death of Kim Il Sung the following month, the United States and North Korea signed the "Agreed Framework" in October 1994, under which Pyongyang pledged to dismantle its existing nuclear reactors and reprocessing equipment in exchange for a promise by the United States and its allies to provide North Korea with modern light water reactors (of a sort less suitable for the manufacture of nuclear weapons) and a supply of fuel oil. South Korea agreed to build the reactors and pay for about two-thirds of their construction costs; Japan and other countries were to pay for the rest.[40]

The Agreed Framework obliges North Korea to resolve all outstanding nuclear safeguards violations—including the status of its undeclared plutonium—before completion of the new reactors. Another important aspect of the agreement is its requirement for direct negotiations between North and South Korea—a provision that Pyongyang has steadfastly avoided. Many analysts fear that North Korea is on the verge of collapse, and that its refusal to satisfy all requirements of the Agreed Framework represents a desperate effort to wring more concessions from the West. Extensive flooding in 1996 and drought in 1997 exacerbated the North's economic woes; reports of malnutrition among the population are common, although North Korea's one-million-man army continues to be adequately fed.

One potential negative effect of North Korea's nuclear program is that it may cause South Korea (and possibly other countries in the region) to reconsider their nuclear options. South Korea operates many nuclear power reactors and clearly possesses the technical capacity to manufacture nuclear weapons, should it decide to do so. In the 1980s, Washington persuaded South Korea to forego a nuclear weapons option and to terminate plans for its own reprocessing facilities.[41] Should the United States reduce its military commitment to South Korea's defense, or if relations with North Korea deteriorate badly, South Korea could reconsider its nuclear options. On the other hand, should reunification occur, Seoul could inherit North Korea's nuclear program—a prospect that surely causes anxiety in China and Japan.

Japan's nuclear prospects also affect the proliferation equation in East Asia. Although Japan's nonproliferation credentials are impeccable, clearly it could build nuclear weapons if it chose to do so.[42] Japan has an extensive nuclear power industry and is building large-scale reprocessing facilities to extract plutonium from spent reactor fuel. These efforts are tied to plans to develop "breeder" reactors that would produce even more plutonium, thus advancing Japan's long-term goal of energy independence. However, critics question Tokyo's costly decision to manufacture plutonium when uranium is so abundant and cheap, and the economic and security risks associated with plutonium are so high.[*] Moreover, a series of accidents in 1996 and 1997 raised fresh questions about the technical and economic feasibility of Japan's plutonium policy. Nevertheless, while most other industrialized nations have gradually abandoned the plutonium fuel cycle, Japan persists in building a large stockpile of plutonium.[43]

South America and South Africa

Events in the Southern Hemisphere demonstrate that it *is* possible to roll back proliferation. Indeed, proliferation threats have all but disappeared in South America and South Africa, mainly in connection with political changes that have taken place in three nuclear threshold states: Argentina, Brazil, and South Africa. In each case, unsafeguarded nuclear facilities associated with nuclear weapons were brought under international safeguards and nuclear weapons free zone treaties were brought into force.

In the 1980s, Argentina and Brazil demonstrated their ability to build and operate reactors and uranium enrichment plants. Much of the technology for these facilities was supplied by West Germany. These nuclear weapons programs, and related ballistic missile projects, prospered with the strong support of military leaders in both countries who valued their nuclear programs as sources of prestige and security. Argentina and Brazil

---

[*] Japan has contracts with French and British firms to extract plutonium from Japan's spent reactor fuel and to ship the plutonium back to Japan. These shipments, carried by ship, have become the focus of controversy—from fear that the plutonium could either be seized by terrorists seeking to acquire nuclear weapons or (through an accident of some sort) leak or spill into the sea and cause massive environmental damage. As a result, some governments have restricted the passage of these shipments through their territorial waters.

also demonstrated a willingness to compete aggressively for a share of the world export market in nuclear and missile technology. Argentina cooperated with Egypt and Iraq to develop the Condor missile, and sold nuclear technology to Algeria; Brazil had prepared a nuclear test site in the Amazon and developed a nuclear submarine program. Neither country was a member of the NPT or a signatory of the Treaty of Tlatelolco, which called for the establishment of a nuclear weapons free zone for South America.[44]

These trends towards proliferation were reversed in the late 1980s. One important factor in the rollback of nuclear proliferation in South America was a shift toward democracy in Argentina and Brazil, endowing civilian leaders with the authority to change the direction of nuclear programs that had had a history of close association with the military. In 1991, the presidents of the two countries announced their intention to cancel their countries' nuclear weapons programs and signed a series of confidence-building measures which led eventually to an agreement with the IAEA to allow inspections of their nuclear facilities. Both countries subsequently signed the Treaty of Tlatelolco, and Argentina signed the NPT.[45]

A somewhat similar situation prevailed in South Africa, which was a nuclear weapons threshold state until it signed the NPT in 1991 and opened its nuclear facilities to international inspection. In 1993, South African President F. W. de Klerk admitted that his country had built six Hiroshima-type nuclear bombs and was working on a seventh, and had prepared a nuclear test range in the Kalahari Desert. South Africa had enjoyed close ties to Israel, and there is evidence of extensive nuclear cooperation between the two countries.[46]

Since South Africa signed the NPT, the IAEA has conducted nearly one hundred inspections to oversee the dismantling of its nuclear weapons program. In 1996, moreover, South Africa joined with fifty-two other countries in signing the Treaty of Pelindaba, making Africa a nuclear weapons free zone. As in Argentina and Brazil, South Africa's decision to abandon the nuclear option and sign the NPT was closely related to the process of political development—in this case, the transition from white minority rule to a democratically elected black majority government. Nevertheless, the closing down of active nuclear weapons programs in these countries could provide a model for rollback of weapons programs in other nuclear threshold states.

PROLIFERATION CHALLENGES
OF THE POST-COLD WAR ERA

Regional proliferation dilemmas will continue to pose major challenges for nonproliferation efforts in the late 1990s and beyond. In addition, several relatively new challenges may arise to further complicate international efforts to control the spread of nuclear weapons. These new challenges will test the will and the capacity of the international community to strengthen and enforce the nonproliferation regime.

Nuclear "Yard Sale" in the Former Soviet Union?

Foremost among these post-Cold War challenges is the risk of nuclear "leakages" from the former Soviet Union. The end of the Cold War and the dissolution of the USSR left Russia and the other ex-Soviet republics with an elaborate nuclear weapons production complex and hundreds of tons of fissionable materials. Western policymakers and analysts worry that the disordered political climate in these countries will facilitate the theft of nuclear materials and technology and their resale to terrorists and so-called rogue regimes in other countries. Indeed, some radioactive materials have been smuggled out of Russia and sold on the black market, although reports of entire warheads being sold to Iran or other proliferators appear to be unsubstantiated.[47] In any case, the ultimate fate of many tons of weapons-grade material creates a major new proliferation problem.

Russia inherited the Soviet Union's nonproliferation commitments along with most of its nuclear weapons. Although some nuclear activities, such as uranium mining and nuclear power plants, are located outside Russia, nearly all of the critical nuclear weapons facilities—including the main nuclear laboratories—are in Russia. Under the START-1 treaty, only Russia (of the former Soviet republics) is to remain a nuclear weapons state; by the end of 1996, all nuclear weapons had been removed from Ukraine, Kazakhstan, and Belarus, which have now joined the NPT as non-nuclear weapons states. Over the past few years, many of the installations that had been involved in the manufacture and storage of nuclear weapons materials have suffered from significant economic decline, producing great uncertainties about the safety and security of these materials. The continuing erosion of political and economic order has created opportunities for thieves, especially those working inside of the nuclear facilities, to acquire and sell nuclear materials to potential proliferators. In fact, Iran reportedly attempted to purchase a supply of six hundred kilograms of highly enriched uranium from a facility in Kazakstan before the material was airlifted to the United States in 1994, as part of a secret U.S. operation called Project Sapphire.[48]

Since 1991, the United States has provided over $2 billion in assistance to improve security for nuclear weapons and materials in the former Soviet Union. This effort, known as the Cooperative Threat Reduction program or Nunn-Lugar (after the two U.S. Senators responsible for its inception), is intended to help the former Soviet states account for nuclear materials, transport them safely, and protect them from theft. Although critics of these programs object to any assistance that could ease the economic burdens of former Soviet weapons makers, most observers support the assistance programs as a useful form of "defense by other means" that reduces dangers to the United States. They point out that more Soviet nuclear missiles have been dismantled by the Nunn-Lugar program than by all other Cold War efforts combined.[49]

Despite these important gains, the dismantlement of nuclear weapons poses a new proliferation problem: what to do with the highly enriched uranium (HEU) and plutonium that was used to make them? The United States is buying five hundred tons of HEU from dismantled Russian warheads to keep it out of circulation. However, the exact amount of HEU in Russia is unknown, and excess plutonium presents a much more difficult issue. The United States and Russia each have about one hundred tons of weapons-grade plutonium; this amount is growing as more nuclear weapons are dismantled in accordance with various arms control agreements.[50] What to do with bomb materials from retired nuclear weapons looms as a major challenge.[51]

Controlling the Spread of Other Weapons of Mass Destruction

The nuclear nonproliferation regime has become increasingly interdependent with the regimes to control the spread of other weapons of mass destruction: chemical weapons, biological munitions, and ballistic missile delivery systems. Several countries, including Iran, Syria, and North Korea, are believed to possess potent chemical warfare capabilities, and many specialists view biological weapons as a major emerging threat.[52] Moreover, an increasing number of countries are able to build and export ballistic missiles capable of delivering nuclear or chemical warheads over long distances.[53] The proliferation of all of these types of weapons tends to reinforce the pressures on threatened nations to enhance their security by deploying their own weapons of mass destruction. The result, in many cases, is a pattern of regional arms races that ultimately reduces security for all.[54] Hence, efforts to control the spread of nuclear weapons must be closely related to the nonproliferation of ballistic missiles and chemical and biological capabilities.

In 1987, the United States initiated a coordinated international effort to control the spread of sophisticated missile technologies by forming a control group called the Missile Technology Control Regime (MTCR). Another informal suppliers association, the Australia Group, coordinates multilateral controls on chemicals and related production equipment that can be used for making chemical weapons. In 1995, a group of industrialized nations established the Wassenaar Arrangement to replace a defunct Cold War export control group called the Coordinating Committee on Multilateral Export Controls (COCOM).[55] These various entities seek to control international sales of "dual-use" commodities such as space-launch systems, chemical processing equipment, and advanced electronics. Many of these dual-use items are in high demand in rapidly developing Third World countries for both civilian and military use; thus, establishing nonproliferation controls that can distinguish between legitimate civilian and illicit military technology transfers is one of the most difficult challenges facing the world community today.

Controls on technology transfers represent but one aspect of a comprehensive approach to nonproliferation. Technology denial has weaknesses, not the least of which is that export controls can never be completely "leakproof"; experience has shown that resourceful proliferators can usually find ways to circumvent export controls. Furthermore, not all supplying countries are equally committed to stopping potentially dangerous exports, especially when very large sums of money in commercial trade are at stake. Very often, when one country refuses to sell a sensitive item to a suspicious buyer, another country gladly steps in to make the deal (as in the case of Russian and Chinese nuclear exports to Iran). Even if export controls are effective at both the national and multilateral level, more and more proliferators may be developing indigenous scientific and industrial capabilities that will enable them to build weapons without outside assistance. Thus, export controls address only one part of the proliferation dilemma.

The United States and other countries have sought to complement informal multilateral export control regimes like the Nuclear Supplier's Group and the MTCR with international conventions that establish recognized norms of nonproliferation. Until recently, treaties for chemical and biological weapons outlawed only the use—but not the *possession*—of such weapons.[56] By contrast, the NPT formally outlaws possession of nuclear weapons by non-weapons states and is reinforced by the IAEA safeguards inspection system. After years of negotiation, a global Chemical Weapons Convention (CWC) with strong verification procedures was signed in 1992 and entered into force in 1997. International efforts are also underway to endow the 1972 Biological Weapons Convention with comparable verification mechanisms.[57] Some analysts also favor a formal, verifiable treaty on missile nonproliferation to back up the MTCR. Efforts to strengthen these various measures will constitute an important aspect of nonproliferation activity in the years to come.

PRESERVING AND STRENGTHENING THE NONPROLIFERATION REGIME

Although formal international commitments undoubtedly add to the effectiveness of international nonproliferation efforts, they may be viewed as a necessary, but not sufficient, component of the global nonproliferation regime. Like export controls, treaties may influence—but, alone, do not always determine—a sovereign nation's decision to acquire weapons of mass destruction. A comprehensive nonproliferation strategy should, therefore, combine unilateral and multilateral export controls, international agreements, and flexible diplomacy to preserve and strengthen the various nonproliferation regimes—the most important of which is, and will remain, the nuclear nonproliferation regime.

The Future of the NPT: The Strengthened Review Process

The NPT is the institutional heart of the nuclear nonproliferation regime. In 1995, at the twenty-five-year anniversary of the treaty, its members voted to extend the treaty indefintely rather than let it lapse. During the course of the NPT review conference, there was much discussion of the original "nuclear bargain" and debate over the extent to which all parties had met their obligations.

One particularly contentious issue was the continuing divide between the five nuclear weapons states and the rest of the parties to the treaty. Article VI of the NPT obligates the weapons states to make "good faith" efforts to end the arms race and to make progress toward complete nuclear disarmament. The United States and Russia argued that the arms race was over and that the deep reductions achieved through the START treaties and other agreements should satisfy the requirements of Article VI. But many countries wanted to keep the pressure on the weapons states for deeper reductions in the future. When the members of the NPT extended the treaty, they agreed to monitor its implementation by holding review conferences every five years to determine if all parties—including the weapons states—are abiding by their obligations. The strengthened review conferences begin in 2000.[58]

International Safeguards, Inspections, and the IAEA

One way to increase confidence in commitments made by NPT states is to improve the international inspection system of the IAEA. The IAEA safeguards system was originally designed to account for nuclear material that was voluntarily identified by each member state. Every non-weapons NPT state must negotiate a "safeguards agreement" with the agency, part of which includes an initial declaration of its nuclear materials and nuclear facilities; periodic inspections are supposed to confirm that declared materials have not disappeared.[59] The IAEA system was not originally designed for the purpose of investigating suspicions about possible undeclared nuclear materials or secret nuclear installations, such as those discovered in Iraq and North Korea. Yet this has turned out to be the major proliferation challenge. IAEA's nonproliferation mission is, therefore, changing in the direction of a more intrusive, more investigative approach to inspections.

To prevent a repeat of Iraq, IAEA has begun to implement reforms of its safeguards system to make civil nuclear programs more transparent, to make its inspections more intrusive, and to ensure access to all relevant locations. The package of reforms, known as the 93+2 program, was proposed in 1993 and presented at the NPT extension conference two years later (hence, "93+2").[60] Since then, several components of 93+2 have been implemented. These include stricter enforcement of initial declaration requirements and the assertion of IAEA authority to conduct more investigative inspections on *all* nuclear sites and materials in non-weapon NPT states. To aid these tasks, IAEA has called on its member states to provide specific intelligence information on suspicious nuclear activities in countries of concern.[61]

However, at a time when IAEA is being called on to inspect more facilities in more countries—including those in Iraq, South Africa, Argentina, Brazil, North Korea, and the newly independent states of the former Soviet Union—the agency's budget remains frozen. As a UN-affiliated international organization, IAEA is dependent on its members for political as well as financial support. IAEA experienced budget shortfalls in 1991 and 1992 due mainly to the inability of Russia and the other new ex-Soviet states to pay their annual assessments to the agency. Thus, implementation of the proposed reforms may depend on the willingness of IAEA member countries to increase its budget.

A Possible Role for the United Nations in Nonproliferation?

Under the IAEA's governing Statute, the organization's director general can report safeguards violations to the UN Security Council, which must decide what (if any) action to take in response. In the case of Iraq, the Security Council established a Special Commission (UNSCOM) to defang Iraq's nuclear, chemical, biological, and missile capabilities. Security Council Resolution 687, which laid the basis for the end of the 1991 Gulf War, directed UNSCOM to work with the IAEA to investigate, destroy (or render harmless), and otherwise dismantle Iraq's nuclear program. This direct linkage between the Security Council and the IAEA established a precedent that some analysts have viewed as a potent international nonproliferation instrument that could be used to impede proliferation in other problem countries. These analysts advocate making the Special Commission (or some similar group) a permanent UN nonproliferation agency.[62] Others, however, argue that the joint UN-IAEA role in Iraq—a nation defeated in war by an unusual international coalition—is a unique circumstance that probably could not be replicated elsewhere.

The UN Security Council has recognized nuclear proliferation to be a severe threat to international security.[63] Whether the Council will, in fact, take decisive action to confront proliferation threats remains to be seen. Areas where the potential is greatest for a vigorous UN role in nonproliferation include: expanding international safeguards and verification procedures to accommodate the vast quantities of fissile nuclear materials being collected from retired nuclear weapons (especially in the new states arising from the former Soviet Union); addressing nuclear safety and environmental hazards; and addressing the root causes of proliferation.

CONCLUSION

Insecurity is a root cause of proliferation. Conventional and/or unconventional weapons provide nations with assurances of their survival. How can nations be persuaded that possession of nuclear weapons will not increase their security? At a fundamental level, nonproliferation policy should offer alternative routes to security. But what are the alternatives?

Collective security alliances can help to control proliferation by extending security guarantees to their members. NATO, the defunct Warsaw Pact, and other superpower military alliances were able to provide security assurances to their members, thus reducing their motivation for acquiring independent nuclear forces. Historically, such guarantees of "extended nuclear deterrence" have not always seemed completely credible, especially if the guarantor would risk destruction of its own society by responding to an attack on one or more of its alliance partners. While military alliances may still offer countries an alternative to proliferation, "extended nuclear deterrence" may also become a Cold War relic.

In some cases, Washington and Moscow tried to prevent their allies from acquiring nuclear weapons by providing them with enough conventional firepower to satisfy their security needs. Yet this approach also embodies significant problems, as demonstrated by the case of Pakistan. In the 1970s and 1980s, the United States provided Pakistan with large quantities of conventional arms for the explicit purpose of capping its covert nuclear weapons program. But not only did Pakistan continue its nuclear program, it also modified U.S.-supplied F-16 fighter aircraft to serve as a nuclear delivery system. Clearly, conventional weapons do not always slake the thirst for nuclear capabilities.

When nonproliferation policies fail, how should other countries respond to a new nuclear power? The alternatives include providing technical assistance to new members of the nuclear club to help them prevent nuclear accidents, as well as preemptive military actions against the weapons facilities of the new nuclear power. Both of these alternatives could actually encourage proliferation. Providing assistance to new nuclear powers could encourage others to follow their lead, while military action for nonproliferation proved largely unsatisfactory against Iraq's hidden facilities.

Another response to proliferation is to develop defenses. Nuclear and missile proliferation has replaced the Soviet threat as the primary justification given by advocates of anti-missile systems for the continuing development and deployment of ground- and space-based strategic defenses. The Department of Defense is also developing new military options against weapons of mass destruction under its "counterproliferation" program.[64] But while such options may prove useful as a last resort in extreme cases, they carry considerable risk of failure.

Arms control offers another alternative to proliferation. Verifiable agreements to hold armaments within specified limits can help reduce pressures to proliferate. Various regional and bilateral security arrangements such as nuclear weapons free zones, nuclear test bans, and nuclear facilities inspection agreements, can help to moderate or avoid arms races that may fuel proliferation. Confidence-building measures, such as officer exchange programs, partial inspections, and mutual declarations of intent, may also contribute to improved relations and thereby pave the way for more substantive agreements or limitations. When these options are combined with multilateral export controls and norm-building treaties like the NPT, the multilayered international nonproliferation regime presents a formidable obstacle to all but the most dedicated proliferators.

QUESTIONS FOR FURTHER STUDY

1. What are the reasons to be optimistic about international efforts to prevent the spread of nuclear weapons technology in the post-Cold War era? To be pessimistic?
2. What is the "nuclear bargain"? What form(s) does it take today? In the current international environment, is this "bargain" an aid or an obstacle to the spread of nuclear weapons technology? Why?
3. What are the basic provisions of the Nuclear Non-Proliferation Treaty? What are the strengths and weaknesses of this treaty? What, in your view, needs to be done to strengthen it?
4. What are the regional dynamics that affect the risk of proliferation in South Asia? In the Middle East? In East Asia? What can be done in each case to reduce the risk of proliferation?
5. What role should the United Nations and the United States play in curbing the spread of nuclear weapons technology?

Notes

1. The gun-type bomb that destroyed Hiroshima produced an explosive force equivalent to between ten and fifteen kilotons of TNT. The implosion-type bomb dropped on Nagasaki produced an explosive force equivalent to about seventeen kilotons of TNT. For comparison, each of the 192 warheads (twenty-four missiles, each with eight warheads) on a Trident submarine missile can produce the equivalent of one hundred kilotons of explosive force; warheads deployed on the Minuteman III missile can produce over three hundred kilotons. For information on nuclear weapons see T. Cochran, W. Arkin, M. Hoenig, *Nuclear Weapons Databook, Volume I, U.S. Nuclear Forces and Capabilities* (Cambridge, MA: Ballinger, 1984).

2. For a history of nuclear diplomacy after World War II see Richard Hewlett and Oscar Anderson, *A History of the United States Atomic Energy Commission, The New World, 1939–1946* (University Park: Pennsylvania State University Press, 1962); and Gregg Herken, *The Winning Weapon* (New York: Alfred Knopf, 1981).

3. See Lawrence Scheinman, *The International Atomic Energy Agency and World Nuclear Order* (Washington: Resources for the Future, 1987).

4. On "Atoms for Peace" see Richard Hewlett and Jack Holl, *Atoms for Peace and War, 1953–1961* (Berkeley: University of California Press, 1989).

5. On the British and French bomb programs see Margaret Gowing, *Britain and Atomic Energy, 1939–1945* (New York: St. Martin's Press, 1964); Gowing, *Independence and Deterrence: Britain and Atomic Energy, 1945–1952, Volumes 1 and 2* (New York: Macmillan, 1974); Wilfred Kohl, *French Nuclear Diplomacy* (Princeton: Princeton University Press, 1971).

6. See John Wilson Lewis and Xue Litai, *China Builds the Bomb* (Stanford, CA: Stanford University Press, 1988).

7. In 1979, U.S. intelligence detected a suspicious flash over the southern Atlantic Ocean. Some people believed it was a nuclear test, conducted jointly by Israel and South Africa. See Seymour Hersh, *The Sampson Option* (New York: Random House, 1991), pp. 271–83. Finally, in 1997, South Africa admitted that the flash was indeed caused by a nuclear test. See Willaim B. Scott, "Admission of 1979 Nuclear Test Finally Validates VELA Data," *Aviation Week and Space Technology,* July 21, 1997, p. 33.

8. NPT review conferences occur every five years. A group of countries has used past review conferences to express their displeasure with the lack of progress on arms control by the weapon states and to link the fate of the NPT to a comprehensive test ban treaty. The test ban issue was especially prominent during the review conferences in 1990 and 1995. On past and future review conferences see Joe Pilat and Robert Pendley, eds., *1995: A New Beginning for the NPT?* (New York: Plenum Press, 1995); *Disarmament,* Vol. XVIII, No. 3, 1995.

9. The treaty allows any nation to withdraw upon giving six months notice. See Leonard Weiss, "Tighten Up on Nuclear Cheaters," *The Bulletin of the Atomic Scientists,* May 1991.

10. Nuclear weapons can be made from two fissile materials, plutonium (Pu) and uranium-235 (U-235). Plutonium is created when natural uranium-238 is irradiated in a nuclear reactor. The Pu is extracted from the spent fuel by a chemical separation method, called reprocessing. Weapons-grade uranium is made by increasing the concentration of U-235 from the 0.7 percent in natural U-238 to over 90 percent using various isotope separation, or enrichment, methods. These include gaseous diffusion, centrifuge, laser, and electromagnetic.

11. There was debate about the suitability of reactor-grade plutonium for use in weapons. Weapons designers prefer nearly pure Pu 239. Reactor-grade plutonium has a higher concentration of Pu 240, which can generate more harmful radioactivity and can cause nuclear reactions to advance too rapidly for efficient detonation. Nevertheless, the U.S. has tested a bomb using reactor-grade plutonium and the IAEA considers it to be a weapon-useable material.

12. For analysis of proliferation trends in the 1980s see Leonard Spector, *Nuclear Ambitions* (Boulder: Westview Press, 1990).

13. The tighter restrictions contained in the Nuclear Non-Proliferation Act of 1978 included the acceptance of full-scope safeguards on all of the peaceful nuclear activities of any country that buys nuclear technology from the U.S. This requirement mandated the renegotiation of all U.S. bilateral agreements for nuclear cooperation. Some countries, including India, Pakistan, Iran, South Africa, and Brazil, did not accept the new standards for U.S. cooperation, and the agreements lapsed.

14. The Glenn-Symington amendment to the Foreign Assistance Act requires that U.S. assistance be cut to countries that acquire unsafeguarded nuclear enrichment or reprocessing technology. The law has focused primarily on Pakistan, which has received considerable sums of U.S. economic and military assistance, even while it was secretly building a nuclear bomb. Another amendment, called the Pressler amendment, placed a condition on continued U.S. aid to Pakistan that required the president to certify to Congress that Pakistan does not possess a nuclear explosive device and that continued aid to Pakistan would advance U.S. nonproliferation objectives. In 1990, President Bush did not make the certification, and aid was cut off. However, in 1996 the Clinton Administration and Congress agreed to restore some aid despite Pakistan's ongoing weapons activities.

15. On Israel's raid on Osirak see Amos Perlmutter, Michael Handel, Uri Bar-Joseph, *Two Minutes over Baghdad* (London: Vallentine, Mitchell and Co., 1982).

16. During the Iran-Iraq War, both sides targeted the other's nuclear reactors, although none of the reactors was operational when attacked and no nuclear materials were released as a result. The U.S. bombed Iraq's Tuwaitha nuclear research center during Operation Desert Storm. Subsequent inspections of the destroyed reactors confirmed that nuclear materials were contained within the immediate compound. On the subject of bombing nuclear reactors, see Bennett Ramberg, *Nuclear Power Plants As Weapons for the Enemy* (Berkeley: University of California Press, 1984).

17. For a full discussion of Israel's nuclear options see Shai Feldman, *Israeli Nuclear Deterrence* (New York: Columbia University Press, 1982).

18. For a comprehensive review of nuclear proliferation in the 1980s see Leonard Spector's books, *Nuclear Proliferation Today* (New York: Vintage Books, 1984); *The New Nuclear Nations* (New York: Vintage Books, 1985); *Going Nuclear* (Cambridge: Ballinger, 1987); *The Undeclared Bomb* (Cambridge: Ballinger, 1988).

19. Rodney Jones, Cesare Merlini, Joseph Pilat, William Potter, *The Nuclear Suppliers and Nonproliferation* (Lexington: D.C. Heath and Co., 1985); William Potter, ed., *International Nuclear Trade and Nonproliferation* (Lexington: Lexington Books, 1990).

20. See David Albright and Mark Hibbs, "Iraq's Shop Till You Drop Nuclear Program," *The Bulletin of the Atomic Scientists* (April 1992); and Albright and Hibbs, "Pakistan's Bomb: Out of the Closet," *Bulletin of the Atomic Scientists* (July/August 1992).

21. Former Director of Central Intelligence R. James Woolsey, testimony before the Senate Governmental Affairs Committee, February 24, 1993.

22. Leonard S. Spector and Mark G. McDonough, *Tracking Nuclear Proliferation* (Washington: Carnegie Endowment for International Peace, 1995), p. 89.

23. On Pakistan's nuclear capability see Albright and Hibbs, "Pakistan's Bomb: Out of the Closet," *Bulletin of the Atomic Scientists* (July/August 1992), p. 38; Spector, *Nuclear Ambitions*, Chapter 7.

24. Senator Larry Pressler, interview on NBC Nightly News, December 1, 1992. Pressler said the Central Intelligence Agency described the Pakistani nuclear program to him. NBC also reported that Pakistan readied a nuclear weapon for delivery and loaded it on a C-130 transport plane during a period of tension brought about by Indian military exercises near the Pakistan border in 1990.

25. The original cutoff is known as the Glenn-Symington amendment, section 669 of the Foreign Assistance Act of 1961. The certification requirement added in 1985 is known as the Pressler amendment, which added a new section to the Foreign Assistance Act of 1961. Recent legislation amended these requirements.

26. In fact, such a crisis may have already occured. In 1990 renewed tensions over the disputed territory of Kashmir triggered a series of actions by Pakistan and India which many analysts interpreted as preparations for a nuclear confrontation. On the 1990 crisis see Seymour Hersh, "On the Nuclear Edge," *The New Yorker* (March 29, 1993). Many Indian and Pakistani analysts dispute this account, however.

27. Estimates of the size of Israel's nuclear arsenal vary according to assumptions about the size and operating record of the Dimona reactor, which is presumed to be the source of Israel's nuclear weapon materials. On Israel's nuclear arsenal see Frank Barnaby, *The Invisible Bomb: The Nuclear Arms Race in the Middle East* (London: I.B. Tauris & Co., 1989); Seymour Hersh, *The Sampson Option* (New York: Random House, 1991); Leonard Spector, *Nuclear Ambitions*, Chapter 9.

28. Shai Feldman, *Nuclear Weapons and Arms Control in the Middle East* (Cambridge: MIT Press, 1996), Chapter 3.

29. Iraqi scientists attended a U.S.-government-sponsored "conference on detonation" held in Portland, Oregon in 1989. Weapons scientists from many countries met to exchange information and ideas directly relevant to nuclear weapons. See Hearings of the Subcommittee on Oversight and Investigations of the Committee on Energy and Commerce, House of Representatives, "Failed Efforts to Curtail Iraq's Nuclear Weapons Program," April 24, 1991 (Washington: Government Printing Office, 1992).

30. The Iraqi bomb scientists renamed their version of the calutron (short for "California magnetron") the "Baghdatron." On the original calutrons see Richard Rhodes, *The Making of the Atomic Bomb* (New York: Simon and Schuster, 1986), p. 601. Iraq's use of calutrons is described in IAEA inspection documents submitted to the United Nations Security Council. The calutron program is also described in an article by David Albright and Mark Hibbs, "Iraq's Nuclear Hide and Seek," *Bulletin of the Atomic Scientists* (September 1991).

31. David Albright and Robert Kelley, "Has Iraq Come Clean at Last?" *Bulletin of the Atomic Scientists* (November/December 1995), p. 53.

32. Analysts who were writing about Iraq's nuclear program in the early 1980s include Leonard Spector, *Nuclear Proliferation Today;* Steve Weissman and Herbert Krosney, *The Islamic Bomb* (New York: Times Books, 1981); and Jed Snyder, "The Road to Osiraq: Baghdad's Quest for the Bomb," *The Middle East Journal* (Autumn 1983). Numerous press reports tracked Iraq's acquisition of nuclear technology in the late 1970s and early 1980s, and the U.S. Congress held regular hearings on the subject.

33. An investigation of U.S. policy toward Iraq by the House Committee on Banking, Finance, and Urban Policy exposed many details of the attempt to use U.S. government credits and loans to lure Saddam Hussein into a more constructive relationship with the West. See Elaine Sciolino, "Iraq Policy Still Bedevils Bush As Congress Asks: Were Crimes Committed?" *The New York Times* (August 9, 1992), p. 18.

34. Testimony of Director of Central Intelligence Robert Gates, before the Senate Governmental Affairs Committee, January 15, 1992. See also Michael Eisenstadt, *Iranian Military Power* (Washington: Washington Institute for Near East Policy, 1996); *Iran's Weapons of Mass Destruction,* Jane's Intelligence Review, Special Report, No. 6 (1995).

35. See Vipin Gupta, "Algeria's Nuclear Ambitions," *International Defense Review* (April 1992).

36. For an analysis of weapons capabilities in the Middle East see Office of the Secretary of Defense, *Proliferation: Threat and Response* (Washington: U.S. Department of Defense, April 1996); Anthony Cordesman, *Weapons of Mass Destruction in the Middle East* (Washington: Brassey's, 1991).

37. For an early post-Cold War analysis of missile proliferation and missile capabilities see Janne Nolan, *Trappings of Power* (Washington: The Brookings Institution, 1991).

38. David Albright and Mark Hibbs, "North Korea's Plutonium Puzzle," *Bulletin of the Atomic Scientists* (November 1992); Joseph Bermudez, "North Korea's Nuclear Programme," *Jane's Intelligence Review* (September 1991), p. 404; Specter, *Tracking Nuclear Proliferation,* p. 108.

39. See *Proliferation: Threat and Response,* Office of the Secretary of Defense (April 1996), pp. 4–7; and testimony before the Senate Armed Services Committee, "Security Implications of the Nuclear Nonproliferation Agreement with North Korea," Senate Hearing (January 26, 1995), pp. 104–188.

40. On the Agreed Framework and U.S. negotiations with North Korea see Mitchell Reiss, *Bridled Ambition: Why Countries Constrain Their Nuclear Capabilities* (Washington: Woodrow Wilson Center Press, 1995).

41. U.S. Foreign Broadcast Information Service, Special Memorandum, "South Korea's Emerging Nuclear Potential" (February 22, 1996).

42. Japan had a nuclear weapons program during the World War II, but its experimental equipment was destroyed by U.S occupation forces. See Richard Rhodes, *The Making of the Atomic Bomb,* pp. 457, 580. See also *The United States, Japan, and the Future of Nuclear Weapons,* Report of the U.S.-Japan Study Group on Arms Control and Non-Proliferation, Carnegie Endowment for International Peace (1995).

43. Robert Manning, "PACATOM: Nuclear Cooperation in Asia," *Washington Quarterly* (Spring 1997), p. 218.

44. On Argentina's and Brazil's nuclear programs see John Redick, *Argentina and Brazil: An Evolving Nuclear Relationship,* Programme for Promoting Nuclear Nonproliferation, Occasional Paper No. 7, (Southampton: Programme for Promoting Nuclear Nonproliferation, 1990); Leonard Spector, *Nuclear Ambitions,* Part IV, Latin America; Paul Leventhal, ed., *Averting a Latin American Nuclear Arms Race* (New York: St. Martin's Press, 1992).

45. See Reiss, *Bridled Ambition: Why Countries Constrain Their Nuclear Capabilities,* p. 45.

46. On South African nuclear cooperation with Israel see Spector, *Nuclear Ambitions,* p. 283; Frank Barnaby, *The Invisible Bomb* (London: I.B. Tauris Ltd., 1989), pp. 16–20.

47. On nuclear smuggling see *The Nuclear Black Market,* Center for Strategic and International Studies, Task Force Report, Washington, D.C., 1996; Graham Allison et al., *Avoiding Nuclear Anarchy: Containing the Threat of Loose Russian Nuclear Weapons and Fissile Material* (Cambridge, MA: MIT Press, 1996).

48. R. Jeffrey Smith, "Kazakhstan Site Had Lax Security," *Washington Post* (November 24, 1994).

49. On the history of Nunn-Lugar programs see Jason Ellis, "Nunn-Lugar's Mid-Life Crisis, *Survival,* Vol. 39, No. 1 (Spring 1997).

50. David Albright, Frans Berhout, and William Walker, *Plutonium and Highly Enriched Uranium 1996: World Inventories, Capabilities and Policies* (New York: Oxford University Press and SIPRI, 1997).

51. On the issue of uranium and plutonium from warheads see John Holdren et al., "Excess Weapons Plutonium: How to Reduce A Clear and Present Danger," *Arms Control Today,* Vol. 26, No. 9 (November/December 1996); Graham Allison, *Avoiding Nuclear Anarchy*; or go to the Department of Energy's Office of Fissile Material Disposition web site at < http://web.fie.com/htdoc/fed/doe/fsl/pub/menu/any> .

52. The prospect of terrorist use of chemical and biological weapons is a particularly vexing problem. On terrorist use of weapons of mass destruction, see John Sopko: "The Changing Proliferation Threat," *Foreign Policy* (Winter 1996/97); Brad Roberts, ed., *Terrorism with Chemical and Biological Weapons* (Alexandria, VA: Chemical and Biological Arms Control Institute, 1997).

53. *The Nonproliferation Review,* published quarterly by the Monterey Institute of International Studies, Monterey, California, regularly published an inventory of global missile capabilities.

54. Another view holds that the spread of nuclear weapons can increase national and international security by creating stable deterrence relationships similar to the deterrence that characterized U.S.-Soviet relations throughout the Cold War. See Scott Sagan and Kenneth Waltz, *The Spread of Nuclear Weapons: A Debate* (New York: W.W. Norton, 1995). The classic formulation of this argument is Kenneth Waltz, *The Spread of Nuclear Weapons: More May Be Better,* Adelphi Paper No. 171, (London: International Institute for Strategic Studies, 1981).

55. "Wassenar Regime Plenary Meeting Adjourns Following Disagreements," *Arms Control Today,* Vol. 26, No. 3 (April 1996), p. 23.

56. The Geneva Protocol of 1925 prohibits the *use in war* of asphyxiating or poisonous gases and liquids, and all bacteriological methods of warfare. The 1975 Convention on the Prohibition of the Development and Stockpiling of Biological and Toxin Weapons and on Their Destruction commits signatories to destroy all stocks of biological weapons and pledge not to transfer such weapons to other countries. Neither treaty has verification provisions.

57. On the chemical weapons convention see Michael Moodie, "Ratifying the Chemical Weapons Convention: Past Time for Action," *Arms Control Today,* Vol. 26, No. 1 (February 1996). On efforts to strengthen the biological weapons convention see Jonathan Tucker, "Strengthening the Biological Weapons Convention," *Arms Control Today,* Vol. 25, No. 3 (April 1995).

58. Tariq Rauf and Rebecca Johnson, "After the NPT's Indefinite Extension: The Future of the Global Nonproliferation Regime," *Nonproliferation Review,* Vol. 3, No. 1 (Fall 1995); Jayantha Dhanapala, "Fulfilling the Promise of the NPT: The CTBT and Beyond," *Arms Control Today* (May/June 1996), pp. 3–6.

59. The frequency of IAEA inspections in a particular country is determined by the quantities of nuclear materials present. Therefore, far more inspections are conducted in countries such as Japan, Canada, and Germany, which operate comparatively more nuclear power plants than countries such as Iraq and Iran, which own just a few reactors.

60. On the 93+2 program, see *IAEA Bulletin,* Vol. 38, No. 4 (April 1997), which contains several articles on the program, or Mohamed El Baradei, "On Compliance with Nuclear Non-Proliferation Obligations," *Security Dialogue,* Vol. 27, No. 1 (March 1996), pp. 17–26. Official IAEA documents are available from the IAEA web site at < http://www.iaea.or.at/>.

61. This proposed reform has encountered resistance from some countries, who suspect most of the intelligence provided to IAEA would come from Western intelligence agencies. Some Third World countries fear that Western intelligence agencies would select certain developing countries such as Iran and Iraq for scrutiny while ignoring others, such as Israel. There has also been concern that sensitive intelligence information cannot be properly protected by an international organization.

62. On the role of the Security Council, see *Confronting the Proliferation Danger: The Role of the UN Security Council,* Report of the United Nations Association of America, New York, 1995.

63. United Nations Security Council Declaration on Disarmament, Arms Control and Weapons of Mass Destruction, January 31, 1992. Each of the nuclear weapons states issued additional assurances against the use of nuclear weapons to support the extension of the NPT in 1995. At that time the Security Council passed resolution 984 affirming those assurances and reinforcing the NPT.

64. On counterproliferation, see William Lewis and Stuart Johnson, eds., *Weapons of Mass Destruction: New Perspectives on Counterproliferation* (Washington: National Defense University Press, 1995).

9 / Fanning the Flames of War: Conventional Arms Transfers in the 1990s

MICHAEL T. KLARE and LORA LUMPE

Despite the end of Cold War conflict and competition, the last decade of the twentieth century has been exceedingly violent. The decade began with Iraq's invasion of Kuwait and the subsequent war in the Gulf. Several other major conflicts followed, including those in Chechnya, Rwanda, Somalia, and the former Yugoslavia. Some of these conflicts have since died down—perhaps only temporarily—while others continue to flare. All told, some twenty-seven major armed conflicts were under way in various parts of the world in 1996, including the deadly and persistent conflicts in Afghanistan, Algeria, Angola, Burma, Kashmir, Kurdistan, Sri Lanka, and Sudan.[1]

All of these occurrences have focused international attention on the international trade in "conventional" weaponry—the tanks, planes, ships, guns, and missiles used in conflicts of every type. Few of the combatants involved in the wars currently under way produce any, let alone all, of their munitions. Rather, they depend on the international arms market for the bulk of their arms and ammunition. At the same time, the massive military production capabilities built up in the United States, Europe, and the former Soviet Union during the Cold War era have proved highly resistant to both closure and conversion—leading arms manufacturers in these countries to seek foreign markets abroad in order to compensate for their own governments' reduced military procurement. This combination of persistent demand and excess supply has fueled a steady flow of munitions to areas of tension and strife. Because this flow is a significant factor in the frequency and intensity of contemporary conflict, it is essential to learn more about the conventional arms trade and consider ways to bring it under effective international control.[2]

When we speak of the conventional weapons traffic, we are normally referring to the transfer, from one country to another, of arms, ammunition, and combat support equipment (radar sets, radios, jeeps, helicopters, and so on). Such transfers are typically conducted on a commercial basis, entailing the exchange of arms for cash or credit; in addition, they can also entail the transfer of arms via military assistance programs. Whether supplied on commercial terms or as part of a military aid package, the recipients of such systems are usually governments or government-related entities; an entirely

160

separate (and illicit) network of black-market channels has arisen to supply insurgents, separatist groups, and other paramilitary formations.

All told, the global arms trade now averages approximately $35 to $40 billion per year—down considerably from the mid-1980s, when annual tallies reached as high as $80 billion per year (in constant 1994 dollars).[3] Although the advanced industrialized nations are the recipients of a significant portion of these transfers, the largest share is consumed by the developing countries. According to the U.S. Arms Control and Disarmament Agency (ACDA), Third World nations accounted for approximately 65 percent of all international arms transfers (in dollar terms) in the 1990s.[4] There are, however, significant regional variations in arms imports by these nations, with some regions receiving a much larger share than others.

Not surprisingly, the major market for arms is to be found in the Middle East, where a combination of oil wealth and regional instability has generated a seemingly insatiable demand for modern weaponry. According to the ACDA, Middle Eastern countries jointly imported $229 billion worth of arms between 1984 and 1994 (in constant 1989 dollars), more than half of all arms acquired by the developing world during this period.[5] Large arms markets have also emerged in South Asia and the Far East. In other areas, such as sub-Saharan Africa and Latin America, the dollar value of arms imports does not reach as high; however, these areas are being deluged with large quantities of small arms and black-market weapons, greatly contributing to the intensity of ethnic and insurgent conflict.

Despite the correlation between high levels of arms imports and chronic instability, control of the conventional arms traffic has been a relatively minor international concern until fairly recently. For most of the Cold War period, arms sales were considered an essential glue to alliance systems and a useful tool in gaining influence in the Third World. Following the Iraqi invasion of Kuwait, however, the world community became much more concerned about conventional arms trafficking. The fact that Saddam Hussein had been able to accumulate a massive military arsenal—consisting of some 5,500 tanks, 3,700 artillery pieces, and 700 combat planes[6]—from external sources led many world leaders to regret their earlier failure to control the arms trade.

Although the United States had not been one of the major suppliers of arms to Iraq, American leaders took the lead in proposing new restraints on conventional arms transfers.[7] Once the Gulf War had ended, President Bush invited leaders of the other major arms-producing countries to join Washington in devising a system of multilateral controls on the conventional arms traffic. Shortly thereafter, in July 1991, representatives of the five Permanent Members (P-5) of the UN Security Council—the United States, the Soviet Union, Great Britain, France, and China—met in Paris to begin work on such a system.[8] (Together, these five countries account for the overwhelming majority of all arms exports, as shown in Table 9.1, page 165.) Three months later, the P-5 representatives drafted a set of guidelines for future management of the arms trade. If adopted by the governments involved, these guidelines would require the P-5 states to consult with one another regarding major military sales and to avoid any transfers that might "prolong or aggravate an existing armed conflict."[9]

In yet another initiative to curb the arms trade, the United Nations voted on December 9, 1991 to establish a voluntary "register" of arms imports and exports. The register, which began functioning in 1993, is designed to reduce the risk of war and aggression by providing early warning of significant arms buildups in areas of recurring conflict.[10] This effort, and the drafting of the P-5 guidelines, suggested that the world community was moving toward the establishment of an arms transfer control regime similar to existing regimes covering the proliferation of nuclear, chemical, and biological weapons.[11]

Unfortunately, subsequent developments soon put the lie to such presumptions. In the two years following the drafting of the P-5 guidelines, the United States announced $71 billion in new military exports, including a $9 billion sale of F-15E bombers to Saudi Arabia, a $4 billion sale of 236 M-1A2 tanks to Kuwait, and a $6 billion sale of F-16 fighter jets to Taiwan.[12] The other major exporters viewed America's selling spree as bestowing carte blanche on their own arms marketing activities. Russia announced the sale of three submarines and ninety-six late-model MiG fighters to Iran, plus several dozen Su-27 fighters to China.[13] China, meanwhile, withdrew from the P-5 talks on the grounds that the F-16 sale to Taiwan had violated a 1982 agreement under which Washington had pledged to refrain from selling advanced weaponry to Taipei; the other four governments then used China's withdrawal as an excuse to suspend the P-5 negotiations altogether.[14]

These developments reflect one of the most conspicuous features of the arms trade: the high degree to which major arms-producing nations have become dependent on weapons exports to maintain domestic arms production at economically sustainable levels and to preserve jobs in critical military industries. These motives took second place to strategic considerations during the Cold War era, when both the United States and the Soviet Union provided large quantities of arms to their allies in Europe and the Third World, but became dominant in the post-Cold War era, when the NATO and former Warsaw Pact countries began to reduce their domestic military spending. With huge supplies of surplus Cold War weapons, and an overabundance of arms-making capabilities, these countries avidly sought foreign customers for their military products.

The election of Bill Clinton as president in November 1992 led some proponents of arms transfer restraint to believe that this pattern would be reversed.[15] However, the Clinton Administration has continued to promote U.S. arms exports with the same fervor as the Reagan and Bush Administrations, while dampening U.S. efforts in the arms control arena. Rather than attempt to restart the P-5 talks, Clinton decided in 1993 to develop a new framework for multilateral arms transfer restraint based on COCOM (the Coordinating Committee on Multilateral Export Controls), a mechanism set up in the Cold War period to restrict technology flows to the Soviet bloc. As a result of Washington's efforts, the United States and thirty-two other nations established the "Wassenaar Arrangement on Export Controls for Conventional Arms and Dual-Use Goods and Technologies" in December 1995.[16] This "Arrangement" is intended to function as a private forum for consultation on military (and military-related) exports among the major military suppliers; in addition, it is expected to provide the basis for "multilateral restraint" in arms trafficking. As of early 1997, however, there had been some preliminary consultations among the Wassenaar members, but little else.[17]

Thus, six years after the Persian Gulf conflict, there had been little progress in curbing the conventional weapons traffic; most of the reductions in arms exports that have occurred were due to market saturation, not legal or diplomatic initiatives. This failure to establish new constraints on conventional arms transfers will have far-reaching consequences. In several regions—particularly the Middle East and East Asia—we can see reinvigorated arms races at higher levels of lethality and sophistication. Such rivalries have periodically ignited armed conflicts in the past, and could easily do so again in the future. The growing traffic in conventional arms will also make it easier for insurgents and separatist groups to siphon off some of this hardware into their own arsenals—thus prolonging the ethnic and sectarian conflicts that are now plaguing many areas of the world.

In order to better appreciate the scale and impact of the conventional arms traffic, it is necessary to understand the basic dynamics of this trade. A greater understanding of the dynamics of the arms trade will also help us to develop control mechanisms when—and if—the world community is prepared to move in this direction.

THE STATE OF THE TRADE

The international arms traffic as it exists today is a composite of a vast number of separate transactions involving individual suppliers and recipients. In 1994, the ACDA found that a total of 101 countries imported at least $5 million worth of military equipment, while 54 countries exported at least that quantity—thereby producing hundreds of individual supplier-recipient transactions.[18] These transactions varied in scale, from the delivery of a few items worth perhaps several tens of thousands of dollars, to major sales involving billions of dollars' worth of advanced military hardware; a host of other transactions were conducted through black-market channels.

Like all other such relationships, the various linkages that make up the global arms trade are shaped and influenced by developments in the international system as a whole. In periods of extreme polarization (such as that which prevailed during the Cold War era), recipients tend to align with one major military power or another, depending on their location and ideological preferences. Thus, the Eastern European countries procured most of their arms from the Soviet Union during the Cold War period, while the Latin American countries procured most of their arms from the United States. Similarly, in times of diminished polarization (such as is the case today), recipients tend to be more eclectic in their buying patterns, seeking arms from several major suppliers. Developments in the global economy can also have an impact on the dynamics of the arms flow: a downturn in global economic activity tends to be accompanied by a decline in arms imports, whereas periods of economic expansion are generally accompanied by an increase in imports.

In studying the arms trade, therefore, we must pay close attention to developments in the international system that might bear upon the direction and magnitude of the arms flow.[19] Indeed, an awareness of changes in the international system is particularly crucial now, as the world continues to experience profound transformations. In examining these changes, it is useful to think in terms of the three key parameters of the arms traffic: (1) the principal *suppliers* of arms, (2) the leading *recipients* of arms, and (3) the specific *commodities* being sold. These three factors are continually interacting with one another and with broad international developments to determine the scale, character, and direction of the global arms flow.

Suppliers

Although many countries now produce and export at least some types of conventional arms, a relatively small number of countries supply most of the weapons being sold on the international market. According to the ACDA, five nations—the United States, Russia/USSR, France, Great Britain, and China—supplied over three-quarters of all weapons transferred on the international market between 1984 and 1994.[20] These five countries are "full service" suppliers, providing a variety of aircraft, ships, missiles, armored vehicles, and artillery pieces, along with a wide range of small arms and other basic combat systems.[21] (See Table 9.1.)

In addition to the major military suppliers, there are a number of "second tier" suppliers that specialize in the sale of particular types of weapons—for example, naval weapons in the case of Holland and small arms in the case of Belgium—or that produce a range of low- and medium-technology weapons for the Third World market. Included in this category are most of the established industrial nations of Europe (notably Austria, Belgium, the Czech Republic, Germany, Italy, the Netherlands, Spain, Sweden, and Switzerland), along with a number of newly industrialized states of the Third World (including Brazil, Israel, Singapore, and South Korea). Although their annual sales tallies rarely match those of the major producers, these countries have captured a distinctive "niche" or segment of the global arms market.[22]

While all of these suppliers are likely to remain significant players in the arms trade for years to come, several developments have affected their relative competitive position. Until 1990, the United States and the Soviet Union

Table 9.1 / Value of Worldwide Arms Shipments, 1991–1995
(in millions of current U.S. dollars)

Supplier	1991	1992	1993	1994	1995	Total
United States						
(government-negotiated)	9,360	10,713	10,685	9,842	12,549	53,149
(industry-negotiated)	5,166	2,667	3,808	2,099	3,620	17,360
Russia	6,200	2,500	3,100	1,500	3,100	16,400
France	2,200	1,800	1,100	1,400	2,200	8,700
U.K.	4,700	4,700	4,600	5,200	4,900	24,100
China	1,400	1,000	1,200	700	600	4,900
Germany	2,400	1,100	1,700	1,400	1,200	7,800
Italy	300	400	400	100	0	1,200
All other Europe	1,800	3,000	1,500	1,300	1,000	8,600
All others	1,900	1,700	2,000	2,400	2,700	10,700
Total	34,426	29,580	30,093	25,941	31,869	152,909

All data based on calendar year except for U.S. industry-negotiated sales, which are on a U.S. fiscal year basis.
Sources: Congressional Research Service, Conventional Arms Transfers 1988–1995; Defense Security Assistance Agency, Foreign Military Sales Facts, 1995.

jointly dominated the international arms traffic, together accounting for approximately two-thirds of all transactions (in dollar terms). Since the end of the Cold War, however, Soviet/Russian sales have declined significantly while the United States has become the dominant supplier. Boosted by the powerful advertising of the Gulf conflict, and aided by active government support, American arms now saturate the international arms flow.[23]

The growing demand for high-tech weapons of the sort used by the United States and its allies in the Gulf has also benefited the major European producers—especially France, Britain, and Germany—which have competed with the United States for sales of advanced military hardware to the Middle East and Asia. Russia, however, has not fared as well. With its factories and supply lines in disarray, it has not been able to offer the sort of backup capabilities that most recipients expect when purchasing costly weapons systems. As a result, Russian sales have dropped considerably in the 1990s, bringing them to the level of the major Western European suppliers.[24]

The lineup of the major military suppliers is also being affected by the changing economic climate. During the Cold War era, each of the major powers sought to maintain a large and diverse arms-production capability; as military spending has dropped in the post-Cold War era, however, it is becoming increasingly difficult for most countries to provide the large subsidies needed to keep all these plants in operation. As a result, many arms companies are seeking alliances or mergers with compatible firms in other countries—thereby producing multinational arms enterprises like Eurocopter, Euromissile, and Panavia.[25] As these enterprises grow in size, it may be that the emerging category of "multinational producers" will surpass many of the individual countries now on the list of major military suppliers.

Finally, when discussing suppliers, it is important to highlight the growing prominence of black-market dealers. Because most non-state actors—insurgents, separatists, brigands, and the like—cannot procure weapons on the commercial arms market, they must rely on black-market sources for most of their equipment. These sources typically involve transnational criminal enterprises that have become adept at transporting arms and ammunition via clandestine channels to remote battle zones in Africa, Asia, and Latin America. Because the demand for black-market arms will remain strong so long as there is a continuing increase in ethnic and insurgent conflict, these suppliers are likely to remain a significant factor in the arms trade.[26]

Recipients

In the final years of the Cold War, a relative handful of countries were responsible for a very large proportion of the total arms traffic. Just fifteen nations—Afghanistan, Angola, Cuba, Egypt, Ethiopia, India, Iran, Iraq, Israel, Libya, Saudi Arabia, Syria, Taiwan, Turkey, and Vietnam—accounted for 72 percent of all Third World arms imports in the 1985–89 period.[27] Analysis of this list indicates that the major Third World importers had several features in common: most were major suppliers of oil (Iran, Iraq, Libya, Saudi Arabia) or favored recipients of superpower military assistance (Afghanistan, Angola, Cuba, Ethiopia, and Vietnam in the case of the USSR; Egypt, Israel, Taiwan, and Turkey in the case of the United States) and all had been engaged in internal or interstate conflicts. This combination of *means*—the cash or credit to buy arms, or the support of one of the superpowers—and *motive*—an acute sense of danger—propelled these nations to the top of the list of major military importers in the 1980s.

As with other aspects of the weapons trade, the end of the Cold War and other changes in the international system have affected the lineup of major recipients. In general, these changes have affected either the means or the motives for arms imports (or, in some cases, both). For some, the issue of means has been paramount: with the Soviet Union no longer in existence, and its successor states in no condition to supply arms on a charitable basis, such long-term Soviet allies as Afghanistan, Angola, Cuba, Ethiopia, and Vietnam dropped off the list of major recipients altogether.[28] Shifts in the motivational side of the equation have also affected the composition of this list: in areas where peace has resumed, or where serious peace talks are now under way, there has been a significant drop in the rank order of the nations involved.

At the same time, however, some nations that were not prominent recipients in the 1980s have emerged as major buyers in the 1990s. Again, means and motives were the key determinants of these reversals. Thus, new

Table 9.2 / Major Third World Recipients of Imported Arms,
1988–1991 and 1992–1995
(in billions of current U.S. dollars)

Rank Order	1988–1991		1992–1995	
	Recipient	Total arms Orders	Recipient	Total arms Orders
1	Saudi Arabia	44.8	Saudi Arabia	22.3
2	Afghanistan	11.5	Taiwan	10.8
3	Iran	8.9	China	6.4
4	Egypt	7.0	Kuwait	6.1
5	South Korea	4.8	United Arab Emirates	4.8
6	Cuba	4.7	Egypt	3.2
7	Taiwan	4.6	Israel	3.2
8	India	4.6	Malaysia	3.2
9	Vietnam	4.0	South Korea	2.4
10	Pakistan	3.8	Pakistan	2.3

Source: U.S. Library of Congress, Congressional Research Service, *Conventional Arms Transfers to Developing Nations, 1988–1995* (Washington, 1996), p. 54.

entrants to this list include Kuwait and the United Arab Emirates—both of which are major oil producers that have increased their arms spending in the wake of the Persian Gulf conflict. Pakistan, which faces military buildups in both India to its east and Iran to its west, has also increased its arms spending. In the Far East, several states, including China, Malaysia, and Taiwan, rose to new prominence among the major recipients of arms. With booming economies and a host of concerns regarding regional stability, these countries devoted considerable sums to the modernization of their military forces and the acquisition of advanced conventional munitions.[29] (See Table 9.2.)

Also likely to emerge as major military recipients in the later 1990s are some of the Third World countries that now face major ethnic or insurgent conflicts in their own or adjacent territories. Among those that may be included in this category are Algeria, Burma, Colombia, India, Indonesia, Morocco, Peru, Sri Lanka, Sudan, Turkey, and Zaire (Congo). Although the purchasing power of these countries will be limited to some extent by domestic economic conditions and the overall decline in foreign military assistance, they are likely to procure large supplies of light weapons and counterinsurgency gear in the years ahead.

Commodities

As now configured, the international arms trade encompasses a broad range of weapons and military systems, ranging from small arms and other light weapons to tanks, aircraft, missiles, and warships. Also included are combat-support systems (communications devices, radar systems, transport vehicles, and so on) and military technology (weapons blueprints, arms-making materials, computer training, and the like). Transfers of all these commodities are occurring all the time, but the relative importance of any particular weapon or product will vary in response to changing international conditions.

In the 1970s and 1980s, major Third World buyers exhibited a strong preference for front-line combat systems: tanks, supersonic jet fighters, guided missiles, and modern warships. Having lacked such systems in the past, these buyers were naturally eager to obtain as large a supply of such systems as they were able. Between 1982 and 1989 alone, Third World countries acquired 10,804 tanks and self-propelled guns (SPGs), 20,870 artillery pieces, 19,966 armored personnel carriers (APCs), 2,840 supersonic combat aircraft, 51 major surface warships, and 2,320 helicopters.[30] Because "big ticket" items of this sort are the costliest items sold on the international arms market, large multiple sales of such products in the 1970s and 1980s pushed the annual tally of global military exports to unprecedented heights.

By the end of the 1980s, however, the demand for major combat systems had begun to decline. Deliveries of tanks and SPGs in the 1992–95 period dropped by 40 percent from the 1988–91 period, while deliveries of APCs dropped by 36 percent and deliveries of supersonic combat aircraft by 55 percent.[31] With fewer big-ticket items being sold, the total value of Third World arms imports also declined during this period—from an average of $35 billion per year in the late 1980s to $28 billion in 1991, $24 billion in 1992 and 1993, and $22 billion in 1994 (in current dollars).[32]

Several factors accounted for this reduction in big-ticket orders. Most important, the global recession of the late 1980s produced a severe fiscal crisis in many Third World countries, forcing them to scale back their spending on imported goods of all types. The disappearence of Soviet subsidies, and the decline in other sources of military aid, also contributed to the decline in big-ticket transfers. In addition, the massive arms transfers of the 1970s and 1980s had so saturated the arms inventories of prominent recipients—often overtaxing their logistical and maintenance capabilities—that they were in no position to absorb additional front-line systems.

Accompanying the decline in transfers of major combat systems in the early 1990s was an increase in sales of "upgrade kits" for existing weapons. Such kits, consisting of advanced propulsion, fire-control, and armament systems, are designed to increase the life cycle and effectiveness of older-model tanks, aircraft, and warships. For a relatively modest investment, the recipients of such kits can significantly enhance the overall capacity of their existing military "platforms." The acquisition of such kits has proved especially attractive to states with large supplies of aging Soviet-type weapons; because these countries often lack the resources to replace all these systems with new American or European platforms, they are increasingly apt to equip them instead with advanced electronics and fire-control systems.[33]

The early 1990s also witnessed a sharp increase in demand for guided missiles, multirole combat planes, and other high-tech weapons of the sort used by the United States and its allies during the Persian Gulf conflict. Such weapons were widely perceived as providing U.S. forces with an extraordinary military advantage in the Gulf, and so those Third World states with the means to do so have procured as many as these systems as possible.[34]

Increasingly, moreover, the arms flow consists of the technology to produce modern weapons, along with weapons themselves. Many Third World countries, especially those with an expanding industrial infrastructure, seek to become self-sufficient in the manufacture of arms rather than to depend indefinitely on the established arms market. These countries with the means to do so are using their economic leverage to compel arms firms in the United States and Europe to supply them with advanced arms-making technologies as part of any major military purchase. Rather than risk losing these countries' business altogether, many firms are now prepared to grant such "offsets" when negotiating new arms transactions. Thus, when arranging the sale of 120 F-16 fighters to South Korea, Lockheed Aircraft (now Lockheed-Martin) agreed to provide the Koreans with the technical know-how to manufacture 72 of the jets under license, and to help them to develop an indigenous training aircraft.[35]

Finally, the character of the arms flow is likely to be influenced by the growing incidence of insurgency, ethnic warfare, criminal violence, and other forms of "low-intensity conflict." To combat these threats, many Third World governments have ordered large quantities of small arms, anti-riot gear, helicopters, and other such systems. And, while sales of such hardware contribute relatively little *in dollar terms* to the annual tally of military sales, they do represent an important and growing segment of the international arms traffic.[36]

TRENDS AND CONSEQUENCES

As we have seen, the arms traffic has been significantly affected by the global transformations of the late 1980s and early 1990s, particularly the collapse of the Soviet Union and the U.S. victory in the Persian Gulf. These developments have resulted in significant realignments among the leading suppliers and recipients of arms, and altered the relative demand for particular military systems. Despite these changes, the weapons trade remains vital and prolific, with new suppliers and recipients eager to replace those that have been forced to curb their arms transfer activities.

As noted, the collapse of the Soviet Union and the drop in demand for major combat systems has produced a significant decline in the annual value of global arms transfers. However, this decline masks several disturbing trends: (1) the reinvigoration of the Middle East arms race, (2) the emergence of a new arms race in East Asia, and (3) the rise of a "buyers' market" in the arms trade. Each of these trends is discussed briefly below.

1. *The reinvigoration of the Middle East arms race.* After booming in the late 1970s and early 1980s, the Middle East arms race slowed down in

the late 1980s as the Iran-Iraq war drew to a close and the global economic recession cut into the military budgets of regional powers. According to the ACDA, total imports into the region dropped from an average of $23.7 billion per year from 1983 to 1990 to approximately $11.5 billion in both 1991 and 1992 (in constant 1993 dollars).[37] Most of this decline was due to the arms embargo against Iraq (in place since 1990) and a reduction in crude oil prices.

Since the end of the Gulf War, however, states in the region (Iraq excepted) have sought to restock their arsenals with large quantities of imported arms. Between 1992 and 1995, Saudi Arabia alone spent $22.3 billion on new weapons, while Kuwait spent $6.1 billion, the United Arab Emirates (UAE) spent $4.8 billion, and Egypt spent $3.2 billion. During this period, states in the region took possession of a total of 2,281 tanks and SPGs, 5,041 artillery pieces, 289 supersonic combat aircraft, and 2,307 surface-to-air missiles.[38]

Aside from their volume and dollar value, recent arms transfers to the Middle East are noteworthy for their high level of sophistication. As discussed earlier, President Bush had made control of the Middle East arms trade a major diplomatic priority in the immediate post-Gulf War period. However, arms-control considerations soon lost out to the economic motives for selling arms, and Washington began to offer late-model equipment to favored clients in the region.[39] In 1992, for instance, the Bush Administration approved the transfer to Saudi Arabia of forty-eight F-15E *Strike Eagle* fighter-bombers, aircraft that had only been introduced into service two years earlier, at the onset of the Gulf War. The Saudi F-15Es will be somewhat less capable than those in the U.S. inventory; nevertheless, this is the most sophisticated combat aircraft that the United States had ever sold to another country—until a year and a half later, when President Clinton agreed to provide Israel with twenty-one F-15Es possessing greater capabilities than the planes sold to Saudi Arabia.[40]

Through these and other such sales, the U.S. government has dramatically raised the standard of combat aircraft and munitions of U.S. allies in the Middle East, many of which are engaged in a "cold peace" with one another. Large-scale exports of advanced conventional weapons to U.S. allies in the region naturally affect the threat perceptions of "unfriendly" states as well, spurring them to seek countervailing weapons from Russia and other major suppliers. The result has been a renewed arms race in the area, with each major recipient citing the military purchases of its rivals as justification for further acquisitions of its own. As in earlier periods of instability, these deliveries are aggravating regional tensions and inhibiting progress toward a regional peace settlement.[41]

2. *The emergence of a new arms race in East Asia.* As in the Middle East, large numbers of high-tech weapons are being sold to the rising powers of the Pacific Rim. With increased funds at their disposal due to rapid economic growth, these countries have have been investing considerable sums in the modernization of their military forces—procuring modern arms

of all types in the process. According to the Congressional Research Service, the nations of Asia jointly spent $34 billion on imported arms between 1992 and 1995, making this the second largest arms market after the Middle East (among the developing nations).[42]

Like their counterparts in the Middle East, the major arms buyers in East Asia seek the latest and most capable weapons available. In particular, these states have sought advanced fighter aircraft, guided missiles, radar patrol aircraft, and major combat ships. Taiwan, for instance, has ordered one hundred fifty F-16 and sixty *Mirage*-2000–5 fighter planes, six French *La Fayette*-class missile frigates, and four E-2C *Hawkeye* radar surveillance planes; South Korea has ordered one hundred twenty F-16s, eighty UH-60 *Blackhawk* helicopters, eight P-3C maritime patrol planes, and nine German Type-209 diesel submarines; and China has ordered forty-eight Su-27 "Flanker" fighters and four Russian "Kilo" class submarines. Similar purchases, although on a more modest scale, have been made by Malaysia, Singapore, and Thailand. Meanwhile Japan, with its more advanced industrial base, has begun producing a wide variety of major weapons under license.[43]

To some extent, these purchases have been spurred by a desire on the part of the region's newly industrialized countries to replace older weapons with systems of the sort fielded by the major Western powers. At the same time, however, most of these countries are engaged in regional conflicts or rivalries, and thus much of this procurement is driven by mutual anxiety over the rising military potential of likely adversaries. In this sense, procurement patterns in the region have taken on the character of classic arms race behavior, with each major acquisition by any one power rivalry likely to trigger similar or countervailing acquisitions by its neighbors. Given this pattern, and the absence of any regional peace talks similar to those now under way in the Middle East, it appears likely that the Pacific Rim area will generate an increasing demand for modern arms in the years ahead.[44]

3. *The rise of a "buyers' market" in the arms trade.* With excess production in much of the industrialized world and a massive supply of surplus Cold War weapons, the international arms trade has become a buyers' market. This means that cash-paying customers are increasingly able to play suppliers off against each other, enabling them to obtain the most sophisticated weapons available, the highest level of technology offsets, the lowest prices, and the most advantageous financing arrangements.

The buyers' market has also resulted in the suppliers' less careful scrutiny of their overseas customers. The vast majority of U.S. arms exports, for instance, are going to countries with a history of authoritarianism, human rights abuses, and military adventurism. Diplomatic and strategic rationales have long been used to justify arms transfers to such countries, with proponents invariably claiming that such sales allow suppliers to gain and maintain "influence" with the leaders of recipient states. Over the years, Congress has attempted to constrain Executive Branch leeway in such matters by imposing human rights restrictions on U.S. military exports. However, these requirements have often been tepidly enforced or blatantly ignored, as

U.S. clients have violated American laws or policies. The government of Turkey, for instance, has repeatedly used American-supplied weapons in attacks on Kurdish communities, in apparent violation of U.S. law.[45]

Another consequence of today's hypercompetitive arms bazaar is the increasing amount of public money being expended to help drum up business for military producers. Despite their dominance of the global weapons market, U.S. arms manufacturers often claim that European competitors receive a higher level of government support.[46] Citing an "unlevel playing field," American industry has sought—and received—many new forms of public assistance to promote and finance U.S. military exports.[47] At the same time, European arms industries seek increased assistance to overcome what they see as unfair competition from American industry. The resulting spiral of initiatives—which make weapons cheaper and easier for customers to finance—calls into question the alleged economic benefits of arms exports. According to one study, the American public paid out an estimated $7.6 billion to underwrite weapons exports in 1995,[48] while new sales contracts signed in that year were valued at only $8.2 billion.[49]

Today, suppliers shy away from even *attempting* to influence prospective buyers' behavior. The arms bazaar is increasingly conducted as a free market, and the global oversupply of munitions means that buyers call the shots. They threaten to turn elsewhere if they cannot obtain the weapons they want or if they dislike conditions attached to a sale. The result is the spread of increasingly sophisticated weapons to areas of instability and turmoil.

A FRAMEWORK FOR POLICY

If these trends persist, we can expect a significant increase in the worldwide flow of arms and ammunition to areas of conflict in the years ahead. The consequences of this continuing military buildup are likely to be severe. Even though the collapse of the USSR and changing economic conditions have cut into sales of major combat systems, the 1990s have witnessed a substantial flow of highly capable weapons to developing areas. As a result, many Third World countries now possess the capacity to conduct wars of great intensity, duration, and reach. And while no one can predict that the growing availability of modern weapons will lead to an increased frequency of armed conflict, there is a high correlation between the growing diffusion of war-making material and the increased tempo of global violence.[50]

Despite widespread recognition of the perils associated with uncontrolled arms exports, the world community does not appear ready at this time to impose tight restraints on conventional arms trafficking. The supposed advantages of such sales—and particularly their perceived economic benefits—outweigh the impulse to regulate arms exports in the interests of global stability. As time goes on, however, the hazards of such neglect will become increasingly evident—and this, one hopes, will prompt world leaders to adopt new multilateral controls on the global arms traffic.

Once the international community sets out to impose new constraints on the arms trade, it will have to exercise great resourcefulness and ingenuity. The extent and complexity of the trade, and the vast number of individual arms-transfer relationships, makes it unlikely that any single treaty or agreement can effectively curb all facets of the weapons traffic. Instead, it will be necessary to combine several approaches into a comprehensive arms transfer restraint system.[51] Many of the components of such a system now exist in embryonic form, but will have to be further developed in the years ahead. These components include transparency, supply-side restraints, barring transfers of especially dangerous weapons, and regional arms control agreements.

Transparency

The first step in imposing greater international control over the weapons trade is to promote greater "transparency" in the reporting of arms transfers—that is, the declaration by states of their military imports and exports. Such openness will counteract the tendency of nations to overarm in response to hazy or incomplete information regarding the arms acquisitions of their rivals—a tendency that often leads to excessive purchases of one's own in order to compensate for "worst case" assumptions regarding an enemy's military capabilities. Transparency can also serve as an "early warning system" to alert the world community of excessive military buildups by potential belligerents.[52]

In line with these views, the UN General Assembly voted on December 9, 1991 to establish an annual "register" of member states' imports and exports of major weapons systems.[53] Although voluntary, many nations have cooperated with the UN register since its formal inception in 1993, and it is hoped that other countries will agree to participate as experience is gained in its operation. Proponents of the register also hope that it will be expanded to include light as well as heavy weapons, along with domestic production of military systems.

Supply-Side Restraints

Although the technology to produce arms has been widely diffused over the past few decades, a handful of nations continue to dominate the trade in high-technology armaments. It is still possible, therefore, to establish supply-side restraints to curb the trade in conventional arms, particularly in advanced weapons. Such measures have generally failed in the past because of nonparticipation by the Soviet Union and China; now that Russia and China are willing to cooperate in such measures (witness the successful UN arms embargoes on Iraq and Libya), it is possible to conceive of supplier agreements that include all of the major military suppliers. This, indeed, was the basis for the arms control talks initiated by the P-5 powers in July 1991 and for establishment of the Wassenaar Arrangement.

The Clinton Administration's preferred approach to such efforts has been to isolate a handful of regimes considered by Washington to be international pariahs, or "rogues." The Administration has sought to build a consensus among major military suppliers on cutting off the flow of arms and military-related technologies to such states as Iran, Iraq, and Libya through the Wassenaar Arrangement, while treating most of the rest of the world as fair game for weapons sales. A more forward-looking U.S. policy would attempt to establish uniform criteria for the sale of arms, barring transfers to *any* nation that has engaged in aggressive military behavior or engaged in a consistent pattern of human rights abuses.

An attractive model for such criteria is contained in the proposed "Code of Conduct on Arms Transfers Act," supported by many Members of Congress. The Code of Conduct would condition U.S. exports on recipients' adherence to internationally-recognized norms of human rights, their participation in the UN Register of Conventional Arms, and their embrace of democracy and nonaggression. The central premise of the Code is that governments that meet these criteria are more likely to be prove stable and responsible allies, thereby ensuring that U.S.-supplied arms are not used for illicit or destabilizing purposes.[54] Similar measures are being considered in other countries, and in the European Union as a whole; in addition, several Nobel Peace Prize recipients, including former President Oscar Arias of Costa Rica, have called for the adoption of an arms trade code of conduct by the United Nations.[55]

Barring Transfers of Especially Dangerous Weapons

In addition to setting performance criteria for prospective arms recipients, the major suppliers should prohibit the export of weapons systems that are particularly destabilizing or that pose an unacceptable humanitarian risk. At present, only two categories of conventional weaponry are subject to multilateral export controls: long-range ballistic missiles and anti-personnel land mines. Exports of the former are banned by the Missile Technology Control Regime (MTCR), established in 1987, while the use of the latter is prohibited by UN General Assembly resolutions. Both cases demonstrate that multilateral export controls are possible to achieve once a particular category of weaponry has been stigmatized through government, media, and public pressure.

Because of the tragic toll they are taking on noncombatants around the world, over one hundred governments have now endorsed the short-term goal of a global ban on the manufacture, export, and use of antipersonnel land mines (small explosive devices that explode when stepped on or ridden over).[56] The export of several other weapons systems that are by nature indiscriminate in their effects, or otherwise violate humanitarian laws of war, should also be barred. Antipersonnel cluster bombs (munitions that open up over the target area and spew out a large number of lethal "submunitions") and fuel-air explosives (bombs that contain a highly volatile incendiary mix that explodes with near-nuclear force when ignited) are other candidates for prohibition on humanitarian grounds. In addition, MTCR-like restrictions could be placed on a number of advanced weapons systems, including diesel attack submarines, deep-penetration bombers, and shoulder-fired antiaircraft missiles.[57]

Regional Arms Control Agreements (by Recipients)

Ultimately, any effort to curb the flow of arms into an area will require the cooperation of recipients, as no supplier-based control system can ever be made 100 percent effective (and may simply generate increased demand for black-market weapons). Supplier cartels are also resented by many Third World governments because of their association with imperial forms of control. Thus, any system for arms control within a region must rely as much on *recipient restraint* as on supplier restraint—with the latter used as a stimulus for the former, or as a substitute when recipient restraint does not appear likely.

The region that is receiving most attention in this regard is the Middle East. A regional arms control agreement in this area could take several forms: restrictions on the acquisition of certain types of high-technology weaponry, annual ceilings on imports of particular categories of basic combat systems (tanks, bombers, artillery, and so on), limits on technology transfers for domestic arms production, and the establishment of "tank-free zones" or "artillery-free zones" along contested borders. Following the example of the Conference on Security and Cooperation in Europe (CSCE), such accords should also include provisions for confidence- and security-building measures such as exchanges of military observers and "open skies" agreements permitting surveillance of military units by unarmed aircraft, as well as regular consultation on matters of regional peace and security.[58]

None of these measures, by themselves, can eliminate all of the dangers associated with uncontrolled arms transfers. Additional measures need to be devised for controlling the trade in black-market arms, and for restricting exports of arms-making technologies. Once joined in a comprehensive arms transfer restraint regime, however, these various measures would screen out many of the most destabilizing arms transfers and constrict the international flow of weaponry. Such a regime would also provide advance warning of dangerous military buildups in areas of recurring conflict, enabling the world community to take timely action to prevent the outbreak of war. The design and implementation of such measures must, therefore, be seen as a major international priority in the years ahead.

Of course, a conventional arms transfer control regime will not eliminate all of the military violence now threatening the international community. Other initiatives, including regional peace agreements, tension-reducing efforts, and international peacekeeping operations, will be needed to reduce the incidence and intensity of warfare in the twenty-first century. (For discussion of such measures, see Chapter 19.) But a concerted effort to curtail the international trade in armaments could help reduce the risk of war and inhibit the escalation of those conflicts that do occur.

QUESTIONS FOR FURTHER STUDY

1. Why, in the view of the authors, has the conventional arms trade proved so resistant to international control in the post-Cold War era?
2. How has the end of the Cold War affected the lineup of major suppliers and recipients of conventional arms?
3. How has the Persian Gulf War affected the market for conventional arms?
4. What are some of the most disturbing trends in conventional arms trafficking today?
5. What sorts of measures do the authors advocate for controlling the international arms trade? Are they likely to work?

Notes

1. For background on these conflicts, see the table of "major armed conflicts" in Stockholm International Peace Research Institute (SIPRI), *SIPRI Yearbook 1997: Armaments, Disarmament and International Security* (Oxford: Oxford University Press, 1997), pp. 23–30. (Hereinafter cited as *SIPRI Yearbook 1996*.)

2. For general background on the structure and dynamics of the international arms trade, see Andrew J. Pierre, *The Global Politics of Arms Sales* (Princeton: Princeton University Press, 1982); and Edward J. Laurance, *The International Arms Trade* (New York: Lexington Books, 1992). See also Michael T. Klare, "Deadly Convergence: The Perils of the Arms Trade," *World Policy Journal*, Vol. 6, No. 1 (Winter 1988/89), pp. 141–68.

3. U.S. Arms Control and Disarmament Agency (ACDA), *World Military Expenditures and Arms Transfers 1995* (Washington: ACDA, 1996), p. 103. (Hereinafter cited as ACDA, *WME&AT 1995*.)

4. Ibid.

5. Ibid., p. 106.

6. For a complete inventory of Iraqi arms holdings prior to the Persian Gulf conflict of 1991, see International Institute of Strategic Studies, *The Military Balance 1990–1991* (London: Brassey's, 1990), pp. 105–106.

7. At the very height of the Gulf conflict, Secretary of State James Baker declared that arms transfer restraint would be a major U.S. priority after the war had been concluded. "The time has come," he told the House Foreign Affairs Committee on February 6, 1991, "to try to change the destructive pattern of military competition and proliferation in [the Middle East] and to reduce the arms flow into an area that is already overmilitarized." Opening Statement by Secretary of State James Baker before the House Foreign Affairs Committee, Washington, D.C., February 6, 1991 (mimeo).

8. In a communiqué issued at the end of the meeting, the P-5 states declared that, as the world's major arms suppliers, they had a special obligation to "observe rules of restraint" when exporting weapons. "Statement of the Five Issued After the Meeting on Arms Transfers and Non-Proliferation," Paris July 9, 1991, *Department of State Dispatch* (July 15, 1991), p. 508.

9. "Communiqué of the Five Countries—London, October 18, 1991," as reproduced in ACDA, *WME&AT-1990*, pp. 24–24B.

10. For discussion of the UN register and text of the enacting resolution, see *SIPRI Yearbook 1992*, pp. 299–301, 305–307.

11. For discussion, see *SIPRI Yearbook 1992*, pp. 291–305.

12. See Arms Control Association (ACA), "ACA Register of U.S. Arms Transfers" (Washington: ACA, October 1996).

13. See "Iran/Russia Wrap Up $2 Billion Arms Deal," *Flight International* (July 21, 1992), p. 13; and Michael R. Gordon, "Moscow Is Selling Weapons to China, U.S. Officials Say," *The New York Times* (October 18, 1992), p. A1.

14. See William D. Hartung, *And Weapons for All* (New York: HarperCollins, 1994), pp. 147–48, 274–76.

15. Clinton himself lent credibility to these views when he told reporters, shortly after the election, that "I expect to review our arms sales policy and to take it up with the other major sellers of the world as part of a long-term effort to reduce the proliferation of weapons of destruction in the hands of people who might use them in very destructive ways." Quoted in *The Washington Post* (November 20, 1992), p. A1.

16. According to a State Department fact sheet on Wassenaar, the Arrangement will primarily be a forum for consultation and transparency, and "where appropriate, multilateral restraint" on weapons and dual-use technology transfers. The regime relies on each participating nation's own laws and policies to monitor and control export of items to be included on the forum's munitions and dual-use technologies lists.

17. Andrew J. Pierre, "The Wassenaar Arrangement," *IISS Strategic Comments,* Vol. 2, No. 7 (August 1996).

18. ACDA, *WME&AT-1995*, pp. 111–51.

19. For further discussion of the systemic determinants of international arms trafficking, see Keith Krause, *Arms and the State: Patterns of Military Production and Trade* (Cambridge: Cambridge University Press, 1992); and Laurance, *The International Arms Trade,* Chapters 3, 6, 7. See also Michael T. Klare, "The Arms Trade in the 1990s: Changing Patterns, Rising Dangers," *Third World Quarterly,* Vol. 17, No. 5 (1996), pp. 857–74.

20. ACDA, *WME&AT-1995,* p. 159.

21. For further discussion of the structure of the arms market, see Krause, *Arms and the State,* Chapter 4; and Laurance, *The International Arms Trade,* Chapters 5, 6. For an annual summary of the arms trade activities of the major suppliers, see the "arms trade register" in the *SIPRI Yearbook*.

22. For discussion of the second-tier producers, see Krause, *Arms and the State,* Chapters 6, 7. For data on the annual value of these countries' arms exports, see ACDA, *WME&AT 1995,* pp. 111–52; for an indication of their product range, see the annual "Arms Trade Register" in *SIPRI Yearbook*.

23. For a complete list of U.S. arms exports since 1990, see the "ACA Register of U.S. Arms Transfers" (note 12). For discussion, see Hartung, *And Weapons for All.*

24. For discussion, see Peter Almquist and Edwin Bacon, "Arms Exports in a Post-Soviet Market," *Arms Control Today* (July/August 1992), pp. 12–17; and *SIPRI Yearbook 1992,* pp. 279–81, 380–90.

25. For discussion, see U.S. Congress, Office of Technology Assessment, *Global Arms Trade* (Washington: U.S. Government Printing Office, 1991), Chapter 4. (Hereinafter cited as OTA, *Global Arms Trade.*) See also *SIPRI Yearbook 1991,* pp. 331–44.

26. For background on the black-market arms traffic, see Michael T. Klare, "Secret Operatives, Clandestine Trades: The Thriving Black Market for Weapons," *Bulletin of the Atomic Scientists* (April 1988), pp. 16–24; Edward J. Laurance, "The New Gunrunning," *Orbis,* Vol. 33, No. 2 (Spring 1989), pp. 225–37.

27. ACDA, *WME&AT 1990,* pp. 131–34.

28. U.S. Library of Congress, Congressional Research Service (CRS), *Conventional Arms Transfers to Developing Nations, 1988–1995* (Washington: CRS, August 15, 1996), p. 54. (Hereinafter cited as CRS, *Conventional Arms Transfers 88–95.*)

29. For annual tallies of arms imports by these countries, see ACDA, *WME&AT-1995,* Table II. For discussion, see Steven Erlanger, "Rush for Resources Impels a New Asia Arms Race," *The New York Times* (May 6, 1990), p. A18; Michael T. Klare, "The Next Great Arms Race," *Foreign Affairs,* Vol. 72, No. 3 (Summer 1993), pp. 136–52; and R. Jeffrey Smith, "E. Asian Nations Intensify Arms-Buying from West," *The Washington Post* (March 9, 1992), p. A1.

30. CRS, *Conventional Arms Transfers 82–89,* p. 66.

31. Ibid., p. 70.

32. Ibid., p. 45.

33. For discussion and examples, see Gerald M. Steinberg, "Recycled Weapons," *Technology Review* (April 1985), pp. 28–38; and *SIPRI Yearbook 1991,* pp. 225–27.

34. For discussion, see *SIPRI Yearbook 1992,* pp. 283–86.

35. For background and discussion, see OTA, *Global Arms Trade,* pp. 131–40.

36. For background and discussion, see Jeffrey Boutwell, Michael T. Klare, and Lora W. Reed, eds., *Lethal Commerce: The Global Trade in Small Arms and Light Weapons* (Cambridge: American Academy of Arts and Sciences, 1995); and Michael Klare and David Andersen: *A Scourge of Guns: The Diffusion of Small Arms and Light Weapons in Latin America* (Washington: Federation of American Scientists, 1996).

37. ACDA, *WME&AT 1993–1994*, p. 94.

38. CRS, *Conventional Arms Transfers 88–95*, pp. 54, 72.

39. For discussion, see Jackson Diehl, "Strategic Plans Giving Way to Mideast Arms Flow," *The Washington Post* (October 4, 1992), p. A24; and Hartung, *And Weapons for All,* Chapters 7, 10.

40. "U.S. Plans to Sell Jet Fighters to Israel," *Washington Times* (April 12, 1994).

41. For discussion of arms race dynamics in the Middle East, see U.S. Congress, Congressional Budget Office (CBO), *Limiting Conventional Arms Exports to the Middle East* (Washington: CBO, 1992), Chapter 2; and Geoffrey Kemp, *The Control of the Middle East Arms Race* (Washington: Carnegie Endowment for International Peace, 1991), Chapters 2, 4, 5.

42. CRS, *Conventional Arms Transfers 88–95*, pp. 48, 54.

43. *SIPRI Yearbook 1995*, pp. 518, 528–31, 545–46.

44. For discussion, see Erlanger, "Rush for Resources"; David A. Fulghum, "Regional Conflicts, Power Shifts Leading to Arms Races Concern Asian Specialists," *Aviation Week and Space Technology* (February 24, 1992), pp. 96–98; Gordon, "E. Asian Nations"; and Klare, "The Next Great Arms Race."

45. For discussion, see Human Rights Watch Arms Project, *Weapons Transfers and Violations of the Laws of War in Turkey* (New York: Human Rights Watch, 1995).

46. See U.S. General Accounting Office (GAO), *Military Exports: A Comparison of Government Support in the United States and Three Major Competitors,* Report GAO/NSIAD-95–86 (Washington: GAO, May 1995).

47. These subsidies have included: U.S. taxpayer guarantees for up to $15 billion of commercial loans for weapons purchases; the systematic waiver of fees included in the price charged buyers of U.S. arms to recover some portion of taxpayer-financed research and development costs for the weapon system being exported; and appearances by U.S. military personnel and equipment at overseas air shows and arms bazaars. For reportage on these and other subsidy issues, see various issues of the *Arms Sales Monitor* (Washington: Federation of American Scientists, 1991–1996).

48. William D. Hartung, *Welfare for Weapons Dealers: The Hidden Costs of the Arms Trade* (New York: World Policy Institute, 1996).

49. CRS, *Conventional Arms Transfers 88–95*, p. 78. This figure excludes arms sales agreements negotiated directly by U.S. arms industry, as such information is not made public.

50. For discussion of the relationship between arms transfers and conflict in the Middle East, see Hartung, *And Weapons for All,* Chapter 10; and Kemp, *Middle East Arms Race,* pp. 101–109.

51. For a discussion and assessment of past efforts to control the arms trade, see Pierre, *The Global Politics of Arms Sales,* pp. 281–90. See also Michael T. Klare, "Gaining Control: Building a Comprehensive Arms Restraint System," *Arms Control Today* (June 1991), pp. 9–13.

52. See United Nations, General Assembly, *Study on Ways and Means of Promoting Transparency in International Transfers of Conventional Arms,* UN Report A/46/301 (New York, 1991), pp. 36–40, 44–46; and United Nations, Department of Disarmament Affairs, *Transparency in International Arms Transfers* (New York, 1990).

53. Paul E. Lewis, "U.N. Passes Voluntary Register to Curb Arms Sales," *The New York Times* (December 10, 1991), p. A11. The register plan is spelled out in UN General Assembly Resolution 46/36 of December 9, 1991, and its accompanying Annex. For texts, see *SIPRI Yearbook 1992*, pp. 305–307.

54. As Rep. Cynthia McKinney said in introducing the bill, "For years we sold weapons to dictators and provided military training for their officers. We armed the Shah of Iran, we armed Iraq, we armed Panama, we armed Somalia and we armed Haiti. We continue to pay for these sales with American tax dollars and American lives. There are presently some restraints on the arms trade. But the failures of the present regimen are all too apparent . . . At the very least, American arms should not be sold and U.S. military training should not be provided to governments that oppose American principles." *Congressional Record* (November 19, 1993), pp. E2939–40.

55. Stephen Kinzer, "Nobel Peace Laureates Draft a Plan to Govern Arms Trade," *The New York Times* (September 6, 1996).

56. Raymond Bonner, "Land Mine Treaty Takes Final Form Over U.S. Dissent," *The New York Times* (September 18, 1997).

57. See John Sislin and David Mussington, "Destabilizing Arms Acquisitions," *Jane's Intelligence Review,* Vol. 7, No. 2 (February 1995), pp. 88–90.

58. For discussion of such measures and of the obstacles standing in the way of such agreements, see Kemp, *Middle East Arms Race,* pp. 119–46.

10 / The Causes of Internal Conflict

MICHAEL E. BROWN

Many policymakers and journalists believe that the causes of internal conflicts are simple and straightforward.[1] The driving forces behind these violent conflicts, it is said, are the "ancient hatreds" that many ethnic and religious groups have for each other. In Eastern Europe, the former Soviet Union, and elsewhere, these deep-seated animosities were held in check for years by authoritarian rule. The collapse of authoritarian rule, it is argued, has taken the "lid" off these ancient rivalries, allowing long-suppressed grievances to come to the surface and escalate into armed conflict. U.S. President George Bush, for example, maintained that the war in Bosnia between Serbs, Croats, and Muslims grew out of "age-old animosities."[2] His successor, Bill Clinton, argued that the end of the Cold War "lifted the lid from a cauldron of long-simmering hatreds. Now, the entire global terrain is bloody with such conflicts."[3] Writing about the Balkans, the American political commentator Richard Cohen declared that "Bosnia is a formidable, scary place of high mountains, brutish people, and tribal grievances rooted in history and myth born of boozy nights by the fire. It's the place where World War I began and where the wars of Europe persist, an ember of hate still glowing for reasons that defy reason itself."[4]

Serious scholars reject this explanation of internal conflict.[5] This simple but widely held view cannot explain why violent conflicts have broken out in some places, but not others, and it cannot explain why some disputes are more violent and harder to resolve than others. It is undeniably true that Serbs, Croats, and Bosnian Muslims have many historical grievances against each other, and that these grievances have played a role in the Balkan conflicts that have raged since 1991. But it is also true that other groups—Czechs and Slovaks, Ukrainians and Russians, French-speaking and English-speaking Canadians, the Flemish and the Walloons—have historical grievances of various kinds that have *not* led to violent conflict in the 1990s. This single-factor explanation, in short, cannot account for significant variation in the incidence and intensity of internal and ethnic conflict.

In this chapter, I will provide an overview of the scholarly literature on the causes of internal conflict, developing four main arguments along the way. First, the literature on internal conflict has focused on the underlying factors or permissive conditions that make some places and some situations more predisposed to violence than others. Four sets of factors have been singled out in this regard: structural factors; political factors; economic/social factors; and cultural/perceptual factors. Second, the scholarly literature is weak when it comes to analyzing the catalytic factors or *proximate* causes of internal conflicts. I contend that internal conflicts can be triggered in four different ways: by internal, mass-level factors (bad domestic problems); by external, mass-level factors (bad neighborhoods); by external, elite-level factors (bad neighbors); and by internal, elite-level factors (bad leaders). Third, the scholarly literature pays insufficient attention to the role played by domestic elites in transforming potentially violent situations into deadly confrontations. Many internal conflicts are triggered by the actions of domestic elites, and these actions therefore merit special attention. Here, too, we need to distinguish between different kinds of conflicts: ideological conflicts, criminal assaults on state sovereignty, and raw power struggles. Fourth and more generally, it is important to recognize that there are many different types of internal conflict, each caused by different things. The challenge for scholars is to identify these different types of conflicts and the different sets of factors that bring them about. The search for a single factor or set of factors that explains everything is comparable to the search for the Holy Grail—noble, but futile.

The first section of this chapter will analyze the scholarly literature on the underlying causes of internal conflict. The second section will examine the proximate causes of internal conflict and develop a framework for analyzing different sets of proximate causes. The third section will focus on the roles played by domestic elites in different types of internal conflicts. I conclude with some observations about the policy implications of this analysis, and with some thoughts on the implications of this analysis for the study of internal conflict.

THE UNDERLYING CAUSES OF INTERNAL CONFLICT

The scholarly literature on internal conflict has tended to focus on the underlying factors or permissive conditions that make some places and some situations more prone to violence than others. More specifically, scholars have identified four main clusters of factors that make some places more predisposed to violence: structural factors; political factors; economic/social factors; and cultural/perceptual factors. (See Table 10.1.)

Structural Factors

Three main structural factors have drawn scholarly attention: weak states, intrastate security concerns, and ethnic geography.

Weak state structures are the starting point for many analyses of internal conflict.[6] Some states are born weak. Many of the states that were carved out of colonial empires in Africa and Southeast Asia, for example, were artificial constructs. They lacked political legitimacy, politically sensible borders, and political institutions capable of exercising meaningful control over the territory placed under their nominal supervision. The same can be said

Table 10.1 / Underlying Causes of Internal Conflict

Structural Factors	Economic/Social Factors
Weak states	Economic problems
Intrastate security concerns	Discriminatory economic systems
Ethnic geography	Economic development and modernization
Political Factors	*Cultural/Perceptual Factors*
Discriminatory political institutions	Patterns of cultural discrimination
Exclusionary national ideologies	Problematic group histories
Intergroup politics	
Elite politics	

of many of the states created out of the rubble of the Soviet Union and Yugoslavia. The vast majority of these new entities came into existence with only the most rudimentary political institutions in place.

In many parts of the world, Africa perhaps most notably, states have become weaker over time. In some cases, external developments such as reductions in foreign aid from major powers and international financial institutions and drops in commodity prices played key roles in bringing about institutional decline. In others, states have been weakened by internal problems such as endemic corruption, administrative incompetence, and an inability to promote economic development. Many countries have suffered from several of these problems.

When state structures weaken, violent conflict often follows. Power struggles between and among politicians and would-be leaders intensify. Regional leaders become increasingly independent and, should they consolidate control over military assets, become virtual warlords. Ethnic groups which had been oppressed by the center are more able to assert themselves politically, perhaps in the form of developing more administrative autonomy or their own states. Ethnic groups which had been protected by the center or which had exercised power through the state find themselves more vulnerable. Criminal organizations become more powerful and pervasive, as we have seen in the Caucasus, Afghanistan, and elsewhere. Borders are controlled less effectively. Cross-border movements of militias, arms, drugs, smuggled goods, refugees, and migrants therefore increase. Massive humanitarian problems, such as famines and epidemics, can develop. Widespread human rights violations often take place. The state in question might ultimately fragment or simply cease to exist as a political entity.

When states are weak, individual groups within these states feel compelled to provide for their own defense; they have to worry about whether other groups pose security threats. This is the second structural factor that has drawn attention in the scholarly literature.[7] If the state in question is very weak or if it is expected to become weaker with time, the incentives for groups to make independent military preparations grow. The problem is that, in taking steps to defend themselves, groups often threaten the security of others. This can lead neighboring groups to take steps that will diminish the security of the first group: this is the internal "security dilemma." These problems are especially acute when empires or multiethnic states collapse and ethnic groups suddenly have to provide for their own security. One group's rush to deploy defensive forces will appear threatening to other groups. Moreover, the kinds of forces most commonly deployed—militia and infantry equipped with light arms—have inherent offensive capabilities even if they are mobilized for defensive purposes; this inevitably intensifies the security concerns of neighboring groups.

The third structural factor that has received attention is ethnic geography.[8] More specifically, states with ethnic minorities are more prone to conflict than others, and certain kinds of ethnic demographics are more problematic than others. Some states are ethnically homogeneous, and therefore face few problems on this score. However, of the more than 180 states in existence today, fewer than 20 are ethnically homogeneous in the sense that ethnic minorities account for less than 5 percent of the population.[9] Some of these states, such as Japan and Sweden, have had a uniform ethnic composition for some time. Others—contemporary Poland, Hungary, the Czech Republic—have few minorities today because of the population transfers and the genocide that took place during World War II, and the way borders were drawn after the war. One of the reasons why Poland, Hungary, and the Czech Republic are relatively stable today is their lack of contentious minorities. It is important to note, however, that ethnic homogeneity is no guarantee of internal harmony: Somalia is the most ethnically homogeneous state in sub-Saharan Africa, yet it has been riven by clan warfare and a competition for power between and among local warlords.

In some states with ethnic minorities, ethnic groups are intermingled; in others, minorities tend to live in separate provinces or regions of the country. Countries with different kinds of ethnic geography are likely to experience different kinds of internal problems.[10] Countries with highly intermingled populations are less likely to face secessionist demands because ethnic groups are not distributed in ways that lend themselves to partition. However, if secessionist demands develop in countries with intermingled populations, ethnic groups will seek to establish control over specific tracts of territory. Direct attacks on civilians, intense guerrilla warfare, ethnic cleansing, and genocide may result. Countries with groups distributed along regional lines are more likely to face secessionist demands, but warfare, if it develops, will generally be more conventional in character.

Most states, particularly those carved out of former empires, have complex ethnic demographics and face serious ethnic problems of one kind or another. In Africa, for example, arbitrary borders have divided some ethnic groups and left them in two or more countries. Most African countries contain large numbers of ethnic groups, some of which are historic enemies.[11] Many of the states of the former Soviet Union inherited borders that were deliberately designed to maximize ethnic complications and cripple the political effectiveness of local leaders with respect to what used to be the center.[12]

Political Factors

Four main political factors have attracted attention in the scholarly literature on internal conflict: discriminatory political institutions, exclusionary
national ideologies, intergroup politics, and elite politics.

First, many argue that the prospects for conflict in a country depend to a
significant degree on the type and fairness of its political system. Closed,
authoritarian systems are likely to generate considerable resentment over
time, especially if the interests of some ethnic groups are served while others
are trampled. Even in more democratic settings, resentment can build if
some groups are inadequately represented in government, the courts, the
military, the police, political parties, and other state and political institutions. The legitimacy of the system as a whole can, over time, fall into question. Internal conflict is especially likely if oppression and violence are
commonly employed by the state or if a political transition is under way.
The latter can take many forms, including democratization, which can be
destabilizing in the short run even if it promises stability in the long run.[13]

Second, it is said that much depends on the nature of the prevailing
national ideology in the country in question. In some places, nationalism
and citizenship are based on ethnic distinctions, rather than the idea that
everyone who lives in a country is entitled to the same rights and privileges.
Although the existence of civic conceptions of nationalism is no guarantee
of stability—civic nationalism prevails in Indonesia—conflict is more likely
when ethnic conceptions of nationalism predominate. Under what conditions are these two conceptions of nationalism likely to emerge? According
to Jack Snyder,

> Civic nationalism normally appears in well institutionalized democracies. Ethnic
> nationalism, in contrast, appears spontaneously when an institutional vacuum
> occurs. By its nature, nationalism based on equal and universal citizenship rights
> within a territory depends on a supporting framework of laws to guarantee those
> rights, as well as effective institutions to allow citizens to give voice to their
> views. Ethnic nationalism, in contrast, depends not on institutions, but on cul-
> ture. Therefore, ethnic nationalism is the default option: it predominates when
> institutions collapse, when existing institutions are not fulfilling people's basic
> needs, and when satisfactory alternative structures are not readily available.[14]

It is not surprising, therefore, that there are strong currents of ethnic nationalism in parts of the Balkans, East-Central Europe, and the former Soviet
Union, where state structures and political institutions have diminished
capacities, and in those parts of the developing world where state structures
and political institutions are weak.

It is important to keep in mind that exclusionary national ideologies do
not have to be based on ethnicity. Religious fundamentalists committed to
establishing theocratic states divide societies into two groups: those who
subscribe to a theologically derived political, economic, and social order;
and those who do not.

Third, many scholars argue that the prospects for violence in a country depend to a significant degree on the dynamics of domestic, intergroup politics.[15] The prospects for violence are great, it is said, if groups—whether they are based on political, ideological, religious, or ethnic affinities—have ambitious objectives, strong senses of identity, and confrontational strategies. Conflict is especially likely if objectives are incompatible, groups are strong and determined, action is feasible, success is possible, and if intergroup comparisons lead to competition, anxiety, and fears of being dominated. The emergence of new groups and changes in the intergroup balance of power can be particularly destabilizing.

Fourth, some scholars have emphasized elite politics and, more specifically, the tactics employed by desperate and opportunistic politicians in times of political and economic turmoil. According to this line of thinking, ethnic conflict is often provoked by elites in times of political and economic turmoil in order to fend off domestic challengers. Ethnic bashing and scapegoating are tools of the trade, and the mass media are employed in partisan and propagandistic ways that further aggravate interethnic tensions. The actions of Slobodan Milošević in Serbia and Franjo Tudjman in Croatia stand out as cases in point.[16]

Economic/Social Factors

Three broad economic and social factors have been identified as potential sources of internal conflict: economic problems, discriminatory economic systems, and the trials and tribulations of economic development and modernization.

First, most countries experience economic problems of one kind or another sooner or later, and these problems can contribute to intrastate tensions. In the industrialized world, problems can emerge even if a country's economy is growing—if it is not growing as fast as it once was, or fast enough to keep pace with societal demands. In Eastern Europe, the former Soviet Union, parts of Africa, and elsewhere, transitions from centrally planned to market-based economic systems have created a host of economic problems, ranging from historically high levels of unemployment to rampant inflation. Many countries in what we would like to think of as the developing world seem to be in a semipermanent state of economic shambles. Others are in an economic free fall. Unemployment, inflation, and resource competition, especially for land, contribute to societal frustrations and tensions, and can provide the breeding ground for conflict. Economic reforms do not always help and can contribute to the problem in the short term, especially if economic shocks are severe and state subsidies for staples, services, and social welfare are cut. In short, economic slowdowns, stagnation, deterioration, and collapse can be deeply destabilizing.[17]

Second, discriminatory economic systems, whether they discriminate on a class basis or an ethnic basis, can generate feelings of resentment and levels of frustration prone to the generation of violence.[18] Unequal economic opportunities, unequal access to resources such as land and capital, and vast differences in standards of living are all signs of economic systems that disadvantaged members of society will see as unfair and perhaps illegitimate. This has certainly been the case in Sri Lanka, for example, where Tamils have been discriminated against in recent decades by the Sinhalese majority. Economic development is not necessarily the solution. Indeed, it can aggravate the situation: economic growth always benefits some individuals, groups, and regions more than others, and those who are on top to begin with are likely to be in a better position to take advantage of new economic opportunities than the downtrodden. Even if a country's overall economic picture is improving, growing inequities and gaps can aggravate intrastate tensions.

Third, many scholars have pointed to economic development and modernization as taproots of instability and internal conflict.[19] The process of economic development, the advent of industrialization, and the introduction of new technologies, it is said, bring about a wide variety of profound social changes: migration and urbanization disrupt existing family and social systems and undermine traditional political institutions; better education, higher literacy rates, and improved access to growing mass media raise awareness of where different people stand in society. At a minimum, this places strains on existing social and political systems.[20] It also raises economic and political expectations, and can lead to mounting frustration when these expectations are not met. This can be particularly problematic in the political realm, because demands for political participation usually outpace the ability of the system to respond. According to Samuel Huntington, "The result is instability and disorder. The primary problem . . . is the lag in the development of political institutions behind social and economic change."[21]

Cultural/Perceptual Factors

Two cultural and perceptual factors have been identified in the scholarly literature as sources of internal conflict. The first is cultural discrimination against minorities. Problems include inequitable educational opportunities, legal and political constraints on the use and teaching of minority languages, and constraints on religious freedom. In extreme cases, draconian efforts to assimilate minority populations combined with programs to bring large numbers of other ethnic groups into minority areas constitute a form of cultural genocide. Aggressive forms of these policies were implemented by Josef Stalin in the Soviet Union in the 1930s and 1940s, particularly in the Caucasus. Similar policies have been pursued by China in Tibet since the 1950s. Somewhat less vicious forms of assimilationist policies have been pursued in Bulgaria with respect to ethnic Turks, in Slovakia with respect to ethnic Hungarians, and in Thailand with respect to members of northern and western hill tribes, for example.[22]

The second factor that falls under this broad heading has to do with group histories and group perceptions of themselves and others.[23] It is certainly true that many groups have legitimate grievances against others for crimes of one kind or another committed at some point in the distant or recent past. Some "ancient hatreds" have legitimate historical bases. However, it is also true that groups tend to whitewash and glorify their own histories, and they often demonize their neighbors, rivals, and adversaries. Explaining away the Hutu slaughter of eight hundred thousand to one million Tutsis in Rwanda in 1994, one Hutu who had been training for the priesthood insisted, "It wasn't genocide. It was self-defense."[24] Stories that are passed down from generation to generation by word of mouth become part of a group's lore. They often become distorted and exaggerated with time, and are treated as received wisdom by group members.

These ethnic mythologies are particularly problematic if rival groups have mirror images of each other, which is often the case. Serbs, for example, see themselves as heroic defenders of Europe and Croats as fascist, genocidal thugs. Croats see themselves as valiant victims of Serbian hegemonic aggression. When two groups in close proximity have mutually exclusive, incendiary perceptions of each other, the slightest provocation on either side confirms deeply held beliefs and provides the justification for a retaliatory response. Under conditions such as these, conflict is hard to avoid and even harder to limit once started.

THE PROXIMATE CAUSES OF INTERNAL CONFLICT

The existing literature on internal conflict does a commendable job of surveying the underlying factors or permissive conditions that make some situations particularly prone to violence, but it is weak when it comes to identifying the catalytic factors—the triggers or proximate causes—of internal conflicts. As James Rule put it in his review of the literature on civil violence, "We know a lot of things that are true about civil violence, but we do not know when they are going to be true."[25] The result is that we know a lot less about the causes of internal conflict than one would guess from looking at the size of the literature on the subject.

However, the existing literature gives us a running start at developing a framework for analyzing the proximate causes of internal conflict because it provides us with a well-rounded set of factors that predispose some places to violence. If we assume that each of these twelve underlying factors can play a more catalytic role if rapid changes take place in the area in question, then we also have a list of twelve possible proximate causes of internal conflict.

In brief, states are especially prone to violence if state structures are collapsing due to external developments (such as sharp reductions in international financial assistance, sharp declines in commodity prices), internal problems (new, incompetent leaders or rampant corruption), or some combination of the above. Under these circumstances, states are increasingly unable to cope with societal demands.[26] When state structures weaken or when new states are created out of the rubble of a larger entity, groups have a heightened sense of potential security problems. They are more likely to take measures to protect themselves which, in turn, are more likely to generate fears in other groups. In situations such as these, security dilemmas are especially intense and arms races are especially likely. Changing military balances—or fears about possible adverse developments—make arms racing and conflict escalation difficult to control.[27] Demographic changes brought about by birth rate differentials, migration, urbanization, or sudden influxes of refugees can aggravate ethnic problems and further complicate the picture by changing the domestic balance of power.

Political transitions brought about by the collapse of authoritarian rule, democratization, or political reforms also make states particularly prone to violence.[28] The emergence and rise of exclusionary national ideologies, such as ethnic nationalism and religious fundamentalism, can be destabilizing as well. The emergence of dehumanizing ideologies, which literally deny the humanity of other ethnic groups, is particularly dangerous because it is often the precursor to genocidal slaughter.[29] The rise of new groups or changes in the intergroup balance of power can intensify intergroup competition and anxieties, making political systems more volatile.[30] The emergence of power struggles between and among elites can be particularly problematic, because desperate and opportunistic politicians are particularly prone to employing divisive ethnic and nationalistic appeals.

Potentially catalytic economic and social problems include mounting economic problems, intensifying resource competitions, growing economic inequities and gaps, and fast-paced development and modernization processes.[31] Industrialized countries, countries attempting to make the transition from centrally planned to market-driven systems, and developing countries generally have to contend with different kinds of problems, but they are all susceptible to economically and socially induced turmoil.

Finally, states are especially prone to violence if discrimination against minorities intensifies, or if politicians begin to blame some ethnic groups for whatever political and economic problems their country may be experiencing. Ethnic bashing and scapegoating are often precursors to violence.

Creating lists of possible underlying and proximate causes of internal conflict is a useful starting point for analyzing these issues, but it does not take us far enough. For starters, this list of twelve possible proximate causes does not distinguish sharply between elite-level and mass-level factors. It is incomplete, moreover, because it does not take into account the catalytic role that neighboring states and developments in neighboring states can play in triggering violence.

I argue that internal conflicts can be categorized according to: (1) whether they are triggered by elite-level or mass-level factors,[32] and (2) whether they are triggered by internal or external developments. There are, therefore, four main types of internal conflicts, and they can be depicted in a

Table 10.2 / The Proximate Causes of Internal Conflict

	Internally-Driven	Externally-Driven
Elite-Triggered	Bad Leaders	Bad Neighbors
Mass-Triggered	Bad Domestic Problems	Bad Neighborhoods

two-by-two matrix. (See Table 10.2.) Put another way, internal conflicts can, in theory, be triggered by any one of four sets of proximate causes.

First, conflicts can be triggered by internal, mass-level phenomena, such as rapid economic development and modernization or patterns of political and economic discrimination. To put it more prosaically, they can be caused by "bad domestic problems." The conflicts in Punjab and Sri Lanka are examples, the former being galvanized by rapid modernization and migration and the latter by long-standing patterns of political, economic, and cultural discrimination.[33] Another example is the conflict over Nagorno-Karabakh, which was triggered by problematic ethnic geography and patterns of discrimination highlighted by the breakup of the Soviet Union.

The proximate causes of a second set of conflicts are mass-level but external in character: swarms of refugees or fighters crashing across borders, bringing turmoil and violence with them, or radicalized politics sweeping throughout regions. These are conflicts caused by the "contagion," "diffusion," and "spill-over" effects to which many policymakers, analysts, and scholars give much credence.[34] One could say that such conflicts are caused by "bad neighborhoods." The expulsion of radical Palestinians from Jordan in 1970 led many militants to resettle in Lebanon, where Muslim-Christian tensions were already mounting. This, one could argue, was the spark that ignited the civil war in Lebanon in 1975.

The proximate causes of a third set of conflicts are external but elite-level in character: they are the results of discrete, deliberate decisions by governments to trigger conflicts in nearby states for political, economic, or ideological purposes of their own. This only works, one must note, when the permissive conditions for conflict already exist in the target country; outsiders are generally unable to foment trouble in stable, just societies. Such conflicts, one could say, are caused by "bad neighbors." Examples include the Soviet Union's meddling in and subsequent 1979 invasion of Afghanistan, which has yet to emerge from chaos, and Russian meddling in Georgia and Moldova in the 1990s.[35] Another example is Rhodesia's establishment of RENAMO in 1976 to undermine the new government in Mozambique.[36]

The proximate causes of the fourth and final type of internal conflict are internal and elite-level in character. Variations include: power struggles involving civilian (Georgia) or military (Nigeria) leaders; ideological contests over how a country's political, economic, social, and religious affairs should be organized (Algeria, Peru); and criminal assaults on the state (Colombia). To put it in simple terms, conflicts such as these are triggered and driven by "bad leaders."

THE IMPORTANCE OF DOMESTIC ELITES

The scholarly literature on the causes of internal conflict is strong in its examination of structural, political, economic, social, and cultural forces that operate at a mass level—indeed, it clearly favors mass-level explanations of the causes of internal conflict—but it is weak in its understanding of the roles played by elites and leaders in instigating violence. The latter has received comparatively little attention. The result is "no-fault" history that leaves out the pernicious effects of influential individuals, which is an important set of factors in the overall equation.

Although mass-level factors are clearly important underlying conditions that make some places more predisposed to violence than others, and although neighboring states routinely meddle in the internal affairs of others, the decisions and actions of domestic elites often determine whether political disputes veer toward war or peace. Leaving elite decisions and actions out of the equation, as many social scientists do, is analytically misguided. It also has important policy implications: underappreciating the import of elite decisions and actions hinders conflict prevention efforts and fails to place blame where blame is due.

The proximate causes of many internal conflicts are the decisions and actions of domestic elites, but these conflicts are not all driven by the same domestic forces. There are three main variations: ideological struggles, which are driven by the ideological convictions of various individuals; criminal assaults on state sovereignty, which are driven primarily by the economic motivations of drug traffickers; and power struggles between and among competing elites, which are driven by personal, political motivations. Admittedly, these compartments are not watertight.[37] It is nonetheless important to make these distinctions, however rough they might be: there are several, distinct motivational forces at work here—several identifiable proximate causes of internal violence. It is important to have an appreciation of the multifaceted nature of the problem, particularly if one is interested in enhancing international efforts to prevent, manage, and resolve internal conflicts.

Ideological Conflicts

First, some internally driven, elite-triggered conflicts are ideological struggles over the organization of political, economic, and social affairs in a country. Some ideological struggles are defined in economic or class terms; others are fundamentalist religious crusades guided by theological frameworks. Ideological struggles over how political, economic, and social affairs should be organized have not gone away with the end of the Cold War, but they have tended to take on new forms. Class-based movements with Marxist agendas have faded from the scene in many parts of the world, including Southeast Asia, the Middle East, Africa, and Latin America, although some rebels in Colombia and Peru have remained largely true to form. Some rebel movements, have mutated and taken on the political agendas of indigenous peoples and ethnic minorities. In many places— Afghanistan, Algeria, Egypt, India, Iran, Sudan—conflicts have formed around new secularist-fundamentalist fault lines. These ethnic and fundamentalist movements draw on many of the same sources that impelled class-based movements in the Cold War era—patterns of political, economic, and cultural discrimination, and widespread dissatisfaction with the pace and equitability of economic development—but they are channeled in different directions. In other words, many of the underlying causes of these conflicts are the same, but their proximate causes have changed.

Criminal Assaults on State Sovereignty

Second, some internally driven, elite-triggered conflicts are in effect criminal assaults on state sovereignty. In several countries in Asia and Latin America, in particular, drug cartels have accumulated enough power to challenge state control over large tracts of territory. This is certainly true, for example, in Afghanistan, Brazil, Burma, Mexico, Tajikistan, and Venezuela. In Colombia, most notably, state sovereignty has been directly challenged by drug barons and their criminal organizations.[38] This problem shows no sign of abating. A related problem is that, with the end of the Cold War and reductions in financial support from Moscow and Washington, many ethnic groups and political movements turned to drug trafficking to finance their activities. This is true, for example, of various groups in Colombia and Peru.[39] In addition to its other pernicious effects, drug trafficking complicates the nature of the conflicts in question and therefore makes conflict management and resolution more difficult.

Power Struggles

Third, some conflicts are in essence power struggles between and among competing elites. Of the three types of internally driven, elite-triggered conflicts outlined here, raw power struggles are clearly the most common. Some are sustained government campaigns to repress ethnic minorities and democratic activists. This would seem to be a fair characterization of the conflicts in Burma, Cambodia, Guatemala, Indonesia, Iraq, and Turkey, for example. Government repression is a prominent feature of other conflicts as well, but power struggles are particularly intense and the "ethnic card" is played very aggressively. Examples abound: Angola, Bosnia, Burundi, Croatia, Kenya, Liberia, the Philippines, Russia/Chechnya, Rwanda, Somalia, and Tajikistan.

One type of power struggle is particularly prominent and particularly pernicious: it accounts for the slaughter in the former Yugoslavia and Rwanda, and has played a role in the conflicts in Azerbaijan, Burundi, Cameroon, Chechnya, Georgia, India, Kenya, Nigeria, Romania, Sri Lanka, Sudan, Togo, Zaire, and elsewhere.[40] The starting point is a lack of elite legitimacy, which sooner or later leads to elite vulnerability. Vulnerabilities can be brought about by weakening state structures, political transitions, pressures for political reform, and economic problems. Those who are in power are determined to fend off emerging political challengers and anxious to shift blame for whatever economic and political setbacks their countries may be experiencing. In cases where ideological justifications for staying in power have been overtaken by events, they need to devise new formulas for legitimizing their rule. Entrenched politicians and aspiring leaders alike have powerful incentives to play the "ethnic card," embracing ethnic identities and proclaiming themselves the champions of ethnic groups.[41]

This produces a shift in the terms of public discourse from civic nationalism to ethnic nationalism and to increasingly virulent forms of ethnic nationalism. Ethnic minorities are often singled out and blamed for the country's problems: ethnic scapegoating and ethnic bashing become the order of the day. When power struggles are fierce, politicians portray other ethnic groups in threatening terms, and inflate these threats to bolster group solidarity and their own political positions; perceived threats are extremely powerful unifying devices.[42] When leaders have control over the national media, these kinds of campaigns are particularly effective: a relentless drumbeat of ethnic propaganda can distort political discourse quickly and dramatically. Political campaigns such as these undermine stability and push countries towards violence by dividing and radicalizing groups along ethnic fault lines. In the former Yugoslavia, Serbian leader Slobodan Milošević and Croatian leader Franjo Tudjman rose to power by polarizing their societies even though Serbs and Croats had coexisted peacefully for decades.

Why Do Followers Follow?

It is easy to understand why desperate and opportunistic politicians in the midst of power struggles would resort to nationalist and ethnic appeals. For many politicians, tearing their countries apart and causing thousands of people to be killed are small prices to pay for staying in or getting power. The more interesting question is: why do followers follow?[43] Given that politicians all over the world employ ethnic appeals of one kind or another, why do these appeals resonate in some places but not others? Why do large numbers of people follow the ethnic flag in some places at some times, but not others?

Two factors are particularly important in this regard: the existence of antagonistic group histories and mounting economic problems. If groups have bad histories of each other and especially if they see themselves as victims of other, aggressive communities, ethnic bashing, and inflated threats seem plausible. If economic problems such as unemployment and inflation are mounting and resource competitions are intensifying, ethnic scapegoating is more likely to resonate and more people are likely to accept a radical change in a country's political course, including armed confrontation. In short, the emergence of elite competition might be the proximate cause of conflicts in places such as the former Yugoslavia and Rwanda, but hostilities escalate only because of the existence of other underlying problems or permissive conditions—problematic group histories and economic problems.

It appears that all three factors—intensifying elite competition, problematic group histories, and economic problems—must be present for this kind of conflict to explode. Russians and Ukrainians, for example, have had to contend with collapsing economies and standards of living, and many Ukrainians do not have benign historical images of Russians. However, Ukrainian politicians have by and large refrained from making the kinds of nationalistic appeals that have caused trouble elsewhere. They undoubtedly recognize that provoking a Russian-Ukrainian confrontation would not bode well for Ukraine or for their own positions as leaders of an independent state. Some Russian politicians have been far less responsible in this regard, but their nationalistic appeals have not yet taken over the Russian national debate. Whether or not nationalistic and pseudonationalistic politicians remain confined to the margins of the Russian political debate is certainly one of the keys to its future and to the stability of a large part of the world.

A few parts of the world have experienced economic turmoil and power struggles, but have been blessed with homogeneous populations and few internal ethnic problems. Finland, for example, has experienced a sharp economic decline since the late 1980s, but has not experienced interethnic strife because minorities are few and small and because intergroup relations are relatively harmonious. Similarly, Poland has gone through a complete political and economic transformation since 1989, but it has few minorities and few intergroup problems: nationalistic appeals have no audience. Poland's hotly contested 1990 presidential election was consequently fought along ideological lines.

Other parts of the world have deeply troubled ethnic histories and leaders who have not hesitated to do whatever was necessary to get and keep power, but they have been spared massive bloodlettings because of their comparatively rosy economic pictures. For example, Malaysia and Thailand experienced considerable turmoil during the Cold War but were quite stable in the early and mid-1990s because of the economic boom that swept through the region. Indonesia has had to contend with simmering conflicts in East Timor, Irian Jaya, and Aceh, but these conflicts have not escalated dramatically, nor has the country as a whole splintered into dozens of ethnic fragments as it might have.[44] Much of this can be traced to a track record of sustained economic growth, which gives groups, even relatively disadvantaged groups, incentives to avoid conflict and destruction of a system that is bringing more and more economic benefits to more and more people.

One can also point to East-Central Europe, which has experienced more than its share of turmoil in the past and which is not blessed with leaders steeped in the principles of Jeffersonian democracy, but which has nonetheless avoided the carnage that has consumed the former Yugoslavia a few hundred miles to the south. East-Central Europe has been comparatively peaceful, even though every country in the region has been going through a political transition of the most profound sort; elites have been jockeying for position ever since 1989. If one had to point to one reason for East-Central Europe's stability, one would point to its comparatively good economic performance and prospects. The fact that the states of this region have a good chance of joining the European Union at some point in the not-too-distant future gives people powerful incentives to ignore nationalistic appeals and not rock the boat. This point is driven home with even greater force when one looks at differences within the region: nationalistic appeals have been less successful in Hungary, which has an ethnic diaspora but one of the region's strongest economies and one of the region's best chances of joining the European Union quickly, than in Romania, which has struggled economically.

Economic developments have also marked important turning points in the Middle East and Africa. The Middle East experienced considerable domestic turmoil in the 1950s and 1960s, when weak states were unable to meet societal demands, but less instability in some places in the 1970s and 1980s, when high oil prices and high levels of foreign aid from the United States and the Soviet Union gave governments more largesse to spread around. Potential opposition forces were pacified and, in essence, bought off. The fact that oil prices and foreign assistance levels have declined sharply in the 1990s does not bode well for the region's future.[45]

Much of sub-Saharan Africa has experienced similar problems for similar reasons. Many governments in West, Central, and East Africa were able to hold their heads above water in the 1970s and 1980s, even though they were riddled with ethnic problems and run by corrupt, incompetent leaders, because they received substantial amounts of financial support from two external sources: the superpowers and Western Europe; and international financial institutions such as the International Monetary Fund (IMF) and the World Bank. In the late 1980s, however, two things happened: the Cold War ended, and international financial institutions changed their ways of thinking about how financial assistance would be handed out. Direct aid from Washington and Moscow dried up, and most aid from Western Europe was redirected to Central and Eastern Europe. In addition, international financial institutions threatened to withhold aid unless governments overhauled their corrupt political systems and ineffective economic systems. This placed many leaders in Africa between a rock and a hard place: if they overhauled their patronage systems they would lose the support of their domestic constituencies and subsequently lose power; if they told the IMF and the World Bank that they would not implement political and economic reforms, they would not get financial assistance from abroad, their governments and economies would collapse, and they would lose power anyway. Many leaders in West, Central, and East Africa failed to resolve this dilemma, and consequently threw their countries into turmoil in the late 1980s and early 1990s.[46] Nigeria, which had substantial oil reserves, suffered similar financial setbacks when oil prices dropped and its government mismanaged the country's oil income. Although parts of Africa, particularly southern Africa, have stabilized since the end of the Cold War, much of the continent has moved in the other direction.

This points to how precarious Russia's position is. Russia is a country with a deeply xenophobic world view; it is comprised of dozens of ethnic groups, many of whom have spent centuries despising each other; with the breakup of the Soviet Union, many Russians now live as minorities in other, contiguous states; and the Russian economy has been in a free fall since the mid-1980s. The fact that rabid nationalistic appeals have not yet taken over Russia's political debate is a minor miracle, attributable in large part to Boris Yeltsin's reluctance to go down this path and his willingness to use force to squelch his opposition. However, there are good reasons for fearing that more formidable nationalists will enter the picture—leaders not burdened with Vladimir Zhirinovsky's self-defeating tendencies. Given Russia's continuing economic crisis and its deeply troubled ethnic picture, the emergence of powerful nationalistic politicians could be the spark that ignites a highly combustible mixture. The key to defusing this situation—and a lever over which outside powers have at least some control—is turning Russia's economy around.

POLICY IMPLICATIONS

My discussion of the causes of internal conflict has three main policy implications. First, conflict prevention efforts should be guided by a two-track strategy. One track should be a series of long-term efforts aimed at the underlying conditions that make violent conflicts more likely. Particular attention should be paid to economic problems, distorted group histories, and patterns of political, economic, and cultural discrimination. A second track should focus on the proximate causes of internal conflict, the catalytic factors that turn potentially violent situations into deadly confrontations.

Second, conflict prevention efforts need to take into account the fact that internal conflicts can be triggered by any one of four sets of proximate causes: internal, mass-level forces; external, mass-level forces; external, elite-level forces; and internal, elite-level forces. Different kinds of conflict prevention efforts will be needed in each case. No single set of preventive actions will suffice.

Third, conflict prevention efforts should focus very aggressively on the decisions and actions of domestic elites, who are often responsible for sparking internal conflicts. Ambitious individuals will always aspire to power; the challenge is to keep power struggles from exploding into civil wars. Those interested in conflict prevention need to think systematically about ways of neutralizing the ethnic bashing, ethnic scapegoating, hate-mongering, and propagandizing that are often the precursors to violence.

One of the implications of this analysis is that distant powers and the international community in general are not as helpless as the conventional wisdom would have us believe. Internal conflicts are often triggered by the decisions and actions of domestic elites, not mass unrest or some uncontrollable form of domestic or regional mass hysteria. Bad leaders and bad behavior are discrete problems that can be identified and targeted for action. These decisions and acts are not necessarily immune to international pressure: they mark moments when distant international powers can try to use their leverage and influence the course of events.

IMPLICATIONS FOR THE STUDY OF INTERNAL CONFLICT

The main message of this chapter is that there are several distinct types of internal conflict. As a result, no single factor or set of factors can explain everything. The problem with "ancient hatreds" theorizing is not that historical grievances are irrelevant but that a single factor is said to be responsible for a wide range of developments. Replacing this single-factor explanation with another—based on economic problems, for example—would not solve this problem. The starting point for advancing our understanding of the causes of internal conflict is identifying different types of conflicts and the different sets of causal factors that are decisive in different settings.

It should go without saying that the framework outlined above does not constitute the final word on this tremendously complex subject. First, the distinctions between and among different kinds of underlying and proximate causes need to be sharpened if we are to refine our classification of conflicts according to their causes. Second, it is entirely possible that other types of conflicts driven by different combinations of factors will be identified as more work is done in this area. Finally, one of the keys to advancing knowledge in this area will be the production of detailed case studies carefully focused on the proximate causes of internal conflicts—more specifically, on the precise moments when political disputes become violent confrontations. Most case histories lack a sharp analytic focus, and the theoretical literature on this subject, as noted above, tends to focus on the permissive conditions of internal conflicts, not the proximate causes of violence. In short, much more work needs to be done.

QUESTIONS FOR FURTHER STUDY

1. What are the four main clusters of factors that scholars have identified as the underlying causes of internal conflict? Which of these clusters, in your opinion, is most significant? Why?
2. What does Michael Brown mean by the "proximate causes" of internal conflict? How does he divide up these causes?
3. Why does Brown emphasize the role of elites in triggering the outbreak of internal conflicts? What are the motivations or policies that

impel elites to engage in behavior that risks the outbreak of internal conflict? Why do the masses often support such behaviors?

4. How accurately does the analysis put forward by Brown accord with your understanding of the causes of the conflict in Bosnia? Of any other internal conflict with which you are familiar?

5. What, in Brown's view, are the policy implications of this analysis? What additional policy implications would you draw?

Notes

1. This chapter is based on Michael E. Brown, "Introduction" and "The Causes and Regional Dimensions of Internal Conflict," in Brown, ed., *The International Dimensions of Internal Conflict* (Cambridge: MIT Press, 1996), pp. 1–31, 571–601.

2. Bush is quoted in Jack Snyder, "Nationalism and the Crisis of the Post-Soviet State," in Michael E. Brown, ed., *Ethnic Conflict and International Security* (Princeton: Princeton University Press, 1993), pp. 79–101 at p. 79.

3. Clinton is quoted in Ann Devroy, "President Cautions Congress on 'Simplistic Ideas' in Foreign Policy," *Washington Post* (May 26, 1994).

4. Richard Cohen, "Send in the Troops," *Washington Post* (November 28, 1995).

5. See, for example, Snyder, "Nationalism and the Crisis of the Post-Soviet State"; Barry Posen, "The Security Dilemma and Ethnic Conflict," in Brown, *Ethnic Conflict and International Security*, pp. 103–124; Susanne Hoeber Rudolph and Lloyd I. Rudolph, "Modern Hate," *New Republic* (March 22, 1993), pp. 24–29.

6. See I. William Zartman, "Introduction: Posing the Problem of State Collapse," in Zartman, ed, *Collapsed States: The Disintegration and Restoration of Legitimate Authority* (Boulder: Lynne Rienner, 1995), pp. 1–11; Gerald B. Helman and Steven R. Ratner, "Saving Failed States," *Foreign Policy*, No. 89 (Winter 1992/93), pp. 3–20

7. See Posen, "The Security Dilemma and Ethnic Conflict." See also Milton J. Esman, *Ethnic Politics* (Ithaca, NY: Cornell University Press, 1994), pp. 244–245.

8. See Posen, "The Security Dilemma and Ethnic Conflict."

9. See David Welsh, "Domestic Politics and Ethnic Conflict," in Brown, *Ethnic Conflict and International Security*, pp. 43–60 at p. 45.

10. See Alicia Levine, "Political Accommodation and the Prevention of Secessionist Violence," in Brown, *International Dimensions of Internal Conflict*, Chapter 9.

11. See Stephen John Stedman, "Conflict and Conciliation in Sub-Saharan Africa," in Brown, *The International Dimensions of Internal Conflict*, Chapter 7.

12. See Matthew Evangelista, "Historical Legacies and the Politics of Intervention in the Former Soviet Union," in Brown, *The International Dimensions of Internal Conflict*, Chapter 3.

13. See, for example, Ted Robert Gurr and Barbara Harff, *Ethnic Conflict and World Politics* (Boulder: Westview Press, 1994), Chapter 5; Arend Lijphart, *Democracy in Plural Societies* (New Haven: Yale University Press, 1977); Edward D. Mansfield and Jack Snyder, "Democratization and the Danger of War," *International Security*, Vol. 20, No. 1 (Summer 1995), pp. 5–38.

14. Snyder, "Nationalism and the Crisis of the Post-Soviet State," p. 86. See also William Pfaff, "Revive Secular Citizenship Above 'Ethnic' Nationality," *International Herald Tribune* (July 20, 1993).

15. See Joseph Rothschild, *Ethnopolitics: A Conceptual Framework* (New York: Columbia University Press, 1981); Donald L. Horowitz, *Ethnic Groups in Conflict* (Berkeley: University of California Press, 1985); Charles Tilly, *From Mobilization to Revolution* (Reading MA: Addison-Wesley, 1978); Charles Tilly, "Does Modernization Breed Revolution?" *Comparative Politics*, Vol. 5, No. 3 (April 1973), pp. 425–447; Lewis Coser, *The Functions of Social Conflict* (Glencoe, IL: Free Press, 1956); Gurr and Harff, *Ethnic Conflict and World Politics*; Van Evera, "Hypotheses on Nationalism and War." For an overview, see Saul Newman, "Does Modernization Breed Ethnic Conflict?" *World Politics*, Vol. 43, No. 3 (April 1991), pp. 451–478; Jack A. Goldstone, "Theories of Revolution The Third Generation," *World Politics*, Vol. 32, No. 3 (April 1980), pp. 425–453.

16. See V. P. Gagnon, Jr., "Ethnic Nationalism and International Conflict: The Case of Serbia," in Michael Brown, ed., *Nationalism and Ethnic Conflict* (Cambridge: MIT Press, 1997);

Human Rights Watch, *Playing the "Communal Card": Communal Violence and Human Rights* (New York: Human Rights Watch, 1995); Warren Zimmermann, "The Last Ambassador: A Memoir of the Collapse of Yugoslavia," *Foreign Affairs*, Vol. 74, No. 2 (March/April 1995), pp. 2–20.

17. For a general discussion and several case studies, see S.W.R. de A. Samarasinghe and Reed Coughlan, eds., *Economic Dimensions of Ethnic Conflict* (London: Pinter, 1991). For a detailed discussion of the economic roots of the wars in the former Yugoslavia, see Susan L. Woodward, *Balkan Tragedy: Chaos and Dissolution After the Cold War* (Washington: The Brookings Institution, 1995), especially Chapter 3. For a discussion of the economic sources of turmoil in South Asia, see Sandy Gordon, "Resources and Instability in South Asia," *Survival*, Vol. 35, No. 2 (Summer 1993), pp. 66–87.

18. For an overview of Marx on this question, see James B. Rule, *Theories of Civil Violence* (Berkeley: University of California Press, 1988), Chapter 2; A. S. Cohan, *Theories of Revolution* (New York: Wiley, 1975), Chapters 4–5. For a discussion of how this applies to the developing world in particular, see Gordon, "Resources and Instability in South Asia."

19. See Samuel P. Huntington, *Political Order in Changing Societies* (New Haven: Yale University Press, 1968); Samuel P. Huntington, "Civil Violence and the Process of Development," in *Civil Violence and the International System*, Adelphi Paper No. 83 (London: International Institute for Strategic Studies, 1971), pp. 1–15; Ted Robert Gurr, *Why Men Rebel* (Princeton: Princeton University Press, 1970); Walker Conner, "Nation-Building or Nation-Destroying?" *World Politics*, Vol. 24, No. 3 (April 1972), pp. 319–355; Walker Conner, *Ethnonationalism: The Quest for Understanding* (Princeton, NJ: Princeton University Press, 1994). For an overview of this literature, see Newman, "Does Modernization Breed Ethnic Conflict?" For critiques of this approach, see Rod Aya, "Theories of Revolution Reconsidered: Contrasting Models of Collective Violence," *Theory and Society*, Vol. 8, No. 1 (July 1979), pp. 1–38; Tilly, "Does Modernization Breed Revolution?"

20. See Chalmers Johnson, *Revolutionary Change* (Boston: Little, Brown, 1966); Mark Hagopian, *The Phenomenon of Revolution* (New York: Dodd, Mead, 1974). For an overview, see Cohan, *Theories of Revolution*, Chapter 6; Goldstone, "Theories of Revolution," pp. 425–434.

21. Huntington, *Political Order in Changing Societies*, p. 5.

22. Many argue that formal, minority rights safeguards are the solution. See, for example, Jonathan Eyal, "Eastern Europe: What About the Minorities?" *World Today*, Vol. 45, No. 12 (December 1989), pp. 205–208; Wiktor Osiatynski, "Needed Now: Bills of Rights," *Time* (December 24, 1990); L. Michael Hager, "To Get More Peace, Try More Justice," *International Herald Tribune* (July 30,1992); Stephen S. Rosenfeld, "Serbs Are the Problem, Minority Rights the Solution." *International Herald Tribune* (September 26–27, 1992).

23. See Van Evera, "Hypotheses on Nationalism and War"; Posen, "The Security Dilemma and Ethnic Conflict," p. 107; Snyder, "Nationalism and the Crisis of the Post-Soviet State," pp. 92–93; Donald Rothchild and Alexander J. Groth, "Pathological Dimensions of Domestic and International Ethnicity," *Political Science Quarterly*, Vol. 110, No. 1 (Spring 1995), pp. 69–82.

24. This Hutu apologist is quoted in "You're Saying We Did It?" *Economist* (June 3, 1995), p. 38.

25. Rule, *Theories of Civil Violence*, p. 265.

26. See Zartman, "Introduction: Posing the Problem of State Collapse," pp. 1–11.

27. See Posen, "The Security Dilemma and Ethnic Conflict."

28. See Mansfield and Snyder, "Democratization and the Danger of War," pp. 5–38.

29. On ethnic nationalism, see Snyder, "Nationalism and the Crisis of the Post-Soviet State." On dehumanizing ideologies, see Helen Fein, "Explanations of Genocide," *Current Sociology*, Vol. 38, No. 1 (Spring 1990), pp. 32–50; Leo Kuper, *Genocide: Its Political Use in the Twentieth Century* (New Haven, CT: Yale University Press, 1981), Chapter 3.

30. See Rothschild, *Ethnopolitics*; Tilly, *From Mobilization to Revolution*; Horowitz, *Ethnic Groups in Conflict*; Gurr and Harff, *Ethnic Conflict and World Politics*; Van Evera, "Hypotheses on Nationalism and War."

31. See, for example, Gordon, "Resources and Instability in South Asia."

32. The utility of the distinction between elite-level and mass-level factors has been noted by others. See Renée de Nevers, *The Soviet Union and Eastern Europe: The End of an Era*, Adelphi Paper No. 249 (London: International Institute for Strategic Studies, 1990), pp. 27–29; Stuart J. Kaufman, "An 'International' Theory of Inter-Ethnic War," *Review of International Studies*, Vol. 22, No. 2 (April 1996), pp. 149–171.

33. See Sumit Ganguly, "Internal Conflict in South and Southwest Asia," in Brown, *The International Dimensions of Internal Conflict,"* Chapter 4.

34. See, for example, John A. Vasquez, "Factors Related to the Contagion and Diffusion of International Violence," in Manus I. Midlarsky, ed., *The Internationalization of Communal Strife* (London: Routledge, 1992), pp. 149–172; Ted Robert Gurr, *Minorities at Risk: A Global View of Ethnopolitical Conflicts* (Washington: U.S. Institute of Peace Press, 1993), pp. 132–135. For an excellent overview of this literature, see Stuart Hill and Donald Rothchild, "The Contagion of Political Conflict in Africa and the World," *Journal of Conflict Resolution,* Vol. 30, No. 4 (December 1986), pp. 716–735.

35. On Afghanistan, see Ganguly, "Internal Conflict in South and Southwest Asia." On Moldova and Georgia, see Evangelista, "Historical Legacies and the Politics of Intervention in the Former Soviet Union."

36. I thank Stephen Stedman for this observation.

37. Some conflicts have mutated over time and have more than one distinguishing characteristic. Most power struggles are characterized by those involved in politically convenient ethnic or ideological terms. Many of these conflicts have powerful ethnic dimensions. These problems make analysis difficult, but not impossible.

38. For a detailed discussion of drug-related problems in Latin America, see Marc Chernick, "Peacemaking and Violence in Latin America," in Brown, *The International Dimensions of Internal Conflict,* Chapter 8.

39. Ibid.

40. See Human Rights Watch, *Playing the "Communal Card."* See also Stedman, "Conflict and Conciliation in Sub-Saharan Africa."

41. See Human Rights Watch, *Playing the "Communal Card."*

42. See Esman, *Ethnic Politics,* p. 244.

43. See Horowitz, *Ethnic Groups in Conflict,* p. 140.

44. See Trevor Findlay "Turning the Corner in Southeast Asia," in Brown, *The International Dimensions of Internal Conflict,* Chapter 5.

45. See Rachel Bronson, "Cycles of Conflict in the Middle East and North Africa," in Brown, *The International Dimensions of Internal Conflict,* Chapter 6.

46. See Stedman, "Conflict and Conciliation in Sub-Saharan Africa."

11 / The Evolution of United Nations Peacekeeping and Peacemaking: Lessons from the Past and Challenges for the Future

MARGARET P. KARNS and KAREN A. MINGST

Iraq's invasion of Kuwait, the breakup of the former Yugoslavia, humanitarian disasters in Somalia and Rwanda, and the chance to rebuild peace in Cambodia have given high visibility to the United Nations' efforts to maintain international peace and security in the post-Cold War era. With extensive experience gained in more than twenty-five peace operations over fifty years, involving the participation of over a half million soldiers, UN peacekeeping continues to evolve with new responsibilities for election oversight, human rights monitoring, humanitarian assistance, and civil administration. The heightened demands for UN peacekeepers have, however, raised a number of important issues for the organization and its member states. These include questions over how and when the United Nations should use military force, whether the UN should intervene only in situations where it has the consent of all parties to a conflict, and the extent to which it can rely on member states for the financing and staffing of such operations. Recognizing the importance of peacekeeping for maintaining international peace and security, the UN Security Council has attempted to enhance its oversight of such activities and its definition of the conditions under which they will be undertaken.

But what is peacekeeping? How does it relate to collective security system embodied in the UN Charter? Where and how has it been used over the years? Why, with the Cold War's end, is it being used so extensively? What factors contribute to successful peacekeeping efforts? And, most significantly, how does peace*keeping*—a supposedly short-term response to crisis and conflict—relate to the larger task of international peace*making*? In this chapter, we examine how UN peacekeeping has evolved over three time periods: the Cold War era; the transition period of 1985–89; and the post-Cold War era of the 1990s. We then analyze the lessons learned from past peacekeeping operations and discuss the challenges to UN action in the future.

THE UN CHARTER AND THE MAINTENANCE OF INTERNATIONAL PEACE AND SECURITY

The founders of the United Nations recognized that the organization they established in 1945 was not likely to abolish war for all time. Nevertheless, they believed that it was "the best mechanism for maintaining international peace and security . . . [they] could devise for the moment."[1] Indeed, maintaining peace and security remains the most important function of the organization. But how the United Nations has undertaken this task has changed over time in ways never envisaged by its founders. In particular, the techniques of peacekeeping were not embodied in the UN Charter; rather, they were developed during the Cold War era when it proved impossible to implement the collective security components of the Charter due to the East-West conflict.

The UN Charter, in Article 2, obligates all members to settle disputes by peaceful means, to refrain from the threat or the use of force, and to cooperate with UN-sponsored peace actions. The Charter invests the Security Council with primary responsibility for the maintenance of international peace and security, and, in Chapter VII, gives it the authority to identify aggressors (Articles 39, 40), to decide what *enforcement* measures—including the use of force—should be taken to resist aggression and restore the peace (Articles 41, 42, 48, 49), and to call on member states to make military forces available to the UN for this purpose (Articles 43–45).

The UN has actually used the enforcement powers in Chapter VII on only six occasions, four of them since 1990. The six include: economic sanctions against Southern Rhodesia (now Zimbabwe) in 1966, an arms embargo against South Africa in 1977, economic sanctions and military action against Iraq in 1990 and 1991, an arms embargo against Yugoslavia in 1991, an air and arms embargo against Libya in 1992, and an arms embargo against Rwanda in 1994. For the most part, the Security Council has relied on the Charter's provisions for peaceful settlement of disputes to deal with the many conflicts placed on its agenda over the years; the Chapter VII provisions for states to earmark military forces for UN use and for the Military Staff Committee to manage UN forces have never been put into effect.

In addition to the Security Council's responsibility for maintaining international peace and security, the Charter also invests the secretary-general with the authority and the responsibility to bring to the Security Council's attention any and all matters that threaten international peace and security (Article 99). Frequently, the secretary-general may be called upon (or seek) to play a formal or informal role as an intermediary between the parties to a dispute. Article 7 also gives him/her broad responsibility for securing and upholding the principles and objectives of the organization. This, combined with Article 99, has been used as a legal basis by the six successive secretaries-general to assume an international political and diplomatic role.

In establishing a system of collective security, the authors of the Charter assumed that the great powers of the post-World War II period would cooperate in the maintenance of peace. Indeed, the effective functioning of the Security Council requires the concurrence of all five permanent members—the United States, the USSR/Russia, China, Britain, and France. The veto power given to these states assures that no collective measures could ever be instituted without their support.[2] Yet, with the outbreak of the Cold War, such concurrence was almost impossible to achieve. Only because the Soviet Union boycotted the Security Council in 1950 (in protest against the UN's refusal to seat the newly established communist government of the People's Republic of China) was it possible to gain initial UN backing for the U.S.-led force to counter the North Korean invasion of South Korea. Once the Soviet Union returned to its seat and exercised its veto, the UN had to devise other means to authorize the continuance of that force and to deal with the breakdown of consensus among the permanent members.

The Charter authorizes the UN General Assembly to discuss any matters within the Charter's purview, so long as the Security Council is not simultaneously dealing with an issue. To circumvent the deadlock produced by the Cold War, the General Assembly in 1950 adopted what was known as the "Uniting for Peace Resolution," a procedural innovation allowing for UN action when the Security Council was prevented from acting by a member's veto. This procedure has been used in a number of subsequent crises, including the Suez and Hungarian crises of 1956 and the Middle East crises of 1958 and 1967. In all, nine emergency special sessions of the General Assembly have been held to deal with threats to international peace when the Security Council was deadlocked.

The development of *peacekeeping*—or the use of UN forces to monitor cease-fires or to otherwise assist in the maintenance of peace—was a second creative response to the breakdown of great power unity and the intrusion of superpower competition into regional conflicts. The technique was first developed in an impromptu fashion to provide observer groups for the monitoring of cease-fire agreements in Kashmir and Palestine in the late 1940s. Later, during the Suez crisis of 1956, it was formally proposed by Lester B. Pearson, the Canadian Secretary of State for External Affairs, as a means for securing the withdrawal of British, French, and Israeli forces from Egypt. The development of peacekeeping and the innovative "Uniting for Peace Resolution" demonstrate that the United Nations has not been a static organization with respect to its role in promoting and maintaining international peace and security; on the contrary, it has developed new strategies and mechanisms for taking action when the measures contained in the Charter could not be invoked.

THE EVOLUTION OF PEACEKEEPING: A TYPOLOGY OF ACTIVITIES

Peacekeeping has taken a number of different forms in the varied circumstances in which it has been applied. Since there is no provision for peacekeeping in the Charter, a broad set of customs, principles, and practices have emerged over time through experience.[3] These principles were formally articulated in 1973 with the establishment of the second UN Emergency Force in the Middle East (UNEF II), and have provided basic guidelines for all subsequent operations. Thus, the UN refers to peacekeeping as "an operation involving military personnel, but without enforcement powers, undertaken by the United Nations to help maintain or restore international peace and security in areas of conflict."[4]

Sir Brian Urquhart, the former UN Undersecretary-General for Political Affairs (and widely regarded as the "father of peacekeeping") summarizes the particular requirements for UN peacekeeping as follows:

- The consent of the parties involved in the conflict to the establishment of the operation, to its mandate, to its composition, and to its appointed commanding officer;
- the continuing and strong support of the operation by the mandating authority, the Security Council;
- a clear and practicable mandate;
- the nonuse of force except as a last resort in self-defense—self-defense, however, including resistance to attempts by forceful means to prevent the peacekeepers from discharging their duties;
- the willingness of troop-contributing countries to provide adequate numbers of capable military personnel and to accept the degree of risk which the mandate and the situation demand;
- the willingness of the member states, and especially the permanent members of the Security Council, to make available the necessary financial and logistical support.[5]

The advantages of peacekeeping operations of this type over collective security measures as envisioned in Chapter VII of the UN Charter are numerous. Because peacekeeping traditionally has required the approval of all parties to the conflict, there was at least a nominal consent to cooperate with the UN forces. In contrast to Chapter VII enforcement action, moreover, no aggressor need be identified and singled out for blame. Also, because most of these operations entail small numbers of observers, the commitment of troops by members in most cases has been relatively modest—a distinct advantage, since the troops involved are volunteered by member nations. Only in the Congo operation of 1960 to 1964 and since 1989 has the UN required large military units for peacekeeping operations.

During the Cold War, peacekeeping units were drawn almost exclusively from the armed forces of nonpermanent members of the Security Council—often from small, neutral, and nonaligned members—in order to keep the superpowers out of regional conflicts or, in the case of postcolonial problems, to keep former colonial powers from returning. Countries which have contributed contingents to a number of operations include Canada, India, Sweden, Norway, Fiji, Ghana, Brazil, Argentina, Bangladesh, Senegal, Togo, and Nepal.[6] Since the end of the Cold War, and especially with the undertaking of much larger operations, major powers have also contributed forces for UN peacekeeping.

The precise form of peacekeeping has varied over time, however, and become increasingly diverse in recent years. This is because operations are tailored to the distinctive requirements of particular crises and conflicts. As Thomas Weiss and Jarat Chopra of Brown University observe, "A typology of peacekeeping is thus largely determined by a typology of conflict."[7] In general, peacekeeping activities can be grouped into five categories: observation, separation of forces, the maintenance of law and order, the use of limited force, and humanitarian intervention. A sixth category, peace enforcement (as defined by Chapter VII), is often included but technically falls beyond the scope of peacekeeping.[8]

Observation

This entails a variety of activities, usually involving small numbers of troops and observers for such purposes as: the supervision of a truce or cease-fire (as, for example, with the 1948 UN Truce Supervision Organization in the Middle East and the UN Iran-Iraq Military Observer Group of 1988); the verification of troop withdrawals (for example, the UN Good Offices Mission in Afghanistan that oversaw the withdrawal of Soviet troops); the monitoring of elections (as occurred in Namibia, Nicaragua, and Haiti); the verification of arms control and disarmament agreements (for example, the Esquipulas II agreement in Central America); and the monitoring of human rights conditions (as with the UN Observer Mission in El Salvador). Observation activities are diverse and the least controversial form of peacekeeping.

Separation of Forces

This requires the interpositioning of lightly armed, neutral referees in a buffer zone between conflicting parties that have agreed to a cease-fire and the mutual disengagement of their forces. It has been most extensively used in the Middle East, notably with the UN Emergency Force (UNEF II) between Israel and Egypt in the 1970s, the UN Disengagement Observer Force (UNDOF) between Israel and Syria from 1973 to the present, and the UN Interim Force in Southern Lebanon (UNIFIL) from 1978 to the present.

Maintenance of Law and Order

This involves actions taken to help establish and maintain domestic law and order in conflict-ridden countries. In the UN Congo Operation (ONUC) of the 1960s, peacekeepers were used to restore order in a civil war situation. More recently, the UN operation in Cambodia (UNTAC) undertook the complex task of rebuilding the country's entire civil administration (including the police) as well as engaging in truce observation, election supervision, and the resettlement of refugees.

Limited Use of Force

On occasion, UN peacekeepers are authorized to use limited force to restore the peace and protect the delivery of humanitarian aid. Such a decision is inevitably fraught with political and legal controversy because of the difficulties of determining how much is limited force, when force is really used defensively, and whether the use of even limited force will cost the UN its diplomatic role as an impartial party to a conflict. Following the Congo operation of 1960 to 1964, when the Security Council authorized ONUC to use force to prevent the dissolution of the country and to remove foreign mercenaries, the UN adopted the general principle that UN peacekeepers use military force only as a last resort and in self-defense. Since the end of the Cold War, however, the UN has become involved in a series of intrastate conflicts and humanitarian operations that have called for the use of force and whose size and scope have raised serious questions about the nature of peacekeeping. These questions remain unresolved today.

Humanitarian Intervention

This new category of UN peacekeeping operations arose from a belief that civilians caught in an area of conflict have an enforceable right to basic necessities of food, medical supplies, and a secure environment. UN peacekeepers have taken action to open vital supply lines, guard food distribution centers, secure law and order in areas of turmoil, and protect those at risk from attack or persecution by providing safe havens. The most notable examples occurred in Somalia, Bosnia, Rwanda, and the Kurdish-occupied portions of Iraq, prompted in part by media attention and public pressure on government leaders and the UN to "do something" about human suffering.

Enforcement Action

This encompasses any steps, including arms embargoes, economic sanctions, blockades, and military action taken in accordance with Chapter VII of the UN Charter to ensure compliance with Security Council directives.[9] Although technically beyond the scope of peacekeeping, enforcement may arise out of more traditional peacekeeping operations, as occurred in Somalia and Bosnia. Enforcement, by definition, eschews the neutrality of traditional peacekeeping and involves UN forces in proactive behaviors intended to produce a particular outcome to a dispute. With the end of the Cold War, there has been a strong temptation to use UN forces in this way to impose solutions to difficult conflicts, especially those intrastate conflicts in which there is no established government able to restore peace and stability on its own. Yet, as we shall see, the UN's experience in Bosnia demonstrates the equally strong reluctance of those states that contribute peacekeeping forces to have their troops involved in military enforcement operations that carry a high risk of casualties.

Many of the tasks that UN peacekeepers have been called to undertake were never specified in the UN Charter, nor were they envisaged by the organization's founders; rather, they are innovations that have enabled the UN to play a useful role in maintaining international peace and security. We turn now to examine the evolution of peacekeeping over three distinct periods: the Cold War era, the transition period of 1985–89, and the post-Cold War era. (See Table 11.1, pages 224–226, for a complete listing of all UN peacekeeping operations, showing their location, size, and duration.)

THE COLD WAR ERA

During the Cold War, UN peacekeeping forces were used most extensively in the Middle East and in conflicts arising out of the decolonization process in Africa and Asia when the interests of the United States and the Soviet Union were not directly at stake. The Suez crisis of 1956 (provoked by the British, French, and Israeli attack on Egypt in response to its nationalization of the Suez Canal and threat to close it to Israeli shipping) marked the first major example of their use. The General Assembly, under the Uniting for Peace Resolution, created the UN Emergency Force (UNEF I) to help defuse the crisis. UN peacekeepers separated the combatants, supervised the withdrawal of British, French, and Israeli forces, and thereafter patrolled the Sinai Peninsula and Gaza Strip.[10] This force was withdrawn just before the Six-Day War of 1967, at Egypt's request.

In 1973, following the Yom Kippur War, UNEF II was established to monitor the Israeli-Egyptian cease-fire and to facilitate the disengagement of forces by supervising a buffer zone between the combatants. A separate force, the UN Disengagement Observer Force (UNDOF), was formed to supervise the disengagement of Israeli and Syrian forces on the Golan Heights. Yet another force, the UN Interim Force in Lebanon (UNIFIL), was established in 1978 to monitor the withdrawal of Israeli forces from southern Lebanon and to assist the government of Lebanon in reestablishing its authority in the area. UNEF II was terminated in 1979 following adoption of the Camp David Accords, whose provisions for disengagement of Israeli and Egyptian forces in the Sinai have been monitored by a non-UN Multinational Force that includes one U.S. battalion; both UNDOF and UNIFIL remain in place despite UNIFIL's inability to prevent repeated Israeli raids and the vulnerability of UN peacekeepers to attack and kidnapping by the various warring groups in southern Lebanon.

UN peacekeeping forces were also deployed in the former Belgian Congo (later Zaire) following its independence in 1960 and the subsequent outbreak of civil violence. The UN Operation in the Congo (ONUC) was originally designed to help the newly independent state establish civil order and to ensure the withdrawal of the Belgian troops that had returned to the

Congo when violence broke out. When the mineral-rich province of Katanga seceded, ONUC's mission was expanded to restore the territorial integrity of the Congo and to avert full-scale civil war. This cost the UN its impartiality among the Congolese and other African states, as well as the support of the Soviet Union; the controversial operation also pushed the UN to the brink of bankruptcy because of disputes over payments from member states for the large force, and it was terminated in 1964.[11]

Another peacekeeping operation, the UN Force in Cyprus (UNFICYP), was established in 1964 to provide a buffer zone between hostile Greek and Turkish populations on the island of Cyprus that were supported respectively by Greece and Turkey. UNFICYP remained in place even during the Turkish invasion of 1974 and continues to patrol a buffer zone between the two communities today. However, the presence of UN peacekeepers and a variety of diplomatic initiatives have failed to produce a long-term settlement of the Cyprus conflict.

Evaluating the relative success of peacekeeping operations during the Cold War period is not an easy task.[12] In several cases, armed hostilities were halted, but permanent resolution of the various disputes proved elusive. UNEF I averted war between the Arabs and Israelis for eleven years, and UNEF II was one of many factors that facilitated the negotiation of the Israeli-Egyptian peace agreement at Camp David. UNDOF can take credit, at least in part, for the tranquillity of the Golan Heights since 1974. ONUC succeeded in preventing the secession of Katanga province and helped restore a modicum of order in the Congo. UNFICYP has averted overt hostilities between the Greek and Turkish communities on Cyprus, but could not prevent the 1974 invasion by Turkish forces nor lay the groundwork for a permanent settlement. Thus, the record of UN peacekeeping during the Cold War is a mixed one: for those whose definition of success entails the peaceful settlement of conflicts, only UNEF II would be deemed fully successful; if success is defined in terms of ending armed hostilities and preventing their renewal, at least for a period of time, then all of the operations except UNIFIL could be deemed successful.

Cold War exigencies meant that the superpowers had to agree before any action was taken, and this meant that many important issues of peace and security, including the Vietnam conflict, never made it to the UN agenda. Nevertheless, the innovation of peacekeeping provided a valuable means for limiting superpower intervention in regional conflicts (with their consent, and in situations where they chose to remain uninvolved) and for coping with threats to peace and stability posed by the emergence of new states and the continuing conflicts in the Middle East. As suggested by Thomas Weiss and Kurt Campbell, the United Nations had to "tiptoe around the Cold War" in order to play a significant role.[13] In doing so, however, it developed a body of practice and experience in peacekeeping that was to prove even more valuable in the transition period of the late 1980s and in the post-Cold War era that followed.

THE TRANSITION PERIOD: 1985–1989

The most striking feature of UN efforts to deal with threats to international peace and security in the late 1980s was the cooperation that developed among the five permanent members of the Security Council. Never before in the UN's forty years of existence had there been such consensus. With the acquiescence of the nonpermanent members of the Council, and enhanced collaboration between the Security Council and the secretary-general, UN peacekeepers chalked up a series of successes in long-standing regional conflicts that led to their being awarded the Nobel Prize for Peace in 1988.

The single most important factor contributing to this set of developments was the dramatic change in Soviet foreign policy initiated by then President Mikhail Gorbachev. In 1987, Gorbachev published an article lauding the valuable role of UN military observers and peacekeeping forces in promoting international peace and security. This reversed the Soviet Union's long-standing skepticism toward UN peacekeeping and was a major factor in moderating the Reagan Administration's own antagonism toward the UN. Also important in changing Soviet and U.S. perceptions of the UN's role was the quiet and increasingly effective diplomacy of then UN Secretary-General Javier Pérez de Cuéllar. This combination of factors facilitated UN efforts to end the Soviet presence in Afghanistan, the war between Iran and Iraq, the long stalemate over Namibia, and the conflict in Central America. Successes in each of these regional conflicts spurred subsequent interest in the possibilities of UN peacekeeping.

Afghanistan

In 1988, nine years after Soviet troops invaded Afghanistan, the persistent efforts by UN mediator Diego Cordovez to engineer a Soviet withdrawal paid off. With counterinsurgency operations against Afghan *mujahedeen* proving increasingly futile and costly, and under pressure to devote more resources to domestic economic needs, Gorbachev agreed to withdraw all Soviet troops from Afghanistan. Fifty UN observers under the UN Good Offices Mission in Afghanistan and Pakistan (UNGOMAP) monitored and verified the withdrawal of over one hundred thousand Soviet troops. It is important to note, however, that although UN peacekeepers helped to secure the withdrawal of Soviet forces from Afghanistan, this did not end the fighting between the various Afghan factions.

The Iran-Iraq War of 1980–1988

In August 1988, with the passage of Security Council Resolution 598, Iran and Iraq agreed to a UN-supervised cease-fire in their eight-year-old conflict—a war that had produced immense damage and killed or wounded over one million people. The resolution was the product of an extended effort by Secretary-General Pérez de Cuéllar to solicit agreement among the permanent members of the Security Council and to secure cooperation from Iran and Iraq to stop the fighting and negotiate their differences. In accordance with Resolution 598, the UN Iran-Iraq Military Observer Group (UNIIMOG) monitored compliance with the cease-fire, investigated violations, and supervised the withdrawal of military forces to internationally recognized boundaries; it completed its task in February 1991.

Angola and Namibia

August 1988 also saw the agreement between Cuba and South Africa allowing for the independence of Namibia. A former German colony administered by South Africa since the end of World War I, Namibia had been the subject of considerable international attention since the 1950s. In the late 1970s, five major Western powers acting outside of (but in close cooperation with) the UN succeeded in persuading South Africa and the main Namibian liberation group, SWAPO, along with the so-called Front Line states in southern Africa, to establish the terms for Namibian independence. These were spelled out in Security Council Resolution 435 of September 1978. The five powers were unsuccessful, however, in getting South Africa to implement the agreement.[14]

In resisting implementation of Resolution 485, South Africa argued that the Soviet-backed Cuban troops that were aiding the Angolan government in its conflict with South African-backed UNITA guerrillas represented a direct threat to its security, and stated that it would not withdraw from Namibia so long as the Cubans were present in the region—a position subsequently endorsed by the Reagan Administration. Efforts to untangle the complex links between the Namibian and Angolan conflicts finally came to fruition in 1988, when Cuba and Angola agreed to the withdrawal of Cuban troops as part of a regional peace settlement. By December, an agreement for implementation of Resolution 435 was in place and the UN moved to initiate a major peacekeeping operation in Namibia and a smaller one in Angola.

The UN Transition Assistance Group in Namibia (UNTAG), deployed in April 1989, was the most ambitious UN undertaking up to that time. Its mandate entailed a diverse set of tasks, including: supervision of the cease-fire between South African and SWAPO forces, monitoring the withdrawal of South African forces from Namibia and the confinement of SWAPO forces to a series of bases, supervising the civil police force, securing the repeal of discriminatory and restrictive legislation, arranging for the release of political prisoners and the return of exiles, and creating conditions for and conducting free and fair elections. With military and civilian personnel provided by 109 countries, UNTAG played a vital role in managing the process by which Namibia moved step-by-step from war to a cease-fire and then to full independence.

Central America

The final peacekeeping operations of the transition period took place in Central America, where they played a key part in the regional peace process. In November 1989, the UN Observer Group in Central America (ONUCA) deployed over one thousand military observers to verify the implementation of the Esquipulas II regional peace agreement. Its mission was to ensure the cessation of outside military aid to the insurrectionist forces, prevent the use of the territory of one state for attacks on any others, and oversee the disarmament and demobilization of combatant forces. Although ONUCA's work covered the territory of five Central American states, most of the peacekeepers were concentrated in Nicaragua and Honduras. ONUCA was complemented by ONUVEN, the civilian UN Observer Mission charged with aiding the electoral process in Nicaragua from August 1989 to February 1990, and by ONUSAL, an observer mission in El Salvador that was given the unprecedented role of monitoring and verifying human rights violations and making recommendations for their future elimination.

The transition period of the late 1980s was marked by the change in the two superpowers' attitudes toward the United Nations and by several innovations in the conduct of UN peacekeeping operations, including verification of troop withdrawals by a superpower, the conduct of elections, and monitoring of human rights violations. These developments made it possible to end a series of long-standing regional conflicts and contribute to peacemaking in a number of war-torn countries. The Nobel Peace Prize for 1988 was awarded to UN peacekeeping forces in recognition of their "decisive contribution toward the initiation of actual peace negotiations."

THE POST-COLD WAR ERA

The fall of the Berlin Wall in November 1989 signaled the advent of a new era in world politics. The post-Cold War era has not, however, been a more peaceful one: regional and ethnic conflicts have, in fact, proliferated. At the same time, the successful experience with UN peacekeeping during the transition period of 1985–89 and the UN's active role in responding to Iraq's invasion of Kuwait increased world leaders' enthusiasm for employing UN peacekeepers in still more tasks in the emerging post-Cold War era. Indeed, many observers believed that the new international climate provided the UN with opportunities for developing and testing new approaches to international peace and security. Between 1989 and 1993, thirteen new peacekeeping operations were launched by the United Nations, equaling the total number of such operations initiated during the previous forty years. Nevertheless, the road to increased prominence has not been an easy one. As we shall see, several of these new operations encountered major difficulties and this, in turn, has generated serious questions about the nature of the UN's future peacekeeping role.

The first challenge to the post-Cold War order came with Iraq's invasion and annexation of Kuwait in August 1990. The Iraqi action triggered a period of unprecedented activity by the UN Security Council as members sought ways to respond effectively to this act of aggression against a UN member state. Unity among the five permanent members of the Security Council, including the Soviet Union (despite its long-standing relationship with Iraq), facilitated the passage of twelve successive resolutions over a four-month period, activating provisions of Chapter VII of the UN Charter. These included, most importantly, Resolution 678 of November 29, 1990, authorizing UN member states "to use all necessary means" to reverse the occupation of Kuwait.

The military operation launched under the umbrella of Resolution 678 was not a peacekeeping operation in the traditional sense, nor did it qualify as a collective security action as defined by Article 42 of the Charter (although it has been portrayed as such). The U.S.-led multinational coalition more closely resembled "a type of 'sub-contract' . . . [by member states] acting on behalf of the organization."[15] At no point in the Kuwait operation was the United States responsible to the authority of the UN through regular reporting to the Secretary-General or through the participation of senior UN personnel in military decision making; nor were UN flags and symbols displayed by coalition forces. Only after the fighting had ceased in late February 1991 was a traditional UN peacekeeping unit, the unarmed UNIKOM force, organized to monitor the demilitarized zone established between Iraq and Kuwait.

Though the U.S.-led military action in the Gulf was widely regarded as exemplifying a new, stronger, post-Cold War United Nations, that action came under critical scrutiny.[16] Because it was conducted under American rather than UN command, most UN members had no say in the operation. Even such key members as Germany and Japan, both of which were expected to contribute monetary resources for Operation Desert Storm, were excluded from important decision-making meetings—a fact that has fueled their interest in permanent membership on the Security Council. Many developing countries, even while endorsing the action, were also troubled by the autonomous nature of the U.S.-led operation. Thus, the Gulf War highlighted an important problem of the post-Cold War era: "The ambivalence of many states toward a stronger UN is now coupled with apprehension about a *pax Americana*, even a UN-centered one, without a Soviet counterweight."[17]

Although significant in the challenge it posed to the world community, the Gulf War was uncharacteristic of other conflicts the UN has dealt with in the post-Cold War era in that it entailed a conflict *between* states rather than *within* them.[18] In the five years following the Gulf War's conclusion, the United Nations launched seventeen new peacekeeping operations, all involving instances of internal conflicts arising from breakdown of central governmental authority, secessionist movements, ethnic clashes, and civil wars of the types seen in Angola, El Salvador, Cambodia, Rwanda, Yugoslavia,

Somalia, Haiti, Liberia, Georgia, and elsewhere. These conflicts have confronted the UN with complex and demanding challenges, requiring further innovations in peacekeeping and peace*building* (that is, the reconstruction of war-torn societies). And, while successful in some instances, these operations have also encountered significant difficulties.

For many observers, the renewed popularity of UN peacekeeping faced its most severe tests in four post-Cold War undertakings: those in Cambodia, Somalia, Rwanda, and Yugoslavia/Bosnia. Each entailed a major commitment of UN resources and each, in its own way, raised significant questions about the future utility of UN peacekeeping.

Cambodia

In October 1991, the Agreements on a Comprehensive Political Settlement of the Cambodia Conflict were signed in Paris with strong UN support. Cooperation between the United States and the Soviet Union provided the impetus for China and Vietnam to support a cease-fire among the rival forces of the Vietnamese-backed Han Sen government, the Khmer Rouge, and former Prince Norodim Sihanouk, along with the demobilization of armies, the repatriation of refugees, and the organization of elections. The agreements also invested the UN with extraordinary and unprecedented responsibility for managing the two-year reconstruction process ending the twenty-year war in Cambodia. As noted by Michael Doyle, "The international community charged the UN—for the first time in its history—with the political and economic restructuring of a member state as part of the building of peace under which the parties were to institutionalize their reconciliation."[19]

The UN's role in implementing the Cambodian settlement began with a small advance mission (UNAMIC) whose mandate was to facilitate communication among the four Cambodian parties in order to implement the cease-fire. This was followed in March 1992 by the deployment of the UN Transition Authority in Cambodia (UNTAC), which incorporated military, police, and civilian personnel. The military component of UNTAC was charged with supervising the cease-fire and disarming and demobilizing the combatants; the civilian component assumed full responsibility for administering the country during the eighteen-month transition period. This included direct control over Cambodia's foreign affairs, defense, finance, public security, and administrative structures to ensure a neutral political environment prior to elections. UN personnel also trained and monitored the local police, promoted respect for human rights, assisted in the return of Cambodian refugees from camps in Thailand, organized the 1993 elections that returned civil authority to the Cambodians, and rehabilitated basic infrastructure and public utilities. Up to 22,000 military and civilian personnel were assigned to UNTAC at its peak, leading Secretary-General Boutros Boutros-Ghali to observe that "nothing the UN has ever done can match this operation."[20]

In some respects, the Cambodia operation can be considered a major success. UNTAC's presence helped put an end to full-scale civil war and brought peace to most of the country. The political system was opened up to opposition parties, 370,000 refugees were repatriated and helped to be resettled, and free and fair elections were organized and conducted under international supervision.[21] At the same time, however, UNTAC was unsuccessful in two key areas of its mandate: it was unable to achieve a complete cease-fire and to effect the demobilization of forces (with the Khmer Rouge, in particular, retaining a significant military capability); and it was unable to complete some aspects of its civil mission, including monitoring civil police and creating stable political institutions. Cambodia thus illustrates the difficulty of carrying out all aspects of a peacekeeping mission when the parties have not fully reconciled themselves to peacefully settling their conflict.

Somalia

In 1991 and 1992, civil order in Somalia totally collapsed as warring clans seized control of various parts of the country. Widespread famine and chaos accompanied the fighting, driving hundreds of thousands of people to the brink of starvation. Control of food was a vital political resource for the Somali warlords and a currency to pay the mercenary gangs who formed their militias. The international community was slow to react because the UN Security Council assumed that it needed the consent of the Somali warlords to provide humanitarian assistance, as in traditional peacekeeping operations. A small (five hundred-soldier) contingent of lightly-armed Pakistani troops (the UN Operation in Somalia, or UNISOM I) was finally deployed in August 1992 with a mandate to protect relief workers, but proved totally inadequate for the task at hand.

In November 1992, with as many as one thousand Somalis dying every day and three-fourths of Somalia's children under the age of five already dead, the Secretary-General informed the Security Council that the situation "had deteriorated beyond the point at which it is susceptible to the peacekeeping treatment" and asserted that the Council had "no alternative but to decide to adopt more forceful measures."[22] On December 3, 1992, under Resolution 794, the Security Council authorized a large, U.S.-led military and humanitarian intervention—the Unified Task Force (UNITAF), known to American audiences as Operation Restore Hope—to secure Somalia's ports and airfields, protect relief shipments and workers, and assist humanitarian aid efforts. The Secretary-General also wanted UNITAF to impose a cease-fire and disarm the factions, but U.S. leaders (in both the outgoing Bush and the incoming Clinton Administrations) were reluctant to enlarge the mission's objectives in this fashion, preferring to commit U.S. forces only to limited humanitarian tasks. This disagreement over objectives produced considerable friction between the White House and the UN leadership in New York, and complicated relations between the various UN contingents on the ground in Somalia.

Despite these problems, UNITAF was largely successful in achieving its humanitarian objectives, supplying food to those in need and imposing a de facto cease-fire in the areas of its deployment. Yet the larger tasks of peace-making remained unfulfilled. This led to recurring problems in 1993, as UNITAF was replaced by UNOSOM II—a larger and more heavily-armed force than a traditional peacekeeping contingent but smaller than UNITAF and lacking much of the heavy equipment and airpower the U.S. had brought to Somalia. UNOSOM II, with 20,000 troops and 8,000 logistical personnel from thirty-three countries, included 5,000 U.S. soldiers (as compared to 26,000 in UNITAF). It was authorized to use force when disarming the factions, but that exposed the peacekeepers to increased risk as some of the militias—especially those led by General Mohamed Farah Aidid—resisted such efforts. When twenty-three Pakistani soldiers were killed by Aidid's soldiers in June 1993, UNOSOM II gave up any pretense of impartiality and targeted General Aidid for elimination. As one observer noted, this converted the UN's role from neutral peacekeeper to active belligerent, putting UNOSOM "in the worst of all possible worlds, which past peacekeepers had scrupulously avoided."[23]

Four months later, in October 1993, eighteen American soldiers were killed by Aidid's soldiers, leading to a public outcry in the United States that echoed unease in other countries over the UN's role in Somalia. Nowhere else was the reaction as abrupt and far-reaching, however, and little note was taken of the hundreds of Somali dead. President Clinton announced that the U.S. contingent in UNOSOM II would be strengthened temporarily, but that all U.S. forces would be withdrawn by March 1994. Peacekeeping operations in Haiti and Bosnia were also affected as the Clinton Administration rethought its commitment to UN peacekeeping, especially those operations that entailed risk of casualties. Within days, in fact, the United States halted the landing of American troops and advisers in Haiti where they were to participate in the UN-aided transition to a democratic government—all because demonstrators in Port-au-Prince threatened to create "another Somalia."

UNISOM remains a controversial and uncertain undertaking.[24] It began at the height of the post-Cold War enthusiasm for UN peacekeeping and later precipitated a significant retreat from such activities. Because the United States wanted to keep the operation short, and was afraid to risk the lives of American soldiers, the Somali warlords gained leverage by targeting U.S. and other UN forces. After the U.S. withdrew its troops in March 1994, it became only a matter of time before all UN forces were withdrawn. UN operations in Somalia finally ceased in March 1995, having succeeded in ending the famine but not in helping the Somalis to reestablish a national government or to end their internal strife.[25]

Rwanda

The UN was still engaged in Somalia when humanitarian disaster on a massive scale erupted in yet another small African country, Rwanda. In April

1994, following the death of Rwandan President Juvenal Habyarimana (a Hutu) in a mysterious plane crash (which also killed the president of neighboring Burundi), Hutu extremists in the Rwandan military and police began slaughtering the minority Tutsi along with moderate Hutus. In a ten-week period, over 750,000 Tutsis were killed, out of a total Rwandan population of 7 million. When Tutsi rebels of the Rwandan Patriotic Front (RPF) seized the capital of Kigali, approximately 2 million Hutus fled their homes in the largest and most rapid human migration of the twentieth century. With media reports of the growing Rwandan tragedy, public outcry in the United States and Europe as well as in Africa put enormous pressure on government leaders and the UN itself to "do something." Yet the UN's painful experience in Somalia produced a pattern of evasion, paralysis, and finally halfhearted action—spearheaded, on this occasion, by France.[26]

The roots of the conflict between the Hutu and Tutsi go back to colonial times when first German and then Belgian rulers favored the minority Tutsi over the majority Hutu. Periodic outbreaks of devastating ethnic violence have occurred in both Rwanda and Burundi (which shares the same ethnic makeup) since each became independent in the early 1960s. In Rwanda, intermittent fighting had broken out in 1990 between the Hutu-dominated government and the RPF, based in neighboring Uganda. An August 1993 peace agreement called for a UN force to monitor the cease-fire and to investigate allegations of noncompliance. In response, the UN Security Council established the UN Assistance Mission in Rwanda (UNAMIR) in October 1993.

The Rwandans (both Hutu and Tutsi) never had much confidence in UNAMIR's impartiality, however, and growing violence in the country made it impossible to undertake its mandated tasks. In April 1994, despite early reports of ethnic violence, the Security Council voted to reduce the strength of UNAMIR from 2,539 to 270. Four weeks later, responding to public pressure for action, the Council voted to deploy 5,500 troops to protect civilians and the delivery of humanitarian aid. Few countries were willing to volunteer the use of their troops, however, and the human tragedy mounted.

Ten weeks after the massacres began, with the RPF having gained control of much of the country and some 2 million Hutus fleeing their advance, the UN finally responded—but only because France (which had established close ties with the former Rwandan government) proposed to send its own troops to provide safe havens for the fleeing Hutu refugees. As it had done in Somalia with the U.S.-led Unified Task Force, the UN Security Council invoked Chapter VII to authorize member states to set up a temporary multinational operation in Rwanda and to pave the way for a reconstituted UNAMIR. Only then, under an onslaught of media coverage, did the United States itself finally send in charter flights of personnel, supplies, and equipment to aid the Rwandan refugees.

UNAMIR belatedly established a humanitarian protection zone in southeast Rwanda in an attempt to ensure the safety of threatened civilians. As UN peacekeepers had done in Somalia, it provided security for relief supply depots and escorts for aid convoys; its personnel also performed a variety of reconstruction tasks, including the rebuilding of roads, bridges, power supplies, and other infrastructure destroyed by the civil war. The Rwandan mission ended in April 1996—not because peace had been restored or humanitarian needs fulfilled, but because the new (Tutsi-led) government requested the departure of UN troops.

Rwanda is linked in many people's minds with Somalia, the two symbolizing the post-Cold War problems of ethnic or factional conflict *within* states and of humanitarian disaster. Yet, their origins were fundamentally different. Somalia was and is a "failed state" with several factions seeking control, none strong enough to prevail over the others. Rwanda's massacres, on the other hand, were clearly the product of a planned campaign of genocide by Hutu extremists, the evidence of which led the Security Council to establish the Rwandan International War Crimes Tribunal in 1995. In both situations, however, earlier action by the international community could almost certainly have reduced the scale of humanitarian disaster.

Both Somalia and Rwanda are also examples of what Secretary-General Boutros-Ghali called "third generation peacekeeping"—military operations to protect the delivery of humanitarian assistance, enforce cease-fires, and assist in reconstruction. Both were launched without the full consent of all parties to the conflicts and, therefore, without a peace to be kept. The UN's failures in Somalia, combined with members' reluctance to risk the lives of their soldiers in combat for other than a vital national interest, dampened the early post-Cold War enthusiasm for peacekeeping. The 1994 change in U.S. policy toward UN peacekeeping was also an important factor shaping the UN's delayed and lukewarm response to the crisis in Rwanda. All of these factors affected the UN's efforts to deal with conflict in the former Yugoslavia, and especially in Bosnia.

Former Yugoslavia and Bosnia

The former Yugoslavia played a unique role in the Cold War competition between East and West and was a country where fault lines of ethnic, religious, and political differences were buried for half a century. The collapse of the Yugoslav Communist Party in 1990 led to the unraveling of Yugoslavia and unleashed ethnic conflicts, the ferocity of which shocked those who imagined that Europe was immune from such horrors. The issues raised by the unraveling of Yugoslavia are central to the nature of the international system in the post-Cold War era, touching questions of self-determination, individual and group rights, and the use of force to serve humanitarian ends. For more than five years, the Security Council devoted a record number of meetings to debate over whether to intervene in Yugoslavia, to what end, and with what means. UN peacekeepers, when finally sent to the region, encountered massive and systematic violations of human rights, intense pressures for more vigorous military action such as bombing, and very little interest by the parties involved in making peace.[27] Yugoslavia thus came to represent a microcosm of problems: with peacekeeping,

Chapter VII enforcement actions, efforts to address human rights abuses, and members' failure to live up to their financial obligations.[28]

The conflict in Yugoslavia was largely brought about by the efforts of Serbian leader Slobodan Milošević to maintain the country's unity in the face of strong separatist movements in Slovenia, Croatia, and Bosnia-Herzegovina. Slovenia and Croatia declared their independence in June 1991, followed by Bosnia-Herzegovina and Macedonia in 1992. The population of Slovenia was fairly homogeneous, and so independence proceeded relatively calmly there; but Croatia and Bosnia-Herzegovina were not: there were large numbers of ethnic Serbs in both, and they were determined not to be a part of either of these new states. Bosnia was even more heterogeneous, with Muslims, Croats, and Serbs intermingled in both rural and urban areas. While nationalistic leaders fueled ancient suspicions and hostilities through manipulation of the media and a selective reading of history, each group's military and paramilitary forces attempted to enlarge their territorial holdings and to create ethnically "pure" entities. The result was a bloody civil war that killed over two hundred thousand people, produced millions of refugees, and subjected others to concentration camps, rape, and torture.

During 1991, the United Nations largely deferred to European efforts to negotiate cease-fires among the warring ethnic groups. This was consistent with Chapter VII of the Charter, which stipulates that regional organizations should make every effort to resolve local disputes before referring them to the Security Council. The Europeans could not agree on what their role should be, on whether sanctions should be applied, on how much force (if any) should be employed, and on whether to grant diplomatic recognition to the newly declared states. Although the European Union continued its efforts to contain the conflict, the many cease-fires that were negotiated rapidly broke down as the fighting escalated.

On September 25, 1991, the UN Security Council appointed former U.S. Secretary of State Cyrus Vance as the Secretary-General's special envoy to Yugoslavia. Vance's chief accomplishment was to secure an agreement from all of the Yugoslav parties on the establishment of a UN peacekeeping operation. Accordingly, the Security Council authorized formation of the UN Protection Force for Yugoslavia (UNPROFOR) in February 1992. UNPRO-FOR was initially deployed in three "Protected Areas" of Croatia, where 14,000 UN military and civilian personnel were expected to maintain a cease-fire, disband the various armed forces (both regular and irregular), ensure protection of basic human rights, and assist humanitarian agencies in returning refugees to their homes.

Meanwhile, fighting broke out in Bosnia-Herzegovina. The Bosnian Serbs, aided militarily by the rump Yugoslavia (composed of Serbia and Montenegro), attacked Muslim villages, shelled the city of Sarajevo (closing its airport), and drove hundreds of thousands of people from their homes. This was accompanied, in many cases, by widespread reports of massacres and atrocities. In June 1992, with pressure building for international intervention, the Security Council authorized the dispatch of peacekeepers to

Sarajevo to reopen the airport and to support humanitarian relief efforts being coordinated by the UN High Commissioner for Refugees (UNHCR). UNPROFOR's mandate did not, however, authorize UN forces to stop the "ethnic cleansing" then being carried out by Bosnian Serb forces in the Muslim-populated areas they had occupied.

With the situation in Bosnia becoming increasingly desperate, the Security Council invoked Chapter VII of the Charter, calling on member states to "take all necessary measures" to facilitate the delivery of humanitarian aid (Resolution 770). It also authorized the creation of UN "safe areas" in six Bosnian cities. Later, Chapter VII was also invoked to authorize enforcement of a "no fly zone" over Bosnia, to secure the withdrawal of heavy weapons from urban centers, to impose economic sanctions on Serbia and Montenegro, and to authorize air strikes against Bosnian Serb forces engaged in attacks on UN-protected "safe areas." However, because UNPROFOR was authorized to use force on a limited basis only, implementation of these measures required the support of individual member countries, especially the United States and its European allies. Acting under NATO auspices, U.S. and European forces were deployed to the region to monitor compliance with economic sanctions, to implement the "no fly zone" over Bosnia, and, eventually, to conduct air strikes against Bosnian Serb positions. Thus began the first experiment in cooperation between UN peacekeepers and a regional military alliance.

Despite NATO air strikes, a tightening of economic sanctions against Serbia, and continued efforts to secure a cease-fire, the war continued in Bosnia. All sides interfered with relief efforts and targeted UNPROFOR and international aid personnel. The UN "safe areas" were anything but safe for the civilians who had taken refuge in them. Peacekeepers and aid workers were taken hostage. Under constant pressure for further action, the Security Council met almost continuously and passed resolution after resolution, progressively enlarging UNPROFOR's mandate and even establishing the International Tribunal for Crimes in the Former Yugoslavia. But resolutions did not produce the greater military, logistical, and financial resources needed to fulfill the enlarged mandate. In other words, the UN membership lacked the political will for a full-scale enforcement action against the Bosnian Serbs and their Serbian backers—they were unwilling to risk the casualties that such enforcement would almost inevitably entail, in a situation where their national interests did not seem directly at stake and the outcome could not be assured.[29]

UNPROFOR began as a classic peacekeeping operation to help implement a cease-fire agreement between Croatian and Serb forces in Croatia. In Bosnia, it was given a humanitarian mandate that began with the consent of the parties and under conditions where the UN was perceived as impartial. However, the atrocities of ethnic cleansing carried out by the Bosnian Serbs led the Security Council to adopt a series of measures that were clearly directed against them, thereby costing UNPROFOR its impartiality. And while the UN Security Council authorized the use of force to help deliver humanitarian relief and protect civilians in the safe areas, it did not provide UNPROFOR with sufficient strength to carry out that mandate. The situation was further complicated by the involvement of NATO—a military alliance that did not regard itself as impartial and was reluctant to take its lead from UN headquarters.

The UN's peacekeeping role in Bosnia and Croatia ended with the U.S.-brokered Dayton Peace Accord of November 1995.[30] In Bosnia and Croatia, UNPROFOR was replaced by a NATO-sponsored Implementation Force (IFOR) of sixty thousand troops, including twenty thousand Americans along with units from almost twenty non-NATO countries, including Russia. IFOR, at least in theory, was freer to use force to prevent a renewal of the fighting. This marked NATO's first effort to do what UN peacekeepers had done so often in the past: separate forces, supervise withdrawals, interpose themselves between parties, and provide a safe environment in which peace might take root.

THE PAST AND FUTURE OF UN PEACEKEEPING

By early 1996, the United Nations had ended all four of its major post-Cold War peacekeeping operations; those that continued after that date have been much smaller in size and scope. Within the UN, member governments, and the academic and policy communities, an extensive reexamination of peacekeeping was underway in an effort to distill the lessons—both positive and negative—of the UN's experiences in Cambodia, Somalia, Rwanda, the former Yugoslavia, and elsewhere. Much of this reassessment is evident in the *Supplement to the Agenda for Peace,* Boutros-Ghali's 1995 follow-up to the far more optimistic *The Agenda for Peace* of July 1992.

The UN's experience with peacekeeping has highlighted a number of issues that represent key questions for the future. These can be grouped into four basic categories: *consent of the parties* as a prerequisite for UN action; peacekeepers' *operational mandate* and the use of force; *political support* of the Security Council and of member states, including the United States; and the *organizational capacity* of the United Nations itself.

Consent of the Parties

"For traditionalists," Weiss and Chopra observe, "no requirement of peacekeeping is clearer than the consent of parties in conflict . . . it is a political and operational imperative."[31] But opinions are changing on both the political and legal necessity of securing the consent of the parties. The plight of Iraq's imperiled Kurdish minority, of Sarajevo's besieged citizens, of Somalia's starving millions, and of Rwanda's countless victims, lent fresh authority to humanitarian intervention *without* consent of the parties.[32] On one occasion after another, the UN bowed to international pressure on this question and authorized intervention despite a lack of consent by one or more of the parties involved.

Clearly, strict adherence to a requirement for parties' consent will prove increasingly problematic if the UN is to play any role in trying to manage or resolve conflicts involving ethnic militias, collapsed states, and large-scale humanitarian disasters. Yet a failure to obtain the consent of all parties, especially of various armed factions, may eventually undermine the UN's involvement even if there is initial success as in Cambodia. For many formerly colonized nations, moreover, the requirement for consent is considered essential if the UN is to retain its neutral status and resist becoming a tool of the great powers and especially of the United States. Thus, the issue of consent is likely to remain a major problem for the UN in the years to come.

Operational Mandate and the Use of Force

The operational mandates for peacekeeping operations constitute the "authorizations for lawful action"[33] that UN-appointed commanders must translate into practicable orders for the various military and civilian contingents under their authority. Traditionally, peacekeeping troops have been authorized to use force only in self-defense. This is realistic in situations like Cyprus where both sides are committed to respecting the cease-fire. But when future peacekeepers are told to disarm local militias, to ensure the delivery of humanitarian relief in war-torn areas, and to protect civilians in the face of armed resistance, they will need clear mandates as to the use of force in carrying out their responsibilities. In particular, they will require precise "rules of engagement" covering when, and under what circumstances, they can employ deadly force in the pursuit of their objectives. More than this, they will require sufficient military strength plus the political support of member states to carry out their tasks under circumstances of adversity.

When UN peacekeepers use force, especially in situations of civil conflict, they risk jeopardizing the UN's impartial position—as was especially clear in Somalia and Bosnia. The line between peacekeeping and enforcement action can be a very fine one. Impartiality is essential when the UN is endeavoring to preserve an agreed-upon peace settlement. But a failure to employ force when the lives of thousands of civilians are at stake, as in Srebrinica and other UN-declared "safe havens" in Bosnia, can also cost the UN its credibility and moral authority.

Member States' Support

Obtaining the necessary financial and logistical support from member states for UN peacekeeping operations has long been a problem. Observer missions are generally funded from the UN's regular budget, whereas full-scale peacekeeping operations have been funded through special peacekeeping assessments. But member states, both large and small, are frequently in arrears. And, as more peacekeeping operations have been mounted, the financial strains on the organization have increased. In 1987, the cost of UN peacekeeping was $233 million; by 1991, it had risen to $421 million, and, by 1994, had jumped to $3.8 billion.[34] In 1996, total arrearages to the UN amounted to $2.3 billion, of which the United States alone owed almost $1.5 billion.

The recruitment of forces for peacekeeping operations has also become a significant problem for the UN. Historically, peacekeeping contingents have been drawn from middle and smaller powers, especially nonaligned and neutral countries; as peacekeeping demands have increased, military units have been drawn from many more countries, including the major powers. Yet participation by the major powers entails certain risks, either because there is a history of past involvement (for example, the United States in Haiti and France in Rwanda) or because the national interests of the major power and the larger interests of the international community may not coincide.[35] Thus, the practice of "subcontracting" the task of organizing a multinational peacekeeping or peace enforcement force, as occurred in Somalia, Rwanda, and Haiti, raises a number of difficult issues; in particular, the leading power is not likely to place its troops under the command of a UN officer, which thus compromises the UN's control over the force's actions.

This issue has particular significance for the United States, since it is the only country that has the political, economic, and military might to lead an effective multinational intervention in large-scale conflicts. Historically, the United States was supportive of traditional UN peacekeeping operations, lending logistical support and equipment to most operations. In the early post-Cold War era, moreover, Washington was strongly supportive of an expanded UN role in international peacekeeping—that is, until the October 1993 debacle in Somalia. Since then, U.S. leaders have been notably reluctant to commit American troops—and, by implication, to risk American lives—to UN peacekeeping operations.

In 1994, the Clinton Administration adopted a constrictive view of the circumstances under which the United States would support such activities. Presidential Decision Directive No. 25 (PDD-25) of May 1994 specifies six preconditions for U.S. participation: (1) general or specific U.S. national interests are advanced by participation, (2) U.S. forces are available without unacceptable impact on U.S. military readiness, (3) U.S. participation is necessary for the success of the mission and to persuade others to join, (4) the command and control relationship is acceptable, (5) the end point of U.S. participation is clearly defined, (6) there is domestic (including Congressional) support for the operation. Clearly, these stringent conditions can be invoked at any time to preclude U.S. involvement in UN operations.

In addition, the U.S. failure to fulfill its financial obligations to the United Nations clearly signals a problem in U.S. support for the organization, particularly from Congress. In 1985, Congress unilaterally reduced U.S. contributions to the UN to below the assessed amounts; since then, U.S.

arrearages have continued to mount with successive reduced appropriations for both the regular UN dues and peacekeeping expenses.[36] Because the United States provides such a large share of the UN's operating funds (25 percent of the regular budget), its failure in this regard has serious consequences for the organization's ability to function. Thus, by setting harsh conditions for participation in future peacekeeping operations and continuing to be in financial arrears, the United States has sowed doubt about the political and financial support that the world's only superpower will contribute to future conflicts.

The Organizational Capacity of the UN

The UN's managerial capacity, especially with respect to peacekeeping operations, has been an increasingly contentious issue as such operations have become larger and more expensive and as the responsibilities they have undertaken have become more complex. No organization could have handled the sudden increase in demand for new peacekeeping operations faced by the UN in the early 1990s without experiencing major strains, nor could it expect success in all that it undertook. As problems emerged, the UN Secretariat took a number of initiatives to provide better coordination of the various facets of complex peacekeeping operations. It has strengthened coordination between the secretary-general and the Security Council, and improved the ability of the secretary-general's office to respond more quickly and flexibly to threats to international peace. Still, much more remains to be done in this regard.

CHALLENGES FOR THE FUTURE

The UN's wealth of experience with over fifty years of peacekeeping has yielded many significant lessons for responding to diverse threats to international peace and security. Meeting these challenges effectively will require further improvement in the UN's organizational capacity for preventive diplomacy, which might avert the need for peacekeeping or enforcement, as well as in its capacity for supporting peacekeeping and peacebuilding operations. It also means addressing the difficult questions of when and how the UN should intervene, when and how UN peacekeepers should use force, when and if operations should be mounted without the consent of the parties involved, and when the UN's members should say no to requests for peacekeepers.

The world has changed in many significant ways since the UN's founding in 1945. Peacekeeping was itself a response to the unforeseen development of the Cold War, which prevented the UN from functioning as it was designed. And, as we have seen, UN peacekeeping has evolved from what are now called "traditional" peace observer missions to complex "third generation" operations involving humanitarian relief, election and human rights monitoring, and reconstruction of war-torn states. With Bosnia and other operations in Africa and Latin America, the UN has begun to collaborate with regional organizations such as NATO, the Organization of American States (OAS), and Organization of African Unity (OAU) in peacekeeping and enforcement activities.

In December 1996, the United Nations elected Kofi Annan as its seventh secretary-general, a man who has spent his career within the UN secretariat focusing on questions of management and served most recently as undersecretary-general for peacekeeping operations. In his December 1996 opening address to the General Assembly, Secretary-General Annan declared, "A new understanding of peace and security must emerge," based on an understanding that conflict has many roots and that "intolerance, injustice, and oppression—and their consequences—respect no national frontiers." He emphasized his own commitment to engaging with member states in a dialogue about the optimal uses of peacekeeping, preventive diplomacy, and postconflict peacebuilding, as well as his commitment to encouraging member states "to develop the sustained will to support the Organization."[37] Still, significant challenges lie ahead for the UN's efforts to build on its long experience with peacekeeping, while working within realistic parameters of what its members and the organization itself can manage.

QUESTIONS FOR FURTHER STUDY

1. How did the technique of "peacekeeping" arise? What are its basic principles?
2. How did UN peacekeeping evolve during the "transition period" of 1985–89? How would you assess the effectiveness of peacekeeping during this period?
3. How did the end of the Cold War affect the evolution of peacekeeping? Is this new era likely to see an increased or diminished need for peacekeeping operations?
4. The United Nations undertook a series of complex and costly peacekeeping operations at the start of the post-Cold War era, including those in Cambodia, Somalia, and Bosnia. To what extent did these operations succeed or fail? What lessons can be derived from these experiences?
5. Do you think that the UN should continue to undertake peacekeeping operations of the sort it has conducted in the past? Should the character of these operations be changed, and if so, how?
6. What policies should the United States adopt toward UN peacekeeping operations? Should U.S. troops participate in such operations? Why, or why not?

Table 11.1 / A Guide to Peacekeeping Operations Listed

Operation	Title	Location	Duration	Maximum Strength
UNTSO	UN Truce Supervision Organization	Egypt, Israel, Jordan, Syria, Lebanon	Jun. 1948–present	572 Military Observers
UNMOGIP	UN Military Observer Group in India and Pakistan	India, Pakistan	Jan. 1949–present	102 Military Observers
UNEF I	First UN Emergency Force	Suez Canal, Sinai Peninsula	Nov. 1956–Jun. 1967	3,378 Troops
ONUC	UN Operation in the Congo	Congo	Jun. 1960–Jun. 1964	19,828 Troops
UNFICYP	UN Peacekeeping Force in Cyprus	Cyprus	Mar. 1964–present	6,411 Military Observers
UNEF II	Second UN Emergency Force	Suez Canal, Sinai Peninsula	Oct. 1973–Jul. 1979	6,973 Troops
UNDOF	UN Disengagement Observer Force	Syrian Golan Heights	Jun. 1974–present	1,450 Military Observers
UNIFIL	UN Interim Force in Lebanon	Southern Lebanon	Mar. 1978–present	7,000 Military Observers
UNGOMAP	UN Good Offices Mission in Afghanistan and Pakistan	Afghanistan, Pakistan	May 1988–Mar. 1990	50 Military Observers
UNIMOG	UN Iran-Iraq Military Observer Group	Iran, Iraq	Aug. 1988–Feb. 1991	399 Military Observers
UNAVEM I	First UN Angola Verification Mission	Angola	Jan. 1989–Jun. 1991	70 Military Observers
UNTAG	UN Transition Assistance Group	Namibia, Angola	Apr. 1989–Mar. 1990	4,493 Troops, 1,500 Civilian Police, and 2,000 Civilian Election Observers
UNOVEN	UN Observer Mission to Verify the Electoral Process in Nicaragua	Nicaragua	Aug. 1989–Feb. 1990	Civilian Election Observers
ONUCA	UN Observer Group in Central America	Costa Rica, El Salvador, Guatemala, Honduras, Nicaragua	Nov. 1989–Jul. 1992	1,098 Military Observers
UNIKOM	UN Iraq-Kuwait Observer Mission	Iraq-Kuwait	Apr. 1991–present	1,440 Military Observers and Troops

Operation	Title	Location	Duration	Maximum Strength
UNAVEM II	Second UN Angola Verification Mission	Angola	Jun. 1991–Feb. 1995	350 Military Observers 90 Police Observers
ONUSAL	UN Observer Mission in El Salvador	El Salvador	Jul. 1991–May 1995	135 Civilian and Military Staff
MINURSO	UN Mission for the Referendum in Western Sahara	Western Sahara	Sept. 1991–present	375 Military Liaison Officers and Civilian Staff
UNAMIC	UN Advance Mission in Cambodia	Cambodia	Oct. 1991–present	380 Military Liaison Officers and Civilian Staff
UNPROFOR	UN Protection Force	Former Yugoslavia-Croatia, Bosnia-Herzegovinia, Macedonia	Mar. 1992–Dec. 1995	30,500 Troops and Civilian Personnel
UNTAC	UN Transition Authority in Cambodia	Cambodia	Mar. 1992–Dec. 1993	15,900 Troops, 3,600 Police Monitors, and 2,400 Civilian Administrators
UNOSOM I, II	UN Operation in Somalia	Somalia	Aug. 1992–Mar. 1995	28,000 Troops and 2,800 Civilian Staff
ONUMOZ	UN Operation in Mozambique	Mozambique	Dec. 1992–Dec. 1994	7,000 Military and Civilian Personnel
UNOMIR	UN Observer Mission Uganda-Rwanda	Uganda-Rwanda border	Jun. 1993–present	81 Military Observers and 24 Civilian Staff
UNOMIG	UN Observer Mission in Georgia	Georgia	Aug. 1993–present	136 Military Observers
UNOMIL	UN Observer Mission in Liberia	Liberia	Sept. 1993–present	374 Military Observers
UNIMIH	UN Mission in Haiti	Haiti	Sept. 1993–present	1,267 Military and Civilian Observers
UNAMIR	UN Assistance Mission for Rwanda	Rwanda	Oct. 1993–March 1996	2,548 Troops with 5,000 additional authorized

Table 11.1 / A Guide to Peacekeeping Operations Listed (continued)

Operation	Title	Location	Duration	Maximum Strength
UNASOG	UN Aouzou Strip Observer Group	Libya/Chad	May 1994–May 1994	N/A
MINUSAL	UN Mission in El Salvador	El Salvador	May 1995–present	N/A
MINUGUA	UN Mission Verification in Guatemala	Guatemala	Jan. 1997–May 1997	N/A
UNAVEM III	UN Angola Verification Mission	Angola	Feb. 1995–June 1997	335 Military Observers, 247 Civilian Police Officers, 246 Staff Officers, 4,103 Troops
UNMOT	UN Observer Mission in Tajikistan	Tajikistan	Dec. 1994–present	87 Military and Civilian Personnel
UNPREDEP	UN Preventive Deployment Force for Macedonia	Macedonia	Mar. 1995–present	1,050 Troops
UNMIBH	UN Mission in Bosnia and Herzgovina	Bosnia	Dec. 1995–present	
UNTAES	UN Transitional Administration for Eastern Slavonia, Baranja, and Western Sirmium	Croatia	Jan. 1996–present	5,587 Military and Civilian Personnel
UNMOP	UN Mission of Observers in Prevlaka	Croatia	Jan. 1996–present	N/A
UNSMIH	UN Support Mission in Haiti	Haiti	Jun. 1996–Jul. 1997	1,587 Personnel

Source: United Nations.

Notes

1. Charles Malik, *Man in the Struggle for Peace* (New York: Harper and Row, 1963), p. 124.

2. For discussion of the veto, see Inis L. Claude, Jr., *Swords into Plowshares,* 4th ed. (New York: Random House, 1984), Chapter 8.

3. Some of the standard works that describe and trace the history of UN peacekeeping include: Indar Jit Rikhye, *The Theory and Practice of Peacekeeping* (London: Hurst, 1984); Jit Rikhye, Michael Harbottle, and Bjorn Egge, *The Thin Blue Line: International Peacekeeping and Its Future* (New Haven: Yale University Press, 1974); Larry L. Fabian, *Soldiers without Enemies: Preparing the United Nations for Peacekeeping* (Washington: The Brookings Institution, 1971); Alan James, *Peacekeeping in International Politics* (London: Macmillan, 1990); United Nations, *The Blue Helmets: A Review of United Nations Peacekeeping* (New York: UNDPI, 1990); Sir Brian Urquhart, *A Life in Peace and War* (New York: Harper and Row, 1987); and Henry Wiseman, ed., *Peacekeeping: Appraisals and Proposals* (New York: Pergamon Press, 1983).

4. United Nations, *The Blue Helmets,* p. 4.

5. Urquhart, *A Life in Peace and War,* p. 198.

6. For a complete listing of contributors to peacekeeping operations, see United Nations, *The Blue Helmets,* Appendix II, pp. 419–49. For the most current information on UN operations, see <http://www.fib.ethz.ch/fib/pko/intro.html>. See also Karen A. Mingst, "State Participation in International and Regional Peacekeeping: A Comparative Analysis," paper presented at the International Studies Association Annual Meeting, San Diego (April 17–20, 1996).

7. Thomas G. Weiss and Jarat Chopra, *United Nations Peacekeeping: An ACUNS Teaching Text* (ACUNS, 1992), p. 8.

8. Ibid, pp. 47–48. See also Leon Gordenker and Thomas G. Weiss, eds., *Soldiers, Peacekeeping and Disasters* (London: Macmillan, 1991) for discussion of humanitarian relief efforts using soldiers.

9. For a particularly good discussion of this point, see the articles on UN peacekeeping in the special issue of *Survival,* No. 3 (May/June 1990).

10. For a history of UNEF I see Gabriella E. Rosner, *The United Nations Emergency Force* (New York: Columbia University Press, 1963).

11. For a history of ONUC, see Ernest W. Lefever, *Uncertain Mandate: Politics of the UN Congo Operation* (Baltimore: Johns Hopkins University Press, 1967).

12. For some systematic attempts to evaluate success, see Ernst B. Haas, "Regime Decay: Conflict Management and International Organizations, 1945–1981," *International Organization,* Vol. 37, No. 2 (Spring 1983), pp. 189–256; and Jonathan Wilkenfeld and Michael Brecher, "International Crises, 1945–1975: The UN Dimension," *International Studies Quarterly,* Vol. 28, No. 1 (1984), pp. 45–68.

13. Thomas G. Weiss and Kurt M. Campbell, "The United Nations and Eastern Europe," *World Policy Journal,* Vol. 7, No. 3 (Summer 1990), p. 577.

14. For an analysis of the Contact Group's efforts, see Margaret P. Karns, "Ad Hoc Multilateral Diplomacy: The United States, the Contact Group, and Namibia," *International Organization,* Vol. 41, No. 1 (Winter 1987), pp. 93–123.

15. See Weiss and Chopra, *United Nations Peacekeeping,* pp. 28–30, for an analysis of the Gulf War.

16. The materials on the Gulf War have proliferated, but few address the UN-related issues. Two helpful sources are Abram Chayes, "The Use of Force in the Persian Gulf," in Lori Fisler Damrosch and David J. Scheffer, eds., *Law and Force in the New International Order* (Boulder: Westview Press, 1991), pp. 3–11; and Ken Matthews, *The Gulf Conflict in International Relations* (London: Routledge, 1993).

17. Edward C. Luck and Tobi Trister Gati, "Whose Collective Security?" *The Washington Quarterly* (Spring 1992), p. 43.

18. For analyses of the issues raised by the UN's involvement in civil wars, see Thomas Weiss, ed., *The United Nations and Civil Wars* (Boulder: Lynne Rienner, 1995).

19. Michael W. Doyle, *UN Peacekeeping in Cambodia: UNTAC's Civil Mandate* (Boulder: Lynne Rienner, 1995), p. 26.

20. "The 'Second Generation:' Cambodia Elections 'Free and Fair,' but Challenges Remain," *UN Chronicle,* Vol. 30, No. 5 (November/December 1993), p. 26.

21. Michael W. Doyle and Nishkala Suntharalingam, "The UN in Cambodia: Lessons for Complex Peacekeeping," *International Peacekeeping,* Vol. 1, No. 2 (Summer 1994), p. 124.

22. United Nations Security Council, "Letter Dated 29 November 1992 from the Secretary-General Addressed to the President of the Security Council" (November 30, 1992) (S/24868), p. 2.

23. "The UN war on Aidid put UNOSOM in the worst of all possible worlds, which past peacekeepers had scrupulously avoided . . . [and] made it one of the players in the conflict." Richard Conroy, "Peacekeeping and Peace Enforcement in Somalia" (Paper presented at the Annual Meeting of the International Studies Association, Washington, D.C., March 30-April 2, 1994), p. 12.

24. For further discussion, see Walter Clarke and Jeffrey Herbst, "Somalia and the Future of Humanitarian Intervention," *Foreign Affairs,* Vol. 75, No. 2 (March/April 1996), pp. 70–85; E. Agnelli and C. Murphy, "Lessons of Somalia for Future Multilateral Humanitarian Assistance Operations," *Global Governance,* Vol. 1, No. 3 (September/December 1995), pp. 339–66.

25. Then UN Undersecretary-General for Peacekeeping Kofi Annan (now Secretary-General Annan) commented presciently: "I don't think the member states have the stomach for this type of operation." Quoted in John L. Hirsch and Robert B. Oakley, *Somalia and Operation Restore Hope: Reflections on Peacemaking and Peacekeeping* (Washington: U.S. Institute for Peace, 1995), p. 150.

26. For one perspective, see Alain Destexhe, "The Third Genocide," *Foreign Policy,* No. 97 (Winter 1994/95), pp. 3–17.

27. Thus, the UN involvement in Yugoslavia came to represent "a microcosm of all the problems that this body faces today: what to do about peacekeeping; when and if to turn to enforcement; where decisions should be taken; how human rights abuses should be dealt with; and who will pay." Rosalyn Higgins, "The New United Nations and Former Yugoslavia," *International Affairs,* Vol. 69, No. 3 (1993), p. 465.

28. For an early assessment of these problems, see ibid.

29. The problem of matching capabilities and resources to mandates was particularly evident in the repeated Security Council resolutions authorizing UNPROFOR to deter attacks against six UN "safe areas" in Bosnia. Where the UN force commander called for 34,000 troops, the Security Council authorized 7,000 and only 3,500 were actually deployed to two of the six areas. This "mismatch of commitments and resources" undermined both UNPROFOR's effectiveness and the UN's credibility. Susan R. Lamb, "The UN Protection Force in Former Yugoslavia," in Ramesh Thakur and Carlyle A. Thayer, eds., *A Crisis of Expectations: UN Peacekeeping in the 1990s* (Boulder: Westview Press, 1995), p. 74.

30. The small contingent of troops (seven hundred), including three hundred U.S. soldiers, that had been deployed to Macedonia in December 1992 to forestall the expansion of conflict to that province remained as a sign of the UN's commitment to ensuring that tensions there not escalate into armed conflict.

31. Weiss and Chopra, *United Nations Peacekeeping,* p. 31.

32. Ibid., p. 32. The discussion on pp. 32–36 regarding legal issues provides an excellent summary of the literature. For discussion of the bases for humanitarian intervention, see Jarat Chopra and Thomas G. Weiss, "Sovereignty Is No Longer Sacrosanct: Codifying Humanitarian Intervention," *Ethics and International Affairs,* Vol. 6 (1992), pp. 95–117; and James A. R. Nafziger, "Self-Determination and Humanitarian Intervention in a Community of Power," *Denver Journal of International Law and Policy,* Vol. 20, No. 1 (Fall 1991), pp. 9–40.

33. Weiss and Chopra, *United Nations Peacekeeping,* p. 40.

34. Address by the Secretary-General, "From Peace-Keeping to Peace-Building," p. 11. Boutros-Ghali discusses various proposals for reform in peacekeeping financing arrangements.

35. For a discussion, see Robert C. Johansen, "Reconciling National and International Interests in UN Peacekeeping," in Ramesh Thakur and Carlyle A. Thayer, eds., *A Crisis of Expectations,* pp. 281–302.

36. For a discussion of the problem of U.S. support for the UN, see Margaret P. Karns and Karen A. Mingst, "The Past As Prologue: The United States and the Future of the UN System," in Gene M. Lyons, Chadwick R. Alger, and John E. Trent, eds., *The United Nations and the Policies of Member States* (Tokyo: UN University Press, 1995).

37. Quoted in "Kofi Annan: The International Civil Servant," *United Nations Chronicle,* Vol. 33, No. 3 (1996), pp. 5, 7.

12 / Global Violence against Women: The Challenge to Human Rights and Development

CHARLOTTE BUNCH and ROXANNA CARRILLO

Increasingly there is acknowledgment in the global arena that human rights and development are interconnected and are essential building blocks for lasting world peace and security.[1] This idea is embedded in the Universal Declaration of Human Rights, approved by the United Nations in 1948. This declaration was adopted on the assumption that achieving human rights in both the socioeconomic and political spheres was necessary to prevent future world conflicts.

During the past two decades, there has been a parallel evolution within the international women's movement as the major concerns of women have come to be seen as interrelated. At the time of the first UN World Conference on Women in Mexico City in 1975, the UN Decade for Women was adopted with the goals of equality, development, and peace. Initially these were perceived as separate issues reflecting the priorities of different political blocs. However, as the Decade progressed, the interconnections of these themes became evident and women's equality and development are now seen as necessary for a lasting peace. Further, the Fourth World Conference on Women, held by the UN in Beijing in 1995, recognized that the realization of the human rights of women necessitates not only equality and development but also freedom from violence—that is, peace—in both the public and private spheres.

Peace, security, and human rights are thus understood not simply as matters of governmental interaction or abstract categories, but as rooted in the everyday lives of women, men, and children. In this regard, peace and violence must be examined as they are reflected at the roots of society—in the home and family as well as in the "public" space of wars and work-places. Thus, the issue of gender-based violence lies at the heart of questions of peace, human rights, and development.

The 1994 *Human Development Report,* published by the United Nations Development Programme (UNDP), elaborated on the meaning of development by introducing the concept of human security as a necessary condition for world peace. "The world can never be at peace unless people have security in their daily lives," the report noted. "Future conflicts may often be within nations rather than between them—with their origins buried deep in growing socioeconomic deprivation and disparities. The search for security in such a milieu lies in development, not in arms."[2]

The need for human security through development is critical to women whose lives often epitomize the insecurity and disparities that plague the world order. As the 1994 UNDP report further stated: "In no society are women secure or treated equally to men. Personal insecurity shadows them from cradle to grave. . . . And from childhood through adulthood they are abused because of their gender."[3]

In this context, gender-based violence emerges as a primary human security concern for women, and thus, as a crucial human rights and development challenge. Women in both North and South live with the constant risk of physical harm. The experience and fear of violence is an underlying thread in women's lives that intertwines with their most basic human security needs at all levels—personal, community, economic, and political. In virtually every nation, violence (or the threat of it) shrinks the range of choices open to women and girls, limiting their mobility and even their ability to imagine having control over their lives.

Violence against women narrows women's choices directly by destroying their health, disrupting their lives, and constricting the scope of their activity; and indirectly by eroding their self-confidence and self-esteem. In all of these ways, violence limits women's exercise of their human rights and hinders their access to full citizenship and participation in the entire spectrum of development efforts. Thus, violence against women remains a steep barrier to securing a culture of respect for human rights and to achieving sustainable development and world peace.

Understanding that violence against women is a human rights issue is important because the concept of human rights is one of the few moral visions ascribed to internationally. Although its scope is not universally agreed upon, it strikes deep chords of resonance among many. The promotion of human rights is a widely accepted goal and thus provides a useful framework for seeking redress of gender abuse. Furthermore, it is one of the few concepts that speaks to the need for transnational activism and concern about the lives of people globally. The Universal Declaration of Human Rights symbolizes this world vision and defines human rights broadly. While not much is said in it specifically about women, Article 2 does entitle all to "the rights and freedoms set forth in this Declaration, without distinction of any kind, such as race, color, sex, language, religion, political or other opinion, national or social origin, property, birth or other status."[4]

Since 1948, the world community has continuously debated varying interpretations of human rights in response to global developments. Little of this discussion, however, has addressed questions of gender, and only recently have significant challenges been made to a vision of human rights that excludes much of women's experiences. The concept of human rights, like all vibrant visions, is not static or the property of any one group; rather, its meaning expands as people reconceive their needs and hopes in relation to it. In this spirit, feminists redefine human rights abuses to include the degradation and violation of women. The specific experiences of women must be added to traditional approaches to human rights in order to make gender-based violations more visible, and to transform the practice of human rights so that it takes better account of women's lives.

The momentum for understanding that women's rights are human rights has grown rapidly in the 1990s, particularly since the World Conference on Human Rights (Vienna, 1993), where this idea first received world exposure. The global conferences convened by the UN during this decade saw an extraordinary mobilization of women from all parts of the world. Through networking, petitions, campaigns, coalitions, tribunals, and fora of all sorts, women used the spaces provided by these events to define a new global agenda that incorporates their lives and experiences.

At the World Conference on Human Rights, the international community recognized that women's rights are human rights, affirming that the human rights of women are universal, inalienable, and indivisible. Further, for the first time in UN history, the Vienna Programme of Action stated clearly that violence against women, whether in public or private, constitutes a violation of human rights. A year later, at the International Conference on Population and Development (Cairo, 1994) the protection of women's human rights was extended to include women's right to reproductive and sexual decision making. The World Summit for Social Development (Copenhagen, 1995) affirmed that equality between women and men is critical to achieving social development, and that this cannot happen in the absence of human rights—including women's human rights. The culmination of these efforts came with the Fourth World Conference on Women (Beijing, 1995), the largest world conference in the history of the UN, where a strong commitment to women's rights as human rights formed the very foundation of the Beijing Platform for Action.[5]

Yet, in spite of these significant advances in rhetorical acceptance of women's rights as human rights and after three decades of development efforts, the violation of the rights of women continues unabated. Women remain disadvantaged in employment, education, health, and government. Gender-based violence is central to the status of women, and understanding how it effects women's participation in society is critical to bringing about change.

GENDER VIOLENCE: A GLOBAL EPIDEMIC

The most insidious myth about women's rights is that they are trivial or secondary to the concerns of life and death. Nothing could be farther from the truth: sexism kills. There is increasing documentation of the many ways in which being female is life threatening. The following are a few examples:

- *Before birth.* Amniocentesis is used for sex selection leading to the abortion of more female than male fetuses at rates as high as 99 percent in Bombay; in China, the most populous nation, significantly more males are born (or survive the first few hours of birth) than females, even though natural birth ratios would produce *fewer* males.

- *During childhood.* In many countries, girls are fed less, breast-fed for shorter periods of time, and taken to doctors less frequently; as a result, the mortality rate of girls aged one to four is higher than boys in forty-three out of forty-five developing countries for which such data is available.[6]
- *In adulthood.* The denial of women's rights to control their bodies in reproduction threatens women's lives, especially where this is combined with poverty and poor health services. In Latin America, complications from illegal abortions are the leading cause of death for women between the ages of fifteen and thirty-nine.[7]

Sex discrimination kills women daily. When combined with race, class, and other forms of oppression, it constitutes a deadly denial of women's rights to life and liberty on a large scale throughout the world. The most pervasive violation of females is gender violence with its many manifestations—from wife battery, incest, and rape, to dowry deaths,[8] genital mutilation,[9] and female sexual slavery. These abuses occur in every country and are found in the home and in the workplace, on streets, campuses, and in prisons and refugee camps. They cross class, race, age, and national lines; at the same time, the forms this violence takes often reinforce other oppressions, such as racism, homophobia, "able-bodyism," and imperialism.

Even a short review of random statistics reveals that the extent of global violence against women is staggering. Official statistics and survey data in the United States, for example, dramatically convey the endemic nature of gender violence. A rape occurs somewhere in the United States every six minutes, and domestic battery is the single most significant cause of injury to women—more than car accidents, rapes, and muggings combined.[10] Moreover, a 1985 FBI report estimates that wife assault is underreported by a factor of at least ten to one. Researchers produce chilling numbers: for example, Strauss, Gelles, and Steinmetz reveal that one in eight couples acknowledged there had been an act of violence between them severe enough to risk serious injury.[11]

Statistics from other industrialized countries are equally disconcerting. Data compiled by the UN Statistical Office indicate that about one in four women in industrialized regions has been hit by an intimate partner. In Austria, 59 percent of women cite violence as the reason for divorce; in Denmark, 25 percent do so.[12] A 1984 study of urban victimization in seven major Canadian cities found that 90 percent of victims were women. One in four women in Canada can expect to be sexually assaulted at some point in their lives, one-half of these before the age of 17.[13]

Although there are fewer studies on gender violence in Third World countries, the patterns there bear a remarkable similarity to those of the industrialized nations. Its manifestations may be culturally specific, but gender-based violence cuts across national boundaries, ideologies, classes, races, and ethnic groups. A 1994 report by the World Bank summarizing the results of thirty-five studies of wife abuse indicates that it occurs at high rates in countries as diverse as Chile, Kuwait, Kenya, Thailand, Nigeria, and Brazil.[14]

In Mexico, it is estimated that domestic violence is present in at least 70 percent of Mexican families, but most cases go unreported. The Mexican Federation of Women's Trade Unions reports that 95 percent of women workers are victims of sexual harassment, and complains that the impunity of these crimes limits women's participation in the workforce.[15] A national survey on domestic violence undertaken by the Papua New Guinea Law Reform Commission showed that, in some areas of the country, as many as 67 percent of wives had experienced marital violence and that 61 percent of people killed in 1981 were women, the majority by their spouses.[16] Over two-thirds of Korean women are beaten regularly by their husbands,[17] and in Nicaragua 44 percent of men admit to having beaten their wives or girl-friends regularly.[18]

Many studies suggest that the abuse of women by intimate male partners is not only pervasive but recurring; most of the victims are subject to escalating abuse over a substantial period of time, often resulting in serious injury or death.[19] For example, a large-scale study conducted in Brazil found that well over a third of domestic battery cases involved serious injury, usually committed by the aggressor's feet and fists.[20] A newspaper survey in Pakistan revealed an astonishingly high incidence of wife battery, and listed the following types of violence committed against women: murdered over land disputes, blinded by husbands frustrated on some issue, kicked to death, burned in anger, abducted, sold, sexually harassed, and raped.[21]

Violence against women not only maims and debilitates; femicide kills women on a large scale from pre-birth to old age. Amartya Sen first calculated the deadly cost of social and economic inequalities by analyzing the sex ratio (of females to males) in the less-developed countries. In countries where both sexes receive similar care, there are about 105 females for every 100 males. But in South Asia, West Asia, North Africa, and China, men significantly outnumber women: there are about 94 women for every 100 men. Roughly 90 million women who should be alive today are "missing" due to the effects of gender discrimination and violence, ranging from female feticide to selective malnourishment and starvation of girls, neglect of health problems, dowry deaths, and various other forms of violence.[22] This is nearly twice the generally accepted figure for military and civilian casualties in World War II.

GENDER VIOLENCE AND HUMAN RIGHTS

Statistics do not reflect the full extent of the problem of violence against women, much of which remains hidden. Yet, rather than receiving recognition as a major site of conflict in the world, this violence is still often accepted as normal, or even dismissed as an individual or cultural matter.

Few governments exhibit more than token commitment to women's equality as a basic human right in domestic or foreign policy, or shape their policies toward other countries on the basis of their treatment of women. However, as a result of the movement for women's rights as human rights in recent years, a few advances have been made in gaining governmental recognition of women's human rights, in matters like refugee policy and the granting of political asylum to women on the grounds of gender-based persecution, as reflected in such behavior as genital mutilation.

Nevertheless, when it is suggested that governments and human rights organizations should respond to women's rights as major concerns that deserve serious attention, traditional attitudes about why this cannot be done are still pervasive. These attitudes tend to follow one or more of these lines: (1) sex discrimination is too trivial, or not as important, or will be addressed only after larger issues of survival have been dealt with; (2) abuse of women, while regrettable, is a cultural, private, or individual issue and not a political matter requiring state action; or (3) even if a matter of serious concern, abuse of women is so pervasive that consideration of it is futile or will dilute the importance of other human rights issues.

One of the problems women face is the prevalence of a narrow definition of human rights, as covering only state violations of civil and political liberties. While important aspects of women's rights do fit into a civil liberties framework, much of the abuse of women is tied to a larger socioeconomic web. Many women are entrapped by circumstances than make them vulnerable to abuses that cannot be delineated as exclusively political or solely caused by the state. The recognition of socioeconomic human rights to food, shelter, and work—clearly delineated as part of the Universal Declaration of Human Rights—is vital to addressing women's concerns.

Furthermore, the assumption that states are not responsible for most violations of women's rights ignores the fact that abuses committed by private citizens are often condoned or sanctioned by the state. As Georgina Ashworth has noted:

> gender relations are already regulated by states, through fiscal arrangements, social security, immigration law, marriage and family law, established religion, [and] military service, and are executed through all the statutory instruments, administrative procedures, and legal and judicial processes, as well as the executive and elective bodies. It is the duty of good governments to enforce respect for women's human rights within them.[23]

State accountability for actively seeking to eradicate violence against women is based on the state's universally recognized responsibility to respect and ensure the fundamental human rights of all individuals in its territory.

Violence against women is a touchstone that illustrates the limited concept of human rights and highlights the political nature of the abuse of women. As Lori Heise states: "this is not random violence . . . the risk factor is being female."[24] Victims are chosen because of their gender. The message is domination: Stay in your place, or expect to be hurt. Contrary to the argument that such violence is only personal or cultural, it is profoundly political. It results from the structural relationships of power, domination, and privilege between men and women. Violence against women is central to maintaining those political relations at home, at work, and in the greater public sphere.

Failure to see the oppression of women as political resulted in the near exclusion of sex discrimination and violence against women from the human rights agenda of the past fifty years. Female subordination runs so deep that it is often viewed as inevitable or natural, rather than as a politically constructed reality maintained by patriarchal interests, ideology, and institutions. But male violation of women is not inevitable or natural. Such a concept reflects a narrow and pessimistic view of men. When violence and domination are understood as elements of a politically constructed reality, it is possible to imagine deconstructing that system and building more just interactions between the sexes.

The physical territory of this political struggle over what constitutes women's human rights is women's bodies. The importance of control over women can be seen in the intensity of resistance to issues that give women control over their bodies: reproductive rights, freedom of sexuality whether heterosexual or lesbian, laws that criminalize rape in marriage, and so on. Homophobia and denial of reproductive rights are thus political means of maintaining control over women and of perpetuating sex roles and power, all of which have human rights implications. The physical abuse of women is a reminder of this territorial domination and is sometimes accompanied by other forms of human rights abuse, such as slavery (forced prostitution), sexual terrorism (rape), imprisonment (confinement to the home), or torture (systematic battery). Some cases are extreme, such as the women in Thailand who died in a brothel fire because they were chained to their beds. Most situations result from more ordinary forms of discrimination, such as denying women decent education or jobs, which leaves them prey to abusive marriages, exploitative work, and prostitution.

This raises, once again, the question of the state's responsibility for protecting women's human rights. Feminists have shown how the distinction between private and public abuse is a dichotomy often used to justify female subordination in the home. Governments regulate many matters in family and individual spheres. For example, human rights activists pressure states to prevent slavery or racial discrimination and segregation, even when these are conducted by nongovernmental forces in private, or proclaimed as cultural traditions, as they have been in both the southern United States and in South Africa. The real questions are: (1) who decides what are legitimate human rights, and (2) when should the state become involved and for what purposes? Riane Eisler argues that:

> the issue is what types of private acts are and are not protected by the right to privacy and/or the principle of family autonomy. Even more specifically, the issue is whether violations of human rights within the family such as genital mutilation, wife beating, and other forms of violence designed to maintain patriarchal

control should be within the purview of human rights theory and action. . . . [T]he underlying problem for human rights theory, as for most other fields of theory, is that the yardstick that has been developed for defining and measuring human rights has been based on the male as norm.[25]

The human rights community has only just begun to move beyond its male-defined norms in order to respond to the brutal and systematic violation of women globally. This does not mean that every human rights group must alter the focus of its work, but it *does* require examining gender biases and acknowledging the rights of women as human rights. Governments must be held accountable for policies that perpetuate the politically and culturally constructed war on women. Every state has the responsibility to intervene in the abuse of women's rights within its borders and to end its collusion with the forces that perpetrate such violations in other countries.

GENDER VIOLENCE AND DEVELOPMENT

The emergence of violence as a crucial issue for development has occurred organically, arising from grass-roots women's endeavors, and has not been dictated by outside authorities or international agencies. For example, reports from projects funded by the United Nations Development Fund for Women (UNIFEM), increasingly identify violence as a priority concern and/or as a problem that limits women's participation in—or capacity to benefit from—development projects. Women have taken leadership in making violence against women visible, and in addressing its causes, manifestations, and remedies. From the Uganda Association of Women Lawyers to the Latin American and Caribbean Network on Domestic and Sexual Violence, women's leadership in the developing world has been struggling to include issues of violence against women on national agendas. As a result, this issue emerged as a major concern from all regions in the preparatory meetings held for the Fourth World Conference on Women.

Within the context of the United Nations Decade for Women, the problem of violence against women has been increasingly acknowledged. At the first three World Conferences on Women—Mexico City (1975), Copenhagen (1980), and Nairobi (1985)—advocates raised the issue of gender-based violence and demanded special attention to the constraints it places on women's full participation in society. At the fourth conference in Beijing (1995), violence against women in the family, in public, and in armed conflict was recognized as a major obstacle to women's enjoyment of their human rights. The official documents produced at these events are powerful indictments of the discrimination that women face in all countries. The Beijing Platform for Action in particular outlines concrete strategies and actions to be taken by governments and international organizations to eradicate violence against women.[26]

One of the most significant UN documents that grew out of the movement for women's human rights is the United Nations Declaration on the Elimination of Violence Against Women, adopted by the General Assembly in 1993.[27] This was a landmark document in three ways:

- *It situated violence against women squarely within the discourse on human rights.* The Declaration affirmed that women are entitled to equal enjoyment and protection of all human rights and fundamental freedoms, including liberty and security of person, and freedom from torture or other cruel, inhuman, or degrading treatment or punishment.
- *It enlarged the concept of violence against women to reflect the real conditions of women's lives.* The Declaration recognized not only physical, sexual, and psychological violence, but also *threats* of such harm; it addressed violence against women within the family as well as within the general community, and confronted the issue of violence perpetrated by the state.
- *It pointed to the gender-based roots of violence.* The Declaration reflected the fact that gender-based violence is not random violence in which the victims happen to be women and girls: the risk factor is being female.

Another major advance made within the UN to address this issue was the appointment in 1994 by the Commission on Human Rights of a Special Rapporteur on Violence Against Women. Her mandate is to report to the UN on issues of violence and to make recommendations for action by both governments and the UN.[28]

The *Human Development Report* (HDR), published annually by the United Nations Development Programme (UNDP) since 1990, has provided another avenue for looking at violence against women. Reassessing the different approaches that marked the three UN Development Decades, this document questions the ability of statistical indicators—such as growth and national income—to measure development adequately. Rather, it suggests the need to focus on other aspects of development that provide more accurate and realistic indicators of human development: nutrition and health services, access to knowledge, secure livelihoods, decent working conditions, security against crime and physical violence, and participation in economic, cultural, and political activities. The goal of development should be to create an environment that enables people to enjoy long, healthy, and creative lives.

Yet, despite three decades of development efforts, nowhere do females enjoy the same standards as males, and in some areas gaps have widened so considerably that one must question whether development attempts are intrinsically gendered to the disadvantage of females. As the 1990 HDR states:

> In most societies, women fare less well than men. As children they have less access to education and sometimes to food and health care. As adults they receive less education and training, work longer hours for lower incomes and have few property rights or none.[29]

Discrimination against females extends to every aspect of life. If women are fed less, have poorer health and less education than males, and their contribution to society's production and reproduction is underestimated, it is no wonder that wide gender gaps between males and females persist in human development indicators.

In order for women to benefit from the development process, a fundamental emphasis must be placed on increasing women's self-confidence, as well as their ability to participate in all aspects of society. Violence against women is in direct contradiction to the securing of human-centered development goals. Violence disrupts women's lives, denies them options, and erodes their self-confidence at every level, physically and psychologically. It destroys women's health, denies their human rights, and hinders their full participation in society. Where domestic violence keeps a woman from participation in a development project, or fear of sexual assault prevents her from taking a job, or force is used to deprive her of earnings, development does not occur.

Women experience violence as a form of control that limits their ability to pursue options in almost every area of life: in homes, schools, workplaces, and most public spaces. Violence is used to control women's labor in both productive and reproductive capacities. For example, case studies of victims of domestic violence in Peru and of garment workers in the Mexican *maquilas* (assembly plants on the U.S.-Mexican border) showed men beating their wives frequently to demand the income women had earned.[30] Indonesian female workers returning to their villages complain of their helplessness in the face of harassment and sexual abuse by their employers; quite often their wages are withheld for months, preventing the possibility of escape or resistance. In the Philippines, women workers in export-oriented industries claim that male managers give female employees the choice of "lay down or lay off."[31]

The socially constructed dependency of women on men is key to understanding women's vulnerability to violence. This dependency is frequently economic, and results from various layers of sexist discrimination. First, much of women's work is unpaid labor at home and in the fields, which is not valued by society nor calculated as part of the gross national product—the productive work of a nation. Second, even in paid jobs, women work longer hours for lower pay, with fewer benefits and less security than men.

Female dependency extends to other areas, as well. Women are trained to believe that their value is attached to the men in their lives—fathers, brothers, husbands, and sons. They are often socially ostracized if they displease or disobey these men. Women are socialized to associate their self-worth with the satisfaction of the needs and desires of others, and thus are encouraged to blame themselves as inadequate or bad if men beat them. This socialization process is reinforced by cultures in which a woman is constantly diminished, her sexuality commodified, her work and characteristics devalued, and her identity shaped by an environment that reduces her to her most biological functions.

Women's socioeconomic and psychological dependency makes it difficult for them to leave situations of domestic violence or sexual harassment. In rural settings it is often physically impossible; women literally have no place to go or the means to get away, and there are no services available. But even in large urban settings, where it may be easier for women to leave abusive relationships, there is often nowhere to go, as illustrated by the links between domestic violence and homelessness. A shelter for homeless women in Boston reports that about 90 percent of its occupants are victims of domestic violence,[32] and New York City shelter workers note a similar trend. Australian sociologist Robert Connell sees the lack of alternative housing as one of the reasons women choose to stay in, or return to, violent marriages.[33]

Violence against women also affects the development and well-being of children. It seems increasingly clear that the best way to reduce infant mortality is through the education of women.[34] The UNDP *Human Development Report* outlines the high social dividend that comes with female literacy, as demonstrated by lower infant mortality rates, better family nutrition, reduced fertility, and lower population growth. Other studies show a connection between women's self-confidence and child mortality. Since the health and psychological well-being of children is connected to the future development of a country, the gender violence implicit in disproportionate female illiteracy is clearly contrary to development. Improving women's self-confidence and education is, therefore, a crucial investment that may have long-lasting effects on children and the future of a nation.

THE COSTS TO SOCIETY

Violence against women deprives society of the full participation of women in all aspects of its activities. Many work hours are lost as a result of violence, not to speak of the costs of providing services to victims. Add to this the work time spent by police, and by others in the legal, medical, mental health, and social-service professions. It is almost impossible to quantify the total costs of the problem, given the limited information available. Beyond such calculable costs lies the price in human suffering, which is vast. And the long-term cost of gender-based violence is the perpetuation of societal structures that keep women politically, economically, and socially subordinate.

Violence against women is often a direct obstacle to women's participation in development activities. For example, in a Mexican project funded by UNIFEM, instances of wife battering increased with women's sense of empowerment through the project. Observers found that men perceived the growing empowerment of women as a threat to their control, and the beatings could be explained as an attempt to reverse the process of empowerment the women experienced, in order to drive them away from the project.[35] Similarly, a revolving-fund project of the Working Women's Forum in Madras, India, almost collapsed when the most energetic participants stopped participating because of the increased incidents of domestic violence they experienced after they joined.[36] Faced with the same problems, the Association for the Development and Integration of Women (ADIM) in Lima, Peru, succeeded by initiating programs that combined income-generating schemes with legal aid to battered wives and women abandoned by their partners.[37]

Another long-term effect of gender violence (and of the cultural atmosphere that demeans women by condoning such violence) is that it denies developing countries the full talents of their female citizens. Family control and violence encourage some of the best-educated women to leave their countries, contributing to the "brain drain" in the Third World and to the loss of highly skilled women who could be contributing to the development process. Women who stay often must comply with the subordinate role that society assigns them, and may be reluctant to be promoted to more visible and productive positions for fear of upsetting their husbands. This problem has recently been seen quite dramatically with the Taliban's control over Afghanistan and their demand that women leave many areas of work.

Health is usually recognized as an important development issue, and one of the clearest facts about gender violence is that it is detrimental to women's physical and mental health, including women's very survival. A 1989 report by the then Surgeon General of the United States C. Everett Koop affirmed that battered women are four to five times more likely than nonbattered women to require psychiatric treatment, and more likely to commit suicide. He reported that, each year, some 1 million women in the United States are sufficiently injured to seek medical assistance at emergency rooms from injuries sustained through battering. These injuries include bruises, concussions, broken noses and teeth, broken ribs and limbs, throat injuries, lacerations and stab wounds, burns, and bites. In view of the extensive evidence, Koop called gender violence "an overwhelming moral, economic, and public health burden that our society can no longer bear."[38]

The AIDS crisis has exacerbated the deadly impact of unequal gender relations. In Africa—where the AIDS epidemic has reached staggering proportions—women are experiencing the effects of male control in multiple and deadly ways. A report of the Health Ministry of Uganda revealed that there were twice as many cases of AIDS among girls between fifteen and nineteen years old as among boys of the same age group in 1990, and the age of new female AIDS victims keeps dropping. These numbers reflect a common belief among sexually active adult men that they will face less risk of being exposed to the AIDS virus if they engage in sexual intercourse with younger women.[39] In some areas where the control of women is reflected in traditional practices like female circumcision and infibulation of the clitoris, the risks of acquiring the disease have multiplied. Deeply entrenched attitudes and traditions around the world justify men's easy access to women's bodies, and result in the transmission of the virus through rape, incest, and other forms of coerced sex.

DIRECTIONS FOR POLICY

The way that societies characterize human rights and development concerns is more than just a question of semantics, because it has practical policy consequences. In virtually every country, human rights (narrowly defined) and economic development are still considered to be more important than women's rights. This distinction perpetuates the idea that the rights of women are of a lesser order than the rights of men, and, as Riane Eisler describes it, "serves to justify practices that do not accord women full and equal status."[40] The failure to address gender violence as part of the developmental process has contributed to the continuing subordination and exploitation of women—at great cost to the goals of development itself.

In order to advance the cause of women's rights and to enhance the well-being of all human beings, it is essential to eliminate the false distinction between human rights and women's rights. Similarly, the eradication of gender-based violence is essential to the goal of sustainable development in all parts of the world. As part of this process, we propose four basic approaches to linking women's rights to human rights and what this might mean for addressing violence against women. These approaches can be applied to many issues, but here they are illustrated primarily in terms of violence against women in order to demonstrate their practical application to a concrete issue. Although these approaches are presented separately in order to identify each more clearly, they often overlap and are complementary.

Women's Rights as Political and Civil Rights

Taking women's specific needs into consideration as part of the already recognized "first generation" human rights, covering political and civil liberties, is the first approach. This involves both raising the visibility of women as victims of traditionally defined human rights violations, as well as calling attention to particular abuses of civil and political rights that women encounter because they are female. Thus, issues of violence against women should be raised when they connect to other forms of violation, such as the sexual torture of women political prisoners.[41] Amnesty International has taken this approach in their campaign on behalf of women political prisoners by addressing the sexual abuse and rape of women in custody, their lack of maternal care in detention, and the resulting human rights abuse of their children.

Documenting the problems of women refugees and developing gender responsive policies are other illustrations of this approach. Women and children make up more than 80 percent of those in refugee camps, where they face a high risk of sexual abuse. Only recently, however, have refugee policies begun to be shaped to meet the needs of these populations. For example, in one camp where the community's rations were allocated to the men, some men gave food to women and their children in exchange for sex; revealing this abuse led to new policies that allocated food directly to the women.[42]

Gender integration into political and civil rights is a useful starting point for many human rights groups; by considering women's experiences, these groups can expand their efforts in areas where they are already working. This approach also raises contradictions that reveal the limits of a narrow civil liberties view, for example, defining rape as a human rights abuse only when it occurs in state custody, and not when it occurs on the streets or in the home. Another contradiction is apparent when human rights groups call it a violation of the right to free speech when someone is jailed for defending gay rights, but do not fight for those who are jailed—or even tortured and killed—for reason of their homosexuality. Thus, although this approach of integrating gender into existing "first generation" human rights categories is useful, it is not enough by itself.

Women's Rights as Socioeconomic Rights

The second approach focuses on the particular plight of women with regard to "second generation" human rights, such as the rights to food, shelter, health care, and employment. This is an approach favored by those who see the dominant Western rights tradition and international law as too individualistic, and who identify women's oppression as primarily economic in origin.

This tendency has its origins among socialists and labor activists who have long argued that political human rights are meaningless to many without economic rights as well. It focuses on the primacy of the need to end women's economic subordination as the key to other issues, including women's vulnerability to violence. This particular focus has led to work on such issues as women's right to organize as workers and opposition to violence in the workplace, especially in settings like the free-trade zones that have targeted women as cheap, nonorganized labor. Another focus of this approach has been highlighting the feminization of poverty, or what might better be called the increasing impoverishment of females. Since females now comprise more than 50 percent of the poor, the right to food is critical to many women's ability to exercise their right to human security.

This approach requires integrating a gender perspective into the movement for development as a human rights issue. Among people working on issues of women in development, there is growing interest in violence against women as both a health and a development issue. If violence is seen as having negative consequences for social productivity, it may get more attention. This type of narrow economic measure should not, however, determine whether such violence is seen as a human rights concern. Violence as a development issue is linked to the need to understand development not just as an economic issue but also as a question of empowerment and human growth.

Women's Rights and the Law

The creation of new legal mechanisms to counter sex discrimination characterizes the third approach to women's rights as human rights. These efforts seek to make existing legal and political institutions work for women, and to expand the state's responsibility for the protection of women's human rights. National and local laws that address sex discrimination and violence against women are examples of this approach. These measures allow women to fight for their rights within the legal system.

The primary international instrument for women's human rights is the Convention on the Elimination of All Forms of Discrimination Against Women.[43] The convention has been described as "essentially an international Bill of Rights for women and a framework for women's participation in the development process . . . [which] spells out internationally accepted principles and standards for achieving equality between women and men."[44] Adopted by the UN General Assembly in 1979, the Convention has been ratified or acceded to by 157 countries as of 1997—with the United States remaining as the only industrialized nation that has not ratified it. In theory, these countries are obligated to pursue policies in accordance with the Convention and to report on their compliance to the Committee on the Elimination of Discrimination Against Women (CEDAW).

While the Convention addresses many issues of sex discrimination, one of its initial shortcomings was a failure to directly address the question of violence against women. Aware of this gap, the CEDAW Committee produced General Recommendation No. 19 in 1992, where it elaborated the meaning of discrimination to include violence against women. This led to an amendment of its reporting guidelines instructing states to include, in their periodic reports to the committee, information about statistics, legislation, and support services in this area.

The 1979 Convention outlines a clear human rights agenda for women that, if carried out by governments, would mark an enormous step forward. However, it is a statute without strong mechanisms for implementation, as illustrated by the difficulty that CEDAW has had in persuading countries to report on compliance with its provisions. Furthermore, it is still treated by governments and many human rights organizations as a document dealing with *women's* (read "secondary") rights, not *human* rights. Nevertheless, it is a powerful statement of principles, endorsed by the United Nations, and as women mobilize to demand its implementation, it can be utilized to help achieve legal and political change.[45]

Feminist Transformation of Human Rights

Transforming the human rights concept from a feminist perspective, so that it will take greater account of women's lives, is the fourth approach. This approach raises the question of how women's rights relate to human rights, by first looking at the violations that women experience and then asking how the human rights concept can change to be made more responsive to them. For example, the Gabriela women's coalition in the Philippines simply stated that "Women's Rights Are Human Rights" in launching one of the earliest such campaigns in 1989. As Ninotchka Rosca explained, coalition members saw that "human rights are not reducible to a question of legal and due process . . . In the case of women, human rights are affected by the entire society's traditional perception of what is proper or not proper for women."[46] While work in the three previous approaches is often conducted from a feminist perspective, this last view is the most distinctly feminist, with its women-centered stance and refusal to wait for permission from some authority to determine what is, or is not, a legitimate human rights issue.

This transformative approach can be taken toward any issue, but those working from this approach have tended to focus most on abuses that arise specifically out of gender, such as reproductive rights, female sexual slavery, domestic and sexual violence against women, and "family crimes" such as forced marriage, compulsory heterosexuality, and female genital mutilation. These are also the issues that are most often dismissed as not really human rights questions. This is, therefore, the most contested area, and one that requires that barriers be broken down between what is considered public and private, and that governments as well as nongovernmental institutions be held responsible for violations by non-state actors.

Those working to transform the human rights vision from this perspective can draw on the work of others who have expanded the understanding of human rights previously. For example, two decades ago there was no concept of "disappearances" as a human rights abuse. However, the women of the Plaza de Mayo in Buenos Aires who protested the disappearance of their loved ones did not wait for an official declaration of this as a human rights matter. They stood up to demand state accountability for these crimes. In doing so, they helped to create a context for expanding the concept of responsibility for deaths at the hands of paramilitary or right-wing death squads—which, even if not carried out directly by the state, were allowed by it to happen. Another example is the developing concept that civil rights violations include "hate crimes," violence that is racially motivated or directed against homosexuals, Jews, or other minority groups. Many accept that states have an obligation to work to prevent such human rights abuses, and identifying violence against women as a hate crime has been useful in some contexts.

Many strategies for change involve elements of more than one of these approaches, and all of them contain aspects of what is necessary to achieve women's human rights. The creative task is to look for ways to connect these approaches and build international acceptance that women's human rights are universal, inalienable, and indivisible.

CONCLUSION

Situating violence against women within the discourse of human rights creates a normative framework in which governments can be held accountable for combating it. This also places such violence on the human rights policy agenda; thus, if governments link foreign aid and policy to human rights concerns, they should take into account the state's treatment of women, including policies on violence against women. Moreover, recognizing women's rights as human rights can lead, and in many nations has led, to more preventative measures, more and better services for victims, and stronger sanctions against perpetrators.

Crosscultural studies on family violence and rape, drawing on data from ninety societies throughout the world, suggest that four factors taken together are strong predictors of the prevalence of violence against women in a society: economic inequality between men and women, a pattern of using physical violence to resolve conflict, male authority and control of decision making, and restrictions on women's ability to leave the family setting.[47] Since violence against women is a function of socially constructed norms of acceptable behavior, it can be reduced and eliminated only through fundamental social and attitudinal change in all four of these levels. This requires formal and informal education, the effective use of media, and a clear commitment from the government not only to condemn such violence legislatively but, even more importantly, to ensure that the legislation is enforced.

In looking at strategies to eradicate violence against women, one underlying challenge stands out: what does it take to make local communities and national governments decide that it is their responsibility to prevent such practices? This requires a profound change in public attitudes, moving away from individual blame toward community accountability for gender-based violence, in which the community assumes responsibility for ending the violence that it has promoted or tolerated by failing to intervene. As a UN expert group recommended, a critical element in any strategy to eliminate violence against women is getting the community to decide not to tolerate such behavior—by strangers or by its own.

Creating a sense of public responsibility for gender-based violence involves examining the ways in which societal institutions currently condone such violence, actively or by passively looking away. Schools, religious institutions, workplaces, advertising and communications media, and families must be challenged about their collusion in the perpetuation of violence against women. In this process, the establishment of human rights standards for state responsibility and of mechanisms for international monitoring can play an important catalyzing role.

The power of education and the media to challenge societal norms and transform cultural values is critical to eradicating violence against women. In many parts of the world there is increasing interest in human rights education and the effort to remove gender bias from school curricula and teaching materials. This includes integrating gender awareness training, parenting skills, and nonviolent conflict resolution into school curricula, as well as providing training to teachers and educators. Moreover, gender awareness training should be institutionalized as part of the basic education of all those engaged in law enforcement, the judiciary, medical and social services, and so on.

Development agencies and programs should conduct their work with increased sensitivity to the issue of violence and to the ways in which development itself brings forth new forms of gendered violence. It is important to address gender-based violence as an aspect of many other development initiatives, including income-generating schemes or housing and transportation plans, and not just those specifically centered on women. International development agencies can also use their leverage and prestige to expand the legitimacy and give voice to groups working on these issues at the national or community level.

The human security of women, and the well-being of their dependents, will rely in large measure on the recognition that societies can alter traditions that include the abuse of women's human rights and develop new norms in their place without sacrificing their identity, stability, or economic well-being. Indeed, attempts to promote a culture of respect for human rights or to achieve sustainable development are doomed to failure if they do not address the issue of global violence against women. This chapter has attempted to build the case for the inclusion of efforts to combat gender-based violence as a major goal of international human rights and development. Likewise, it maintains that policies and programs that deal with violence toward women are building blocks for a more comprehensive, empowering, and therefore sustainable effort to achieve human security.

QUESTIONS FOR FURTHER STUDY

1. Why, in Bunch and Carrillo's view, should the "false distinction" between women's rights and human rights be eliminated? Do you agree or disagree with this view? On what basis?
2. Bunch and Carrillo identify attacks by men against women as a *global,* rather than a purely local or national problem. On what basis do they make this claim? Do you agree with their interpretation of the problem?
3. How, in the author's view, does violence against women impact on the prospects for socioeconomic progress in developing countries?
4. What role can the international community play in reducing the global epidemic of violence against women? Should efforts to combat global violence against women be incorporated into U.S. foreign policy? If so, how?

Notes

1. Although this chapter includes some updated material, it is primarily based on an earlier version that condensed two essays by Bunch and Carrillo from their pamphlet, *Gender Violence: A Development and Human Rights Issue* (New Brunswick, NJ: Center for Women's Global Leadership, Douglass College, Rutgers University, 1991).

2. United Nations Development Programme, *1994 Human Development Report* (New York and Oxford: Oxford University Press, l994), p. 1.

3. Ibid., p. 31.

4. Universal Declaration of Human Rights, adopted December 10, 1948, G.A. Res. 217A(III), Doc. A/810 (1948).

5. Reports and documents on the Beijing conferences are available from the UN Department of Public Information and on the World Wide Web at <http://www.un.org/womenwatch>.

6. Sundari Ravindran, *Health Implications of Sex Discrimination in Childhood* (Geneva: World Health Organization, 1986); UNICEF (United Nations Children's Fund), *Statistical Review of the Situation of Children of the World* (New York, 1986); Shushum Bhatia, "Status and Survival," *World Health* (April 1985), pp. 12–14.

7. Debbie Taylor, ed., *Women: A World Report: A New International Book* (Oxford: University Press, 1985), p. 10. For more statistics on the effects of sex discrimination see *The World's Women 1995: Trends and Statistics* (New York: United Nations, 1995).

8. Frequently, a husband will disguise the death of a bride as suicide or an accident in order to collect the marriage settlement paid to him by the bride's parents. Although dowry is now illegal in many countries, official records for 1987 showed 1,786 dowry deaths in India alone. See Lori Heise, "International Dimensions of Violence Against Women," *Response*, Vol. 12, No. 1 (1989), p. 5.

9. For more information see Center for Women's Global Leadership, *Gender Violence and Women's Human Rights in Africa* (New Brunswick, NJ: CWGL, 1994); Nahid Toubia, *Female Genital Mutilation: A Call for Global Action* (New York: RAINBO, 1993); Alison T. Slack, "Female Circumcision: A Critical Appraisal," *Human Rights Quarterly*, Vol. 10 (1988), p. 439.

10. National Center on Women and Family Law, Information Package on Battered Women, No. 47 (1988).

11. N.A. Straus, R. Gelles, and S.K. Steinmetz, *Behind Closed Doors: Violence in the American Family* (New York: Doubleday, 1981).

12. United Nations, *Women: Challenges to the Year 2000* (New York: United Nations, 1991), p. 67.

13. L. MacLeod, *Women and Environment*, Vol. 12, No.1 (Fall 1989/Winter 1990), p. 12.

14. Lori L. Heise, Jacqueline Pitanguy, and Adrienne Germain, *Violence Against Women: The Hidden Health Burden* (Washington: World Bank Discussion Papers, No. 255, 1994), pp. 6–10.

15. Instituto Latinoamericano de Estudios Transnacionales (ILET), *Mujer/Fempress*, No. 97 (November 1989), No. 100 (February/March 1990), No. 104 (June 1990); also the special issue on "Contraviolencia" (December 1988).

16. C. Bradley, "Wife-Beating in PNG—Is it a Problem?" *Papua New Guinea Medical Journal* (September 1988).

17. Asian Women's Research and Action Network (AWRAN), Report prepared for the Nairobi World Conference on Women (Philippines, 1985).

18. ILET No. 104 (June 1990) (see note 15).

19. *The World's Women: Trends and Statistics* (New York: United Nations, 1995).

20. Human Rights Watch, *Criminal Injustice: Violence Against Women in Brazil* (New York, Human Rights Watch, 1991).

21. AWRAN Report (1985) (see note 17).

22. Amartya Sen, "Gender and Cooperative Conflicts," in Irene Tinker, ed., *Persistent Inequalities: Women and World Development* (New York and Oxford: Oxford University Press, 1989), pp. 123–149. See also Stephen Klasen, "'Missing Women' Reconsidered," in *World Development*, Vol. 22, No. 7 (1994), pp. 1061–1071.

23. Georgina Ashworth, "Women and Human Rights," background paper for the Development Assistance Committee/Women in Development (DAC/WID) Expert Group on Women in Development, of the Organization for Economic Cooperation and Development (OECD) (Paris, 1992), p. 22.

24. Lori Heise, "International Dimensions of Violence Against Women," p. 3.

25. Riane Eisler, "Human Rights: Toward an Integrated Theory for Action," *Human Rights Quarterly*, Vol. 9 (1987), p. 297. See also Alida Brill, *Nobody's Business: The Paradoxes of Privacy* (New York: Addison-Wesley, 1990).

26. Fourth World Conference on Women, *Platform for Action and the Beijing Declaration*, UN Department of Public Information, Doc. No. DPI/1766/Wom-95–39642 (February 1996). Also available on the World Wide Web at <http://www.un.org/womenwatch>.

27. United Nations, *Declaration on the Elimination of Violence Against Women* (New York: United Nations, 1993).

28. The reports of the Special Rapporteur on Violence Against Women, its causes and consequences, can be found in the documentation of the annual sessions of the Commission on Human Rights since 1995.

29. United Nations Development Programme, *Human Development Report 1990* (New York and Oxford: Oxford University Press, 1990), p. 31.

30. R. Vasquez and G. Tamayo, *Violencia y Legalidad* (Lima: Concytec, 1989); J. Bruce and Dwyer, *A Home Divided* (Stanford: Stanford University Press, 1990).

31. AWRAN Report (1985) (see note 17).

32. "Women's Shelter Wants Women Only on Its Board," *The New York Times* (August 26, 1990).

33. Robert W. Connell, *Gender and Power* (Stanford: Stanford University Press, 1987), p. 11.

34. See Report of the White House Task Force on Infant Mortality, cited in *The New York Times* (August 12, 1990); M. Buvinic and S.W. Yudelman, *Women, Poverty, and Progress in the Third World* (New York: Foreign Policy Association, 1989).

35. Unpublished UNIFEM report (1990).

36. H. Noponen, "Grassroots Women's Worker Organization: Rhetoric and Reality," unpublished essay (1989).

37. Buvinic and Yudelman, *Women, Poverty, and Progress*, p. 44.

38. C.E. Koop, "Violence Against Women: A Global Problem," address at a seminar of the Pan American Health Organization, Washington, D.C. (May 22, 1989), pp.5–6.

39. Jane Perlez, "Toll of AIDS on Uganda's Women Puts Their Roles and Rights In Question," *The New York Times* (October 28, 1990).

40. Eisler, "Human Rights: Toward an Integrated Theory for Action," p. 297.

41. Ximena Bunster describes this in Chile and Argentina in "The Torture of Women Political Prisoners: A Case Study in Female Sexual Slavery," Kathleen Barry, Charlotte Bunch, and Shirley Castley, eds., *International Feminism: Networking Against Female Sexual Slavery* (New York: International Women's Tribune Center, 1984).

42. Report given by Margaret Groarke at Women's Panel, Amnesty International New York Regional Meeting (February 24, 1990).

43. United Nations, Convention on the Elimination of All Forms of Discrimination Against Women, UN Doc. A/Res/34/180 (1980).

44. "The Convention on the Elimination of All Forms of Discrimination Against Women," Summary of CEDAW prepared by the International Women's Rights Action Watch, Humphrey Institute of Public Affairs, Minneapolis (1988).

45. During the 1990s, efforts to strengthen the women's convention have been the focus of considerable organizing, and proposals to this effect were included in both the Vienna 1993 and the Beijing 1995 programs for action. They include a call for universal ratification of the convention, efforts to remove the reservations made by countries that have ratified which are contrary to the spirit of the convention, and the drafting of an optional protocol to the convention. The optional protocol is a mechanism that would allow the CEDAW Committee to receive interstate and individual complaints related to noncompliance with the convention and to initiate investigations of country violations of it.

46. Speech given by Ninotchka Rosca at Amnesty International New York Regional Conference (February 24, 1990), p. 2.

47. David Levinson, *Violence in Cross-Cultural Perspective,* (Newbury Park, CA: Sage, 1989).

13 / Transnational Criminal Organizations and International Security

PHIL WILLIAMS

To understand the causes of turbulence and disorder in the post-Cold War world it is necessary to examine subnational and transnational forces as well as interstate relations. There is, of course, a danger that consideration of new security challenges will encourage the fabrication of enemies or security threats. This, however, should not inhibit efforts to rethink the nature of challenges to national and international security, and to identify nontraditional threats when these have a valid empirical basis. In particular, it is necessary to analyze the threat posed by transnational criminal organizations (TCOs).[1]

There are several reasons why one might object to treating TCOs as an international security problem: they are economic rather than political; they do not appear to pose the same kind of overt or obvious challenge to states as do terrorist organizations; crime is usually viewed as a domestic problem; and law enforcement and national security are based on very different philosophies, organizational structures, and legal frameworks. The contention of this essay, however, is that TCOs pose serious threats to national and international security and are extremely resistant to efforts to contain, disrupt, or destroy them. The first section of the essay discusses the changing international conditions that have led to the emergence of TCOs; the second section looks at the structure and operations of TCOs, with particular attention given to some of the major examples; and the third analyzes the threats that TCOs pose to national and international security. The article concludes with an assessment of the problems faced by states in trying to control TCOs.

THE CHANGING INTERNATIONAL ENVIRONMENT

Organized crime has a long history, and traditionally has been seen as a domestic law-and-order problem—largely confined to particular societies such as Sicily, the United States, Japan, and Hong Kong. Over the past two decades, however, crime has taken on new international dimensions and criminal organizations have evolved to resemble transnational corporations. Although these TCOs are usually based partly on familial ties and kinship—

at least at the top level—their structures make them highly proficient, adaptable, and able to "treat national borders as nothing more than minor inconveniences to their criminal enterprises."[2]

The emergence of TCOs is partly a result of underlying changes in global politics and economics that have proved conducive to the development of *all* transnational organizations. The emergence and development of the "global village" in the second half of the twentieth century has fundamentally changed the context in which both legitimate and illegitimate businesses operate. Increased interdependence between nations, the ease of international travel and communications, the permeability of national boundaries, and the globalization of international financial networks have all facilitated the emergence of what is, in effect, a single global market for both licit and illicit commodities. This has created unprecedented opportunities for international criminal activity.

The past fifty years have witnessed a vast increase in transnational activity—the movements of information, money, physical objects, people, or other tangible or intangible items across state boundaries—in which at least one of the actors involved in the transaction is nongovernmental.[3] As Edward Morse has noted, virtually all tangible items involved in such transactions can be treated as a commodity or service to which a monetary value can be attached.[4] It is not surprising, therefore, that we have seen the development of TCOs that transport illicit commodities across national jurisdictions against the wishes of governments.[5]

With the globalization of trade and of consumer demand for leisure products, it is only natural that criminal organizations should become increasingly transnational in character. The very things that have made it possible to move goods, people, and money through the global economy have also facilitated the movement of "dirty money" and contract killers, as well as the transportation of drugs, arms, and illegal aliens. Indeed, transnational organized crime can be understood as the dark side of interdependence and globalization. Just as borders no longer provide an impediment to licit business activity, they are no longer a barrier to illicit activities. For TCOs, the formalities of sovereignty remain important only in terms of hindering government responses to criminal activities.

The scale of these activities largely reflects the opportunities resulting from changes in both international relations and the conditions within states. The second half of the twentieth century has not only witnessed a great increase in transactions across national boundaries that are neither initiated nor controlled by states, but has also seen a decline in effective state control over its own territory. TCOs are both contributors to, and beneficiaries of, these changes.

The speed and ease of international transport has greatly increased the ability of people and products to cross national boundaries. In a 1970s discussion of the underlying conditions that had led to the emergence of transnational corporations, Raymond Vernon noted that "between 1960 and 1974 . . . passenger volume on international commercial flights rose from 26 billion passenger miles to 152 billion."[6] By 1992, the figure had increased to between 600 and 700 billion passenger miles;[7] two years later, it had exceeded 850 billion passenger miles.[8] Other statistics underline the phenomenal growth that has taken place in transnational travel and movement. In 1984, for example, 288 million people entered the United States; by 1990 the figure had increased to 422 million; by 1992 it had gone up to 447 million.[9] In many areas, moreover, there has been a significant increase in both legal and illegal immigration.

Closely related to the increased mobility of populations has been the growth of international trade. Facilitated by the free-trade system of the postwar period, there has been a vast global increase in the import and export of goods and services. The increase in the value of world exports in the twenty years from 1970 to 1990 was immense. Using 1990 U.S. dollars as the base, global exports in 1970 totaled $1.27 trillion. By 1980 the figure had reached $2.2 trillion, and by 1990 it had increased to $3.3 trillion. Nor was the expansion complete: by 1995, the figure had climbed to approximately $4.3 trillion.[10]

The increase in transnational economic activity has made it easier to hide illicit transactions, products, and movements within the mass of licit transactions, products, and movements because law enforcement agencies and customs services are unable to inspect more than a small proportion of the cargoes and people coming into their territories. Moreover, the scale of the problem is constantly increasing. In 1990, for example, the number of dry cargo containers in use worldwide was a little under 6,000,000; by 1994 it had expanded to over 8,339,000. It is clear, therefore, that national borders have become increasingly porous.

Linked to the development of transport, communications, and international trade has been the growth of global financial networks. As Lawrence Krause has noted, this partly reflects the particular qualities of money: "Money is the most fungible of all commodities. It can be transmitted instantaneously and at low cost . . . It can change its identity easily and can be traced only with great effort if at all. These characteristics work to the disadvantages of governments in their efforts to tax, regulate, and control economic activity."[11] Indeed, the development of a perpetually active global financial system with multiple points of access and incomplete regulation is ideal for TCOs, which are thus able to move the profits from their illegal transactions with speed, ease, and relative impunity. In a sense, money laundering is simply one subset of the much larger problem of maintaining even a semblance of state control over global financial networks, which operate according to the logic of a global market and are not very responsive to the dictates of state economic policies or national legal requirements.

Global financial centers are associated with cities rather than countries—London, Frankfurt, New York, Tokyo, and Hong Kong. Yet this is part of a much broader phenomenon: the rise of world cities that are closely linked by advanced communication and transportation systems and act as the key nodes in the global economic system. This is reflected in the cosmopolitan nature of major cities throughout the world. Cities are the repositories not only of capital and wealth but also of technological innovation and advancement.[12] Along with corporations, they are major facilitators of transnational transactions. It is not coincidental, therefore, that large, global cities are also now the major loci for criminal organizations.[13] The cocaine trade, for example, has been dominated by cartels in two Colombian cities—Medellin and Cali. Similarly, Chinese criminal organizations based in Hong Kong play a major role in the distribution of heroin from Southeast Asia, and Istanbul acts as a clearinghouse for heroin being transshipped from Southwest Asia to Western Europe.

While changing international conditions have contributed to the rise of these illegal activities, and continue to facilitate them, criminal organizations have also taken advantage of the new markets that have resulted from the development of industrial and postindustrial "mass consumption" societies. The period since 1945 has seen unprecedented demands for goods and services, with surplus wealth creating new opportunities for recreation and leisure. While expenditure of wealth for pleasure is not new, there is an unprecedented number of people who are now able to engage in such spending.

Linked to this is the communications revolution, which has created a degree of global transparency that has both accentuated inequalities between societies and led to developing countries' emulation of patterns of consumption seen in economically advanced societies. Indeed, the growing ease of travel and the expansion of international communications has led to a convergence of consumer tastes in many different countries. Although "truly universal products are few and far between," we have seen the emergence of a global marketplace in which consumers "have access to information about goods and services from around the world."[14] Entrepreneurs have recognized the opportunities this presents for global marketing and the successful corporations are those which have acknowledged the emergence of global markets and effectively sought to exploit them.

It is in this connection that illegal narcotics have emerged as a global commodity of immense significance—and TCOs have developed to meet the demands of what has become, if not a single global market, a series of large regional markets in drugs. This is not new, of course, as during the nineteenth century opium was a key component of the international commodity trade (albeit a trade dominated largely by governments). Now, however, TCOs control what has become a global industry in heroin and cocaine production and distribution. Although the drug of choice differs from region to region, illicit drugs have become one of the few truly global products. Determining the scale of the global drug trafficking industry has proved elusive, primarily because of its illicit nature. Some estimates, however, have suggested that it is worth $500 billion per year—larger than the global trade in oil.[15] Although this is one of the more generous estimates, illicit drug trafficking is clearly a major worldwide economic activity.

Furthermore, it is likely that illicit drugs will become an even more significant commodity in the future. The turbulence that has arisen with the end of the Cold War, the resurgence of ethnic and regional conflicts, and the rise of subnational groups challenging existing states have created a growing number of groups and actors requiring armaments. Engaging in criminal activity—especially drug trafficking—is often an efficient way to obtain the funds needed to buy arms. Examples of this range from the Tamil Tigers of Sri Lanka to several of the factions involved in the Balkans conflict. In the future, therefore, the development of the drug trade is increasingly likely to be influenced by political as well as economic motives.

One important implication of all this is that there are likely to be new opportunities for criminal activities that are regional and global rather than local or national in scale. Furthermore, the incentives for engaging in such activities are likely to increase rather than decrease in the future. Continued inequalities—both within and between societies—combine with poverty to encourage individuals and groups to engage in illicit activities as a source of income. This is as true of the Peruvian and Bolivian peasants who grow coca as it is of the young African Americans who sell drugs in U.S. cities.

If opportunity and incentives are important in the globalization of crime, so too are capabilities: the criminal groups that have developed into transnational criminal corporations have displayed both organizational skill and entrepreneurial flair. The next section offers a discussion of these groups and their activities, and suggests that they rival many transnational corporations in the scale and sophistication of their activities, in their search for and penetration of global markets, and in their disregard for national boundaries.

THE RISE OF TRANSNATIONAL CRIMINAL ORGANIZATIONS

Just as the modern industrial economy and the rise of mass consumer markets encouraged the growth of organized crime in the United States, so growing opportunities for transnational activities have facilitated the growth of TCOs. Not only is transnational economic activity as open to criminal groups as to legitimate transnational corporations, but the character of criminal organizations also makes them particularly suited to exploit these new opportunities. Since criminal groups are used to operating outside the rules, norms, and laws of domestic jurisdictions, they have few qualms about crossing national boundaries illegally. In many respects, therefore, TCOs are transnational organizations par excellence. They operate outside the existing structures of authority and power in world politics, and have developed sophisticated strategies for circumventing law enforcement efforts both in individual states and in the global community of states.

Samuel P. Huntington of Harvard University has described transnational organizations as entities that conduct centrally directed operations in the territory of two or more nation-states, mobilize resources and pursue optimizing strategies across national boundaries, are functionally specific, and seek to penetrate but not acquire new territories.[16] This is also true of TCOs. Criminal enterprises, however, differ from legal transnational organizations in one crucial respect: transnational organizations seek access to territory and markets through negotiation with states,[17] while TCOs obtain access not through consent but through circumvention. They engage in systematic activities to evade government controls—a process made all the easier by the fact that the conditions which have given rise to the TCO's emergence also make it very difficult for governments to counter them.

TCOs vary considerably in size, scale, and degree of sophistication. Some, like the Colombian cartels, focus almost exclusively on drug trafficking, while others like the Chinese triads or Japanese Yakuza, engage in a whole series of criminal activities, including extortion, credit card fraud, and control of prostitution, along with drug trafficking. Both the common and the idiosyncratic features of these organizations are evident in the following overview of the major TCOs.

The Italian Mafia

Until very recently, the very notion of organized crime was almost synonymous with the Italian Mafia, whether in Italy itself or the United States. In the United States, however, the Italian Mafia has declined in importance—partly because of the inroads made by the FBI (using electronic surveillance techniques and effective use of informants), partly because of the growing assimilation of Italian Americans into the economic, political, and social mainstream, partly because of the rise of ruthless competitors in the form of other ethnic criminal organizations, and partly because of the "altered structure of urban politics and policing" which has reduced the opportunities for corruption.[18] In addition, a continued reliance on brute force rather than sophisticated business strategies has placed the Mafia at a competitive disadvantage compared with other groups.

Indicators of the Mafia's decline in the United States include a drop in membership of the five major New York Mafia families from 3,000 in the early 1970s to 1,200 in the mid-1990s, and the fact that twelve Philadelphia Mafiosi requested representation by the public defender rather than using more expensive mob lawyers.[19] The extent of this decline, however, has been a matter of considerable controversy, with some experienced observers claiming that celebrations of the Mafia's demise are premature. The willingness of Russian criminal organizations engaged in gasoline fuel scams to share the proceeds with Italian criminal groups in New York suggests that the Mafia is still a force to be reckoned with.

If Italian-American criminal organizations remain an important component of what one commentator has termed a new criminal mosaic, they are no longer clearly the overwhelming or dominant presence.[20] Chinese, Colombian, Dominican, Vietnamese, African-American, Russian, Albanian, Jamaican, and Nigerian organizations have all become participants in a much more complex and competitive criminal environment.[21] In some cases, these new groups are both more ruthless and more violent than the Italians. They are also more difficult targets for U.S. law enforcement agencies, which spent years developing expertise on Italian criminal organizations and were able to use the Racketeer Influenced and Corrupt Organizations Act (more commonly known as RICO) and electronic surveillance to very good effect. The overall result has been that Italian organized crime in the United States has had to accommodate the newcomers; to some extent, in fact, it has been surpassed by them.

In Italy, by contrast, the Mafia continues to dominate criminal activities in what still remains its exclusive domain (although even here, it has suffered some major setbacks). While the term Italian Mafia is used very widely, in many respects it is inadequate to describe an organized crime world encompassing four distinct groups:

- The Sicilian Mafia, or Cosa Nostra, which consists of some 180 criminal groups and 5,000 "men of honor." Since the early 1980s, it has been dominated by the Corleonesi family.[22]
- The Neapolitan Camorra, made up of a number of gangs which sometimes band together but more often engage in bloody wars."[23] The Camorra engages in various criminal activities, ranging from extortion to drug trafficking and cigarette smuggling, and exerts considerable influence on municipal councils—with the result that, in the mid-1990s, thirty-two of seventy-five councils in Campania had to be dissolved.[24]
- The Calabrian 'Ndrangheta, a federation of families engaging in contraband tobacco smuggling, drug trafficking, and kidnapping, with some 160 criminal groups and over 6,000 personnel.[25] Factional differences within the 'Ndrangheta made Calabria the most violent region in Italy, and led in the early 1990s to the creation of a "provincial commission" to provide peaceful arbitration among the various factions.[26]
- The "Sacra Corona Unita" in Apulia, which is based on breakaway factions from the Camorra and 'Ndrangheta and is less powerful than the other three branches.

While each of these organizations has its own specialization, all four are founded upon the law of silence (*omerta*) and upon close associations that are partly functional, partly personal and familial, and partly based on fear. Of the four groups, the Sicilian Cosa Nostra remains the most powerful and has successfully transformed itself from a predominantly rural phenomenon to a transnational criminal enterprise based on "industrial and business cultures."[27]

Although many of its activities are still regional, and its power base remains Sicily and Southern Italy, the Cosa Nostra has spread its influence to the United States, Germany, and other European countries. It is in Italy itself, however, that the Cosa Nostra has had the greatest impact, partly because, in the aftermath of World War II, it succeeded in establishing a remarkably durable symbiotic relationship with segments of the political elite. "The Mafia entered the world of politics, commerce, and public administration as a direct participant," providing political support for politicians—who, in turn, helped to ensure a continuing flow of contracts, franchises, and jobs.[28] The symbiosis between the Mafia and the Christian Democrats allowed the Cosa Nostra to flourish.

For a variety of reasons, this collusive relationship began to unravel during the 1980s. Factional fights, the defection of Tommaso Buscetta (a well-informed Mafia member), the investigations by magistrates who could be neither bought nor intimidated, and the Maxi-trials (a series of trials of large numbers of Mafia members) led the Cosa Nostra to conclude that its protectors had reneged on their agreement. The result was a war against the Italian state. However, after the assassinations of the two leading anti-Mafia magistrates, Falcone and Borsellino, the Italian state initiated "its most vigorous anti-Mafia campaign in decades."[29] The campaign had remarkable results, including the arrest of Salvatore Riina, the apparent leader of the Cosa Nostra, and of Giovanni Brusca, the killer of Falcone.

Pressure from the government and particularly its encouragement of "turncoats," or *pentiti,* has also eroded what were once sacrosanct norms and conventions. As the law of silence has broken down, wives and families have become targets of vendettas. There has also been a significant deterioration in the political power of the Mafia—and a closely associated decline in profit levels. An assessment in *Il Mondo* in 1995 suggested that falling revenues from drug trafficking, a sharp drop in public works spending, stagnation in the market for new construction, increased asset seizure by courts, *pentiti* information that helped law enforcement to target Mafia assets, and increasing legal expenses had all created unprecedented financial problems for the Mafia.[30]

In spite of these setbacks, however, Italian organized crime should not be counted out. Patron-client relations are deeply embedded in Italian political life and, although old political affiliations have dissolved, new ones can be created. Moreover, the four major groups have forged new ties with one another, a development characterized by one shrewd observer as "the syndication of Italian organized crime, a form of internal *pax mafiosa* directed at maximizing profit and minimizing conflict."[31] In addition, the Mafia continues to operate extensively in other countries in Europe. In 1994, for example, members of Italian groups accounted for about 5.7 percent of individuals from criminal organizations apprehended in Germany.[32]

Equally significant, both the Cosa Nostra and the other major criminal organizations have developed close ties with their counterparts in Colombia and Russia. The Mafia's cooperative arrangements with the Colombian cartels allowed the latter to break into the European drug markets while allowing the Italians to diversify from heroin distribution and sales into the cocaine market and to assist with money laundering. Such cooperation has several levels:

At the lowest level are simple buyer-seller deals involving relatively small investments, little advance planning, and relatively little interaction between the parties . . . [while] at the highest level is what might be called strategic cooperation,
which encompasses the principles of long-term agreements, large volume shipments of both drugs and money, and the creation of specialized infrastructure to
facilitate these flows.[33]

Whatever the level, it is clear that such cooperation enhances the capacity of
criminal organization to circumvent and to challenge governments, and also
opens up new criminal opportunities.

Similarly, Italian Mafia linkages with Russian criminal organizations
have provided new ventures in money laundering, trafficking in counterfeit
currency, munitions trafficking, and drug smuggling. There have also been
persistent reports that Italian criminal organizations have been active in
acquiring nuclear materials from the former Soviet Union—although
whether this was for their own use or resale is not clear. Whatever the case,
these foreign activities provide not only new sources of profit but also a
cushion that helps the Mafia to absorb its losses within Italy. The Italian
Mafia has proven very resilient in the past. In view of its extensive criminal
activities, its vast (if diminished) earning power, and its known capacity to
corrupt the political system, celebrations of its demise would be premature.

Russian Organized Crime

The rise of Russian organized crime has been remarkable. Although the
Russian Mafiya had antecedents in the black market operators of the
centralized economy and in a criminal underworld dominated by "thieves
professing the code"—professional criminals who lived by a code which
included a complete lack of cooperation with the authorities and which
ascribed high status to those who served time in prison—crime in the Soviet
Union was circumscribed and contained by the state. There were symbiotic
relationships between the criminal underworld and the state, but these were
dominated by the latter. However, the collapse of centralized power in the
Soviet Union completely altered the relationship between the state apparatus and criminal organizations. Although some symbiotic relationships persist, organized crime, rather than the state, is now the dominant partner.

According to published Ministry of Interior figures on Russian organized crime, there has been a constant growth in the number of criminal
organizations. The figures have inexorably moved upward, from 3,000 in
1992 to 5,700 in 1994 and about 8,000 in early 1996. At first glance, these
figures seem to reveal an ever increasing threat from an expanding criminal
empire. It is equally plausible, however, that the increase reflects looser criteria for categorizing groups as criminal organizations and, in particular, the
inclusion of small and unimportant street gangs. The higher numbers could
also reflect fissiparous tendencies in many Russian criminal organizations,
which have led to fragmentation into smaller groups, threat inflation on the

part of Russian law enforcement authorities eager for more Western assistance, or simply increased visibility of criminal organizations as a result of more efficient policing and better intelligence analysis. Moreover, the official figures do not reveal the process of consolidation among individual organizations that has led well-informed observers to claim that there are about two hundred major criminal organizations with widespread geographical and sectoral influence. According to a detailed analysis by Guy Dunn of Control Risks, there are six large groups in Moscow—three Chechen groups (the Tstentralnaya, Ostankinskaya, and Avtomobilnaya) plus the Solntsevskaya, the Podolskaya, and the Twenty-First Century Association—four more major groups in St. Petersburg, two major gangs in Yekaterinburg (the Uralmashkaya and the Tsentralnaya), and nine major gangs in Vladivostok.[34]

Even with the consolidation process, organized crime in Russia remains fractured, with divisions based on ethnicity, territorial and sectoral control, and generational shifts—although conflict among groups has not precluded cooperation when it was obviously beneficial. Indeed, one important characteristic of Russian organized crime has been the *obshak,* or common pool of resources, used for bribery and corruption, to generate new enterprises, and to support the families of those in prison. More often than not, however, such cooperation has been outweighed by competition among the groups. A major split has emerged between "thieves professing the code" and the new generation of criminals who do not respect established traditions, are more entrepreneurial and, in some cases, have become "authorities" because of wealth, rather than status accrued through time in prison. As a result, the "thieves" have suffered considerable attrition. Overlapping this particular rift is a continuing struggle for dominance between the Russian or Slavic groups and those from the Caucasus.

From the perspective of Russian law enforcement, this diversity is an advantage: competition among criminal organizations is preferable to further consolidation. At the same time, the very diversity and complexity of Russian criminal organizations make concerted action against them difficult. So does the fact that many of the groups have infiltrated licit businesses and established inroads in key sectors of the legal economy. In August 1995, the MVD All-Russia Scientific Research Institute estimated that criminal groups control over four hundred banks. More pessimistic assessments suggest that as much as 70 to 80 percent of the private banks in Russia are controlled by organized crime. Although it is uncertain what such control means in this context, it is clear that criminal organizations exert considerable influence over the banking sector as well as other parts of the Russian economy. Extortion has become pervasive and contract killings are often used to remove those who resist or to settle disputes.

Drug trafficking in Russia has become a major activity, involving not only well-publicized links with Colombian cocaine traffickers, but also the supply of opium, heroin, and marijuana from Central Asia and the Golden Crescent of Southwest Asia. In addition, clandestine laboratories have appeared, producing synthetic drugs—something that is hardly surprising given the combination of technical and scientific expertise on the one side and unemployment and inflation on the other. While some organizations specialize in drug trafficking, others combine this with other activities such as car theft, prostitution, extortion, and fraud. Indeed, one of the strengths of organized crime in Russia is that it has so many different dimensions and engages in such a wide range of activity.

The issue that has aroused the greatest trepidation, however, is that of nuclear-material smuggling. Lack of security at some nuclear facilities as well as poor inventory management has provided criminal opportunities for disgruntled workers in the nuclear industry. The possibility that such workers, either through economic need or intimidation, could offer weapons-grade material to criminal organizations provides the basis for nightmare scenarios that range from large-scale environmental damage to nuclear terrorism or nuclear extortion. What remains unknown, however, is the extent to which such trafficking is a core activity of Russian criminal organizations. For the most part, such trafficking has been the preserve of amateur smugglers rather than well-established criminal groups. Yet there is some evidence that criminal organizations have been involved in this activity on a limited basis. One arrest seems to have involved twelve members of the Solntsevskaya in possession of radioactive material; in another case, a group of criminals from Yekaterinburg was involved in the smuggling of large amounts of zirconium to the United States and Cyprus. Nuclear-material trafficking is not yet a core activity of Russian organized crime—not least because the risks are high and the profits uncertain—but could become increasingly significant, especially as more Russian criminal organizations become transnational.

Indeed, many of the Russian criminal organizations have already established branches in other countries. In the United States, Russian criminals have been involved in fuel tax evasion schemes, health care and insurance fraud, extortion, car theft, and contract murders. Elsewhere, Cyprus has become a major recipient of the profits of Russian criminal activity, while in London there is concern about money laundering through British financial institutions. Russian criminal organizations have also established a limited presence in Germany, which has become a source of stolen luxury cars for the Russian market, a battleground for intergroup rivalries, and a market for both illicit products and for licit products that have been obtained through illegal means.[35]

One of the problems for law enforcement agencies combating Russian criminal organizations is that these organizations operate from what is, in effect, a sanctuary or safe haven. Through a mixture of corruption and coercion they are able to ensure that this home base in Russia remains a congenial environment *in* which, and *from* which, they can operate with a high degree of impunity. And, unless the Russian state is able to develop both a greater capability and will to tackle criminal organizations, the situation could worsen. Indeed, if domination by the Communist Party is ultimately replaced not by democratic politics and the free market, but by the domination of organized crime, then Russia will become an even more important base for transnational criminal activities.

Chinese Criminal Organizations

If Russian criminal organizations are becoming increasingly transnational in scope, Chinese criminal organizations have traditionally had this character- istic. The Chinese diaspora has provided global networks that have helped to facilitate both licit and illicit business. It has also provided an excellent environment for the overseas activities of Chinese "triads" (secret societies which have become criminal organizations) based in Hong Kong and Taiwan. Details of these criminal societies make sobering reading. Law enforcement estimates suggest that there are currently about fifty triad societies (with at least 80,000 members) in Hong Kong, of which fifteen are very active. The largest triad is the Sun Yee On, with an estimated 25,000 members. The Wo Group, including the Wo Hop To and at least nine other subgroups, has more than 20,000 while the 14K (and its various subgroups) also has over 20,000 members. There are also two major triads based in Taiwan: the United Bamboo Gang, with an estimated membership of over 20,000, and the Four Seas Gang, which has about 5,000 members. All of these groups are augmented by a considerable, although uncertain, number of overseas members.

Details of triad membership do not convey the unique duality in Chinese organized crime. On the one hand, there are the formal organizational structures—triads, tongs (chambers of commerce in many Chinatowns), and street gangs—that provide a framework for Chinese criminal activities. On the other, it is clear that much Chinese crime is transaction based rather than organization based—that is, individuals and small groups come together for particular criminal activities, disperse, and then reassemble according to needs and opportunities. This is not to deny the importance of the triads, which act like alumni associations, facilitating trust and providing introduc- tions and assistance. Although triads have formal structures, with a dragon head and specialists such as enforcers and administrators, much of Chinese criminal activity takes place among triad members who operate on an ad hoc basis and establish fluid networks that are based partly on membership and partly on *guanxi*—a concept of reciprocal obligation, based on family and social relationships, that can span generations.[36]

This mixture of formal structure and informal activities complicates the tasks of law enforcement. It also makes it more difficult to identify career criminals and to differentiate between legal and illegal enterprises. An important consequence of this is the very considerable scope of independent criminal entrepreneurship.[37] In Australia, for instance, Chinese criminal net- works engage in a wide variety of organized criminal activities and have become the most important heroin importers in that country—operating largely at the wholesale level and leaving the drug retail business to others, including Vietnamese groups.[38]

In short, Chinese criminal enterprises are highly flexible and able to exploit new opportunities as they arise. In recent years, one of the most significant opportunities has stemmed from the desire of many Chinese to migrate from China to the West. While there has been considerable legal migration, a lucrative business has developed in bringing illegal immigrants to the United States and Western Europe. Most of the illegal migrants coming to the United States travel by air, often by circuitous routes, using false documentation—a requirement that has generated a cottage industry in the production of false passports, visas, and the like. About 10 percent are smuggled in by sea, often enduring months of hardship and ill treatment at the hands of the smugglers. In those cases where the migrants are unable to pay the remainder of the fee—and fees generally range from $25,000 to $30,000—they are made to work in sweatshops or recruited into criminal activities such as drug trafficking or prostitution.

The comprehensive nature of Chinese criminal activities, the difficulties faced by law enforcement in attempting to infiltrate closely knit ethnic groups, the Chinese takeover of Hong Kong, and the vast upsurge of organized crime and corruption in China itself suggest that the Chinese organized crime problem is likely to increase rather than decrease. For one thing, China has once again become a major consumer of heroin, most of which is smuggled across the border from Burma. In addition, the rapid expansion of capitalism in China provides enormous opportunities for criminal organizations, as "old systems and ideas have broken down and new social guarantees and prevention forces are not yet in place."[39] The extent of the problem was evident in 1993 when Chinese authorities reported that they had disrupted over 150,000 criminal groups with over 570,000 members.[40] Although these figures may include political activists as well as criminals, they nevertheless reveal that Chinese criminal organizations are a significant problem inside China.

Japanese Yakuza

The Japanese umbrella term for organized crime is Yakuza or Boryokudan (violent ones). Like the term "Mafia," however, the Yakusa actually encompasses several distinct organizations, the most important of which is the Yamaguchi-gumi, which a few years ago had an estimated membership of over 26,000. The second largest gang is the Inagawa-kai, which had over 8,600 members, while the third largest, the Sumiyoshi-kai, had over 7,000.[41] In the mid-1990s these groups were the target of an intense crackdown by Japanese law enforcement agencies using new anti-Boryokudan laws and a strategy that encouraged defection. The result has been a marked decline in membership of the Yamaguchi-gumi, Inagawa-kai, and Sumiyoshi-kai to about 34,600.[42] In addition, Japanese authorities reported that in 1993 they succeeded in dissolving 222 smaller criminal organizations with over 2,600 members.[43]

Nevertheless, the Yakuza remains active in a variety of criminal enterprises, including racketeering and extortion. Japanese criminal organizations have made extensive use of front companies to penetrate the licit economy, especially in the areas of construction, financing and insurance, and real estate.[44] Although they have been less international than many other such entities, the Yakuza have been involved in significant criminal activities across national borders, including trafficking methamphetamine into Hawaii and California and smuggling guns from the United States into Japan. In addition, the Yakuza has moved into gambling, fraud, and money laundering. Yakuza members have been deeply involved in the sex and drug trades and have also invested heavily in real estate in Hawaii. Elsewhere in the United States, Japanese criminal organizations have invested in real estate (especially golf courses) and legitimate American corporations.[45]

The Yakuza also has a significant presence throughout much of Southeast Asia, where Japanese criminals have became a major force in the sex industry. This is certainly the case in the Philippines, which has also been used by the Yakuza as a base for production and smuggling of amphetamines and handguns.[46] Another major target for investment has been South Korea, where Japanese Yakuza organizations have purchased or invested in hotels, gambling establishments, and, in at least one case, a department store.[47] As part of what is clearly a more diversified criminal portfolio, Japanese criminal organizations have also helped smuggle Chinese illegal migrants into Japan.[48] Thus, even though they are under considerable pressure in their home base, Japanese criminal organizations have developed an important reservoir of resources and profits through their transnational activities.

Colombian Drug Cartels

Unlike most other transnational criminal organizations which tend to engage in a range of illegal activity, the Colombian cartels focus almost exclusively on drug trafficking. At the same time, however, they have diversified their markets to include Western Europe in addition to the United States, and expanded their products to include heroin as well as cocaine. Some of the major organizations within the drug industry in Colombia have amalgamated corporate and criminal cultures, using sound management principles (such as specialization and division of labor) while also employing classical criminal techniques of violence and corruption.

During the 1980s, Carlos Lehder and other members of the Medellin Cartel led the way in applying industrial-style transport to the drug trafficking business, increasing the amounts of cocaine transported into the United States by air. The Cali Cartel took this a stage further and applied successful business management techniques and meticulous accounting procedures to its activities. Although the Medellin Cartel is still active in drug trafficking—and there have been allegations that the Ochoas (two of the cartel's top leaders) are still running their drug business from prison—the killing of Pablo Escobar (another key leader) by government forces both highlighted and accentuated the shift in power from the Medellin Cartel to the Cali Cartel. For its part, the Cali Cartel adopted a strategy of co-option rather than confrontation, and tried to establish a modus vivendi with the Colombian government through high-level corruption.

Under pressure from Washington, the Colombian government initiated a major crackdown on the cartels in the mid-1990s, resulting in the captivity or death of key cartel leaders. While the cartels have not been completely destroyed, the Medellin and Cali organizations are clearly no longer the force they once were. These successes against Medellin and Cali have not destroyed the drug industry in Colombia, but have neutralized—at least temporarily—the threat to the state posed by powerful criminal organizations with large disposable resources and a substantial capacity for both violence and corruption. In the long term, however, successor trafficking organizations could come to pose an equally formidable threat to the government.

Nigerian Criminal Organizations

The emergence of Nigerian criminal organizations is often traced to the collapse of oil prices in the early 1980s and the dislocation this caused to an economy that, by the late 1970s, had come to rely on oil for 95 percent of its export earnings.[49] At that time, many sophisticated and college-educated Nigerians located in other countries were effectively deprived of their source of income. In some cases they turned to crime, often with spectacularly successful results. Indeed, Nigerians have developed large-scale drug trafficking activities and have been identified as second only to the Chinese in the import of heroin into the United States. Once again, this was facilitated by the fact that they were able to operate from a relatively safe home base, characterized by an unstable government, a high level of corruption, and few resources to devote to the fight against organized crime.

The Nigerian criminal organizations have proved to be very adept in finding alternative trafficking routes, concealment techniques, courier profiles, and choice of product, and have progressed from simply being drug couriers for other TCOs to becoming major players in their own right. Although there is little evidence of a formal Nigerian cartel, a loose network of drug barons has been identified and it is clear that even the activities of couriers are carefully orchestrated. In October 1996, the United States Department of Justice announced the arrest of thirty-four members of a transnational heroin network that was run largely by Nigerian women. The arrests were made primarily in Chicago, New York, and Detroit, but one person was arrested in Bangkok and one in Pakistan; the key distributor of the heroin in the United States proved to be a Nigerian woman who used her Chicago boutique as a front.

Nigerian criminal activities in the United States have not been limited to drug trafficking. Deputy Assistant Secretary of State Jonathan Winer described Nigerian criminal enterprises as "adaptable, polycrime organizations" that are active in at least sixty countries. "They launder money in Hong Kong, buy cocaine in the Andes, run prostitution and gambling rings in Spain and Italy, and corrupt legitimate businesses in Great Britain with their financial crimes."[50] There is also a large number of fraudulent proposals emanating from Lagos and directed at wealthy businessmen. It has been estimated that America loses $250 million a year in "4-1-9 schemes, a term that refers to the section of the Nigerian criminal code dealing with advance fee frauds. Individual losses range from around $10,000 to about $4 million."[51] Those perpetrating the frauds are very skilled, ensuring that all the documentation looks official. Nigerian organizations have also engaged in fraudulent activities related to credit cards, commercial banks, and government assistance programs. They have proved adept at obtaining the documentation for false identities that have facilitated check kiting, student loan fraud, social services fraud, insurance fraud, and electronic funds transfer fraud.

The members of these organizations tend to live modestly and ship money back to Nigeria, where few, if any, questions are asked about its origin. Although legislation has been passed against money laundering, it is far from clear that this is being vigorously implemented. This provides opportunities for leaders of these organizations to accumulate considerable wealth. Not surprisingly, the success of Nigerian criminal organizations has bred imitation elsewhere in Africa, as individuals and groups from Ghana, Benin, and Sierra Leone have become involved in transnational crime, especially drug trafficking.

Although law enforcement agencies have had some success in curbing their activities, the Nigerian organizations have several built-in defense mechanisms. The use of a variety of different dialects, for example, reduces the usefulness of wiretaps and other electronic surveillance devices; in essence, they have found a nontechnological method of circumventing high-tech policing. The fact that these organizations tend to be based on family or tribal ties also makes them very difficult to infiltrate. Although the threat they pose in terms of corruption and violence in Western countries is less than that of most other groups, they are a particular threat to states in transition. For instance, Nigerian criminal organizations are very active in drug trafficking in Russia, and in South Africa their activities have done much to create large heroin and cocaine markets—a particularly damaging process in a country facing the formidable tasks of nation-building and state-building.

Other Criminal Organizations

This survey of TCOs, limited by space considerations, has omitted Turkish criminal groups, Jamaican posses, African-American criminal organizations, Mexican drug trafficking families, Dominican organizations, and Pakistani drug barons, among others. Even so, it highlights the growing scope and penetration of organized crime into virtually all regions of the world. This process has been accompanied by a growing interconnectivity among criminal organizations. In Belgium, for example, indigenous criminal groups have links with Chinese and Italian groups as well as with Turkish networks; in the Czech Republic, meanwhile, law enforcement authorities complain that indigenous criminal groups have been relegated to "service" organizations for stronger organizations from elsewhere.[52]

The nature of these linkages extends from transient one-off connections to much more permanent cooperative arrangements that can legitimately be described as strategic alliances. These alliances enhance the capacity of TCOs to circumvent control efforts by states and law enforcement agencies, facilitate risk-sharing, neutralize or co-opt potential competitors, and enable trafficking organizations to exploit differential profit margins in different markets. They also suggest that TCOs constitute an increasingly formidable adversary for states. The extent to which their activities constitute a threat to national and international security is examined next.

THE THREAT TO SECURITY

It is tempting to say that the activities of transnational criminal organizations have little impact on world security. Unlike revolutionary or terrorist groups, TCOs have predominantly economic objectives. Moreover, it is arguable that even illicit enterprises add to national wealth, create jobs, and provide a safety net of sorts against recession. The profits from their activities are enormous and at least some of them are ploughed back into local and national economies, usually with some multiplier effects. In these circumstances, one might conclude that TCOs do not pose a threat to national and international security.

Such an assessment is based on a narrow military conception of security. If security is defined not simply in terms of defense against external military threats but as pertaining to all challenges to the effective functioning of society, then drug trafficking and organized crime are much more serious than many other problems that have traditionally been viewed as security threats. Drug trafficking, for example, poses one of the most serious challenges to the fabric of society in the United States and Western Europe, and even in many of the drug-producing countries (which have also become consumers of their product). In recognition of this, drug trafficking was designated a national security threat by the Reagan Administration in 1986, and subsequent administrations have concurred with this assessment. The Clinton Administration has gone even further, defining international organized crime as a significant threat to U.S. national security. Taking this further, it is clear that TCOs pose threats to security at three levels—the individual, the nation-state, and the international system of states.[53]

At the individual level, security can be defined as the provision of a relatively safe and secure environment in which citizens do not fear harm or intimidation and are able to pursue their right to life and property without danger of organized violence. TCOs have had a profound impact on these aspects of security. Indeed, if individual security is inversely related to the level of violence within society—the greater the violence, the less the security enjoyed by citizens—then transnational organized crime, drug trafficking, and associated activities pose a very real security threat. This is partly because of the close connection between drugs and violence. There are, in fact, three kinds of violence usually associated with the drug industry: violence by criminal organizations to protect their "turf" and profits, crimes against people and property by drug users who need to pay for illicit drugs, and violence perpetrated by individuals under the influence of mind-altering substances.[54] It has been estimated, for example, that the average heroin user commits two hundred crimes a year to feed the habit.[55]

Transnational criminal organizations can also pose serious threats to the security of both their home and their host states. Their willingness to use force against the state and its agents challenges the state monopoly on organized violence, and can be more destructive or destabilizing than the activities of revolutionary or terrorist groups. In some cases, their power rivals that of the state itself. This has certainly been the case in Colombia and Italy, where TCOs have resisted state control and engaged in extensive violence and terrorism. In Colombia, the Medellin Cartel posed a direct threat to the Colombian government and, despite the death of Pablo Escobar, the devastation has been enormous. The Colombian judiciary has been decimated, the level of violence has at times reached levels characteristic of small civil wars, and Colombian political and economic activity has been dominated by the threats posed by the *narcotrafficantes*. The cartels have eroded the country's democratic values, killing journalists critical of their activities and corrupting the institutions of the state.

Similar problems have been experienced in Italy, where the Mafia has launched attacks on the judiciary and proved to be a far more formidable enemy than terrorist organizations such as the Red Brigades. This is partly so because the Mafia created an illicit but effective parallel authority structure, with its own territory, population, laws, and armed forces.[56] Having gained tremendous power and wealth through its involvement in the heroin trade from Southeast Asia and the cocaine trade from Latin America, the Mafia has routinely used both corruption and violence to further its aims. Although its violence ultimately proved counterproductive, events in Italy revealed the vulnerability of even advanced industrialized states to the challenge posed by powerful TCOs.

These challenges to state authority may be unavoidable. As one eminent criminologist has noted, "each crime network attempts to build a coercive monopoly and to implement that system of control through at least two other criminal activities—corruption of public and private officials, and violent terrorism in order to enforce its discipline."[57] This would certainly apply to Russia, where criminal organizations have used violence and intimidation not only against each other, but also against bankers, businessmen, journalists, and those politicians and administrators not easily susceptible to corruption. Contract killings have become frequent occurrences, eroding the willingness and ability of the government to take decisive action against criminal organizations that are becoming a dominant force in Russia's society and economy. By their very nature, TCOs undermine civil society, destabilize domestic politics, challenge the effectiveness of government, and undercut the rule of law.

Transnational criminal organizations sometimes create chaos, but they also exploit the uncertainty created by other domestic and international developments. Not surprisingly, TCOs flourish in states with weak authority structures and dubious legitimacy—whether derived from economic inequalities, the dominance of traditional oligarchies, the lack of congruence between nation and state, poor economic performance, ethnic divisions, or a combination of the above. In such circumstances, the development of parallel political and economic structures is almost inevitable. In some instances, government institutions may be so corrupt that they no longer have either the incentive or the capacity to reassert control. Indeed, if TCOs often emerge where the state is weak, they have a vested interest in perpetuating that weakness—and in encouraging acquiescence, connivance, or even involvement in their activities by government and law enforcement officials.

It is important not to overstate the importance of TCOs in causing political upheaval, because whenever states lose legitimacy and political authority, the problems have deep and extensive roots. Nevertheless, there is an important link between the rise of TCOs on one hand, and the crisis of governance and decline in civil society, which have become such familiar features of the post-Cold War world, on the other. Whatever the underlying reason for the breakdown in authority structures, political chaos provides a congenial environment for criminal activity. Moreover, a key feature of TCOs is that they link "zones of peace" and "zones of turbulence" in the international system—that is, they transport illicit products from one zone to another (e.g., arms in, drugs out).[58] They take advantage of the chaos that exists, for example, in countries such as Myanmar and Afghanistan, both of which lack an effective, legitimate government, are the world's main producers of heroin, and are internationally isolated, yet linked to other areas through clandestine criminal networks.

Threats to the integrity of states generate challenges to the international state system as a whole. Although the field of security issues has traditionally focused on military relations between states, in the future it will also have to consider the relationship between states and powerful non-state actors. The traditional dominance of governments has increasingly been challenged by the emergence of such actors, especially those with transnational ties. Lacking the attributes of sovereignty is often an advantage, rather than a constraint, for such transnational actors—they are sovereignty free rather than sovereignty bound—and they use this freedom and flexibility to engage in activities that are difficult for states to regulate.[59] The issue is control versus autonomy: states want control and transnational actors want autonomy.

Transnational criminal organizations challenge aspects of state sovereignty and security that have traditionally been taken for granted. They demonstrate the permeability of national borders and readily penetrate societies that are nominally under the control of established nation-states. The states may retain formal sovereignty in such circumstances, but if they are unable to control the importation of arms, people, and drugs into their territory, it loses much of its significance. Sovereignty may remain a useful basis for the international society of states, but it no longer reflects real control over the territorial dimension of statehood. The concept of sovereignty and the permeability of national boundaries do not make easy bedfellows.

It can be argued, of course, that the operations of many transnational corporations also undermine national sovereignty. Most of these organizations, however, obtain access to national markets and operate on a state's territory only with the permission of the government, a process that revalidates state power and authority.[60] TCOs are different because they obtain access through clandestine methods, minimize the opportunities for state veto of their activities, and prevent real sovereignty from being exercised. Although the main purpose of their activities is to make a profit, an inevitable by-product is an implicit challenge to state authority and sovereignty. The threat is insidious rather than direct: it is not a threat to the military strength of the state, but to the governmental prerogatives that are an integral part of statehood.

This does not mean that all states oppose TCOs. Alliances of convenience between "rogue" or "pariah" states and TCOs could pose serious international security threats, especially those that include trafficking in nuclear material. As soon as a transnational trafficking network is functioning effectively, product diversification is easy. Organizations that deal in drugs can also traffic in technology and components for weapons of mass destruction. Whether the recipients of such transfers are terrorist organizations or "pariah" states, the link between criminal activities and security is obvious. If nonproliferation and other regulatory regimes are to function effectively in the future, it will be necessary to curb the activities of transnational criminal organizations. This will not be easy.

CONCLUSION

In a contest between governments and TCOs, governments can achieve significant results, as they have in Colombia and Italy. Yet, these countries may be the exceptions rather than the rule. In both cases, the criminal organizations directly challenged the authority of the state, compelling it to mobilize all its energies and resources in the struggle to defend itself. In most other cases, where criminal organizations do not directly threaten the state, governments suffer from several disadvantages. First, they have a multiplicity of purposes and constituents. Transnational crime is simply one item on a very crowded agenda—one that does not always enjoy a high priority.

Governments have also found it difficult to pursue a consistent and coherent set of policies in which the activities of different parts of the bureaucracy complement, rather than undercut, one another. The battle against criminal and trafficking organizations is, therefore, a battle of unequals: it is a struggle between a government composed of multiple organizations and constituencies, with diverse objectives and interests, and an organization with a single purpose or goal—the maximization of profits. As TCOs become more prominent, more information will be needed about their major characteristics, strengths, and weaknesses. This, in turn, requires improved intelligence and more effective bureaucratic integration. Unfortunately, intelligence about drug trafficking and other transnational crimes is often jealously guarded, bureaucratically compartmentalized and fragmented, and disseminated without any clear sense of purpose or direction. These problems are particularly acute in the United States, where the horizontal and vertical divisions in government enable individual agencies to conduct their activities with considerable autonomy; they are not, however, wholly absent in other states.

Although not all governments are as fragmented as that of the United States, most of those in the democratic countries are forced to work within a framework of rules. TCOs, by definition, work outside the rules, can be ruthless in carrying out their policies, and are not accountable to constituents for their behavior. Ironically, these organizations often use nationalism and the sovereignty of the home government as a defensive measure against multilateral law enforcement efforts, even though most of their activities undermine the sovereignty of their own and other states. The Colombian cartels, for example, tried to mobilize national support by depicting Colombia's extradition treaty with the United States as a violation of Colombian sovereignty.

Another problem faced by governments is their lack of experience in dealing with TCOs. States are well equipped to deal with security threats from other states, but when faced with transnational, sovereignty-free actors, they are unsure as to which instruments of influence to employ, and whether strategies aimed at the TCOs themselves, or at putting pressure on their home governments, are likely to be more effective.

There is a marked contrast, therefore, between the seriousness of the challenge posed to security by TCOs and the nature of the response by governments. Criminal organizations are sophisticated, adaptable, and highly resilient. To redress the balance, governments have to acknowledge the scale and complexity of the problem, engage in more extensive functional cooperation with each other, and mobilize legitimate transnational organizations such as banks, airlines, and freight transportation companies to assist them. Although progress has been made in some of these .areas, especially in Western Europe, much more has to be done if one of the most insidious and long-term threats to national and international security is to be contained.

QUESTIONS FOR FURTHER STUDY

1. What characteristics of the current international environment are particularly conducive to the emergence of transnational criminal organizations (TCOs)?

2. How do TCOs mimic the operations of licit transnational corporations?

3. In what respects are major TCOs like the Italian Mafia, the Colombian drug cartels, and the Japanese Yakuza similar to each other? How are they different?

4. Williams argues that TCOs represent a threat to world security every bit as potent as that posed by such traditional threats as international terrorism and revolutionary warfare. What are his reasons for making this claim? Do you agree with his assessment? Why, or why not?

5. Based on what you have learned about TCOs, what steps do you think the international community should take to curb their operations?

Notes

1. The author would like to thank Jack Karns of the Graduate School of Public and International Affairs, University of Pittsburgh, and Paul Stares of the Brookings Institution for their helpful comments on many of the issues raised in this paper. He is also grateful to Michael Brown for his suggestions on an earlier draft of this paper.

2. Senator Roth quoted in *The New International Criminal and Asian Organized Crime,* Report made by the Permanent Subcommittee on Investigations of the Committee on Governmental Affairs, United States Senate, 102nd Congress, Second Session, S. Print 102–129 (December 1992), p. 2.

3. Robert Keohane and Joseph Nye, *Transnational Relations and World Politics* (Cambridge: Harvard University Press, 1971), p. xii.

4. Edward Morse, "Transnational Economic Processes," Ibid., pp. 23–47 at p. 25.

5. John A. Mack and Hans-Jurgen Kerner, *The Crime Industry* (Lexington, MA: Heath, 1975), pp. 6, 13.

6. R. Vernon, *Storm over the Multinationals* (Cambridge: Harvard University Press, 1977), p. 2.

7. See *World Air Transport Statistics,* No. 37 (Geneva: International Air Transport Association, 1993), pp. 8–11.

8. *World Air Transport Statistics,* No. 39 (Geneva: International Air Transport Association, 1995), p. 8.

9. Commensurate increases have occurred in the number of carriers (aircraft, trains, boats, ships, buses, trucks, and cars). From 90 million in 1984 the number increased to 125 million in 1990 and 131 million in 1992. See U.S. Customs Service, *Customs USA Fiscal Year 1988,* pp. 38–40; and *U.S. Customs Update 1992,* pp. 21–22.

10. See Lester R. Brown, Christopher Flavin, and Hal Kane, *Vital Signs 1996: The Trends That Are Shaping Our Future,* (New York: W. W. Norton, 1996), p. 77.

11. L. Krause, "Private International Finance" in Keohane and Nye, op. cit., pp. 173–190 at p. 175.

12. See Jane Jacobs, *The Economy of Cities* (New York: Random House, 1969) for a fuller discussion.

13. Ports, in particular, have been favorite bases for organized crime. See, for example, Peter Lupsha, "Organized Crime: Rational Choice Not Ethnic Group Behavior: A Macro Perspective" in *The Law Enforcement Intelligence Analysis Digest* (Winter 1986), pp. 1–7.

14. Kenichi Ohmae, *The Borderless World* (New York: Harper Business, 1990), pp. xiii, 18–26.

15. See Louis Kraar, "The Drug Trade," *Fortune* (June 1988), pp. 27–38.

16. See Samuel Huntington, "Transnational Organizations in World Politics," in *World Politics,* Vol. 25, No.3 (April 1973), pp. 333–368.

17. Ibid., p. 355.

18. See Peter Reuter, "The Decline of the American Mafia," *Public Interest,* No. 120 (Summer 1995).

19. Charles Rogovin and Frederick Martens, "The American Mafia Is Alive and Kicking," *Trends in Organized Crime,* Vol. 1, No. 3 (Spring 1996), pp. 35–36.

20. William Kleinknecht, *The New Ethnic Mobs* (New York: Free Press, 1996).

21. Ibid.

22. G. de Genaro, "The Influence of Mafia Type Organizations on Business and Industry," *Trends in Organized Crime,* Vol. 1, No. 2 (Winter 1995) pp.36–42.

23. Ibid.

24. Ibid.

25. Ibid.

26. Ibid.

27. Adolfo Beria di Argentine, "The Mafias in Italy" in Ernesto Savona, ed., *Mafia Issues,* pp. 19–32, provides an excellent overview of the various Mafias. The quote is from page 20.

28. See Alison Jamieson, "Mafia and Institutional Power in Italy," *International Relations,* pp. 1–23 at p. 3.

29. Alexander Stille, *Excellent Cadavers* (New York: Pantheon, 1995), p. 7.

30. See Enzo d'Antona, "The Mafia in the Red," *Il Mondo,* September 11–18, 1995, pp. 12–16.

31. Alison Jamieson, "The Transnational Dimension of Italian Organized Crime," *Transnational Organized Crime,* Vol. 1, No. 2 (Summer 1995), pp. 151–172.

32. Ibid.

33. P. Clawson and R. Lee, *The Andean Cocaine Industry* (New York: St. Martin's Press, 1996), p. 75.

34. See Guy Dunn, "Major Mafia Gangs in Russia," in *Transnational Organized Crime* special double issue on "Russian Organized Crime: The New Threat?", Vol. 2, Nos. 2 and 3 (Summer/Autumn 1996), pp. 63–87.

35. While German arrest figures indicate that only 1.8 percent of those involved in organized crime in Germany are Russian—compared with 14.6 percent Turks, 7.5 percent Yugoslavs, and 5.7 percent each for Italians and Poles—this figure might be deceptively small. These figures are taken from a report by the BKA discussed in "A Chronic Problem," *Munich Focus,* (June 17, 1996), p. 34. They refer to 1995. For the 1994 figures see "Organized Crime in the Federal Republic of Germany: Summary of the Situation in 1994," reproduced in "Global Proliferation of Weapons of Mass Destruction," Hearings before the Permanent Subcommittee on Investigations of the Committee on Governmental Affairs, United States Senate, 104th Congress, Second Session, Part II, (March 13, 20, and 22, 1996), pp. 741–757.

36. See Willard H. Myers III, "Orb Weavers—The Global Webs: The Structure and Activities of Transnational Ethnic Chinese Criminal Groups, *Transnational Organized Crime,* Vol. 1, No. 4 (Winter 1995), pp. 1–36.

37. As one report on Asian organized crime activity in Australia noted: "Whatever criminal triads exist in Australia do not operate as branches that are subject to control from some overseas headquarters. Indeed, it may be overstating things to regard them as enduring entities at all. In recent years in Australia, loosely organized syndicates appear to have been the predominant form in which Chinese organized crime has manifested itself. Some syndicate members may belong to a particular triad, others may belong to different triads, and some syndicate members may not have any triad connections." Report on Asian Organized Crime in Australia, by Parliamentary Committee (1994).

38. Ibid.

39. "Expert Interviewed on Criminal Syndicates," FBIS Daily Report (March 8, 1995).

40. "Minister Warns of International Organized Crime," FBIS Daily Report (November 21, 1994).

41. See "Asian Organized Crime: The New International Criminal Hearings Before the Permanent Subcommittee on Investigations of the Committee on Governmental Affairs," United States Senate, 102nd Congress, Second Session, (June 18 and August 4, 1992), p. 125.

42. "White Paper on Police 1994," reproduced in *Trends in Organized Crime,* Vol. 1., No. 3 (Spring 1996), pp. 49–56.

43. Ibid.

44. On Yakuza involvement in the banking crisis of the mid-1990s, see "Of Note: Asia," ibid., p. 69.

45. See "Asian Gangs Greatest Future Organized Crime Threat," *Organized Crime Digest,* Vol. 15, No. 13 (September 28, 1994), pp. 1–3 at p. 2.

46. David E. Kaplan and Alec Dubro, *Yakuza* (New York: Macmillan, 1986), p. 208.

47. "As their typical method of infiltration, Korean resident members of Yakuza organizations use their relatives in Korea. Of the total ninety thousand Yakuza members in Japan it is estimated that about nine thousand, or 10 percent, are Korean residents," "Article Views Struggle with International Crime," FBIS Daily Report (July 27, 1995).

48. See White Paper on Police (1994).

49. This section draws heavily upon *Nigeria: A County Overview* (Johnstown, PA: National Drug Intelligence Center, March 17, 1994).

50. Pat Griffith, "Nigerian Scams Costing Americans Millions," *Pittsburgh Post Gazette* (September 22, 1996), p. A10.

51. Ibid.

52. J.S., "Attention Mafia," *Prague Respekt* (May 21, 1995).

53. The three levels follow Barry Buzan, *People, States and Fear* (Brighton, U.K.: Wheatsheaf, 1983).

54. P. Goldstein, H.H. Brownstein, P. Ryan, and P. Bellucci, "Crack and Homicide in New York City, 1988: A Conceptually Based Event Analysis," *Contemporary Drug Problems,* Vol. 16, No. 4 (Winter 1989), pp. 651–687.

55. The Majority Staffs of the Senate Judiciary Committee and the International Narcotics Control Caucus, *The President's Drug Strategy: Has it Worked?* (September 1992), p. vi.

56. "The Sicilian Mafia," *The Economist* (April 24, 1993), pp. 21–24 at p. 22.

57. R. J. Kelly, "Criminal Underworlds: Looking Down on Society from Below" in R. J. Kelly, ed., *Organized Crime: A Global Perspective* (Totowa, NJ: Rowman and Littlefield, 1986), pp. 10–31 at p. 17.

58. The concept of the two zones is developed in M Singer and A. Wildavsky, *The Real World Order* (Chatham, NJ: Chatham House, 1993)

59. James Rosenau, *Turbulence in World Politics* (Princeton: Princeton University Press, 1991), p. 253.

60. See Huntington, op. cit., p. 363.

14 / The Global Divide: Socioeconomic Disparities and International Security

MICHAEL RENNER

The vast majority of armed conflicts in the world today involve fighting within, rather than between, sovereign states. Civilians account for perhaps 90 percent of all war-related deaths during the current decade. The predominance of civil war as opposed to interstate war is, in a sense, nothing new—indeed, since 1945, more than three-quarters of all warfare has been of an internal nature—but Cold War perceptions and priorities had long clouded this reality.[1] It seems that only since the onset of the post-Cold War era has the foreign policy establishment (and, likewise, the public at large) come to terms with this fact.

The internal clashes of the new era were quickly labeled "ethnic" conflicts. But the by-now-ritual reference to "resurfacing ancient hatreds" has led policymakers to conclude that we have been witnessing outbreaks of essentially irrational fighting that can be neither prevented nor mediated. A corollary is the widely used term "failed state"—the idea that certain societies are made up of such irreconcilable population groups that they are virtually condemned to failure.[2] It is not that ethnic tensions do not play a role in current conflicts; rather, the problem is that the term "ethnic conflict" describes the symptom instead of the root of the problem. The popular focus on ethnic identity masks the underlying stress factors that generate or deepen rifts within societies. A toxic brew of growing disparities in wealth, increasing unemployment and job insecurity, population growth, and environmental degradation is provoking social disintegration and political strife in many countries, sometimes leading to devastating violence.[3]

All of these trends are taking place in the context of a rapid economic globalization that promises enormous wealth and power for some, but uncertainty and vulnerability for many others. Commenting on the change from the Cold War's security preoccupations to those of today, Juan Somavia, Chile's UN Ambassador and Secretary-General of the 1995 World Social Summit in Copenhagen, Denmark, observed: "We have less insecurity in the military sphere and more insecurity in the personal and community spheres. We've replaced the threat of the nuclear bomb with the threat of a social bomb."[4]

Social, economic, demographic, and environmental challenges increasingly erode state capacity and authority, and expose the weakness of many political systems—wholly illegitimate in some countries, designed to serve the demands of only a narrow constituency in others, incapable of attending to broad public needs in yet others. As people turn to ethnic, religious, or other group-based organizations for assistance, protection, and identity, their relations with other groups often deteriorate and intergroup friction and competition rises. The more intense the competition, moreover, the greater the likelihood that social friction will turn into mass violence—especially given the easy availability of large quantities of weapons. The immense proliferation of weapons of all calibers—but particularly of small arms—makes it more likely (though not inevitable) that conflicts will be carried out by violent means, that fighting will be of greater intensity and carry on for far longer, that greater havoc and destruction will be wrought in the process, and that peace—after fighting comes to an end—will rest on shaky foundations.[5]

PERSISTENT POVERTY AND GROWING ECONOMIC DISPARITIES

Measured by a traditional yardstick, the world is getting steadily richer from year to year. Since 1950, the gross global product has grown from $3.8 trillion to $20.8 trillion (in 1987 prices), strongly outpacing the population growth rate. Statistically speaking, the average person has thus grown richer. Indeed, orthodox economic theory has it that "a rising tide lifts all boats" or that "a growing pie gives everyone a larger slice"—that is, economic growth improves the livelihoods of everyone.[6]

But while there have been undeniable improvements in human well-being over the past few decades, large numbers of people remain mired in excruciating poverty. Some 1.5 billion people worldwide—a quarter of the global population—are considered poor, with some of their most basic needs unmet. (See Table 14.1.) An even larger number of people—some 1.6 billion people in developing countries alone—are considered "capability-poor" (as defined by the 1996 *Human Development Report*), lacking adequate nourishment, health care, and education to escape poverty and lead decent, productive lives.

By far most of the poor—some 86 percent of the global total—live in developing countries.[7] Poverty is especially concentrated among the countries of South Asia, with about 560 million people in poverty, and sub-Saharan Africa, with 400 million. (See Table 14.2.) Relative to the total population of these regions, however, sub-Saharan Africa stands out: two-thirds of its people are poor, compared with roughly 40 percent in South Asia and about 45 percent in Latin America.[8]

For people at the bottom of the global economic heap, particularly in developing countries, the day-to-day reality is less one of dazzling possibilities than of innumerable hardships and chronic insecurity. They contend with meager incomes despite long hours of backbreaking work, insufficient amounts of food and poor diets, lack of access to safe drinking water, sus-

Table 14.1 / Dimensions and Magnitude of Human Insecurity, Early 1990s

Source of Insecurity	Observation
Income	1.3 billion people in developing countries live in poverty; 600 million are considered extremely poor; in industrial countries, 200 million people live below the poverty line.
Literacy	900 million adults worldwide are illiterate.
Land	More than 1 billion rural people are landless or near-landless; 400 million people in developing countries living on degraded, ecologically fragile lands.
Water	1.3 billion people in developing countries lack access to safe water; more than 700 million people live in countries where per-capita water supplies are inadequate or barely sufficient for food self-sufficiency.
Food	800 million people in developing countries have inadequate food supplies; 500 million of them are chronically malnourished, and 175 million are children under the age of five.
Jobs	120 million people worldwide are unemployed and 700 million more are underemployed.
Housing	100 million urban dwellers worldwide (out of 2.4 billion) are homeless; another 400 million live in inadequate housing.
Preventable Death	15–20 million people die each year due to starvation and disease aggravated by malnutrition; 10 million people die annually due to substandard housing, unsafe water, and poor sanitation in densely populated cities.
Cultural Status	300 million indigenous people in seventy countries are subject to discrimination and marginalization.

Sources: UNDP, *Human Development Report,* various editions; UN Department of Public Information (UNDPI) fact sheets: "The Faces of Poverty" (March 1996), "The Geography of Poverty" (March 1996), and "Poverty: Casting Long Shadows" (February 1996); UN Research Institute for Social Development (UNRISD), *States of Disarray: The Social Effects of Globalization* (Geneva: 1995); United Nations, "Backgrounder—Global Report on Human Settlements Reveals: 500 Million Homeless or Poorly Housed in Cities Worldwide" (February 9, 1996); Sandra Postel, *Dividing the Waters: Food Security, Ecosystem Health, and the New Politics of Scarcity,* Worldwatch Paper 132 (1996); Alan B. Durning, *Poverty and the Environment: Reversing the Downward Spiral,* Worldwatch Paper 92 (1989).

ceptibility to preventable diseases, and housing that provides few comforts and scant shelter.

The world's wealth is very unevenly distributed. A good deal of this inequality is embodied in the persistent North-South disparity: the developing world accounts for three-quarters of the world's population, but receives only 16 percent of global income. The gap between rich and poor has grown to almost unimaginable proportions. The one-fifth of the world's population that lives in the richest countries now receives 82.7 percent of global income, while the fifth that lives in the poorest countries has to make do with 1.4 percent. This makes for a ratio of about 60 to 1, double the ratio in 1960.[9]

Table 14.2 / World Poverty by Region, Early 1990s

Region	Number of Poor People[1] (millions)
South Asia	560
Sub-Saharan Africa	400
East/Southeast Asia and Pacific	170
Latin America and Caribbean	110[2]
Middle East and North Africa	73
Subtotal, developing countries	1,300
Western industrial countries	100
Former communist countries	100
World	1,500

[1] People living below the official poverty line in their country of residence, which may substantially understate the severity of the problem.

[2] A study by the Institute for Economic Research at the National Autonomous University of Mexico found that the incomes of some 192 million Latin Americans are below the poverty line, with almost half of them being extremely poor. See "Mexico and Latin America: Poverty and Integration," NAFTA and Inter-American Trade Monitor (Institute for Agriculture and Trade Policy, December 1995).

Source: UNDP, Human Development Report, various editions.

And yet, this comparison understates true global disparity, because these statistics are based on national averages—that is, they assume that all inhabitants of the richest countries are rich and all inhabitants of the poorest countries are poor. But this obviously is not the case: in fact, the richest 20 percent of humanity, irrespective of the country they live in, enjoy an income 150 times as large as the bottom 20 percent. A different statistic underscores this reality: the world's 358 wealthiest individuals (distinguished by possessing at least $1 billion in assets) had a combined wealth of $762 billion in 1994—the equivalent of the income of 2.4 billion people at the bottom of the scale, or 45 percent of the global population.[10]

Equally important, gaps exist within countries of both the South and the North, and they seem to be growing in many countries. (See Table 14.3.) There is now a "Third World" of impoverished communities even within the richest countries, just as there is a "First World" of wealthy enclaves within poorer ones. Inequality, marginalization, and the resulting polarization in society appear to be on the rise virtually everywhere. Many societies, including those misleadingly called "developed," are confronting the paradox of a growing GNP and stagnating or eroding incomes and living standards.

As a group, Latin American countries have long displayed the most unequal income distribution in the world—disparities that grew even larger during the 1980s. In Argentina, Brazil, Costa Rica, Uruguay, and Venezuela, for example, the richest 5 percent of the population gained during the 1980s at the expense of the bottom 75 percent. A front-page New York Times

Table 14.3 / Ratio of Richest 20 Percent of Population to Poorest 20 Percent
in Selected Countries, 1981–1992

South Africa	45
Brazil	32
Guatemala	30
Senegal	17
Mexico	14
United States	13[1]
Malaysia	12
Zambia	9
Algeria	7
China	7
South Korea	6
Germany	6
India	5
Japan	4

[1] Data for 1993.
Sources: UNDP, Human Development Report 1995; David Dembo and Ward Morehouse, The Underbelly of the U.S. Economy (1995); Reinhold Meyer, "Waiting for the Fruits of Change. South Africa's Difficult Road to Equality," Development + Cooperation (July/August 1996).

headline in late 1994 summarized the situation well: "Latin Economic Speedup Leaves Poor in the Dust." Income inequality has also risen sharply in many countries in Eastern Europe and the former Soviet Union. Among Asian countries, income distribution in India, Malaysia, Singapore, Hong Kong, and Taiwan has become more balanced, but in Bangladesh and Thailand it has deteriorated.[11]

The Western industrial nations have vastly greater resources to "lift all boats," but, even so, some 100 million of their inhabitants—more than 10 percent—live below the poverty line, and more than 5 million are homeless. About 15 percent of Americans—39 million people—were officially considered poor in 1993. And 100 million people in formerly communist industrial countries live in poverty. Inequality has also increased in many rich nations: in the United Kingdom, the ratio between the top and bottom 20 percent of the population went from 4 to 1 in 1977 to 7 to 1 in 1991; in the United States, which has the widest income gap among the industrial nations, it went from 4 to 1 in 1970 to 13 to 1 in 1993. Between 1975 and 1990, the top 1 percent of the U.S. population increased its share of all assets from 20 to 36 percent.[12]

Rich-poor disparities are about much more than just the inability to accumulate material wealth: they are often a matter of life and death. The 1991 edition of the Human Development Report noted that the life expectancy of the poorest Mexicans—53 years—was 20 years less than that of the richest of their compatriots. And in rural Punjab, a region straddling India and Pakistan, babies born to landless families have infant mortality rates one-third higher than those born to landowning families.[13]

In some countries, there is a growing spatial segregation between the poor and rich into virtually separate communities and societies. Where the wealthy are located physically close to the poor, one can see the emergence of walled-in, guarded compounds for the affluent, supplied with electricity, drinking water, and other social amenities through private networks, while the poor have to depend on public systems that are unreliable and decrepit, if present at all.

The growing gap between rich and poor—conspicuous wealth in the midst of misery and hardship for the poor, and growing economic uncertainty for portions of the middle class—generates discontent and resentment, fueling social conflict. As the *New York Times* asked rhetorically in a 1994 report on the seemingly sanguine macroeconomic trends in Latin America:

> But if things are so rosy, why did peasants rise up this year in southern Mexico? Why has Venezuela had two coup attempts and continued unrest? Why have Bolivian workers staged national strikes? And why, in Argentina, considered a stellar example of economic transformation, did workers burn a provincial government building last December and march on the capital this summer?[14]

Conflict, where it arises, does not necessarily take place across the class spectrum. Those who struggle to get just a few crumbs from the pie frequently see themselves in competition with others who are equally hard-pressed. And the beleaguered part of the middle class often perceives the less well-off to be the source of their troubles—ostensibly by competing for the same scarce jobs and by burdening public social services. Under such circumstances, people often organize and mobilize in ways that are intended to benefit the immediate group they feel loyal to, rather than the community at large. It is the splintering and breakdown of communities, of mutual dependence and trust, that may be the most worrisome trend in terms of the potential for social conflict and violence.

THE IMPACT OF THE GLOBAL ECONOMY

The champions of rapid economic globalization point to the immense potential for stepped-up economic growth as national borders are thrown open to outside investment and regulations torn down. But we need to look past the aggregates of gross national product and trade to assess the implications for social stability and peace. In this regard, the *Human Development Report 1996* expresses concern about several aspects of the global economic growth process: that growth is increasingly jobless, ruthless, voiceless, rootless, and futureless. (See Table 14.4.)

The future of wealth and poverty increasingly depends on the ways in which the accelerating process of economic globalization proceeds. This process is characterized by increasing moves toward free trade and capital

Table 14.4 / Destructive Growth Processes and Conflict Potential

Phenomenon	Policies That Promote Growth, but:
Jobless growth	fail to generate a commensurate rise in employment (unemployment, job insecurity, competition for jobs)
Voiceless growth	suppress unions and human rights (political oppression, lack of democracy)
Ruthless growth	fail to invest in human capital and distribute the benefits fairly (poverty and income inequality)
Rootless growth	marginalize or eliminate cultural diversity (homogenization)
Futureless growth	diminish or destroy the environment (habitability, sustainability) ·

Source: Compiled by author, based on UNDP, *Human Development Report 1996*.

mobility, privatization, and deregulation. It is principally a corporate-driven process that goes hand in hand with an erosion of the welfare state. Given the relative ease of relocating factories and shifting investment resources across the planet, the pressure on countries and communities to remain competitive and offer an inviting investment climate is tremendous. In part, this means downward pressure on wages and a trend toward a low-common-denominator world with regard to working conditions, social welfare, and environmental regulations.

The human consequences of all this can be seen in the spread of sweat-shop factories in countries from El Salvador to Indonesia, in which workers are paid a pittance and treated like disposable items—their dignity trampled upon, their human rights denied, and their efforts to unionize (to gain even minimal improvements in their daily lives) countered with often severe repression. These conditions present fertile ground for severe conflict. Ordinary consumers in rich countries may "benefit" from this blatant exploitation—in the form of cheap clothing and other products—but as workers themselves, they cannot possibly compete with a labor force paid hunger-level wages. The corporate search for ever cheaper labor is a constant threat to workers. The intensity of recent strikes in France, Germany, and South Korea clearly demonstrates the stakes involved.

In the absence of strong rules and norms, economic globalization could turn into a free-for-all, an intensifying competition among and within communities everywhere over jobs, income, and economic well-being. By generating deep apprehension and feelings of insecurity, the very unevenness and uncertainty of the globalization process is itself becoming a source of conflict.

This sort of globalization primarily benefits the relatively few countries, communities, companies, and individuals with adequate capital, technological know-how, infrastructure, and entrepreneurial skills. The vast majority of countries and their populations are relatively powerless to affect the central workings and dynamics of the emerging global system, and are often highly vulnerable to its vagaries. This is particularly true for countries that rely primarily on exports of commodities. They have precious little influence over the markets that, by determining the demand for their raw materials and the prices their exports will fetch, control their economic fortunes.

Globalization affects individual regions of the world in vastly different ways. The rapidly industrializing states of East and Southeast Asia are poised to take advantage of the opportunities that further global economic integration promises, rapidly shedding the status of "developing" countries and joining ranks with the "old" industrial nations. Although Latin America has been able to attract substantial flows of foreign investment— the region saw a fourfold increase between 1990 and 1993—a good deal of this has involved portfolio, short-term, and speculative investment. Much of sub-Saharan Africa, meanwhile, remains a marginal and extremely vulnerable player in the global economy; the region is increasingly being bypassed by the global economy. Of the total of $585 billion in private capital flow to developing countries from 1989 to 1994, 40 percent went to East Asia and 30 percent to Latin America; South Asia received only 3 percent, and sub-Saharan Africa a bare 1 percent.[15]

For many developing countries in Latin America and Africa, the sharp increases in what were already large social and economic discrepancies were a consequence of "structural adjustment programs" imposed by the International Monetary Fund (IMF) and the World Bank since the early 1980s. These typically require recipients of adjustment loans to implement measures such as: lowering trade and investment barriers; devaluing the currency; reducing or eliminating subsidies, price controls, and social programs; and privatizing state enterprises.

There is little doubt that many of these economies needed adjustment— although the type of adjustment most suitable is very much in contention. Typically, they suffered from a combination of homegrown and external problems, including distorted economic structures, wrongheaded economic policies, careless borrowing of foreign funds, soaring interest rates in the late 1970s, and plunging world market prices for their commodity exports in the 1980s. This drop in world prices led to a significant erosion of the terms of trade—that is, the ratio of export prices measured against import prices on a unit-per-unit basis. In several countries, warfare worsened problems by absorbing large amounts of money and disrupting local economies. The upshot of all these factors was that foreign debt of developing nations soared from $217 billion in 1970 to $1.1 trillion in 1980 (expressed in 1993 dollars)—the equivalent of 88 percent of the Third World's annual exports, or 27 percent of these countries' GNP.[16]

By the mid-1990s, some seventy-five countries had signed on to structural adjustment programs with the IMF and World Bank. In most cases, this proved to be exceedingly bitter medicine for the poor and even for large parts of the middle class. Yet the severe shock therapy failed to accomplish what in theory it should have done: the installation of more successful and sustainable economic structures. The UN Research Institute for Social

Development concluded in 1995 that most structural adjustment experiences had been failures, and that even those that yielded some of the expected macroeconomic results had detrimental social consequences.[17]

One reason for the failure of adjustment was itself structural: it initiated a vicious cycle of retrenchment and disinvestment that led to economic stagnation or decline, rather than putting in place the building blocks for a new beginning. In sub-Saharan Africa, for instance, investment declined by 50 percent during the 1980s. Nor did structural adjustment loans lighten the debt burden; because these loans were intended to help debtor countries service their debts (and hence protect lenders from the perils of default), they essentially kept them on the debt treadmill. Total Third World foreign debt climbed from $1.1 trillion in 1980 to close to $2 trillion in 1994 (in 1993 dollars). Walden Bello of Focus on the Global South notes that "between 1982 and 1986, Third World countries received $25 billion more from official creditors than they paid out to them, while they paid the commercial banks $183 billion more in interest and amortization than they received in new bank loans." The U.S.-based organization Bread for the World notes that African governments spend more than twice as much servicing their debts as they do on health and primary education combined.[18]

As a result of all this, most people in highly indebted African and Latin American countries suffered a severe drop in living standards during the 1980s—hence the term "the lost decade." In sub-Saharan Africa, per capita income by the end of the 1980s was no higher than in the early 1960s, when many of these countries gained independence.[19] For all of Latin America, per capita income fell by 11 percent in the 1980s. In Mexico, real wages declined by more than 40 percent from 1982 to 1988. In Nicaragua, declining incomes led to a 15 percent drop in per capita consumption of such basic staples as corn and beans between 1990 and 1993. Observers might simply chalk this up to the difficulties associated with an economy still reeling from years of warfare. But even neighboring Costa Rica, widely regarded as an island of stability in a troubled region, has suffered: in a sharp reversal of its historical record, real wages there declined 17 percent between 1980 and 1991, and poverty increased from 21 to 28 percent from 1987 to 1991.[20]

Not surprisingly, the hardships and deepening disparities have triggered or reopened political rifts within these societies and provoked a wave of urban protests. In Mexico, impoverished peasants in the southern state of Chiapas rose up in revolt in early 1994, while increasing numbers of residents chose illegal migration to the United States as their ticket to a better life. In Nicaragua, desperate workers have unleashed a wave of strikes since 1990. Many ex-Contra guerrillas and former Sandinista government soldiers have taken up arms again—sometimes joining forces—to press their demand that the government honor social and economic commitments made under the country's peace agreement. And in Costa Rica, increasing economic polarization may begin to jeopardize the country's social stability and democratic tradition.[21]

Observing a spiral of violence in Latin American countries that results from a variety of sources, "ranging from drug trafficking . . . to income inequality, megacities without services, and corrupt police and courts," *The Economist* reports that the region as a whole spends 13 to 15 percent of its GDP on public and private security measures—more than it devotes to social welfare. The magazine points out that civilian governments that are still weak after years of military dictatorship are increasingly giving special powers to the military in order to contain the strain that their societies are under.[22]

Structural adjustment policies are part of a larger, neoliberal model of development that sees privatization, deregulation, trade liberalization, and world market integration as the road to economic salvation for all. As countries liberalize their economies, however, it is the stronger states that reap the most gains from the new opportunities that arise in connection with world market integration—partly because they are already poised to do so, and partly because government policy helps them more than it does others. In many countries—China, Sri Lanka, Mexico, and Chile, among others—privatization and world market integration has led to a rapid rise in inequality.[23]

LAND DISTRIBUTION AND RURAL MARGINALIZATION

In most developing countries, where agriculture is a mainstay of the economy and key to people's livelihoods, land distribution is an indicator as important as the distribution of wealth. It, too, tells a story of immense imbalances. Together with population growth, which forces peasants to subdivide plots into smaller and smaller parcels from one generation to the next, unequal land tenure is causing increasing landlessness. In 1981, an estimated 167 million rural households worldwide, containing 938 million people, were landless or near-landless, and their numbers are expected to increase to nearly 220 million by the turn of the century.[24] On the whole, Latin American land tenure patterns are much more inequitable than those found in Asia and Africa. (See Table 14.5.)

In addition to unequal land ownership, the mechanization and modernization of agriculture—particularly in the context of growing world market integration—has brought new social pressures to the countryside. Millions of subsistence peasants and small-scale farmers (who are often seen by technocratic leaders as inefficient and an obstacle to modernization) are being marginalized by cash-crop farmers (who are typically more oriented toward lucrative export markets and nonstaple and perhaps even nonfood crops, such as cut flowers). In the Sudan, for instance, it is estimated that 90 percent of the marketable agricultural production is controlled by fewer than 1 percent of its farmers.[25]

Governments often give priority to the larger commercial crop producers in a variety of ways. In many countries, small farmers are losing access to

Table 14.5 / Land Distribution and Landlessness, Selected Countries or Regions[1]

Country/Region	Observation
Brazil	Top 5 percent of landowners control at least 70 percent of the arable land, the bottom 80 percent have only 13 percent of the cultivatable area; 12 million rural Brazilians are landless or near-landless, yet enough land is currently left idle by large landowners to provide the 12 million with more than 2 hectares of land each.
Peru	Three-quarters of the rural population is landless or near-landless.
Central America	In Guatemala, 2 percent of farmers control 80 percent of all arable land; in Honduras, the top 5 percent occupy 60 percent; in El Salvador, the top 2 percent own 60 percent, and almost two-thirds of the farmers are landless or near-landless; in Costa Rica, the top 3 percent have 54 percent of the arable land.
India	40 percent of rural households are landless or near-landless. The 25 million landless households of 1980 are expected to reach 44 million by the end of the century.
Philippines	3 percent of landowners control one-quarter of the land; 60 percent of rural families have too little or no land.

[1] Near-landlessness means that a rural family or household possesses too little land to sustain its members' livelihoods with farming alone.

Sources: Norman Myers, *Ultimate Security: The Environmental Basis of Political Stability* (1993); UNDPI, "The Geography of Poverty" (March 1996); Myriam Vander Stichele, "Trade Liberalization—The Other Side of the Coin," *Development + Cooperation* (January/February 1996).

credits, extension services, and other forms of support, such as guaranteed prices. Typically, 40 percent of the people in developing countries receive less than 1 percent of the total credit disbursed.[26]

There is also evidence that large, often export-oriented, commercial operators rather than small farmers are being given priority access to fertile land and water. In Colombia, flower production for foreign markets has caused groundwater levels to fall, harming local food production. In Senegal and Mali, fruit and vegetable export plantations were developed to the detriment of the local peasant economy. In the Jodhpur district of Rajasthan, India, increasing use of scarce groundwater to cultivate chili peppers and other water-intensive cash crops has caused village wells used by the rural poor to go dry. Villagers have seen their land degrade, their herds die, and their communities fall apart. And, in a case that has gained worldwide attention, a huge dam-building and irrigation project in India's Narmada valley has triggered massive opposition, in part because a small number of wealthy farmers who cultivate water-intensive export crops would be the principal beneficiaries, while small peasants would bear the brunt of the project's social and environmental burden.[27]

International markets no doubt hold considerable opportunities for some wealthier farmers, but many small commercial farmers and particularly subsistence peasants are struggling to survive; they often lack access to credit and do not have the resources required to modernize and intensify their operations in order to compete in the brave new world of globalized agriculture. With import tariffs being lowered (now that agriculture is to be opened up more to international trade), these small-scale producers compete with an increasing flood of cheap grain imports from other countries. Some 5 million poor Brazilian peasant households, for example, see their very existence threatened in this manner: Brazil's wheat imports surged sixfold between 1988 and 1995, now supplying 79 percent of the country's consumption; small domestic grain producers often cannot compete against this flood of imports.[28]

Unjust patterns of land distribution, population growth, soil erosion due to overly intensive land use, the marginalization of small-scale agriculture, and the conversion of cropland to cattle ranching (to supply the growing demand for beef in the wealthier countries) are among the factors that cause many rural areas to be in crisis and rife with social conflict. These factors are driving millions of rural people into more marginal areas, such as steep hillsides and rainforests.

Though nobody knows the precise numbers, anywhere from 250 to 500 million farmers worldwide are being pushed onto marginal lands, and their numbers are likely to rise steadily in the future. In Mexico, for example, more than half of all farmers are eking out a living on small plots on steep hillsides that now account for one-fifth of all Mexican cropland. But hillsides and rainforests are easily susceptible to soil erosion, producing floods and mudslides during periods of heavy rain, and their limited soil fertility soon forces settlers to move on to other, equally precarious plots.[29] Others join the trek to urban areas, where jobs are already scarce, social services overtaxed, and the gaps in wealth and comfort growing. Still others seek a better life in another country, adding to the legions of illegal migrants— many of whom encounter hostility and violence in the receiving country.

On the other hand, some of the land-poor decide to stay put, because they see little alternative elsewhere. One young peasant from Chiapas, Mexico, summed it up: "The land is all we have, all we know. Without the land . . . we will be begging on the streets of Mexico City or work as *peones* like our grandfathers did." In Mexico and in a number of other countries, movements have arisen of people who occupy the unused properties of large landowners; very often, however, the owners strike back with the help of state police and military forces or with their own private armies. The upshot is an unending series of bloody land skirmishes. In Brazil, for example, land distribution is so unequal and so much land is left idle by absentee landlords that redistributing it could virtually eliminate landlessness. At least 85,000 landless families are currently involved in land occupations, and more than 1,000 peasants have been killed in confrontations with landowners during the past ten years.[30]

In the southern Mexican state of Chiapas, large landowners resisted or evaded government land redistribution efforts over several decades. More than one hundred thousand hectares of idle land remain to be distributed, making Chiapas the repository of 30 percent of the total land reform backlog in Mexico. But as it became evident that the Mexican government has all but abandoned the pursuit of land reform, the landless and near-landless have increasingly resorted to the occupation of idle estates. The pace of land takeovers in southern Mexico has exploded since the early 1970s, and skirmishes with militias hired by wealthy landowners have become a chronic feature of rural security. This was one of the factors that propelled the 1994 Zapatista uprising in Chiapas.[31]

THE GLOBAL JOBS CRISIS

Another cause for rising inequality and poverty—and a major threat to social cohesion and stability—is what various observers have termed the "global jobs crisis." Out of the global labor force of about 2.8 billion people, at least 120 million people are unemployed, while 700 million are classified as "underemployed"—a misleading term because many in this category are actually working long hours but receiving too little in return to cover even the most basic of needs. The record shows that economic growth per se does not ensure that everyone who is willing to work will find a job: between 1975 and 1990, economic output worldwide grew 56 percent, but employment grew by only half as much.[32]

Unemployment, underemployment, the threat of job loss, and the specter of eroding real wages are challenges for hundreds of millions of workers across the globe, though the particular conditions and circumstances diverge widely in rich and poor countries. In advanced industrial countries, three phenomena can be observed. First, technological development (particularly the rise of microelectronics) has dramatically reduced the need for labor—so much so that a substantial share of unemployment in these countries now is structural rather than governed purely by the growth-recession cycle. This has given rise to the notion of "jobless growth."

Second, many companies are embracing various measures—such as smaller and more flexible production units, extensive subcontracting, and temporary or part-time hiring—that allow them to adapt rapidly to fast-changing market conditions but render job security more tenuous and insecure. Third, due to modern communications and transportation networks, the ability to parcel out components of the work process, and increased capital mobility, corporations are increasingly able to tap into a large pool of cheap labor in developing countries, replacing a much higher-paid domestic work force. Initially, only unskilled or semiskilled jobs were at risk in this manner, but recent evidence suggests that skilled workers are now facing similar pressures.[33]

A key effect of this cheap labor strategy is strong downward pressure on wages, as evidence from the United States makes clear. Between 1973 and

1990, real wages for production or nonsupervisory workers (excluding agriculture) declined by more than 20 percent. Although the loss of 43 million jobs between 1979 and 1995 was numerically more than offset by some 70 million newly created jobs, two-thirds of those who found new employment now earn less. In fact, an estimated 18 percent of all full-time U.S. workers now have jobs that pay wages at or below the poverty level.[34]

Many other industrial countries have not—so far, at least—embraced the low-wage strategy seen in the United States, for fear of rapidly growing economic inequality among their populations and the implied threat to the social and political health of their societies. But they face high and growing unemployment rates that not only burden the welfare state, but also gnaw at the foundations of social stability. In 1996, unemployment stood at above 10 percent in the member countries of the European Union.[35] Among members of the Organization for Economic Cooperation and Development (OECD), Japan alone has managed to keep joblessness low, at slightly above 3 percent; this is, nevertheless, the highest it has been since the end of World War II.[36]

The social and psychological impacts of these employment patterns are often traumatic. People unable to find work, or who work only at substantially lower wages than they are accustomed to, suddenly see their middle-class existence evaporate: their careers are interrupted or brought to a premature end, their incomes are no longer sufficient to meet the bills, and their retirement security is beset by uncertainty.

In modern societies, a job not only provides the means to pay the bills but often helps people define who they are. Joblessness carries a heavy stigma in a success-oriented, materialistic society. While some cope well, others become depressed, develop illnesses, or abuse alcohol or drugs; frequently, their relationships with spouses, children, and friends suffer. The threat to jobs is such that even those who survive one round of layoffs feel insecure, wondering if they are to suffer the ax next.[37] And even though workers in OECD countries are clearly the global "elite" in terms of wages and benefits, the threat to their job and wage security has triggered significant political reactions, including calls for protectionist policies against imports from countries where labor is cheap and hostility toward immigrants seen as taking jobs or social benefits away from domestic workers.[38]

Whereas Western countries have experienced a gradual rise in unemployment during the past two decades, the formerly communist countries of Eastern Europe and the Soviet Union have had to contend with rapidly emerging mass unemployment and dramatic increases in poverty and inequality. They continue to undergo a wrenching and uncertain transition to what must seem like a highly uncertain future from a system that, although highly inefficient and even demoralizing, provided a sheltered kind of employment and a sense of steadiness. Suddenly being forced to compete on world markets with more efficient Western companies, many enterprises in these countries have gone bankrupt. From 1990 to early 1992 alone, the ranks of the unemployed in these countries rose from one hundred thousand to more than 4 million. From virtually zero in the late 1980s, unemployment rates had by 1993 climbed to 14 percent in Poland, 11 percent in Hungary, and about 5 percent in Russia. Real wages declined some 30 percent in Poland between 1989 and 1993, and by 27 percent in Russia between 1991 and 1993.[39]

In the developing world, the impact of unemployment has been sharply divergent in different areas. The dynamic economies of East and Southeast Asia have experienced high growth in productivity, output, employment, and real wages. Unemployment rates ranged between 2 and 3 percent during the late 1980s and early 1990s. Employment and wage levels in most countries in Latin America and Africa, by contrast, have suffered from stagnation and structural adjustment, as discussed earlier.[40]

Many of those unable to find regular jobs drift to the informal sector—the underbelly of the economy in many developing countries. According to the International Labor Organization (ILO), the informal sector in sub-Saharan Africa employed more than 60 percent of the urban work force in 1990, and its share of the nonagricultural work force in Latin America rose from 40 to 53 percent during the 1980s. However vibrant, this area is characterized by low skills, productivity, and pay (though some talented entrepreneurs do well), and offers no form of social protection. In Africa, the ILO finds that "the majority of workers in the informal sector would be very fortunate to earn even the official minimum wage."[41]

The global job crisis is likely to command increased attention. With continuing population growth, the numbers of job seekers will continue to climb steadily. The world's labor force is projected to grow by almost 1 billion people during the next two decades, mostly in developing countries that are already hard-pressed to generate anywhere near adequate numbers of jobs. During the 1990s, an additional 38 million people will seek employment each year in these countries.[42]

Perhaps most unsettling is the presence of large-scale youth unemployment. Virtually everywhere, youth unemployment is substantially higher than the rate for the labor force as a whole. (See Table 14.6.) One survey of fifteen African countries found youth unemployment rates to be triple those for adults. Even in most industrial countries, youth unemployment is an enormous challenge: in the early 1990s, it reached 14 percent in the United States, 15 percent in the United Kingdom, 26 percent in Italy, and 36 percent in Spain. (Japan and Germany are the principal exceptions, with rates of 5 and 6 percent, respectively.[43])

High rates of population growth and the resulting disproportionately large share of young people in many developing countries translate into much greater pressure on job markets. Roughly 20 percent of the population in industrial countries is age fifteen or younger. But in China, the figure is 27 percent; in Latin America, 34 percent; in South and Southeast Asia, 38 percent; and in Africa, 45 percent. The uncertain and often discouraging

Table 14.6 / Unemployment Rates, Total Labor Force and Youth Labor Force, Selected Countries,[1] 1991–1993

Country	Total (percent)	Youth[2] (percent)
Spain	22.4	36
Italy	11.5	26
Poland	14.0	25
Israel	10.0	21
Canada	11.1	20
Colombia	9.1	20
Sweden	8.2	20
Venezuela	6.4	19
Turkey	7.4	17
United States	6.7	14
Philippines	6.7	11
Chile	4.5	10
Indonesia	2.7	8
Germany	5.8	6
Japan	2.5	5

[1] For many developing countries, no youth unemployment data are available.
[2] Age 15 to 24.
Source: International Labour Organisation, World Labour Report 1995 (Geneva: 1995), Table V.

prospects that many young adults encounter are likely to provoke a range of undesirable reactions: they may trigger self-doubt and apathy, cause criminal or deviant behavior, feed discontent that may explode in street riots, or foment political extremism.[44]

In Rwanda, for instance, the extremist Hutu leaders who planned and carried out the 1994 genocide of Tutsis and moderate Hutus relied strongly on heavily armed militias. Members of these militias were recruited primarily from among the uneducated, the unemployed, and the alienated. These were the people who had insufficient land to establish and support a family of their own, and little prospect of finding a job outside agriculture. Their lack of hope for the future and low self-esteem were channeled by the extremists into an orgy of violence against those who supposedly were to blame for these misfortunes.[45]

The search for jobs is a major factor in the continuing migration of people from the countryside to the cities. But their journeys often do not stop at national borders: in many cases, this search leads the poor and unemployed to travel to other countries—legally if they can, illegally if they cannot. The search for jobs is, in fact, a principal cause of the growing migration of people from the poorer countries of the South and the East to the richer countries of the North and the West. (See Chapter 18.)

It is difficult to predict the full consequences of the current international jobs crisis. Whether the current situation is compared to the Industrial

Revolution or the tumultuous Depression Era, the implication is clear: a failure to deal appropriately with sharpening social problems could have devastating political consequences. People whose hopes have worn thin, whose discontent is rising, and whose feelings of security have been stripped away are more likely to support extreme "solutions," and it is clear that some politicians stand ready to exploit the politics of fear. Although alarmism may be premature, it is prudent to remember that the hardships and dislocations of the Great Depression resulted in the rise of fascism and the onset of World War II.[46]

CONCLUSION

The highly uneven and unequal process of economic globalization is generating unprecedented wealth for some and continued poverty or new marginalization for others. Communities that may be far apart geographically are brought into intensifying competition with one another and sometimes into conflict when their vital interests—their need for jobs, income, and a sense of economic security—clash head on. Globalization also has its impact within individual communities, sometimes eroding the sense of commonality of interest that its inhabitants have long enjoyed.

Inequality and poverty are, of course, nothing new. But today's polarization takes place when traditional support systems are weakening or falling by the wayside. In many developing countries, there is an erosion of the bedrock of stability—the webs and networks of support found in extended family and community relationships (although admittedly, these are often paternalistic and exploitative). It is unclear what will replace these support systems as rural communities are weakening, urban populations are rapidly expanding, and the state is increasingly unable to provide anything near adequate services for growing populations.

In Western industrial countries, the post-World War II welfare state substituted or supplemented many family and community support functions. This, along with steadily rising wages, provided an extraordinary degree of social stability in the 1945–70 period. Since the 1970s, however, the welfare state has come under growing attack, both because of ideological objections and because of stagnating public revenues in the face of growing welfare costs. This is happening just as structural unemployment worsens and downward pressures on wages strengthen.

Among former Eastern bloc states, the political upheaval of the late 1980s succeeded in loosening and then largely demolishing the grip of authoritarian institutions; creating viable alternatives, however, has proved far more elusive. Unemployment is rising fast and growing inequality is threatening to tear apart an already weak social fabric.

Privatization and economic globalization have unleashed entrepreneurial energies and led to the emergence of vast new markets and opportunities.

Yet this type of progress has also brought profound disquiet. Uncertainty about what the future holds and fears of losing a job or livelihood are now endemic. Many people have no real chance to take advantage of beckoning opportunities and instead fear being left behind.

No country, company, community, or individual can rest on past success, and many are struggling hard just to avoid losing ground. "Global markets [are permitted to] wreak havoc with the livelihoods of many of the world's people," concluded a 1995 UN report entitled *States of Disarray*.[47] As growing numbers of people and communities are in the grip of the world market's gyrations, competition becomes more than just a market inter-action—it becomes a struggle for survival. The social fabric of many soci-eties, whether affluent or destitute, is under increasing strain as the paths of rich and poor diverge more sharply and as the stakes of economic success or failure rise.

QUESTIONS FOR FURTHER STUDY

1. How, in Renner's view, does economic globalization lead to the per-sistence and even growth of extreme poverty in many parts of the world? Is his analysis persuasive?
2. What are "structural adjustment programs?" Why do poor countries agree to initiate such programs? What are their social and economic consequences?
3. How do patterns of land ownership in poor Third World countries contribute to poverty and unrest? How do global market forces affect agricultural patterns in such countries?
4. What is the "global job crisis?" What are its causes and effects?
5. Renner argues that the persistence of poverty in many parts of the world represents a significant threat to international peace and stabil-ity. Do you agree or disagree with his assessment? On what basis?

Notes

1. Share of civilian victims from Ernie Regehr, "A Pattern of War," *Ploughshares Monitor* (December 1991). Internal conflicts since 1945 from Aaron Karp, "Small Arms: The New Major Weapons," in Jeffrey Boutwell, Michael T. Klare, and Laura W. Reed, eds., *Lethal Commerce: The Global Trade in Small Arms and Light Weapons* (Cambridge: American Academy of Arts and Sciences, 1995).

2. Gerald B. Helman and Steven R. Ratner, "Saving Failed States," *Foreign Policy* (Winter 1992/1993).

3. For an overview of ethnic groups and strife, see Ted Robert Gurr, *Minorities at Risk: A Global View of Ethnopolitical Conflicts* (Washington: U.S. Institute of Peace Press, 1993). A broad discussion of the various challenges mentioned here can be found in Michael Renner, *Fighting for Survival: Environmental Decline, Social Conflict, and the New Age of Insecurity* (New York: W.W. Norton, 1996).

4. Somavia quoted in Barbara Crossette, "Despite the Risks, the UN Plans a World Conference on Poverty," *New York Times* (January 23, 1995).

5. Christopher Louise, "The Social Impacts of Light Weapons Availability and Proliferation," Discussion Paper No. 59, UN Research Institute for Social Development (March 1995).

6. Lester R. Brown, "World Economy Expanding Steadily," in Lester R. Brown, Christopher Flavin, and Hal Kane, *Vital Signs 1996: The Trends That Are Shaping Our Future* (New York: W.W. Norton, 1996).

7. United Nations Development Programme (UNDP), *Human Development Report 1996* (New York: Oxford University Press, 1996).

8. Calculated on basis of ibid. Latin America from UN Economic Commission for Latin America and the Caribbean, *Social Panorama of Latin America 1994* (Santiago, Chile: 1994).

9. UNDP, op. cit., note 7; UN Department of Public Information (UNDPI), "Poverty and Development: An (Im)balance Sheet" (February 1996); UNDPI, "The Geography of Poverty" (March 1996).

10. True disparity from David Korten, *When Corporations Rule the World* (West Hartford, CT: Kumarian Press, and San Francisco: Berrett-Koehler, 1995). Billionaires from Marcos Arrudal, "Education for Whose Development?" in the APC electronic conference igc: econ.saps on November 18, 1995.

11. North-South gap from UNDP, *Human Development Report 1995* (New York: Oxford University Press, 1995). Latin America most unequal from "Mexico and Latin America: Poverty and Integration," *NAFTA and Inter-American Trade Monitor* (Institute for Agriculture and Trade Policy, December 1995). Richest 5 percent gaining at expense of poorest 75 percent from International Labour Organisation (ILO), *World Labour Report 1993* (Geneva, 1993); Nathaniel C. Nash, "Latin Economic Speedup Leaves Poor in the Dust," *New York Times* (September 7, 1994); Asia from UNDP, op. cit., note 7.

12. Number of poor people in western industrial countries from UNDP, op. cit., note 11. Formerly Communist industrial countries from UNDP, *Human Development Report 1991* (New York: Oxford University Press, 1991). Western nations from United Nations, *World Social Situation in the 1990s* (New York: United Nations, 1994), and from UNDP, op. cit., note 7. United Kingdom from UN Research Institute for Social Development (UNRISD), *States of Disarray; The Social Effects of Globalization* (Geneva, 1995). United States calculated from David Dembo and Ward Morehouse, *The Underbelly of the U.S. Economy* (New York: Apex Press, 1995).

13. UNDP, op. cit., note 12.

14. Nash, op. cit., note 11.

15. "New Debt Crisis in Latin America?", *Development + Cooperation* (May/June 1995); UNDP, op. cit., note 7.

16. For data on debt, commodity prices, and terms of trade, see International Monetary Fund, *Financial Statistics Yearbook 1995* (Washington: 1995); World Bank, *Commodity Trade and Price Trends, 1989–91* (Baltimore: John Hopkins University Press, *International* 1993); World Bank, *World Debt Tables 1994–1995*, Vol. 1 (Washington: World Bank, 1994).

17. Number of countries signed on to structural adjustment programs from Carlos Heredia and Steve Hellinger, "Getting to the Root of the Mexico Crisis," in the APC electronic conference igc:twn.features on September 25, 1995; UNRISD, op.cit., note 12.

18. Vicious cycle from UN Conference on Trade and Development, *The Least Developed Countries 1993–1994 Report* (New York: United Nations, 1994). Fall in sub-Saharan Africa investment from ILO, op. cit., note 11. Debt development from World Bank, *World Debt Tables,* op. cit., note 16, and from Hal Kane, "Third World Debt Rising Slowly," in Lester R. Brown, Hal Kane, and Ed Ayres, *Vital Signs 1993* (New York: W.W. Norton, 1993); Walden Bello with Shea Cunningham and Bill Rau, *Dark Victory: The United States, Structural Adjustment and Global Poverty* (London: Pluto Press, 1994). African debt servicing from Bread for the World, "Easing Africa's Debt Burden," in the APC electronic conference igc:africa.news on March 6, 1996.

19. Samuel A. Morley, *Poverty and Inequality in Latin America: Past Evidence, Future Prospects,* Policy Essay No. 13 (Washington: Overseas Development Council, 1994). Sub-Saharan Africa from Bello, op. cit., note 18.

20. Anthony de Palma, "In Mexico, Hunger for Poor and Middle-Class Hardship," *New York Times* (January 15, 1995). Drop in real wages from Carlos Heredia and Mary Purcell, "Structural Adjustment in Mexico: The Root of the Crisis," from Karen Hansen-Kuhn, "Structural Adjustment in Nicaragua: Sapping the Social Fabric," and from Karen Hansen-Kuhn,

"Structural Adjustment in Costa Rica: Sapping the Economy," all in the APC electronic conference igc:econ.saps on March 7, 1995.

21. Michael Renner, "Chiapas: An Uprising Born of Despair," World Watch (January/February 1997), pp. 12–24; Hansen-Kuhn, "Structural Adjustment in Nicaragua," op. cit., note 20; Hansen-Kuhn, "Structural Adjustment in Costa Rica," op. cit., note 20.

22. "The Backlash in Latin America," The Economist (November 30, 1996), pp. 19–21.

23. UNDP, op. cit., note 7.

24. Landless trends from Alan B. Durning, Poverty and the Environment: Reversing the Downward Spiral, Worldwatch Paper 92 (Washington: Worldwatch Institute, November 1989).

25. Sudan surplus from John Prendergast, "Greenwars in Sudan," Center Focus (July 1992).

26. Michel Chossudovsky, "The Causes of Global Famine," in the APC electronic conference igc:dev.worldbank on October 16, 1995; UNDP, Human Development Report 1994 (New York: Oxford University Press, 1994).

27. Colombia from Ekkehard Launer, Zum Beispiel Blumen (Göttingen, Germany: Lamuv Verlag, December 1994). Senegal and Mali from Chossudovsky, op. cit., note 25. Rajasthan from Sandra Postel, "Forging a Sustainable Water Strategy," in Lester R. Brown, et al., State of the World 1996 (New York: W.W. Norton, 1996). Narmada from Volker Böge, "Das Sardar-Sarovar-Projekt an der Narmada in Indien. Gegenstand ökologischen Konfliktes," Occasional Paper No. 8, Environment and Conflicts Project (Bern, Switzerland: June 1993).

28. Threat to Brazilian peasants from Myriam Vander Stichele, "Trade Liberalization: The Other Side of the Coin," Development + Cooperation (January/February 1996). Brazilian imports from U.S. Department of Agriculture, Economic Research Service, "Production, Supply, and Distribution" (electronic database), (Washington: November 1995).

29. Norman Myers, Ultimate Security: The Environmental Basis of Political Stability (New York: W.W. Norton, 1993).

30. Peasant quoted by Tom Barry, Zapata's Revenge: Free Trade and the Farm Crisis in Mexico (Boston: South End Press, 1995). On Brazil: Diana Jean Schemo, "Violence Growing in Battle over Brazilian Land," New York Times (April 21, 1996); "Brazil: Agrarian Reform Proposed to End Violence," NAFTA & Inter-American Trade Monitor (November 3, 1995).

31. See Michael Renner, "Chiapas: An Uprising Born of Despair," World Watch (January/February 1997), pp. 12–24.

32. Ray Marshall, "The Global Jobs Crisis," Foreign Policy (Fall 1995); Richard J. Barnet, "Lords of the Global Economy," The Nation (December 19, 1994). Disparity in growth of GNP and employment from Hal Kane, The Hour of Departure: Forces That Create Refugees and Migrants, Worldwatch Paper 125 (Washington: Worldwatch Institute, June 1995).

33. UNRISD, op. cit., note 12; United Nations, op. cit., note 12. Labor pool from Barnet, op. cit., note 30. Skilled labor in danger from Keith Bradsher, "Skilled Workers Watch Their Jobs Migrate Overseas," New York Times (August 28, 1995), and from Louis Uchitelle, "U.S. Corporations Expanding Abroad at a Quicker Pace," New York Times (July 25, 1994).

34. Declining real U.S. wages from Dembo and Morehouse, op. cit., note 12. U.S. job statistics from Louis Uchitelle and N. R. Kleinfield, "On the Battlefields of Business, Millions of Casualties," New York Times (March 3, 1996). Poverty-level wages from Barnet, op. cit., note 30.

35. "Gimme a Job," The Economist (January 4, 1997), p. 48.

36. Rejection of cheap labor strategy from Marshall, op. cit., note 30. Unemployment rates from ILO, World Labour Report 1995 (Geneva: 1995), and from Associated Press, "G-7 Nations Fail on Jobs Plan," in CompuServe's AP Online on April 2, 1996. Discussion of the measurement of U.S. unemployment from Dembo and Morehouse, op. cit., note 12.

37. See, for example, Uchitelle and Kleinfield, op. cit., note 32 (the lead article in a seven-piece New York Times series on "The Downsizing of America").

38. Global wage differentials from World Bank, World Development Report 1995 (New York: Oxford University Press, 1995).

39. Ibid.

40. Marshall, op. cit., note 30.

41. United Nations, op. cit., note 12; ILO, op. cit., note 11.

42. Projected growth of global labor force from Kane, op. cit., note 30. Developing countries' annual job creation needs from United Nations, op. cit., note 12.

43. Youth unemployment rates from UNDPI, "The Faces of Poverty" (March 1996), from ILO, op. cit., note 11, and from ILO, op. cit., note 33.

44. Under-15 population shares from Population Reference Bureau, "1995 World Population Data Sheet" (wallchart) (Washington: May 1995). Possible reactions from UNDPI, op. cit., note 40, and from Peter Gizewski and Thomas Homer-Dixon, "Urban Growth and Violence: Will the Future Resemble the Past?", The Project on Environment, Population, and Security, American Association for the Advancement of Science and University of Toronto (1995).

45. Human Rights Watch, *Slaughter Among Neighbors: The Political Origins of Communal Violence* (New Haven: Yale University Press, 1995); Howard Adelman and Astri Suhrke, "Feilschen Während Ruanda Brennt," *Der Überblick* (March 1996).

46. Sanford A. Marcus, "Downsizing: The Trashing of America's Soul" (letter to the editor), *New York Times* (March 8, 1996).

47. UNRISD, op.cit., note 12.

15 / The Global Trading System and International Politics

VINCENT FERRARO, ANA CRISTINA R. SANTOS, and JULIE GINOCCHIO

From 1686 to 1759, French law prohibited the importation of printed calicoes. Some sixteen thousand people lost their lives as a result of this law, being either executed for violating the law or killed in riots driven by opposition to the law.[1] It is difficult now to imagine the intensity of feelings generated by trade disputes in the past: it is unlikely that the U.S. Congress will mandate the death penalty for driving an imported Toyota. Nonetheless, trade disputes continue to raise high emotions. As the Cold War recedes as the principal focus of international relations, trade conflicts will become more frequent and intense.

From a theoretical perspective, trade disputes should not exist. After all, economic doctrine assumes that nations freely exchange goods and services, and that the impersonal forces of supply and demand determine the allocation of these resources. The pursuit of a more efficient allocation of resources, guided by the doctrine of comparative advantage, is held by many to be a genuinely universal objective, shared by all nations regardless of culture or history, time, or space.

Nations, however, like individuals, are motivated by values sometimes quite different and even inconsistent with economic efficiency.[2] Trade complicates the ranking of values: it forces nations to make trade-offs between efficiency and other possible values such as economic equity, social stability, environmental protection, or political representation. A nation cannot easily afford high wages for its workers if those workers produce goods that can be imported from low-wage economies. The intrusiveness of trade on the domestic affairs of states accounts for its political significance.

In the early modern period, most governments in Europe vigorously controlled trade so that its intrusiveness could be rigidly managed. The term *mercantilism* is generally used to describe this system of control.[3] Mercantilist policies were designed to stimulate exports and depress imports so that the country would always have a favorable balance of trade—policies that were possible largely because of the heavy state involvement in economic activity, through trading companies and the like. The favorable balance of trade represented an accumulation of wealth by the nation, which could then serve as a resource for the political and military aspirations of the state. At this time, there was no meaningful distinction between political and economic objectives—or, as Jacob Viner described it, between power and plenty.[4]

The policies used to support mercantilist objectives were quite straightforward: the importation of certain products would be forbidden by law; the production of certain products in colonies governed by mercantilist states would be banned; subsidies would be granted to the producers of favored exports; and the state would take the necessary steps to assure a viable merchant fleet for the transportation of exports. Beyond these general policies, every state had specific measures reflecting its unique circumstances, but all mercantilist policies from this period reflect the strong political and economic interests of the state. As argued by Edward Meade Earle in 1943:

> In short, the ends of mercantilism were unification of the national state and development of its industrial, commercial, financial, military, and naval resources. To achieve these ends the state intervened in economic affairs, so that the activities of its citizens or subjects might be effectively diverted into channels as would enhance political and military power.[5]

As capitalism matured and economic and political rights began to adhere to individuals, the direct intervention of the state in administering economic activity became both less necessary and less desirable. In *The Wealth of Nations* (1776), Adam Smith articulated an economic system driven by the private interests of individuals, not the public ones of the state. More importantly, Smith argued that a "hidden hand" of market behavior would actually transform these private and selfish interests into public benefit—greater economic activity and an economic surplus into which the state could tap, through taxation, for its security requirements. In other words, the "free" market (that is, a market substantially free of governmental controls and regulations) could more efficiently channel economic activity than the state in ways that actually enhanced the power of the state: the private pursuit of plenty could also result in the public acquisition of power.

The struggle to realize this framework domestically was difficult, and has yet to be fully resolved except in some of the advanced industrialized countries. Internationally, the struggle to create a free market has been significantly more difficult. In 1817, British economist David Ricardo wrote *The Principles of Political Economy and Taxation,* which extended Smith's argument to international commerce and advocated the adoption of free trade on the basis of comparative advantage. Ricardo tried to prove that if two countries engage in trade, each should specialize in those goods it produces relatively well: even if one of the countries is better at producing every product, it can still benefit from trade by emphasizing the products it produces best and importing those products it which it is only *relatively* inefficient at producing. Since Ricardo's time, mainstream economic doctrine has accepted this proposition and has argued that unrestricted trade results in vastly expanded production—and, hence, greater wealth.

The fight to implement and impose free-trade practices globally was led first by Great Britain and subsequently by the United States. Because of domestic opposition to the uneven and stringent effects of international competition, neither state has, in fact, subscribed completely to the principles of free trade. Nevertheless, the rhetorical support that each provided to the principles was almost religious, as well described by Lord Maynard Keynes:

> I was brought up, like most Englishmen, to respect free trade not only as an economic doctrine, which a rational and instructed person could not doubt, but also almost as a part of the moral law. I regarded ordinary departures from it as being at the same time an imbecility and an outrage. I thought England's unshakable free trade convictions, maintained for nearly a hundred years, to be both the explanation before man and the justification before Heaven of her economic supremacy.[6]

In fact, these principles were often violated: the British maintained a very elaborate and sophisticated set of trade preferences within its Empire, favoring its colonies at the expense of non-Empire producers of the same goods. Likewise, the United States has often manipulated trade to secure advantages for domestic producers of certain goods, such as its use of the oil import quota in 1959 to protect the oil companies that pumped oil within the United States against the cheaper oil flowing in from the Middle East.

THE POST-WORLD WAR II TRADE REGIME

Even in light of these deviations from the principles of free trade, one could scarcely argue that nineteenth century Britain and late-twentieth century America were protectionist states. Adherence to free trade is largely a matter of degree, and both states implemented free-trade policies to a substantial degree. The doctrine of free trade is an unquestionably powerful idea; since the end of World War II, it has been championed by the United States and has served as the measure of determining governmental policy for many states in the international system. Moreover, in the late twentieth century, a very strong movement toward freeing trade even further has gained momentum: the policies of some of the more protectionist states in the system—Brazil, China, India, Russia, and France—have moved to reduce their tariffs, quotas, and other barriers to trade. This movement is not irreversible; historically, attitudes toward trade have changed very rapidly. But at this particular point in time, there is little question that free trade is aggressively being pursued by most of the major economic powers.

The idea of free trade is seductively simple: barriers to the free flow of goods and services, such as tariffs and quotas, should be reduced to zero. Individual entrepreneurs would invest their capital in those areas in which they would make the most profit. Global production would then increase dramatically as greater efficiencies of production are realized and, as a result, the wealth of the world would increase.

Increased trade among nations shows a clear correlation with increased wealth on a global scale. In 1820, the world gross domestic product (GDP) was estimated to be around $695 billion; by 1992, the world GDP had increased to $27,995 billion. World exports were about $7 billion in 1820, and by 1992 they had increased to about $3,786 billion (all data in constant 1990 U.S. dollars).[7] Stated another way, exports accounted for only about 1 percent of the world product in 1820. By 1913, exports accounted for about 8.7 percent, and by 1992 the figure was about 13.5 percent.[8] These statistics suggest that increased trade is a critical component of the dramatic increase in global wealth in the last two centuries.

International trade is also heavily concentrated. The top ten exporters accounted for over 60 percent of global exports; the top ten importers accounted for almost 58 percent of world imports. (See Table 15.1.) Indeed, the top fifty exporters accounted for 96.1 percent of all world exports in 1995, which means that approximately 135 countries account for only 3.9 percent of world exports. This concentration of trade reflects the concentration of global economic activity and does not suggest that trade cannot be of crucial importance to small countries.

There is strong international support for free trade because its alternative, protectionism, is viewed by many as a dangerous policy. The commitment of the United States to free trade can be partially explained by the disastrous experience of the Great Depression. The decisions by the U.S. Congresses during the late 1920s and early 1930s to erect significant tariff barriers against foreign products as a way of stimulating internal demand were entirely counterproductive and led instead to a deepening of the Depression. While the decision to raise tariffs, most dramatically in the case

Table 15.1 / Top Ten Global Exporters and Importers of Merchandise in 1995 (in billions of U.S. dollars)

Exporter	Value	Share of World Exports	Importer	Value	Share of World Imports
United States	583.9	11.6	United States	771.3	14.9
Germany	508.5	10.1	Germany	443.2	8.6
Japan	443.1	8.8	Japan	336.0	6.5
France	286.2	5.7	France	274.5	5.3
United Kingdom	242.1	4.8	United Kingdom	265.3	5.1
Italy	231.2	4.6	Italy	204.0	3.9
Netherlands	195.3	3.9	Hong Kong*	196.1	3.8
Canada	192.2	3.8	Netherlands	175.9	3.4
Hong Kong*	173.9	3.5	Canada	168.4	3.3
Belgium-Luxemb'g	168.3	3.3	Belgium-Luxemb'g	154.2	3.0

* Hong Kong had domestic exports of $29.9 billion and reexported $143.9 billion. Its retained imports in 1995 totaled $52.1 billion.

Source: World Trade Organization, Focus, No. 14 (December 1996), <http://www.wto.org/wto/Whats_new/focus14.pdf>, p. 5.

of the Smoot-Hawley tariff of 1930, was consistent with most of American economic history, the leaders of the United States decided that its post-World War II economic policies would be quite different, and they adopted a strong free-trade position as the hallmark of American power. Thus, the United States helped create and maintain the Bretton Woods System, whose institutions—the International Monetary Fund (IMF), the World Bank, and the General Agreements on Tariffs and Trade (GATT)—were committed to the principle of free trade.

Although not the most powerful of these institutions, the GATT was the organization most centrally concerned with establishing the global free-trade regime. In 1945, the United States invited twenty-two other nations to join it in drafting an agreement that would multilaterally reduce tariffs and other barriers to trade. The negotiations held in Geneva in 1947 resulted in the GATT, which at that time was only provisional. The plan was to eventually incorporate the GATT into the proposed International Trade Organization (ITO). However, the ITO never came into being because of strong opposition, primarily generated by the United States, to its powers of regulating trade. Ultimately, the GATT took over some of the duties of the stillborn ITO (such as settling disputes and providing information about tariffs and quotas).

Over the years more countries joined the GATT, and the contracting parties felt the need to meet in what came to be known as trade negotiating rounds. Eight such rounds have taken place since 1947, the last three being the longest and most important: the Kennedy, Tokyo, and Uruguay Rounds.

The Kennedy Round was initiated in 1962 and concluded in 1967. Its major contribution was the introduction of multilateral trade negotiations. Previously, the common practice had been to settle tariffs item by item. The new procedure introduced by the Kennedy Round was to group items generically (by type of product according to an agreed upon classification system): if an item was not listed as an exception by a country, its tariff would be set automatically at the generic rate. This procedure greatly simplified the process of tariff reduction. Additionally, four main issues were discussed at the Kennedy Round: industrial tariffs, agriculture, nontariff barriers, and the integration of developing countries into the global economy through trade.

Progress on reducing industrial tariffs at the Kennedy Round was quite successful: the value of trade covered by the talks was about $40 billion, and the final agreements affected about 40 percent of the goods imported by industrialized countries. Progress was more limited in the remaining three issue areas. Agricultural restrictions proved intractable due to the political significance of farming constituencies in many countries. Nontariff barriers, such as quality standards and labeling regulations, were difficult to identify and assess. Finally, the problems of overcoming poverty in developing countries by facilitating their trade (by asymmetrically reducing tariffs on the exports of poorer countries) involved concessions the industrialized countries were unwilling to make.

Despite the successes in reducing industrial tariffs, the Kennedy Round failed to meet the expectations of many of the participants. One of its biggest drawbacks was that the negotiators continued to rely upon the reciprocity clause: a country would reduce its tariffs only if its trading partners did likewise. Nations were unwilling to import more unless their exports increased by a similar amount. Moreover, developing countries were not treated as full participants in the negotiations; the United States, the European Economic Community, and Japan dominated the discussions.

The Tokyo Round opened in 1972, triggered by the withdrawal of the United States from the gold standard in 1971. Ninety-nine countries—including both members and nonmembers of GATT—participated in the extensive negotiations that would finally be concluded seven years later. The Round resulted in the reduction of hundreds of tariffs and in steps toward the quantification and elimination of nontariff barriers to trade. Six major Codes of Conduct were articulated, including the Standards Code, which attempted to restrict nontariff barriers such as quality controls or governmental subsidies to specific industries. As was the case with the Kennedy Round, actual adherence to these new standards has been quite spotty; and, again, developing countries were not offered structural concessions.

By this point, the world community had come to recognize that poorer countries need different treatment in the area of trade. In particular, it was recognized that trade was only beneficial to poor countries if they had access to the manufacturing markets of the rich countries. There are two major trading institutions that try to compensate for the difficulties faced by poorer countries: the Generalized System of Preferences (GSP) and the tariff preferences extended to seventy African, Caribbean, and Pacific countries through the European Union's Lome Regime, which was officially recognized by GATT in 1994. These two systems grant lower tariffs and, in some cases, duty-free status to developing countries. The system of preferences certainly made it easier for poor countries to export their traditional (usually agricultural) products by reducing the tariffs on those products, but it also made it difficult for them to diversify their exports, particularly toward manufactured and semimanufactured products. As the world moves closer toward a lowering of all tariffs, however, the advantages that these two systems offer to poorer states will decline.

The Uruguay Round was the most important and most comprehensive of all the negotiating rounds. Initiated on September 20, 1986 in Punta del Este, it was stalled for three years due to conflicts between the United States and the European Union over agricultural trade. The very credibility of multilateral negotiations was at stake during those years; if the disputes had not been settled, the global framework of international trade might have succumbed to protectionism and bilateral agreements. However, a compromise was reached in December 1993 in Geneva, and the final text was signed the following March in Marrakesh, Morocco.

The Uruguay Round was a watershed in the history of the GATT. The jurisdiction of the agreement was extended to issues that many countries had reserved to their national sovereignty: services, textiles, and agriculture. Most important, the Uruguay Round established the World Trade Organization (WTO). The WTO has the power to resolve trade disputes, putting an end to further multilateral rounds of negotiations. Unlike GATT decisions, those made by the WTO are binding. More complex and far-reaching than GATT, the WTO is both the successor to GATT and the reincarnation of the ITO.

Established in Geneva on January 1, 1995, the WTO already has over 120 members. Its additional functions include implementing all multilateral trade agreements and monitoring national trade policies. In December 1996, the WTO held its first biennial Ministerial Conference in Singapore, and concluded the Information Technology Act, which dealt with matters concerning protection of intellectual property rights associated with new electronic technologies. The Ministerial Conference is the WTO's highest authority, and is composed of the trade ministers of every member state. Several bodies and committees work around a General Council in the Geneva headquarters of the WTO.

So far, only minor issues have been turned over to the WTO for resolution.[9] For example, a dispute has arisen between the United States and the European Union over the exportation of bananas from the Caribbean. The European Union has restricted some imports of bananas from the region to exporters licensed in Europe (which, not coincidentally, happen to be European firms). The United States insists that Europe should be forced to import bananas from any firm (the largest of which happen to be American). The dispute hardly seems to be one of great strategic significance. One should remember, however, that the issues are crucially important to the producers and exporters of bananas. More important, the issue cannot be resolved without setting a precedent for future disputes concerning these distinctions.

At this stage it is impossible to assess the effectiveness of the WTO: the question of whether it will be able to enforce its decisions will be discussed in greater detail.

EXCEPTIONS TO A GLOBAL FREE-TRADE REGIME: REGIONAL TRADING BLOCS

The WTO is ostensibly operating in a global environment, but trade is increasingly being organized along regional lines. Article XXIV of the GATT allowed for regional institutions to establish their own free-trade areas as potential way stations to a global regime:

> The contracting parties recognize the desirability of increasing freedom of trade by the development, through voluntary agreements, of closer integration between the economies of the countries parties to such agreements.

There are many such agreements, but they are far from uniform in scope. There are also different levels of integration in the world, and each regional organization deals with the issue of national sovereignty differently. A free-trade area (FTA) is the simplest form of trade alliance: barriers to trade are lowered only among member states, and each country remains independent with respect to nonmembers of the FTA. Custom Unions go one step further: they establish a common external tariff (CET) which applies uniformly to all nonmembers. At the most sophisticated level of regional integration, nations form a common market in which there is, in addition to free mobility of the factors of production (capital and labor), a common trade policy and the harmonizing of national economic legislation.

The process of regional integration has grown steadily since the end of World War II. In the early 1950s, many believed that the political tensions between France and Germany could only be reduced if the two were tied together economically. The European Coal and Steel Community (ECSC) was created as a result, providing a stepping-stone to the Treaty of Rome (1957) and to the European Economic Community (EEC) which it established. The EEC has evolved over the years and now, as the European Union (EU), is still involved in arduous negotiations to achieve a higher level of political and economic integration, including the creation of a common currency. From an initial group of six, the EU currently consists of fifteen countries, and other nations have applied for membership.

The North American Free Trade Agreement (NAFTA) and Mercosur are more recent regional trade alliances. NAFTA was signed by the United States, Canada, and Mexico in 1992, and entered into force on January 1, 1994. The Treaty of Asunción, which created Mercosur, was signed by Brazil, Argentina, Paraguay, and Uruguay in March 1991, and was implemented on January 1, 1995. As of now, both agreements are free-trade areas, which aim to withdraw all barriers to the exchange of goods, services, and capital only among the member nations. Mercosur, however, plans to eventually become a common market and follow the European example; at present, however, it is only a semifunctioning customs union.

Both·NAFTA and Mercosur are currently reviewing membership applications from other Latin American nations and, at the Summit of the Americas in 1994, thirty-four countries supported the creation of the Free Trade Area of the Americas (FTAA). However, the path toward such integration will not be an easy one, especially because the area involved is much more heterogeneous than Europe. Some initial efforts have been made, but it remains to be seen if the United States in particular is willing to pursue and support some form of hemispheric integration. The most likely new member of NAFTA would be Chile, but domestic opposition within the United States toward NAFTA has made the Clinton Administration quite cautious about pursuing further agreements. Moreover, negotiating such agreements is politically very sensitive. The Administration had the authority to negotiate what are known as "fast-track" agreements (which are agreements subject only to a "yes or no" vote by Congress), but opposition by labor and environmental groups to further expansion of free-trade arrangements has slowed down efforts toward greater regional integration in the western hemisphere. "Fast-track" authority lapsed due to this opposition in 1995, though President Clinton has sought to get it reinstated.

Overall, regional trading blocs account for about 61 percent of all trade, a very high percentage. C. Fred Bergsten of the Institute for International Economics estimates the different shares for the main blocs in the world today as shown in Table 15.2. Quite clearly, the regional trading blocs are highly significant actors in world trade. However, while they are expected to be mere way stations to a global free-trade regime, they also represent institutional interests that may actually restrict trade. The banana dispute between the United States and the European Union suggests how regional interests can define policies distinctly at odds with the principles of free trade.

More interestingly, regional groups represent concentrated and focused political power. The economic consequences of action taken at a regional, as opposed to a national, level are substantially higher. The world is essentially divided now among three trading blocs centered in North America, Western Europe, and the Asian-Pacific region, and sharp disputes among any of these three centers would have serious effects upon the global economy. Moreover, countries not directly aligned with any of the three blocs (most significantly, a large majority of the African and Caribbean nations) are at risk of being further excluded from the global system. For example, a World Bank study concluded that Mexico, as a member of NAFTA, could replace "one-third of the Caribbean's $12.5 billion in exports to the United States."[10]

The WTO is clearly concerned about the long-term consequences of regionalism. Its Director-General, Renato Ruggiero, described two scenarios: a "closed" regionalism where the groups practice free trade internally and protected trade with outsiders, and an "open" regionalism where the trading blocs gradually open up their markets to outside competition. His language is stark:

> The choice between these alternatives is a critical one; they point to very different outcomes. In the first case, we would arrive at a division of the trading world into two or three intercontinental preferential areas, each with its own rules and with free trade inside the area, but with external barriers still existing among the blocs. The second alternative, on the other hand, points toward the gradual convergence on the basis of shared rules and principles of all the major regional groups. In this case, at the end we would have one global free market with rules and disciplines internationally agreed and applied to all . . . [11]

Obviously, the WTO will be monitoring the degree to which the rules implemented by each trading bloc are "open" to outside influence, but, at this stage, it is too early to speculate on which of Ruggiero's scenarios are most likely to pan out.

Table 15.2 / Regional Free-Trade Arrangements
(share of world trade, 1994)

European Union	22.8
European Union and the Mediterranean (EUROMED)	2.3
North American Free Trade Agreement (NAFTA)	7.9
Mercosur	0.3
Free Trade Area of the Americas (FTAA)	2.6*
ASEAN Free Trade Area (AFTA)	1.3
Australia–New Zealand	0.1
Asia Pacific Economic Cooperation (APEC)	23.7
TOTAL	61.0

*Represents share that would be added to FTAA by countries not in NAFTA or Mercosur.
Source: C. Fred Bergsten, "Competitive Liberalization and Global Free Trade: A Vision for the Early Twenty-First Century, Institute for International Economics, APEC Working Paper 96–15 (1996). <http://www.iie.com:80/9615.htm>.

EXCEPTIONS TO A GLOBAL FREE-TRADE REGIME: ECONOMIC PROTECTION

By far the most important exceptions to free trade come from pressures to protect a domestic economy from international competition. The techniques for such protection include tariffs, quotas, export subsidies, government procurement policies, quality, and health regulations, and a whole host of other pricing mechanisms. In 1993, the World Bank and the Organization for Economic Cooperation and Development (OECD) estimated that protectionist measures of this sort cost the global economy about $450 billion a year.[12]

At the global level, the arguments supporting free trade are probably unassailable: free trade unquestionably stimulates more efficient production and, as we have seen, greater wealth. Nations, however, are not asked to defend a global perspective; they are expected to defend national interests. While free trade may actually create jobs by stimulating demand and lowering prices, free trade cannot guarantee that those who lose their jobs to lower-priced imports will be hired to fill the new jobs created by the economic stimulus for increased exports. It is this *asymmetry of benefits,* their unequal distribution among different countries (and among different products and different workers) that creates powerful opposition to free trade.

Quantifying the effects of freer trade is extraordinarily difficult, as demonstrated by the problems in determining the effects of NAFTA on the U.S. and Mexican economies. A recent study conducted by the University of California at Los Angeles suggests that the overall effects of NAFTA since it was signed in 1994 have been quite modest:

Using a new model of how exports and imports influence jobs in various product categories and regions, the study estimated that the net job gain to the United States since the agreement took effect at the beginning of 1994 has been just 2,990 jobs. The net figure, however, masked a much greater level of both job losses and gains among different companies. Increased imports to the United States killed an estimated 28,168 jobs the last three years, the study said, while increased exports supported creation of 31,158 jobs.[13]

Obviously the people who lost their jobs or their businesses feel that NAFTA was a bad decision, while the people who gained jobs or who benefited from lower prices for the products they purchased feel that NAFTA was a good decision. The difficulty for a policymaker is determining freer trade's overall effect on the national economy, including the costs of addressing the needs of those who lose their jobs or businesses.

Those who support greater protection against economic competition from abroad argue that domestic producers will move to countries where cheaper labor is available, or where regulations—such as environmental or safety controls—are minimal. Indeed, the logic of free trade is that producers *ought* to move to places in which higher profits can be made and so, to the extent that such considerations are important, one would expect changes of this nature. It is difficult, however, to determine the extent to which such considerations are decisive. For example, there has not been a documented systematic shift of manufacturing from the United States to Mexico or to any other country in which labor costs are substantially lower than in the United States. The manufacturing share of the U.S. economy has not drastically changed in the past thirty years (21 percent of the U.S. economy).[14] It is clear, then, that lower labor costs or reduced regulations are not the sole determinants of business decisions to relocate: in some cases they may be, but it other cases, access to skilled labor or the presence of a sophisticated infrastructure may be more important.

What is clear is that appeals for protection from free trade constitute a powerful political issue. There is no question that some jobs have been lost because of NAFTA and many within the United States believe that the U.S. government has a responsibility to protect Americans from job erosion. Presidential aspirant Pat Buchanan made this issue a central part of his campaign in 1996:

> To "conservatives of the heart," even if NAFTA brings an uptick in GNP it is no good for America. No matter the cash benefits, we don't want to merge our economy with Mexico. We don't want to force American workers to compete with dollar-an-hour Mexican labor. That's not what America is all about.[15]

In many countries there are provisions for helping workers whose jobs are lost due to trade, but it is hard to assert that those programs are especially successful. By and large, trade-displaced workers are older, less educated, and less mobile than workers who are attractive to the more dynamic sectors of an economy, and so it is particularly difficult to find work for them in other fields.

Additionally, one should always be aware that justifications for trade protection are also defenses of relative inefficiency. Tariffs and quotas are costs to an economy, ones usually borne by the consumer. They can protect workers, but, in the process, they can also protect the private corporate interests of those who hire the workers. In the early 1980s, the automobile industry in the United States was at a competitive disadvantage to Japanese producers and lobbied for protection against imported automobiles. After a quota was implemented, the prices of automobiles went up rather dramatically. The American industry announced that the quota saved about 22,000 jobs. The quota also increased the profits of the industry. However, the price increase led to a sales drop of about 1 million cars, which in turn led to a loss of about 50,000 jobs in the industry.[16]

EXCEPTIONS TO A
GLOBAL FREE-TRADE REGIME:
NATIONAL SECURITY CONCERNS

The ideal of global free trade faces a challenge when viewed in light of national security concerns. Nations do not wish to export to their adversaries products that might have the effect of enhancing the latter's relative power, even if the private companies producing those products have an interest in increasing their sales. During the Cold War, the economic benefits of free trade were overridden in many cases by national and multilateral export controls on strategically sensitive products such as turbines, supercomputers, and nuclear-related technology. The formal agency responsible for maintaining these controls was the Coordinating Committee for Multilateral Export Controls (COCOM), which aimed to protect the West's security interests by placing restrictions on sales of technologies and equipment that might have strengthened the Soviet Union's military position in the Cold War. COCOM, established in 1949, included Japan and all of the NATO countries except Iceland.[17]

COCOM restrictions on strategic trade were partially effective in limiting the transfer of strategic materials to the Soviet bloc, but were never wholly successful. It proved to be extremely difficult to identify which products were of strategic value. For example, in 1972 the United States gave the Bryant Grinder Corporation authorization for a shipment of precision miniature ball-bearing grinders to the Soviet Union, which later proved to be used in Soviet guided ballistic missiles. Other COCOM states had also shipped similar types of equipment to the Soviet Union.[18] Similarly, computer technology proved to be extraordinarily difficult to define in strategic terms: many items could be used for military purposes, and it was impossible to define those items that could not somehow be adapted for strategic purposes.

The end of the Cold War has diminished support for multilateral controls over strategic exports, and COCOM was dissolved on March 31,

1994.[19] However, international efforts to prevent the spread of ballistic missiles and weapons of mass destruction require the maintenance of some form of control over strategic technologies and materials. Currently, such nonproliferation controls are exercised by a number of multilateral entities, including the Nuclear Suppliers Group (a consortium of advanced industrial powers that seeks to restrict the spread of weapons-related nuclear technology), the Australia Group (a similar consortium concerned with the spread of chemical and biological weapons technology), and the Missile Technology Control Regime (MCTR, a more formal arrangement limiting the commerce in missile and space technology). In each case, the members of these groups have worked out a system of information exchange and joint controls over particular types of materials and equipment considered particularly sensitive from a proliferation perspective. The MTCR, for instance, is described by the Arms Control and Disarmament Agency in these terms:

> The MTCR is neither a treaty nor an international agreement but is a voluntary arrangement among countries which share a common interest in arresting missile proliferation. The Regime consists of common export guidelines applied to a common list of controlled items. Each member implements its commitments in the context of its own national export laws.[20]

In addition, a group of thirty-three industrial powers has agreed to establish a similar regime covering dual-use commodities (that is, products with both military and civilian applications) along with advanced conventional weapons. This regime, known as the Wassenaar Arrangement, is intended to replace the now-defunct COCOM system.

Such controls have never been regarded as inconsistent with a free-trade regime, but if the definition of strategic commodities were to expand significantly to include many computer and information technologies, the effects on international trade might be considerable. These controls affect many high-technology items, and many poorer countries are concerned that these restrictions have the effect of denying them access to more productive and efficient economies. For example, the restrictions on nuclear technology make it more difficult for countries to develop nuclear energy as an alternative to energies based on hydrocarbons. Restricted access to computer technology can slow down the integration of the information technologies—which are proving to be so important in human affairs—into poorer economies. The inability of the advanced industrial countries to define exactly what they mean by security concerns raises doubts as to whether the issue is really one of security, or rather one concerned with preserving the power of the wealthy countries vis-à-vis the poorer ones.

The plasticity of the term "national security" is no more apparent than in the recent dispute between the United States and many other countries over the international legitimacy of the Cuban Liberty and Democratic Solidarity (LIBERTAD) Act, more commonly known as the Helms-Burton Act. This law came into effect in March 1996, and it essentially codified the almost complete trade embargo by the U.S. against Cuba, which has been in effect since the early 1960s. However, there are several provisions to this law which affect the trade interests of many other countries, most specifically the "creation of a private right of action in U.S. courts that will allow U.S. nationals whose property was confiscated by the Cuban government to sue Cuban governmental entities or foreign investors who use or profit in any way from those properties."[21] In this manner, the Helms-Burton Act uses U.S. domestic law to force other nations to join the embargo against Cuba.

Many nations have objected to this extension of U.S. law, and the European Union formally challenged the Helms-Burton Act before the WTO (the challenge was suspended in April 1997 pending further negotiations between the U.S. and the EU). The United States indicated that it would refuse to participate in the WTO proceedings, arguing that the Helms-Burton Act is not a trade issue but rather a national security issue.[22] The Europeans argue that trade sanctions are unquestionably a matter of trade policy and that if the United States wishes to address the national security threat posed by Cuba, it should use nontrade sanctions. The dispute was quite heated in early 1997, but both sides pulled back in April rather than force a confrontation that probably would have seriously damaged the WTO. While this issue is still unresolved, it is a good illustration of how the issue of national security is held to be a clear exception to the principles of free trade—but also how ambiguous that exception can actually be.

EXCEPTIONS TO A GLOBAL FREE-TRADE REGIME: HUMAN RIGHTS

Trade is often used as a mechanism for influencing the policies of states. The United States signaled its displeasure at the Japanese invasion of Manchuria in 1931 by cutting off vital exports to Japan, including oil and iron ore. This action simply reinforced the position of those in Japan who argued that further armed expansion was the only solution to the vulnerability of a relatively resource-scarce island. On the other hand, the trade embargo against the apartheid regime in South Africa, while far from complete, ultimately succeeded in persuading the Nationalist Government that continued isolation from the rest of the world was more costly to South Africa than the establishment of majority rule. In both cases, trade was manipulated as a diplomatic instrument to achieve a certain objective.

Many simply disagree with the use of trade as a policy tool. For them, economics should follow its own logic and its purposes should not be subordinated to the political interests of the state. This position suggests that, over time, the forces of economics will slowly persuade states to cooperate more effectively, no matter what the ideological or political differences among them. Many people argue, moreover, that using trade as a lever for inducing change is simply ineffective. The failure of the long-term U.S. trade embargo against Cuba to force a change in the Cuban government is a case in point.

There is probably no way to separate trade from politics, and it would be naïve to suggest otherwise. Trade restrictions are more often reflections of domestic politics within states than they are actually well-crafted mechanisms of change. Perhaps the most visible case of trade politics in recent years has been the dispute between the United States and the People's Republic of China over a U.S. extension of Most-Favored-Nation (MFN) status to the Chinese. (MFN status simply means that the restrictions on trade between two nations will be no more onerous than the least restrictions offered to any other single state with whom trade occurs. The status does not confer any special advantage: it merely prohibits a specific disadvantage that could possibly be directed against a single state. MFN is a crucially important status because it allows states to compete more or less equally within the global trading network.)

As China has become one of the most significant partners in United States trade, importing in 1995 about $12 billion from the United States and exporting about $45 billion to the United States, the question of whether China should be granted MFN status has become critically important. There are some who oppose granting MFN status to China simply because they believe that the United States cannot compete with Chinese products due to the very low wages typically paid to Chinese workers. According to these analysts, an influx of Chinese goods would cost Americans jobs— arguments similar to those developed earlier in the section on protectionism. There are others, however, who argue that the absence of political freedoms in China renders China an unfit trading partner. They suggest that the United States should threaten to restrict Chinese exports to the United States unless China adopts a system of human rights more compatible with Western values.

There is very little question that China has a profoundly different system of politics than the United States. Moreover, there is little question that many Americans find Chinese practices—particularly the treatment of political dissidents—to be abhorrent. At the same time, however, it is difficult to accept the proposition that American political practices should be the standard by which all nations should be judged, and most nations in the world would repudiate such a standard. (Indeed, the United States itself might be found lacking in adherence to its own principles in many respects.) The Chinese argue, moreover, that its internal political and economic system accurately reflects the values of its society, and that its internal politics are not subject to evaluation or judgment by outsiders. This position is similarly difficult to accept: the precedents established by the Nuremberg and Tokyo War Crimes Tribunals after World War II effectively dismissed the possibility of politics ever being a purely "domestic" matter—the position was only reinforced by the subsequent UN sanctions imposed on South Africa.

Which side is right? Initially, the United States took the position in 1993 that MFN status would not be conferred unless human rights practices in China changed dramatically. Subsequently, however, the United States changed its position, and, in 1996, granted China MFN status for a year. Presumably, that status will be renewed unless Chinese actions change dramatically for the worse.

In some sense, one could conclude from this that the Chinese had clearly won a victory over United States policy—trade would flow freely between the two nations, and no conditions were imposed on Chinese behavior. Nonetheless, this interpretation of the outcome is overly simple. United States pressure certainly discomfited the Chinese, and the publicity surrounding certain dissidents in China and the possibilities of prison labor for profit damaged China's reputation globally. The more important point, however, was much simpler: the United States decided that its ability to influence Chinese domestic political practice through trade was minimal. This pragmatic observation led to the decision that opening trade further might lead to political changes within China more rapidly than a coercive approach, punishing China for its human rights practices. The position of the Clinton Administration was well articulated by its National Security Advisor, Samuel Berger, on June 6 before the Council on Foreign Relations:

> The need for capital to fuel China's growth—for which China must compete with other compelling new markets around the world—increases the need for greater rule of law and predictability, at least in its commercial affairs. And the fellow travelers of the new global economy—computers and modems, faxes and photocopiers, increased contacts and binding contracts—carry with them the seeds of change. Can China successfully make the next great leap toward a modern economy in the Information Age without producing the result of empowering its people, further decentralizing decision making, and giving its citizens more choices in their lives? Possible—but I doubt it.[23]

As is the case with most pragmatic decisions, time will tell.

EXCEPTIONS TO A GLOBAL FREE-TRADE REGIME: ENVIRONMENTAL PROTECTION

The most recent exceptions to the free-trade system revolve around the growing concern over how corporations may subvert environmental regulations by moving their operations to states with lax environmental controls (so as to avoid paying for costly pollution cleanup measures at home). There is scant systematic evidence to document how extensive this problem may be, but there are a number of examples that suggest that the problem may be widespread. Arlene Wilson of the Congressional Research Service observed that "a number of studies have shown that trade liberalization may reduce a country's overall welfare if environmental resources are incorrectly priced."[24] It is difficult, however, to know how to correctly price environmental protection—particularly since, in the international arena, attitudes toward balancing the values of economic development and environmental protection may differ profoundly.

In making environmental standards a part of NAFTA, the United States, Canada, and Mexico have set the stage for increased debate between environmental activist organizations and advocates for freer trade. As part of the negotiations leading up to the establishment of NAFTA, the three countries set up a "side agreement" known as the North American Agreement on Environmental Cooperation (NAAEC). This agreement was not part of the central trade agreement but was included as a specific guarantee against the abuse of the free trade area to avoid environmental regulation. It provides a mechanism in which disputes over environmental regulations may be settled outside of the NAFTA framework.[25]

In opposing NAFTA, many environmentalists feared that American businesses would flock to Mexico to produce more cheaply by avoiding costly U.S. environmental regulations. There is not yet sufficient information to assess whether this fear was or is justified. There seems to be widespread consensus that "dirty" (i.e., heavily polluting) industries "have expanded faster in developing countries than the average rate for all industries over the last two decades—and faster than in industrial countries. It is uncertain, however, whether this international pattern merely reflects growth—or industrial migration as well."[26]

The creation of the side agreement was clearly an initiative sparked by domestic concerns within the United States, and the rhetorical level of support for environmental protection was quite high. Former Secretary of State Warren Christopher affirmed in 1996 that the United States is "striving through the new World Trade Organization to reconcile the complex tensions between promoting trade and protecting the environment—and to ensure that neither comes at the expense of the other."[27] Whether this balance can be attained remains to be seen. It is unlikely that freer trade would substantially increase the opportunities for new environmental degradation; it might, however, intensify current problems.

THE CRITIQUE OF THE FREE-TRADE REGIME

The exceptions to the practice of free trade listed above are generally regarded as practical concessions to the political realities of the international system. They are, in some respects, modifications or reforms designed to accommodate interests that find the demands of the free market inconsistent with other values such as equality and justice. There are many, however, who believe that free trade cannot be reconciled with these other values. These critics argue that the free-trade regime is in fact a political system—indeed, an imperialist system—engineered to maintain the power of the advanced industrialized countries at the expense of the poorer countries.

There are a number of variations to this argument and limited space prohibits their development in any detail in this essay. Marxists, dependency theorists, and liberal reformers all share some basic elements of the critique.[28] What separates their analyses is the extent to which the system can be changed, what the nature of those changes ought to be, and whether the changes have to involve the fundamental premises of the capitalist system.

The analysis of the problem is straightforward: free trade favors the more developed economies and this bias channels wealth from the poor to the rich. The rich countries will always be producing the goods with the highest value; the poor countries will always be consigned to producing raw materials and providing cheap labor. This division of labor, according to the critics of free trade, is inherently unequal. This process has been going on for centuries and the cumulative effect of the bias is the growing income gap between rich and poor. Powerful states adopt free trade precisely because it increases their relative power over other states. Bismarck once noted:

> England had the highest protective duties until she had been so strengthened under the protection that she came forward as a Herculean fighter and challenged everybody with, "Enter the lists with me." She is the strongest pugilist in the arena of competition, and is ever ready to assert the right of the strongest in trade.[29]

From this perspective, free trade is nothing more than a mercantilist policy designed to enhance the power of a rich state relative to others.

The critics of free trade argue that the openness of the free-trade regime exposes poorer countries to intense competition, which they view as patently unfair. Rich countries have access to capital, technology, transportation, and large, affluent markets—all of which are generally unavailable to poorer countries. The poor countries can sell their labor and their land in the form of primary commodities; both of these factors of production are in great supply and therefore the prices for them are low. Free trade thus creates a context in which poor countries have few avenues of escape: their products are less valuable than the products of the rich countries and their relative poverty only increases the more they participate in the free-trade regime.

The critics of the free-trade regime stand solidly on their description of the international distribution of wealth. Since the mid-1800s, wealth and income have become increasingly concentrated in the industrialized nations. There is little question that poor countries have had a more difficult time catching up to the rich countries as free-trade practices have become more global. The liberalizing of trade after the Tokyo Round did not significantly improve the status of poorer countries:

> Since the end of the Tokyo Round in 1979, the average level of industrial tariffs in developed countries has fallen by nearly a half to 6.4 percent and the value of total world merchandise trade has grown by a remarkable 4.8 percent per year. This growth is mainly confined to the industrialized countries: in the 1980s, developing countries' exports grew by only 1.6 percent, and their share of world trade fell from 28 to 21 percent.[30]

There is no question that some developing countries have benefited from the expansion of trade opportunities in the post-World War II period. Many countries in East Asia—Singapore, Thailand, Malaysia, Taiwan, and South Korea—deliberately pursued an export-led strategy that resulted in impressive growth in their gross domestic products. However, other countries have not been able to use trade as an "engine of growth." These countries, many of them in Africa, export primary commodities for which demand has been declining over time. The expansion of free trade into the agricultural sectors of these economies poses serious threats to the farming communities in many of these areas. While it is probably safe to say that free trade will always benefit the wealthy, one must be more cautious in advocating free-trade commitments for the poor. For them, trade will never be enough unless their exports include high-value manufactured products.

CHALLENGES TO THE FUTURE OF THE WORLD TRADING SYSTEM

There are three primary concerns that have emerged out of the recent expansion of the free-trade regime. The first is over the ways in which the trade system is connected to the larger economic process of globalization. The WTO, in its Annual Report for 1995, notes the significance of the connection:

> In virtually every year of the postwar period, the growth of world merchandise trade has exceeded the growth of world merchandise output. Overall, the volume of world merchandise trade is estimated to have increased at an average annual rate of slightly more than 6 percent during the period 1950–94, compared with close to 4 percent for world output. This means each 10 percent increase in world output has on average been associated with a 16 percent increase in world trade. During those forty-five years, world merchandise output has multiplied 5½ times and world trade has multiplied 14 times, both in real terms.[31]

In other words, the vast increase in global wealth in the second half of the twentieth century represents "shared" wealth: world economic output has soared primarily because market expansion has occurred due to increased international trade. The United States is a good example of this expansion: in 1970, the value of U.S. trade represented about 13 percent of the GDP. In 1992, the percentage was 25 percent. In 1997, trade accounted for nearly 30 percent of the U.S. GDP.

Nations trade because there are differences in production possibilities and costs among nations. While some of these factors are fixed, others, like the cost of labor, are not. When production changes location because of these differences in costs, the demand for these factors of production changes as well. For example, the demand for high-wage labor may be reduced because of the availability of low-wage labor somewhere else, which then leads to a reduction of the high wages in the original country. We know that this transformation has in fact occurred, since trade is increasing at a faster rate than production.

The fear that freer trade will depress high wages and lead to a mass exodus of jobs from the industrialized countries to the lower-wage poorer countries is genuine, and manifests itself in a nightmare of a global system of sweatshops. There is little systematic or global evidence to document the extent to which this fear is legitimate, although the anecdotal evidence is horrific. But the most important issue facing the WTO is the internationalization of standards—labor and environmental—implicit in the process of globalization. If the global economy becomes truly universal, then one would expect a tendency for prices and wages to converge. But will that convergence be at the levels now experienced in the advanced industrial countries? Or will it settle down at the levels now characteristic of the poorer countries in the system?

The issue is extremely complicated. Evening out the differences in factors of production vitiates the efficiencies gained by comparative advantage; ignoring the differences assures strong political opposition to opening up markets. Further, there is no way to accurately measure the quality-of-life standards referred to by questions concerning wages and environmental protection: What is a decent, living wage? What is a "clean" environment? How does one account for the cultural variations in the definitions of these criteria? Finally, the internationalization of these standards poses a serious challenge to the idea of state sovereignty. When an international organization such as the WTO or the International Labor Organization (ILO) begins to dictate working conditions within a country, serious questions arise about the ability of states to manage their own domestic affairs. Indeed, one begins to wonder if there is really any meaning to the terms "foreign" and "domestic" in a truly global economy.

The second major challenge facing the world trading system is whether the free-trade regime can remain politically coherent and consistent. Free-trade principles have typically been articulated and enforced by powerful states, especially Great Britain and the United States. In the post-World War II period, GATT reflected the interests of the United States, Western Europe, and Japan. As such, GATT enforced no rules that were in any way inconsistent with the interests of the major powers. The conclusion of the Uruguay Round and the creation of the WTO, however, reflect the economic and political power of "new" entrants to the global economy, most importantly China and the states of the former Soviet Union. Additional impetus for the new structures came from two states that changed their trade policies toward more liberalized trade: India and Brazil. The more traditional supporters of free trade—the United States and several of the European states— actually saw domestic support for free trade decline.

In others words, the presumed universality of the doctrine of free trade itself will become increasingly subject to political and cultural critique. This critique is at the present time somewhat muted because most of the new nations participating in the system have enjoyed vigorous economic growth: in good economic times, free trade typically expands. The real strength of the new trade regime will be tested when an economic downturn occurs. Under conditions of economic stress, domestic pressures for protectionist measures undoubtedly increase, and the ideological coherence of the commitment of the advanced industrial nations will be significantly diluted.

In the absence of a strong ideological and political commitment, enforcement of the rules and principles of free trade become problematic. The WTO has a Dispute Settlement Body and an Appellate Body to enforce the rulings of the WTO, but the general effect of these enforcement mechanisms thus far has been to persuade nations to resolve their disputes "out of court." Such resolutions of trade disputes are important and should not be discounted; nonetheless, it remains to be seen whether the WTO has the ability to enforce unpopular decisions in powerful states. The response of the United States to challenges to its Helms-Burton Act suggests that enforcement is going to be exceedingly difficult.

The third and final challenge to the world trading system is the presence, persistence, and expansion of global poverty. It is a mistake to think that the WTO can address this problem on its own. It is also a mistake, however, to think that an uncritical pursuit of free trade will help all countries equally. One of the clear characteristics of trade is that it rather faithfully represents the distribution of economic power in the international system. That some poor countries have been able to use trade to stimulate their economies to grow at rather rapid rates is an important reason to support free trade in principle. But it cannot be used as a blanket justification for policies that expose very poor societies to economic competition that undermines their long-term viability.

The current distribution of wealth is not defensible, either in moral or in practical terms. There are far too many people on the planet who lead lives of total desperation: over a billion people are malnourished, ill housed, and cut off from adequate education, medical care, clean water, and a safe environment. Free trade will not, on its own, pull these people into prosperity. Moreover, in a free-trade regime, the economic fortunes of the rich countries are inextricably linked to the fortunes of the poor. This is so because free trade has a convergence effect on wages, although the power of that effect is not clearly measurable. If industries do migrate to low-wage areas, then the tendency will be for high wages to fall. At some point, the reduction in wages will have a depressing effect on demand for products and this reduction will unquestionably lead to lower rates of economic growth—perhaps even negative growth rates.

This challenge to the free-trade regime is not dramatic or immediate, but it is inexorable. Nor does it suggest that free trade itself should be abandoned as a general principle. But the challenge of global poverty demands that richer countries think about trade as a way of helping poor nations integrate more successfully into the global economy. Such integration will require concessions, primarily ones of access to markets as well as the transfer of capital and technology, to protect the weak economic infrastructures of many countries from the rather unforgiving rigors of free trade.

QUESTIONS FOR FURTHER STUDY

1. What are the arguments traditionally made in favor of a global free trade system? What is the evidence to support these arguments?
2. How has the principle of free trade been embedded in international economic institutions since World War II? How effective have these institutions proved to be in practice?

3. How do the requirements of national security impact on a state's trade policies? How does the quest for human rights affect trade policy? The quest for environmental protection? Which of these, if any, do you believe should take precedence over the principle of free trade?

4. How does the global trading system affect the prospects for economic development in the world's poorest countries? Do you think that the trading system should be modified in some fashion to enhance the prospects for economic growth in these countries, and if so, how?

Notes

1. Eli Hecksher, *Mercantilism*, Vol. 1 (London: George Allen & Unwin, 1935), pp. 172–3.

2. As Susan Strange puts it: "Efficiency never has been, *and never can be,* the sole consideration in the choice of state politics." Susan Strange, "Protectionism and World Politics," *International Organization,* Vol. 39, No. 2 (Spring 1985), p. 236 [italics in the original].

3. The literature on historical mercantilism is quite large. Hecksher (op. cit.) remains the most extensive treatment of the subject. See also: Philip W. Buck, *The Politics of Mercantilism* (New York: Octagon Books, 1974); Charles Woolsey Cole, *French Mercantilism, 1683–1700* (New York: Octagon Books, 1971); James Breck Perkins, *France under Mazarin* (New York: G. P. Putnam's Sons, 1902).

4. Jacob Viner, "Power versus Plenty As Objectives of Foreign Policy in the Seventeenth and Eighteenth Centuries," *World Politics,* Vol. 1, No. 1 (October 1948), pp. 1–29.

5. Edward Meade Earle, "Adam Smith, Alexander Hamilton, Friedrich List: The Economic Foundations of Military Power," in *Makers of Modern Strategy: Military Thought from Machiavelli to Hitler* (Princeton: Princeton University Press, 1943), p. 118.

6. John Maynard Keynes, "National Self-Sufficiency," *The Yale Review,* Vol. 22, No. 4 (June 1933), p. 755.

7. Angus Maddison, *Monitoring the World Economy, 1820–1992* (Paris: Development Centre of the Organisation for Economic Co-operation and Development, 1995), p. 19.

8. Maddison, op. cit., p. 37.

9. The *Wall Street Journal* reported that "only sixty-two quarrels have been sent there for resolution." *The Wall Street Journal* (December 3, 1996), p. A1.

10. Peter Passell, "Economic Analysis: Doubts Grow About Regional Trade Pacts," *New York Times* (February 4, 1997).

11. Renato Ruggiero, "Multilateralism and Regionalism in Trade," United States Information Agency, *Economic Perspectives,* USIA Electronic Journals, Vol. 1, No. 16 (November 1996), < http://www.usia.gov/journal/sites/1196/ijee/ej4rugg.htm>.

12. Ian Goldin, Odin Knudsen and Dominique van der Mensbrugghe, *Trade Liberalisation: Global Economic Implications* (Paris: Organisation for Economic Co-operation and Development, 1993), p. 13.

13. Richard W. Stevenson, "NAFTA's Impact on Jobs Has Been Slight, Study Shows," *New York Times* (December 19, 1996).

14. Bryan T. Johnson, "The Truth About Free Trade and Protectionism," The Heritage Foundation (April 25, 1996), <http://www.heritage.org/heritage/commentary/op-bj2.htm>.

15. Patrick J. Buchanan, "America First, NAFTA Never" (November 7, 1993), <http://www.buchanan.org/never.htm>.

16. Robert Crandell, "The Effects of U.S. Trade Protection for Autos and Steel," *Brookings Paper on Economic Activity,* No. 1 (1987), as quoted by Johnson, op. cit.

17. Panel on the Impact of National Security Controls on International Technology Transfer, *Balancing the National Interest: U.S. National Security Export Controls and Global Economic Competition* (Washington: National Academy Press, 1987), pp. 70–71.

18. Gary K. Bertsch, *East-West Strategic Trade: COCOM and the Atlantic Alliance* (Paris: The Atlantic Institute for International Affairs, April 1983), p. 38.

19. "Controlling a Deadly Trade: COCOM," *The Economist,* Vol. 330, No. 7856 (March 26, 1994), p. 52.

20. "The Missile Technology Control Regime," United States Arms Control and Disarmament Agency (November 7, 1994), <http://members.aol.com/mehampton/ACDA/mtcr-94.txt>.

21. "Fact Sheet on the Cuban Liberty and Democratic Solidarity Act," United States Information Service (April 1, 1996), <http://www.usia.gov/topical/econ/libertad/libdosfs.htm>.

22. David E. Sanger, "U.S. Rejects Role for World Court in Cuba Trade," *New York Times* (February 21, 1997).

23. Remarks by Samuel R. Berger, Assistant to The President for National Security Affairs, Council on Foreign Relations (New York: June 6, 1997).

24. Arlene Wilson, Congressional Research Service, "GATT, Trade Liberalization, and the Environment: An Economic Analysis," Report No. 94–291 E (April 5, 1994), <http://www.cnie.org/nle/econ-3.html>.

25. Pierre Marc Johnson and André Beaulieu, *The Environment and NAFTA: Understanding and Implementing the New Continental Law* (Washington: Island Press, 1996), pp. 121–130.

26. "International Trade and the Environment," *World Bank Policy Research Bulletin*, Vol. 4, No. 1 (January/February 1993), <http://www.worldbank.org/html/dec/Publications/Bulletins/PRBvol4no1.html>.

27. Warren Christopher, "American Diplomacy and the Global Environmental Challenges of the Twenty-First Century," Address and Question-and-Answer Session by Secretary of State Warren Christopher, Stanford University (Palo Alto, CA: April 9, 1996), <http://www.usis.usemb.se/speeches/christopher/ENVIRO.html>.

28. The literature on this subject is vast. For Marxist analyses, see V.I. Lenin, *Imperialism: The Highest Stage of Capitalism* (New York: International, 1939); Paul Baran, *The Political Economy of Growth* (New York: Monthly Review Press, 1957); Rosa Luxemburg, *The Accumulation of Capital* (New York: Monthly Review Press, 1964). For dependency theorists, see Johan Galtung, "A Structural Theory of Imperialism," *Journal of Peace Research*, Vol. 13, No. 2 (1971), pp. 81–118; Theotonio Dos Santos, "The Structure of Dependence," in K.T. Fann and Donald C. Hodges, eds., *Readings in U.S. Imperialism,* (Boston: Porter Sargent, 1971), pp. 225–236; Andre Gunder Frank, *Capitalism and Underdevelopment in Latin America* (New York: Monthly Review Press, 1969). For the liberal reformer view, see J. Gallagher and R. Robinson, "The Imperialism of Free Trade," *Economic History Review,* Vol. 6, No. 1 (1953), pp. 1–15; Bernard Semmel, *The Rise of Free Trade Imperialism* (Cambridge: Cambridge University Press, 1970).

29. Made in a speech before the Reichstag on June 14, 1882, as quoted in William Harbutt Dawson, *Protection in Germany: A History of German Fiscal Policy during the Nineteenth Century* (London: P.S. King & Son, 1904), p. 37.

30. Goldin, op. cit., p. 21.

31. "International Trade Trends and Statistics," prepared by the Economic Research and Analysis Division and the Statistics and Information Systems Division (World Trade Organization, 1995), <http://www.wto.org/htbin/htimage/wto/map.map?449,256>.

16 / International Environmental Cooperation as a Contribution to World Security

JANET WELSH BROWN

Anticipating the collapse of the Soviet empire, George Kennan wrote in *Foreign Affairs* in 1985 of the "two unprecedented and supreme dangers" facing the world: the prospect of nuclear war and the "devastating effect of modern industrialization and overpopulation on the world's natural environment."[1] The latter was a shockingly new idea at the time, especially because it came from the pen of the old cold warrior. His warning fell largely on deaf ears, exciting no public debate and not meaningfully changing the way in which most academic analysts researched, published, and taught security studies, nor the way in which security policy was made in Washington and other capital cities.

A mere ten years later, one could see an enormous increase in international activity around environmental issues. It is perhaps the fastest growing field in international politics. According to the Register of International Treaties of the United Nations Environment Programme (UNEP), more than 170 treaties affecting the environment have been negotiated, most of them since 1980. They are remarkable documents in several respects. Some are near universal, having up to 170 signatory states. They cover environmental issues comprehensively—whaling, climate, marine pollution, trade, endangered species, protection of Antarctica, desertification, trade in hazardous wastes, acid rain, and so on. These international agreements are dynamic, designed to be responsive to changing science and politics. They include a variety of players in the negotiations—international organizations, financial and business institutions, regional organizations, substate entities, and especially nongovernmental organizations (NGOs)—as well as states. These treaties, even after signing and ratification, undergo constant evolution that strengthens the basis for international cooperation.

As a result, there is now a substantial body of international environmental law, widely agreed to, requiring extensive international cooperation. Indeed, powerful nations and ministates alike have willingly given up modest degrees of sovereignty because doing so is thought to be in their national interests. They have rendered their own domestic policies on pesticide runoff, fishing in international waters, national energy policy, and a range of other national decisions open to international scrutiny. They are account-able now in many areas to international standards and agreements.

Despite this worldwide recognition of the seriousness of environmen-tal problems, the notion that environmental degradation could threaten national security is still struggling for precedence in security policy circles. The 1996 U.S. National Security Strategy recognizes, among the nonmili-tary risks, an "emerging class of transnational environmental and natural resource issues," and declares a need to address both domestic and interna-tional environmental problems.[2] The Clinton Administration has also cre-ated environmental offices in both the Department of State and the National Security Council. But the concept of environmental security—that is, the notion that environmental, population, and natural-resource issues may affect key U.S. interests[3]—has not necessarily penetrated the ranks of policy makers and implementers. Indeed, specializing in the environment is not considered a promising career path in the State Department, where, even in the post-Cold War era, it is considered better to have expertise on the for-mer Soviet countries than on the environment if one hopes to make ambas-sador rank.

Nor is there yet wide public understanding of the importance of the role of the environmental treaties in protecting of ecosystems and assuring sus-tainable human development. Even in the United States, where the environ-mental conscience and rhetoric is as well developed as in any state, key treaties go unratified without public outcry, media coverage, or political debate. The biggest of the international meetings, such as the Kyoto 1997 Conference of Parties (COP) to the Climate Treaty, get coverage only in the most sophisticated U.S. dailies and perfunctorily on television news, while some of the less spectacular convention meetings, such as the Biodiversity COP in 1996, are barely mentioned in daily news reports. On the other hand, there is an explosion of regular, specialized publications on specific treaty areas—wildlife, energy, biodiversity, waste—and some that cover the whole range of issues, such as the *International Environment Reporter, Earth Negotiations Bulletin, Earth Times,* and *Greenwire.* At the time of actual negotiations, there is a further swell of publications in the form of detailed electronic reporting on each day's development and politics—often put out by NGOs such as the International Climate Network, but used as well by official government delegations and the news media.[4]

The lack of widespread public understanding is not surprising, given the number, frequency, and complexity of the international negotiations. Even specialists in related fields have little time to contemplate the connections among their own particular interests. Thus, the analysts writing about envi-ronmental and demographic topics in this book scarcely acknowledge the importance of democracy or military expenditures to the fulfillment of envi-ronmental goals, nor do we often recognize the importance of cultural diver-sity to the maintenance of biological diversity. And though there are notable exceptions, rarely do human-rights activists sit down with environmental-ists, or environmentalists share a platform with military security advisers, unless (in recent years) at the invitation of the military analysts.[5] It therefore behooves us to do a better job in educating our colleagues and sharing more widely our understanding of the importance of international environmental cooperation to the nation's (and the planet's) well-being.

It is simply no longer possible for any one country, no matter how rich and powerful, to address global environmental problems alone. Various levels of international cooperation are required. In some cases, as with atmospheric problems such as depletion of the ozone layer and global warming, all countries contribute and all will be affected—albeit in different ways, and not necessarily in proportion to their contributions to the problem. Australians and Argentineans, for instance, suffer higher skin-cancer rates as a result of atmospheric ozone depletion, despite their playing a lesser role in ozone-layer destruction. Or a problem such as tropical deforestation may be concentrated in a few countries, but have an adverse impact on the rest of the world, through the loss of biological diversity and accelerated global warming (due to the release, through fires, of the carbon stored in the forests). In still other cases, such as the overfishing of international waters, it does the U.S. and Canadian fishing communities no good to curb their harvest of dwindling North Atlantic fish stocks if Portuguese vessels are hauling in migratory fish stocks from just outside our territorial waters. American fishermen, manufacturers, and farmers naturally want assurance that they will not be at a disadvantage with international competitors if they are required to meet high environmental standards. International environmental cooperation, required in a whole series of treaties, is meant to protect a wide variety of U.S. interests by assuring that all countries play by the rules on a level playing field.

Citizens should find the progress on international environmental issues to be encouraging, for developments are moving in a positive direction. The questions remaining are whether the progress being made can keep up with the accumulation of problems, and whether there exists sufficiently determined international leadership—especially U.S. leadership—to keep ahead of the trends of environmental deterioration. Despite much progress, there continues in most areas an acceleration of pollution of the earth, damage to the atmosphere, and the harvest of renewable resources—forests, fish, wildlife—at a rate that is not sustainable in view of increasing population and consumption. Despite the many hopeful signs, there are many worrying ones.

CHALLENGES

For almost two decades now, citizens and their leaders all over the world have been aware of ominous, well-documented trends of increasing pollution of the environment and degradation of the resource base. Public opinion shows awareness is growing and concern is worldwide—indeed, citizens often seem to be ahead of their political leaders in their recognition of the urgency of environmental threats and in their willingness to deal with them.[6] Books crowd the shelves, warning of ozone depletion, disappearing species and habitats, global warming, international legal trade in (and illegal dumping of) hazardous wastes, overfishing, deforestation, the pollution and drawing down of key water sources, industrial accidents, nuclear plant breakdowns, and vast oil spills. In extreme cases, some biospheres have been so damaged as to have collapsed, to an irretrievable extent. The Aral Sea (in the former Soviet Union), once the world's fourth largest lake, is now one-third its original volume and heavily salinated—destroyed primarily by the diversion of water for the irrigation of cotton. In other cases, such as the drawing down of important aquifers in North Africa shared by Libya and Egypt, or the Ogallala aquifer in the American Southwest, restoration is so far in the future as to make the present condition seem permanent. In other cases, such as global warming, the damage is technically remediable, but adequate steps have yet to be taken and problems will grow more severe before they get better.

Organizations that track these environmental changes assert that "most of the trends show a worsening of environmental problems, suggesting that many national and international environmental goals will not be met without extensive policy reform and significant changes in current practices and strategies."[7] The current trends in carbon dioxide (CO_2) emissions from fossil fuels are especially discouraging. Energy use, already high in the industrialized countries, is growing rapidly in developing countries. Recent studies predict increases in global energy use, mostly from fossil fuels, in the range of 34 to 44 percent by 2010 and 54 to 98 percent by 2020, with the highest growth in Asia and Latin America.[8] The result will be large increases in local air pollution, with its insidious effects on morbidity and materials damage, and significant further CO_2 emissions (up 30 to 40 percent by 2010). All kinds of energy use—residential heating and cooling, power generation, manufacturing, mining, and transportation—will contribute emissions, but the expected increase in motor vehicles, spurred largely by urban growth in developing and industrialized countries, is among the most startling.

Worldwide, as the level of industrial activity increases along with economic growth, the production of wastes from industrial processes is on the increase. Degradation occurs when natural resources are extracted and processed (causing the release of effluents into the water and soil and gaseous substances and particles into the air), and through the use and disposal of manufactured products.

Most highly industrialized countries—except the former Soviet states—have environmental regulatory systems that curb the worst effects. On the other hand, developing countries—especially those that are undergoing rapid growth and industrialization—experience some of the worst pollution problems in the world. Indeed, in countries such as Mexico and China, industrial pollution has become a political liability for governments. But despite regulations and the enlightened intentions of many corporations, the problems continue to grow. The scale is enormous: each year the United

States—the world's largest producer and consumer of industrial products and among the highest producers of waste—devours nearly 2.7 billion metric tons of raw materials (not including stone, sand, and gravel), and creates 6.9 billion tons of solid waste from extraction processes, 7.7 billion tons of solid waste from metal and mineral processing, 120 million tons of conventional air pollutants, and 4.9 billion tons of CO_2. The World Resources Institute concludes, "Few would argue that current industrial practice is sustainable."[9]

Some portion of the hazardous wastes from these processes crosses boundaries and becomes the subject of international politics. Acid rain, crossing boundaries from Britain, France, and Germany to Scandinavia, became the object of one of the earliest international efforts (1979) to control transboundary pollution. A proportion of the hazardous waste produced in the world enters into international trade, and about one-fifth of that is shipped from highly industrialized to developing countries.

Similar destructive trends can be charted in many other areas, including forest loss, fishery depletion, habitat and biodiversity loss, coastal pollution from onshore sources, overharvesting of whales, and the dangerous thinning of the Earth's protective ozone layer. Only the last two are sufficiently under international control—through broadly supported treaties—to offer hope that the damage may be undone. In most areas, international efforts to ameliorate environmental destruction are not yet able to stay ahead of the curve.

All these trends in environmental deterioration are exacerbated, of course, by rapid population growth, especially in developing countries, and by increasingly high rates of consumption, especially in highly industrialized countries, but also by the increasingly affluent classes in developing countries. The 20 percent of the world's population that lives in the highly industrialized countries consumes an inordinate share of the world's resources. With respect to fossil fuels, for instance, which are the worst contributors to global warming, the industrialized countries use almost half of the total, which is nine times the per capita consumption of the developing countries. And the gap will not easily be closed because the new technologies that promise greater efficiency in the use of all materials are owned mostly by institutions in the North.[10]

RESPONSES

Even while environmental problems were advancing, the world gained experience with technologies and policies to deal with them: techniques to conserve water and shelter crops from wind in arid areas, to conserve energy by using it more efficiently, and to harvest food and fiber and medicinal plants from the forests without leveling the forests themselves; and national policies to get prices right, to reduce destructive subsidies, and to provide incentives for new techniques. These policies and techniques, in different combinations in every country, are the stuff of *sustainable development,* defined in 1987 by the World Commission on Environment and Development (the Brundtland Commission) as "development that meets the needs of the present without compromising the ability of future generations to meet their own needs."[11]

The concept of sustainable development was legitimized in 1992 by 180 nations at the United Nations Conference on Environment and Development (UNCED) in Rio de Janeiro when they produced the grand blueprint *Agenda 21,* and the *Declaration of Principles.* Inherent in the Rio documents—hammered out in perhaps the longest, most comprehensive, and most inclusive international negotiations in history—is the understanding that economic development and environmental protection must go hand in hand if the planet is to survive and sustain 10 billion people in the next century. Delegates recognized their nations' shared but differentiated responsibilities for global environmental problems. They further acknowledged the incompatibility of poverty and environmental protection and the need for *equity*—that is, more equitably shared resources and opportunities—within and between countries and between generations, and declared that environmental issues are handled best when citizens are given access to information and participate fully in decision making.

These understandings are the basis for scores of international agreements. Some treaties are quite broad in scope—they may express a determination to cooperate to stem desertification or produce a plan to meet the peculiar development needs of small-island developing states in the Caribbean, South Pacific, and Indian oceans. Others zero in on the production and use of particular chemicals, such as the chlorofluorocarbons and related compounds that destroy the ozone layer. Some are based on more complete scientific information than others, but the level of knowledge underpinning these agreements is rising in all areas. Whereas the earliest of the treaties tended to deal with exploited species (e.g., whales) and endangered species, the more recent ones—on climate, biodiversity, and international trade in hazardous waste—affect the core economic activities of the nations involved.

Nor are decisions on trade and international assistance unaffected, for environmental obligations raise fundamental questions about the ways in which nations order their economic development and growth. The multilateral banks and bilateral-assistance agencies increasingly condition their grants and loans on environmental protection and conservation demands. Governments, too, are obligated—through their own national plans developed as follow-ups to the Rio Conference—to organize their energy strategies, forestry policies, and other development investments in ways that break out of the traditional nonsustainable ways of "growing" their economies.

Trade, which has a far greater impact on countries' development patterns than international development assistance, is no longer immune to environmental considerations either. While there are currently great expectations (especially among the great trading nations) that lowering trade barriers and lifting investment restrictions will stimulate economic growth and create jobs, there is also concern that increased trade and investment, pursued along the old lines—that is, without respect for environmental and equity considerations—could cause further environmental damage and create even larger gaps between rich and poor.[12] For that reason, environmental considerations—weak though they are—have been introduced into the North American Free Trade Agreement and the World Trade Agreement, and can be expected to be part of all multilateral trade negotiations from now on.[13] The environment is no longer a side issue in international relations; environmental considerations now impinge upon negotiations covering every issue.

Collectively, these environmental treaties constitute a system in the making—a system that is witnessing new high levels of international cooperation to achieve environmental protection and sustainable development. A brief analysis of three representative treaties and the politics surrounding their negotiations and implementation follows.[14] They illuminate the way national self-interest propels negotiations—or holds them back—and dictates the compromises. They illustrate the role that science plays, the way that popular pressures or politics within a country can affect outcomes, the variety of new players (especially NGOs), the leadership of certain nations, and the remaining stubborn controversies.

A TREATY TO PROTECT THE OZONE LAYER

In the 1960s and early 1970s, scientists working in Europe and North America began raising questions about depletion of the stratospheric layer of ozone that protects the Earth from the intense ultraviolet radiation of the sun. The thinning of this protective layer and the resulting damage to human health and to the survival of other animals and plants did not become an issue in international politics, however, until after 1975. At this time the United Nations Environment Programme funded a study by the World Meteorological Organization (WMO) to investigate the theory that depletion of the Earth's protective ozone layer could be caused by chlorofluorocarbons (CFCs), a group of chemical compounds used heavily by industrialized countries (and increasingly by developing countries as well) as refrigerants in air conditioners, refrigerators, freezers, and other cooling equipment, and as an ingredient in plastic foams, solvents, and aerosols. Despite the fact that the United States was the foremost producer and consumer of CFCs (the annual production of goods and services involving CFCs was worth $28 billion and the chemicals were also used in installed equipment worth $128 billion[15]), the United States, along with Canada, Finland, Norway, and Sweden, asked UNEP in 1977 to consider international protection of the ozone layer. Later that year, a UNEP-sponsored meeting of experts produced a plan of action. At this point the scientific evidence on ozone depletion was not definitive, however, and this potential threat to the atmosphere seemed remote to most laypersons.

An international working group of twenty-four nations began meeting in 1982 to consider measures for addressing the problem, but there was no sense of urgency. The resulting treaty, the 1985 Vienna Convention for the Protection of the Ozone Layer, established basic principles, but required no commitments to specific actions. Proposals from the United States and the Nordic states for a simultaneously negotiated protocol, calling for specific obligations, were rejected. Basically, governments agreed only to cooperate on monitoring, research, and information exchange. But they did agree, at the urging of the United States, to meet again in 1986 to work on a binding protocol. At this early stage, CFC-producer nations (the United States, Great Britain, France, Germany, Italy, and Japan) controlled the process. No developing country was active in the negotiations. The larger ones—India, China, Indonesia, Brazil, and Mexico—used CFCs and, although they produced less than 5 percent of the world total, their production was rapidly increasing.

Adoption of the ozone convention, which had taken ten years, constitutes a fine example of the "precautionary approach" often taken in the face of scientific uncertainty about the seriousness or extent of a particular threat to the environment. That there was a treaty at all was the result of persistence by UNEP, the United States, and smaller "lead" states (states that exercise leadership on a particular environmental issue). What followed after this was an example of treaty goals being adjusted, very quickly, as the science and the economic concerns changed.

The 1987 Montreal Protocol on Substances That Deplete the Ozone Layer (which, significantly, is how the 1985 ozone treaty has been known ever since) was a compromise between the lead states and the European Community. In the Protocol, which was in effect an amendment to the 1985 Vienna Convention, the industrial countries agreed to a 50-percent reduction of their 1986 levels of production of CFCs by 1999. Developing countries would be allowed to increase production modestly for ten years. The treaty still had no financial provision to ease their transition to alternative chemicals, as demanded by the developing countries. It was mute also on the subject of acceptable substitutes, had no adequate provisions for monitoring production and use, and incorporated no penalties for noncompliance. Some developing countries signed the Protocol (among them Mexico and Indonesia, perhaps because they were subject to trade pressures from the United States), but China, India, and Brazil—all key states—refused to sign, stating that they were a very small part of the problem and claiming that they could not afford to convert to the safer substitutes without a special fund to help defray the costs of doing so.

Within months, British scientists discovered a seasonal "hole" in the ozone layer over Antarctica. This discovery was followed in 1988 by another report documenting the thinning of the ozone shield over the northern hemisphere, and then one report followed another, year after year, as scientists documented rapidly increasing damage to the ozone layer. Within a few years, new reports documented a higher incidence of skin cancer, especially in Australia, along with reports of other possible health effects, such as suppression of human immunological systems.

In 1990, the European countries and Japan, in a major shift, voted with the lead states at the London Conference of the Parties to the treaty for a complete phaseout of CFCs by 2000—the earliest date the producer states would agree to. Their agreement this time dealt also with other ozone-depleting chemicals—carbon tetrachloride and methyl chloroform. In 1992, negotiators shortened the timetables set for themselves and added hydrochlorofluorocarbons (HCFCs) to the list, though only after the usual argument over each new chemical proposed for restriction. Pressed by U.S. NGOs, the parties also agreed in 1993 to phase out methyl bromide, which was used in pesticides (mostly in industrialized countries, but increasingly in developing countries). The United States had already frozen production of this compound (with the intent of ending production altogether in 2001) and primary European producers had phased out agricultural use because of contamination of water supplies.

The 1990 changes in the Protocol, in a bargain that assured major developing-country participation, also established a Multilateral Fund—the only one of its kind attached to an environmental treaty—to help fund the developing countries' transition from CFCs to safer substitutes. Industrialized countries pledged a modest $740 million over six years and agreed to a disbursing authority in which donor and recipient countries would be equally represented. The developing countries' demand for international financial assistance to help them meet their international environmental obligations was just the first of similar demands since made in all environmental-treaty negotiations, and the refusal of the major donor states to meet that demand continues to be an obstacle to international efforts to control environmental damage.

There remain, of course, other legitimate arguments over timetables, new chemicals, and choice of substitutes. Not all countries are on schedule with their commitments. Russia says frankly that it cannot meet its commitments because of economic hardships. The fund is still too small to meet developing-country needs, and annual subscriptions lag behind schedule or are withheld—as was done by the 104th U.S. Congress, some of whose members seemed in denial about the threat to the ozone layer, and many of whom were willing to reduce U.S. international environmental obligations in the name of balancing the budget. As CFC prices have risen at the end of the phaseout, worrisome illegal trade has created a lucrative black market. And there are still opposition forces trying to undo specific commitments, such as the efforts of the 104th Congress to renege on the U.S. promise to phase out methyl bromide. But, on the whole, the treaty works, and there is cautious optimism among experts that international cooperation within the treaty framework will be able to reverse the damage done to the ozone layer since the 1960s. The ozone treaty is therefore held up as the model of successful international cooperation to control substances harmful to the global commons.

How did this happen? Can this success be replicated? On the ozone issue, science was clearly on the side of regulation, but is unlikely to be so unequivocal in the case of other destructive substances or practices. United States leadership—persistent during conservative administrations in spite of corporate opposition at home—was very important. Business had predicted that moving away from CFCs would be expensive, eliminate jobs, and result in a lower quality of goods and services, but none of that happened. The government held firm, and corporate technological innovation and adaptation met the challenge. Indeed, U.S. firms have gained a significant market share in CFC substitutes. A combination of regulatory and market-based policies, including tradable consumption permits and a tax on ozone-depleting chemicals, accelerated the process. Experience with this treaty demonstrated that specific goals and timetables are more effective than voluntary measures and that modest international funds, over which recipient nations share control, can provide incentives to developing countries. Indeed, on January 1, 1996, well ahead of schedule, the United States stopped production of all CFCs, evidence that "Smart policies will drive technology innovation and bring compliance costs down."[16]

A CLIMATE TREATY

The Climate Treaty, signed at the Rio "Earth Summit," as the 1992 UN Conference on Environment and Development came to be called, attempts to deal with the problem of global warming. It is an excellent example of a generation of new global environmental problems. The buildup of greenhouse gases—largely CO_2 from the burning of fossil fuels, but also from methane generation and forest loss—creates a greenhouse effect that is warming the planet, heading the world toward climate shifts and a rise in the sea-level. Every country is affected by it and every country contributes to it—albeit in different ways and different amounts—making it a perfect candidate for international cooperation and regulation. It is, on the other hand, a complex and difficult problem, stemming from multiple sources. There is unusually broad consensus on the basic science of global warming, but questions remain over the rate at which such warming is occurring and the ability of ecosystems to adapt. Widely varying scenarios, made on the basis of competing modeling techniques and vociferous cries of "wolf" from a handful of dissenting scientists, continue to confuse the public—for most of whom global warming still seems an abstract and remote threat.[17]

Because energy use is required in all human activity, it is central to governments' economic development plans and concern about energy availability and cost shapes their negotiating positions. Historically, the highly industrialized countries, led by the United States, the former Soviet Union, and the European Union, have been and still are the biggest users of fossil fuels; however, the developing countries' share of the total has been growing in the last twenty years and will continue to grow. Among the latter—especially China, India, Thailand, and Indonesia—the use of large supplies of domestic coal (the worst offender among fossil fuels) is increasing, fueling rapid economic growth. In addition, the developing countries tend to be inefficient in the use of energy, unnecessarily increasing their contributions of CO_2. Thus, from the beginning of international climate discussions in the mid 1980s, views of the global-warming problem have diverged along North-South lines.

The North-South disjunction also affects how different governments measure their greenhouse gases. For instance, India makes its calculations by adding up the accumulated CO_2 emissions of the great industrial powers over the years and expresses them in terms of current per capita contributions—which emphasizes the immense historical contributions of the industrialized states to global warming and underlines India's own small per capita contribution to the problem. The Northern nations, on the other hand, prefer to count current annual national contributions, and include not only CO_2 emissions but also the CO_2 equivalents of methane and deforestation—which puts two developing countries, China and Brazil, right up at the top with the biggest emitters: the United States, the former Soviet Union, and the European Union. (See Table 16.1.)

Table 16.1 / Thirty Countries with the Highest Industrial Emissions of Carbon Dioxide, 1992

Rank	Country	Total CO_2 Emissions (million metric tons)	Rank	Country	Total CO_2 Emissions (million metric tons)
1	United States	4,881,349	16	South Korea	289,833
2	China	2,667,982	17	Australia	267,937
3	Russian Federation	2,103,132	18	North Korea	253,750
4	Japan	1,093,470	19	Iran	235,478
5	Germany	878,136	20	Spain	223,196
6	India	769,440	21	Saudi Arabia	220,620
7	Ukraine	611,342	22	Brazil	217,074
8	United Kingdom	566,246	23	Indonesia	184,585
9	Canada	409,862	24	Turkey	145,490
10	Italy	407,701	25	Netherlands	139,027
11	France	362,076	26	Czech Republic	135,608
12	Poland	341,892	27	Uzbekistan	123,253
13	Mexico	332,852	28	Romania	122,103
14	Kazakhstan	297,982	29	Argentina	117,003
15	South Africa	290,291	30	Venezuela	116,424

Source: World Resources Institute, World Resources, 1996–97 (New York: Oxford University Press, 1996), p. 318.

But there have been sharp divisions within the industrialized countries as well. Even before the scientific consensus was reached, the United States had signaled its opposition to specific binding commitments to targets and timetables. At a 1989 conference in the Netherlands, the United States, the Soviet Union, China, and Japan (which together accounted for more than half the world's CO_2 emissions from fossil fuels) declared that the goal of reducing CO_2 emissions required "further study." Although Japan waffled, these states were the basis of a coalition that would block a strong treaty. Consistent leadership for control of emissions has come from some of the Western European countries—notably the Netherlands and the Scandinavian countries. During the Bush Administration, the United States was the most recalcitrant of negotiating states, reflecting a corporate concern about profits, the American public's addiction to the automobile, and a historic entitlement to low-cost oil. During the pre-Rio negotiations, the United States (backed by Canada, which shared the same carbon culture), the Soviet Union (which was on the brink of collapse and economic chaos), and sporadically Japan (which was afraid to offend the United States), held out in a battle over targets and timetables and degrees of commitment—an argument that continues to this day. (See Figure 16.1.)

Although formal negotiations of the Climate Treaty took less than two years, the issue was a long time developing. Scientists had long understood that a buildup of CO_2 in the atmosphere could cause warming by means of the greenhouse effect, but it was not until the World Meteorological Organization and UNEP secured scientific consensus at a 1985 conference in Villach, Austria, that global warming was considered to be sufficiently serious to warrant international action. The next year, reports by the WMO, the U.S. National Aeronautics and Space Administration (NASA), and other agencies found that warming was indeed already taking place. And a very hot summer in Washington in 1988 finally got American politicians' attention. The WMO and UNEP established the International Panel on Climate Change (IPCC), in which scientists from both highly industrialized and developing countries participated, to provide the basis of common factual understanding on which to base the negotiations. The IPCC hammered out a report by August 1990 that gave its collective judgment on the state of scientific understanding, the social and economic impacts, and possible response strategies. The IPCC has continued to serve as the authoritative international body on the technical issues, and offers a good model for sifting through scientific uncertainties that are the subject of highly political negotiations.[18]

Despite growing pressure from Europe and a determined campaign by the small-island states which feared inundation by sea-level rise, the United States prevailed in the two years of negotiations. The Climate Treaty, formally known as the United Nations Framework Convention on Climate Change, was signed by 154 states in Rio in 1992. It expressed only voluntary intentions to stabilize CO_2 emissions by 2000 to unspecified "earlier" levels (interpreted by the Europeans to mean 1990 levels), and applied only

Figure 16.1a / Cumulative Carbon Dioxide Emissions, 1992

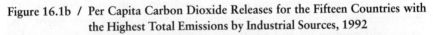

Source: World Resources Institute, *World Resources, 1996–97* (New York: Oxford University Press, 1996), p. 319.

Figure 16.1b / Per Capita Carbon Dioxide Releases for the Fifteen Countries with the Highest Total Emissions by Industrial Sources, 1992

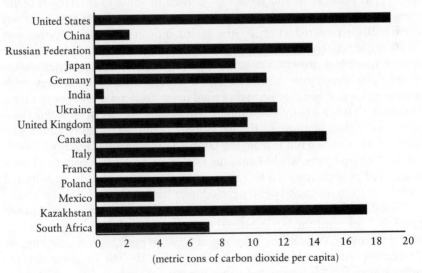

Source: World Resources Institute, *World Resources, 1996–97* (New York: Oxford University Press, 1996), p. 319.

to the highly industrialized countries. It was a weak treaty, and only the parties' agreement to provide regular national reports on emissions held promise of meaningful international regulation. A compelling treaty was not possible without cooperation of the biggest emitter. By the time the treaty came into force two years later with the minimum 50 states having ratified it, the new Clinton Administration had declared its commitment to reduce emissions to 1990 levels, but the struggle over targets and timetables continues.

The Climate Treaty was disappointing to environmentalists everywhere, but the 1992 document was hardly the end of the battle. The treaty had provisions for interim meetings even before ratification was complete, and for regular conferences of the parties since 1994. At the Berlin Conference of the Parties (COP) in 1995, knowing that substantial reduction of emissions *below* the 1990 levels—perhaps as much as 60 percent below—was necessary, the parties (now joined by representatives of the Clinton Administration) agreed in principle to the need for further reductions. So far, compliance is all voluntary, and the goals and plans of some countries are highly unrealistic: emissions in the United States, Japan, and most countries of the European Union are still increasing. Emissions from the former Soviet Union are flat, but only because of economic depression. In 1996, at the second meeting of the parties in Geneva, the United States admitted that the nonbinding structure was not working.

There remains the problem of large developing-countries' growing CO_2 contributions. The 1992 treaty requires no commitment from them, and with rapid population and economic growth in some of the largest countries, emissions are steadily creeping upward, at rates sufficient to offset even a 20-percent reduction by the major industrial powers by the year 2010. So, for the treaty to succeed, the developing countries must *slow* their rate of fossil fuel growth, while the highly industrialized countries *reduce* theirs. The developing countries could realize enormous savings with greater efficiency, but they want and need more financial assistance to do so. Unlike the Ozone Treaty, the Climate Treaty has no special fund for these purposes, although some of the developing countries, notably China and India, have obtained funds from the Global Environmental Facility (a modest fund set up by the World Bank, the UNDP, and UNEP to help fund environmental projects required by environmental treaties) and some additional assistance from the multilateral development banks.

The developing countries are not going to take serious measures to curb fossil-fuel use until the big industrial emitters do so. The European Union, led by Germany, decided in the spring of 1997 to push for a legally binding 15-percent reduction in emissions by the year 2010. The Japanese government argued for "differentiated commitments," based on different starting points and targets that would give Japan and other energy-efficient countries credit for efficiency already achieved, but the United States is recalcitrant, willing only to make *voluntary* commitments. At the June 1997 UN General Assembly Special Session observing the fifth anniversary of the Rio Conference, President Clinton acknowledged the serious implications of global warming and endorsed the underlying science, but continued to eschew commitment to specific targets and timetables. In this, the United States was supported only by Canada, Australia, and Japan, and faced a barrage of criticism from NGOs and European and developing-nation leaders.

It appeared likely in mid-1997 that a deadlock would emerge at the Kyoto COP in December 1997 and that no targets or timetables that are commensurate with the scale of the problem will be set. But other incremental steps could be taken. Stronger voluntary targets and timetables could be agreed to in 1997, perhaps even voluntary curbs on the growth of developing-country emissions. And the reporting mechanisms could be greatly strengthened allowing greater comparability and transparency, which would make it possible for the European lead states and NGOs to publicize the inadequacy of some countries' plans and possibly embarrass them into greater efforts. Some European nations have already started taxing carbon emissions (through levies on fuels) as an incentive to use fossil fuels more efficiently or to switch to renewable energy sources. Although their experience provides good examples, carbon taxes will not be adopted on a large enough scale and in sufficient amounts in Europe and Japan until the United States does it also. Other possible steps include the development of international standards by which to certify a variety of private voluntary efforts by industry. Host-country Japan, with its enormous potential as a technological leader and a generous donor of development assistance, may want to provide some leadership, rather than sit quietly on the sidelines as in the past.[19]

Agreement may also be reached at Kyoto on the "joint implementation" (JI) provisions included in the treaty, whereby industrialized countries can obtain credit against their own reduction of emissions by assisting developing countries in introducing emission controls and through what is known as "carbon sequestration"—that is, preventing the release into the atmosphere of the carbon stored in trees, by protecting forests from destruction and by reforesting denuded areas. Although there are some pilot projects underway, JI projects remain controversial. The United States and some Europeans favor them in the expectation that, over time, such projects would multiply and their impact would grow. JI is opposed, however, by significant developing-country players and by Northern NGOs, who contend that its implementation will postpone the tough decisions that the United States and others need to take to reduce their own fossil-fuel use—because it will be so much cheaper for large corporations to finance the easier first steps toward efficiency in notoriously inefficient countries.

All of these efforts will push the United States—the key player on this issue—along, but it will probably take some large natural or political disaster in the United States to jolt it (and the rest of the world) onto a more rapid track of emissions reduction. The whole Climate Treaty process, no matter how frustrating or how haltingly it responds to still growing problems, is nevertheless a very good illustration of how even the most powerful and recalcitrant country cannot stop international movement completely, even when that country's participation is necessary.

A TREATY TO CONTROL INTERNATIONAL TRADE IN WASTES

Most international environmental regimes have been initiated and championed by the major industrialized countries, often in collaboration with UNEP. They are likely to have well-developed environmental regulatory systems and effectively organized environmental NGOs. They bring strong expert teams to the negotiating table and seem more confident that they can control the process in their own interests. The developing countries, on the other hand, face strong internal political pressures favoring economic growth over environmental protection, have poorly functioning regulatory systems, and in international negotiations are wary of being dominated by more powerful industrial states. An exception concerns the issue of international shipment of hazardous wastes, where developing countries, being the most affected parties, have taken the lead in campaigning for an international regime.

The amount of industrial wastes produced by societies has exploded along with everything else in the enormous world economic growth since the 1950s. Most hazardous wastes are disposed of domestically or are traded among the industrialized countries themselves, but about 20 percent have been shipped from Europe and the United States to developing countries—mostly to poor countries in Africa, Central America, and the Caribbean. Most of the trade is legal—the poor countries need the payments—but some is illegal, dumped on beaches or private property for illicit payments. Most of it, legal or illegal, has been shipped to countries that do not have the technological or administrative resources to deal with it safely. In the 1980s, the United States, despite the fact that only 1 percent of its wastes was shipped overseas (and that mostly to Canada), led the exporting states in opposition to meaningful international control because the government was opposed in principle to any restrictions on U.S. trade. The U.S. government perhaps also feared that it could be held liable for damages done by any U.S. company that broke the law.[20]

Once again it was UNEP, in 1984 and 1985, that began the fact-finding process and came up with some international guidelines that specified notification of and consent from the receiving state, and verification by the exporting state that the recipient country had requirements for disposal and treatment at least as stringent as their own. But these guidelines, describing a process known as "informed consent," did not alter practice, and African states, backed by other developing countries, demanded a full ban on shipping to their countries and recognition by the exporting nations of their liability if the ban were violated. When treaty negotiations took place in Basel, Switzerland, in 1989, the industrialized countries remained firm and offered their informed-consent mode, or nothing. And that was all the African lead states could get at Basel, despite the support of the Non-Aligned Movement and elected parliamentarians of Europe. The treaty, known as the Basel Convention on Control of Transboundary Movements of Hazardous

Wastes and Their Disposal, offered no improvement over the status quo—a classic example of international recognition of a problem without an agreement to address it.

But the African states and their allies continued their pressure, and, in 1989, a split developed in the blocking coalition when the European exporting states shifted sides in the debate. The European Community agreed to ban shipment of wastes to sixty-eight former colonial states—largely in response to pressure from their former colonies. Early in 1991, twelve African states, meeting in Bamako, banned all shipment of waste to their countries. These two acts in effect became a regime that was stronger than the Basel Convention, which came into force in 1992 without the ratification of any of the industrial exporting states necessary to ensure the bland terms of the treaty—a very weak treaty, indeed.

Within two years, more than one hundred states had joined the Bamako countries in banning wastes, but they could still not enforce their wishes. In the meantime, Greenpeace had investigated one thousand egregious cases of illegal dumping, adroitly using the national press in both exporting and recipient countries to expose the venality of the traffickers.[21] The organization deserves much of the credit for helping to create, in two years' time, a worldwide moral climate that would no longer countenance waste shipments to impoverished, defenseless developing countries.

By the time the parties to the Convention met in Geneva in 1994, U.S. NGOs had persuaded the Clinton Administration to drop its opposition to a ban, and even though the United States had not yet ratified the Basel agreement and therefore appeared at the conference as an observer only, the U.S. shift was very helpful in turning the tide in favor of a law. The argument then became one to determine which categories of waste were to be banned and the timetable for doing so. The U.S. delegation went to Geneva proposing an immediate ban on hazardous wastes to all developing countries and a ban on shipments to all countries in five years, but they sought to exclude glass, metal, textiles, and paper wastes that were traded for recycling purposes. But world public opinion had outstripped even Washington's big leap forward. Opponents to the U.S. exception argue that the exclusion of recyclable materials (which were, in fact, often dumped rather than recycled anyway) would just postpone the day when the industrial countries would fully recycle their own wastes. Parties to the treaty reached a consensus on a total immediate ban on shipping hazardous wastes from the industrialized nations of the Organization for Economic Cooperation and Development (OECD) to non-OECD countries (including Russia and other former Soviet states that had been willing to accept almost any waste for pay), and to end all exports, including "recyclables," by the end of 1997.

Despite efforts by Australia, the United States, Canada, Japan, and New Zealand to limit the ban they had just agreed to, the 1995 COP of the Basel Convention, with full support of the European Union, referred to its Technical Working Group the task of recommending which categories of wastes should be banned. Those decisions have since been made to the satisfaction of the developing countries, and formal amendment of the Basel Convention to include the ban is as expected at the 1997 COP.[22] The United States still has not ratified the treaty, and there is some evidence that some OECD companies are rushing to ship questionable wastes before the 1998 deadline, but the negotiations stand out as a clear victory for the developing countries. The struggle to end international trade in hazardous wastes offers clear lessons: when developing countries stick together on an issue and persist, no matter how weak their collective economic and political power, they *can* prevail; also, a very well-focused public information campaign by an international NGO can help shift world opinion.

Regarding other selected issues, developing countries have also tasted victory, though not so decisively as the ban on hazardous-waste trade. The International Convention to Combat Desertification (1994) and the Small Island Developing States Action Plan (1994) were both negotiated within two years, fulfilling promises made at UNCED. These agreements recognize the peculiar nature and urgency of development in tiny island states and in arid countries, especially in Africa, and call for international assistance. They are important expressions of worldwide responsibility to development in the most vulnerable countries, but they created no implementing funds and made no specific commitments, and so they must be categorized along with some others as treaties of good intentions.

The United Nations Convention on Biological Diversity, signed in 1992 in Rio by almost all states except the United States, represents a different kind of victory for the developing countries. Throughout the negotiations, the developing countries sought guarantees that they would share in the benefits of products developed by other countries from fauna and flora harvested in their territories, focusing debate on intellectual property rights, control of biotechnology, and financing. As in the parallel negotiations on the Climate Treaty, the United States, ostensibly under pressure from corporations, held out for stronger protection of intellectual property and declined to make any concessions on technology transfer. Despite its singular great-power status and its preeminence in biotechnology, the United States was unable to hold up the treaty—precisely because the developing countries, not the United States, owned most of the biological diversity whose protection the treaty addresses. But neither did the developing countries achieve their aims with respect to financing and technology transfers. The Clinton Administration, under pressure from NGOs who were joined this time by industry, found that U.S. corporate interests would best be protected within the treaty, and signed it in 1993.

Other issues on which developing countries have played significant roles are endangered species (through the Convention on International Trade in Endangered Species, 1973) and efforts to negotiate a forestry treaty. Here again, their cooperation is essential to the working of the treaty, and even the most powerful states cannot expect international agreement without the cooperation of at least the most relevant among them.

THE POLITICS AND PLAYERS OF THE EMERGING GLOBAL ENVIRONMENTAL SYSTEM

It is in the ongoing struggle to negotiate international standards, mechanisms, regulations, and institutions that one can so clearly see the politics—and the continuing though uneven progress toward an international environmental protection system. One can gauge the overall sentiment, concern, and commitment on a particular issue, and chart the interests and shifts of particular parties. Several things become clear. Although there are consistent environmental leaders (the Netherlands and the Scandinavian countries), and those with conspicuously low profiles (China, Japan, the former Soviet states) there are no 100-percent good guys or bad guys. The position of most states on environmental issues, though conditioned by an identifiable philosophy and history of involvement or noninvolvement, will vary with the issue and how important it is to key constituent interests within the country.

Size, power, and influence—for example, of the United States, China, India, Germany—do matter, but not to the degree one would expect in matters of traditional security concerns. Some very small countries have achieved a high profile in international environmental politics. It is quite possible for a very small country like the Netherlands to wield disproportionate influence on international environmental issues because of its consistent moral position, its good example in domestic policy, its bilateral development assistance programs, and its willingness to take developing-country needs into account. Similarly active, but on the other side of the issues, are countries such as Malaysia, whose determined defense of "development first" and its articulate resistance to big-power blandishments have often made Malaysia the voice of developing countries in their demand for concessions and financial assistance—giving this small country influence that far outweighs its size and power. And the small-island developing states of the South Pacific, Caribbean, and Indian oceans have, by organizing around particular issues such as development and climate change, made a mark that far outstrips their actual numbers and power.

Although participation in treaty negotiations is near universal these days, there are some important nations that appear not to play much of a part. I am referring not to small developing countries that often find themselves severely disadvantaged by their lack of sufficient staff to attend and effectively participate in complex international negotiations, but to the large industrialized nations, some of them major powers, who attend all sessions and join all treaties, but contribute little or nothing to the debate.

Japan is one such country. It is a nation with an admirable record on most domestic environmental issues (especially on energy efficiency and waste management) and an extensive, if not so admirable, history in dealing with developing countries, where Japanese firms have supported the most rapacious cutting of tropical forests. Japan is clearly changing: it is now the largest single international donor of development assistance, playing a leadership role in the Asian Development Bank and in some UN agencies. Japan has been sensitive to international public opinion and reversed its earlier opposition to restricted trade in endangered species and sharply curtailed its whaling. It could be a leader and champion of sustainable development and international cooperation on environmental protection, but it is retiring and bashful. Some reticence can be explained by patterns of culture, but often one suspects that Japan's primary consideration is not to offend its most important trade and security partner, the United States.

China's representatives also sit at every environmental negotiating session, sign all conventions, but say almost nothing during the process. They actually carry out their treaty obligations fairly well. Some say it is because delegates come to negotiations with orders that do not allow them flexibility and compromise during the process. But I think their nonactive participation reflects their long isolation from international politics and their discomfort with the free give-and-take of political argument, as well as the sometimes rapid shifts that occur in environmental negotiations. One has to hope they are working their way into a new stage of greater activism. China is the most populous state in the world and is growing very fast economically, and its development has major global consequences—especially with respect to climate, but also on a wide variety of pollution problems where cooperation with their neighbors is essential. The Chinese government is already concerned about severe domestic environmental problems, and there are signs at the grassroots level of a nascent national environmental movement.[23] China's fuller participation in international environment politics would bolster their domestic cleanup efforts, as it would also ensure the success of international cooperation on key global issues.

The countries of the former Soviet Union—especially Russia, as the most significant heir to the empire—also play a nonrole in international environmental politics. The Soviet Union and its successor states have attended all negotiations, occasionally joining a blocking coalition (for example, on waste, climate, and ozone), but its delegates also have little to say during the proceedings. In Soviet days, the contravention of treaty obligations was often deliberate and secret. The world now knows of the Soviet Union's reckless dumping of nuclear wastes in international waters. Nowadays, Russia signs on to treaties and then pleads economic chaos as an excuse for not implementing them. The latter is real enough, and other treaty parties are more worried about Russia's transition to a market economy and political stability than about their dereliction of environmental duty. European and American friends do not therefore call them on their lapses, although they have offered the former Soviet states some international aid to correct their worst offenses against nature and human health. For the time being, the recession has cut into the most flagrant of Russia's international practices—overfishing, whaling, ocean-dumping, and high CO_2 emissions—but the country retains its huge potential, for good or ill, on the international environmental scene.

It is clear from examination of these three giants (and of some developing countries, too) that there is a clear relationship between a nation's degree of international environmental participation and responsibility, and the degree of political debate, dissent, and freedom in those countries. We are referring here not so much to the phenomena of electoral democracy and tolerance of dissidence, as to the organization and involvement of the civil society and the public's access to information and debate. Even in Japan, with its well-established free elections and press, the people's impact on public affairs is limited by strong cultural prohibitions against bucking authority and by a weak, albeit now growing, NGO sector. These conditions at home limit even Japan's official participation in international environmental issues and minimize the participation of Japanese NGOs in international NGO networks. The much more formidable barriers—political and economic—to free speech, information, organization, and public participation in debate and decision making in China and Russia are paralleled by a near exclusion of their representatives, both official and NGO, in meaningful decision making on the international level.

The European Union presents an example of effective regional cooperation on environmental protection. Over more than twenty years, member states have concluded a range of legislation, regulations, and common standards on such topics as recycling, emissions control, and pesticide use. They are still struggling over a carbon tax, and working in new areas such as noise control. Though they cannot always reach a common position in treaty negotiations, once they have, it is binding. And even when they have not been able to achieve unanimity, individual countries or coalitions have often been lead states in the advocacy of progressively stronger international control.

But, as the foregoing treaty discussion made clear, the United States remains the single most important player in the international environmental-protection system—as it is regarding military security and economic matters. Although it never holds all of the cards and cannot dictate its will to others, it has tremendous power, for good or ill, in negotiations around each of these issues. Historically, the American record is pro-environment, but its stance has varied from issue to issue and from administration to administration—and not strictly along party lines. The Clinton 1997 position on targets and timetables for the Climate Treaty, for instance, is not perceptibly different from President Bush's holdout stance in 1991 and 1992. But the U.S. role as the single remaining superpower is crucial to the outcome of international environmental issues. That is often a scary prospect. On the other hand, it means that American substate players (state and local governments) and nongovernmental organizations, which have tended to be pro-environment, operate in an arena where they can have worldwide influence if they succeed at home.

LOOKING AHEAD

What can we expect in the decade ahead? More treaties, protocols, and conferences of the parties—more continuing negotiations, not less. Progress
toward greater international cooperation will surely be uneven, as illustrated by the nations' inability to agree on key climate and financial issues at
the UN Special Session in June 1997, but it will lurch on in a forward direction. In some cases, startling new information may provide the impetus to
increased cooperation—as occurred in the ozone negotiations—but incremental progress is much more likely in most issue areas. The push-and-pull
effect of the treaties will continue—that is, the forward steps required by
treaties will pull some nations along faster than they might otherwise move,
and the politics and needs of coalitions of determined leading countries will
push the treaty process further along.[24] So-called natural disasters, horrific
accidents, crop failures, epidemics, an electoral change—any of these could
act as a catalyst and a spur to move events more decisively.

Whether the international remedies thus hammered out will keep the
planet ahead of the curve of environmental deterioration is not yet clear.
Despite the energetic environmental diplomatic activity of the last fifteen
years, and especially since preparation for UNCED began, most global environmental problems are not yet under control. At the same time, the
demand for goods—for basic food, shelter, and jobs, as well as the amenities
that rising expectations demand—continues to grow with the population,
the globalization of taste, and the spread of the consumption ethic. Since the
growth of population and consumption is inevitable even under the most
optimistic of population scenarios, the challenge of keeping ahead of the
environmental-destruction curve will be with us for some time.

I do not believe the world can get ahead and stay ahead of that curve
without the leadership of the United States and other major powers, and
without the key players from the developing world—especially China,
India, Indonesia, Nigeria, Mexico, and Brazil. The direction of China's and
India's growth is especially important. By 2025 they will have, between
them, 2.9 billion people, or 35 percent of the world's population. If they aim
to produce and consume on a U.S. model, there is no way that the global
environmental system will not be severely impaired. But of all the nations,
U.S. leadership is most important. If the well-endowed United States cannot
shift its production and consumption to a more sustainable path, what
nation can? As we have seen, the United States cannot prevent environmental progress in the face of other determined nations, but because of its size
and power, the sheer size of its market, and its prestige, it has become the
world's setter of fashion.

The United States now has an excellent blueprint for change in the 1996
Report of the President's Council on Sustainable Development. This
thoughtful document reflects the consensus of a mix of government, corporate, and NGO members. It examines all sectors of the American economy
and persuasively sets forth a list of proposals for government, the private

sector, and individuals to undertake.[25] Its recommendations for the government include the purchase of environmentally superior products, the elimination of environmentally damaging subsidies, and a shift in taxes to encourage employment opportunities and economic opportunities, while discouraging environmentally damaging production and consumption. For industry, the Council proposes extended product responsibility through a variety of take-back, buy-back, and reuse/recycling measures. Together, the Council's comprehensive recommendations make eminent good sense, but they will require intensive continuing education, leadership, and investment to bring them into being.

One suspects the world is going to have to live with chaos for a while yet. The path to sustainability will not be orderly. There will be many simultaneous efforts in parallel. It is unlikely that we will see the creation of a UN Economic and Environmental Security Council or a super-UN environmental protection agency to centralize and coordinate efforts, nor any superorganization of NGOs—and that, in my opinion, is just as well. No megainstitution, neat and orderly as it might look on paper, is any more desirable than it is likely. It is probably impossible to build one single institution that could have the great range of expertise necessary to manage so many different kinds of pollution and resource management issues. In this period of rapid change, sustainable development requires many different efforts and experiments.

Each of the environmental treaties is building processes and institutions to carry out its purpose, and is developing lasting habits of international cooperation at the same time. We do need to strengthen the process by providing adequate funds: to UNEP for monitoring, data collection and dissemination, and an early-warning system, and to the UN Development Program (UNDP) and other development agencies that can provide technical assistance to poor countries to aid them in their development transitions. And we need to achieve much higher investment in sustainable development, especially through better applications of funds from the multilateral development banks. With more experience—and determined political leadership and support—these separate efforts will sort themselves out, and lessons learned in one area will be transferred to another. If processes are fully transparent and broadly participatory, progress will continue at a faster rate. Eventually—and, one hopes, in time—the world will have an adequately developed system of international environmental protection and the necessary institutions to ensure the planet's security.

QUESTIONS FOR FURTHER STUDY

1. What is meant by "sustainable development"? Why do Janet Brown and others argue that "economic development and environmental protection must go hand in hand" if the planet is to survive into the next century?

2. What do efforts to adopt an international regime for protecting the ozone layer tell us about the process of negotiating international environmental treaties? Can—and should—this process be replicated in other areas of environmental decline?

3. To what extent has the international community succeeded in addressing the problem of global warming? To what extent has it failed? What must still be done to slow the increase in global temperatures?

4. How can rapidly industrializing countries like India and China be persuaded to abide by international environmental agreements? Do the affluent countries of the North have an obligation to subsidize the adoption of environmentally friendly practices by the developing nations of the South?

Notes

1. George F. Kennan, "Morality and Foreign Policy," *Foreign Affairs* (Winter 1985/86), pp. 205–218.

2. *U.S. National Security Strategy,* 1996 (Washington: The White House, January 1996), p. 12.

3. Secretary of State Warren Christopher, "Memorandum to All Under and Assistant Secretaries, Subject: Integrating Environmental Issues into the Department's Core Foreign Policy Goals" (February 14, 1996).

4. For instance, the respected Canadian International Institute for Sustainable Development covers all major international environmental negotiations and reports in detail on a daily basis via the Internet, and at the end of such sessions produces a balanced summary of the proceedings. Their *Earth Negotiations Bulletin* is available in print and also in an electronic version at either <gopher.igc.apc.org> or, in hypertext, at <http://www.iisd.ca/linkages/>. Further information may be obtained by inquiring at <kimo@pipeline.com>.

5. Over the last six years, the National Defense University has hosted a series of conferences to which environmental activists have been invited, and the Defense Department has financed a number of studies and conferences such as the Leadership Workshop on Environment and Security at Yale University, in September 1994. In 1995, the Pew Foundation funded the Environmental Change and Security Project at the Woodrow Wilson Center, Smithsonian Institution, Washington, D.C., which publishes an annual *Report.*

6. Riley E. Dunlap, George H. Gallup, Jr., and Alec M. Gallup, *Health of the Planet* (Princeton: Gallup International Institute, 1993). In this survey of thirty thousand people in twenty-four nations, majorities in twenty-one countries gave priority to environmental protection, even if that slowed economic growth, and in seventeen of those countries, citizens were willing to pay more for environmental protection. See especially p. 8 and Tables 14a–e.

7. World Resources Institute, *World Resources, 1996–97* (New York: Oxford University Press, 1996), p. ix, and Chapters 9–14; and United Nations Development Programme's annual *Human Development Report,* published by Oxford University Press. Current information on a wide variety of environmental trends can be found on the World Resources Institute's web site <http://www.wri.org> and through Friends of the Earth at <http://www.foe.org>.

8. Ibid., p. xiii, 273–81.

9. World Resources Institute, *World Resources, 1994–95* (New York: Oxford University Press, 1994), p. 214.

10. See President's Council on Sustainable Development, *Population and Consumption: Report of a Task Force of the President's Council on Sustainable Development* (Washington: U.S. Government Printing Office, 1996) and World Resources Institute, *World Resources, 1994–95,* Chapters 2, 15, and 16.

11. The World Commission on Environment and Development, *Our Common Future* (New York: Oxford University Press, 1897), p. 43.

12. Latin American and Caribbean Commission on Development and Environment, *Our Own Agenda* (Inter-American Development Bank, Washington, and United Nations Develop-

ment Program, New York, 1990), especially Chapter II; and the New World Dialogue on Environment and Development in the Western Hemisphere, *Compact for a New World* (Washington: World Resources Institute, 1991), pp. 19–21.

13. For a short dissertation on the politics of trade and development, see Gareth Porter and Janet Welsh Brown, *Global Environmental Politics,* 2nd ed. (Boulder: Westview Press, 1995), pp. 129–141.

14. For a fuller discussion of these and other environmental treaties, see Porter and Brown, *Global Environmental Politics,* 2nd ed., Chapter 3. For current developments on negotiations see the *Earth Negotiations Bulletin,* op. cit., note 4.

15. Elizabeth Cook, ed., *Ozone Protection in the United States. Elements of Success* (Washington: World Resources Institute, 1996), p. 1.

16. Ibid., p. 9.

17. Robs Gelbspan, "Hot Air, Cold Truth: Why Do We Pay Attention to Greenhouse Skeptics?" *The Washington Post* (May 25, 1997). For help in sorting out competing predictions, see Robert Repetto and Duncan Austin, *The Costs of Climate Protection: A Guide for the Perplexed* (Washington: World Resources Institute, 1997).

18. Intergovernmental Panel on Climate Change, *The Science of Climate Change,* Vol. 1 of *Climate Change in 1995, IPCC Second Assessment Report* (Cambridge: Cambridge University Press, 1996). Volumes 2 and 3 deal with impacts, adaptation and mitigation, and economic and social dimensions of climate change. Summaries of the documents of the working groups are available on the Worldwide Web <http://www.UNEP.ch/IPCC/IPCC-0html>.

19. For a fuller discussion of these possibilities, see Christopher Flavin and Odil Tunali, *Climate of Hope: New Strategies for Stabilizing the World's Atmosphere* (Washington: Worldwatch Institute, 1996), pp. 53–68.

20. For greater detail on the politics of waste, see Porter and Brown, *Global Environmental Politics,* 2nd ed., pp. 84–88.

21. Greenpeace, *The International Trade in Wastes: A Greenpeace Inventory,* 5th ed. (Washington: Greenpeace, 1990).

22. Marcelo Furtado, "Basel Ban Here to Stay," (Greenpeace) *International Toxics Investigator* (First Quarter, 1996), p. 7; and Van Hernandez, "Technical Working Group Moves Basel Ban One Step Further," *Internanonal Toxics Investigator* (Third Quarter, 1996), pp. 10–12.

23. Impressions gathered by the author in interviews with national and municipal officials, party officials, academics, and NGO leaders during a trip to China in November, 1995.

24. Readers can follow negotiations daily via the Internet, by checking the reports filed by the Winnipeg-based International Institute for Sustainable Development. See details in note 4.

25. The President's Council on Sustainable Development, *Sustainable America: A New Consensus for Prosperity, Opportunity, and a Healthy Environment for the Future* (Washington: U.S. Government Printing Office, February, 1996). E-mail address <pcsd@igc.org>.

17 / Environmental Scarcity and Intergroup Conflict

THOMAS HOMER-DIXON

By the year 2025, the planet's human population will soar from 1992's 5.3 billion to a figure probably over eight billion.[1] Global economic output—the total production of goods and services traded in markets around the planet—will also skyrocket from around $20 trillion to perhaps $60 trillion in current dollars. Largely as a result of these two global trends, environmental change will occur much faster, and be much more widespread and severe. Around the planet, human beings will face a steady decline in the total area of high-quality agricultural land. Much of the planet's remaining virgin forests will vanish along with the wealth of species they shelter. We will also see the exhaustion and pollution of many rivers, aquifers, and other water resources; the collapse of key fisheries; further ozone depletion in the stratosphere; and maybe significant climate change due to global warming.

We can think of these environmental changes as "scarcities" of vital renewable resources such as soil, water, forests, fish, the stratospheric ozone layer, and an equable climate.[2] Although people have long speculated that such scarcity could contribute to intergroup conflict, little clear evidence was available. But in the last three years, various researchers have gathered enough information to reach a disturbing conclusion: scarcities of renewable resources (or "environmental scarcities," as I call them here) are already contributing to very violent conflicts in many parts of the developing world. Moreover, these conflicts may be the early signs of an upsurge of violence in the coming decades—especially in poor countries—that is caused or aggravated by environmental change.[3]

Experts have proposed numerous possible links between environmental change and conflict. Some have suggested that environmental change may shift the balance of power between states either regionally or globally, causing instabilities that could lead to war.[4] Another possibility is that global environmental damage might increase the gap between rich and poor societies, with the poor then violently confronting the rich for a fairer share of the world's wealth.[5] Severe conflict may also arise from frustration with countries that do not go along with agreements to protect the global environment, or that "free-ride" by letting other countries absorb the costs of environmental protection. Warmer temperatures could lead to contention over more easily harvested resources in the Antarctic. Bulging populations and land stress may produce waves of environmental refugees, spilling across borders and disrupting relations among ethnic groups. Countries might fight among themselves because of dwindling supplies of water and the effects of upstream pollution.[6] A sharp decline in food crop production and grazing land could lead to conflict between nomadic tribes and sedentary farmers.

Environmental change could in time cause a slow deepening of poverty in poor countries, which might open bitter divisions between classes and ethnic groups, corrode democratic institutions, and spawn revolutions and insurgencies.[7] In general, many experts have the sense that environmental problems will "ratchet up" the level of stress within states and the international community, increasing the likelihood of many different kinds of conflict—from war and rebellion to trade disputes—and undermining possibilities for cooperation.

Which of these scenarios are most plausible, and why? In the following pages, I discuss why environmental issues have become prominent in recent years, and provide a framework for understanding them. I then identify the likely links between environmental change and violent conflict, and illustrate these links with several case studies. The chapter concludes with a discussion of international environmental negotiations culminating in the 1992 United Nations conference in Rio de Janeiro, and with a series of recommendations for action by both rich and poor countries.

The case studies discussed in this chapter reflect the results of a three-year research project on "Environmental Change and Acute Conflict" jointly organized by the Peace and Conflict Studies Program at the University of Toronto and the American Academy of Arts and Sciences in Cambridge, Massachusetts. This project brought together a team of thirty researchers from four continents. We found that poor countries are likely to be affected sooner and more harshly by environmental scarcity than rich countries. This is because they usually do not have abundant financial, material, and intellectual resources, and because their economic and political institutions are often weak and inflexible. Poor societies, therefore, are less able to buffer themselves from environmental scarcity and the social crises it can cause.

Our research also suggests that violence arising from environmental change will generally not follow the age-old pattern of conflicts over scarce resources, where one group or nation tries to seize the water, oil, or minerals of another. This is partly because some environmental resources—such as the climate and the ozone layer—are held in common. It is also because the social effects of environmental scarcity are often insidious, such as slow population displacement and economic disruption, that can in turn lead to clashes between ethnic groups and to social rebellion. But, while these types of conflict may not be as conspicuous or dramatic as wars between countries over scarce resources, they may have critical implications for the security interests of rich and poor nations alike.

UNFORESEEN THRESHOLDS

Why are people suddenly paying attention to environmental issues? Clearly, the end of the Cold War has given the public and its leaders a chance to think about problems other than U.S.-Soviet hostility. But there is another factor at work: during the last decade there has been a genuine shift in experts' perceptions of global environmental problems. Experts used to perceive environmental systems as relatively stable and resilient, in spite of the fact that humans were harvesting resources and dumping wastes on a massive scale. They thought that these systems would change only slowly in response to human insults. But now scientists have discovered that these systems may exhibit sudden changes or "threshold" effects, which means that it may be much easier than was previously thought to push a system from one equilibrium state to a very different equilibrium state. Thus, in 1987, geochemist Wallace Broecker noted that recent polar ice-core and ocean-sediment data indicate that "Earth's climate does not respond to forcing in a smooth and gradual way. Rather, it responds in sharp jumps which involve large-scale reorganization of Earth's system. . . . We must consider the possibility that the main responses of the system to our provocation of the atmosphere will come in jumps whose timing and magnitude are unpredictable."[8]

A dramatic example of such a threshold effect in a complex environmental system was the discovery of the Antarctic ozone hole in the mid-1980s.[9] The scientific models of ozone depletion used to that point had, for the most part, assumed that ozone depletion would increase in steady, constant steps as chlorofluorocarbon (CFC) emissions increased. But it turns out that, if the conditions are right, massive depletion can occur at lightning speed, stripping the ozone from mile-thick layers of the stratosphere in a matter of days. The Antarctic ozone hole was startling evidence of the instability of environmental systems in response to human inputs, of the ability of humans to significantly affect the ecosystem on a global scale, and of our inability to predict exactly how the system will change.

This new perception of the nature of the environmental system has percolated out of the scientific community into the policymaking community. It may also be influencing the broader public's view of environmental problems. Scientists, political leaders, and the general public are beginning to interpret data about environmental change in a new light: constant, step-by-step degradation of environmental systems is not as tolerable as it was once considered to be. We do not know where and when we might cross a threshold and move to a radically different and perhaps very undesirable system.

KEY VARIABLES AND RELATIONSHIPS

The environmental problems facing humankind might seem overwhelming. They are large-scale, long-term, and poorly understood. They strike directly at our most intimate links to the biosphere, including our ability to get the food and water we need for survival and for the stability of our societies.[10] But we must avoid slipping into simpleminded "environmental determinism"; in other words, we must not assume that the environment surrounding us determines, inescapably and inevitably, our behavior and degree of happiness. Our societies are often very flexible; human beings can be very creative; and many factors often permit great variability and adaptability in human-environmental systems.

Some of these factors are identified in Figure 17.1. It shows that the total effect of human activity on the environment in a particular ecological region is a function of two main variables: first, the product of total population in the region and physical activity per capita; and, second, the vulnerability of the ecosystem in that region to those particular physical activities.[11] Activity per capita is a function of available physical resources in the region (including nonrenewable resources, such as minerals, and renewable resources, such as water, forests, and agricultural land) along with social and psychological factors (such as institutions, social relations, preferences, and beliefs). The figure also shows that environmental change, such as the degradation of agricultural land, might cause certain types of social effect, such as the large-scale migration of people out of the affected region. This could in turn lead to various kinds of conflict, especially ethnic conflict as newcomers of one group come in contact with local residents of a different group. There are important feedback loops from social effects and conflict to the social and psychological factors at the top of the figure, and then back to activity per capita and population. For example, migration could alter relationships among classes and ethnic groups in a society, which might in turn affect its economic activity.

The factors at the top of Figure 17.1 are particularly important. This social and psychological context is broad and complex. It includes the

Figure 17.1 / Main Variables and Causal Relations

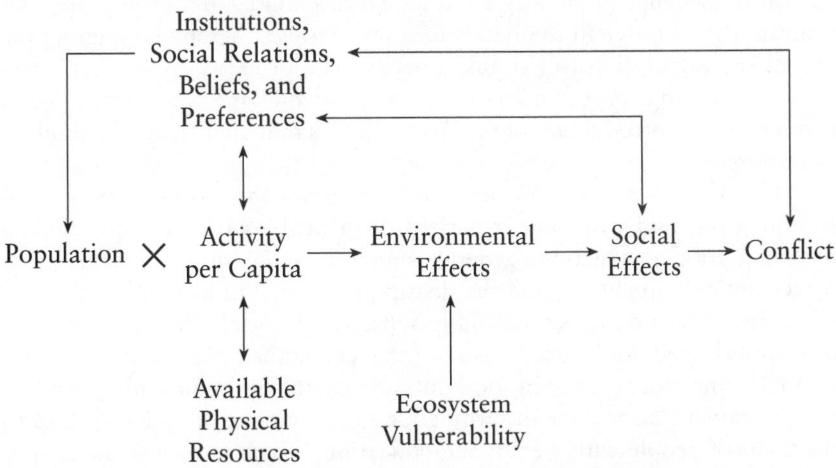

degree of inequality of land and wealth distribution in a society; the system of property rights and markets that encourages or discourages the production of goods and services within the economy; family and community structures; perceptions of the chances of long-run political stability within the society; historically rooted patterns of trade with other societies; the distribution of power among countries in the international system; and beliefs about the relationship between humans and nature.

Without a deep understanding of these factors we cannot begin to grasp the true nature of the relationships between human activity, environmental change, and its social effects, or the vulnerability, adaptability, and flexibility of societies when faced with environmental stress.[12]

ENVIRONMENTAL SCARCITY AND ITS SOCIAL EFFECTS

We have used the term "environmental scarcity" in our discussion to this point without a precise definition. There are three main sources of human-induced environmental scarcity. First, human activity can either reduce the quantity or degrade the quality of an environmental resource faster than the resource is renewed. Experts often refer to this process using terms similar to those we use for money in a bank, where we talk about "capital" and the "interest" or "income" it earns. The capital of a renewable resource is the resource stock (say, a forest) that generates a flow of income (the annual wood production through normal growth of the forest) that can be tapped for human consumption and well-being. A "sustainable" economy should not produce an average annual loss of the resource greater than this income.

The second main cause of environmental scarcity is population growth, which can reduce the amount of a renewable resource available per person. For example, a given flow of water or a given area of cropland might, over time, have to be divided among more and more people.

Third, a change in the way a resource is distributed in a society can concentrate the resource in the hands of a few people, thereby consigning the rest of the population to extreme scarcity. The property rights that affect resource distribution often change as a result of large-scale development projects or the introduction of new technologies that alter the relative values of resources.

These three sources of environmental scarcity can operate singly or in combination, and can have a variety of critical social effects, including declining food production, general economic stagnation or decline, displacement of population, and the disruption of institutions and traditional social relations among people and groups. These social effects, in turn, are often interlinked, and sometimes reinforce each other. For example, migration resulting from a drop in food output may further reduce food production by causing a shortage of farm labor. Or, economic decline may lead to the flight of people with wealth and education, which in turn weakens universities, courts, and institutions of economic management—all of which are crucial to a healthy economy.

Agricultural Production

Experts often suggest that constrained food output is the most worrisome possible result of environmental scarcity.[13] Around the world, agricultural land is decreasing in availability and quality. Currently, total global cropland amounts to about 1.5 billion hectares, which is roughly twice the area of the lower forty-eight states. Optimistic estimates of potential cropland on the planet range from 3.2 to 3.4 billion hectares, but nearly all of the best land has already been used. What is left is either less fertile, not sufficiently rain fed or easily irrigated, infested with pests, or harder to clear, plow, and plant. During the 1980s, cropland grew in the developing countries at just 0.26 percent a year, less than half the rate of the 1970s. More important, cropland per capita dropped by 1.9 percent a year.[14] Without a major increase in the amount of cropland in developing countries, experts expect that the world average of 0.28 hectares per capita will decline to 0.17 hectares by the year 2025, given the current rate of world population growth.[15] Moreover, large areas of land are being lost each year to a combination of problems, including encroachment by cities, erosion, depletion of nutrients, acidification, compacting, and salinization and waterlogging from overirrigation.[16] For certain regions, the drop in the availability of good cropland may in time sharply limit food output, depending upon the ability of societies to increase the "intensity" of their agricultural practices (that is, to increase yields per hectare through mechanization, greater fertilization and irrigation, and the use of new seeds).

But there are many other factors besides land availability that may influence agricultural production, including deforestation, depletion of water supplies, global warming, and increased ultraviolet radiation from ozone depletion. The Philippines provides a good illustration of deforestation's impact on food output.[17] Across the archipelago, logging and land clearing have accelerated erosion, changed regional hydrological cycles (the cycles of water among the atmosphere, land, and plants), and decreased the land's ability to hold water during rainy periods. The resulting flash floods have damaged irrigation works while plugging reservoirs and irrigation channels with silt.

Global warming and climate change may also affect agricultural production, although this is a contentious issue.[18] Coastal croplands in countries such as Bangladesh, Egypt, and China are very vulnerable to storm surges. Such events could become more common and devastating, because global warming will cause sea levels to rise and could intensify storms. The greenhouse effect will also change rainfall patterns and soil moisture; while this may benefit some agricultural regions, others will suffer. Countries at special risk from climate change will be those—such as the nations of the Sahel in sub-Saharan Africa—with an imbalance between population and food growing ability, and with little money to fund changes in their agricultural systems. As some areas become too dry to grow food, while others, formerly dry, suddenly have enough water, many poor countries will not be able to afford the new dams, wells, irrigation systems, roads, and storage silos that they need in order to adjust.

Many plants grow faster and larger in a warm environment rich in carbon dioxide, and they often use water more efficiently. Some scientists therefore conclude that greenhouse warming will increase global agricultural output. But optimistic estimates of increased crop yields have been based on laboratory experiments under ideal growing conditions, including ideal amounts of soil nutrients and water. In addition, these estimates have ignored the influence on yields of more frequent extreme climate events (especially droughts and heat waves), increased insect infestation, and the decreased nutritional quality of crops grown in a carbon-dioxide enriched atmosphere.[19]

In general, the magnitude of climate change is likely to be less of a problem for poor countries than the *rate* of change. Around the world, human beings and their agricultural systems have adapted to differences in temperature far greater than the maximum warming predicted for the next one hundred years. But the rapid rate expected for this change will produce new pressures on human society at a time when they are already stressed by other population and resource problems. These changes may be too fast and complex for societies that have limited buffering capacities.

Economic Decline

A very important social effect of environmental scarcity is the further poverty it causes in already poor countries. A country's ability to produce wealth may be affected directly by environmental stress, or indirectly by lower food output and population movements caused by environmental problems. There are numerous possible mechanisms. For instance, the higher ultraviolet radiation caused by stratospheric ozone depletion is likely to raise the rate of disease in humans and livestock, which may cost poor societies dearly. Similarly, logging for export markets—as in Southeast Asia, West Africa, and Central America—may produce short-term economic gains for a country's elite, but the resulting deforestation can also greatly affect longer-term economic productivity. The increased water runoff caused by deforestation damages roads, bridges, and other valuable infrastructure; and extra siltation reduces the capacity of rivers to generate hydroelectric power, as well as their usefulness as transport routes for ships and barges. As forests are destroyed, moreover, wood becomes scarcer and more expensive, and it takes up more of the household budget of poor families using it for cooking and heating fuel.

Farming is the source of a large share of the wealth generated in poor societies. It is not uncommon for nearly 50 percent of a country's GNP to be generated by farming, and for 60 percent or more of its population to depend on agriculture for jobs. Food output has soared in many regions over the last decades because expanded irrigation, fertilizer use, and new agricultural technologies (such as high-yielding varieties of grain) have produced a "green revolution" that has more than compensated for the declining soil fertility and depth.

In many poor countries, the effects of land scarcity and degradation will probably become much clearer as the gains from green-revolution technologies are fully realized. But, despite the extravagant claims of some commentators, there is no new generation of agricultural technologies waiting in the wings to keep food productivity rising. Genetic engineering may in time help scientists develop salinity-resistant, drought-resistant, and nitrogen-fixing grains, but their wide use in poor countries is probably decades in the future.

Damage to the soil is already producing a harsh economic impact in some areas. Unfortunately, measuring the actual cost of land degradation is not easy. Current national income accounts—statements of GNP—do not include measures of resource depletion. The economist Robert Repetto comments: "A nation could exhaust its mineral reserves, cut down its forests, erode its soils, pollute its aquifers, and hunt its wildlife to extinction—all without affecting measured income."[20] Such weak measures of economic productivity reinforce the belief of government officials in poor countries that there is a direct trade-off between economic growth and environmental protection; this belief, in turn, encourages societies to generate present income at the expense of their potential for future income.

A more realistic assessment of the economic consequences of environmental damage would challenge these beliefs. Thus, after a careful analysis of soil types, cropping practices, logging, and erosion rates in upland areas of Java in Indonesia, Repetto concludes that the country's national income accounts "significantly overstate the growth of agricultural income in Indonesia's highlands." Taking lost future income into account, Repetto calculates the one-year cost of erosion in Indonesia to be $481 million, which is about 40 percent of the annual value of upland cropland production. He also estimates that costs downstream from eroded hillsides, including the higher expense of clearing waterways and irrigation channels of silt, come to $30 to $100 million a year.[21]

A similar assessment emerges from recent research on China, in which Vaclav Smil has estimated the combined effect of environmental problems on current economic productivity. The main economic burdens he identifies are reduced crop yields caused by water, soil, and air pollution; more human sickness from air pollution, farmland loss because of construction and erosion; nutrient loss and flooding due to erosion and deforestation; and timber loss arising from poor harvesting practices. Smil calculates the current cost to be at least 15 percent of China's gross domestic product, and he is convinced that the economic toll will become much heavier during the coming decades.[22]

Population Displacement

Some commentators have claimed that environmental degradation may produce vast numbers of "environmental refugees."[23] For example, sea-level rise due to global warming may drive people back from coastal and delta areas in Egypt; soil degradation and desertification may empty countries in the African Sahel as their populations move south; and Filipino fishermen may leave their ruined fishing grounds for the cities. But the term "environmental refugee" is misleading, because it implies that environmental scarcity will be the direct and sole cause of refugee flows. Usually, it will be only one of a large number of interacting physical and social factors that *together* force people from their homelands. The term also does not distinguish between people who are genuine "refugees" from disaster and acute hardship, and those who are "migrants" for a variety of less urgent reasons. In general, migrants are motivated by a combination of "push" and "pull" factors, while refugees are motivated primarily by "push" factors.

The northeast region of the Indian subcontinent provides a good example of population displacement arising from environmental scarcity. Over the last three decades, land scarcity has been a key factor causing the large-scale movement of people from Bangladesh to the Indian state of Assam. In the future, people may be driven from Bangladesh by other environmental problems, including rising sea levels combined with cyclones (made worse by climate change), and by terrible flooding due to deforestation in watersheds upstream on the Ganges and Brahmaputra rivers. Similarly, Vaclav Smil predicts that, over the coming decades, tens of millions of Chinese will try to move from the country's impoverished interior and northern regions, where water and fuelwood are desperately scarce and the land often badly damaged, to the booming cities along the coast. In all likelihood, bitter disputes will develop among these regions over water sharing and migration.

Disrupted Institutions and Social Relations

All societies are held together by a thick fabric of institutions, organizations, rules, customs, and habitual behavior. Environmental scarcity will tear this fabric, mainly as a result of the social effects described above. Falling agricultural output will weaken rural villages through malnutrition and disease, and by encouraging people to leave. Economic decline will corrode confidence in the national purpose, and undermine financial, legal, and political institutions. And mass migrations of people into a region will drive down wages, shift relations between workers, peasants, and land owners, and upset the long-standing balance of economic and political power among ethnic groups.

We must pay particular attention to how environmental scarcity affects the state in developing countries.[24] Environmental scarcity sharply raises financial and political demands on government by requiring huge spending on new infrastructure. It also drives up the number of "marginal" people who barely survive on the edges of society and who are desperate for government help. Simultaneously, the loss of renewable resources, from fish and fertile land to abundant forests, can reduce tax revenues to local and national governments. We have, then, the potential for a widening gap between demands on the state and its financial ability to meet these demands. Such a gap could in time boost frustration within a poor society, erode the state's legitimacy, and increase competition between cliques and factions within its elite as they struggle to protect their shares of the economic pie.

ENVIRONMENTAL SCARCITY AND VIOLENT CONFLICT

If food production stagnates, if developing societies slide further into poverty, if large numbers of people leave their homelands, and if institutions and social relations are disrupted, what kinds of conflict are likely to develop?

We do not have much data with which to answer this question. This may be partly because environmental and population pressures have not yet passed a critical threshold of severity in many poor countries. Also, until recently, there was little good research on the conflicts caused by environmental scarcity. But three types of conflict seem most likely: scarcity, group-identity, and deprivation conflicts.

Scarcity Conflicts

Scarcity conflicts are those we intuitively expect when countries calculate their self-interest in a world where the amount of resources is fixed. Such conflicts will probably arise over three types of resource in particular: river water, prime fisheries, and good cropland. These are likely to spark conflict because their scarcity is increasing swiftly in some regions, because they are often critical to human survival, and because they can be physically seized or controlled.

The controversy over the Euphrates River illustrates how scarcity conflicts can arise. On January 13, 1990, Turkey began filling the giant reservoir behind the new Ataturk Dam in eastern Turkey. For one month, Turkey held back the main flow of the Euphrates River, which cut the downstream flow in Syria to about a quarter of its normal rate. By early in the next century, Turkey plans to build a huge complex of twenty dams and irrigation systems along the upper reaches of the Euphrates. This will reduce the annual average flow of the Euphrates within Syria by more than a third. Syria is already desperately short of water: almost all water for its towns, industries, and farms comes from the Euphrates, and the country has been chronically vulnerable to drought. Syria's population growth rate, at 3.6 percent per year, is one of the highest in the world, which gives a further push to the country's demand for water.

Turkey and Syria have exchanged angry threats over this situation. Syria gives sanctuary to guerrillas of the Kurdish Workers Party (the PKK), which has long been waging an insurgency against the Turkish government in the eastern part of the country. Turkey suspects that Syria might be using these separatists to gain leverage in bargaining over Euphrates water. Thus, in October 1989, then prime minister Turgut Ozal said that Turkey might cut off the river's water if Syria did not restrain the PKK. Although he later retracted the threat, the tensions have not been resolved, and water issues remain a major source of friction in Syrian-Turkish relations.

Clearly, the problem of Euphrates water is tangled up with issues of territorial integrity and relations between government and ethnic minorities in both Syria and Turkey. Although water scarcity is a source of serious tensions between Syria and Turkey, and may produce interstate violence in the future, this dispute is not a pure example of a scarcity conflict. Truly pure examples may be impossible to find.

Experts in international relations who address the security implications of environmental scarcity usually emphasize the potential for interstate scarcity conflicts.[25] Yet, our research shows that these conflicts will not be the most common to arise from environmental stress. Indeed, ethnic disputes and corrosive conflict within countries deserve greater attention from analysts.

Group-Identity Conflicts

Group-identity conflicts are likely to arise from the large-scale movements of populations caused by environmental scarcity. As different ethnic and cultural groups are pushed together by these migrations, we should expect people in these groups to see themselves and their neighbors in terms of "we" and "they"; in other words, they will use the identity of their own group to judge the worth of other groups, often negatively.[26] Such attitudes can lead to violence. The situation in the Bangladesh-Assam region is a good example: Assam's ethnic strife over the last decade has apparently been catalyzed by in-migration from Bangladesh (see the case study in this chapter).[27]

As population and environmental stresses grow in poor countries, we can also expect surging immigration to the industrialized world. People will seek to move from Latin America to the United States and Canada, from North Africa and the Middle East to Europe, and from South and Southeast Asia to Australia and Japan. This migration has already shifted the ethnic balance in many cities and regions of the richer countries, where governments are struggling to contain a backlash against "foreigners." Such racial strife will undoubtedly become much worse.

Although it seems probable that environmental scarcity will cause people to move in large numbers, thereby producing conflict, several qualifications are needed. First, refugees tend to be weak, which limits their ability to organize and to make demands on the government of the receiving society. Rather than provoking overt violence, therefore, a common result will be silent misery and death, with little destabilizing effect. Second, displaced groups often need the backing of a state (either that of the receiving society or an external state) before they have sufficient power to cause conflict. And, finally, we must remember that migration does not always produce negative results. It can, for instance, ease labor shortages in the receiving society—as has been the case, for instance, in Malaysia. We only have to look to countries as diverse as Canada, Thailand, and Malawi to conclude that the capacity of societies to absorb migrants without conflict is often substantial.

Deprivation Conflicts

As poor societies produce less wealth because of environmental problems, their citizens will probably become increasingly angered by the widening gap between their actual standard of living and the standard they feel they deserve. The rate of change is key: the faster the economic deterioration, the greater the discontent. Lower-status groups will usually be more frustrated than others, because elites will use their power to maintain, as best they can, the same standard of living despite a shrinking economic pie. At some point, the frustration and anger of some groups may cross a critical threshold, and they will act violently against those groups perceived to be the agents of their economic misery, or those thought to be benefiting from an unfair distribution of economic rewards in the society.[28]

In general, experts on conflict within societies tell us that rebellion, revolution, and insurgency are likely when: (1) there are clearly defined and organized groups in a society; (2) some of these groups regard their level of economic achievement, and in turn the broader political and economic system, as wholly unfair; and (3) these same groups believe that all peaceful opportunities to achieve change are blocked, yet regard the balance of power within the society as unstable—in others words, they believe that there are opportunities for overthrowing authority in the society.[29]

Environmental scarcity helps produce both the second and third of these conditions. As we have seen, a key social effect of this scarcity in poor countries is the disruption of institutions, such as the state. Thus, environmental problems may not only increase the frustration and anger within poor societies (through increased deprivation); in addition, by weakening the state and other institutions, environmental problems may open up opportunities for angry groups to overthrow existing authority.

CASE STUDIES

We can now review several case studies of environmental conflict in today's world. Earlier, I identified three sources of environmental scarcity: degradation and depletion of renewable resources, population growth, and changes in resource distribution among groups. In this section, I will show how these

Figure 17.2 / Some Sources and Consequences of Environmental Scarcity

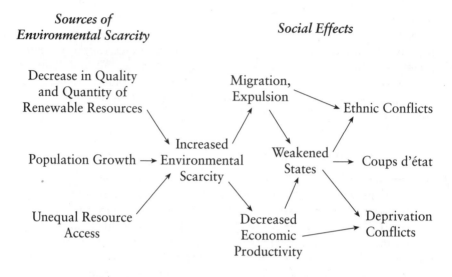

three sources operate singly or in combination to produce the types of conflict just discussed. The case studies below, which deal in particular with shortages of good agricultural land, suggest that group-identity and deprivation conflicts will be especially common outcomes of environmental scarcity. (See Figure 17.2.)

Bangladesh-Assam

In some cases, population growth by itself will be a key source of social stress and conflict. Bangladesh, for instance, does not suffer from critical degradation or loss of agricultural land, because the normal floods of the Ganges and Brahmaputra rivers lay down a layer of silt every year that helps maintain the fertility of the country's vast plains. But the United Nations predicts that Bangladesh's current population of 115 million will grow to 235 million by the year 2025. Cropland is already desperately scarce at about 0.08 hectares per capita, but since all of the country's good agricultural land has already been exploited, population growth will cut this figure in half by 2025. Land scarcity and the brutal poverty and social turmoil it produces have been made worse by extreme floods and the susceptibility of the country to cyclones.

Over the last four decades, these stresses have caused millions of people to migrate from East Pakistan/Bangladesh to neighboring areas of India. Detailed data are scarce; the Bangladeshi government is reluctant to admit that there is significant out-migration, since the question has become a major source of friction with India. But Sanjoy Hazarika, an investigative journalist who reports for the *New York Times* from South Asia, has pieced together demographic information and experts' estimates. He concludes that migrants from Bangladesh and their descendants have increased the population of neighboring areas of India by 15 million people, of which only 1 or 2 million can be attributed to migration caused by the 1971 war between India and Pakistan that resulted in the creation of Bangladesh. He estimates that the population of the Indian state of Assam has swelled by at least 7 million people, of Tripura by 1 million, and of West Bengal by about 7 million.[30]

This enormous movement of people has produced sweeping changes in the politics and economies of the receiving regions.[31] It has altered land distribution, economic relations, and the balance of political power between religious and ethnic groups, and it has triggered serious intergroup conflict in Assam. Members of the Lalung tribe, for instance, have long resented Muslim Bengali migrants, and they accuse the newcomers of stealing the area's richest farmland. In early 1983, violence finally exploded during a bitter election for federal offices in the state. In the village of Nellie, Lalung tribespeople used machetes, knives, and spears to hack to death nearly 1,700 Bengalis in one five-hour rampage.

In the neighboring Indian state of Tripura, the original Buddhist and Christian inhabitants now make up only 29 percent of the state's population, with the rest consisting of Hindu migrants from East Pakistan/Bangladesh. This shift in the ethnic balance precipitated a violent insurgency between 1980 and 1988 that was called off only after the government agreed to return land to dispossessed Tripuris and stop the influx. But as the migration has continued and the agreement is not fully implemented, the insurgency has continued.

The Senegal River Basin

Elsewhere in the world, population growth and damage to renewable resources often encourage large-scale development projects that can alter access to resources. This, in turn, can produce dire environmental scarcity for poorer and less powerful groups whose claims to resources are opposed by elites, and this may lead to violence. A good example is the dispute that began in West Africa in 1989 between Mauritania and Senegal over the Senegal River basin that defines their common border.[32]

Senegal has fairly abundant agricultural land, but much of it suffers from high-to-severe wind and water erosion, loss of nutrients, salinization, and compaction caused by agriculture. The country has an overall population density of 380 people per square kilometer and a population growth rate of 2.7 percent, giving a doubling time of about twenty-five years. Except for the Senegal Valley along its southern border and a few oases, Mauritania is largely arid desert and semiarid grassland. Although its population density is very low at about twenty people per square kilometer, the growth rate is 2.8 percent. This combination of factors led the UN Food and Agriculture Organization (FAO), in a 1982 study, to include both Mauritania and Senegal in their list of "critical" countries whose croplands cannot support their current and projected populations without a large increase in agricultural inputs, such as fertilizer and irrigation.

The floodplains fringing the Senegal River are broad and fertile, and support a productive economy—farming, herding, and fishing—based on the river's annual floods. During the 1970s, a serious drought and the prospect of a chronic food shortfall in the region encouraged the region's governments to seek international financing for the high Manantali Dam on the Bafing River tributary in Mali and for the Diama salt-intrusion barrage near the mouth of the Senegal River between Senegal and Mauritania. These dams were designed to regulate the river's flow to produce hydropower, expand irrigated agriculture, and provide river transport from the Atlantic Ocean to landlocked Mali. But as anthropologist Michael Horowitz has found, anticipation of the new infrastructure sharply increased land values along the river where irrigation could be installed. This led the white Moor elite in Mauritania to rewrite legislation governing land ownership, effectively stripping black Africans of their rights to continue farming and herding along the Mauritanian bank of the river.

There has been a long history of racism by white Moors in Mauritania toward their non-Arab black compatriots. In the spring of 1989, tensions in the river basin triggered an explosion of black Senegalese hostility toward the Moors. Within a few weeks, almost all of the 17,000 shops owned by Moors in Senegal were pillaged or destroyed, several hundred people had been killed and thousands injured in ethnic violence in both countries, nearly two hundred thousand refugees fled in both directions across the border, and the two countries were nearly at war. The Mauritanian regime used this occasion to activate the new land legislation, declaring the black population along the Mauritanian portion of the river basin to be "Senegalese," stripping them of their citizenship, and seizing their properties and livestock. Many of these blacks were forcibly expelled to Senegal, and some launched cross-border raids to retrieve expropriated cattle.

We see here the interaction of the three sources of human-induced environmental scarcity I have identified. Agricultural shortfalls, caused in part by population pressures and degradation of the land resource, encouraged a large development scheme. These factors together raised land values in one of the few areas in either country offering the potential for a rapid move to high-intensity agriculture. The result was a change in property rights and resource distribution, a sudden increase in resource scarcity for an ethnic minority, expulsion of the minority, and ethnic violence.

The Philippines

In many parts of the world, we see a somewhat different process: unequal resource access combines with population growth to produce environmental damage. This can lead to economic deprivation that spurs insurgency and rebellion. In the Philippines, Spanish and American colonial policies left behind a grossly unfair distribution of land. Since the 1960s, the introduction of green-revolution technologies has permitted a dramatic increase in lowland production of grain for domestic consumption and of cash crops that has helped to pay off the country's massive external debt. This modernization has raised demand for agricultural labor. Unfortunately, though, the gain has been overwhelmed by a population growth rate of 2.5 to 3.0 percent. Combined with the maldistribution of good cropland and an economic crisis in the first half of the 1980s, this growth produced a surge in agricultural unemployment. With insufficient rural or urban industrialization to absorb excess labor, there has been unrelenting downward pressure on wages.

Economically desperate, millions of poor agricultural laborers and landless peasants have migrated to shantytowns in already overburdened cities, such as Manila; millions of others have moved to the least productive, and often most ecologically vulnerable territories, such as steep hillsides.[33] In these uplands, settlers use fire to clear forested or previously logged land. They bring with them little money or knowledge to protect their fragile ecosystems, and their small-scale logging, production of charcoal for the cities, and slash-and-burn farming often cause horrendous environmental damage—particularly water erosion, landslides, and changes in the hydrological cycle. This has set in motion a cycle of falling food production, the clearing of new plots, and further land degradation. Even marginally fertile land is becoming hard to find in many places, and economic conditions are often precarious for the peasants (see Figure 17.3).[34]

Figure 17.3 / Some Sources and Consequences of Enviromental Scarcity in the Philippines

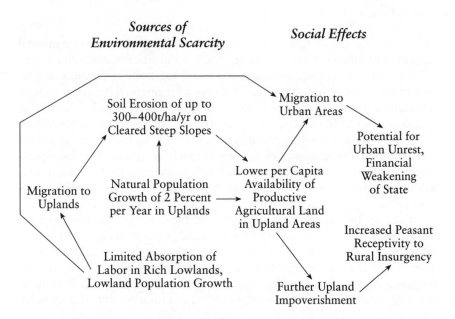

The Philippines has suffered from serious internal strife for many decades. But Celso Roque, the former undersecretary of the environment of the Philippines, and his colleague Maria Garcia have concluded that resource stress appears to be an increasingly powerful force driving the present communist-led insurgency. Some senior Filipino politicians have reached the same conclusion. Daniel Lacson, the governor of the province of Negros Occidental under President Aquino, identifies two sources of poverty and injustice behind the insurgency: the accumulation of land in the hands of a few who have failed to deal with the problems of the poor; and land degradation that affects small farmers and is not alleviated by government action.

The upland insurgency is motivated by the economic deprivation of the landless agricultural laborers and poor farmers displaced into the hills, where they try to eke out a living from failing land; it exploits opportunities for rebellion in the country's peripheral regions, which are largely beyond the effective control of the central government; and it is helped by the creative leadership of the cadres of the insurgent New People's Army and the National Democratic Front. During the 1970s and 1980s, these groups found upland peasants very receptive to revolutionary ideology, especially where the repression of landlords and local governments left them little choice but to rebel or starve. The revolutionaries have built on local understandings and social structures to help the peasants define their situation and focus their discontent.[35]

THE LONG-TERM IMPLICATIONS FOR NATIONAL AND INTERNATIONAL SECURITY

In the coming decades, a poor country faced with severe environmental scarcity will follow one of four paths. Most optimistically, the country may be able to supply enough technical and social ingenuity to permit substitution of relatively plentiful resources for scarce resources, or to allow societal adaptation to scarcity. If this is not possible, the country might be able to "decouple" itself from dependency on its own environmental resources by making goods and services that can be traded on the international market for the environmental resources it needs (such as grain). The decoupling might, in fact, be achieved by rapidly exploiting the country's environmental resources, which allows it to accumulate enough money, industrial equipment, and education to permit a shift to other forms of production.

If the country is unable to do either of these things, the government's instruments to manage society—its financial, bureaucratic, and political machinery—may eventually be so damaged by environmentally induced social stress that chronic protest and violence arise. The country may then fragment, as peripheral regions come under the control of renegade authorities and "warlords." Such a weakening of government control over outer regions is already underway in the Philippines, and environmental scarcity may be a strong contributor to this process.

Finally, and most pessimistically, the state may avoid fragmentation by becoming a "hard" regime, that is, by resorting to authoritarian measures against internal opposition. A hard regime may also launch military attacks against neighboring countries to distract its people's attention from their rising grievances. External aggression may also result after a new government comes to power through civil violence: governments born of revolution, for example, are particularly adept at mobilizing their citizens and resources for war.[36]

Whether or not a given country will follow the third or fourth path above depends, in part, on the level of remaining resources and wealth in the country's economic system that can potentially be appropriated by the state for its own uses. This suggests that the countries with the highest probability of becoming "hard" regimes (and potential threats to their neighbors) in the face of environmental and economic stress are large, relatively wealthy developing countries that are dependent on a declining environmental base, such as Indonesia, Brazil, and perhaps Nigeria. In contrast, resource-poor countries, such as Bangladesh, Haiti, the Philippines, Ethiopia, and the Sudan, are more likely to fragment.

If many developing countries evolve in the direction of extremism, the military interests of rich countries may often be directly threatened. Of special concern here is the growing gap between rich and poor nations that may be widened by environmental scarcity. Some poor nations may be heavily armed, and may possess weapons of mass destruction; such regimes could be tempted to use nuclear blackmail to induce rich countries to transfer their wealth to the Third World. However, it is likely that environmental stress and the social disruption it produces will so weaken the economies of poor countries that they will be unable to build sizable armed forces. But the North would surely be unwise to rely on poverty and disorder in the South for the preservation of its security.

WHAT CAN BE DONE?

The global environmental situation is critical, and is already causing social disruptions and intergroup conflict. But we are not powerless to alter these processes. We know a great deal about what we are doing to our environment, about which kinds of social systems damage the environment least, and about how we can best adapt to ecological stress.

Over the last few years, there have been some heartening moves in the right direction by national governments and international agencies. For example, countries and chemical companies have moved aggressively to limit and eventually stop the production of the CFCs that destroy the ozone layer. The international agreements to do this include novel ways of transferring funds from rich to poor countries to help them move to technologies that do not use CFCs. This may be a precedent for transfer mechanisms to help poor countries develop energy technologies that produce less carbon dioxide.

International financial agencies, like the World Bank, the Asia Development Bank, and the International Monetary Fund, have become much more aware of the intricate relationship between economic development and environmental scarcity. They are more cautious about funding large-scale, centralized development projects, such as hydroelectric dams, and they have begun to subject their financing to more careful environmental review. In addition, they are providing substantial funding for sustainable development projects around the world.

Without question, the most important event in recent years was the United Nations Conference on Environment and Development (UNCED) in Rio de Janeiro, Brazil, in June 1992. This was the largest and most inclusive international negotiation in history. In arduous meetings leading up to the conference, delegates from rich and poor nations tried to work out preliminary agreements to protect biodiversity, control carbon dioxide emissions, and slow deforestation. Some environmentalists were disappointed by the final results of the conference: the United States refused to sign the biodiversity treaty; the carbon-dioxide agreement was significantly weakened (again, as a result of U.S. pressure); and some poor nations objected to the deforestation agreement. Nonetheless, the Rio conference was a milestone in humankind's efforts to meet the environmental challenge. It brought worldwide attention to the crisis, and it showed politicians and policymakers that good environmental policy can be a source of political authority and moral legitimacy.[37]

Our research project on "Environmental Change and Acute Conflict" has produced some recommendations for action in rich and poor countries to reduce the chances of environmentally induced conflict. Some of these recommendations are very general and will need elaboration by experts as well as continuing negotiation among governments; others are quite specific. Importantly, some recommendations do *not* require huge financial investments but may, nonetheless, make a great difference to the future well-being of our world.

While circumstances differ across the developing world, poor countries should in general act to control population growth, they should implement a fairer distribution of land and wealth within their societies, and they should encourage sustainable economic growth to provide employment for surplus labor. In the short-term, the leaders of many poor countries see a trade-off between economic growth and environmental protection, and this encourages overuse and the degradation of environmental resources. But the real trade-off is between short-term unsustainable prosperity and long-term growth potential. This is an answer to the common argument from poor countries that rich countries are using environmental issues to deny them the opportunity to grow: it is in the developing world's self-interest to prevent environmental decline. Policymakers in both rich and poor countries must, therefore, change their understanding of development to emphasize the true value of natural resources and the importance of efficiencies in production as a way of conserving resources. Scholars and researchers in universities, think tanks, and public agencies can play an important role in educating policymakers about these realities.

More thorough environmental impact assessments of resource-development projects, such as dams and irrigation systems, are needed. Principles of sound resource management should be incorporated into contracts between development agencies, financial institutions (such as development banks), and developing countries that receive resource-related aid. Unfortunately, many international development agencies do not yet have adequate internal capability for thorough assessments. Moreover, it is impossible to accurately and completely predict the effects of a given resource-development project; and, even if it were possible, a project's social costs and benefits often cannot be compared. Policymakers should therefore be humble about the potential gain from environmental impact assessments.

In general, environmental problems require regional or "ecosystem-wide" solutions, rather than policies based at the national level. This point also applies to the management of the social effects of environmental scarcity: for instance, large-scale migration caused by environmental change can be most effectively limited and managed through regional accords. Some successful solutions of regional environmental problems may be transferable from one region to another. A good example is the International Joint Commission between Canada and the United States that manages disputes over water. Another example is the 1960 Indus Water Treaty that apportions the waters of the Indus River basin between India and Pakistan.

Population stabilization is key to limiting environmental stress, and it clearly requires collaboration between rich and poor countries. Wealthy countries can usefully supply financial aid and technology to slow population growth, although ideological reasons have caused the United States to sharply curtail support for such programs since the mid-1980s. Unfortunately, poor countries may also resist family planning for political and ideological reasons; Islamic fundamentalists and the Roman Catholic Church, for example, are opposed to birth control. In addition, leaders of poor countries sometimes perceive that a large population will enhance military security.

Rich countries can additionally support land reform in developing countries, reduce the debt burden of these countries, and promote—through aid and transfers of appropriate technology—rural industrialization projects. Poor nations, under pressure from banks and international lending agencies to pay their foreign debts, often use their best lands to grow cash crops for export. As people are displaced from these lands, governments and development agencies can work to provide them with jobs. Ideally, land reform combined with labor-intensive rural industries will boost incomes and stem the flow of people into ecologically vulnerable areas and into cities that are increasingly unmanageable.

In addition, rich countries can help poor countries overcome their lack of expertise on environmental management. In the developing world, inequality in national expertise translates into inequality in national power. Countries with advantages in technical expertise can dominate their neighbors; they have the edge in negotiations over resource management, and this can lead to misperceptions, rivalry, and conflict. Charles Okidi, an international lawyer at Moi University in Kenya, notes that there are only three Ph.D.-level hydrologists in his country. The addition of four per country in East Africa would greatly improve prospects for regional water management. It is cost-effective for rich countries to provide funds for the training of environmental experts in the developing world, including hydrologists, soil and agricultural scientists, energy-systems engineers, and fisheries specialists. If research and teaching centers in poor countries were adequately equipped and staffed, the "brain drain" to rich countries could be stemmed. Moreover, networks of such centers established across national borders could start wider cooperation among a region's countries.

Beyond these policy recommendations, certain changes of attitude are needed. This was one of the main lessons of the recent United Nations conference in Rio. Rich countries must recognize that global environmental problems are, in important ways, problems of global fairness. Deep poverty in the developing world often causes activities and strengthens economic structures that harm the environment. Moreover, as poor countries industrialize, they will need massive financial and technological help to leapfrog over the environmentally damaging technologies and practices that were used by today's industrialized countries. Poor countries also argued at the Rio meeting that environmental degradation is often driven, not by large populations, but by the high consumption and waste production of wealthy countries. Poor countries are not the main causes of, yet may be most vulnerable to, the large-scale environmental problems getting most attention in the developed world, such as global warming and ozone depletion. For all these reasons, widespread environmental scarcity may force humankind at last to deal with the wrenching economic differences that plague our planet.

QUESTIONS FOR FURTHER STUDY

1. What does Homer-Dixon mean by "environmental scarcity?" What factors are likely to produce such scarcity?
2. Homer-Dixon argues that conflicts brought about by "environmental scarcity" are different from traditional interstate conflicts over scarce resources like oil and rare minerals. What is the basis for this distinction? Do you agree that such a distinction exists?
3. How, in Homer-Dixon's view, can environmental scarcity lead to violent conflict? To what extent do the case studies cited in the chapter confirm or disprove his thesis on the relationship between environmental scarcity and violent conflict?

4. How does environmental scarcity impact on the stability of Third World governments? How might unstable Third World governments respond to environmental perils? What can be done to help such governments avert collapse or fragmentation?

Notes

1. Portions of this article originally appeared in Thomas Homer-Dixon, "Environmental Scarcity and Global Security," *Headline Series* (New York: Foreign Policy Association, 1992); in Thomas Homer-Dixon, "On the Threshold: Environmental Changes As Causes of Acute Conflict," *International Security*, Vol. 16, No. 2 (Fall 1991) pp. 76–116; and in Thomas Homer-Dixon, Jeffrey Boutwell, and George Rathjens, "Environmental Change and Violent Conflict," *Scientific American* (February 1993). Permission for republication has been granted by MIT Press and the Foreign Policy Association.
2. A renewable resource has both a "stock" and a "flow." A stock is the quantity or quality of the resource that is available for consumption or that maintains a useful service; and a flow is the incremental addition to, or restoration of, the stock per unit of time. See David Pearce and Kerry Turner, *Economics of Natural Resources and the Environment* (Baltimore: Johns Hopkins University Press, 1990), pp. 52–53. A "nonrenewable" resource consists only of a stock that is not replenished or restored over time; these include fossil fuels, metals, and minerals.
3. Although scarcities of nonrenewable resources may also contribute to conflict (for example, some people claim that the need for oil was a motivating factor behind the 1991 Persian Gulf war), I do not address this question in this chapter. For theory and historical analysis of nonrenewable resource conflicts, see Nazli Choucri and Robert North, *Nations in Conflict* (San Francisco: Freeman, 1975), and Ronnie Lipschutz, *When Nations Clash: Raw Materials, Ideology, and Foreign Policy* (Cambridge: Ballinger, 1989).
4. For example, see David Wirth, "Climate Chaos," *Foreign Policy*, Vol. 74 (Spring 1989), p. 10.
5. Robert Heilbroner, *An Inquiry into the Human Prospect* (New York: Norton, 1980), pp. 39 and 95; William Ophuls, *Ecology and the Politics of Scarcity: A Prologue to a Political Theory of the Steady State* (San Francisco: Freeman, 1977), pp. 214–217.
6. Peter Gleick, "Climate Change and International Politics: Problems Facing Developing Countries," *Ambio*, Vol. 18, No. 6 (1989), pp. 333–339; Gleick, "The Implications of Global Climatic Changes for International Security," *Climatic Change*, Vol. 15, No. 1/2 (October 1989), pp. 309–325; and Malin Falkenmark, "Fresh Waters As a Factor in Strategic Policy and Action," in Arthur Westing, ed., *Global Resources and International Conflict: Environmental Factors in Strategic Policy and Action* (New York: Oxford, 1986), pp. 85–113.
7. Ted Gurr, "On the Political Consequences of Scarcity and Economic Decline," *International Studies Quarterly*, Vol. 29, No. 1 (March 1985), pp. 51–75.
8. Wallace Broecker, "Unpleasant Surprises in the Greenhouse?" *Nature*, Vol. 328, No. 6126 (July 9, 1987), pp. 123–126.
9. J. C. Farman, B. G. Gardiner, and J. D. Shanklin, "Large Losses of Total Ozone in Antarctica Reveal Seasonal CO_2/NO_2 Interaction," *Nature*, Vol. 315, No. 6016 (May 16, 1985), pp. 207–210.
10. Readers interested in technical background on environmental issues should consult *World Resources 1994–95* (New York: Oxford University Press, 1994) and *World Resources 1996–97* (New York Oxford University Press, 1996). This publication, produced biennially by the World Resources Institute (WRI) in collaboration with the United Nations Environment Programme and other organizations, is widely regarded as the most accessible, accurate, and comprehensive source for information on global change issues. The more popular *State of the World* report, published annually by the Worldwatch Institute, is useful but sometimes selective and tendentious.
11. In 1971, Ehrlich and Holdren introduced a product formulation similar to that in Figure 17.1. They proposed that $I = P \times F$, where I is the total negative impact on the environment, P is the population, and F is a function that measures per capita impact on the environment. See Paul Ehrlich and John Holdren, "Impact of Population Growth," *Science*, Vol. 171 (March 26, 1971), pp. 1212–1217.
12. Numerous writers, especially those considering the social impact of climate change, have generated diagrams similar to Figure 17.1. See, in particular, the excellent survey article by

Richard Warrick and William Riebsame entitled "Societal Response to CO_2-Induced Climate Change: Opportunities for Research," *Climatic Change,* Vol. 3, No. 4 (1981), pp. 387–428.

13. See, for example, Lester Brown, "Reexamining the World Food Prospect," in *State of the World 1989* (New York: Norton, 1989), pp. 41–58.

14. Nafis Sadik, *The State of the World Population 1990* (New York: United Nations Population Fund, 1990), p. 8.

15. WRI, et al., *World Resources 1990–91,* p. 87.

16. See Vaclav Smil, *Energy, Food, Environment: Realities, Myths, Options* (Oxford: Oxford University Press, 1987), pp. 223 and 230.

17. For a thorough account of the Filipino environmental crisis, see World Bank, *Philippines: Environment and Natural Resource Management Study* (Washington: World Bank, 1989).

18. There is scientific debate about the likely magnitude, rate, and timing of global warming, and about its climatic, ecological, and social impacts. The current consensus is summarized in the reports prepared by Working Groups I and II of the Intergovernmental Panel on Climate Change under the auspices of the World Meteorological Organization and the United Nations Environment Program. The complete report of Working Group I has been published as *Climate Change: The IPCC Scientific Assessment,* eds. J. T. Houghton, G. J. Jenkins, and J. J. Ephraums (Cambridge: Cambridge University Press, 1990). For a thorough assessment of climate change and agriculture, see M. L. Parry, T. R Carter, and N. T. Konijn, eds., *The Impact of Climatic Variations on Agriculture, Volume 1: Assessments in Cool Temperate and Cold Regions; Volume 2: Assessments in Semi-Arid Regions* (Dordrecht, Netherlands: Kluwer, 1989).

19. See R. A. Warrick, R. M. Gifford, and M. L. Parry, "CO_2, Climatic Change, and Agriculture: Assessing the Response of Food Crops to the Direct Effects of Increased CO_2 and Climatic Change," in Bert Bolin, et al., eds., *The Greenhouse Effect, Climatic Change, and Ecosystems,* SCOPE 29 (New York: Wiley, 1986), pp. 393–474. See also Fakhri Bazzaz and Eric Fajer, "Plant Life in a CO_2-Rich World," *Scientific American,* Vol. 266, No. 1 (January 1992), pp. 68–74.

20. Robert Repetto, "Wasting Assets: The Need for National Resource Accounting," *Technology Review* (January 1990), p. 40.

21. Robert Repetto, "Balance-Sheet Erosion—How to Account for the Loss of Natural Resources," *International Environmental Affairs,* Vol. 1, No. 2 (Spring 1989), pp. 103–137.

22. Vaclav Smil, "Environmental Degradation As a Source of Conflict and Economic Losses in China," Occasional Paper of the American Academy of Arts and Sciences and the Peace and Conflict Studies Program of the University of Toronto (December 1993).

23. Jodi Jacobson, *Environmental Refugees: A Yardstick of Habitability,* Worldwatch Paper 86 (Washington: Worldwatch Institute, 1988).

24. For an illuminating account of how population growth and resource shortages undermined state capacity in the past, see Jack Goldstone, *Revolution and Rebellion in the Early Modern World* (Berkeley: University of California Press, 1991).

25. One theory of war arising from resource scarcity is provided by Choucri and North in *Nations in Conflict* (San Francisco: Freeman, 1975).

26. Theoretical perspectives on group-identify conflict are provided by M. Sherif, *Group Conflict and Cooperation: Their Social Psychology* (London: Routledge & Kegan Paul, 1966); Henri Tajfel, *Human Groups and Social Categories: Studies in Social Psychology* (Cambridge: Cambridge University Press, 1981); and Donald Horowitz, *Ethnic Groups in Conflict* (Berkeley: University of California Press, 1985).

27. Myron Weiner, "The Political Demography of Assam's Anti-Immigrant Movement," *Population and Development Review,* Vol. 9, No. 2 (June 1983), pp. 279–292.

28. See John Dollard, et al., *Frustration and Aggression* (New Haven: Yale University Press, 1939); James Davies, "Toward a Theory of Revolution," *American Sociological Review,* Vol. 6, No. 1 (February 1962), pp. 5–19; and Ted Gurr, *Why Men Rebel* (Princeton: Princeton University Press, 1970). Gurr explicitly attempts to apply deprivation theories of civil strife to situations of environmental crisis in "On the Political Consequences of Scarcity and Economic Decline," *International Studies Quarterly,* Vol. 29, No. 1 (March 1985), pp. 51–75.

29. The importance of changes in the perceived "opportunity structure" facing challenger groups is emphasized by Doug McAdam, *Political Process and the Development of Black Insurgency, 1930–1970* (Chicago: University of Chicago Press, 1982); see also Charles Tilly, *From Mobilization to Revolution* (Reading, MA: Addison-Wesley, 1978).

30. Sanjoy Hazarika, "Bangladesh and Northeast India: Land Pressure, Migration, and Ethnic Conflict," Occasional Paper No. 3 of the Project on Environmental Change and Acute Conflict (February 1993).

31. Weiner, "The Political Demography of Assam's Anti-Immigrant Movement."

32. For a full account, see Michael Horowitz, "Victims Upstream and Down," *Journal of Refugee Studies,* Vol. 4, No. 2 (1991), pp. 164–181.

33. A full account of these processes in the Philippines can be found in Maria Concepcion Cruz, et al., *Population Growth, Poverty, and Environmental Stress: Frontier Migration in the Philippines and Costa Rica* (Washington: World Resources Institute, 1992).

34. Gareth Porter and Delfin Ganapin, Jr., *Resources, Population, and the Philippines' Future: A Case Study,* WRI Paper No. 4 (Washington: World Resources Institute, 1988).

35. Gary Hawes, "Theories of Peasant Revolution: A Critique and Contribution from the Philippines," *World Politics,* Vol. 42, No. 1 (January 1990), pp. 261–298.

36. See Theda Skocpol, "Social Revolutions and Mass Military Mobilization," *World Politics,* Vol. 40, No. 2 (January 1988), pp. 147–168.

37. For further information on the Rio summit, see Peter Hass, Marc Levy, and Edward Parson, "Appraising the Earth Summit: How Should We Judge UNCED's Success?" *Environment,* Vol. 34, No. 8 (October 1992), pp. 7–11, 26–33. A summary of the treaties and documents produced by UNCED, including Agenda 21 (a plan for global sustainable development into the next century), is provided in Edward Parson, Peter Haas, and Marc Levy, "A Summary of the Major Documents Signed at the Earth Summit and the Global Forum," *Environment,* Vol. 34, No. 8 (October 1992), pp. 12–15, 34–36. The concept of "sustainable development" was given wide currency by the final report of the World Commission on Environment and Development (popularly called the Brundtland Commission) in *Our Common Future* (Oxford: Oxford University Press, 1987).

18 / Demographic Challenges to World Security

DENNIS PIRAGES

Large-scale population changes are disruptive forces that often create international or domestic insecurity. Rapid population growth is the demographic change factor most commonly linked to domestic disorders and various kinds of tensions among nations; but migration, differential growth patterns, and even rapid leveling of growth can all create various kinds of disorders. All of these will be major factors associated with political, economic, social, and military problems in the next century.

Homo sapiens, like most other species, lives in biological populations that, in the case of human beings, can be identified by use of a shared language and by frequency of interaction. Sometimes human populations are coincident with state boundaries, but most of the time states encompass two or more of them. Like those of other species, human populations usually grow until they run up against resource limitations. Many historical and contemporary military conflicts and civil disturbances have their origins in growth-driven quests to move beyond these environmental limits and seize additional territory and resources.

While warfare among human populations has always been a factor in trimming their size, there are many other significant threats to human security that cause societal devastation, human injuries, and premature deaths. Most of these are ecological factors such as environmental degradation, famines, floods, pestilence, and disease. An ecological approach to security, focusing on these factors, raises a broader set of concerns not yet commonly addressed in policy forums. Given traditionally accepted purposes of national security policy, the protection of the state and prevention of large-scale premature loss of human lives and potential, this ecological approach suggests looking well beyond cross-border military incursions when assessing future threats to human well-being.

Historically, security policy has been mainly concerned with preventing deaths and damage due to the predation of other human populations. This was the case because threats from others were readily understood, and because there was always the hope that credible defense measures could thwart future attacks. But such predation hasn't been the only, or even the major, threat to state security and human well-being. For example, while defense efforts against viruses have not traditionally been part of security thinking, one of the deadliest battles ever fought was the struggle between

Homo sapiens and the influenza virus that began in Kansas in 1918 and spread around the world during World War I. It is estimated that more than 20 million people lost their lives during this struggle.[1]

Human populations have co-evolved with various other species and microorganisms over time within an ever changing physical environment. Ecological security for human beings has been maximized when the following four kinds of balances have been maintained between:

- the demands of human populations and the sustaining capabilities of environmental systems,
- the size and growth rates of various human populations,
- the demands of human populations and those of other species, and
- human populations and pathogenic microorganisms.

Significant disturbances of any of these four balances can have serious social consequences. In the past, security policies have focused largely on only one of these dimensions—events associated with disruptions of balances among human populations—largely because the threats of premature deaths from other sources, such as plagues, were poorly understood and not easily remedied. But the size, growth patterns, and changing habits of interacting human populations are at the base of all four aspects of ecological security.

DEMOGRAPHIC CHANGE AND INSECURITY

Four types of rapid demographic changes can lead to various kinds of insecurity. Significant population growth, large-scale population movements, differential patterns of growth, and even the aging of populations can present challenges to social stability. Rapidly growing human populations obviously require increasing quantities of resources in order to maintain or augment existing living standards. Therefore these growing populations often press close to the ecological carrying capacity of territories they occupy, thus leading to environmental degradation, increased vulnerability to disease, and even to violent conflict.[2] If needed resources cannot be obtained locally, moreover, and if capabilities exist to get them elsewhere, lateral pressure to obtain resources from other populations is likely to develop.[3]

For long stretches of history, Homo sapiens lived in relative harmony with nature. The total number of people grew very slowly and, while the local environmental impact of individual populations might have been considerable, the global impact of human beings was relatively small.[4] During the early stages of the Industrial Revolution, however, the world's population began to expand rapidly. In 1650, there were only 500 million human beings on the Earth. This number doubled to 1 billion in two hundred years. Only eighty years later, by 1930, the world's population had doubled once again. The next doubling, to four billion, took only forty years. Today, there are nearly six billion people occupying an ever more densely populated world.

While rapid population growth is most frequently identified as a cause of political, economic, and even military insecurity, three other kinds of demographic change can also create problems. People in motion—whether migrating from rural to urban areas within a country or from one country to another—often trigger resentment when they settle at their destinations. For example, migrants have recently poured into Germany from Central and Eastern Europe, into France from North Africa, into Zaire (Congo) from Rwanda, and into the United States from the Caribbean and Latin America—in each case, meeting with various kinds of challenges ranging from discrimination to massacres. And when neighboring populations or populations that share territory grow at different rates, such as Islamic and non-Islamic neighbors, various kinds of tensions and conflicts are likely to arise.

Paradoxically, even a significant slowing of population growth—moving to or beyond zero population growth—can have political, economic, and military ramifications. The United States, Japan, and most European countries have recently experienced declining birthrates that, combined with life-prolonging technologies, are shaping "graying," or entitlement societies and a set of potentially divisive intergenerational conflicts. The so-called birth dearth in these countries threatens to pit economically productive young people—who will have to pay for future social programs—against those who will be the beneficiaries of Social Security and Medicare payments. A dwindling future workforce could be faced with picking up the costs of swelling entitlement programs that were created when economies were rapidly expanding and labor forces were growing.[5]

A DEMOGRAPHICALLY DIVIDED WORLD

The contemporary world is very much a demographically divided one.[6] On the less affluent, Southern side of this demographic divide, rapid population growth and related urbanization are creating insecurities by overwhelming the sustaining capabilities of social and physical systems. On the more affluent, Northern side of the divide, graying populations are increasingly confronting problems of chronic diseases and sociopolitical arteriosclerosis. And large-scale traffic across the North-South divide often provokes the wrath of those who see migrants as potential economic threats.

The industrialized countries have mostly completed a period of *demographic transition* in which reproductive values have changed and birth rates have fallen in response to rising affluence. In this more developed part of the world, several countries have even dropped below zero population growth. In the less-industrialized portions of the planet, however, a young and restive population continues to grow rapidly. The result is a kind of active demographic fault line separating the two. On the industrial, or Northern side of the fault, declining population growth rates are raising concerns about the future socioeconomic impact of graying populations, while on the less industrialized, Southern side of the divide, the Malthusian drama associated with rapid population growth grinds on.

These demographic differences can be attributed to an incomplete demographic transition. According to demographic transition theory, which is based on the historical experience of the first industrialized countries, there are three demographic phases through which industrialized societies have passed.[7] The first, or preindustrial, phase is characterized by both high birth and death rates, producing populations in equilibrium. In the second, industrializing phase, death rates plummet while birth rates remain high—resulting in rapid population growth. In the third, mature phase, birth rates drop to match the lower death rates and population equilibrium is reestablished.

Societies unaffected by industrialization, of which there are now very few, have historically exhibited high infant mortality. Thus, pro-natalist norms and values, which favor large numbers of offspring, have evolved in such societies to reflect this experience. Couples adhering to traditional values in these types of societies have felt that they were doing the right thing by having numerous children, since previous experience indicated that a large percentage of them would never reach adulthood.

Many countries on the Southern side of the demographic divide are now well into the second stage of transition. Having benefited from extensive transfers of lifesaving medical technologies such as vaccines and antibiotics, these countries have experienced a substantial drop in infant mortality and a related increase in life expectancy. But birth rates remain high because traditional, pro-natalist norms and values still govern reproductive behavior. Thus, in countries such as Tanzania and Haiti, birth rates are now well above death rates because people continue to behave reproductively as if present infant mortality rates were the same as those experienced by their grandparents. (See Table 18.1.)

Countries in the second stage of the demographic transition face an additional problem of *demographic momentum* inherent in the youthfulness of these rapidly growing populations. In countries such as Uganda, Libya, and Zambia, nearly one-half of the population is under fifteen while only 2 percent is over sixty-five. This means that a very large proportion of the population is about to enter prime childbearing age. Even if by some demographic miracle couples in these countries were to cut back to a two-child family immediately, there would still be considerable population growth. The reproductive momentum inherent in such societies, with so many people yet to pass through the years of maximum reproduction, would reverberate in the form of population surges through succeeding generations.

In stark contrast, on the Northern side of the demographic divide, most countries have already worked their way well into the third phase of the demographic transition. In this phase, industrial modernization and related

Table 18.1 / The Demographic Divide

	Births per 1,000	Deaths per 1,000	Natural Increase (percent)	Population 1996 (millions)	Population 2025 (millions)
DEVELOPED COUNTRIES					
Russia	9	15	−0.5	147.7	153.1
Bulgaria	9	13	−0.4	8.4	7.9
Hungary	11	14	−0.3	10.2	9.3
Germany	9	11	−0.1	81.7	79.3
Italy	9	10	0.0	57.3	54.4
United States	15	9	0.6	265.2	335.1
ALL DEVELOPED	12	10	0.6	1,171.0	1,268.0
DEVELOPING COUNTRIES					
Iraq	44	7	3.7	21.4	52.6
Libya	45	8	3.7	5.4	14.4
Cote d'Ivoire	50	15	3.5	14.7	33.4
Uganda	52	19	3.3	22.0	37.4
Ethiopia	46	16	3.1	57.2	129.7
Zambia	45	15	3.0	9.2	18.5
ALL DEVELOPING	27	9	1.9	4,600.0	6,925.0

Source: "1996 World Population Data Sheet," Population Reference Bureau, Washington, D.C.

value shifts have produced a change toward much smaller families. Thus, Danish demographic data for 1950 indicate that the statistically average woman was producing 2.58 children during her lifetime; by 1985, this had dropped to 1.45. In West Germany in 1950 the figure was at 2.10, and it dropped to 1.29 by 1985.[8] For the industrialized world as a whole there is now an average of twelve births and ten deaths per one thousand people, yielding a population growth rate of only 0.2 percent annually. But on the less industrial side of the divide there are still twenty-seven births and only nine deaths per thousand, yielding a population growth rate of 1.9 percent.[9]

A smooth progression through the second phase of the transition by the presently less-industrialized countries cannot be assumed. It is unclear whether many of the less-industrialized countries can avoid a "demographic trap" resulting from a combination of large numbers of young people and little economic growth, which would prevent their move on to the third stage. Many of these countries now appear to be economically bogged down and unable to move forward rapidly enough to avoid ecological and economic deterioration brought about by persisting high birth rates.[10] Further, lack of economic progress has shaken faith in a secular, industrial way of life and has led to a resurgence of pro-natalist religious fundamentalism in many parts of the world.

GROWTH PRESSURES AND INSECURITY

As human numbers on the Southern side of the demographic divide have rapidly grown, ecological insecurity has increased apace and there are now abundant signs of stress. For example, the contemporary densely populated world is experiencing increasing numbers of so-called natural disasters as burgeoning human populations press into areas—river basins, coastal lowlands, earthquake areas, and so on—that can be occupied only at great risk.[11] And the number of people continues to grow. The world is projected to have 8.2 billion occupants by the year 2025, with 85 percent of them living in the presently less-industrialized countries.[12] It is estimated that 60 percent of the less-industrialized world's poorest people now live in ecologically vulnerable areas.[13] Thus, trees that can be used for firewood are rapidly disappearing before the demands of growing populations, and the related deforestation is increasing soil erosion and flooding.

Water is another source of insecurity in many areas of the world. Rapidly growing populations in the Middle East are competing for very limited supplies. Israel and the Palestinians are perpetually at odds over control of water, and Jordan and Syria have repeatedly accused each other of stealing water from the small river running between the two countries. Similarly, Syria, Turkey, and Iraq are constantly feuding over withdrawals from the Tigris and Euphrates rivers.[14]

Population pressures on land and water are also responsible for considerable malnutrition and even starvation. While growth in worldwide food production has slightly exceeded world population growth over the last decade, this has not been the case in many countries. When data for the period of 1982–84 are compared with that of 1992–94, food production per capita actually declined in seventy-two countries.[15] And some experts, such as Lester Brown, claim that world food markets in the next century will be under even greater pressure due to urbanization (which often leads to a loss of cropland as cities spread out in all directions), environmental deterioration, and demands for food imports from rapidly developing states like China.[16]

A widening gap in economic opportunity also parallels the demographic divide. The richest fifth of the world's population now produces 83 percent of the gross world product while the poorest fifth produces only about 1 percent.[17] And the income gap seems to be widening: between 1960 and 1989 the per person income difference between the average person in the top 20 percent of the world's population and the bottom 20 percent grew from $1,864 to $15,149.[18] And between 1980 and 1993 there was a decline in real per capita GDP in fifty-three countries on the Southern side of the demographic divide.[19]

Economic stagnation and decline in these countries is related, in turn, to political turmoil and insecurity. There is a strong relationship among population growth, poverty, environmental deterioration, social violence, political instability, and authoritarian forms of government.[20] When politics can only be concerned with allocations of deprivations, it is difficult for democratic regimes to survive. In Haiti, for example, the combined birth and death rates are unmatched in the western hemisphere and the pattern of authoritarian regimes and political violence there led to an intervention by the United States to establish some semblance of order. Similarly, authoritarian governments and violence have been commonplace in economically stagnant African countries such as Angola, Ethiopia, Liberia, Somalia, Sudan, Uganda, and Zaire.

PEOPLE IN MOTION

Rapid population growth on one side of the demographic divide and the potential for a birth dearth on the other are now associated with two kinds of large-scale population movements. The pressures of rural population growth in less-industrialized countries combined with perceived, and often illusory, economic opportunities in urban areas are driving and luring large numbers of people into cities. And others, driven by the pressures of population growth, declining economic opportunity, and political instability, are moving (legally and illegally), across flimsy bridges spanning parts of the international demographic divide.

Migrants are swarming into the United States from Asia, the Caribbean, and Latin America at a rate in excess of six hundred thousand annually. Western Europe is being pressured from several directions: estimates indicate that between 1991 and 2000 as many as 4 million Eastern Europeans, 3.5 million people from the former USSR, 2.5 million North Africans, 2 million sub-Saharan Africans, and 1 million Asians will have arrived in Western Europe seeking jobs.[21]

People migrate for a variety of reasons. Historically, the largest share of them has moved in search of better economic conditions. But contemporary migration is also populated by refugees from military conflict, ethnic violence, and the collapse of states. It is very difficult to estimate the numbers and types of migrants and refugees in the world today. The largest share remains in the countries of origin; the next largest portion crosses boundaries only within the less-industrialized world; and an even smaller share crosses the demographic divide into the industrialized nations. But millions of migrants cross borders quite legally each year, and there are several million contract laborers living abroad at any given point in time.

It is illegal migrants, asylum-seekers, and refugees that create political conflict. By definition, illegal migrants are very difficult to count. It is roughly estimated that between one hundred thousand and three hundred thousand people slip into the United States illegally each year.[22] Most industrialized countries, with the clear exception of Japan, have recently seen a large increase in people claiming political asylum. In many of these countries the wheels of justice turn very slowly, permitting those seeking asylum to stay for long periods or to quietly blend into the population.[23]

The most troublesome political and moral dilemmas are associated with refugees. While precise data on migrants and refugees are difficult to obtain because of the ever changing nature of population movements, the United Nations conservatively estimates that there are now about 23 million refugees who have crossed national borders.[24] There is probably a similar number of internally displaced persons. Thus, protracted conflicts, civil wars, ethnic cleansings, and a variety of human tragedies have created a large population of semipermanent refugees, most of whom live dreary and hopeless lives under primitive conditions. Afghanistan tops the list of countries creating refugees with 3 million Afghans registered as refugees abroad. Rwanda follows closely behind with 2.1 million refugees.[25] The pieces of the former Yugoslavia have collectively created similar numbers of migrants and refugees.

RAPID URBANIZATION

Intense urbanization within less-industrialized countries can also lead to various kinds of insecurity. Worldwide, 36 percent of the world's population lived in cities in 1965. By 1990 the portion living in cities had increased to 50 percent. In the low-income countries, however, the percentage living in cities more than doubled, growing from 18 to 38 percent. In China, the percentage increased from 18 to 56 percent; in Tanzania, it jumped from 5 to 33 percent.[26]

The number of people living in urban areas is expected to double to more than 5 billion people between 1990 and 2025. About 90 percent of this growth will take place in the less-industrialized countries.[27] Many of those moving to urban areas become squatters, having little money to buy land or a home of their own. More than 2 million people in Calcutta live in slums and squatter settlements, as do more than 1 million people in Rio de Janeiro, Jakarta, Manila, Bogota, Lima, Casablanca, and Istanbul.[28] It is estimated that by the year 2000, 90 percent of the poorest people in Latin America and the Caribbean, 40 percent of the poorest in Africa, and 45 percent of the poorest in Asia will live in cities.[29]

Rapid urbanization is closely associated with a parallel problem of growing "megacities." Projecting urbanization trends forward to the year 2034, Mexico City and Shanghai could each have populations of 39 million; Beijing could have 35 million; Sao Paulo, 32 million; and Bombay, 31 million.[30] Providing adequate housing, sanitation, transportation, jobs, security and other amenities for rapidly growing numbers of new urban dwellers will be a staggering undertaking. So will the task of maintaining order and preventing outbreaks of disease among the restless army of unemployed in these crowded and polluted megacities.

Rio de Janeiro is typical of many large and growing cities. Urban crowding, combined with the lack of economic opportunities, threatens to destroy the social fabric. On a typical weekend, there are dozens of murders in the metropolitan region. Holdups along Rio's beaches are so common that diplomats refer to them as "tourist taxes." Kidnappings of wealthy children for ransom are commonplace. A psychiatrist living in Brazil describes the breakdown as "living in an era where each call for social responsibility is made fun of, as a moralizing fable or the kind of prayer an orphan might make on Christmas Eve."[31]

Growing cities also require large quantities of food, water, and other resources, thus creating a large "ecological footprint" in the surrounding countryside.[32] Large quantities of food must be "imported" by cities in order to keep up with demands of the ever increasing numbers of urbanites. But growing cities also need large quantities of water for drinking and sewage treatment—water which is often not available. In Dhaka, Bangladesh, for example, only one-fifth of the population is served by a sewage system. And in Bangkok, Thailand, growing demand is depleting the groundwater in much of the city with parts of it sinking by between five and ten centimeters per year. Experts estimate that the center of Mexico City has dropped about eight meters over the last fifty years due to groundwater extraction.[33] In addition, urban sprawl often destroys much of the fertile agricultural land surrounding cities. It is estimated that 476,000 hectares (1 hectare = 2.47 acres) of arable land is being transformed to urban uses annually in the less-industrialized countries.[34]

Mexico City, which is expected to be the largest of the world's cities by the middle of the next century, is already experiencing many environmental insecurity problems associated with large and dense urban populations. Located in a mountain-ringed basin at an altitude of 7,300 feet, Mexico City lacks sufficient fresh air to meet the competing needs of people, automobiles, and industry. Ozone levels reached such high levels in the early 1990s that the government expanded a one-day-per-week ban on each urban automobile to two days per week, thus keeping 40 percent of the region's automobiles off the streets on any given weekday. But even in the face of such tragic evidence of environmental decay, the population continues to grow, and is expected to increase from its present 20 million to 26 million by the year 2000.[35]

POPULATION, POVERTY, AND PLAGUES

Remarkable progress has been made in the twentieth century in reducing suffering due to the many diseases that afflict human beings. But there are now indications that rapid growth in human numbers, the greater density of urbanized populations, increasing poverty, and global ecological changes are making human populations much more vulnerable to disease-bearing microorganisms.[36] The World Health Organization (WHO) estimates that one-quarter of the world's population is subject to chronic intestinal parasitic infections. Nearly 20 million annual deaths now occur due to communicable diseases; tuberculosis annually kills 3 million people; malaria,

2 million; and hepatitis, 1 million. In addition, millions of others die prematurely from a myriad of other diseases.[37]

The AIDS virus, which is estimated to have infected more than 1.2 million people in North America, has afflicted about 17 million people worldwide. More than 9.7 million people are HIV-positive in sub-Saharan Africa, and 3.5 million in Asia. By the year 2005, it is projected that 2.4 million people will be dying from AIDS annually, representing nearly 5 percent of deaths from all sources.[38]

There is also a growing risk of other epidemics spreading rapidly through an increasingly integrated "global village." Microorganisms that emerge in one neighborhood can quickly spread to others. An acceleration of international air travel as well as an increasing volume of international trade are opening up new possibilities for the rapid movement of various kinds of microorganisms. Between 1950 and 1990, the number of passengers on international air flights grew dramatically from 2 million to 280 million annually.[39] Nasty influenza viruses named after Asian cities of origin—such as the recent Wuhan (China) virus—may soon be replaced by much more deadly relatives.

Many of the bacteria and viruses that pose future threats to ecological security are not new. They have coexisted with Homo sapiens in various parts of the world for long periods of time. But changes in human behavior, patterns of residence, poverty levels, and transportation systems are now altering the people-microbe balance.[40] In the words of Nobel Laureate Joshua Lederberg, "Some people think that I am being hysterical, but there are catastrophes ahead. We live in evolutionary competition with microbes—bacteria and viruses. There is no guarantee that we will be the survivors."[41] Thus, the greatest threat to future world security may not come from thermonuclear explosions, but from microorganisms too small to be seen by the human eye.

AGING AND SOCIAL INSECURITY

As the industrialized countries move further into the third stage of the demographic transition, the portion of these populations under fifteen years of age is shrinking while the portion beyond retirement age—thanks to longer life spans—continues to grow. In the industrial countries as a group, 14 percent of the population is now over sixty-five and only 20 percent is under fifteen. In Germany and Italy, the portion under fifteen and over sixty-five is nearly equal.[42] The growing numbers of elderly and the unprecedented decline in the younger population will have significant implications for future social stability.

The economic, political, social, and health implications of this "graying" have not yet been adequately explored, both because the greatest impact of this demographic shift still lies ahead, and because of the potentially explosive nature of the associated distributional issues. As Michael Boskin, former chairman of the U.S. Council of Economic Advisers, forewarned more than a decade ago, "A confrontation between workers and retirees will arise that will create the greatest polarization along economic lines in our society since the Civil War."[43]

Aging in these countries will undoubtedly ignite various kinds of intergenerational skirmishes as unfunded liabilities from entitlement programs established during a period of rapid population and economic growth will be paid for during a period of relative austerity. A growing elderly population expects to receive continued extensive pension and medical benefits—benefits that are presently unfunded or underfunded—at a time when a shrinking working-age population will be hard-pressed to pay the bills.

The Organization for Economic Cooperation and Development (OECD) has examined some of the long-term social policy implications of "graying" within its member countries. It projects that by the year 2030, 27 percent of the population of Switzerland and 26 percent of the population of Germany will be over sixty-five. In the United States and Japan, 20 percent will be over sixty-five.[44]

This "graying" of the population will dramatically alter future *aged dependency ratios* in the industrial countries. An aged dependency ratio refers to the number of people over sixty-five compared to those of working age (fifteen to sixty-five). In the United States, the ratio now stands at about .20, meaning that one elderly person could be theoretically supported by about five people in the labor force. But not all people of working age are employed, and currently there are only four workers supporting each retired person.[45] In France, where truckers and transit workers have been agitating for full retirement benefits at age fifty-five, there are now only two workers in the labor force for every retiree.[46]

By the year 2030, the aged dependency ratio in the United States will have reached .32, meaning that each person over sixty-five could be potentially supported by only three active workers. In Switzerland the ratio will rise from the current .21 to .47 and in Germany from .22 to .44.[47] Thus, in both of these countries, there will be only about two potentially active workers for each retiree in the year 2030. These numbers bring visions of a future proletariat toiling long hours in order to pay taxes necessary to keep politically organized retirees in the style to which they have become accustomed. Since most of these future obligations are woefully underfunded, the two or three workers supporting each retiree will have to provide the bulk of entitlement funding—a situation that is politically explosive. In fact, in the 1996 U.S. presidential campaign, President Clinton aggressively courted the senior citizen vote by charging that his opponent, Bob Dole, would cut Social Security benefits.

The population of Japan is aging faster than that of the United States, and the Japanese Economic Planning Agency is concerned about the future impact of "graying" on economic growth. The portion of Japan's gross domestic product devoted to social expenditures is projected to mushroom from 14 to 27 percent between 1983 and 2025.[48] This is a consequence of the extraordinary portion of the population that will be over seventy-five in 2025: nearly half of Japan's elderly will be seventy-five or over, and among them there will be one hundred women for every seventy-five men.[49] Japanese planners are particularly concerned about the impact of these changes on the future labor force, especially given existing stringent regulations governing immigration. Thus, robots increasingly will be needed to meet a significant portion of future needs for labor.[50]

Insecurities associated with aging are not limited to the industrially advanced nations. In China, a vigorous family-planning policy stressing one-child families has led to more rapid "graying" than is taking place in many other countries. Estimates indicate that by the year 2040, fully 35 percent of the population could be over the age of sixty. This is five times the present ratio.[51] The dilemma facing Chinese leaders is that the one-child-per-family policy, made necessary in order to preserve some semblance of balance with nature, is resulting in an older population long before enough economic growth has taken place to support extensive retirement programs. Similar issues will be faced by the former socialist countries of Central Europe where a demographic transition has been completed without a prior period of rapid economic growth.

Adding together future retirement obligations and medical burdens associated with "graying," it is very likely that the generous systems of social protection, which evolved in an era of population growth, economic expansion, and social exuberance, are increasingly going to be the subject of political controversy. Unfunded and underfunded pension systems and growing medical care costs will place heavy financial demands on governments in more slowly growing economies, and doing "more with less" will become a common admonition in the next century.

Governments in the industrial countries have begun to grapple with these issues, but action has been less than resolute. In the United States, a presidential bipartisan panel set up to make suggestions for preserving the future social security system reported itself to be hopelessly deadlocked on these issues in early 1997. In France, where only 38 percent of men over fifty-five are now working, transit workers went on strike in January 1997 in order to force the government to lower their retirement age to fifty-five, a move that would cost between $11 billion and $20 billion a year. In Germany, a government panel recently suggested reforming the social security system so that Germans retiring in 2030 would get only 64 percent of their average wages, down from 70 percent in 1997; this would be financed at that time by a combined employee-employer contribution of nearly 23 percent of wages.[52]

Since future generations do not vote, one of the first casualties of budget crunches may well be education and other programs for the dwindling number of politically unprotected young people. It is somewhat ironic that on the Southern side of the demographic divide, the educational and employment needs of the large and growing number of young people pose a threat to future stability, whereas on the Northern side the growing number of retired persons presents such a challenge.

THE HAZARDS OF DIFFERENTIAL GROWTH

Rapid population growth contributes to ecological insecurity by disrupting the balance between human beings and nature, but differential population growth among neighboring human populations can be an even greater precipitant of conflict. Population pressures often force people from high-growth areas to neighboring areas of lesser growth. Such dynamics can precipitate conflict within states shared by two or more ethnic groups, or can create conflicts among states.

People in countries with low population growth rates often perceive themselves to be potential targets of rapidly growing neighbors. Israel, with an annual rate of natural population increase of 1.5 percent, feels threatened by Arab neighbors with populations growing at more than twice that rate. Israel has attempted to compensate for this by encouraging large-scale immigration, much of it from the former Soviet Union. This migration, in turn, has increased insecurity among Palestinians in the West Bank and Gaza areas, who fear that the migrant influx will increase political pressure on their lands. As former Israeli Prime Minister Shamir once put it succinctly, "A big immigration needs a big Israel."[53] Similar fear dynamics operate within countries. In countries as diverse as Rwanda, India, Somalia, and Canada, friction between differentially growing ethnic or religious groups has caused political instability, ethnic conflict, and even massacres.

The rapid growth of Islamic populations compared to their non-Islamic neighbors is also a potential source of future instability. There are now forty countries in which more than half of the population is Islamic, and another seven in which Moslems are a very significant minority. In recent years these forty-seven Islamic countries had an average population growth rate of 2.8 percent annually, while their similarly situated non-Islamic neighbors were growing at a rate of only 2.3 percent.[54] Given a seeming surge of Islamic fundamentalism, neighbors of Islamic countries are understandably insecure in the face of these burgeoning populations.

The demographic fault line stretching the length of the Mediterranean is one of the areas in which rapidly expanding Islamic populations—in this case in North Africa—are seen as a threat by more stable non-Islamic populations. On the European side of this fault, almost all countries are close to zero population growth; the Islamic countries of North Africa, by contrast, are growing at about 2.6 percent annually. The total population of North Africa, 164 million in 1996, is expected to grow to 272 million by 2025, while the European countries are expected to grow hardly at all.[55] In France and Italy, total fertility rates are 1.7 and 1.2 children per woman, respectively, well below replacement rate; in Northern Africa, by contrast, large families are still the rule. In Algeria, the total fertility rate is 4.3 children per woman, and in Libya it is about 6.4 children.[56]

Given its historical ties to North Africa, France has been most directly affected by surges of immigrants from that region. Migration is now a major issue in French politics. The National Front—the right-wing political party headed by Jean-Marie Le Pen—has gained an increasing share of the national vote by suggesting that all immigrants should be returned to their countries of origin. Germany has also been affected by large-scale immigration from the South and the East. Discontent with immigration laws and the influx of foreigners has been manifested in deadly violence against foreigners in several parts of the country.

In the United States, although violent conflict based on differential population growth is unlikely, such growth will be an important force in reshaping the political map of the country over the next few decades. The so-called WASPs (White, Anglo-Saxon Protestants) that controlled American politics for a long period are nearing zero population growth, while the former minority populations, reinforced by immigration, are growing much more rapidly. This demographic shift is of great interest to both major political parties as they reassess their traditional bases of support. Thus, the growing Hispanic vote was ardently courted by both presidential candidates in the 1996 U.S. election, and was thought to have had a decisive impact on the outcome of a number of close Congressional races.

Differential population growth will also reshape politics on a global scale. By the year 2025, there will be six people living South of the demographic divide for every person in the industrialized North.[57] The less-industrial countries will have young, growing, and potentially restive populations, whereas industrial ones will be stable, older, and more likely conservative. Various kinds of new challenges to global stability are likely to come from this potentially volatile mix of growing populations, radical doctrines, and revolutionary movements arising within large poverty pockets in the South, such as in the fundamentalist Islamic movements of North Africa, and growing conservatism among the stable or even shrinking (and increasingly older) populations of the North.

BUILDING ECOLOGICAL SECURITY

Building ecological security requires a commitment to sound policies designed to restore the equilibrium among human populations, between human populations and nature, and between humans and other organisms. This means taking measures to stem population overshoot in poorer countries when the demands of growing populations are clearly causing environmental degradation. But it also means that the industrial countries must reevaluate their own excessive resource consumption. A more sustainable world can only be created if people take responsibility for living within nature's constraints. Building a more sustainable world implies redirecting so-called defense spending from treating the visible symptoms of insecurity to attacking the causes—many of which are closely related to patterns of demographic change. It is much more cost-effective to spend a billion dollars promoting family planning or AIDS education in potentially unstable countries than it is to engage in far more expensive police actions later on.

Building ecological security requires a major long-term shift in thinking about the purpose of foreign and defense policies that can only be briefly explored here. Curbing rapid population growth is an obvious place to begin. But even attempts to reduce population growth rates have become politically difficult because many politicians are unwilling to confront the politically powerful pro-natalist forces and values that originated during a period of history when the future survival of Homo sapiens could be ensured only through vigorous reproduction. As John Weeks has put it, "It must be remembered that all nations that have survived to the present day did so by overcoming high levels of mortality."[58] Thus, in the United States and around the world, population policy has vacillated from one administration and leadership group to the next.

One of the biggest barriers to reducing population growth is a growing emphasis on human rights and privileges at the expense of human responsibilities. In the industrialized countries the policy emphasis has been on individual freedoms with little focus on obligations to the rest of society. Thus, if a married couple wants to have six children, or to own several cars and homes, it is considered their right to do so, whatever the impact on the global environment. But particularly in countries with rapidly growing populations, couples have some responsibility to society to limit the number of offspring for the common good; all societies, moreover, have a responsibility to conserve the earth's vital resources.

Because of the widespread emphasis on rights and freedoms, there is a tendency to duck the tough issues of responsibilities for behavioral changes that must take place in many areas of the world in order to restore ecological security. Thus, at the 1994 UN conference on Population and Development, the program was dominated by various interest groups pressing their own agendas at the expense of resolute action on family planning. As Lindsey Grant has put it, nowhere does the resulting UN Action Program state "that population growth should stop. Nowhere are growing countries urged to give high priority to stopping (or even slowing) population growth."[59]

Another roadblock to resolute action is persistent quibbling among population scholars over the depth and impact of these demographic problems. While there is a preponderance of scholarly opinion that the world's population is now much too large, many academic hairs have been split over its optimum level.[60] Growth advocates, such as economist Julian Simon, only muddy the waters when they declare that the human population is the ultimate resource and "that population growth, along with the lengthening of human life, is a moral and material triumph."[61] These demographic ideologues, for the most part living in comfort in the industrial countries, can easily ignore the suffering of the growing numbers of starving and malnourished in the less-affluent neighborhoods on the disadvantaged side of the demographic divide.

Finally, the timid and contentious domestic and international politics of family planning also hinders efforts to deal resolutely with the perils of rapid population growth. A political split between countries of the North and South first became apparent in 1974 at the World Population Conference in Bucharest, Romania. The industrial countries, led by the United States, sought the adoption of a World Population Plan of Action which would have made family planning a central part of economic development efforts. But many representatives from less-industrialized countries portrayed this as an intrusion into their internal affairs and argued that economic development is the "best contraceptive." This split persisted over the next decade and surfaced again at the 1984 International Population Conference in Mexico City. And, at the Rio de Janeiro "Earth Summit" of 1992 and the 1994 Cairo population conference, the core population issues were very much ignored because of pressure from fundamentalist religious organizations, various women's groups, and politicians from poor countries who sought to blame the bulk of the world's ills on the industrial countries.

Discontinuities in U.S. policies have also been a significant part of the problem. The United States has historically been at the forefront of family planning activity. Throughout the 1940s, noted demographers such as Dudley Kirk, Frank Notestein, and Kingsley Davis called attention to the impact of colonialism and the eventual independence movements on population growth. These insights influenced U.S. policy, and every Secretary of State from Dean Rusk to George Schultz supported family planning. The United States began to encourage population limitation as a central tenet of development policy under the Kennedy Administration, and this emphasis persisted through the Carter Administration.[62]

Since the mid-1980s, however, this support has been wavering—held hostage to partisan politics associated with the new conservatism. In 1984, the United States astonished family planning advocates when the former Secretary of State James Baker, addressing the World Population Conference in Mexico City, declared population growth to be a natural phenomenon that neither advanced nor hindered economic growth, in spite of the stagnation experienced in dozens of poor countries with rapidly growing populations.[63]

The United Nations Population Fund (UNFPA) is the largest multilateral agency providing family planning services, with programs in 130 countries. The United States used to fund about 20 percent of the UNFPA budget. Although the UNFPA precludes the funding of programs that encourage abortion, in 1985 the agency gave a $10 million grant to China—a country that includes abortion as a method of family planning—to support maternal and health care as well as contraceptive research. The Reagan Administration, seeking to placate domestic anti-abortion forces, seized upon the China issue and began withholding the U.S. contribution to UNFPA.

When George Bush became president in 1989, there was hope that the U.S. contribution to UNFPA would be restored. Bush had been an outspoken advocate of family planning in the 1960s and 1970s, and even advocated making contraceptives available worldwide on a massive scale.[64] When he was appointed Ambassador to the United Nations in 1971, Bush called existing population trends a prescription for tragedy and chaos, and expressed the hope that greater UN efforts would have a major impact.[65] But family planning assistance under Bush continued to be held hostage to political infighting between liberals, who favor family planning, and conservatives, who often oppose such policies for religious reasons, and the cuts were not restored. The Clinton Administration has taken a more vigorous position on population growth issues and restored some funding for international family planning, but a Republican Congress has continued to limit administration flexibility.

There is international consensus on the need for population stabilization. In 1989, seventy-nine countries, including the United States, met in Amsterdam and drew up a plan to stabilize population growth and to extend the availability of contraceptives to 75 percent of the world's women. The resulting Amsterdam Declaration called for worldwide family planning assistance to increase to $10.5 billion by 1991, a goal that was never even approached. Moving rapidly to reach the goals set forth in the Amsterdam Declaration would certainly be a major step toward increasing population stability and world security. The United States could fund a significant part of such a program simply by diverting some spending from the production of expensive and exotic weapons to foreign assistance.

The Clinton Administration has given population policy a higher profile. Clinton restored the U.S. contribution to UNFPA early in his first term. But congressional cuts in the foreign affairs budget in 1996 resulted in a 35-percent reduction in resources for international population assistance. Anti-abortion forces in Congress argue that there is no way to keep family planning money that goes overseas separate from abortion money and have continued to obstruct efforts to release birth-control funding.[66]

Dealing with global migration pressures is also a thorny issue, but slowing population growth in economically depressed societies would eliminate many of the problems that result in large-scale migration. Reducing or reversing the worldwide influx of people into densely packed cities requires local action and, with the exception of China, has not been a high priority in most countries. Again, this problem would be addressed by more successful family planning in rural areas. But future sustainable development will require educational efforts and creative alternatives to stem the tide of people migrating to already crowded and polluted cities. Such alternatives might include policies to redirect economic growth to smaller cities, as well as increasing economic incentives to farmers in order to keep more people in agricultural occupations.

Other demographic shifts that are likely to create future insecurity, particularly the growing impact of aging in the industrial countries, require resolute action, including raising taxes to fund future pension and medical benefits. But politicians run for office on promises of tax cuts and are hesitant to address entitlement issues for fear of alienating the growing number of elderly voters. In the United States, even technical changes in the setting of the consumer price index (CPI), which is used to index inflation for social security payments, have become politically contentious because they might reduce the size of future pensions. Obviously problems of financing future entitlements will force action on this set of issues, and compromises will be required in order to avoid open intergenerational conflict.

It is unfortunate that grappling with these ecological security issues, which require major shifts in values and behavior, takes place at a time when governments worldwide are already coping with budget crises. Thus, it is becoming more difficult to provide the family planning and economic assistance necessary to help affected countries spring out of their demographic traps. Coping with these emerging demographic changes and uncertainties will require anticipatory thinking and action on an unprecedented scale, as well as new policy approaches aimed at preserving ecological security and thereby the welfare of future generations on both sides of the demographic divide.

QUESTIONS FOR FURTHER STUDY

1. What does Pirages mean by "ecological security"? How is that security threatened by human behaviors at the end of the twentieth century?
2. What is meant by the "demographic transition"? What is the normal course that this transition takes in industrializing countries? Why is there a risk that some of the developing nations will not make a successful transition to the third, mature phase of the transition?
3. What are the problems associated with rapid urbanization in the Third World? What can be done to reduce the impact of these problems?
4. What are the problems associated with the "graying" of the population in advanced industrial nations? How does the graying of the North combine with rapid population growth in the South to produce global friction and instability?
5. What, in your view, should the world community do to promote global ecological security?

Notes

1. See Alfred Crosby, *America's Forgotten Pandemic: The Influenza Epidemic of 1918* (Cambridge: Cambridge University Press, 1990).
2. See Thomas F. Homer-Dixon, "On the Threshold: Environmental Changes As Causes of Acute Conflict," *International Security* (Fall 1991); Thomas F. Homer-Dixon, "Environmental Scarcities and Violent Conflict: Evidence from Cases," *International Security* (Summer 1994).
3. See Nazli Choucri and Robert North, *Nations in Conflict* (San Francisco: W. H. Freeman, 1975); Nazli Choucri, *Population Dynamics and International Violence* (Lexington, MA: D. C. Heath, 1974).
4. See J. Donald Hughes, *Ecology in Ancient Civilizations* (Albuquerque: University of New Mexico Press, 1975).
5. See Ben Wattenberg, *The Birth Dearth* (New York: Pharos Books, 1989); The World Bank, *Averting the Old Age Crisis* (New York: Oxford University Press, 1994).

6. The term comes from Lester Brown and Jodi Jacobson, *Our Demographically Divided World* (Washington: Worldwatch Institute, 1986).

7. The term demographic transition was developed by Frank Notestein in 1945. Frank Notestein, "Population: The Long View," in T. W. Schultz, ed., *Food for the World* (Chicago: University of Chicago Press, 1945).

8. Dirk J. van de Kaa, "Europe's Second Demographic Transition," *Population Bulletin* (March 1987), p. 19.

9. Figures from The Population Reference Bureau, "1996 World Population Data Sheet" (Washington: 1996).

10. *Our Demographically Divided World,* pp. 32–34.

11. See Anders Wijkman and Lloyd Timberlake, *Natural Disasters: Acts of God or Acts of Man* (London: Earthscan, 1984).

12. "1996 World Population Data Sheet."

13. *World Resources 1992–93* (New York: Oxford University Press, 1992), p. 30.

14. Jonathan Randal, "A Dwindling Natural Resource," *The Washington Post* (May 13, 1992). See also Peter H. Gleick, "Water and Conflict: Fresh Water Resources and International Security," *International Security* (Summer 1993).

15. *World Resources 1996–97* (New York: Oxford University Press, 1996), Table 10–1.

16. See Lester Brown, *Who Will Feed China?* (New York: W.W. Norton, 1995).

17. United Nations Development Program, *Human Development Report 1995* (New York: Oxford University Press, 1995), p. 14.

18. United Nations Development Program, *Human Development Report 1992* (New York: Oxford University Press, 1992), p. 35.

19. Data from The World Bank, *World Development Report 1995* (New York: Oxford University Press, 1995), Table 1.

20. See Dennis Pirages, "Political Stability and Conflict Management," in Ted Gurr, ed., *Handbook of Political Conflict* (New York: The Free Press, 1980), pp. 432–441.

21. "The Floodgates Are Bursting," *Business Week* (September 9, 1991). See also Myron Weiner, *The Global Migration Crisis: Challenge to States and to Human Rights* (New York: HarperCollins, 1995), Table 5.

22. Susan Kalish, "Immigration: IRCA Tops Out," *Population Today* (November 1992).

23. See Doris Meissner, "Managing Migrations," *Foreign Policy* (Spring 1992).

24. United Nations figures cited in Hal Kane, *The Hour of Departure: Forces That Create Refugees and Migrants* (Washington: Worldwatch Institute, 1995), pp. 18–19.

25. *The Hour of Departure,* p. 24.

26. Data from The World Bank, *World Development Report 1992* (New York: Oxford University Press, 1992), Table 31.

27. *World Resources 1996–97,* p. 3.

28. Figures from *World Resources 1988–89* (New York: Basic Books, 1988), pp. 36–37.

29. *World Resources 1988–89,* p. 37.

30. Leon Bouvier, "Planet Earth 1984–2034," *Population Bulletin* (February 1984).

31. Eugene Robinson, "Crime Is Choking Rio," *The Washington Post* (October 4, 1990).

32. Ecological footprint is the term used to describe the impact of demand for resources on surrounding environments, in Mathis Wackernagel and William Rees, *Our Ecological Footprint* (Philadelphia: New Society, 1996).

33. *World Resources 1988–89,* p. 45; *World Resources 1996–97,* pp. 64–65.

34. *World Resources 1996–97,* p. 59.

35. Edward Cody, "Mexico City Choked by Pollution Emergency," *The Washington Post* (March 26, 1992).

36. See Laurie Garrett, *The Coming Plague: Newly Emerging Diseases in a World out of Balance* (New York: Farrar, Straus and Giroux, 1994).

37. World Health Organization, *The World Health Report 1995* (Geneva: World Health Organization, 1995), Chapter 1.

38. John Bongaarts, "Global Trends in AIDS mortality," *Population and Development Review* (March 1996).

39. Laurie Garrett, op. cit., p. 571.

40. See Dennis Pirages, "Microsecurity: Disease Organisms and Human Well-Being," *The Washington Quarterly* (Autumn 1995).

41. Taken from "Emerging Viruses, Emerging Threat," *Science* (January 19, 1990).

42. Figures from "1996 World Population Data Sheet."

43. Quoted in Steven Mufson, "Debt Poses Politicians Staggering Challenges," *The Washington Post* (September 29, 1992).

44. *Aging Populations: The Social Policy Implications* (Paris: OECD, 1988), p. 22.

45. Steven Pearlstein and Clay Chandler, "Medicare: After the Rhetoric, a Reality Check," *The Washington Post* (November 3, 1996).

46. Anne Swardson, "French Transit Workers Press Retirement at 55," *The Washington Post* (January 25, 1997).

47. *Aging Populations: The Social Policy Implications*, p. 32. The German figures are for West Germany.

48. Linda Martin, "The Graying of Japan," *Population Bulletin* (July 1989), p. 6.

49. Japan Institute of Population Problems, *Population Projections for Japan: 1985–2025* (Tokyo: Ministry of Health and Welfare, 1987).

50. Fred Hiatt, "Japanese Robots Reproducing Like Rabbits," *The Washington Post* (January 2, 1990).

51. Jean-Claude Chesnais and Wang Shuxin, "Population Aging, Retirement Policy and Living Conditions of the Elderly in China," *Population*, Vol. 2, p. 7. See also H. Yuan Tien, et al., "China's Demographic Dilemmas," *Population Bulletin* (June 1992).

52. Anne Swardson, op. cit.; Matt Marshall, "German Panel Proposes to Cut Pension Levels," *The Wall Street Journal* (January 31, 1997).

53. Quoted in Jackson Diehl, "Exodus of Soviet Jews May Alter Israel's Fate," *The Washington Post* (June 10, 1990).

54. John Weeks, "The Demography of Islamic Nations," *Population Bulletin* (December 1989), p. 13.

55. Figures are from "1996 World Population Data Sheet."

56. Data from "1996 World Population Data Sheet."

57. "1996 World Population Data Sheet."

58. "The Demography of Islamic Nations," p. 18.

59. Lindsey Grant, *Juggernaut: Growth on a Finite Planet* (Washington: Island Press, 1996), p. 240.

60. See Paul Ehrlich and Anne Ehrlich, *The Population Explosion* (New York: Simon and Schuster, 1990); William Catton, *Overshoot: The Ecological Basis for Revolutionary Change* (Urbana, IL: University of Illinois Press, 1980); S. Fred Singer, ed., *Is There an Optimum Level of Population?* (New York: McGraw-Hill, 1991); Robert Goodland, "The Case That the World Has Reached Limits," *Population and Environment* (Spring 1992).

61. Julian Simon, *The Ultimate Resource* (Princeton: Princeton University Press, 1981), p. 9.

62. See Peter Donaldson, "On the Origins of the United States Government's International Population Policy," *Population Studies* (November 1990).

63. Reported in Chet Atkins, "International Family Planning: Where's the Leadership?" *Washington Post* (August 27, 1991).

64. Jessica Mathews, "World Population: As the President Turns," *The Washington Post* (November 1, 1990).

65. Richard Gardiner, "Bush, the UN and Too Many People," *New York Times* (September 22, 1989). See also Barbara Crane and Jason Finkle, "The United States, China, and the United Nations Population Fund: Dynamics of U.S. Policymaking," *Population and Development Review* (March 1989).

66. John F. Harris, "Clinton Requests Release of Birth Control Funds," *The Washington Post* (February 1, 1997).

19 / Building World Security: The Need for Strengthened International Institutions

ROBERT C. JOHANSEN

OVERCOMING INTELLECTUAL AND INSTITUTIONAL INERTIA

If we want to enhance U.S. and global security in the midst of the extraordinary political, economic, and environmental changes occurring throughout the world, we would do well to heed the historians who have warned that generals (and others) tend to overlook inconvenient yet threatening realities and prepare defenses that are more appropriate for the last war than for the next one. One might expect that mental inertia would not be a problem during a time of major change, such as the end of the Cold War and dissolution of the Soviet Union, because obvious transformations can hardly be ignored. Yet, most governments have not responded adequately to the new security needs of the post-Cold War era. Moreover, they have failed to take advantage of the opportunities that arose after 1989 for institutionalizing fundamental changes in how countries relate to one another—even though these have been rare opportunities that human civilizations seldom encounter.

Although many people in North America and Western Europe in the 1990s have felt smugly assured that the United States (with the help of an expanded NATO alliance and other allies) can solve future security problems by clever adaptations of policies used during the Cold War period, they are, as previous chapters in this book demonstrate, sorely mistaken. Merely extending past policies into the future will not solve the deep-seated security problems lurking beneath the apparent peace and prosperity of the industrialized nations. The world's peoples have become so functionally interdependent that the existing political fragmentation of the planet, based on autonomous nation-states, simply provides inadequate forms of governance. As the international Commission on Global Governance concluded, "Instead of coming together around a common vision of the way forward, the world seems in danger of losing its way."[1]

While many governments have adopted new rhetoric extolling the need for multilateral cooperation, most have refused to institutionalize a new code of international conduct that is more peaceful, just, and environmentally sound. Because there have been no serious strategic military threats to global stability or to U.S. leadership in recent years, we have been living in the midst of the most significant opportunity for changing the international system to have occurred in many decades, if not in several centuries. I am convinced that we are witnesses to a tragedy of unimaginable proportions as we continue to allow the extraordinary opportunities for establishing more effective international institutions to slip through our fingers. *If* there were good leadership, and *if* there were strong public pressures to do so, it would be possible to build a radically more just and peaceful global society, with reliable governing institutions—at costs that are far more manageable than what the future is likely to extract if fundamental changes are not made now.

Policymakers in many capitals seem snared in perhaps the oldest and most widely honored maxim of international relations: "If you want peace, prepare for war." This is not the place to debate whether preparations for war throughout history have more often lead to war than to peace.[2] But it seems increasingly clear—at least to those people not closely wedded to the vested interests of traditional policies—that *if we want peace we must prepare for peace.* This can be done by strengthening international norms and institutions *against* war and by eliminating conditions that give rise to violence—*not* by fine-tuning institutions and arsenals for the conduct of war.

At the heart of a new security concept must be a transformation of views on the role of military power. This transformation was anticipated, even before the end of the Cold War, by such noted world leaders as Willy Brandt of Germany and Olaf Palme of Sweden, and carried forward in reports of well-known international commissions that were chaired by them and by Gro Harlem Brundtland of Norway, Julius Nyerere of Tanzania, Ingvar Carlsson of Sweden, and others.[3] These international commissions suggested many positive measures—most of which have not been integrated into any major government's policies—to revamp the customary code of international conduct and to strengthen international institutions by equipping them with sufficiently attractive representation and accountability at the global level, so that they may manage the pressing economic, military, and environmental problems that no national government can handle separately.

In particular, these commissions have introduced two vital concepts for the construction of future world security policies: *common security* and *comprehensive security.* Common security is rooted in the recognition that a country either holds security in common with other nations or simply cannot achieve it.[4] Given widespread access to extremely destructive technologies and weapons, nations "can no longer hope to protect their citizens through unilateral military measures." Indeed, "all states, even the most powerful, are dependent in the end upon the good sense and restraint of other nations."[5] To be successful, new security policies must also be far more comprehensive in addressing nonmilitary problems. Comprehensive security suggests that, if the first duty of government is to guarantee safety for its people, then new forms of governance must protect people against whatever endangers them—be it environmental jeopardy, economic deprivation, unwanted migratory pressures, or "ethnic cleansing," as well as the threat of foreign armies.

Despite some reductions in world military expenditures since the height of the Cold War, U.S. and world security priorities fall far short of a new orientation that would attempt to encompass the security of all nations and reduce the role of military power in international affairs generally. In the mid-1990s, U.S. military spending measured in constant dollars *exceeded* the average annual expenditures during the Cold War in the decade preceding the Reagan Administration's massive buildup.[6] Most national security managers still do not, in their practices, acknowledge that people's security in the future will rest on finding alternatives to the military postures that have characterized the nation-state system up to now. Symptomatically, more attention in Washington has been devoted to identifying a future alternative to the former communist security threat than to finding an alternative to the international security system that has produced recurring military threats throughout its existence, since the Peace of Westphalia in 1648. This system never has prevented war permanently and presumably never will. Yet, permanent prevention of major war must be the aim of any serious security policy today.

Although U.S. policy now includes more sensitivity to multilateral diplomacy than in the 1980s, it still relies too much on military power and traditional bilateral diplomacy, and too little on launching a multilateral diplomatic program to denuclearize and then demilitarize the global system with reliable institutions for the maintenance of peace. Policies seem blind to the possibility that even the large U.S. arsenals of the future—although unequaled elsewhere—may still be outflanked by equity-seeking desperate societies with crude weapons of mass destruction, or by nonmilitary security threats (such as environmental degradation, economic decline, or migratory pressures) that simply cannot be managed by even enormous military might or flawless bilateral diplomacy from a single superpower.

If the United States replaces the East-West conflict of the Cold War era with North-South conflict between the rich and poor countries, or with intercivilizational conflict (as, for example, between Christians and Muslims) without aiming in the long run to replace the balance of military power with a legally constituted balance of political power, little will be done to reduce the likelihood or costliness of violence in the long run. Nor will the maintenance of the present international system be an effective bulwark against new nonmilitary challenges to security that are likely to arise in the future. The way to make international relations more peaceful in the long run is to *institutionalize* a more peaceful code of conduct and the means to maintain it. New global institutions are needed to prevent backsliding once gains have been made, and to provide incentives to engage reluctant governments in a more pacific code of conduct.

What policies and institutions could truly come to grips with the many security challenges that press upon people throughout the world? In the preceding chapters of this volume, the authors have recommended a variety of specific initiatives to enhance security; in this chapter, I will attempt to integrate these recommendations and move beyond them, by charting the long-range direction that policies and institutions must follow if the people of the United States and the rest of the world are to survive with dignity for themselves and respect for each other. My intention is to develop guidelines that can inform the policies of *all* nations, and also to show how the United States, in particular, can change its own direction to chart a fundamentally new path.

A PRINCIPLED WORLD POLICY

To interrupt the inertial tendency to remain unresponsive to changing security problems, we need a *principled* world policy—one designed to implement and institutionalize clearly desirable values that serve not just one or several national interests, but what might be called the "human interest."[7] To embrace key principles for the conduct of nations can produce several positive results. First, an awareness of central principles gives constancy to policy and reduces the damage arising from partisan politics when elected officials or opportunistic candidates, in the interest of obtaining public support, fan the flames of adversarial nationalism, reinforce exaggerated fears of foreigners or those of a different ethnicity or religion, or suggest that jingoism, militarism, economic exploitation, and the stifling of dissent are congruent with patriotism.

Moreover, just as a principled policy may reduce the disruption of narrow-minded nationalism and domestic political partisanship, so, too, the establishment of a principled policy can alleviate the conflict-generating tendency in international relations to believe that one's own nation may legitimately give higher priority to its own *interests* than to other peoples' *rights*. This tendency is one manifestation of what could be called "national partisanship" in an age of global interdependence. In a world where the entire human species becomes an important constituency in decision making, any exclusively national perspective—however bipartisan it may be from the standpoint of domestic politics—is partisan from a global perspective.

Finally, by following an explicitly principled code of conduct, policymakers could more readily encourage all governments to follow suit and to institutionalize diplomatic progress. To have a peaceful and just world order, people and governments must increasingly move away from an us-versus-them mentality toward common standards of conduct and fair play for all. The expansion of human identities that this implies need not be seen as an unwise sacrifice of legitimate national interests; as in domestic society, one person can willingly give up his or her "right" to disregard the law in return for other persons' compliance with it. Washington can advance legitimate U.S. rights most effectively, amidst the claims of other governments, when all operate within a global political structure that requires disputes to be settled in a principled manner through political and legal means.

Five basic principles, each suggesting innovations in international institutions, are useful in defining the human interest and shaping policies that will enhance security for people in the United States and all other nations: *reciprocity, equity, environmental sustainability, democratization,* and *demilitarization*. Each is described below.

Reciprocity

Reciprocity, the first and most fundamental principle, simply means that a government willingly evaluates its own actions by the same standards that it applies to other states' behavior. A national government that respects the principle of reciprocity does not insist on a right for itself that it does not willingly grant to others, nor does it specify a duty for others that it does not accept for itself.[8] This principle is almost universally endorsed by people regardless of nationality, religion, or ideology; in practice, however, it is violated frequently, in part because the world lacks institutions to encourage respect for it. In any case, its universal endorsement provides a basis for attempting to hold governments accountable to a fundamental ordering principle that transcends cultural differences.

If rigorously implemented, this principle could by itself eliminate most wars and dampen arms buildups. Since no nation or group wants to be the target of military aggression, no group can legitimately act aggressively itself. Moreover, if the United States and other nuclear powers claim a right to retain and develop new weapons of mass destruction, they can hardly find persuasive grounds on which to deny a similar "right" to others. If Washington seeks to prevent the spread of nuclear weapons, it will be more likely to succeed by advocating *universal* constraints, applicable to itself as well, and by establishing international monitors and enforcement to uphold the principle of nonproliferation for all.

A rigorous respect for reciprocity also discourages one of the most serious dangers associated with a principled foreign policy: namely, that its proponents may assume a moralistic attitude, based on the assumption that their policies are more holy or virtuous than the policies of other governments. They may insist on their own way, evangelize for the "right" point of view, and rationalize military threats to implement their policies. To nullify this common, yet poisonous tendency, reciprocal rights and obligations should be authoritatively upheld wherever possible by multilateral institutions representing the human interest rather than a single national, ethnic, or religious interest.

Equity

The second principle, to enhance equity throughout global society, arises from a moral desire for human justice and equal opportunity, from an economic need for greater economic rationality and productivity, and from a political need to generate global cooperation and a willingness to sacrifice for the good of all. This principle aims to expand economic opportunity in ways that meet basic human needs, promote social integration among potentially hostile ethnic or religious groups, and achieve a fairer distribution of economic resources and political influence throughout the world.

The unaddressed negative consequences of world capitalist markets now harm all nations, rich and poor alike. Today's economic structures leave more than a billion people living in poverty, facing serious shortages of food, and often leading unproductive lives. In part because the world community has not eliminated glaring inequities, the North's industrial capacity remains underutilized while the South urgently needs—but cannot afford—goods that the North could easily produce. In addition, poverty adds pressures on limited food resources, tillable land, and timber supplies. Overfishing, overgrazing, desertification, and loss of topsoil eventually cause a declining standard of living for the human species everywhere. Poverty also stimulates unwanted population growth that could be reduced if oppression of women and economic insecurity were reduced throughout the world.

From the standpoint of pragmatic global politics, poverty needs to be abolished because the worldwide cooperation required to build a durable security system cannot be achieved with the planet divided, economically half slave and half free. Poverty also leads to degradation of the biosphere, because poor governments often feel compelled to reduce domestic environmental standards to promote development and attract foreign capital and to destroy rain forests in order to obtain hard currencies. Accordingly, the abolition of global poverty would serve the security interests of the rich and middle classes even if they have little moral concern for justice or the well-being of the poor.

Sustainability

The third principle, environmental sustainability, emphasizes that a deeper respect for nature is essential to maintaining a healthy biosphere, without which lives of human dignity will not be possible. Environmental decline poses planet-enveloping dangers capable of causing such irretrievable damage that they constitute one of the most serious long-range security problems facing the world today. As country after country declared at the World Conference on Environment and Development in Rio de Janeiro in 1992, life-support systems for the human species face severe danger from pollution, resource depletion, and population pressure.[9] These dangers obviously cannot be addressed through the traditional security instruments of military strength; only more effective international institutions, with legally binding powers and the transfer of financial resources and brainpower from military to environmental purposes, will enable the species to enhance its long-term security.

The idea of global sustainability suggests that the current flurry of fragmented international activity should be orchestrated within an integrated global program to set permissible levels for the emission of pollutants, to apply money and technology throughout the world at the points where they are most likely to produce substantial international benefits (regardless of the host society's ability to pay), and to enforce agreed-upon standards and financial obligations. The goal is to achieve a sustainable world society that "satisfies its needs without jeopardizing the prospects of future generations." From now on, each generation must take responsibility for ensuring "that the next one inherits an undiminished natural and economic endowment."[10] This third principle thus dovetails with the second, because the goal of sustainability takes root in the desire to achieve *intergenerational* equity.

Democratization

Democratization, the fourth principle, aims to increase every government's accountability to the people who are affected by its decisions, regardless of whether those people live inside or outside of that particular country's territory. Ensuring that all governments become and remain accountable to the people who are affected by their decisions is not merely a desirable moral value; immediate steps in that direction are also essential for pragmatic security policies. Without governmental accountability, major decisions—whether made at the national, regional, or global level—will lack sufficient legitimacy and support to avoid unacceptable risks, costs, and violations. To enhance global security through deepening democracy therefore requires progress in both "horizontal" and "vertical" accountability.

"Horizontal accountability" refers to a government's responsibility for activities that extend across national borders. Traditionally, scholars and politicians alike have not recognized a need for any horizontal accountability beyond what would occur through normal diplomatic representation. Increasingly, however, more representative international institutions are needed to enable citizens to influence the decisions that directly affect them, even if they are made in another country. This is so because, as global interdependence increases, the number of decisions made outside the United States that directly affect U.S. citizens also increases. For example, the economic security of the U.S. public depends on decisions made in Tokyo or Brussels as well as in New York and Chicago; to erect a tariff wall of economic protection, or engage in Japan-bashing, will not eliminate this reality.[11] Likewise, if people in other lands pollute the atmosphere, then U.S. citizens suffer environmental degradation without representation.[12] Clearly, if the political, economic, and environmental decisions that affect U.S. people increasingly occur outside the United States while U.S. and global political institutions remain unchanged, then the element of democracy in U.S. political life declines—even though fair elections, a free press, and competing political parties remain operational within the United States as they have in the past.

As military force becomes less applicable to problem solving and less widely accepted as legitimate, and as economic power becomes more widely diffused throughout the world, the United States will want to ensure that its voice is heard in international institutions that are reliable and democratic—and that guarantee rights for global minorities as well as majorities. The society relevant to our lives is now international, as well as national and local, so supporters of democracy must reconstruct sovereignty and transform the profoundly inadequate institutions (in terms of their representativeness, authority, and power) that now exist at the global level.

A healthy concern for cross-border government accountability also entails concern for accountability *within* national domestic contexts—or "vertical accountability"—because global representation cannot fully implement the democratic principle unless the structures beneath it facilitate fair representation. Authoritarian governments are less likely to serve the interests of their people—including security, in the broadest sense—than are more popular, responsive governments. The growth of internal democracy also aids the growth of peace because democratic societies have related more peacefully to each other than they have to authoritarian societies or than authoritarian societies have to each other.[13]

Demilitarization

The fifth and final principle, global demilitarization, is inspired by the desire to reduce the role of military power in international relations generally, not merely to reduce arms of one sort or another. To be sure, one way of constraining the use of military force is to reduce and eliminate weapons that exacerbate insecurities, so demilitarization includes the gradual reduction of armaments; however, it goes far beyond arms control to effect the gradual elimination of all countries' offensive military capabilities. In addition, demilitarization includes steps to free national economies from dependence on military spending, to inform political and educational institutions more accurately about the human interest in enforcing peace through peaceful means, and to nurture changes in the social and psychological patterns that sustain collective violence. Demilitarization aims at dismantling national and international military culture and replacing it with a culture of legal obligation and nonlethal forms of dispute settlement.

Demilitarization is necessary because nations are unlikely to achieve a lasting and just peace within a balance-of-power system, characterized by national armed forces that may be employed unilaterally at any time, along with the continued development of ever more destructive weapons. In addition, demilitarization is required because military institutions, regardless of their ethnic or ideological setting, organize and train people, and shape economic and political institutions, in ways that are antithetical to democratic processes and the other four principles described above.[14] To reduce the role of military power in world affairs while simultaneously addressing people's legitimate fears of potential adversaries will, of course, also require the strengthening of world security institutions.

INSTITUTIONALIZING A PRINCIPLED WORLD POLICY

These five precepts—reciprocity, equity, environmental sustainability, democratization, and demilitarization—form the basis of a principled world policy for the twenty-first century. If followed, they would guide policymakers in shaping policies that would enhance security for all. But embracing these principles is not enough: it is essential that they be *institutionalized* to preclude a return to older, dysfunctional modes of behavior. In the following section, I illustrate the forms that such institutionalization should take to be effective over the long run.

Representative International Institutions

The most reliable path for implementing reciprocity in world affairs is to move toward a more just representation of all people in increasingly democratic international institutions capable of mediating national partisanship. Such institutions could enable or require societies to be less narrowly focused on unfair, selfish interests and to share responsibility for deciding global issues such as how to limit arms, avert global warming, and use scarce global resources for the good of all. Every country's legitimate security interests can be better served by more effective UN institutions for peacekeeping and enforcement, as such institutions broadly share the burdens of global policing, increase the legitimacy of such policing, and constrain negative behavior, while motivating positive policies by other countries.[15]

Most people also have a strong (though seldom acknowledged) self-interest in securing balanced representation in international organizations and courts, where reciprocity can be impartially defined, because such procedures are virtually the only way to increase all peoples' claim to freedom in an increasingly interdependent world in which one person's freedom can easily encroach on another's. Indeed, representation is so strongly related to freedom that Thomas Paine, one of the revered leaders of the American Revolution, wrote that "representative government is freedom."[16] The rejection of broadly representative international institutions to adjudicate disputes and enforce multilateral settlements will lead to future violence or gross injustices, as the strong or ruthless dictate to the weak or fair-minded.

From now on, national societies will, if they remain viable, rely increasingly on international institutions to facilitate major decisions regarding military security, environmental protection, economic well-being, and human rights. Yet such institutions cannot be effective unless they represent fairly the people affected by their decisions, because societies will not implement multilateral decisions unless they have been well represented in the decision-making process.[17] In addition to gradually expanding the representation of those people who are now underrepresented in the operation of global markets and existing international organizations (such as the UN

Security Council and the World Bank), the world community should widen the use of existing impartial political institutions (such as the World Court) and create several new bodies to meet specific needs.

Institutions to Abolish Poverty

The achievement of greater equity will require several institutional innovations. First, the international community should commit itself to eradicate hunger within ten years and extreme poverty within the next twenty-five years, through a determined effort to achieve sustainable development. A systematically replenished World Development Fund is needed to divert financial resources from wasteful, unnecessary spending into the reduction of poverty. States should cooperate in establishing and contributing to such a fund that could be financed through what would amount to an element of universal taxation based on a country's ability to pay.[18] Until such a system is in place, all industrialized nations should publicly commit themselves to set a date by which they will reach the goal of providing at least 1 percent of their GNP for development assistance to the poorest countries.

Second, a World Economic Council, representing the economic ministries of approximately two dozen of the world's economies, should be established to administer the proposed development fund and to coordinate exchange, trade, and development policies affecting the global political economy. Such a body should be more representative of the world's people than the G-7 meetings of the major industrialized powers. The Council should shape global economic policies to give highest priority to meeting human needs and to undertake "preventive development," or efforts to promote social cooperation among different ethnic, religious, and racial groups, among which historic antagonisms are likely to worsen without economic policies aimed at social integration and peacebuilding.[19] Once established, the Economic Council should aim at two long-term goals: the elimination of gross poverty, and the establishment of sustainable economies. Neither of these can be achieved by simply leaving them to the workings of global markets and the profit motive alone.

Third, the International Monetary Fund (IMF), the World Bank, and the General Agreement on Tariffs and Trade (GATT) should be reformed to increase the portion of their aid that is devoted to reducing poverty, as opposed to projects that do not meet basic human needs. International lending institutions should aim to achieve more equitable burden sharing by establishing stable exchange rates, adjusting balance-of-payment deficits, expanding international liquidity, and eradicating the debt that keeps many societies buried in poverty. In addition, the decision-making procedures of these institutions should incorporate expanded representation, both of poor countries' governments and of nongovernmental organizations (NGOs), with a demonstrated success in managing development programs that are sensitive to both equity issues and environmental protection.

With a serious international program to share and conserve resources, abject poverty could be abolished within twenty-five years by using only a portion of total world military expenditures or a modest fraction of the likely increase in income of the richest one-third of the world's population. Greater equity also would encourage the world's peoples—many of whom are now alienated from prevailing political and economic institutions—to support what would become a more fair and stable international political system.

Institutions for Environmentally Sustainable Societies

To cope effectively with the environmental perils it now faces, the world community should establish a new Environmental Council, within the United Nations system, to unify presently scattered efforts to avert climate change and ozone depletion and to manage all other major transnational environmental problems.[20] A new agency is required to speed the treaty-making process (so that a new forum does not need to be created every time another treaty is to be negotiated), to build world political consensus for protecting the biosphere, to implement treaties and ensure compliance with the ozone convention and the more than 170 other existing environmental treaties (most of which have completely inadequate monitoring and enforcement provisions), to address the need for slowing population growth and conserving scarce resources throughout the world, and to provide incentives (primarily financial) to encourage reluctant states to join a unified environmental effort. Such an agency, directly responsible to the UN General Assembly, could have much higher visibility than a haphazard collection of diverse organizations, each focused on only a single aspect of the environmental crisis.

The Council might be made up of representatives from the environmental ministries of a score of national governments, and, building upon the example set by representation in the International Labor Organization, could include representatives from business, labor, and environmental NGOs such as Friends of the Earth, Greenpeace, and EarthAction. Citizens' groups need to be represented in the Council's proceedings because they help enormously in monitoring compliance with global norms, in carrying grievances to governments at all levels, and in building public support for needed environmental measures.

With the proper representation and authority, the Council could set global emission standards for a number of substances, including chlorofluorocarbons and carbon dioxide, that pose especially severe threats to human security. Acting as a truly representative global body, it could help equalize the burden of such standards so that all countries will receive fair treatment. The benefits of experience gained by the existing United Nations Environment Program (UNEP) could be utilized by reconfiguring this body—which now has no authority to enforce compliance with treaties—as a permanent secretariat for the proposed Environmental Council.[21]

Should a government violate international environmental standards, its case could be referred to an environmental mediation service established by the Environmental Council, or referred to the International Court of Justice (World Court). In such cases, the Court should have compulsory jurisdiction and binding authority. Although the implementation of this proposal would constitute a significant departure from past state practice, precisely such a departure is necessary. In 1989, more than thirty countries expressed support for proposals such as these in the Hague Declaration, calling for the establishment of an international body empowered to render legally binding decisions on vital issues affecting the biosphere through veto-free voting procedures.[22] Citizens have yet to press their governments to turn their promising proposals into living reality.

Security enhancement also requires that substantial funds be raised to encourage sustainability. Probably the best mechanism for this would be for the international community to establish a tax on atmospheric releases of carbon dioxide, a step that would begin to pay for a small portion of the enormous environmental damage that fossil fuel consumption has caused. More broadly, charges should be considered for any use of the global commons, including: permissible waste disposal in the atmosphere and oceans; satellites orbiting in space; airplane, ship, and submarine use of airspace and sea lanes; and harvesting of fish from the oceans.

Successful environmental management could nurture networks of cooperation across existing adversarial boundaries, suggest models of representation and veto-free deliberations in strengthened international institutions, establish exemplary instruments of community-wide adjudication and enforcement, and distribute financial assistance in a manner that would encourage compliance with desirable international standards.

Nurturing Democratic Institutions

Because all human beings are entitled to influence the decisions that affect their lives, and because people throughout the world need to feel ownership of UN decisions if they are to honor them, a citizens' chamber or World Assembly should be convened to complement the existing representation of national governments in the General Assembly and Security Council. To expand representation in this way would, in the long run, increase the UN's reliability and integrity. The United Nations could then begin to gain a modest degree of autonomy from national capitals while giving citizens a direct connection with the UN's main political organs, so people would no longer see them only as extensions of the diplomatic community.

A World Assembly might begin, in its first stage, as an "assembly of parliamentarians,"[23] consisting of representatives from national legislatures who have been chosen by the representatives themselves (much as the European Parliament emerged in the European Union); later, it could evolve into a directly elected assembly. Until a World Assembly is established, a "forum of civil society"[24] could easily be held preceding the opening of the annual session of the General Assembly, enabling citizens' groups already accredited to the United Nations as NGOs to articulate their agendas and provide assistance to official delegations interested in promoting a more effective transnational political process.

To nurture democracy at the national level, the world community should also institutionalize, within the United Nations, an electoral monitoring agency to help administer elections (when invited to do so) and to certify whether election results have been fair. Such services, provided on an ad hoc basis in the past, have already contributed to the advancement of peace and stability in Nicaragua, El Salvador, Namibia, Haiti, and elsewhere. Since 1989, the United Nations has received more than ninety requests for electoral assistance of this sort, but it has been unable to respond satisfactorily to all of them.[25] To perform electoral monitoring expeditiously, and with an indisputable reputation for impartiality, can contribute enormously to the prevention of political violence and the growth of democracy, especially in a world where more and more conflict stems from ethnic or religious disputes within countries. The existence of a well-known, reputable electoral agency would also put pressure, through a concrete and unambiguous procedural test, on authoritarian leaders to rise to international electoral standards.

Protecting People's Rights

The advancement of democracy also entails stepped-up efforts to protect people's basic human rights. This can best be achieved over the long run by implementing existing human rights treaties and by upgrading human rights institutions. Drawing upon widely accepted norms, such as those contained in the Universal Declaration of Human Rights, the Covenant on Civil and Political Rights, and the Covenant on Economic, Social, and Cultural Rights, the UN High Commissioner for Human Rights should prepare more detailed reports on states' human rights performance and designate special rapporteurs to investigate gross violations of such rights.[26] To encourage more widespread compliance, priority in the disbursement of economic assistance might be given to those states making serious efforts to implement these covenants.

Centuries of political experience demonstrate the need to maintain strong protection for minorities. Reinforcing such protection at every opportunity will not only encourage minorities to accept and support majoritarian procedures associated with democracy, but also prevent the deepening of fears and hostilities among ethnically diverse populations, such as occurred with tragic consequences in the former Yugoslavia, several republics of the former Soviet Union, and Rwanda, Burundi, Sudan, and elsewhere in the early 1990s. To prevent a spiral of negative reactions that descend into genocidal violence, it will be necessary to strengthen monitoring of human rights by the UN High Commissioner for Human Rights and human rights NGOs, and to establish a permanent international criminal court.

Because most wars in recent years have been primarily intrastate conflicts, and because these conflicts have often entailed massive abuses of human rights, the international community needs to establish clear criteria for deciding when UN intervention is justified. These should combine the Security Council's well-established duty to maintain peace and security with its more recent willingness to consider intervention to stop gross violations of human rights, as in its effort to protect the delivery of food assistance to starving people in Somalia, to restore democracy in Haiti, and to halt "ethnic cleansing" and genocide in Bosnia.[27]

Many governments now recognize a "'duty to intervene' in cases where a government's actions are creating a humanitarian catastrophe"; however, some critics have warned against the expansion of the UN's interventionary mandate.[28] Many governments fear the UN may assume a neo-imperial role in which the great powers intervene in the affairs of less-powerful societies. These legitimate fears can be addressed by ensuring that UN interventions are initiated on principled grounds, that reform of the Security Council gives fairer representation to all societies, that the interests of local people are served wherever UN peacekeeping deployments occur, and (unlike the case in traditional colonialism) that the UN brings resources into the society involved rather than taking them out.

Three issues need to be resolved by international treaty or authoritative UN action: What sorts of emergencies warrant collective intervention? What form of collective authorization is required to justify intervention? And, what interventionary actions are permissible? Intervention probably should be attempted only if it is authorized by the UN (rather than a unilateral act), enjoys wide international support, and is shaped by a desire to avoid loss of life. Of course the Charter legitimizes military enforcement only as a last resort, so preventive measures and positive incentives should be given priority over more forceful instruments.

Decreasing the Role of Military Power

To promote the concept of common security, the United States could chart a new path in permanently reducing the role of military force. A carefully orchestrated diplomatic program should focus on these goals: to reduce all armed forces and reorient all remaining military power toward nonoffensive defenses; to establish clear standards against the spread of all weapons of mass destruction and to undertake negotiations aimed at the complete abolition of nuclear weapons; to support an international treaty curtailing arms transfers and making mandatory the existing voluntary reporting of arms sales to the United Nations' Register of Conventional Arms; and to develop international peacemaking, monitoring, and enforcing institutions to establish and enforce norms of permissible military conduct.

Because the end of bipolar confrontation between Moscow and Washington has not eliminated the danger of nuclear catastrophe, a high-level commission of military and political leaders, convened by the Australian government in Canberra, has called for "immediate and determined efforts . . . to rid the world of nuclear weapons." These leaders concluded that "the proposition that nuclear weapons can be retained in perpetuity and never used—accidentally or by decision—defies credibility." The only effective defense, they asserted, "is the elimination of nuclear weapons" and the development of reliable verification measures.[29] A very similar policy has been advocated by the former Commander-in-Chief of the U.S. Strategic Air Command, General Lee Butler. Along with more than sixty other retired generals and admirals from the United States and Russia, he urged that governments base their security policies on "the declared principle of continuous, complete, and irrevocable elimination of nuclear weapons."[30]

The views of the Canberra Commission and many military officials were buttressed by the opinion of the International Court of Justice, announced in 1996, that (1) the threat or use of nuclear weapons is "contrary to the rules of international law," and (2) all nuclear powers are legally obligated "to pursue in good faith and bring to a conclusion negotiations leading to nuclear disarmament in all its aspects under strict and effective international control."[31] A commitment by the nuclear powers to the abolition of nuclear weapons would also underscore the precept that a strengthened nuclear nonproliferation regime must not be inequitable, with the nuclear "haves" enjoying privileges over the non-nuclear "have nots," thus meeting India's explicit condition for ratifying the Non-Proliferation Treaty and encouraging other undeclared or nuclear powers to forego nuclear weapons programs.

Until nuclear arsenals are dismantled, nuclear-weapon-free zones (NWFZs) should be created wherever possible and expanded as a means of confining nuclear deployments. The establishment of two new NWFZs in 1996—one in Southeast Asia (under the Treaty of Bangkok) and the other in Africa (under the Treaty of Pelindaba)—advanced a far-reaching, desirable South African recommendation that African states cooperate with governments in the existing South Pacific and Latin American NWFZs to establish a "southern hemisphere-wide" nuclear-free region.[32] Creating such a zone in Central and Eastern Europe now takes on urgent importance as countries there are understandably concerned about regional stability after the dissolution of the Soviet Union and Washington's unimaginative, needless commitment to expand NATO eastward despite the evidence that expansion will stimulate Russian nationalism and feelings of insecurity.

To address the violence-inducing perils of conventional arms exports, the international community should establish an arms control agency to integrate, encourage, and monitor diverse efforts to constrain arms transfers. As suggested by Michael Klare and Laura Lumpe in Chapter 9, the components of such a regime should include more transparency by exporters and importers, supplier agreements to ban export of weapons and technologies that are highly destabilizing, regional arms control agreements to curtail competitive buildups, and programs for economic conversion to alleviate the economic disruption and political opposition arising from reduced military production.

Developing Effective Peacemaking and Enforcement

Effective demilitarization also requires the establishment of robust war-prevention and peacemaking instruments. In particular, the world community needs to be better prepared to reduce tensions before they explode, to monitor closely governments' compliance with agreements leading toward a less-militarized code of international conduct, and to enforce compliance with agreed-upon rules when necessary.

As a start, the UN Security Council must become far more serious about serving as the world's crisis management center. Toward that end, the Council and the secretary-general need more timely information, communication, and negotiation capabilities. The Security Council should authorize the secretary-general to employ more roving ambassadors to observe conflicts, report back to the UN Secretariat, and mediate disputes. In addition, the Council and secretary-general should establish standing conflict-resolution committees in each region of the world, to make and implement recommendations for dampening local conflicts before they get out of hand.

In addition, an international monitoring agency under UN auspices is needed to integrate diverse verification functions and to bring the weight of the entire world community behind efforts to ensure compliance with arms control and nonproliferation agreements, environmental standards, and other international rules. Such an agency, equipped with various technical means of surveillance and reconnaissance, could perform a wide variety of vital tasks, including: monitoring of compliance with international agreements restricting the acquisition and use of nuclear, chemical, biological, and conventional weapons; deterring clandestine testing of missiles or war-heads anywhere on earth; observing cease-fire lines, monitoring implementation of economic sanctions, and assisting UN peacekeeping and enforcement missions; discouraging illegal technology shipments, infiltration of arms across borders, and covert operations; gathering evidence for prosecution of those charged with "ethnic cleansing" and other war crimes; and helping resolve questions of fact that national intelligence services by themselves are incapable of resolving to the satisfaction of each other, thereby allowing UN decisions to be made without relying on secondhand (and possibly biased) intelligence reports from member governments.

Improved capabilities for surveillance and negotiation need to be complemented with several other instruments to deter those who might pose a threat to the peace. First, the Security Council should give the secretary-general blanket authority, in advance of any particular crisis, to dispatch unarmed UN observers at any time within a limited corridor along borders anywhere in the world. After the world community grows accustomed to this practice, the Council might extend similar advance authority for the secretary-general to send UN observers not only to borders, but to any place in the world where he or she determines that their presence is needed to contribute to peace.

Second, the more sophisticated conflict management and peace enforce-ment[33] needed in the future can be aided enormously by the creation of permanent UN civilian police and peacekeeping forces. Until now, the United Nations has been handicapped in its reliance on ad hoc peacekeeping forces, because the Secretary-General cannot dispatch a standing, UN-commanded force to a trouble spot immediately. If better-trained and more numerous UN personnel were available for earlier deployment, and if they were highly skilled in relating to local populations and carrying out sophisticated enforcement under unified UN command, they could help avert the eruption of violence, possibly elicit sufficient local consent for UN operations to work with local law-enforcement authorities, and enforce international law on individuals rather than against an entire society. A permanent volunteer force could more effectively transform potentially violent regional conflicts into peacebuilding processes by working collaboratively among local, national, and international authorities. Even in its infancy, a permanent UN force could help (as have the ad hoc UN peacekeeping forces) to deter intrastate collective violence, interstate border violations, and small-scale aggression by militarily adventurous countries.

What is proposed here differs from past UN peacekeeping not only in its permanence, but also in its composition of individually recruited persons instead of military units drawn from various national armed forces. Direct recruitment by the UN from volunteers of all countries would enable personnel burdens to be shared more equitably than at present, without raising fears that any government's national military units would play a partisan role underneath the UN flag, or take orders from national capitals instead of UN headquarters. To have highly trained young people of many nationalities working side by side, regardless of their homelands' former or current animosities, would powerfully symbolize the prospects for enforcing norms on behalf of the world community without prejudice to any nationality. Such a force would help set the institutional stage for educating publics and governments about the possibilities for gradually curtailing national uses of military power by impartially enforcing key rules against armament and aggression.[34]

A standing UN force would also permit the concept of "UN-protected countries" to become a realistic possibility. Small countries could feel some reassurance if UN forces were always ready to come to their aid in time of need. By having an opportunity to draw upon UN peacekeepers, small UN-protected countries, which are unable in any case to protect themselves militarily against larger aggressors, would be able to relieve themselves of the financial burden of maintaining their own armed forces. This, in turn, would free them of the danger that their own military would threaten democracy (or the prospects for it) at home. As the UN role in maintaining security for small states increased, the temptation for external military powers to intervene would decline; incentives for international arms sales, foreign bases, and the projection of military power abroad would also decrease.

Until such a permanent force is established, *standby* UN forces, made up of selected national units contributed by member states, should be readied so that they can respond quickly if needed. Supportive governments should respond favorably to the Secretary-General's request for as many countries as possible to train and prepare earmarked units of their armed forces to be on call for UN service within twenty-four hours.[35] The United Nations should also establish its own training center for officers and specialists who are earmarked by member states for service in UN peacekeeping units.

Making the Security Council More Representative and Effective

With the Security Council frequently rendering critical decisions for the first time in its fifty-year history, it should not perpetuate the disproportionate representation of the victorious powers in World War II, as the framers of the Charter in 1945 understandably required. Instead, the Council's membership should be changed to reflect current political and economic realities. Specifically, it should be expanded by six to eight members to include influential countries and regions that were not well represented at the founding of the organization.

Japan, for example, does not have a permanent seat in the Security Council, yet Japan is a major source of investment capital and operates the world's second largest economy; it also contributes the second largest amount of money to the UN budget and donates more overseas development aid than any other country.[36] For Japan not to be represented among the permanent members is politically unfair, economically unwise, and morally unjustifiable. Strong cases can also be made for Germany, also a major economic power, and for India, the world's largest democracy, to hold permanent seats.

Equity also requires broader representation from less-industrialized segments of world society, including states in Africa, Latin America, and South Asia. In order to avoid extending the veto power of permanent members to additional states (which would undoubtedly impede timely decision making), a new category of five "reserved seats" might be developed for such countries as Japan, Germany, India, Brazil, and Nigeria (or South Africa). The other nonpermanent, rotating members should be increased by two or three, thus broadening representation while still enabling the Council to remain small enough to function well. If the Council's permanent and reserved membership were expanded to fairly represent all major cultural regions and well over half of the world's population and economic productivity, the Council's legitimacy would increase substantially. Such a body would possess power and authority far beyond the present Council, enabling it to speak more truly for the people of the world and to exert enormous pressure for assuring compliance with its decisions.

Because the veto power enjoyed by the five permanent members (Britain, China, France, Russia, and the United States) is a glaring example of inequity, and allows a country to place itself outside the law by blocking criticism or enforcement action against itself, use of the veto should be circumscribed so that no member can prevent the world community from trying to hold it accountable to existing international norms. As a first step, negative votes from two permanent members, rather than one, could be agreed upon as a requirement before a negative decision would be made. When the veto can be phased out entirely, positive decisions might require a three-fourths vote of all members.

As the Security Council increases its enforcement role it should establish clearer guidelines for employing economic sanctions and other coercive measures. Such guidelines would help prevent excessive use of force by national officials pursuing their own goals within a UN operation, as occurred during Operation Desert Storm (when the UN relinquished control over the scale of destruction exerted by the coalition forces it uncritically endorsed), and should ensure that UN forces are not deployed without widespread political support, adequate size, and special training.

Utilizing International Law

As part of the process of demilitarization, the world community should extend into the international domain the use of those instruments that are most widely accepted in the domestic arena for solving disputes between individuals and groups: processes of impartial adjudication and legal settlement. Security Council members should remind themselves and other states of their Charter obligation to settle disputes "in conformity with the principles of justice and international law."[37] Although many disputes are characterized as political rather than legal, any conflict can be amenable to legal analysis based on equity and customary international law, if the parties are willing to be bound by adjudication.

The International Court of Justice (ICJ), often called the World Court, is handicapped at present because many states have not accepted its compulsory jurisdiction and it cannot compel states to appear before it. In addition, the Security Council often has not taken action to ensure that states abide by court decisions. In order to institutionalize a larger role for the ICJ, the United States should, after itself accepting the compulsory jurisdiction of the Court without any reservation, press other states to do the same. Future treaties should give the Court more automatic jurisdiction and also allow international organizations and nongovernmental organizations the right to initiate suits. In addition, a special environmental chamber of the World Court might be created to handle a rising caseload.[38]

To enforce, at acceptable cost, the international laws prohibiting genocide and military aggression, the Security Council needs to prepare itself and the world community to move as rapidly as possible toward holding *individuals* accountable to the law, rather than trying to enforce norms through military combat against an entire society. To discourage hostility against an entire nationality or ethnic group, with the attending likelihood of sowing the seeds of resentment and future violence, laws should be enforced on the particular individuals who commit heinous crimes rather than on entire societies (in which many people are usually innocent of any wrongdoing).

To succeed in applying international law to individuals, thereby helping to deter future genocides, enforcement must be strictly impartial. Yet the temporary nature of the existing ad hoc tribunals to prosecute war crimes in Rwanda and the former Yugoslavia gives the impression that the law against genocide will be applied in some cases, against certain nationalities, and not in other cases, or for all nationalities. The international community should not tolerate such inequity, because it enables those who commit misdeeds to claim that, if prosecuted, their nationality is being discriminated against, thereby fueling the existing flames of group prejudice and hostility. In contrast, a permanent court with the authority to investigate and prosecute any genocidal acts by persons of any nationality would add greatly to the deterrent strength of existing international norms. To this end, an international criminal court—now being widely discussed in UN proceedings—should be established as soon as possible.[39] This would provide a mechanism for prosecution that could systematically gather information about alleged crimes, prepare indictments, issue international warrants for arrest, and hold impartial trials under due-process procedures.

Financing Demilitarization

No threatened people or government will take seriously the existing international prohibitions of genocide and aggression unless a UN police force, monitoring agency, and permanent international criminal court, as well as other peacebuilding initiatives recommended here for preventive development and sustainable economies, have substantial financial backing to make them effective in action. It is obvious, therefore, that effective demilitarization requires that sufficient funds be made available, to carry out the various initiatives described above and to further strengthen international efforts on behalf of peace, equity, sustainability, and human rights.

At present, national governments are calling upon the United Nations and its agencies to undertake more extensive and varied forms of peacekeeping and enforcement—yet, in case after case, member states have refused to authorize sufficient financial support for the UN to mount an optimal effort. When the UN is insolvent (yet has been harnessed to carry new responsibilities), those countries that do not pay their dues (yet have the ability to do so) scarcely conceal their own moral bankruptcy. The United States—now the biggest offender—has for several years owed the United Nations approximately $1 billion in past dues, an amount roughly equal to the UN's entire regular budget for one year. Although Washington has withheld payment ostensibly to encourage UN reform, the U.S. refusal to pay violates both domestic and international law (such nonpayment violates a duly ratified treaty that is constitutionally defined as the law of the land) and undermines UN effectiveness.[40]

One of the most equitable and practical ways to generate such revenue would be to charge an extremely modest fee of, say, five-hundredths of 1 percent (0.05 percent) on all transactions on the world's international currency exchanges. A fee of this type would generate over $150 billion per year that could be divided among three essential international functions: peace operations (preventive diplomacy, monitoring, peacekeeping and enforcement, and establishment and operation of an international criminal court); preventive development and peacebuilding activities to promote social integration and eliminate conditions that give rise to violence; and programs for environmental sustainability.

Of course, other approaches to generating revenue should also be considered, including fees for the use of the global commons and "green taxes" on selected uses of the atmosphere, such as the emission of greenhouse gases that contribute to global warming. In addition, governments might reconsider the Brandt Commission's recommendation that an international fee be levied on national military spending, on profits of arms manufacturers, or on international arms transfers to help offset the costs of peacekeeping.

EMPHASIZING SPECIES SECURITY

The contributors to this volume have demonstrated that a fundamental transformation of policies and world security institutions must occur to bring real safety to people in the postmodern world. As many highly regarded world leaders have concluded, the current world reality "requires us urgently . . . to establish a new order of global governance."[41] A large share of the responsibility for this task will fall on citizens' organizations, because the major world powers have shown little inclination to lead in the right direction. Recognizing this in the domain of nuclear policy, the former Commander of the U.S. Strategic Air Command observed recently: "The risks entailed by nuclear weapons are far too great to leave the prospects of their elimination solely within the province of governments."[42] To chart a purposeful course toward common security and comprehensive security, citizens everywhere should seek to implement the five basic principles of a just and peaceful world security policy: reciprocity, equity, sustainability, democratization, and demilitarization.

Commitment to these values helps not only to shape the most effective means for their attainment, but also to inspire and motivate people to make the necessary changes. Focusing on a principled world security policy can help recast our understanding of how to relate to other peoples and to nature. If we honor these principles in our personal and national lives, we will demonstrate that security can be maintained with greater justice and far less violence. One of the severe weaknesses of U.S. foreign policy in recent years has been that no leadership has articulated a positive vision of the U.S. role in the world. Yet a strong, clear call by citizens for positive action in the human interest, based on the five principles articulated here, could be heard above the aimless din of "politics as usual" in Washington.

A truly effective world policy, which can be distilled from the preceding chapters, not only must set new policy directions and create new institutions. It must also draw upon moral inspiration to guide its direction and to enhance its political strength. To serve the human interest in justice and in peace does not compromise national prudence; it is prudence of the long run. In the current era, as never before in history, what is ethically desirable in our relations with our neighbors converges with what is politically prudent for all. That is the full meaning of the preceding chapters' emphasis on the mutuality and comprehensiveness of security.

In the final analysis, a truly realistic security policy recognizes that *species security*[43] provides the firmest foundation for national security. Such a policy can be pursued effectively through legal, political, economic, environmental, psychological, and educational means, but not, as in the past, through chronic preparations for war.

QUESTIONS FOR FURTHER STUDY

1. Why does Johansen fault U.S. and other Western leaders for their actions following the end of the Cold War? Do you agree or disagree with his assessment of their behavior?

2. What, in Johansen's view, constitutes the basic components of a "principled" world policy? Do you think that principles of this sort should govern U.S. and world policy? What basic principles would you add to and/or subtract from Johansen's list of five?

3. What steps, in Johansen's view, should be taken by the world community to enhance global economic equity? Environmental sustainability? Democratic institutions? World peace? Do you believe that his proposals would effectively promote these goals? What else needs to be done by the world community to attain these goals?

4. What does Johansen mean by "species security"? Do you believe that this is a valid concept?

Notes

1. Commission on Global Governance, *Our Global Neighborhood* (New York: Oxford University Press, 1995), p. 2. This commission, which included three dozen high-level officials or former officials from all regions of the world, was co-chaired by Ingvar Carlsson, former prime minister of Sweden, and Shridath Ramphal, former secretary-general of the Commonwealth and minister of foreign affairs from Guyana. The commission was aided in its work by advice from many other experts and scholars of worldwide reputation.

2. Although one nation or another may benefit for a limited time from high levels of military preparedness, international society as a whole suffers in the long run from chronic preparations for war. For documentation, see Robert C. Johansen, "Do Preparations for War Increase International Peace and Security?" in Charles W. Kegley, ed., *The Long Postwar Peace* (Glenview, IL: Scott, Foresman, 1990), pp. 224–244.

3. See Independent Commission on International Development Issues, Willy Brandt, chairman, *North-South: A Programme for Survival* (Cambridge: MIT Press, 1980); Independent Commission on Disarmament and Security Issues, Olaf Palme, chairman, *Common Security: A Blueprint for Survival* (New York: Simon and Schuster, 1982); World Commission on

408 WORLD SECURITY: CHALLENGES FOR A NEW CENTURY

Environment and Development, Gro Harlem Brundtland, chairman, *Our Common Future* (New York: Oxford University Press, 1987); South Commission, Julius Nyerere, chairman, *The Challenge to the South* (Oxford: Oxford University Press, 1990); Stockholm Initiative on Global Security and Governance, Ingvar Carlsson, chairman, *Common Responsibility in the 1990's* (Stockholm: Prime Minister's Office, 1991); and Commission on Global Governance, Ingvar Carlsson and Shridath Ramphal, co-chairmen, *Our Global Neighborhood* (New York: Oxford University Press, 1995).

4. Whether a security threat resembles the nuclear arsenal of the former Soviet Union or the danger of nuclear proliferation in Iraq, no country can, in the long run, increase its own security while ignoring or increasing the insecurity of other societies, because insecurity for one's adversaries eventually rebounds into added threats against oneself. Even if continually advancing U.S. technologies of destruction move into space and remain beyond the capabilities of U.S. adversaries, in the absence of security policies designed to reduce reliance on the threat-system of international relations, one adversary or another in the future will be able to bring catastrophe home to U.S. citizens by launching nuclear weapons, delivering suitcase bombs, or engaging in chemical, radiological, biological, environmental, economic, or "migratory warfare." The world's societies are so intertwined and easily despoiled that more armaments do not lead to more security. On the contrary, competitive arms buildups and arms transfers undermine the growth of security by often increasing tensions and taking resources and attention away from addressing nonmilitary security threats.

5. The Palme Commission on Disarmament and Security Issues, *A World at Peace: Common Security in the Twenty-First Century* (Stockholm: The Palme Commission, 1989), pp. 6–7.

6. See U.S. Department of Commerce, *Statistical Abstract of the United States 1996*, (Washington: U.S. Bureau of the Census, 1996), p. 351. This astonishing reality, despite the enormous reduction of strategic threats to the United States, provides evidence to support Paul Kennedy's finding that mature great powers over the last five hundred years have declined because they relied too much on military power and spent excessively for military purposes, thereby undermining the economic health and nonmilitary strengths on which their power ultimately depended. For extensive historical evidence, see *The Rise and Fall of the Great Powers: Economic Change and Military Conflict from 1500 to 2000* (New York: Vintage, 1987).

7. These ideas build upon the concept of the human interest developed in Robert C. Johansen, *The National Interest and the Human Interest: An Analysis of U.S. Foreign Policy* (Princeton: Princeton University Press, 1980), pp. 3–37.

8. This principle represents a modest international expression of Immanuel Kant's categorical imperative, in which each person should behave in ways that, if everyone else behaved in the same way, would result in his or her own happiness.

9. See Gareth Porter and Janet Welsh Brown, *Global Environmental Politics* (Boulder: Westview Press, 1996).

10. Lester R. Brown, Christopher Flavin, and Sandra Postel, "Picturing a Sustainable Society," in Lester R. Brown, ed., *State of the World 1990* (New York: Norton, 1990), pp. 173–190.

11. Similarly, the security of U.S. citizens depends on military decisions in Moscow or Tel Aviv, in Berlin or Baghdad, as well as in Washington.

12. Alternatively, if U.S. economic policies cause worldwide inflation, then people in other lands suffer inflationary "taxation" without representation.

13. See Bruce Russett, "Toward a More Democratic and Therefore More Peaceful World," in Burns Weston, ed., *Alternative Security* (Boulder: Westview Press, 1990); Michael Doyle, "Liberalism and World Politics," *American Political Science Review*, Vol. 80 (1986), pp. 1151–1161.

14. These points are elaborated in Robert C. Johansen, "Military Policies and the State System As Impediments to Democracy," *Political Studies*, Vol. 40 (1992), pp. 99–115.

15. See Joseph Nye, "What New World Order?" *Foreign Affairs*, Vol. 71 (Spring 1992), pp. 83–96.

16. Quoted by Louis Henkin, *The Rights of Man Today* (Boulder: Westview Press, 1978), p. 20, from Thomas Paine, *The Rights of Man*, edited by Henry Collins (Harmondsworth: Penguin, 1969), p. 223.

17. Indeed, the need for building more effective international institutions has been so pressing that an international commission of widely respected leaders from throughout the world declared, in a far-reaching (but largely ignored) statement in 1991, that "a World Summit on Global Governance" should be called, "similar to the meetings in San Francisco and

at Bretton Woods in the 1940s" that created the UN, World Bank, and IMF. The Stockholm Initiative on Global Security and Governance, *Common Responsibility in the 1990's* (Stockholm: Prime Minister's Office, 1991), p. 45.

18. Independent Commission on International Development Issues, *North-South: A Programme for Survival* (Cambridge: MIT Press, 1980), p. 274.

19. A possible model for such efforts is the European Coal and Steel Community, which promoted cooperation between Germany and France after many decades of hostility and recurring wars.

20. The Commission on Global Governance recommended that the Trusteeship Council, having finished its original tasks, "should be given a new mandate: to exercise trusteeship over the global commons." *Our Global Neighborhood*, p. 301.

21. The decision at the Rio summit to create a UN Commission on Sustainable Development was a positive step because it can encourage governments to focus resources on environmentally sound development policies. But it is far too limited in purpose to cover the functions that the above proposals embody. It could either report to an Environmental Council, once created, or be transformed into an organization along the lines recommended here.

22. The group included Australia, Brazil, Canada, Egypt, Germany, France, Hungary, the Ivory Coast, India, Indonesia, Italy, Japan, Jordan, Kenya, Malta, New Zealand, the Netherlands, Norway, Senegal, Spain, Sweden, Tunisia, Venezuela, and Zimbabwe. The original twenty-four nations have been joined by Austria, Belgium, Czechoslovakia, Denmark, Ireland, Luxembourg, Pakistan, Portugal, and Switzerland. See Hilary F. French, "An Environmental Security Council?" *World Watch*, Vol. 2 (September/October 1989), p. 7.

23. See the Commission on Global Governance, p. 257.

24. See the Commission on Global Governance, p. 301.

25. Michael Renner, *Remaking UN Peacekeeping: U.S. Policy and Real Reform* (Washington: National Commission for Economic Conversion and Disarmament, 1995), p. 27.

26. For these documents see Ian Brownlie, ed., *Basic Documents on Human Rights* (Oxford: Oxford University Press, 1989). See also the Convention on the Rights of the Child and the Convention on the Elimination of All Forms of Discrimination Against Women.

27. Indar Jit Rikhye approvingly notes that "the balance of opinion in the Security Council seems to be swinging toward greater preparedness to intervene in domestic conflicts, especially when they threaten the stability of neighboring states or involve gross human rights violations." Indar Jit Rikhye, *Strengthening UN Peacekeeping: New Challenges and Proposals* (Washington: U.S. Institute for Peace, 1992), p. 12.

28. French officials quoted by Edward C. Luck and Toby Trister Gati, "Whose Collective Security?" *The Washington Quarterly* (Spring 1992), p. 53.

29. Canberra Commission on the Elimination of Nuclear Weapons, *Report of the Canberra Commission on the Elimination of Nuclear Weapons: Executive Summary* (Canberra: Commonwealth of Australia, 1996), p. 7. The report outlines practical steps to achieve the verifiable elimination of nuclear weapons and the safeguarding of weapons-grade fissile materials. The Canberra Commission included high-level former political and military officials, such as former Secretary of Defense Robert McNamara, former Chief of the U.S. Strategic Air Command General Lee Butler, former Chief of the UK Defense Staff, Field Marshall Lord Carver, and former Brazilian Foreign Minister Celso Amorim.

30. "A Major New Drive to Eliminate Nuclear Weapons," *Disarmament Times* (December 17, 1996), p. 4.

31. Quoted in the Canberra Commission *Report*, p. 4.

32. "General Assembly Debate," *Disarmament Times* (November 7, 1996), p. 4.

33. "Peace enforcement" occurs when the UN Security Council, acting under authority granted by Chapter VII of the Charter, authorizes deployment of UN forces to implement a cease-fire or other legally binding Security Council decision without the consent of the target government. In contrast, peacekeeping occurs with the consent of the host country.

34. For elaboration of this point, see Robert C. Johansen, "The Reagan Administration and the UN: The Costs of Unilateralism," *World Policy Journal*, Vol. 3 (Fall 1986), pp. 601–641.

35. Boutros Boutros-Ghali, *An Agenda for Peace: Preventive Diplomacy, Peacemaking, and Peace-keeping*, A/47/277; S/24111 (June 17, 1992), (New York: United Nations, 1992), pp. 20–21.

36. Jeffrey Laurenti, *The Common Defense* (New York: United Nations Association of the United States of America, 1992), p. 49.

37. UN Charter, Article 1.

38. On these topics see Hilary F. French, "From Discord to Accord," *World Watch,* Vol. 5 (May/June 1992), pp. 26–32.

39. See M. Cherif Bassiouni, and Christopher L. Blakesley, "The Need for an International Criminal Court in the New International World Order," *Vanderbilt Journal of Transnational Law,* Vol. 25 (1992) pp. 151–179; Representative James A. Leach, "The Case for Establishing an International Criminal Court," Address for the American Bar Association Annual Convention, Atlanta, Georgia (August 11, 1991), unpublished manuscript.

40. Even if all states paid their dues, the small size of the UN regular and peacekeeping budgets underscores national priorities: For every dollar that national governments contributed to UN peacekeeping since 1948, they have spent $3,000 for national military purposes. See Michael G. Renner, "A Force for Peace," *World Watch,* Vol. 5 (July/August 1992), p. 39.

41. The Stockholm Initiative on Global Security and Governance," *Common Responsibility in the 1990's* (Stockholm: Prime Minister's Office, 1991), p. 37.

42. As the Commander in Chief of the U.S. Strategic Command, General Lee Butler possessed responsibility for all U.S. Air Force and Navy nuclear forces. "Excerpts from an Address to the State of the World Forum," *Vital Signs,* Vol. 10, No. 1 (1996), p. 11.

43. That is, security for the *entire* human species, rather than a national or ethnic segment of it, and, by extension, for all species.

Index